THE**G**REEN**G**UIDE

San Francisco

Transamerica Pyramid and Sentinel Building © Pascal Ducept/hemis.fr

THEGREENGUIDE **SAN FRANCISCO**

Editorial Director	Cynthia Clayton Ochterbeck
Editor	Sophie Friedman
Principal Writer	Meesha Halm; Julie E. D. Meade; Barabara Rockwell
Production Manager	Natasha George
Cartography	Peter Wrenn
Picture Editor	Yoshimi Kanazawa
Interior Design	Chris Bell
Cover Design	Chris Bell, Christelle Le Déan
Layout	Natasha George

Contact Us
Michelin Travel and Lifestyle North America
One Parkway South
Greenville, SC 29615
USA
travel.lifestyle@us.michelin.com

Michelin Travel Partner
Hannay House
39 Clarendon Road
Watford, Herts WD17 1JA
UK
✆01923 205240
travelpubsales@uk.michelin.com
www.viamichelin.co.uk

Special Sales
For information regarding bulk sales,
customized editions and premium sales,
please contact us at:
travel.lifestyle@us.michelin.com

HOW TO USE THIS GUIDE

PLANNING YOUR TRIP

The blue-tabbed PLANNING YOUR TRIP section gives you **ideas for your trip** and **practical information** to help you organize it. You'll find tours, practical information, a host of outdoor activities, a calendar of events, information on shopping, sightseeing, kids' activities and more.

INTRODUCTION

The orange-tabbed INTRODUCTION section explores San Francisco's **Nature** and geology. The **History** section spans from the Gold Rush to the 20C rise of progressive politics. The **Art and Culture** section covers architecture, art, literature and music, while **The City Today** delves into the modern region.

DISCOVERING

The green-tabbed DISCOVERING section features Principal Sights by region, featuring the most interesting local **Sights**, **Walking Tours**, nearby **Excursions**, and detailed **Driving Tours**. Admission prices shown are normally for a single adult.

ADDRESSES

We've selected the best hotels, restaurants, cafes, shops, nightlife and entertainment to fit all budgets. See the Legend on the cover flap for an explanation of the price categories. See the back of the guide for an index of hotels and restaurants.

Sidebars

Throughout the guide you will find blue, orange and green-colored text boxes with lively anecdotes, detailed history and background information.

😊 A Bit of Advice 😊

Green advice boxes found in this guide contain practical tips and handy information relevant to your visit or sight in the Discovering section.

STAR RATINGS★★★

Michelin has given star ratings for more than 100 years. If you're pressed for time, we recommend you visit the ★★★ or ★★ sights first:

★★★   **Highly recommended**
★★   **Recommended**
★   **Interesting**

MAPS

😊 Regional Driving Tours map, Places to Stay map and Sights map.
😊 Region maps.
😊 Maps for major cities and villages.
😊 Local tour maps.

All maps in this guide are oriented north, unless otherwise indicated by a directional arrow. The term "Local Map" refers to a map within the chapter or Tourism Region. A complete list of the maps found in the guide appears at the back of this book.

PLANNING YOUR TRIP

INTRODUCTION TO SAN FRANCISCO

CONTENTS

DISCOVERING SAN FRANCISCO

© Jon Arnold Images/hemis.fr

YOUR STAY IN SAN FRANCISCO

Welcome to San Francisco

Globally recognized as a center of high technology and finance, the San Francisco Bay Area also boasts world-class cuisine, diverse cultural offerings, and a well-deserved reputation as being eco-friendly. With its agreeable climate and incomparable geographic setting, the vibrant "City by the Bay" is a most desirable place to live and an unparalleled destination for visitors.

DOWNTOWN *(pp64–111)*

In the northeast corner of the city, San Francisco's bustling downtown encompasses its major financial, retail, and civic centers: the skyscraper-filled Financial District, the fashionista-beloved Union Square, and the Beaux Arts-style Civic Center. Also downtown are vastly diverse historic neighborhoods. North Beach recalls its early heritage with Italian restaurants, bakeries and cafes, while Nob Hill retains an upper-class cachet from the late 19C, housing many of the city's most grand hotels. To the east, Cantonese and the smells of roast duck fill the air in colorful Chinatown.

THE EMBARCADERO AND THE WATERFRONT *(pp112–151)*

The bay front is home to several of San Francisco's most popular attractions. Fisherman's Wharf draws throngs to its colorful array of piers, docks, carnival amusements and seafood eateries. The Embarcadero offers a 3mi waterfront promenade from Fisherman's Wharf to Oracle Park, with expansive bay views, public art, and the Ferry Building. West of Fisherman's Wharf, the Marina District is home to Fort Mason, The Palace of Fine Arts, and dozens of trendy boutiques and restaurants. Further west is the Presidio, a 1,480-acre former military base with trails and great views of the Golden Gate and San Francisco Bay. Of course, the Golden Gate Bridge itself is a prime bayside attraction as well.

CENTRAL NEIGHBORHOODS *(pp152–173)*

San Francisco's central districts are anchored by sprawling Golden Gate Park, which stretches 52 blocks from the Pacific Ocean to the Haight-Ashbury district, and houses the California Academy of Sciences, the de Young museum, and the Conservatory of Flowers. To the north is Pacific Heights, which has been San Francisco's most fashionable residential neighborhoods for more than a century. Nearby Japantown is a compact neighborhood centered on the Japan Center, a shopping, hotel, and restaurant complex.

SOUTHERN NEIGHBORHOODS *(pp174–194)*

The lively Castro District forms the heart of San Francisco's LGBTQ community. Bars, restaurants, and boutiques crowd along Castro, Market and 18th Streets, while residential side streets are lined with refurbished Victorians. To the east, the sunny Mission District is both a Latino enclave and a magnet for the city's arty, hipster, and techie crowds. Farther east, SoMa is dominated by warehouses and office buildings, but is also a prime cultural and nightlife district, especially in the vibrant

Shop front, Haight-Ashbury

© Jon Arnold Images/hemis.fr

Napa valley vineyards, St. Helena

© Philippe Renault/hemis.fr

museum-filled blocks around Yerba Buena Gardens, where you'll find the massively expanded San Francisco Museum of Modern Art, one of the city's top sights.

OCEANFRONT *(pp195–209)*
Where the Richmond and Sunset districts meet the ocean, sit the San Francisco Zoo, the Cliff House, the ruins of Sutro Baths, and the Legion of Honor museum. Follow the Coastal Trail along the shoreline for spectacular views of the Golden Gate Bridge and Marin Headlands, or head to Fort Funston to watch hang-gliders. South of the Sunset District, Lake Merced and Sigmund Stern Grove offer further opportunities for various recreation activities.

EAST BAY *(pp210–239)*
The dynamic university city of Berkeley has an appetite for political activism, energetic intellectualism, and cultural diversity, not to mention a long history of serving up top-quality California cuisine. Up in the Berkeley Hills, the city boasts beautiful neighborhoods with stunning views of San Francisco. Oakland, Berkeley's ultra-cool neighbor to the south, is a diverse and growing city with a revitalized waterfront and civic center district, an exceptional museum, and ambitiously restored mid-19C to 20C residential and commercial buildings.

MARIN COUNTY *(pp240–263)*
Scenic Marin County combines the sophisticated charm of Sausalito and the breezy maritime ambience of Tiburon with the ancient redwoods of Muir Woods and the stunning seascapes of Point Reyes and the Marin Headlands. While some 260,000 suburbanites reside in this county, most settlement is on the eastern side of Mt. Tamalpais, leaving the coastal precincts in a largely natural state.

WINE COUNTRY *(pp264–289)*
Within an hour's drive north and northeast of San Francisco, the hills and valleys of Sonoma and Napa thrive on the abundant sunshine and fertile soil that produce grapes for some of North America's finest wines. The temperate climate, natural beauty, and acclaimed wineries, plus a reputation for excellent dining, make the Wine Country one of California's top tourist destinations.

SOUTH BAY AND PENINSULA *(pp290–307)*
Located in the Santa Clara Valley, San Jose is now California's third-largest city. The self-proclaimed capital of Silicon Valley bustles with high-tech prosperity and offers numerous cultural attractions, such as the Tech Museum of Innovation. Further north, Palo Alto is home to Stanford University.

Financial District with Transamerica Pyramid,
Alcatraz and Coit Tower in the background
© Mlenny/iStockphoto.com

When and Where to Go

WHEN TO GO

The San Francisco Bay Area enjoys a temperate climate year-round. Although temperature variation from season to season is slight, weather conditions can change quite suddenly in the course of a day, and from area to area. Inland temperatures are usually higher than those along the bay and oceanfront. Nighttime lows tend to stay between 45° and 55°F.

The key to comfort when visiting the region is dressing in layers. Shorts and other light clothing are rarely practical. In the **spring** and **summer**, daytime highs average in the 60s, although the rare fog-free day can bring sunny skies and temperatures in the 80s. July and August generally bring the busiest tourist season; visitors should make advance reservations whenever possible and expect long lines for the more popular attractions. The region's glorious views are at their finest during the clear days of **fall**, when daytime temperatures in the 70s make exploring the area quite comfortable. 80 percent of the annual precipitation occurs between November and April, and temperatures hover between 45° and 60°F throughout the day. However, California's long drought has led to unpredictable drier and warmer winter days.

Fog is an important weather determinant: its presence causes temperatures to drop, making a sweater or jacket necessary. Spring fog occurs in the early morning and generally lifts by midday. Fog persists throughout the day in coastal areas during summer, though it may burn off over inland areas before returning in the evening. Fall and winter days, though often crisp, are relatively clear and fog-free.

Guided Tours

If your schedule permits, a **guided tour** is a good way to get an in-depth look at a specific area of the city that piques your interest. Knowledgeable guides can illuminate the mysteries of Chinatown, the colorful history of the Castro District, the tastes and aromas of North Beach or the bustling waterfront. *See Sightseeing* in *What to See and Do* or check the San Francisco Convention & Visitors Bureau website (*www.sftravel.com*) for information on themed tours and walking tours in San Francisco and the Bay Area.

WHERE TO GO
SUGGESTED TWO-DAY ITINERARY
FIRST DAY
FISHERMAN'S WHARF AND CHINATOWN

Morning – Ride the Powell-Hyde cable car to **Fisherman's Wharf★★★**. Have an Irish coffee at the Buena Vista Café. Visit historic ships at **Hyde Street Pier★★** or rent a bike and ride the **Bay Trail★★** over the **Golden Gate Bridge★★★** to **Sausalito★**, returning to Fisherman's Wharf on the ferry.

Lunch – Dungeness crab at street

SAN FRANCISCO TEMPERATURE CHART *(recorded at San Francisco International Airport)*			
Month	avg. high	avg. low	Precipitation
Jan	56°F (13°C)	41°F (5°C)	4.6in (11.7cm)
Apr	63°F (17°C)	47°F (8°C)	1.5in (3.8cm)
Jul	71°F (21°C)	53°F (12°C)	0.04in (0.1cm)
Oct	70°F (21°C)	51°F (10°C)	1.0in (2.5cm)

stands or clam chowder in a sourdough bowl at Fisherman's Wharf.
Afternoon – Walk down **Lombard Street★★★**, "the world's crookedest street"; view the Depression-era murals at **Coit Tower★★★**; then have a cappuccino and cannoli at an Italian cafe in **North Beach★★**. Browse the beat poetry section at **City Lights Bookstore**. Shop in **Chinatown★★★**.
Evening – Dine in Chinatown and see a show in the **Theater District**.

SECOND DAY
ALCATRAZ, UNION SQUARE AND SOMA
Morning – Take a morning ferry to **Alcatraz★★★** (be sure to reserve ahead). On returning, take the F-Market streetcar line along the **Embarcadero** to the **Ferry Building** for some **shopping★★**.
Lunch – At the Ferry Building.

Afternoon – Explore South of Market, including the newly expanded **Museum of Modern Art★★** and the **Yerba Buena Center for the Arts★** (take kids to the Rooftop at Yerba Buena Center for the **Arts★★**). Shop in **Union Square★★★**.
Evening – Dine in the **Union Square** area. Have a cocktail with a **view★★★** at the **Top of the Mark** in Nob Hill or go dancing at **Harry Denton's Starlight Room**.

IF YOU HAVE FIVE DAYS...

THIRD DAY
GOLDEN GATE PARK AND OCEAN BEACH
Morning – Grab a coffee in the **Haight-Ashbury** before going to the **California Academy of Sciences★★** or the **de Young★★★** in **Golden Gate Park★★★**.
Lunch – At the de Young museum.

California Academy of Sciences

Japanese Tea Garden, Golden Gate Park

© RobertPlotz/iStockphoto.com

Afternoon – Visit the **Japanese Tea Garden**★★ and the **Conservatory of Flowers**★★, then rent a paddle boat at **Stow Lake**★.
Continue to **Ocean Beach**, stopping by the buffalo paddock and the Dutch windmills. Enjoy the sunset from the **Beach Chalet** or the restored **Cliff House**★★.
Evening – Dine in the **Castro District**★ or the **Mission District**★★, then see a movie at the historic **Castro Theatre**★.

FOURTH DAY
PRESIDIO AND LEGION OF HONOR
Morning – Breakfast on **Chestnut Street** in the **Marina District**★, snap photos by the **Palace of Fine Arts**★★ and then walk along Crissy Field close up view of the Golden Gate Bridge.
Lunch – Grab lunch at **Arguello** at the Officer's Club in **The Presidio**★★.
Afternoon – Visit the **Legion of Honor**★★★; walk the **Coastal Trail**★★ to the **Sutro Baths Ruins**★.
Evening – Dine in **Hayes Valley**; attend an opera, play, symphony, dance or ballet performance at the vast **War Memorial** and **Performing Arts Center**★★ or catch a show at the **SFJAZZ Center**★.

FIFTH DAY
CIVIC CENTER & PACIFIC HEIGHTS
Morning – Visit the expanding **Asian Art Museum**★★★ and **City Hall**★★.

Lunch – In Hayes Valley.
Afternoon – Browse independent boutiques in **Hayes Valley** and **Pacific Heights**★★; take a walk in Pacific Heights to see the stately mansions. Proceed south to **Alamo Square** for a photo of the Painted Ladies on **Postcard Row**★★★.
Evening – Dine in one of the new culinary destinations on **Divisadero Street**, see an art film at the **Kabuki Theatre** in **Japantown**, roots music at the **Boom Boom Room** or rock 'n' roll at **The Fillmore**.

IF YOU HAVE A CAR
In the Bay Area there are many outstanding scenic excursions and driving tours. ⬤*See the Principal Sights Map on the inside back cover.*
Listed below are the sights within the *Excursions* section of the guide, where you can find directions from the city and local driving tours.
- East Bay Area
- Marin Headlands
- Mount Tamalpais
- Point Reyes National Seashore
- Sausalito
- Napa Valley
- Sonoma Valley
- Upper Sonoma- Russian River Region
- Palo Alto
- San Jose
- San Mateo County Coast
- Santa Cruz

What to See and Do

OUTDOOR FUN

A mild climate promotes recreational opportunities year-round, most in the city or within an hour's drive of its limits. Hikers, bikers and equestrians avail themselves of trails throughout Marin County, the East Bay and the San Francisco Peninsula. Lovers of water sports take to the waves for surfing, windsurfing and sea kayaking, though swimming in most places is unsafe. Jogging, roller-blading, hang-gliding, kite-flying and sportfishing are other recreational possibilities. Golden Gate Park, Marin County and units of the Golden Gate National Recreation Area (GGNRA) are good places to start when seeking outdoor recreation information.

Trail maps, facility hours and other information are available at the **San Francisco Recreation & Park Department** (*McLaren Lodge, 501 Stanyan St.; 415-831-2700; www. sfrecpark.org*) and the **GGNRA** (*Fort Mason, Building 201; 415-561-4700; www.nps.gov/goga*). The **Marin County Visitors Bureau** (*1 Mitchell Blvd. Ste. B, San Rafael, CA 94903; 415-925-2060; www.visitmarin.org*) also provides maps and visitor's guides.

Hiking – The Bay Area is a hiker's paradise, with extensive trails exploring its valleys, scaling its peaks, tracing its coastlines and penetrating its forests. Contact the GGNRA or the San Francisco Recreation & Park Department (*above*) for trail maps and information. Within the city, there are several beautiful hikes, including the **Golden Gate Promenade** (3.5mi) from Aquatic Park to Fort Point below the Golden Gate Bridge, and the **Coastal Trail** (9mi) from the Golden Gate Bridge to Fort Funston, afford lovely ocean and cityscape views.

Biking – Mountain biking is an especially popular sport among the hills and valleys of Marin County and in the Presidio and Land's End areas of San Francisco. Most trails are accessible to both hikers and bikers, though some are restricted to hikers only. Routes within San Francisco include the Golden Gate Promenade and the Coastal Trail (*left*). In addition, many streets have designated bike lanes. The SFMTA (www.sfmta.com) offers a bicycle trip planner and maps for cyclists. Bicycle rental outlets include:

- **Avenue Cyclery:** Bikes: 756 Stanyan St. at Waller St. 415-387-3155. www.avenuecyclery.com.
- **Blazing Saddles Bike Rentals:** Bikes, tandems, and guided tours: eight locations including 465 Jefferson St. at Hyde St., Fisherman's Wharf; and 112 Market St., at Steuart St., Embarcadero. 415-202-8888. www.blazingsaddles.com.
- **Ford GoBike**: San Francisco's public bike-share program offers 24- and 72-hour passes for visitors. Download the app to use bicycles at any of the program's 540 stations in San Francisco, San Jose, and the East Bay. www.fordgobike.com.

Golf – There are several public courses within the city of San Francisco; all rent clubs and other equipment. You'll find others throughout the area.

- **Lincoln Park**, *Open daily 7am–sunset,* 34th Ave. & Clement St., Outer Richmond. 415-221-9911. www.lincolnparkgolfcourse.com.
- **Golden Gate Park Golf Course**, *Open daily 7am–4pm,* 47th Ave. & Fulton St. 415-751-8987. goldengateparkgolf.com.
- **Presidio Golf Course**, *daily dawn–dusk,* 300 Finley Rd. & Arguello Gate, the Presidio. 415-561-4661. www.presidiogolf.com.

SELECTED BAY AREA BEACHES	Price	Swimming	First Aid	Camping	Wheel	Beachwalking
Aquatic Park Cove		swimming			disabled	
Baker Beach						surfing
Bolinas Beach		swimming				surfing
China Beach		swimming	lifeguard	camping		surfing
Drakes Beach		swimming			disabled	
Fort Funston		swimming				surfing
Kehoe Beach		swimming				surfing
Land's End		swimming				
Lighthouse Field State Beach					disabled	surfing
Limantour Beach		swimming			disabled	
McClures Beach		swimming				
Montana State Beach		swimming				
Muir Beach		swimming			disabled	
North Beach & South Beach	fee			camping		
Ocean Beach					disabled	surfing
Rodeo Beach					disabled	surfing
Stinson Beach		swimming	lifeguard		disabled	surfing
Tomales Bay State Park	fee	swimming		camping	disabled	

Windsurfing – Consistent westerly winds from March to October make San Francisco Bay a prime spot for windsurfing and kiteboarding, particularly at Crissy Field, Candlestick Point, and Lake Merced. A few organizations offer instruction and rental equipment, including the **Boardsports California** (April–Sept only; San Mateo and Alameda; ℘415-385-1224; boardsportscalifornia.com/).

Swimming and Beachwalking – Waters of the Pacific shore and Golden Gate can be dangerous. Tides sweep in suddenly and powerfully and "sneaker waves" may appear without warning. Never turn your back to the ocean. Avoid walking along coastal cliffs; keep to established trails. Rip tides (strong, narrow seaward flows), sudden dropoffs, and strong currents make most areas dangerous for swimming and even wading. Besides, water temperatures average a chilly 55°F (13°C) year-round. Exercise caution when swimming at all times, and obey posted warnings.
Symbols on the chart above indicate: ∞admission/parking fee; swimming; ✚lifeguard; △camping; disabled facilities; surfing.

Sportfishing – The cold, upwelling waters off the coastal shelf north and south of San Francisco bring salmon, tuna, sturgeon, halibut and various types of rockfish near shore. Charter boats abound for both experienced and novice fishers; many provide equipment and tackle, and sell fishing licenses.

For information and recommendations, visit www.norcalfishreports.com. Good ones to try: the **Salty Lady** (*415-674-3474; www.saltylady.com*) or the **Blue Runner** (*415-458-8700; www.bluerunnercharters.com*).

Horseback Riding – The historic equestrian center in Golden Gate Park is in the process of reopening. Until then, there are stables and ranches throughout the Bay Area, which cater to riders of every experience level, with lessons, horse rentals and organized trail rides. Contact **Bay Area Equestrian Network** (*925-484-0395, 800-943-8883; www.bayequest.com*) for information. **Miwok Livery Stables** (*701 Tennessee Valley Rd., Mill Valley; 415-383-8048; www.miwokstables.com*) offers public riding on GGNRA lands.

Hang-gliding – The cliffs of Fort Funston rank among the finest hang-gliding sites in the US (*main season Mar–Oct*). Several hang-gliding shops, located near the fort, offer rentals and instruction. Contact the **San Francisco Bay Area Paragliding Association** for a list of shops, current conditions and hang-gliding events (*www.sfbapa.org*).

ACTIVITIES FOR KIDS 👪

With cable cars and boats to ride, barking seals to visit, beaches to run on, bridges to cross, towers to climb and whales to watch, to say nothing of excellent museums and attractions to entice youngsters' interest, San Francisco is a giant funhouse for kids. Most attractions offer discounted admission for visitors under the age of 18, and some restaurants offer special kids menus. The family-oriented website www.sffamilies.org has an updated list of special events and activities for youngsters living in and visiting the city. Throughout this guide, sights of particular interest to kids are indicated with a 👪 symbol.

SIGHTSEEING

The free publication *Where San Francisco* offers information on events, attractions, shopping and dining. It's available at hotels and visitor kiosks. In addition, the **San Francisco Convention & Visitors Bureau** publishes the free magazine *San Francisco Traveler;* download or order the current issue at www.sftravel.com, or pick one up at the Bureau's **Visitor Information Center**, located on the lower level of Hallidie Plaza (*900 Market St., at Powell St.; open year-round Mon–Fri 9am–5pm, Sat–Sun, holidays 9am–3pm, closed Sun Nov–Apr and on Jan 1, Thanksgiving Day, and Dec 25. l 415-391-2000; www.sf.travel.com*). The center has helpful multilingual staff and stocks brochures for restaurants, hotels, clubs and attractions. It also sells Muni maps and passes and cable car tickets.

TOURS
CITY AND BAY AREA BUS TOURS

Several operators tour the main attractions of San Francisco and the surrounding Bay Area by mid-size coach.

♦ **Big Bus San Francisco:** Hop-on, hop-off double-decker bus tours. Open year-round daily 9am to 8pm, 2 hrs 30 min. complete loop, 21 stops. $50, $40 children. ♿ 855-854-8687 www.bigbustours.com.

♦ **Gray Line of San Francisco Hop-on, Hop-Off:** Double-decker bus tours. Open year-round daily 9am to 5pm. Pass valid 24 hours, $55, $38 children. ♿ 415-434-8687. graylineofsanfrancisco.com.

♦ **Great Pacific Tour Co.:** Van tours of San Francisco. Open year-round daily 9am, 11am, 2pm. 3hrs 30min. $79, $66 children. ♿ 415-626-4499. www.greatpacifictour.com.

♦ **Tower Tours:** City bus tours. Open year-round daily 9am, 2pm. 3hrs 30min. $59 half day. ♿ 415-345-8687. www.towertours.com.

HISTORICAL & ARCHITECTURAL TOURS

San Francisco City Guides, a nonprofit organization, offers dozens of free historical walking tours led by volunteer docents *(year-round daily, start times vary; check website for schedule & departure points. ♿ ☎415-557-4266; www.sfcityguides.org).*

The **San Francisco Museum and Historical Society** leads several popular Barbary Coast Trail walking tours *(2hrs; reservations required; $15; call or consult website for schedule and departure points. ♿ ☎415-775-1111; www.sfhistory.org).*

The **Victorian Home Walk** unveils the city's past through the treasured "painted lady" architecture of Pacific Heights. Depart from the corner of Powell and Post streets in Union Square *(open year-round daily 11am; 2hrs 30min; $25 cash only; ☎415-252-9485; www.victorianhomewalk.com).*

NEIGHBORHOOD TOURS

All About Chinatown Walking Tours depart from Old St. Mary's Cathedral at California St. at Grant Ave *(Open year-round daily 10am; 2hrs; reservations required; $35 tour; $65 including dim sum lunch noon–1pm; ♿ ☎415-982-8839; www.allaboutchinatown.com).*

Cruisin' the Castro's Historical LGBTQ Tour highlights the history of San Francisco's LGBTQ community. Tours, run by locals, depart from Harvey Milk Plaza at Castro and Market Sts. *(open year-round Mon–Sat 9am or by appointment; 2hrs; reservations required; $25, ♿ ☎415-550-8110; www.cruisinthecastro.com).*

The **Haight-Ashbury Flower Power Walking Tour** departs from Stanyan & Waller Sts. opposite Stanyan Park Hotel *(open year-round Tue & Sat 10.30am, Fri 2pm; 2hrs 30min; $20; www.haightashburytour.com).*

The **Precita Eyes Mural Arts Center** leads the Classic Mural Tour along six blocks in the Mission District *(depart from 2981 24th St. near Harrison St., open year-round Sat–Sun 1.30pm; 2hrs; $20; ☎415-285-2287; www.precitaeyes.org).*

HobNob Walking Tours explore the robber-baron legacy of Nob Hill; they depart from the Fairmont Hotel *(open year-round Mon–Sat 10am & 1.30pm, Sun 9.30am & 1.30pm; 2hrs; reservations required; $30; ☎650-814-6303; www.hobnobtours.com).*

The **Pacific Heights Walking Tour** is offered by San Francisco Architectural Heritage. It departs from Haas-Lilienthal House, 2007 Franklin St. *(open year-round Sun 12.30pm; 2hrs; $8; ☎415-441-3000; www.sfheritage.org).*

SCENIC CRUISES & FERRIES

Bay cruises offer views of the skyline, Golden Gate Bridge, Alcatraz, and the hills of Marin County and the East Bay. Some companies offer evening and dinner/dance cruises. Following are some popular cruises; for additional ferry information, ⛴see By Ferry in Getting There and Getting Around.

Blue & Gold Fleet Bay Cruise Adventure: frequent departures from Pier 39. Check website for schedule *(1hr; $33; ✗♿ ☎415-705-8200; www.blueandgoldfleet.com).*

Red & White Fleet Golden Gate Bay Cruise: frequent departures from Pier 43½. Check website for schedule *(round trip 1hr; commentary; $30; ✗♿🅿 ☎415-673-2900; www.redandwhite.com).*

Hornblower Dining Cruises: brunch, lunch, and dinner cruises depart from Pier 3 *(frequent departures year-round; 2-3 hours; starting at $69; ✗♿🅿 ☎888-467-6256; www.hornblower.com).*

BOOKS

See also Introduction to San Francisco

REFERENCE

San Francisco Architecture. Sally B. Woodbridge, John M. Woodbridge and Chuck Byrne (2005).
Comprehensive and portable guide to the city's built environment by recognized experts in the field.
The Barbary Coast: An Informal History of the San Francisco Underworld (2002)
A history of the city's underbelly, from the Gold Rush to the 1920s.

LITERATURE

San Francisco Noir (2005). Peter Maravelis, ed. A collection of short stories with a dark twist by San Francisco writers.
San Francisco Stories. John Miller, ed. (2004). Vivid accounts of life in the city by 25 well-known literary lights including Mark Twain, Jack London and Tom Wolf.
The World of Herb Caen: 1938–1997. Barnaby Conrad (1999).
Recent history of the city as seen through the life and times of the SF *Chronicle's* beloved columnist.

FILMS

See also Introduction to San Francisco

The Graduate. (1967).
Social commentary laces this coming-of-age comedy about a young man in need of direction and the women who provide it.
Vertigo (1967). Alfred Hitchcock murder mystery about an alcoholic detective in pursuit of a glamorous socialite with something to hide.
Harold and Maude (1971).
Cult classic rife with black humor about a morbid young man and his redemptive relationship with a life-loving woman in her 70s.
The Times of Harvey Milk (1985).
Insightful documentary about the career and assassination of San Francisco's first openly gay city supervisor.
The Rock (1996).
Thriller about a plot to seize Alcatraz and threaten San Francisco with biological weapons
Blue Jasmine (2013).
New York socialite moves in with her modest sister and tries to pull her life back together.

Calendar of Events

Listed below is a small selection of popular annual events in the Bay Area; dates often vary from year to year. For more information about events taking place during your visit, contact the **San Francisco Travel Visitor Information Center** (*415-391-2000; www.sftravel.com*).

JANUARY
early Jan.
San Francisco Restaurant Week
Citywide
www.sfrestaurantweek.com

Jan
Fog Design + Art
Fort Mason Festival Pavilion
415-745-3315
fogfair.com

late Jan–Feb
Southwest Chinese New Year Festival & Parade
Chinatown.
415-982-3000
www.chineseparade.com

FEBRUARY
Noise Pop Music & Arts Festival
Various locations.
www.noisepopfest.com

JUNE: North Beach Festival

© Steven Restivo Event Services, LLC

MARCH

2nd or 3rd Sun in Mar
St. Patrick's Day Parade
Embarcadero to Civic Center.
www.uissf.org.

APRIL

Easter Sunday
Union Street Spring Celebration & Easter Parade
Union St. between Gough & Fillmore Sts.
mid-Apr
Cherry Blossom Festival
Japantown.
☎415-563-2313.
www.sfcherryblossom.org.
mid-late Apr
San Francisco International Film Festival
various locations.
☎415-561-5000
www.sffilm.org.

MAY

Sun closest to May 5
Cinco de Mayo Festival
Mission District.
mncsf.org/sfcincodemayo
early May
CAAMFest (Formerly the Asian American International Film Festival)
San Francisco and Oakland
caamedia.org
3rd Sun in May
Bay to Breakers
Embarcadero to Ocean Beach.
www.baytobreakers.com.

late May
Carnaval San Francisco
Mission District.
www.carnavalsanfrancisco.org.
late May
BottleRock Napa Valley
Napa
www.bottlerocknapavalley.com

JUNE

2nd Sunday in Jun
Haight-Ashbury Street Fair
Haight-Ashbury.
www.haightashburystreetfair.org.
3rd weekend in Jun
North Beach Festival
Washington Square Park.
☎800-310-6563
www.sresproductions.com.
mid-Jun–mid-Aug
Stern Grove Festival
19th Ave. & Sloat Blvd.
☎415-252-6252
www.sterngrove.org.
Jun
San Francisco Jazz Festival
Hayes Valley.
☎866-920-5299 www.sfjazz.org.
last weekend in Jun
San Francisco Pride Celebration
Market Street & Civic Center.
☎415-864-0831. www.sfpride.org.

JULY

late Jun-early July
Fillmore Jazz Festival
Fillmore District.
☎800-310-6563.
www.sresproductions.com.
July 4
July 4 Celebration at the Pier
Pier 39
www.pier39.com.
early July
Marin County Fair
Marin County Fairgrounds
☎415-473-6400
www.marinfair.org

AUGUST

early-Aug
American Craft Council Show
Fort Mason Center.
www.craftcouncil.org.

SEPTEMBER: Opera in the Park

© Cory Weaver/San Francisco Opera

mid Aug
Outside Lands
Golden Gate Park.
www.sfoutsidelands.com

SEPTEMBER
Labor Day weekend
Sausalito Art Festival
Marinship Park, Sausalito.
☏415-332-3555.
www.sausalitoartfestival.org.
Sunday after Labor Day
Opera in the Park
Golden Gate Park.
☏415-864-3330.
www.sfopera.com.
mid-late Sept
Autumn Moon Festival
Chinatown.
www.moonfestival.org.
late Sept
Folsom Street Fair
SoMa. ☏415-552-3247.
www.folsomstreetfair.org.

OCTOBER
early-Oct
Litquake
Various locations.
☏415-440-4177. www.litquake.org.
1st weekend in Oct
Hardly Strictly Bluegrass
Golden Gate Park.
www.hardlystrictlybluegrass.com.
1st Sun in Oct
Castro Street Fair
Castro District.
www.castrostreetfair.org.

2nd weekend in Oct
Fleet Week
Embarcadero & Fisherman's Wharf.
☏415-306-0911.
www.fleetweeksf.org.
mid Oct
Treasure Island Music Festival
Oakland
www.treasureislandfestival.com
2nd Sun in Oct
Italian Heritage Parade & Festival
Fisherman's Wharf & North Beach.
sfitalianheritage.org
mid-Oct–mid-Nov
ArtSpan Open Studios
Citywide
☏415-861-9838. www.artspan.org.

NOVEMBER
Nov 2
Dia de los Muertos
Mission District.
www.dayofthedeadsf.org.
Nov
San Francisco Auto Show
Moscone Center
www.sfautoshow.com

DECEMBER
Dec
San Francisco Ballet's Nutcracker
War Memorial Opera House.
☏415-865-2000 www.sfballet.org.
Dec. 24
Home for the Holidays,
San Francisco Gay Men's Chorus
Castro Theater
www.sfgmc.org

Know Before You Go

USEFUL WEBSITES

www.sftravel.com
The official site of the San Francisco Travel Association maintains ample information on hotels, dining, tours, shopping, and local events.

www.sfgate.com
The *San Francisco Chronicle* site has sections describing neighborhoods and nightlife, plus restaurant reviews, news, weather and traffic information.

www.sfbg.com
A digital-only offshoot of the now-deunct progressive weekly *San Francisco Bay Guardian* runs articles on the arts, nightlife and an annual Best of the Bay section.

www.sfweekly.com
Articles about offbeat and underground happenings in the city. Includes an extensive list of blog links.

sf.eater.com and www.tablehopper.com
San Francisco restaurant news.

sf.funcheap.com
Current listing of free and cheap things to do in the San Francisco Bay Area.

www.yelp.com
Reviews of local businesses, including restaurants.

LOCAL TOURIST OFFICES

Visitors may contact the following agencies to obtain maps and information on points of interest, accommodations and seasonal events.

- **San Francisco Convention & Visitors Bureau**
  900 Market St.
  San Francisco CA 94102
  ☎415-391-2000.
  www.sftravel.com

- **Berkeley Convention & Visitors Bureau**
  2030 Addison St., Berkeley CA 94704. ☎510-549-7040.
  www.visitberkeley.com

- **Marin County Visitors Bureau**
  1 Mitchell Blvd. Ste B, San Rafael CA 94303, ☎415-925-2060
  www.visitmarin.org

- **Napa Valley Welcome Center**
  600 Main St., Napa CA 94559.
  ☎707-251-5895.
  www.visitnapavalley.com

- **Oakland Convention & Visitors Bureau**
  481 Water St., Oakland CA 94607. ☎510-839-9000.
  www.visitoakland.org

- **San Jose Convention & Visitors Bureau**
  408 Almaden Blvd., San Jose CA 95110. ☎408-792-4511
  www.sanjose.org

INTERNATIONAL VISITORS

In addition to the agencies listed here, visitors from outside the US can contact the San Francisco Convention & Visitors Bureau's seven foreign-language pages (French, German, Italian, Korean, Spanish, Mandarin and Japanese) www.sftravel.com.

Embassies and Consulates

Visitors from outside the US can obtain information by contacting the San Francisco Convention & Visitors Bureau (☎415-391-2000; www.sftravel,com) or the US embassy or consulate in their country of residence. Major international consulates in San Francisco include:

- **Australia** 575 Market St.
  ☎415-644-3620
- **Canada** 580 California St.
  ☎415-834-3180
- **China** 1450 Laguna St.
  ☎415-852-5900
- **France** 88 Kearny St.
  ☎415-397-4330
- **Germany** 1960 Jackson St.
  ☎415-775-1061.
- **Japan** 275 Battery St.
  ☎415-780-6000.

- ◆ **Mexico** 532 Folsom St.
  ☎415-354-1700.
- ◆ **United Kingdom** 1 Sansome St.,
  Ste. 850.
  ☎415-617-1300.

ENTRY REQUIREMENTS

Citizens of countries participating in the **Visa Waiver Program** (VWPP) are not required to obtain a visa to enter the US for visits of fewer than 90 days, but must present a machine-readable passport upon arrival. Residents of visa-waiver countries must apply ahead for travel authorization online through the **ESTA program;** *www.cbp.gov/esta.* Travelers may apply any time ahead of their travel; at least three days before departure is strongly recommended. Beware private sites charging extravagant fees which are not affiliated with the US government. Upon entry, nonresident foreign visitors must present a valid passport, a visitor's visa and round-trip transportation ticket. Canadian citizens need a passport to enter the US. All travelers (including infants and children) entering the US from countries participating in the **Western Hemisphere Travel Initiative** (Canada, Mexico, Bermuda and the 17 Caribbean regions) must carry a passport if traveling by air. US citizens entering the US from WHTI countries by any means must present a passport, passport card or another WHTI-compliant document.

🄸 For information on entry requirements, see **http://travel. state.gov** or contact the US consulate in your country of residence.

CUSTOMS REGULATIONS

All articles brought into the US must be declared at the time of entry. Items **exempt** from customs regulations are: personal effects; one liter of alcoholic beverages; either 200 cigarettes, 100 cigars; gifts not exceeding $100 in value. **Prohibited items** include plant material; firearms

and ammunition; meat or poultry products.
For further information, contact the US embassy or consulate before departing or go to the US Customs and Border Protection website: www.cbp.gov.

HEALTH

The United States does not have a national health program. Before departing, visitors from abroad should check with their insurance company to determine if their medical insurance covers doctors' visits, medication and hospitalization in the US, and to purchase private insurance if necessary. The European Health Insurance Card is not valid in the US. Prescription drugs should be identified and accompanied by a copy of the prescription.

ACCESSIBILITY

Throughout this guide, full wheelchair accessibility is indicated in sight descriptions by a ♿ symbol.
All **BART** trains and stations and all **Muni** lines are wheelchair accessible. The *Muni Access Guide* gives helpful hints for disabled persons using the system *(free from Muni Accessible Services, 1 South Van Ness Ave., 3rd Floor, San Francisco CA 94103;* ☎*415-701-4485, TTY 415-701-4730; www.sfmta.com/access).*
San Francisco Paratransit provides door-to-door van and taxi service for those who are unable to use Muni's accessible buses or trains *(www. sfparatransit.com).*
Other useful publications include Access Northern California (ANC, *1427 Grant St., Berkeley, CA 94703; t510-524-2026; www.accessnca.com) and San Francisco Access Guide (San Francisco Convention & Visitors Bureau; t415-391-2000 or 415-392-0328 TDD; www. sftravel.com).* The Mayor's Office on Disability has resources at www.sfgov. org. You can also contact the Society for Accessible Travel and Hospitality, 347 Fifth Ave., Suite 605, New York NY 10016 (☎*212-447-7284; www.sath.org).*

Getting There and Getting Around

BY PLANE

San Francisco is served by two major airports, one south of downtown and one in Oakland. Plan to arrive at the airport two hours before departure time for domestic flights and three hours ahead for international flights. As airport security and baggage regulations change frequently, it is always advisable to check the rules before you fly. Visit www.tsa.gov for more information on what not to carry. Airlines serving Bay Area airports include:

Air Canada www.aircanada.com
Air France www.airfrance.com
American Airlines www.aa.com
British Airways
www.britishairways.com
Delta Airlines www.delta.com
Southwest Airlines
www.southwest.com
United Airlines www.united.com

SAN FRANCISCO INTERNATIONAL AIRPORT (SFO)

13.5mi south of San Francisco via Rte. 101. ☎*650-821-8211. www.flysfo.com.* Most international and domestic flights arrive and depart the Bay Area from SFO. The airport's **Travel Agency** *(open daily 7am–11pm)* is located in the International Terminal's main hall. **Airport Information Booths** are located throughout all terminals, both before and after security. A **medical clinic** is located in the main hall of the International Terminal *(open Mon–Fri 8.30am–5pm; Sat 9am–1pm;* ☎*650-821-5601).*

OAKLAND INTERNATIONAL AIRPORT (OAK)

www.oaklandairport.com. ☎*510-563-3300. 7.5mi south of downtown Oakland; 17mi southeast of downtown San Francisco via I-880 and I-80.* This smaller airport handles both domestic and international flights.

Information booths are located near main entrances. If you're driving from San Francisco, allow at least 1hr, especially during rush hours.

AIRPORT TRANSFERS

Visitors have a variety of public and private transportation options for getting to and from San Francisco and the airports. Taxis, buses, and shuttles depart from outside the baggage-claim areas; for information, call 511 or log on to www.511.org, which provides consolidated transit information for the entire Bay Area.

BY SUBWAY

The most popular means of getting to and from the airports via public transportation is **BART (Bay Area Rapid Transit)**, the commuter rail system that links San Francisco with cities in the East Bay and South Bay. The trip from SFO to downtown San Francisco costs $9.65 and takes about 35min; there are three to four trains per hour, departing from the international terminal. It's a 40min, $10.95 trip from OAK to downtown San Francisco; in Oakland, the BART train departs from a station directly outside the baggage claim area in Terminal 1. More info at www.bart.gov.

BY TAXI

There are taxi stands outside the baggage claim areas at both airports. Taxi service to downtown San Francisco from SFO takes approximately 20–30min and costs around $45; from OAK the ride takes around 45min and costs roughly $80.

BY SHUTTLE

Numerous companies offer door-to-door van service between SFO and OAK and private residences and hotels all over the Bay Area. Service is available on a walk-up basis, but it's best to make reservations if you are arriving after 11pm. Try **Airport Express** (☎415-775-5121; www.airportexpresssf.com) or **Super Shuttle** (☎800-258-3826; www.supershuttle.

com). Cost to Downtown San Francisco is about $19 from SFO and $75 (Super Shuttle) from Oakland.

BY RENTAL CAR

♿ *See also By Car.*
At SFO, the free AirTrain Blue Line operates 24 hrs connecting to the Rental Car Center from every terminal. At Oakland, buses leave baggage claim area every 10min for the Rental Car Center, where agencies serving the airport have counters.

BY FERRY

♿ *See Sightseeing in What to See and Do.*
Several ferry services link San Francisco with Marin County, East Bay and North Bay cities. Most depart from the Ferry Building or Pier 41, offer parking near terminals, accept bicycles, and provide discounted fares for children, seniors and disabled passengers.
Blue and Gold Fleet *(✗♿ ☎415-705-8200; www.blueandgoldfleet.com)* operates ferries between Pier 41 and Tiburon (45min; $12.50), Sausalito ($12.50), and Angel Island (25mins; 30-45min; $9.75), with some boats making multiple stops. The fleet also offers sightseeing cruises.
San Francisco Bay Ferry *(♿ ☎877-643-3779; sanfranciscobayferry.com)* serve San Francisco and Vallejo (60min; $14.60), as well as transport to the dock at Oracle Park.
Golden Gate Ferries *(✗♿ ⓟ ☎415-455-2000; www.goldengateferry. org)* runs commuter routes between the San Francisco Ferry Building and Larkspur (30min; $11) and Sausalito (25min; $11.75); as well as event service to Oracle Park.

BY TRAIN

The **Amtrak** rail network serves the East Bay city of Emeryville; a free shuttle bus (20min) transports passengers to downtown San Francisco. Fares are comparable to air travel. The **California Rail Pass** ($159) allows seven days of unlimited rail travel in the state during a consecutive 21-day period. A **USA**

RailPass allows 15 or 30 days of unlimited travel within designated regions. Advance reservations are required for passholders. Schedule and route information: ☎800-872-7245; www.amtrak.com.
CalTrain offers service between San Francisco and San Jose, with stations along the route in Palo Alto, Menlo Park, and Santa Clara, among others. Schedule and route information: ☎888-660-4287; www.caltrain.com. In the North Bay, the **Sonoma-Marin Area Rail Transit**, or SMART train, links Marin County to Petaluma, Santa Rosa, and the Santa Rosa airport (sonomamarintrain.org).

BY BUS

Greyhound buses arrive at and depart from the Transbay Temporary Terminal, *(200 Folsom St.)*. Fares are generally lower than rail or plain. Advance reservations advised. Schedule, fare and route information: ☎800-231-2222; www.greyhound.com.

BY CAR

Major interstate highways into San Francisco include US-101 and I-280 from the south; I-80 from the east across the Bay Bridge *(see below)*; and US-101 from the north, across the Golden Gate Bridge *(see below)*. Visitors with a valid driver's license are not required to obtain an International Driver's License to drive in the US. Drivers must carry vehicle registration and/or rental contract, and proof of automobile insurance at all times. Vehicles are driven on the right-hand side of the road in the US. Distances are posted in miles (1mi=1.62km); gasoline is sold by the gallon (1 gal=3.8 liters).

DRIVING IN SAN FRANCISCO

San Francisco Road Conditions: ☎511. Given the efficiency of public transportation, a car is not necessary in the city proper, though it can be useful to drive to Marin and surrounding areas. **Peak transit times** for business commuters are generally weekdays 6am–9am and 3pm–7pm.

CAR RENTAL		
Rental Company	✆Reservations	Website
Alamo	800-651-1223	www.alamo.com
Avis	800-230-4898	www.avis.com
Budget	800-218-7992	www.budget.com
Dollar	800-800-4000	www.dollar.com
Enterprise	800-736-8222	www.enterprise.com
Hertz	800-654-3131	www.hertz.com
National	800-227-7368	www.nationalcar.com
Thrifty	800-847-4389	www.thrifty.com

(Toll-free numbers may not be accessible outside of North America.)

ROAD REGULATIONS

The **speed limit** on most major expressways is 65mph in rural areas and 55mph in and around cities. The speed limit in the city is generally 25mph. **Seat belts** are mandatory for all riders. It is against the law to use **handheld wireless phones** while driving. Child safety seats are required for children under 4 years old or weighing less than 40 pounds (seats available from most rental car agencies). Drivers must always yield the **right of way** to cable cars and pedestrians.

PARKING

When parking on a hill, drivers must block front wheels against the curb (facing downhill turn wheels *toward* curb, facing uphill turn wheels *away* from curb); use of the parking brake is mandatory. Restricted parking is indicated by the color of curb: **red** (no standing or parking), **yellow** (loading zone), **white** (limited to 5min), **green** (limited to 10min), **blue** (reserved for the disabled). Check street signs carefully and don't block driveways.

BRIDGE TOLLS

Tolls are required to cross the Golden Gate Bridge ($7.50), the Oakland Bay Bridge ($5), and the Richmond–San Rafael Bridge ($5). You can no longer pay cash on the Golden Gate Bridge; don't stop at toll booths. For single crossings, the electronic tolling system

FasTrak identifies your vehicle by its license plate number. You can pay the fee online before or after your trip at www.bayareafastrak.org. Almost all rental cars have FasTrak transponders, allowing you to cross any bridge in the Bay Area.

BY PUBLIC TRANSPORTATION

Information on routes and fares for all transportation systems in the Bay Area, including traffic, is available free from anywhere in the Bay Area at 511 (✆*511 ; www.511.org*). Muni's NextBus app provides real-time schedule information.*(www.nextbus.com)*. Public transportation carriers within San Francisco include **San Francisco Municipal Railway (Muni)** (☝*see below)*; and **Bay Area Rapid Transit** (☝*see right)*. Bus and ferry service to other areas is provided by **Golden Gate Transit** (✆*415-455-2000; goldengateferry.org)*, serving Marin and Sonoma Counties; **SamTrans** (✆*800-660-4287; www.samtrans.org)*, serving San Mateo County; **AC Transit** (✆*511; www.actransit.org)*, serving Alameda and Contra Costa Counties.

SAN FRANCISCO MUNICIPAL TRANSPORTATION (MUNI)

✆*311. 415-701-2311; www.sfmta.com.* Muni operates an extensive network of transportation lines using buses, light rail and cable cars. System maps are available on the SFMTA website or at newsstands and at three SFMTA kiosks (Powell & Market Sts., Hyde & Beach Sts. and Bay & Taylor Sts.). In this guide, recommended transit lines are indicated with the ᴍᴜɴɪ symbol.

Buses – Muni buses operate daily 5.30am–12.30am, every 4–20min; some routes on major run 24hrs/day (**owl service** designates late-night schedule). Route maps are posted in bus shelters and real-time screens. All Muni buses are accessible to riders with disabilities via wheelchair lifts, ramps and kneelers (Muni Accessible Services ℘415-701-4485).

Metro Streetcars – Muni's light-rail system includes the J-Church, K-Ingleside, M-Oceanview and T-Third Street lines (daily 5:30am–12:30am) and the L-Taraval and N-Judah lines (24hrs/day; buses provide owl service) with service every 5–15min weekdays and every 10–20min evenings and weekends.

Cable cars – ♿see NOB HILL. Three lines operate daily 6am-12:30am. The **Powell-Hyde** (PH) and **Powell-Mason** (PM) lines zigzag from Powell and Market Streets in the Union Square Area over Nob Hill to Fisherman's Wharf. The **California** (C) line runs along California Street through Chinatown from Market Street to Van Ness Avenue. Brown-and-white signs along the route indicate stops.

Historic Streetcars – Muni operates a fleet of historic streetcars along the F-Market line from the Castro District to the Ferry Building, then along the Embarcadero to Fisherman's Wharf.

Fares – You can buy single rides or day passes on buses and cable cars using the **MUNI Mobile** app on your smartphone (more info at www.sfmta.com), paying for one or multiple riders. Alternatively, you can use a **Clipper Card** (www.clippercard.com) to pay for public transit. Clipper Cards are accepted on Muni, Bart, and Golden Gate Transit systems; unlike Muni Mobile, they can be used by only one rider at a time. You can buy or add value to a Clipper card online, at most Whole Foods or Walgreens, at Muni light rail and Golden Gate Ferry ticket machines, and in the Ferry Building (see website for all retail locations). Bus and streetcar fares are $2.75 if paid in cash (exact change only), and $2.50 per ride with a Clipper Card or on Muni Mobile. Cable cars are $7 per ride. Muni Mobile offers a $5 all-day bus pass (cable car not included), as well as the **Muni Passport,** which allows unlimited rides on buses, streetcars, and cable cars for one ($12), three ($29), or seven ($39) consecutive days. Muni Passports can purchased via Muni Mobile, on a Clipper Card, or at retail locations across the city, including Bay Crossings in the Ferry Building (℘415-362-0717) and at SFMTA kiosks listed above (see SFMTA website for all retail locations).

BAY AREA RAPID TRANSIT (BART)

℘415-989-2278 or 510-465-2278. www.bart.gov.
This fast commuter rail system links the city with East Bay cities and SFO and provides local service within the city itself. BART runs Mon–Fri 4am–midnight, Sat 6am–midnight and Sun 8am–midnight. Ticket machines are located in each station and Clipper Cards are accepted. Fares are determined on a per-mile basis; keep your ticket handy, as it must be swiped before and after every ride. In this guide, recommended stations are indicated with the ʙᴀʀᴛ symbol.

BY TAXI

All San Francisco taxis charge $3.50 for the first fifth of a mile and 55 cents each additional fifth of a mile. Two companies are **Yellow Cab** ℘415-333-3333 and **SF Green Cab** ℘415-626-4733.

BY RIDE SHARING SERVICES

Services such as Uber (www.uber.com) and Lyft (www.lyft.com) provide on-demand pick up location using an app on your smartphone.

Basic Information

BUSINESS HOURS

Most businesses operate Mon–Fri 10am–6pm. Banks are usually open Mon–Fri 9am–6pm. Department stores and shopping centers operate Mon–Sat 9.30am–8pm, Sun 11am–6pm; many extend their hours between Thanksgiving and Christmas. Stores near Fisherman's Wharf have longer summer hours. Smaller shops and stores (except in Chinatown) may be closed on Sundays or Mondays.

DISCOUNTS

Most public transportation providers (Muni, BART, ferry companies) offer discounted fares of up to 50% for seniors, youth and disabled riders. Many museums and other attractions also offer reduced admission fees for children, students and seniors.

ELECTRICITY

Voltage in the US is 120 volts AC, 60 Hz. Foreign-made appliances may need AC adapters and North American flat-blade plugs.

EMERGENCIES

In the event of injury or emergency, telephone the police, ambulance or fire department by dialing 911. Visitors should immediately report a lost wallet or passport to the local police, then contact banks and credit card issuers (see Money) to prevent unauthorized access to credit or personal information. Lost passports should be reported to the nearest embassy or consulate of the country of residence.

EARTHQUAKE PRECAUTIONS

Although severe earthquakes are infrequent, they are also unpredictable. If an earthquake strikes when you are outside, move away from trees, buildings or power lines. If you are in a vehicle, pull to the side of the road and stop. Do not park on or under bridges; sit on the floor of the vehicle if possible. If you are in a building, stand within a doorway or sit under a table. Stay away from outside walls and be prepared for aftershocks.

LIQUOR LAW

The legal minimum age for purchase and consumption of alcoholic beverages is 21. Proof of age is normally required. Almost all packaged-goods stores sell beer, wine and liquor; legal hours of sale are 6am–2am.

MAIL/POST

Post offices located throughout the San Francisco Bay Area operate Monday–Friday 8am–5pm (some have extended weekday and Saturday hours). First-class rates within the US: letter 47¢ (1oz), postcard 34¢. Overseas: letter, postcard or

IMPORTANT NUMBERS	
Police/Ambulance/Fire (emergency, 24hrs)	☎**911**
Police (non-emergency, 24hrs)	☎415-553-0123
Physician Referrals (24hrs)	☎415-353-6566
Dental Emergencies (24hrs)	☎415-421-1435
Medical Emergencies (24hrs)	☎4 15-206-8000
24hr Pharmacies	
Walgreens 3201 Divisadero St. (Marina District)	☎415-931-6417
Walgreens 498 Castro St. (Castro District)	☎415-861-3136
Weather	☎831-656-1725

aerogramme generally $1.15 (1oz). Stamps and packing material may be purchased at many convenience and drugstores, and at post offices. Businesses offering postal and express shipping services are located throughout the city (*see Yellow Pages of phone directory under Mailing Services or www.yp.com*). Postal Service Information Line (*Mon–Fri 8am–6pm; 800-275-8777; www.usps.com*).

MEDIA
NEWSPAPERS AND MAGAZINES

San Francisco's main daily newspapers are the *San Francisco Chronicle* and the *San Francisco Examiner*. The Sunday and Thursday *Chronicle* features an extensive arts-and-entertainment supplement. *SF Weekly* features diverse and comprehensive entertainment sections, while the *Bay Area Reporter* and the *San Francisco Bay Times* cater to the gay community. All are available in newspaper boxes and cafes.

MONEY

The American dollar is divided into 100 cents:
a penny = 1 cent
a nickel = 5 cents
a dime = 10 cents
a quarter = 25 cents

CURRENCY EXCHANGE

Most Financial District and downtown branches of Bank of America (*1 Powell St., t415-837-1394; www.bofa.com*) and Wells Fargo Bank (*1 California St.; 415-396-2779; www.wellsfargo.com*) offer foreign currency exchange. Visitors can also exchange currency at Travelex (*www.travelex.com*) branches throughout San Francisco and at the airport (International Terminal).

BANKING

Most banks are members of the network of Automatic Teller Machines (ATMs), allowing visitors to withdraw cash using bank cards and major credit cards 24hrs a day. ATMs can be found at banks, airports, grocery stores and

MAJOR TV NETWORKS	
ABC	Channel 7
FOX	Channel 2
CBS	Channel 5
NBC	Channel 4
CNN	Channel 3
PBS	Channel 9

MAJOR RADIO STATIONS	
88.5 FM	Public Radio
102.1 FM	Classical
680 AM	Sports/talk
93.3 FM	Country
103.7 FM	Jazz
810 AM	News/talk
107.7 FM	Rock
104.5 FM	Alternative

malls. Networks (Cirrus, Star, Plus) serviced by the **ATM** are indicated on the machine. For cash transfers, **Western Union** (*800-325-6000; www.westernunion.com*) has agents throughout the Bay Area.

CREDIT CARDS, TRAVELERS CHECKS

Few business besides banks accept **travelers checks** (picture identification required); credit and debit cards are the preferred form of payment. **American Express Travel** is located at 455 Market St. (*415-536-2600*).
To report a **lost or stolen credit card**: American Express 800-528-4800; Diners Club 800-234-6377; MasterCard 800-307-7309; Visa 800-336-8472.

TAXES

Prices displayed or quoted in the US do not include sales tax (8.75% in California). Hotel tax is 14% (not included in quoted hotel rates). Tax percentages in other areas may vary.

PUBLIC HOLIDAYS

Most banks and government offices in the San Francisco area are closed on the following legal holidays: *Many retail stores and most restaurants stay open on these days.*

January 1	New Year's Day
3rd Monday in January	Martin Luther King Jr.'s Birthday*
3rd Monday in February	Presidents' Day*
Last Monday in May	Memorial Day
July 4	Independence Day
1st Monday in September	Labor Day*
2nd Monday in October	Columbus Day*
November 11	Veterans Day*
4th Thursday in November	Thanksgiving Day
December 25	Christmas Day

SMOKING

California law prohibits smoking in enclosed spaces, including bars and restaurants. In addition, San Francisco ordinance prohibits smoking outdoors in city-owned parks and public spaces.

TELEPHONES

Wireless calling has made public telephones nearly obsolete in San Francisco. Local calls cost 50¢. Some accept credit cards, and all will accept long-distance calling cards. Most hotels add surcharges for telephone

AREA CODES	
San Francisco (including Marin County)	☎415
Peninsula cities (including San Mateo County)	☎650
East Bay (including Berkeley and Oakland)	☎510
East Bay (including Contra Costa County)	☎925
Wine Country	☎707

calls. For long-distance calls in the US and Canada, dial 1 + area code + number. To place an international call, dial 011 + country code + area code + number. You'll find a list of country codes in the local phone directory. Unless otherwise indicated, telephone numbers that start with 800, 866, 877 or 888 are toll-free in the US only. Visitors using mobile phones compatible with GSM networks can avoid roaming charges by purchasing a prepaid local SIM card for use in their phones. SIM cards are available online and at service-provider outlets; vouchers to add minutes to your account are available at most newsstands and convenience stores. Another option for mobile calling is a pay-as-you-go phone, available from many local service-provider outlets.

TIME

San Francisco is on Pacific Standard Time (PST), 3hrs behind Eastern Standard Time (EST) and 8hrs behind Greenwich Mean Time (GMT). Daylight Savings Time (clocks advanced 1hr) is in effect for most of the US from the second Sunday in March until the first Sunday in November.

TIPPING

In restaurants, it is customary to tip the server 18–20% of the bill. In addition, many restaurants add a "health surcharge" or "SF mandate" fee (anywhere from $1 to three-five percent of the total), to offset the costs of the city's mandated health care program. A growing number of restaurants in San Francisco, including several listed in this book, are "tipless," meaning they've stopped allowing gratuities altogether, bundling the cost of service into the menu price and paying workers a living wage.

At hotels, porters should be tipped $1 per suitcase and hotel housekeeping a minimum of $1 per day. Taxi drivers should be tipped $1-2; it's easiest to round up and then add a dollar (i.e. a fare of $5.30 is $7 including tip).

CONVERSION TABLES

Weights and Measures

🇪🇺	🇺🇸	🇬🇧	
1 kilogram (kg)	**2.2 pounds (lb)**	**2.2 pounds**	*To convert*
6.35 kilograms	14 pounds	1 stone (st)	*kilograms*
0.45 kilograms	16 ounces (oz)	16 ounces	*to pounds,*
1 metric ton (tn)	**1.1 tons**	**1.1 tons**	*multiply by 2.2*
1 litre (l)	**2.11 pints (pt)**	**1.76 pints**	*To convert litres*
3.79 litres	1 gallon (gal)	0.83 gallon	*to gallons, multiply*
4.55 litres	1.20 gallon	1 gallon	*by 0.26 (US)*
			or 0.22 (UK)
1 hectare (ha)	**2.47 acres**	**2.47 acres**	*To convert*
1 sq kilometre	**0.38 sq. miles**	**0.38 sq. miles**	*hectares to*
(km²)	**(sq mi)**		*acres, multiply*
			by 2.4
1 centimetre (cm)	**0.39 inches (in)**	**0.39 inches**	*To convert metres*
1 metre (m)	**3.28 feet (ft) or 39.37 inches**		*to feet, multiply*
	or 1.09 yards (yd)		*by 3.28; for*
			kilometres to miles,
1 kilometre (km)	**0.62 miles (mi)**	**0.62 miles**	*multiply by 0.6*

Clothing

Women	🇪🇺	🇺🇸	🇬🇧		Men	🇪🇺	🇺🇸	🇬🇧
	35	4	2½			40	7½	7
	36	5	3½			41	8½	8
	37	6	4½			42	9½	9
Shoes	38	7	5½		**Shoes**	43	10½	10
	39	8	6½			44	11½	11
	40	9	7½			45	12½	12
	41	10	8½			46	13½	13
	36	6	8			46	36	36
	38	8	10			48	38	38
Dresses	40	10	12		**Suits**	50	40	40
& suits	42	12	14			52	42	42
	44	14	16			54	44	44
	46	16	18			56	46	48
	36	6	30			37	14½	14½
	38	8	32			38	15	15
Blouses &	40	10	34		**Shirts**	39	15½	15½
sweaters	42	12	36			40	15¾	15¾
	44	14	38			41	16	16
	46	16	40			42	16½	16½

Sizes often vary depending on the designer. These equivalents are given for guidance only.

Speed

KPH	10	30	50	70	80	90	100	110	120	130
MPH	6	19	31	43	50	56	62	68	75	81

Temperature

Celsius (°C)	0°	5°	10°	15°	20°	25°	30°	40°	60°	80°	100°
Fahrenheit (°F)	32°	41°	50°	59°	68°	77°	86°	104°	140°	176°	212°

To convert Celsius into Fahrenheit, multiply °C by 9, divide by 5, and add 32.
To convert Fahrenheit into Celsius, subtract 32 from °F, multiply by 5, and divide by 9.
NB: Conversion factors on this page are approximate.

The City Today

Ethnically diverse, well-educated, tech-savvy, food-loving San Francisco is one of North America's most desirable cities.

COSMOPOLITAN SAN FRANCISCO
AN ECCENTRIC, ENCHANTING PLACE

With much of its economy dependent on tourism, finance, and high-tech, San Francisco attracts and nurtures a diverse, largely well-educated population with strong interests in the arts, social experimentation and good living. Well over half of the city's residents are unmarried, while over 50 percent of residents over the age of 25 have attended college. The arts thrive at all levels of society, from grand opera productions to neighborhood cultural centers. Eating well is a passion for San Franciscans, who are forever on a quest for new cuisines and restaurants, yet well-disposed toward traditional regional specialties. They enjoy working off their calories with outdoor exercise; weekends find them by the thousands jogging, biking and sailing, taking advantage of the waters and parks surrounding the city. San Franciscans actively guard their architectural heritage, subsidizing the archaic cable-car system and supporting zoning restrictions and retrofitting projects that preserve buildings. Strong supporters of the conservation movement, they have preserved an unparalleled system of parklands in and around the city. Though a reputation for tolerance holds sway, San Franciscans value individualism over universality. Residents are notorious throughout the Bay Area (as the surrounding region is known) for their stubborn political coalitions and special-interest groups that make consensus difficult, and neighborhoods that trenchantly guard their ethnic or cultural flavor.

Despite their preservationist attitudes, denizens pride themselves for being at the forefront—though others might call it a sideline—of American social experimentation. Set in motion by its eccentric birth and history, the city's penchant for flamboyant eccentricity attracts an eclectic mix of people and ideas. Freethinkers, poets, artists, counterculture gurus and revolutionaries have always thrived here, as have the many idealistic civic organizations, such as the Sierra Club and the congregation at Grace Cathedral, that were established here. This same rule-breaking spirit makes it a hospitable home to a flourishing new industry of distruptive and innovative businesses .

PEOPLE AND POPULATION

With a population of 884,363 (2017 estimate) inhabiting an area of only 46.9 square miles confined on the tip of a peninsula, San Francisco has the second highest population density in the U.S. after New York. Surprisingly small, it ranks as the fourth most populous city in California after Los Angeles (3,971,833), San Diego (1,394,928) and San Jose (1,394,928). The city forms the cultural and financial hub of the San Francisco Bay Area, a nine-county region of 7.56 million people.

San Francisco led the region in population, culture and economic influence throughout the 19C and early 20C. Within months of the discovery of gold in 1848, the town's population of about 800 doubled, quadrupled and septupled with young men (who outnumbered women by 10 to 1) from every American state and European country, especially England and Ireland, France, the German states and Scandinavia. Great numbers came from China and Mexico, and sizable minorities from Hawaii, Australia, Chile and other Latin American countries. The population rocketed to 34,776 within four years and exploded between 1860 and 1870 from 56,802 to 149,473. Though the rate of growth slowed in the financial depression of the 1870s, by the turn of the 20C San Francisco was still the largest city west of St. Louis, with a population of 342,782. Population briefly peaked at 775,357 in the mid-20C, followed by a slow decline as the city's lost industry and port facilities to

Alamo Square

Oakland and other Bay Area cities. A post-recession boom in the mid-21C has reversed that trend, with the city growing by 8,000–14,000 residents every year from 2011 to 2017. Today, the region's population is home to a diverse array of immigrants from Europe, the Americas and Asia, and close to 38 percent of San Franciscans are foreign-born.

Latinos

People of Spanish and Mexican ancestry have formed an important segment of the Bay Area's population since the arrival of Europeans in 1776. Politically dominant until the American conquest of 1846, the established Californio families contributed greatly to the founding and development of the village of Yerba Buena, though their political and economic power dwindled considerably with the influx of newcomers from the U.S. Even as generations of Latino families acculturate to American society, the continuing arrival of new immigrants, documented and undocumented, keeps Latino cultures robust over much of California. Latinos today comprise about 15 percent of the city's population.

Chinese

Forming about 21 percent of the city's population, the largest of any single ethnic group, the Chinese have constituted a substantial minority since the Gold Rush. Though historically perse-

cuted, the Chinese were instrumental in countless enterprises that developed the West, not least in construction, agriculture and the fishing industry.

The numbers of Chinese in San Francisco dwindled after passage of the Chinese Exclusion Act of 1882, reaching a low of 1.5 percent, or 7,744 people, in the 1920 census. Repeal of the act during World War II heralded a second wave of immigrants, greatly diversifying the Chinese community with wealthy families from Hong Kong and Taiwan, poorer families from China, refugees from Southeast Asia, and students.

Although Chinatown has prospered from this influx, most Chinese Americans dwell in widely scattered and well-integrated neighborhoods of San Francisco (especially North Beach, Nob Hill, Russian Hill, the Richmond District and the Sunset District) and the Bay Area.

Italians

After the Chinese were expelled from the fishing wharves in the 1870s, Fisherman's Wharf became known as a Genoese harbor, although Sicilians would later hold it. By the early 20C the heart of North Beach was referred to as Little Italy. Although the nickname has since disappeared, the neighborhood still houses Italian cafes, restaurants, and bakeries. With declining immigration rates, rapid acculturation and movement to the suburbs, the numbers of

Napa valley vineyards

FOOD AND DRINK

San Franciscans are curious and demanding diners. Their adventurous willingness to experiment with new cuisines and interpretations of traditional favorites has earned the city a well-deserved reputation for fine dining, which in 2019 has more 3-star Michelin restaurants than New York. Innovation and quality abound at every price point. The region's multi-ethnic restaurants happily coexist with white-tablecloth restaurants, and even the average food truck slings food with more pedigree and panache than most high-end restaurants in less cosmopolitan cities.

LOCALLY GROWN

Thanks to California's mild climate and fertile soil, a year-round abundance of locally grown fruits, vegetables, meats and dairy products flows into the city daily. This produce, often grown within a 100-mile radius, stocks not only grocery stores and restaurants, where their provenance is frequented name-checked on the menu, but also farmers' markets throughout the Bay Area. A stroll through these markets enables food-loving visitors to behold, taste or purchase seasonal delights such as juicy white peaches, exotic herbs, and a dizzying variety of heirloom tomatoes. Much of this produce is organically or sustainably grown. Shoppers will also find fresh eggs, local cheeses, and nuts from the Central Valley agricultural region.

Local waters no longer provide most of the city's seafood, but an enormous variety is flown or trucked in daily—salmon and oysters from Washington state, sea bass from Chile, mussels from New Zealand, halibut from Canada. One notable exception are local oysters, harvested from Tomales Bay in Point Reyes, which you'll see on menus across the city. From November through April, **Dungeness crab** appears on menus and in fish markets; this famed San Francisco treat is often served with sourdough bread and a glass of crisp white wine.

San Francisco's renowned **sourdough bread** remains a beloved local treasure. True devotees swear it cannot be pro-

immigrants have retrenched, but the influence of Italian Americans is still felt in many aspects of city life.

Other Cultures

Many of the city's most prominent movers and shakers of the 19C and early 20C were of English, German and Scandinavian stock. Large numbers of working-class Irish families settled in the Mission District from the 1870s, becoming more than 23 percent of the population by 1910. Other ethnic enclaves around the turn of the 20C included the Maltese and the Japanese, who settled after the 1906 earthquake in the present neighborhood of Japantown.

The African American population burgeoned during World War II, when thousands of Southern blacks came to work in Bay Area shipyards. Many settled along Fillmore Street (vacated by the incarcerated Japanese) in the Western Addition. Thousands of Filipinos have settled in the Bay Area since World War II, particularly in Daly City on San Francisco's southern border, and in the East Bay. The old Russian community in the Richmond District, which burgeoned after the 1917 Revolution, then dwindled through acculturation, is once again thriving under a new wave of immigrants.

Molinari Delicatessen, North Beach
© Brigitta L. House / Michelin

duced anywhere but in the city. Dating from the 19C gold-mining days, the recipe for this tangy loaf calls for a yeast-like starter, no sugar, and microbes that apparently float only in San Francisco air. California's phenomenally successful **wine** industry produces an array of vintages to suit any palate or budget, from good, hearty table wines to world-class award-winners. Most San Francisco wine lists prominently feature vintages from the Wine Country of the Napa and Sonoma valleys to the northeast, though fine wines also come from Mendocino County, to the north, and from Monterey and the Central Coast, to the south. Many restaurants also stock high-quality selections from Europe.

Locally brewed beers experienced a popular resurgence in the late 20C. Well worth sampling are brews from the San Francisco-based Anchor Brewing Company, whose Steam Beer traces its recipe from the Gold Rush era, and such respected microbreweries as Sierra Nevada, Mendocino Brewing and Anderson Valley Brewing Company, whose Boont Amber is a rich, creamy ale.

INTERNATIONAL FLAVORS

As in many port cities, San Francisco's abundant restaurants proffer cuisine from around the globe. In North Beach, a fragrant array of bakeries, trattorias, delicatessens and cafes dish up glorious **Italian** treats. Besides espresso, cannoli, pasta, pizza and other Italian

fare, look for the local specialty *cioppino,* a tomato-based seafood stew. **Chinese** restaurants are so plentiful, there seems to be one on every street corner, especially in Chinatown and the Richmond District. A Cantonese specialty, favored at lunch or brunch, is *dim sum,* a selection of sweet or savory dumplings filled with meat, seafood or vegetables. Lovers of other Asian cuisines (including Japanese, Vietnamese, Thai and Cambodian) can as easily sample sushi, coconut-milk curries, peanut noodles or teriyaki dishes.

Mexican food may be found all over the city but particularly in the Mission District, where a plethora of restaurants serve up large portions of tacos, burritos, enchiladas, tamales and *carne asada.* At Salvadorean restaurants, *papusas* are a popular Central American treat.

CALIFORNIA CUISINE

Drawing on California's polyglot heritage, and taking advantage of high-quality, readily available ingredients, a new approach to eating was introduced in 1971 when Alice Waters opened her Chez Panisse restaurant in Berkeley. Reacting to the prepackaged, mass-marketed food that had come to dominate American menus, and drawing on her experiences in France's Provence region, Waters developed a method of cooking based on fresh, seasonally varying, wild and locally grown produce. Presented in a visually appealing manner, **California**

Cuisine, as it was called, transformed American gastronomy and reawakened the American palate. Even today, it remains a powerful influence in San Francisco's farm-to-table dining scene. California Cuisine also gained a reputation for small portions at high prices. In the late 1980s, the pendulum swung in the opposite direction, with restaurants suddenly luring customers with "New American" fare, heartier portions of traditionally American foods, which were still often made with fresh, locally grown produce and innovative twists.

By the late 90s, some chefs began incorporating Asian ingredients and techniques into their food, resulting in what was often called Asian fusion cusine. More recently, a small but influential group of Bay Area chefs have embraced innovative modern techinique such as sous vide and liquid nitrogen, popularized in advant garde restaurants in Europe. Still San Francisco's farm-to-table ethos, based on sustainable, local and organic ingredients, is still the reigning principle, across culinary genres.

RESTAURANTS WITH ATTITUDE

San Francisco's restaurant culture thrives on residents' fascination with the experience of dining out. Local newspapers and web sites exhaustively cover the restaurant scene. Chefs of successful eateries are feted as celebrities, and followed religiously on social media. In keeping with this heightened sense of importance, restaurateurs pay close attention to style and design. Interiors, table settings, waitstaff attire and music are carefully choreographed to complement cuisine and maximize its camera-readiness. "Open kitchens" that allow customers to watch the proceedings, along with post-industrial interiors replete with exposed lightbulbs and communal tables where strangerwithout reservations share impromptu meals, are the order of the day. While celebrants still dress up at high-end spots, dress codes are rare and casual clothing is the norm at most places.

ECONOMY

San Francisco's early economy was shaped by its location. Isolated on the western edge of the continent, without easy access to other U.S. cities until the transcontinental railroad was completed in 1869, mid-19C San Franciscans built their own economy from scratch. The discovery of gold on the American River in 1848 transformed the settlement from the sleepy center of an active trade in cattle hides and tallow to a boomtown of commerce and manufacturing. Guarding the mouth of its great bay, San Francisco also became the premier West Coast shipping hub, a bustling outpost that benefited greatly from the millions of dollars worth of gold, silver and grain ("green gold") that flowed down two inland rivers and out through the Golden Gate.

In more than 150 years that have passed since the Gold Rush, San Francisco has made the slow, sometimes painful transition from small working-class boomtown to large international business center. In recent decades Oakland has assumed most of San Francisco's port activity, and heavy industry and factories have relocated to the East Bay's Alameda and Contra Costa Counties, while San Francisco has fashioned itself as a business and finance headquarters. The mid-90s were a giddy time for the Bay Area, with the economy swelling 24 percent over the period, almost twice as fast as the rest of the nation. The technology sector accounted for nearly a third of that growth. At the top of the market, in December 2000, San Francisco was rated "the No. 2 Best City for Business in the U.S." (after New York) by *Fortune* magazine. The bubble burst shortly thereafter, resulting in the loss of some 350,000 jobs during the period of 2001–2003. A gradual recovery eventually took place, with a greater emphasis on building a diversified economy. While technology— a mix of gaming, social media, peer-to-peer service transactions, information services and the sharing economy —has had the greatest impact, banking, tourism, biomedical research, legal services and real estate are also high on the list of thriving local industries. And the growth shows no sign of stopping. Between 2011 and 2016, San Francisco added 76,000 new jobs.

BUSINESS AND FINANCE

San Francisco's Financial District has been called the "Wall Street of the West" since the mid-19C. Although its ability to generate capital remains as dynamic as ever, the city's ranking as the nation's third-largest financial market was challenged in the late 1990s as mergers and acquisitions forced three of its largest banks (Bank of America, Montgomery Securities and Robertson Stephens) to move their headquarters to other cities. The Pacific Exchange, founded here in 1882, was the nation's fastest growing stock exchangeand a key player in the booming U.S.–Asia trade until it merged with the Chicago Board Options Exchange in 1998.

Today San Francisco has the headquarters of Wells Fargo, a bank with roots in the American West; the brokerage firm Charles Schwab & Co., Bechtel engineering and Visa, and apparel makers such as Gap and Levi Strauss & Co. South of the city, Silicon Valley is home to tech heavyweights such as Adobe Systems, Apple, Cisco, eBay, Facebook, Google, Hewlett-Packard, Intel, and Oracle, and continues to be a source of venture capital. The greater Bay Area region took in $8 billion of venture capital funding in Q3 2015, which represents almost 50% of the venture capital investments in the country.

CONVENTIONS AND TOURISM

Tourism is San Francisco's number-one industry. In 2015, the city attracted 24.6 million tourists, business travelers and conventioneers, who together spent $9.3 billion on goods and services. Those dollars sustain over 71,000 local jobs. San Francisco hosts several hundred conventions, meetings and trade shows each year.

The largest local facility, the Moscone Center contains over 990,000 square feet of exhibit space and over 100 meeting rooms, plus over 150,000 square feet of prefunction lobbies.

RETAIL AND RESTAURANTS

More than 7,000 retail establishments, employing upward of 95,000 workers, vie for San Franciscans' and visitors' dollars. Shoppers spend some $8 billion a year here, both in independently-owned neighborhood shops and in Union Square Area department stores.

Leisure and hospitality jobs make up 14% of San Francisco's economy. With more than 4,800 establishment employing over 60,000 workers, San Francisco boasts the highest number of restaurants per capita in the U.S., and makes up over 50% of the sales tax generated in the retail sector.

INFORMATION TECHNOLOGY AND ELECTRONICS

Home to more than 300 IT firms alone, innovative technologies continues to drive the region's economic revival. Silicon Valley, situated near the Bay Area city of San Jose, represents the epicenter of U.S. high-tech growth. Some of the biggest names in computers, such as Apple, Hewlett-Packard, Intel and Sun Microsystems, got their starts here, while Bay Area start-ups such as Oracle, Adobe, Autodesk, and Salesforce, have become big players on the international software scene.

In San Francisco proper, the South of Market area has grown into a technology hub in recent years. In 2011, the city became even more startup-friendly by approving a 6-year tax break on stock options taxes for companies that go public in an effort to prevent them for leaving town, and a growing number of companies, such as Twitter and Salesforce, have built massive headquarters within city limits.

DIGITAL ENTERTAINMENT AND SOCIAL MEDIA

The Bay Area's IT industry expertise, paired with its tradition for the creative arts has helped turn San Francisco into a hub for digital entertainment companies. More than 300 innovative digital media companies operate in the Bay Area—among them are Youtube, Electronic Arts, Zynga, Twitter, Dolby Laboratories, Pixar, Sony and PDI Dream-Works SKG.

SHIPPING AND TRANSPORTATION

Most of the shipping that goes on in San Francisco today consists of bits and bytes flowing over fiber-optic cables, but from the Gold Rush until well into the 20C, San Francisco's waterfront thrived. In its 1880s heyday, the San Francisco port, which employed thousands of longshoremen and sailors, handled 99 percent of all West Coast imports and 83 percent of all exports. Through the 19C the city was the whaling headquarters of the Pacific coast, but shipping declined with completion of the trans-continental railroad. Although the ship-yards came alive briefly during World War II, in the 1960s San Francisco quietly ceded the bulk of its industrial shipping business to Oakland, which had made a sizable investment in up-to-date loading equipment and dredged its harbor to accommodate the latest generation of deep-draft ships.

Today San Francisco Bay maintains three major international ports: San Francisco, Oakland, and Richmond. Asia accounts for two-thirds of its shipping trade, with the remainder split between Latin America, New Zealand, and the South Pacific, British Columbia, and Europe. The Port of Oakland, the fifth-busiest container port in the country, handles 99 percent of the containerized cargo that passes through the Golden Gate. San Francisco International Airport (SFO) hosted more than 41 million passengers in 2015, making it among the busiest nationwide. SFO also handles over 90 percent of the Bay Area's international air-cargo trade and is a major trade hub with South Korea, Japan, and Taiwan.

BIOTECHNOLOGY

Employing one third of the global work-force in this sector, the Bay Area is the world capital of biotech, which creates marketplace applications for scientific innovations—from genetically engineering plants to provide higher crop yields, to manufacturing human insulin for diabetics. Since 1976, when Genentech was founded just south of the city, biotech companies have been flooding the region, complemented by some of the top health education and medical research facilities in the nation at UC San Francisco, UC Berkeley and Stanford University. The recent transformation of the desolate Mission Bay area into a thriving biotechnology and heatlthcare hub, with the opening of QB3, an bio-tech incubator in 2013, a new UCSF medical facility in 2015, and forthcoming centers for bio-entreneurship and innovation, continues to draw life science innovation to San Francisco.

SERVICES

As in most densely populated cities, the service industry accounts for the lion's share of jobs in San Francisco. Fueling the operations of the booming innovation industries, securities and investment and legal services firms represent the largest cluster of the city's professional workforce. The Bay Area boasts the largest aggregation of research universities and federal research institutions in the nation, and some 8,200 people are employed at area colleges and universities. Government agencies employ more than 28,000 workers and, and, and and there are nearly 46,000 health-care workers in San Francisco and San Mateo counties. Meanwhile, commerical projects such as the new Salesforce Tower and the construction of 3,654 units of housing in 2014 (a 50% increase from 2013) and the authorization of another 3,834 more over the next three years, promises to swell the ranks of local construction companies, which now support 16,000 workers.

LOCAL GOVERNMENT

The City and County of San Francisco are administered jointly as a consolidated unit. The executive branch of government is headed by the **mayor**, who is elected every four years and may serve a maximum of two consecutive terms. The mayor's office oversees more than 50 offices and agencies including the police and fire departments, the civil service, and the offices of economic development and public works. The current mayor **Edwin Lee** will complete his second term of office in 2020.

The 11-member **Board of Supervisors** constitutes the legislative branch of city and county government. The Board considers legislation, confirms mayoral appointments and approves the city budget (projected to be $9 billion in 2016). Supervisors are elected every four years, and must live in the districts they represent. In the event of the death or resignation of the mayor, the Board President assumes the mayor's duties for the remainder of the term, as happened when Dianne Feinstein served as mayor

following the assassination of George Moscone in 1978, and Edwin Lee served in 2011 after Gavin Newsom resigned to become Lieutenant Governor.

San Francisco is a major center of U.S. government activity. Federal agencies maintaining offices here include the Army Corps of Engineers, the Federal Reserve Bank, the Federal Bureau of Investigation (FBI) and the U.S. Mint. More than 30 foreign countries operate consular offices in the city.

San Franciscans participate in California's legislative process through **ballot initiatives**, a form of direct democracy by which legislation is introduced for consideration through petition of registered voters. Recent initiatives have addressed same-sex marriage, handgun ownership, minimum wage and the legalizatoin of recreational marijuana.

History

Although it is a young city even by American standards, few places on the globe have changed as dramatically as San Francisco has in the past 250 years. Containing just two permanent structures at the time of the Declaration of Independence, it exploded with gold-seeking dreamers in 1849, only to be decimated by the 1906 earthquake. In the ensuing century it has steadily grown into one of the country's most desirable cities.

TIME LINE

c. 10,000 BC   Native Americans first settle in the Bay Area.

1579   Explorer Francis Drake anchors near Point Reyes to repair his ship and claims Alta California for England.

1769   Expedition led by **Gaspar de Portolá** and **Junípero Serra** sets out from Mexico to establish the mission chain in Alta California. Sgt.

José Ortega first sights San Francisco Bay.

1775   **Lt. Juan Manuel de Ayala** and his crew are the first Europeans to explore and map the bay.

1776   First mass is celebrated near the site of Mission Dolores. The first building on The Presidio is completed on September 17.

1791   Mission San Francisco de Asís (Mission Dolores) is completed.

1833   Following Mexican independence from Spain (1821), the mission chain is secularized.

1834   First town council is organized near Mission Dolores, with **Francisco de Haro** appointed as *alcalde,* or mayor.

1835   William Richardson and his wife build the first structure in Yerba Buena.

1846 American settlers in Sonoma declare the **Bear Flag Republic;** less than a month later, the U.S. flag is raised in San Francisco.

1847 California's first newspaper, *The California Star,* is published by **Sam Brannan**. Yerba Buena is renamed San Francisco.

1848 First commercial bank and first American public school open in San Francisco.

1849 California **Gold Rush** begins.

1852 **Wells Fargo** begins stagecoach service for passengers and freight.

1857 California's first commercial winery, Buena Vista, is founded in Sonoma by Hungarian **Agoston Haraszthy**.

1859 The **Comstock Lode** silver deposits are discovered in Nevada.

1865 Charles and Michael de Young found the *San Francisco Dramatic Chronicle,* later dropping the word dramatic.

1868 The College of California in Oakland is taken over by the state, chartered and renamed the **University of California**. The campus is moved to Berkeley in 1873.

1869 The Central Pacific and Union Pacific railroads are joined at Promontory Point, Utah, creating the first **transcontinental railway** link between San Francisco and the East Coast.

1873 Andrew Hallidie successfully tests the first **cable car** on Clay Street. **Levi Strauss** patents riveted blue jeans. Pacific Coast Stock Exchange is founded.

1882 Enactment of the federal **Chinese Exclusion Act** restricts immigration of Asians to the U.S. It is not repealed until 1943.

1891 **Stanford University** is established in Palo Alto.

1892 **Sierra Club** is founded, with **John Muir** as president.

1904 Produce wholesaler A.P. Giannini founds the Bank of Italy, later renamed **Bank of America**, pioneering branch banking in the state.

1906 **Great Earthquake and Fire** devastate San Francisco; the quake is estimated at 8.3 on the Richter Scale.

Postcard from the Panama-Pacific International Exposition 1915

1915 **Panama-Pacific International Exposition** in San Francisco celebrates the city's recovery from the 1906 earthquake.

1917 Architect Willis Polk completes **Hallidie Building**, the world's first skyscraper clad in a glass curtain wall.

1919 **Ina Coolbrith** is California's first Poet Laureate.

1936–37 The **San Francisco-Oakland Bay Bridge** and the **Golden Gate Bridge** link San Francisco to the East Bay and Marin County.

1945 **United Nations** charter is drafted at the Fairmont Hotel and signed at the Civic Center.

1958 The New York **Giants** move to San Francisco, becoming the Bay Area's first major-league baseball team.

1964 **Free Speech Movement** sit-ins at the University of California, Berkeley, lead to mass arrests of student protesters.

1965 Promoter **Bill Graham** opens Fillmore Auditorium, staging legendary rock-and-roll concerts.

1967 Haight-Ashbury's "**Summer of Love**" establishes San Francisco as the hippie capital of the world.

1971 Alice Waters opens Chez Panisse restaurant in Berkeley, beginning the rage for **California cuisine.**

1973 First **BART** train travels through the transbay tube from the East Bay to the Montgomery Street station.

1978 San Francisco Mayor **George Moscone** and gay supervisor **Harvey Milk** are assassinated by ex-supervisor Dan White. His sentence of just five years' imprisonment starts riots.

1989 **Loma Prieta earthquake**, measuring 7.1 on the Richter Scale, rocks the entire Bay Area from an epicenter near Santa Cruz.

1993 When Bay Area politicians **Dianne Feinstein** and **Barbara Boxer** are elected to the U.S. Senate, California is the first state to have two women senators simultaneously in office.

1995 San Francisco 49ers win an unprecedented fifth **Super Bowl.**

1998 State law bans smoking from public areas, including restaurants and bars.

2001 After five years of spiraling technology stock prices, the bubble bursts; 30,000 San Franciscans leave the city to find work elsewhere.

2004 Early in the year, nearly 4,000 **same-sex marriages** are performed at San Francisco City Hall. The California Supreme Court declares the marriages void in August.

2006 Study finds San Francisco to be the second-most-expensive city in the U.S.

2007 San Francisco Giants' **Barry Bonds** slams his 756th career home run, breaking the record set in 1974.

2008 California Supreme Court overturns ban on **same-sex marriages**. Voters then pass Prop 8, overturning the court ruling.

2009 San Francisco buys former naval base **Treasure Island** from the U.S. government for $55 million, with plans to develop a cutting-edge green community.

2010 San Francisco Giants win the World Series, breaking a 52-year drought. They'd go on to win again in 2012 and 2014, propelling a popular "even year" theory for winning championships.

2011	Oakland police fired tear gas into a crowd of several hundreds of protesters who had sought to retake an Occupy Oakland encampment.
2013	New eastern span of the San Francisco-Oakland Bay Bridge opens, six years behind schedule and five times over budget.
2014	Community activists escalate their protests against so-called "Google buses", luxury shuttle buses that transport high-paid tech workers from San Francisco to Silicon Valley.
2015	The Golden State Warriors take the NBA title and go on to set the record for most regular season wins in NBA history the following year.
2016	SFMOMA reopens in Yerba Buena Gardens with a vastly expanded collection.
2016	49ers quarterback Colin Kapernick refuses to stand for the national anthem at Levi's Stadium to protest racial inqualitys.
2017	Mayor Ed Lee dies suddenly on December 12, 2017.
2018	The Salesforce Tower, San Francisco's tallest building, officially opens.
2018	London Breed is elected mayor of San Francisco in an election using ranked-choice ballots.

PEOPLE AND EVENTS
BEGINNINGS

Native Americans began settling the Bay Area around the 11C BC, building small villages of brush and tule bulrush. They enjoyed a rich and varied diet of seeds, ground acorn meal, shellfish, deer and other game. Although regional residents spoke various dialects and distinguished themselves by different tribal names, historians group them into three distinct peoples.

The **Coast Miwok** dwelt north of the city, in present-day Marin and western Sonoma counties. The **Wintun** lived north of the Carquinez Straits in modern Solano, Napa and eastern Sonoma counties. The **Ohlone**, or Costanoans, inhabited areas east of the bay, on the San Francisco Peninsula and south to Big Sur. Though discussion of death was taboo among the Ohlone, they believed their dead souls transmigrated westward across the sea to the Farallon Islands, which they called the Islands of the Dead.

Despite small-scale but merciless feuds between some villages, trade and intermarriage promoted a generally peaceful and prosperous existence, as did the region's remoteness from the more bellicose cultures of Mexico and the Great Plains, and from the sea lanes of Europe and Asia. By the time the Spanish arrived in the 18C, the Bay Area supported between 7,000 and 10,000 people, and was North America's most densely populated region north of Mexico.

After conquering Mexico in 1521, the Spanish Crown was eager to expand its influence in the New World, especially over territories that could supply gold and other transportable treasure to subsidize the costs of colonization and war. In 1542 Spain dispatched a sea expedition, commanded by **Juan Rodríguez Cabrillo**, up the coast of Alta California in search of a passage connecting the Pacific Ocean to the Atlantic. Although he made the first documented visit by a European to California, Cabrillo failed to find either the fabled Northwest Passage or the very real passage into San Francisco Bay that John C. Frémont—almost three centuries later—would christen the Golden Gate.

In 1579 English privateer **Francis Drake** put in for repairs at a sheltered bay in northern California—possibly present-day Drakes Bay, in the lee of Point Reyes. He claimed the land for Queen Elizabeth I as Nova Albion, but the English did not follow up on their claims, leaving California to gradual conquest by Spain.

In 1602 **Sebastián Vizcaíno** dropped anchor in Monterey Bay, 85 miles south of the Golden Gate. Although he traveled no farther north, his glowing but inaccurate description of the cove inspired the Sacred Expedition and the first European sighting of San Francisco Bay 167 years later.

HISPANIC ENCLAVE

Mexico dispatched stalwart soldier **Gaspar de Portolá** in 1769 with orders to plant colonies in Alta California, with a provincial capital at the acclaimed Monterey Bay. He was accompanied by a religious contingent, headed by Franciscan friar **Junípero Serra**, charged with founding a chain of coastal missions. While searching for Monterey Bay, but having overshot their mark, a scouting party led by **Sgt. José Ortega** stumbled upon San Francisco Bay in November of that year. Mistaking it for Drakes Bay, which the Spanish had renamed for St. Francis, the great inlet was incorrectly—but permanently—called San Francisco.

Commissioned by the colonial government in Mexico, an expedition led by **Juan Bautista de Anza** arrived at San Francisco Bay in 1776 and formally established the Presidio on a hill overlooking the entrance to the bay. De Anza also selected a site for a mission church near a small lagoon in the sheltered valley to the south, naming the lagoon for Our Lady of Sorrows (*Nuestra Señora de los Dolores* in Spanish). On October 9, 1776, Padre Serra officially dedicated the new mission to St. Francis of Assisi, although it wasn't completed until 1791. Today it is known as Mission Dolores.

The Spanish mandate was to colonize the land and the natives, converting them to Catholicism and teaching agriculture. Overawed by Spanish bravado and firepower, and initially believing the newcomers to be ancestors returned from the Islands of the Dead, the native Ohlone and Wintun allowed themselves to be pressed into mission society. They labored in the fields, lived in barracks segregated by sex, and received religious instruction. Resisters fled to the hills and the marshes of the Solano Delta, from where they mounted raids

and were in turn hunted by Spanish and native soldiery. The old ways of life quickly disappeared as the Church seized land around the bay for grazing, eventually establishing three missions in Ohlone territory, and one each in the Miwok (at San Rafael) and Wintun (at Sonoma) homelands. Thousands of natives died of European diseases, especially after smallpox was contracted from a trading expedition to the Russian settlement at Fort Ross in 1837.

After Mexico declared independence from Spain in 1821, the missions were secularized. The government decreed that half of their lands go to indigenous peoples, the remainder to be sold or doled out to soldiers and civilians as private land grants in lieu of pensions or payments. The demoralized and undercapitalized natives, however, failed to work their lands, which were readily absorbed by the private landholders; the natives either went to work for them or drifted into vagabondage.

Among the largest landholders around the bay were the ranching families of **Noe**, **De Haro** and **Bernal** on the tip of the San Francisco Peninsula; **Peralta** and **Martinez** in the East Bay and—most powerful of all—**Mariano Vallejo** to the north of the bay. Another ambitious settler was **John Sutter**, a Swiss adventurer who built extensive workshops and a fort on his land grant in the Sacramento Valley. With little interference from the Mexican government, the Californios, as they called themselves, lived self-sufficient lives. Served by small armies of cheap, native labor, they prospered by selling hides and tallow to visiting ships, many of them Yankee traders who carried glowing reports of the harbor's size and excellence to U.S. East Coast.

YANKEE VILLAGE

Until 1835, most of the San Francisco Peninsula's residents lived near the mission. In June of that year, an English sailor named **William Richardson,** who had married the daughter of the Presidio *comandante,* erected a tent dwelling and trading post on a hill overlooking Yerba Buena Cove. This inlet on the northeastern shore of the peninsula had long been an anchorage for visiting ships, for it provided both sheltering hills and deep-water mooring close to shore.

The Richardsons improved their homestead with adobe buildings and drew up simple plans for a village called **Yerba Buena** (Spanish for "good herb"). Attracted by the prospect of trade with U.S. whalers and other vessels, more American settlers set up trading posts, hotels, shops and other services. Hides and tallow were the biggest commodities, but the Yankees also began stocking a wider supply of ships' provisions, including sailors' grog. Among the most prominent settlers were Ohio trapper-turned-shopkeeper Jacob Leese; Hawaiian traders Nathan Spear and William Heath; **Sam Brannan**, a business leader and renegade agent of Brigham Young's Church of Latter-day Saints; and **William Leidesdorff**, a mulatto entrepreneur from the West Indies, who served as the first U.S. vice consul and was the town's largest landowner at the time of his death in 1848. The focus of the settlement was the sleepy town plaza, where goats were tethered and sailors and vaqueros from the neighboring ranches slept off their hangovers.

Goaded by impending war with Mexico, politicians in Washington sent adventurer **John C. Frémont**, guided by Kit Carson, to assess (and encourage) local interest in joining the Union. Frémont's efforts bore fruit in 1846 when a party of Yankees in Sonoma declared California's independence from Mexico, establishing it as the **Bear Flag Republic**. Less than one month later, Commodore John Sloat claimed California as American territory at Monterey. On July 9, 1846, 70 U.S. marines and sailors, commanded by Captain John Montgomery, raised the Stars and Stripes above Yerba Buena plaza, renaming it Portsmouth Square.

As real-estate speculation boomed, other amenities followed, including the town's first school and newspaper. **Washington A. Bartlett**, the town's first American *alcalde* (mayor), changed Yerba Buena's name to San Francisco in 1847, a decision he rightly believed would associate the little town with the growing fame of this huge port. Bartlett also hired Irish engineer **Jasper O'Farrell** to draw up a new town plan. O'Farrell laid out rectangular street grids, cut diagonally by the broad thoroughfare of Market Street.

GOLD RUSH BOOMTOWN

Boosters celebrated San Francisco's promising future, but none could have predicted the extraordinary kismet that was shortly to befall it. This fate was unwittingly set in motion by good-natured John Sutter, whose prospering empire in the Sacramento Valley required timber. Dispatched to build a sawmill on the American River in the Sierra Nevada foothills, Sutter's foreman, James Marshall, noticed a glitter of metal in the mill's tailrace on January 24, 1848: it was gold! Sutter tried to keep a tight lid on the discovery, fearful that a rush of prospectors might

"We sailed down the magnificent bay with a light wind, the tide, which was running out, carrying us at the rate of four or five knots… We passed directly under the high cliff on which the Presidio is built, and stood into the middle of the bay, from whence we could see small bays, making up into the interior, on every side; large and beautifully wooded islands; and the mouths of several small rivers. If California ever becomes a prosperous country, this bay will be the centre of its prosperity. The abundance of wood and water, the extreme fertility of its shores, the excellence of its climate, which is as near to being perfect as any in the world, and its facilities for navigation, affording the best anchoring-grounds in the whole west coast of America, all fit it for a place of great importance… "

Richard Henry Dana, *Two Years Before the Mast* (1835)

overwhelm his enterprise. Rumors did leak out, but San Franciscans remained skeptical until May, when Sam Brannan displayed a bottle full of gold dust and nuggets in Portsmouth Square. "Gold!" he cried. "Gold from the American River!" Much of the city emptied as gold-seekers headed for the mines, and in 1849, the first wave of gold-seekers from the outside world—the **Forty-niners**—hit San Francisco.

As thousands of treasure-hungry prospectors stormed ashore, the town exploded within months from a population of 800 into a boomtown serving 90,000 anxious transients. New American shopkeepers and old-time Californios rubbed shoulders with a floating population of men from Mexico, Hawaii, Australia, China, Chile and all the countries of Europe. Tents crowded the slopes of Telegraph and Rincon Hills, and abandoned ships were winched ashore to serve as hotels and warehouses. New buildings rose daily and burned down with alarming frequency: the city center was virtually destroyed by fire six times in four years. After the May 1851 San Francisco Fire (the most destructive before 1906), the business district was rebuilt of masonry.

By 1852 San Francisco had 30,000 residents, a library, restaurants, hotels, churches and hundreds of saloons and gambling halls, and was the fourth-largest harbor city in the U.S. Enthusiastic audiences filled new theaters to cheer stage companies from thousands of miles away. New piers extending into the bay rapidly became obsolete as Yerba Buena Cove was filled to create a new business district. A few speculators, Brannan among them, became millionaires by selling provisions to miners. Crime bred furiously in the manic society as gangs robbed and extorted from the general public. Brannan mobilized vigilante action, prodding frustrated citizens to dole out exile and even lynching to brazen criminals. From their make-shift stronghold popularly known as Fort Gunnybags, a Committee of Vigilance lynched corrupt city councilman James Casey and seized control of the

Stamp commemorating the California Gold Rush of 1849

city, staging torchlight parades, secret trials and summary executions.

Though the crime rate declined, the governor, mayor, legislature, responsible citizens and newspapers spoke out against the militia tactics, and the committee disbanded after two months.

SILVER METROPOLIS

Just as the Gold Rush seemed to be ending, the 1859 discovery of the **Comstock Lode**, a fabulously rich vein of silver at what would soon become Virginia City, Nevada, brought a new boom. As investors' profits flooded San Francisco, ostentatious new millionaires vied to build spectacular mansions on Nob Hill. To provide service to the precipitous slopes, engineer **Andrew Hallidie** developed the **cable car**, which took the city by storm, opening new tracts of steep or remote land for development. By 1890 San Francisco had 21 cable car lines and more than 100 miles of track.

Foremost among city boosters was **William Ralston**, founder and president of the Bank of California. Ralston had resurrected the profitability of the Comstock mines at a point when their fortunes seemed to be failing. With the help of his ambitious agent in Virginia City, William Sharon, Ralston earned millions and used his boundless capital to elevate San Francisco into a world-class city of economic dynamism and cultural refinement. Among the projects that Ralston helped capitalize were Golden Gate Park; the Spring Valley Water Company; the Palace Hotel, largest in the world in its day; and **Adolph Sutro**'s famous tunnel in the Comstock.

City's Victorian houses

© Jon Arnold Images/hemis.fr

San Francisco investors were almost universally convinced that a plan to link the city to the Eastern seaboard by a transcontinental railway would enrich California. So in 1861 an ambitious route was plotted across the treacherous Sierra Nevada by engineer **Theodore Judah**.

An army of laborers, including thousands of Chinese men, laid tracks. Driving eastward to meet the Union Pacific Railway at Promontory Point, Utah, the Central Pacific Railway was financed by a quartet of ambitious and cunning small businessmen in Sacramento: **Leland Stanford**, **Mark Hopkins**, **Collis P. Huntington** and **Charles Crocker**. Known as "the Big Four," they leveraged federal railroad right-of-way grants into a vast empire of real-estate holdings under the auspices of the Southern Pacific Corporation. Reaping vast personal fortunes, the Big Four turned the Southern Pacific into the most powerful political and economic force in the West.

Their power and reach, likened to the inescapable tentacles of an octopus, excited popular, passionate hatred and inspired the well-known proletarian novel by Frank Norris, *The Octopus*.

ON THE WRONG TRACK

But rather than a boon to the state, the transcontinental railway, completed in 1869, proved a bust. Cheap goods from eastern factories flooded California, causing factory closures, unemployment and widespread financial ruin in the 1870s. Overextended by $5 million, William Ralston was forced to close the Bank of California; he was found dead the same day, a probable suicide.

Factory owners cut production costs by hiring Chinese workers at reduced wages, bestowing upon them resentment from the unemployed. As militant labor grew stronger, strikes became common. Anti-Chinese riots spread across the West, bringing violence to San Francisco's Chinatown. Political pressure resulted in the federal Chinese Exclusion Act of 1882, which severely limited Chinese immigration until the act was repealed in 1943. Closed off from protection by the broader society, Chinatown fell prey to the **Tong Wars**, violent power struggles between gangs. Despite an undercurrent of unrest, San Francisco's restaurants, hotels and mansions set the style to which other Western towns of the Victorian period aspired, and fed its reputation as the Paris of the West. Ostentation gilded the lives of the wealthy and infiltrated the flamboyant character of a city that cultivated notoriety as well as distinction. Arts and entertainment flourished in this prosperous and stimulating climate. While the **Barbary Coast**, a rough and licentious neighborhood of gambling clubs, saloons and brothels, thrived at the southern foot of Telegraph Hill, great European opera companies and world-famous stage performers routinely played in the glittering footlights of downtown theaters.

Distinguished writers like Mark Twain, Rudyard Kipling, Robert Louis Stevenson and Oscar Wilde celebrated its unique and rambunctious character in novel and essay. A fledgling bohemian movement, nurtured by Ina Coolbrith, Charles Stoddard, Gellet Burgess and Joaquin Miller, cultivated artistic tastes from ramshackle cottages on Telegraph and Russian hills, and at Miller's retreat in the Oakland hills. Architects A. Page Brown, Bernard Maybeck and Willis Polk cut their teeth on Bay Area projects. Photographer Arnold Genthe set up his studio in the city and began taking pictures of old Chinatown. Home from the mountains, John Muir scribbled the essays that would spark the early American conservation movement.

As in many American cities of the era, corruption crept into San Francisco politics, climaxing under Mayor **Eugene Schmitz**, who was elected to office in 1901. Under the pernicious influence of his adviser **"Boss" Abe Ruef**, Schmitz exchanged favors for bribes, leading to his conviction on 27 charges of graft and bribery in 1906. He was ousted from office the following year.

EARTHQUAKE AND FIRE

On the morning of April 18, 1906, San Franciscans were jolted awake by a massive earthquake on the San Andreas Fault. Residents of most neighborhoods were relieved and even bemused to find the most extensive damage to be fallen chimneys, broken water and gas mains, shattered windows, cracked plaster and smashed crockery. Downtown, however, and in the shoddily built neighborhood south of Market Street, the devastation was frightening. Although the modern skyscrapers had withstood the tremor with flying colors, fissures gaped in the streets and wooden tenement row houses listed dangerously, or lay in ruins. The colonnaded walls of City Hall had fallen away, leaving its mag-nificent dome hovering on a weakened steel frame, the most prominent victim of Abe Ruef's reckless fund-siphoning. The Central Emergency Hospital had collapsed, crushing medical staff and patients. Scores of people were hurt or killed by falling bricks.

By noon, 52 fires were burning with impunity around the city. Unable to restore the water supply, firefighters watched helplessly as the conflagration spread alarmingly through the tenements south of Market Street. Hundreds evacuated by ferry to Oakland, which had survived relatively unscathed. By night, the flames of the burning city lit up the skies around the Bay Area.

Mayor Schmitz hastened to the newly finished Fairmont Hotel atop Nob Hill to form disaster plans. Coordinating with Brigadier General **Frederick Funston**, army troops from the Presidio began patrolling for looters (seven of whom were indeed shot) and dynamiting broad fire lines along Van Ness Avenue. By dawn on April 19, the fire crested Nob Hill, destroying the "hill of palaces" and gutting the Fairmont. Prisoners were moved to Alcatraz, and thousands of refugees streamed westward to makeshift tent camps on the Presidio grounds and in Golden Gate Park.

By the third day, the fire had burned south into the Mission District and clear to the northern wharves. Then the wind changed, pushing the flames back onto themselves. The fire was stopped at Van Ness Avenue, sparing the western half of the city. Some 250,000 people were left homeless and 674 were dead or missing. The city center was destroyed, some 514 blocks of offices, homes, warehouses, factories, saloons, churches, and public buildings. Yet a plucky atmosphere prevailed in the refugee camps.

A PHOENIX FROM THE ASHES

Relief funds poured in from around the world and record-breaking reconstruction proceeded. By 1915, the city was ready to celebrate its recovery. Building an enchanting "city" lit by electrical lights on newly filled land in the Marina District, San Francisco hosted the **Pan-**

ama-Pacific International Exposition, the highest regarded city world's fairs. The momentum of reconstruction culminated in an era of epic civil-engineering projects. The Civic Center was rebuilt on a grand scale in the Beaux-Arts style. Mayor **James "Sunny Jim" Rolph** cleared the way for residential development of the Richmond District by ordering the city's many cemeteries closed and all human remains removed to Colma, south of the city limits. The electric streetcar began replacing the cable car as the premier form of public transport. San Francisco's financial institutions—particularly A.P. Giannini's Bank of Italy (later the Bank of America)—regained the central role in a new California "rush" that outstripped the gold and silver bonanzas of the previous century by capitalizing new farms and agricultural towns and building the state's role as the nation's fruit and vegetable garden.

To secure a dependable source of good water, the city dammed the Tuolumne River at Hetch Hetchy Canyon, 150 miles east in Yosemite National Park, carrying the river water by aqueduct to the Crystal Springs reservoirs on the peninsula. Most spectacularly, in spite of the Great Depression, the city simultaneously built two of the largest bridges in the world—the Bay Bridge, connecting the long-isolated peninsula eastward across the bay to Oakland, and the Golden Gate Bridge north across the Golden Gate to Marin County. To again celebrate its vigor in flamboyant San Francisco style, the city threw another world's fair, the **Golden Gate International Exposition**, which rose on newly completed Treasure Island, the largest artificial island in the world.

Labor problems plagued the city throughout these decades. Springing from resentment against the "robber barons" of the 19C, the 20C labor movement reorganized into an effective, if sometimes corrupt, political force, winning an eight-hour workday and turning San Francisco into a "union town." Labor strikes became a fixture in local politics. Longshoremen staged the largest strike

in American history in 1930, eventually winning better pay after strikebreakers stormed their lines, sparking riots that injured scores and left two dead. The century's most notorious unionist court case was the **Mooney Trial**. A rabble-rousing socialist named Tom Mooney was railroaded through court for a bombing that left ten dead at a parade on the eve of World War I. Found guilty, Mooney was pardoned in 1939 after witnesses admitted they lied under oath.

WAR AND UNEASY PEACE

World War II brought another boom to the Bay Area as shipyards at Hunters Point and Sausalito tooled up for wartime production. Thousands of Japanese-American citizens were rounded up from Bay Area cities and expelled to internment camps. While the army built bunkers and batteries in the Marin Headlands to fend off a Japanese invasion that never came, 1.5 million soldiers, sailors, and marines embarked for the Pacific theater from San Francisco. The population continued to grow after the war, but with most of the new residents settling in Bay Area suburbs, the city began to lose its luster as a commercial hub. As Los Angeles became the manufacturing center of the West Coast, tourism became big business in San Francisco. North Beach became the national focus of a bohemian movement, the Beat Generation, during the 1950s, when nonconformist writers like Jack Kerouac, Allen Ginsberg and Lawrence Ferlinghetti, encouraged by a society tolerant of unconventional behavior, frequented the Italian coffee houses, wrote poetry and "dug the scene." Curious tourists eventually drove the Beats from North Beach but the city generated another bohemian movement in the 1960s, this time in the Haight-Ashbury: Thousands hippies and "flower children" gathered to experiment with drugs, music and libertine society.

The Bay Area soon acquired a national reputation for what some might call political and social idealism, others left-wing radicalism. Huey Newton founded

San Francisco Pride Celebration

the Black Panther Party in Oakland, as neighboring Berkeley, home of the University of California, became a national center of student protest against the Vietnam War and other issues. When thousands of gay men and women moved to San Francisco, the Castro District became the capital of the American gay community. Relaxed immigration laws led to an influx of larger numbers of Asian and Hispanic immigrants, changing the ethnic makeup of the city.

THE NEW MILLENNIUM

Urban problems like homelessness and crime compounded in San Francisco during the 1980s, but the 1990s witnessed a renaissance in many city institutions with the building of the new San Francisco Museum of Modern Art and a new main library, the birth of an arts center at Yerba Buena Gardens, and the refurbishment of City Hall, the War Memorial Opera House, and the California Palace of the Legion of Honor, as well as along the Embarcadero. The burgeoning internet industry took root in San Francisco, with thousands of entrepreneurs and investors exploiting the newly formed medium for financial gain. Many of dotcommers became millionaires before the inevitable crash of 2001, which led to the exodus of some 30,000 people from the city.

The two-term election of Gavin Newsom (2003 and 2007) demonstrated San Franciscans commitment to their progressive politics despite the downturn. A champion of small business and the environment, Newsom authorized the marriage of over 4,000 same-sex partners in 2004, eleven years before the U.S Supreme Court made it the rule of law. When Newsom left San Francisco to take the lieutenant governorship in Sacramento, he was replaced by Edwin Lee, the city's first Asian American mayor, who put a pro-business agenda into action, including generous tax breaks to revitalize the mid-Market area. Unemployment dropped from nearly 9 percent when he took office to 3.1 percent in 2016. On December 12, 2017, Mayor Lee unexpectedly died of cardiac arrest. He was provisionally replaced by San Francisco Board of Supervisors President London Breed, a San Francisco native, who was in 2018 elected mayor in an election that used ranked-choice ballots, a first for San Francisco. With tech on the rise in the city again, one of the main challenges for Mayor Breed's administration is the lack of affordable housing for city residents.

Architecture

San Franciscans are well known for their warm embrace of new cultures, attitudes and ideas, and that goes for art and architecture too. While there is a bedrock of tradition, San Francisco artists are eager to innovate. And judging by the number of performances and exhibits on any given night, audiences are equally eager to devour the outcome.

The oldest major U.S. city west of the Rockies, San Francisco revels in examples of many eras and styles of buildings. The city's built environment has been shaped by various entrepreneurial, artistic and political forces, all of which have contributed to its distinctive architectural legacy. San Francisco's role as a commercial and financial nexus continues to attract new and innovative forms of architecture.

NATIVE AMERICANS AND THE MISSION PERIOD

Before the arrival of Europeans, many small Ohlone and Miwok communities dotted the shores of San Francisco Bay. The natives lived in cone-shaped structures made of reeds and trees lashed together. As these natural building materials had a limited life span, no constructions remain from this era, although archeologists have recorded scores of shell mounds marking village sites around the bay shore, as well as acorn-grinding rocks in oak woodlands where the native peoples made seasonal camps comprising many dwellings.

The earliest extant structures in the Bay Area date from the mission period. The center of each mission community was a simple church and monastery, built of thick walls of whitewashed adobe capped by gabled red-tile roofs, supported upon heavy rough-hewn timbers. Spanish friars designed the missions along classical lines, using elements such as pilasters, niches and arcades to embellish the exteriors, and ornate reredos, tiled floors and colorful frescoes to ornament the interior spaces. Much of the interest in mission decoration comes from the folk-art flavors imparted by the Native American laborers who did the construction work. San Francisco's oldest building, the chapel at Mission Dolores, remains the finest example of the architecture of this period, while the surrounding Bay Area holds a variety of others, most notably the well-preserved mission and town plaza of Sonoma.

THE VICTORIAN ERA

From 1860 to 1900, as wealth poured into the city from the gold mines and the silver deposits of Nevada's Comstock Lode, San Francisco's downtown commercial district grew in stature. Grand hotels were constructed to house visitors to the burgeoning metropolis, the most opulent of which was the Palace Hotel, completed in 1875. The U.S. Mint, now called the Old Mint, was built nearby around the same time. By the 1890s, Chicago School office towers such as the Mills Building and the Chronicle Building had begun to rise along the bustling streets. The landmark Ferry Building was begun in 1894, and the Victorian era also saw the construction of elaborate resorts, most notably the second Cliff House and the now-ruined Sutro Baths complex near Seal Rocks on the city's Pacific shoreline.

The best-known and most enduring legacies of the Victorian era remain the many blocks of homes erected in the distinctive sub-styles of this romantic period. Throughout Pacific Heights, Haight-Ashbury, the Castro District and other residential neighborhoods, streets are lined with abundantly decorated wooden houses, most of them built between 1870 and 1906. Using redwood, fir, and pine lumber from the dense forests of the northern California coast, contractors could produce homes quickly and inexpensively for San Francisco's burgeoning middle class. Closely crowded on narrow lots and built to standardized floor plans, these houses were adorned with an almost endless catalog of decorative sidings, elaborately milled

Italianate Style

Queen Anne

moldings and bay windows with carved frames. Some were accented with fanciful turrets, false gables and intricate art-glass windows.

Most Victorian homes were designed not by architects but by home owners, builders and property developers. They often followed general principles laid down by "pattern books" that outlined design precepts of each of the main Victorian "styles." Most prevalent in San Francisco were **Italianate** (1860–80), marked by Neoclassical ornament and pedimented false gables; **Stick** or Eastlake (1870–90), epitomized by comparatively flat wall surfaces and more angular, geometric forms; and **Queen Anne** (1870–1906), the most free-form and asymmetrical of the Victorian styles, often incorporating corner towers, turrets and a sometimes-frenzied variety of wall sidings, all on the same facade. The free spirit of these "painted ladies"—so called because, though once mainly gray, they had flamboyant color schemes

applied—has captured the fancy of visitors and locals alike. Thousands of Victorian homes march up and down San Francisco's streets, imposing a distinctive and colorful stamp on the city's architectural signature. One of them has been preserved for public viewing: the imposing Queen Anne-style Haas-Lilienthal House in eastern Pacific Heights.

The latter part of the Victorian era saw the emergence of the **Arts and Crafts** movement, which in San Francisco brought together a loose grouping of artists and architects interested in the bohemian, "back-to-nature" teachings of local preacher Joseph Worcester. The Swedenborgian Church epitomizes the movement's rustic approach to architecture, adapted by such diverse and prolific architects as A. Page Brown, Willis Polk, Ernest Coxhead and Bernard Maybeck, all of whom built numerous residences around the Bay Area. Using dark-stained shingles of redwood lumber and creating innovative spatial arrangements that took advantage of the picturesque topography and mild climate, these architects satisfied a Bay Area taste for cultivated rusticity.

THE CITY BEAUTIFUL

At the turn of the 20C, San Francisco's civic government considered altering the city's layout along the lines of an ambitious plan proposed by Chicago architect Daniel Burnham. **The Burnham Plan** called for wide boulevards and Baroque public spaces like those of Paris or Washington DC, ideals

Stick Style

at the forefront of the Beaux-Arts-inspired "City Beautiful" movement. The earthquake and fire of 1906 left a clean canvas upon which to implement Burnham's ideas, but urgency propelled the rebuilding of the city according to its previous layout. The only aspect of the Burnham Plan to be constructed after the earthquake was the new Civic Center. This monumental rectangle of libraries, theaters and other public buildings, centered upon the landmark Baroque-style dome of City Hall, forms a grand, dignified public space.

Some of San Francisco's most impressive commercial buildings, including the Bank of California and the grand Fairmont Hotel, date from the post-earthquake period, as do many of the mansions of Pacific Heights. The city's main architectural gesture of recovery was the **Panama-Pacific International Exposition of 1915**, which filled the reclaimed lands of the modern Marina District with a celebratory fairground of eclectic architecture. The sole survivor is Bernard Maybeck's stately Palace of Fine Arts. Across the bay, the Neoclassical campus buildings of the University of California, Berkeley, were erected by John Galen Howard and others, including Julia Morgan.

The growing economy of the 1920s supported another building boom in the Financial District. The city's first skyscrapers sprouted at the end of that decade, including Timothy Pflueger's Art-Deco PacBell Building, the Mayan-style tower at Four Fifty Sutter, and George Kelham's 31-story, Gothic-style Russ Building, then the tallest on the West Coast.

DEPRESSION AND POSTWAR ERA

Commercial construction slowed considerably during the Great Depression. Following World War II, San Francisco underwent a long period of suburbanization, with freeways constructed to reach new tract-housing suburbs of the outlying Bay Area. Through the late 1950s and early 60s, urban renewal

caused the demolition of vast tracts of older buildings, in turn inspiring a movement to preserve the city's architecture. At the same time, a rash of new construction in the Financial District transformed the city's skyline. The first distinctive new project was the 1959 Crown Zellerbach Building, now One Bush Street, an International-style glass box supported on piers above a paved plaza. More skyscrapers continued to be built, culminating in the city's two tallest—Skidmore, Owings & Merrill's monolithic Bank of America, in 1971, and William Pereira's unique Transamerica Pyramid, in 1972.

Public outcry against the pace of growth, which critics claimed had "Manhattanized" the attractive city skyline, resulted in stringent planning controls encoded in the **Downtown Plan** of 1985. This put a cap on the amount of square footage of new construction permitted in the Financial District and effectively shifted future growth to the less densely developed area South of Market.

CONTEMPORARY ARCHITECTURE

Recent years have brought a number of internationally renowned architects to design projects in San Francisco and the Bay Area, among them Philip Johnson, Mario Botta, Daniel Libeskind, James Ingo Freed and Michael Graves, whose signature contemporary take on the Classical style may be seen at Clos Pegase Winery in the Napa Valley. San Francisco has witnessed a renaissance in public architecture through major projects like the expanded Moscone Convention Center and the adjacent Yerba Buena Gardens. In 1995, Botta's new home for the San Francisco Museum of Modern Art opened, followed in 1996 by Freed's striking new San Francisco Public Library at Civic Center. Herzog & de Meuron's copper-clad de Young Museum, unveiled in 2005, is one of the most daring buildings in decades, rivaled by Renzo Piano's California Academy of Sciences, opened in 2008 with a "Green Roof" of 1.7 million native plants.

Visual Arts

The visual arts of San Francisco reflect the history, diversity and excitement of the entire Bay Area, making it one of the art capitals of the American West.

EARLY ARTISTIC LANDSCAPE

San Francisco's rich, multilayered art history began with the Ohlone, Wintun and Coast Miwok Indians, who maintained a beautiful ceremonial culture. Today, baskets produced by native Californians are treasured for their geometric designs and precise weaving; many are on view at the Oakland Museum of California and other collections.

Mission Dolores stands as the primary reminder of the city's Mexican period: Walls and ceilings of the old chapel reveal replicas of beautiful geometric patterns designed by native artisans. The population explosion during and after the Gold Rush introduced European values and aesthetics. Important pioneer artists began visiting San Francisco, including landscape painters Albert Bierstadt and William Keith. Early photographers Carleton Watkins and Eadweard Muybridge (who helped settle a bet about horse racing with his groundbreaking photographic studies of animal locomotion) paved the way for one of the area's most enduring obsessions. The San Francisco Art Association, precursor of today's San Francisco Museum of Modern Art, was founded in 1871 by members Bierstadt, Keith, Muybridge and others to display art publicly and offer classes. Railroad magnates Leland Stanford and Mark Hopkins assembled major collections of European art in the late 19C.

In the early 20C, important developments in the arts took root in San Francisco, including the California **Arts and Crafts** movement in painting, furniture and decorative arts, led by Arthur and Lucia Matthews. **Tonalist** painting, incorporating the colors of the city's distinctive foggy palette, was exemplified by Gottardo Piazonni and Xavier Martinez. Following the influential Panama-Pacific International Exhibition of 1915, where works by European and New York modernists were displayed at the Palace of Fine Arts, an explosion of color appeared in the work of Bay Area painters Clayton S. Price and Selden Gile. The latter was a member of the **Society of Six**, an informal association of artists who practiced a painterly, figurative style during the 1920s. In the 20s and 30s, several artists of Japanese and Chinese ancestry blended aspects of Asian art traditions with Western practices to create innovative Asian-American styles.

Photographers Ansel Adams, Edward Weston, Imogen Cunningham and others founded the **Group f.64** in 1932 and exhibited together the following year. Reacting against the blurred-focus work of their "pictorialist" contemporaries, they embraced a sharp-focus, "precisionist" depiction of forms and textures. Social themes characteristic of the Great Depression are movingly rendered in the works of painter Maynard Dixon and his wife, photographer Dorothea Lange, as well as in pieces by African-American sculptor Sargent Johnson.

Diego Rivera made repeated visits to the city with his wife, Frida Kahlo, during the 1930s; the Mexican muralist executed several works here, engendering mural projects by other artists in public locations across the city.

ABSTRACT AND FIGURATIVE

After World War II, Clyfford Still and Mark Rothko of the San Francisco Art Institute inspired an explosion of abstract expressionist painting by their students, including Sam Francis and Robert Motherwell. Painters Elmer Bischoff, Richard Diebenkorn and David Park responded with a representational movement known as **Bay Area Figurative**, a motif that Berkeley-based painter Joan Brown and sculptor Manuel Neri later personalized. Beat culture and Zen philosophy helped inspire the work of individualists like Bruce Conner, William Wiley and Jay de Feo. Popular culture of the 1960s is recorded in the work of painters Wayne Thiebaud and Robert Bechtle. The lat-

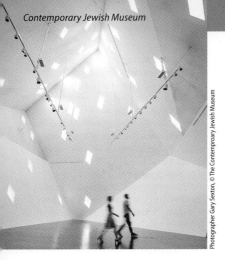

Photographer Gary Sexton, © The Contemporary Jewish Museum

ter counterculture movement also saw unique developments in poster art around Haight-Ashbury, as the cartoon art of R. Crumb and others gained worldwide exposure.

Artists working in craft media have continued to challenge the boundaries of their materials—ceramists Robert Arneson, Viola Frey and Peter Voulkos are known internationally, and textile-based sculptors Kay Sekimachi and Ruth Asawa have helped redefine their medium. Asawa is also the creator of fountains at Ghirardelli Square and at the Grand Hyatt Hotel near Union Square. Sculptor Beniamino Bufano created a menagerie of rounded and evocative animal forms and symbolic human figures that populate city parks and public squares.

THE CONTEMPORARY SCENE

Today, the greatly expanded San Francisco Museum of Modern Art is dedicated to showcasing works by Bay Area artists along with cutting-edge works by international artists. Exhibits at the nearby Yerba Buena Center for the Arts, The Contemporary Jewish Museum, and Gagosian Gallery continue to bring new art to the public eye, as do thrice-yearly Open Studios, when galleries and artists' studios citywide hold open houses.

The city has a high concentration of nonprofit spaces and artist cooperatives, including S.F. Camerawork, Artists' Television Access, Hunters Point Studios, Galeria de la Raza, the Minnesota Street Project, Southern Exposure, The Kadist Art Foundation and the Headlands Center for the Arts in Marin County. Commercial galleries, many of them clustered in near Union Square, present a range of contemporary and historical art. Worth looking into are Hang, John Berggruen, Gallery Wendi Norris and Fraenkel Gallery, located within blocks of one another. The work of performance and conceptual artists such as Guillermo Gomez-Pena, painters Enrique Chagoya and Oliver Jackson, muralists Juana Alicia and Daniel Galvez, and photographers Richard Misrach and Linda Connor continue to infuse the city's arts with new ideas and vitality.

"The Mission School" of young artists, a term invented by the San Francisco Bay Guardian to describe the avant garde in the 1990s and 2000s, include such influential new-gen artists as Margaret Kilgallen, Barry McGee, Clare Rojas, and Rigo 23. You can still frequently find their work in contemporary San Francisco galleries.

CINEMA

San Francisco's quirky film history began in 1872 when Eadweard Muybridge, a Bay Area photographer, put together a rapid succession of still photographs to prove that a running horse at one period of his stride has all four feet off the ground. Through the 20C the film industry flourished here as directors from Erich von Stroheim to John Huston to Alfred Hitchcock to Francis Ford Coppola used San Francisco's glorious cityscapes as the backdrop for numerous productions. Fisherman's Wharf, Lombard Street, the Presidio and Pacific Heights have all served as film sets at one time or another. The San Francisco Film Commission is charged with developing policies and incentives to keep the city attractive to production companies; since 2006, over 400 films or television series were partially or completely shot here, including *Memoirs of a Geisha* (2005), *Contagion* (2011), *Blue Jasmine* (2013), *Ant Man* (2015), *San Andreas (2015)* and *Steve Jobs* (2016).

Performing Arts

Famed for its cultural diversity, San Francisco has always been a hotbed for the performing arts. A city of immigrants, it has nurtured the European traditions of opera, symphony and ballet while making room for Chinese opera, Latin jazz and ethnic dance. A haven for nonconformists, it has been the birthplace of new strains of rock-and-roll music and postmodern dance.

OPERA

Of all the musical arts, opera is the one that has most enduringly won a place in San Francisco's heart. Even when the city was but a small, gritty mining outpost, luxuriant operas were staged on a regular basis in some of the most sumptuous theaters in the nation. Beginning with Bellini's *La Somnabula* in 1851, some 5,000 operatic performances were given by more than 20 companies prior to the 1906 earthquake.

In 1923 pianist-producer Gaetano Merola founded the **San Francisco Opera** with a production of *La Bohème*. It was not until 1934, though, that the company christened the War Memorial Opera House, its permanent home, with a performance of Puccini's *Tosca*. The company has presented such greats as Luciano Pavarotti, Angela Gheorghiu and Birgit Nilsson. Smaller companies such as the Lamplighters, a Gilbert and Sullivan company formed in 1952, and Pocket Opera, a troupe that has performed classic works in English since 1968, illustrate opera's mass appeal with their inventive, accessible productions.

CLASSICAL MUSIC

San Francisco's taste for orchestral music is well established. Founded in 1911, the **San Francisco Symphony Orchestra** hosted the adolescent debuts of violinists Yehudi Menuhin (1926) and Isaac Stern (1936) and developed a repertory rooted in the classical and romantic traditions. However, with the 1995 installation of Leonard Bernstein protégé Michael Tilson Thomas as its director, the symphony has undergone a renaissance. Tilson Thomas has challenged his musicians and his audiences with an array of difficult, under-recognized 20C masterpieces by Copland, Debussy, Varese and onetime Bay Area composers Lou Harrison and Darius Milhaud.

Among chamber-music groups, the **Kronos Quartet**, founded in San Francisco in 1977, stands out for crystallizing the city's ethos of experimentation and fun with its original, often-playful arrangements of contemporary works. The male choir **Chanticleer**, a full-time classical a cappella group, has performed an eclectic array of new and ancient music since its inception in 1978, including rare Renaissance choral pieces, vocal jazz and gospel.

JAZZ AND ROCK

San Francisco and Oakland enjoyed a brief flowering as jazz hubs in the 1940s and 50s. Breaking from the Dixieland tradition parlayed locally by Crescent City musicians, Bay Area native Dave Brubeck pioneered a new sound, characterized by syncopated rhythms, percussive piano and classical song structures. Brubeck's runaway success with his albums for Fantasy, a local label, made San Francisco one of the world centers for jazz recording. In the 1990s, a "new jazz" style, grounded in bebop but inflected by rock and funk,

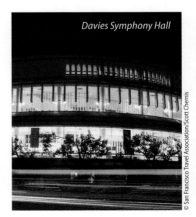

Davies Symphony Hall

© San Francisco Travel Association/Scott Chernis

developed by younger San Franciscans, most notably guitarist Charlie Hunter. Today, the best place to experience jazz is at the SFJAZZ Center in Hayes Valley. San Francisco's place in the rock-and-roll canon was clinched in the 1960s when local bands the Grateful Dead, Jefferson Airplane and Big Brother and the Holding Company (featuring Janis Joplin) wrote the soundtrack for a decade of political protest and cultural revolution. Free concerts in Golden Gate Park and all-night jam sessions at the Family Dog, Fillmore and Avalon ballrooms drew thousands to hear what became known as the **San Francisco Sound**. In the 1970s political folk singers like Joan Baez and bands like Country Joe and the Fish emerged. Crooner Chris Isaak, whose stylish music has been described as rhythm-and-blues with roots in country and folk, burst onto the scene in the late 1980s. Around the same time, a hardcore punk scene coalesced around Jello Biafra's Dead Kennedys, leading the way for a punk-pop explosion in the East Bay that hurtled the band **Green Day** to platinum status in the 90s. Today's popular Bay Area bands include Counting Crows, Third Eye Blind, Train and Michael Franti.

THEATER

Demonstrating its flair for the dramatic, San Francisco has always supported the theater. In the 1850s, 22 of Shakespeare's 38 plays were staged, but circus acts and minstrel shows were equally popular. In the 1860s some of the most sumptuous playhouses in the nation were built here as Barbary Coast melodeons were gaining a toehold. Audacious local stars like Lola Montez, Adah Isaacs Menken and Lotta Crabtree achieved mythic status. Once the transcontinental railroad was completed in 1869, San Francisco became a must-stop on the national touring circuit but it was not until the mid-20C, that it regained a strong local theater community. In 1951 San Francisco State University professors Jules Irving and Herbert Blau founded the

Actors' Workshop, introducing the works of Harold Pinter, Samuel Beckett and Edward Albee to local audiences. The **San Francisco Mime Troupe** was founded in 1959 and now travels the world with its self-styled political satires. In 1967, actor and director William Ball established the **American Conservatory Theater** (ACT), today considered one of the best regional theaters and drama schools in the U.S. Over 100 professional companies mount everything from the local camp classic *Beach Blanket Babylon* to Shakespeare, and SHN presents traveling Broadway tours.

DANCE

Second only to New York in the diversity and quality of its troupes, San Francisco is at the forefront of classical and modern dance in the U.S. Founded in 1933, the **San Francisco Ballet** is the oldest resident classical ballet company in the U.S. The ballet presented the first full-length American productions of such classics as Tchaikovsky's *Swan Lake* and *The Nutcracker,* in addition to a repertoire of 20C works by George Balanchine, Jerome Robbins and resident choreographers like Lew Christensen. Other notable local troupes are Smuin Ballet and Alonzo King LINES Ballet. In the East Bay, the Oakland Ballet is known for reviving classic 20C ballets by Vaslav Nijinsky and others. Modern dance is also well established in San Francisco. One of its foremothers, Isadora Duncan, was born here in 1877, though she spent most of her life abroad and performed in the city only twice. Anna Halprin emerged in the late 1950s as an influential choreographer; her explorations of ritual, physicality and the creative process sparked groundbreaking postmodern work in the 1960s. Today, ODC, Margaret Jenkins, Robert Moses' Kin, and Joe Goode Performance Group masterfully combine dance with theater and live music, and dance companies explore everything from butoh and belly dancing to flamenco and capoeira.

Literature

Born in the wake of the Gold Rush, San Francisco's literary tradition began as a torrent of local magazines and newspapers that has since broadened and expanded. Today a host of renowned and up-and-coming journalists, novelists and poets make the city their home and source of inspiration.

THE GOLDEN FIFTIES AND SILVER SIXTIES

Legendary Mormon entrepreneur Sam Brannan founded San Francisco's first major newspaper, the *California Star,* in 1847. By the mid-1850s San Francisco boasted a dozen dailies and nearly 40 weeklies—more publications than in London at the time. While most of these were political organs or advertisers, they also encouraged some of the city's literary voices. Nearly every paper carved out room for a "poet's corner" on the front page, thereby nurturing the talents of miner-bards such as Alonzo Delano and John Rollin Ridge, who wrote under the noms-de-plume Old Block and Yellow Bird, respectively.

Through the 1860s, literary journals such as *The Pioneer,* the *Golden Era, The Californian* and the *Overland Monthly* flourished, as did the unconventional culture that aided and abetted them. Bret Harte and Joaquin Miller drew from their experiences working in mining towns for their early essays, short stories and poems. Others, like Ina Coolbrith and Charles Stoddard, found inspiration in nature and the emotions. Ambrose Bierce and Mark Twain made their reputations writing irreverent satires and burlesques. As the decade wore on, Bierce grew increasingly misanthropic and cynical, earning himself the nickname "Bitter Bierce" by becoming a vociferous champion of suicide and attacking progressive issues such as women's suffrage and the eight-hour workday. Twain, on the other hand, sharpened his skills and applied them to the picaresque fiction that would later assure his place in the American literary canon.

During the financial depression of the 1870s, many publications foundered and talents such as Harte, Miller, Twain, Bierce and Stoddard relocated elsewhere. A steady stream of writers came through the city in the next couple of decades, however. Poet Robert Frost was born in 1874 near the Embarcadero and lived there 11 years; Robert Louis Stevenson wrote in a flat near Union Square in 1879 and 1880; and in the late 1880s British Indian writer Rudyard Kipling tried, unsuccessfully, to publish his stories in the city's major journals. Across the bay Gertrude Stein lived in Oakland from 1880 to 1891 before going east to Radcliffe College and subsequently founding her salon in Paris. Of the 1860s bohemians, only Ina Coolbrith remained in San Francisco, hosting literary salons and encouraging the next generation of writers in their pursuits.

SOCIAL REALISM

One of Coolbrith's many acolytes, Jack London wrote in the tradition of Twain and Harte, using his adventures to fuel his fiction. And like many writers of his time, London addressed larger social and philosophical issues in his work. His story "South of the Slot" contains a sharp critique of class differences in San Francisco (the title refers to Market Street, which once sharply divided the rich from the poor). London's contemporary, Frank Norris, also saw contradictions in San Francisco society; his acclaimed naturalistic novel *McTeague* (1899), set in the Polk Gulch area, explores such themes as greed and social Darwinism from the point of view of a beleaguered dentist. Taking a different tack, poet George Sterling wrote torrid romantic poems and famously described the city as a "cool, grey city of love." Other writers and artists of the era belonged to the fun-loving group Les Jeunes (the Young Ones), which published its work in *The Lark* (1895–97), "a magazine of humorous anarchy." Most members of Les Jeunes did their best-known work after the group's breakup, although founder

City Lights Bookstore, North Beach

© San Francisco Travel Association/Scott Chernis

Gellett Burgess remains famous for his frivolous poem "The Purple Cow," which appeared in *The Lark*.

From 1920 to 1929 crime writer Dashiell Hammett made San Francisco his home; the fog-cloaked slopes of Nob Hill provided a noir backdrop for the nighttime ramblings of Sam Spade, Hammett's hard-boiled detective hero of *The Maltese Falcon*. John Steinbeck also lived in the city in the late 1920s, although he drew from the environs of nearby Salinas and Monterey for his acclaimed novels *East of Eden* and *Cannery Row*.

BEAT HAPPENING

In the 1950s San Francisco underwent a literary renaissance as the Beat Generation came of age in North Beach. From the early to mid-1950s, Jack Kerouac churned out more than a dozen books about wanderlust, love and longing. Kerouac typed *On the Road* as one very long paragraph in 20 days of April 1951; upon publication in 1957, the book catapulted him and his Beat Generation cohorts to fame. According to poet and City Lights bookstore founder Lawrence Ferlinghetti: "The emergence of the Beat Generation made North Beach *the* literary center of SF—and it nurtured a new vision that would spread far beyond its bounds." Poet Allen Ginsberg, one of that vision's most articulate proponents, gave birth to the San Francisco poetry renaissance in 1955 when he read his poem "Howl" (first published by City Lights) to a standing-room-only audience in the Marina District.

In 1960 and 1961 Ken Kesey wrote *One Flew Over the Cuckoo's Nest*, his best-seller about a mental institution, from his home in Palo Alto. Journalist Tom Wolfe captured the psychedelic counterculture in his 1969 book *The Electric Kool-Aid Acid Test*. In the 1970s Armistead Maupin followed the lives of young drifters in his long-running *San Francisco Chronicle* column, later published as the book *Tales of the City*. Before he died of AIDS in 1994, *Chronicle* journalist Randy Shilts *(And the Band Played On)* gained renown in writing about city politics, gay liberation and the AIDS epidemic. For six decades until his death in 1997, Pulitzer Prize-winning *Chronicle* columnist Herb Caen entertained a huge and faithful following of avid readers with his witty blend of gossip and news about the city he loved. Today the San Francisco Bay Area boasts a wide range of resident writers, including Amy Tan *(The Joy Luck Club)*, Alice Walker *(The Color Purple)*, Dave Eggers *(A Heartbreaking Work of Staggering Genius)*, Lemony Snicket *(A Series of Unfortunate Events)*, Michael Pollan *(The Omnivore's Dilemma)*, Rebecca Solnit *(Men Explain Things to Me)* and regular public readings by local novelists, essayists and poets.

Nature

San Francisco boasts an incomparable setting of mountains, hills and water at the tip of a long peninsula forming the western boundary of a 496-square-mile bay. Its dramatic topography, its agreeable climate and the pervasive presence of the sea have invited exploration and provided enjoyment for centuries. San Francisco Bay itself was immensely important in the city's early development as the commercial and cultural hub of the western United States.

LANDSCAPE

The hills and valleys that characterize San Francisco and the Bay Area form part of the **Coast Ranges**, a low but rugged belt of mountains extending from Santa Barbara County north to Oregon. Prominent Bay Area summits include **Mt. Tamalpais** (2,571ft), which looms over Marin County to the north; **Mt. Diablo** (3,849ft), which backdrops the hills of Oakland to the east; and **Mt. Hamilton** (4,213ft), which lies southeast of the city near San Jose. Peaks within the city include Mt. Davidson (929ft), Twin Peaks (922ft and 904ft) and Mt. Sutro (908ft).

San Francisco's owes its famed steep streets to surveyor Jasper O'Farrell, who in 1847 laid out a perpendicular street grid in keeping with the standards of the day. The result: byways that abruptly ascend a hill, crest, then plummet vertiginously down the other side. Several commanding hilltops remained squatter settlements until the invention of the cable car made it possible for the well-to-do to get up and down. Later development in the region took topography into account, so that in Berkeley, Oakland and other Bay Area towns, most streets sensibly follow the natural contours of the land.

The great **San Francisco Bay** bisects the Coast Ranges, serving not only as a coastal inlet but as an estuary through which the rivers draining the western slope of the Sierra Nevada and the plains of the Central Valley join and pass to the sea. The bay itself submerges a large, northwest/southeast-running valley that would have been visible 20,000 years ago when a vast amount of water was frozen in continental glaciers.

AN UNSTABLE FOUNDATION

The Bay Area lies atop a complex system of tectonic faults created by the motion of the Pacific and North American plates, giant solidified sections of the earth's crust that move about atop the molten material of the earth's mantle. The two plates slide past each other at an average speed of two inches per year. Movements along faults occur frequently and, under normal conditions, impercepti-

Mount Diablo, looking towards west

© yhelfman/iStockphoto.com

bly. Occasionally, however, the slide is impeded by rigid material, and pressure increases as the plates strain to move. When the obstruction gives way, the pent-up pressure is released in a sudden lurch, accompanied by shuddering and trembling known as an **earthquake**.

The most notorious fault is the **San Andreas Rift Zone**, extending from the Imperial Valley in southeastern California to Cape Mendocino on the north coast, passing en route beneath the seabed west of San Francisco. Along the San Francisco Peninsula, the long valley of the Crystal Springs reservoirs just west of Interstate 280, marks the zone, as does the valley that separates Point Reyes from the rest of Marin County. In the famous 1906 earthquake, more than 16ft of movement occurred along this fault in a few seconds. Another major quake, with its epicenter in the Santa Cruz Mountains near San Jose, occurred on this fault in 1989.

The San Andreas Fault is the best known in this shear zone. Most ominous is the Hayward Fault, which runs along the base of the Oakland and Berkeley hills, an area that has become densely populated since its last major earthquake.

CLIMATE

San Francisco's cool, dry summers and mild, wet winters are characteristic of a Mediterranean climate—accentuated by the peculiarities of the city's location. The Sierra Nevada mountains to the east block frigid air masses that sweep across the rest of the United States.

The Pacific Ocean has a regulating effect on temperature extremes: San Francisco registers the lowest mean summer temperature of any city in the U.S. outside of Alaska, and rarely sees a winter frost. Snow has accumulated in the downtown area only twice in the city's recorded history.

Although seasonal temperature variation is remarkably slight, weather within the city—and throughout the Bay Area—is greatly affected by microclimates that result from the hilly topography. The dip of a mountain ridge or change in proximity to the ocean can create pronounced variations in weather between neighborhoods; temperatures may vary as much as 35°F between coast and inland areas. The staggered ridges of the Coast Ranges confine the chilling effect of the Pacific to a rather narrow frontage along the coast.

One of the principal factors in San Francisco's cool summers is the city's renowned **fog**, created when westerly winds, laden with moisture from the Pacific, cross the cold California Current. The moisture condenses, creating dramatic rivers and banks of fog that invade the city from the west, turning a brilliant day into a gloomy one within minutes. This "advection fog" often forms a dense layer that hugs the ground and leaves higher elevations clear. In summer, fog typically builds during the day over the coast, then pours over the hills and through the Golden Gate, shrouding the Sunset District and other coastal areas in a dense gray mist while leaving other neighborhoods with blue skies.

Most rain falls between November and April. In summer, atmospheric circulation creates a cell of high pressure that deflects fronts and storms into the Pacific Northwest. In winter, the high-pressure cell moves south and allows storms in, bringing rain, sometimes for days on end. In recent years, Mother Nature has thrown a wrench into the equation. Since 2012, drought has led to record-breaking warm and dry weather.

FLORA AND FAUNA

As with the human population, much of the Bay Area's plant life originated elsewhere. The grasses that shroud the "golden hills" are mostly European wild oats, seeds of which stowed away in bags of wheat sent to Spanish missions. The eucalyptus trees that perfume many a park, campus and backyard were imported from Australia in the 1860s. Most palms in the Bay Area come from the Canary Islands and other places.

Indigenous features of the plant landscape include stately **live oaks**, which grow widely spaced on grassy hillsides. Coast redwoods, which live more than 2,000 years and grow to heights above 300ft, thrive near the ocean.

Also typical of Bay Area landscapes are dense thickets of **chaparral**, formed not of a single plant but of an association of native species. The shrubby plants grow during wet winters then dry out in late summer, a perfect fuel for brush fires that periodically sweep over the hills. The plants then grow back quickly from burls below ground level.

The Bay Area's salt marshes, mud flats, beaches, tidepools and baywaters are home to a vast array of native **wildlife** species. The rocky coastal areas harbor sea lions, seals and sea otters while dolphins and porpoises frolic offshore. Humpback, gray and blue whales and orcas swim by on annual migrations, and the region lies on the Pacific Flyway, a north–south route for migratory birds. The demise of wildlife habitats, thanks to urban development and a number of disastrous oil spills by passing tankers, has given rise to public and private organizations dedicated to preserving species at risk. The **San Francisco Bay National Wildlife Refuge Complex** administers seven refuges, including the 30,000-acre Don Edwards Refuge in South San Francisco Bay. **Año Nuevo State Reserve** in San Mateo County protects a rookery of northern elephant seals. Rescue organizations such as the Marin Headlands' **Marine Mammal Center** concentrate efforts on rehabilitating injured animals and returning them to the wild.

Elephant seals, Año Nuevo State Reserve

© JasonDoiy/iStockphoto.com

Golden Gate Bridge
© Robert Harding/hemis.fr

Contrary to its laidback image, San Francisco has a bustling and vibrant downtown area. The Financial District ranks among the largest business centers in the nation and is an increasingly important locus for the tech industry. The city's retail heart, Union Square, is packed with department stores and high-end boutiques. The elegant Beaux Arts-style Civic Center draws city government workers by day and chicly clad concertgoers by evening. Chinatown teems with tiny temples, outdoor markets and dim sum restaurants; just above it, Nob Hill retains its Old World charm and upper class cachet. To the north, lively North Beach boasts a history filled with Italian heritage and literary greats.

Highlights

1 Stroll down lively Chinatown's **Grant Avenue** (p67)

2 Explore the fine **Asian Art Museum** with an audio tour (p76)

3 Sip a cocktail with a view atop Nob Hill at **Top of the Mark** (p95)

4 Browse **City Lights Books** and lounge in a **North Beach cafe** (p97, p103)

5 Climb parrot-filled steps to mural-adorned **Coit Tower** (p100, p102)

The Changing Face of Downtown

In 1846 Captain John Montgomery officially claimed the small settlement of Yerba Buena for the U.S., raising an American flag at Yerba Buena's central plaza. This plaza, later renamed Portsmouth Square after Montgomery's ship, now rests in the heart of San Francisco's downtown, on the border of Chinatown, the Financial District and North Beach. During the 19C California Gold Rush, these neighborhoods boomed, drawing thousands of treasure hunters who ventured up toward Sutter's Mill in search of gold.

The face of downtown changed drastically in 1906, when a massive earthquake and fire razed the district. By 1909, the area was largely reconstructed, with many of the new buildings showing off the Classical style. Today, Chinatown teems with ethnic eateries, old world pharmacies and outdoor produce markets. In North Beach, the flavors and fragrances of the neighborhood's Italian roots still predominate, as evidenced by dozens of well-patronized trattorias, cafes and delicatessens.

West of the Financial District and Chinatown, Nob Hill also changed after the 1906 disaster, with decimated mansions of San Francisco's elite replaced by posh hotels. Today, residential Nob Hill is peppered with upscale restaurants, apartment buildings, and several of the city's most historic hotels.

Retail and Civic Centers

The first place any self-respecting shopper heads in San Francisco is Union Square, the area bordering the formal park of the same name. Named on the eve of the Civil War, Union Square lies at the center of the city's ritziest retail district. The Westin St. Francis Hotel presides over its western edge, with upscale department stores Saks, Macy's and Neiman Marcus completing the square.

Up Market Street from Union Square, San Francisco's Civic Center remains the sole remnant of a 1905 plan to remake San Francisco according to the principles of the City Beautiful movement—replete with wide boulevards and grand monuments that borrowed heavily from the aesthetics of the then—contemporary Beaux Arts movement. Among the movement's crowning achievements, San Francisco's magnificent City Hall stands out with its sparkling gold-leaf dome. This area is also home to several of the city's grandest performance spaces and cultural institutions, including the San Francisco War Memorial and Performing Arts Center, the gleaming granite San Francisco Public Library, and the stellar Asian Art Museum.

Chinatown★★★

A colorful fusion of Cantonese market town and American Main Street, San Francisco's Chinatown spreads along the lower slope of Nob Hill overlooking the Financial District. One of the largest Chinese settlements outside Asia and the first in North America, Chinatown ranks among the country's most densely populated neighborhoods. Over 100,000 people live in the 24-block core bounded by Broadway and Montgomery, California and Powell Streets. Many residents are immigrants who maintain their native traditions and language, but Chinatown is unique in that it also absorbs and refashions diverse American influences.

A BIT OF HISTORY

Among the thousands who flocked to California during the 1849 Gold Rush were Cantonese men intent on striking bonanzas and returning to China. Few bothered to learn English or assimilate Western culture. As China's ruling Manchu dynasty decayed through the 19C, however, and conditions worsened, ever-greater numbers of Chinese chose to settle in the American West.

By 1870 more than 63,000 Chinese, mostly men, were living in the U.S. In demand as laborers for construction projects, they built much of the western half of the first transcontinental railroad, pioneered the fishing industry on San Francisco Bay, and farmed California's farmlands. In many Western towns, Chinese entrepreneurs opened small businesses such as laundries, retail shops, and grocery stores.

As the premier point of entry for Asian immigrants, San Francisco harbored North America's oldest and largest Chinese community. Settlements formed around the city, but by the 1860s, most Chinese immigrants had established themselves along Sacramento Street a block south of Portsmouth Square.

Surviving Troubled Times – Waves of anti-Chinese sentiment swept the West

Powell-Hyde or Powell-Mason. Bus 30–Stockton, 511.org.

Info: www.sanfrancisco chinatown.com.

Location: Chinatown is bounded by Broadway, Montgomery, California and Powell Streets. To fully experience Chinatown's vibrant, intense character, explore on foot. Steep hills may be a challenge, but Grant Avenue and Stockton Street, the main thoroughfares, are largely flat. To explore in more depth, take a guided tour (☏415-982-8839; www. allaboutchinatown.com).

Kids: The dragons, colorful floats, and firecrackers of the **Chinese New Year Festival and Parade** in late January–mid-February (☾see Calendar of Events).

Timing: Temples and businesses typically open after 10am, but Chinatown can be interesting any time of day. Visit Portsmouth Square before 8am to see locals practicing t'ai chi. Saturday morning is particularly busy, especially along Stockton Street.

Parking: Parking garages are at St. Mary's Square (433 Kearny St.; ☏415-434-4400; ☜$2.50-4/hr), Portsmouth Square (733 Kearny St.; ☏415-982-6353; ☜$3/hr), and Vallejo Street (766 Vallejo St.; ☏415-989-4490; ☜$3/hr), but given its proximity to buses and cable cars, we recommend public transportation.

Don't Miss: A meal at one of Chinatown's restaurants.

Chinatown Temples

Among the most illuminating and evocative manifestations of Chinatown life are its many religious temples. Conventional Western scholarship may categorize Chinese religion as Confucianism, Taoism or Buddhism, but the truth is complex. Most Chinese adhere to elements of all three philosophies:

Confucianism is more an ancient state doctrine than a religion. Its prescribed rites constitute a symbolic pact upholding an ideal of harmonious social order and stability. Its hierarchy traditionally was headed by the emperor, with each member of society happily ensconced in his or her appropriate niche.

Chinatown Temples

Taoism, a mystical religion, might be characterized as a way of organizing the enormous array of Chinese gods and natural forces into a formal system. Among the most popular Taoist deities worshipped in Chinatown temples are Guan Di, the god of warriors and poets, and Tin How (also known as Ma-Tsu), the Queen of Heaven.

Buddhism, carried into China from India more than 1,700 years ago, has been shaped over the centuries into a distinctively Chinese belief system, markedly different from traditional south Asian Buddhism. In China, a pantheon of different Buddhas and faithful disciples is worshiped. A less materialistic form of Chinese Buddhism is Ch'an, better known in the West by its Japanese name of Zen.

Since ancient times, the Chinese have paid reverence to their ancestors and propitiated the forces of nature through sacrifice and prayer. In every temple, worshipers can be seen offering sacrifices of fruit, rice wine, roast meats and flowers, burning incense to resident deities or to tablets inscribed with names of recently deceased relatives. After the spirits are thought to have consumed the essence of the sacrifice, the worshiper will remove the now-sanctified offering and freely partake of it at mealtime. Symbolic offerings of paper cars and houses, "cash" and even paper servants are sometimes burned in a temple furnace, by which means they are sent to deceased loved ones believed to be residing in the spirit world. The person sending the offering will often hit a drum announcing his or her sacrifice to the spirit.

Although Buddhist temples normally house only Buddha images, many Taoist temples freely mix Buddhist statues among figures of several deities. As long as beliefs do not interfere with social harmony—as long as the Confucian doctrine is upheld—the Chinese are very tolerant in matters of religion.

☺ *Visitors are welcome in most temples, though it may be necessary to ring a doorbell to gain admittance. Courtesy is expected; photography is not permitted. Contributions left in marked donation boxes are appreciated.*

after the economic depression of 1872. As bankruptcies erased jobs, tycoons bolstered profits by hiring Chinese workers at low wages. Mobs of unemployed men stormed Chinese communities, including San Francisco's Chinatown in 1877, beating (and often killing) people and destroying property. Labor organizers pushed passage of the Chinese Exclusion Act of 1882, barring Chinese laborers from entering the U.S. The act prevented thousands of men already in the U.S. from sending for brides, thus preserving Chinatown's male-dominated society well into the 20C.

Chinese immigrants sought security in *tongs* ("associations" or "companies") whose memberships were usually based upon clan name or members' province of origin. These organizations often paid new arrivals' passage to San Francisco, assuming the roles of labor guild, insurance company, social club, legal advisor, protection agent and undertaker, in return for dues. A few tongs were little more than criminal gangs. By the late 19C, Chinatown had a villainous reputation as a haven for opium dens, gambling halls, and brothels. Violent tong wars erupted between fractions seeking to control profits. To restore order and to represent Chinese interests, men from the six most powerful tongs in 1882 agreed to form a confederation. Known as the **Chinese Six Companies**, it remains an active, if diminishing, force in modern Chinatown.

The repeal in 1943 of the Chinese Exclusion Act and a further relaxation of immigration laws in the 1960s heralded a new influx of immigrants from Hong Kong, China, and Southeast Asia. Families moved to other areas of the city. So many have settled in adjacent North Beach since the 1960s that sections of that neighborhood long known as "Little Italy," are now culturally an extension of Chinatown. Parts of the Richmond and Sunset Districts have also been transformed into "new" Chinatowns inhabited by wealthier, younger, and better-educated Chinese. Old Chinatown, however, remains the heart and soul of the far-flung Chinese

Chinatown

community. Chinese from around the Bay Area flock here to shop, eat, and socialize in the lively markets, restaurants, bookstores, and cultural centers. Tourists come by the thousands to wander Grant Avenue, Stockton Street, and the warren of side streets between them, visiting temples and herb shops, dining in the many restaurants, and shopping for Chinese groceries, embroidered linens, artwork, jewelry and souvenirs. The Central Subway project, expected to be completed by 2019, will only increase access, connecting Chinatown to Union Square, South of Market and the 4th St Caltain station.

WALKING TOUR

.7mi.

▶ Begin at the intersection of Bush St. & Grant Ave. and walk north.

Grant Avenue★★

The eight blocks of Grant Avenue between Bush Street and Broadway comprise Chinatown's principal thoroughfare for visitors. The street abounds in architectural chinoiserie—painted balconies, curved tile rooflines and predominantly red, green and yellow color schemes—applied during the 1920s and 30s to give the neighborhood an exotic cachet. Ceramic carp and dragons on the roof of the **Chinatown Gate** (*Grant Ave. at Bush St.*) symbolize auspicious

CHINATOWN

some Catholic church served as the cathedral for Archdiocese of San Francisco.

The Gothic Revival structure was redesignated a church following construction of a new St. Mary's Cathedral on Van Ness Avenue in 1891. The church serves as the venue for popular noontime concerts of classical music *(year-round Tue 12.30pm; $5; for schedule ℘415-777-3211; www.noontimeconcerts.org)*.

Across California Street from the cathedral lies St. Mary's Square, a small, serene park that has become the site of international controversy since **Comfort Women: Pillar of Strength (1)** was erected here in September 2017. A tribute to the hundreds of thousands of women, predominantly Korean, who were enslaved in Japanese military brothels during World War II, the statue depicts three women joining hands, while Korean human rights activist Kim Hak-sun looks on. The statue has caused intense friction with the Japanese government, particularly San Francisco's sister city of Osaka. Another notable statue here is the steel and granite tribute to **Sun Yat-sen (2)** (1938) by sculptor Beniamino Bufano. Considered the founding father of the Republic of China, Sun visited San Francisco's Chinese community several times around the turn of the 20C to raise support to overthrow China's Qing Dynasty.

▷ Return to Grant Ave. and continue north, turning right on Clay St.

fortunes. Taiwan's government donated materials for the gateway, which was designed in 1970 by Clayton Lee. North of the gate, shops selling curios, souvenirs, jewelry, furniture, cameras and electronics draw visitors in droves, while hardware stores, banks, markets and small cafes cater to a local clientele. Numerous authentic Taoist, Buddhist and Confucianist temples are tucked away on upper floors behind unassuming doors throughout the neighborhood. Visitors are welcomed at the **Ching Chung Temple★** *(615 Grant Ave., 4th floor; ⊙open daily; ℘415-433-2623)*, where portraits of the founders of three Taoist sects distinguish the main altar.

Old St. Mary's Cathedral★
660 California St., at Grant Ave. ⊙Open Mon–Fri 7am–4.30pm, Sat 10am–6pm, Sun 8am–3.30pm. ♿ ℘415-288-3800. www.oldsaintmarys.org.

The largest building in the state at the time of its dedication in 1854, this hand-

Portsmouth Square★
Formerly the central plaza of the Mexican settlement of Yerba Buena, this broad square is today Chinatown's most important outdoor gathering point. In 1846 Captain John Montgomery officially claimed Yerba Buena for the

Chinatown Herb Shops

Along Stockton Street and the side streets leading down to Grant, visitors can find many traditional Chinese herb shops. These shops are recognizable for the collections prominently displayed in the front windows: bottled snakes, preserved ginseng roots that parody an almost human shape, medical charts of the human body, pieces of tree bark, elk horn, dried seahorse and other sundries. These are the stuff of an ancient Chinese system of pharmacology, a lore gathered by early Taoist monks and herbalists, chronicled, tested, and refined over thousands of years.

Entering any shop, visitors will find a counter backed by wooden cabinets with drawers containing hundreds of dried herbs and other medicinals. Most by far are vegetable in origin: ginkgo for tuberculosis, mulberry leaves for colds and headaches, sumac for laryngitis, loquat leaf for coughs, climbing dogbane for rheumatoid arthritis, winter cherry leaf for diabetes, Job's tears for lobar pneumonia. Among the items most exotic to Western medicine might be dried centipedes, a remedy for infantile convulsions, spasms, cramps, and lockjaw; dead silkworm for sore throats and headaches; snakeskin for abscesses; and decoction of silkworm cocoon to relieve exhaustion.

The herb most familiar to Westerners is ginseng, a root sliced and steeped to make a tea celebrated for its curative virtues. The finest examples of ginseng root grow wild in the mountains of north China and Korea, but these can be quite expensive and probably will not be casually displayed in the herbalist's shop. Less expensive grades of ginseng powders and teas, including a popular variety of American ginseng from Wisconsin, make popular gifts.

U.S. by raising the American flag above the plaza, later renamed for his ship. California's first public school opened here in April 1848, and the square was the site of Sam Brannan's announcement that gold had been discovered some 100 miles east of San Francisco. During the Gold Rush, Portsmouth Square served as center of the boom-town. As commercial activity shifted, Portsmouth Square was left on the periphery. Today elderly men congregate in the square to socialize and play cards or Chinese chess. In the center of the square stands a **statue (3)** of the Goddess of Democracy, a memorial to the 1989 Tiananmen Square massacre in Beijing. On the north side stands a sailing-ship **monument (4)** to Robert Louis Stevenson, who enjoyed the square during his extended visit of 1879–80. To the east, a pedestrian bridge leads across Kearny Street to the **Chinese Culture Center** (Hilton Hotel, 750 Kearny St., 3rd

floor; ⊙ open Tue–Sat 1-am–4pm, Sat , closed major holidays ✆ 415-986-1822; www.c-c-c.org), featuring exhibitions of Chinese and Chinese-American art, programs on Chinese culture and heritage, and musical performances.

▷ Leave the square and walk uphill on Washington St.

Old Chinese Telephone Exchange
743 Washington St.
The neighborhood's most exuberant example of chinoiserie rises in three graceful pagoda-like tiers above a glossy, red-pillared pediment. Now a branch of East West Bank, the one-story building was opened as the Chinatown Telephone Exchange in 1909 to serve the community's 800 telephones. Switchboard operators had to know how to speak Cantonese, Sze Yup and three other Chinese dialects, as well as English.

▷ Turn right on Grant Ave., walk one block and turn right on Jackson St. Walk half a block down the hill and turn left on Beckett street.

Ma-Tsu Temple of USA★

30 Beckett St. ○*Open daily 9.30am–4.30pm.* ✎*Donation requested.* ♿ ☎*415-986-8818. www.matsuusa.org.*

This bright, attractive temple honors the Queen of Heaven using her title as known in Guangdong and Taiwan. The central statue is guarded by figures of two ferocious warriors—the blue-faced Shun Feng Er ("Ear of Favorable Wind") on the left and the red-faced Chien Li Yen ("Eye of 1,000 Li") on the right—noted respectively for their prodigious powers of hearing and sight (a *li* is a unit of distance; hence the guards can detect evil from 1,000 *li*.).

▷ Return to Jackson St. Turn right up the hill, across Grant Ave., to Ross Alley; turn left and continue to Washington St.

Jackson Street, Ross Alley and Washington Street between Grant Avenue and Stockton Street traverse a densely populated enclave of herbalists, jewelers, restaurants, small groceries and fragrant bakeries. These side streets retain the dark, intriguing ambience of old Chinatown. Many turn-of-late-19C tong war clashes occurred here, and **Ross Alley** is still known among old residents as "Lu Song Hang" or "Spanish Lane," a reference to Hispanic prostitutes in the alley's 19C brothels. Today you'll find a shop purveying shrines, lanterns and religious statuary; several clothing factories hum behind closed doors. Step inside the charming **Golden Gate Fortune Cookie Company★** *(56 Ross Alley;* ○*open daily 9am–6pm;* ☎*415-806-8243)*, where you'll see cookies being baked and stuffed with fortunes by workers seated at rotating griddles. Pick up a bag of 40 fresh cookies for $5.

▷ Cross Washington St., walk a few steps downhill; turn right on Waverly Pl.

Waverly Place★

This two-block alley is dubbed "the Street of Painted Balconies" for the handsome chinoiserie gracing the buildings. The colors are symbolic—red stands for happiness, green for longevity, black for money, yellow for good fortune. Among older Chinatown residents, Waverly Place is known as "Tin How Miu Gai" or "Queen of Heaven Temple Street." From the street, pedestrians may hear drums booming from upper floors as youth groups practice lion-dance drills and other festival activities.

Tin How Temple

125 Waverly Pl., 4th floor. ○*Open daily 9am-5pm.* ✎*Donation requested.*

The present building of Chinatown's oldest temple dates from 1911. It is devoted to Tin How, a Chinese woman of Fujian Province (AD 960–987) now revered as the Queen of Heaven and protector of seafarers. The worship came to the U.S. with immigrants who fell under her care when they crossed the Pacific Ocean. Red paper lanterns cover the ceiling in the incense-filled interior, above a wooden statue of Tin How.

▷ Turn right on Sacramento St., walk uphill to Stockton St. and turn right.

Chinese Six Companies

843 Stockton St.

⚤ *Interior not open to the public.*

The Chinese Six Companies still wields influence among Chinatown's businesses. The building's colorful facade is one of Chinatown's most elaborate.

Kong Chow Temple★

855 Stockton St., 4th floor (elevator entrance to left of post office).
○*Open Mon–Sat 9am–4pm.*

The Kong Chow temple first opened on Pine St. in 1857. Among the original furnishings transferred to the present building (1977) are excellent examples of Chinese wood carving. At the main altar, the swarthy-faced statue with a black beard represents Guan Di, a figure seen all over Chinatown in shrines an shop windows. A general in the Three Kingdoms period (AD 220–280), Guan Di fought ferociously and loyally for his lord, a contender for the imperial throne. Killed by treachery, he was elevated into the Taoist pantheon, becoming patron saint of a host of disparate professions, including soldiers, poets, prostitutes, police and gangsters. The figure of Guan Di is flanked by his bearded warrior "brother" Zhang Fei and his gentler son, together symbolizing Guan Di's balanced devotion to both the civil government and the military.

▶ Turn left on Clay St. for one block.

Chinese Historical Society of America Museum (R)

965 Clay St., between Stockton and Powell Sts. 🕐*Open Tue–Fri noon–5pm, Sat-Sun 10am–4pm.* 🕐*Closed Jan 1, July 4, Dec 25 and Lunar New Year.* 🎫*$15.* ☎*415-391-1188. www.chsa.org.*
The Chinese Historical Society of America occupies a 1932 red-brick YWCA building designed by famed architect Julia Morgan. A pair of pagoda-like towers rise above a roofline crenellated with imported Chinese tiles, and a cast-stone arch with leaded glazing surmounts the entrance doors.
The main gallery tells the story of the Chinese in America with photographs and artifacts. Two other rooms have rotating art and history exhibits.

▶ Return to Stockton St. and continue north to Broadway.

Stockton Street★

The four blocks of Stockton Street between Clay Street and Broadway feature Chinatown's greatest concentration of markets. The street draws crowds of shoppers from all over the city, especially on weekend mornings. Savory Chinese specialties like pressed or roast duck or barbecued pork and soy-sauce chickens hang in the windows. Mounds of vegetables and fruits (including the aromatic durian), displayed on sidewalk stands, vie for space with vendors peddling live poultry or fresh produce. Market cries and vigorous bargaining contribute to the colorful, amiable havoc.

ADDRESSES

🍴EAT

China Live – *816 Sacramento St. at Waverly Pl.* ☎*415-788-8188. chinalivesf.com.*
A sleek multistory culinary and shopping center, China Live has a lively market-style restaurant, a 25-seat tea counter, a cocktail bar, and a home and kitchenwares shop downstairs. Upstairs, find swanky bar Cold Drinks and ultra-exclusive Chinese fine-dining restaurant Eight Tables.

City View – *662 Commercial St.* ☎*415-398-2838. cityviewdimsum.com.* Considered one of the top spots for traditional dim sum in San Francisco, this unassuming restaurant is always packed at lunchtime, when carts circle the dining room with Shanghai dumplings, barbecue pork buns, and shu mai.

SHOPPING

Kim+Ono *729 Grant Ave. 415-989-8588. kimandono.com.* This contemporary-feeling boutique by second-generation Chinatown merchants sells a proprietary line of hand-painted kimonos, in both silk and synthetics, and luxe Asian bath products.

The Wok Shop – *718 Grant Ave. Open daily 10am–6pm.* ☎*415-989-3797. wokshop.com.* Iron woks, tea pots, bamboo steamers, and other Asian kitchen- and tableware are stocked floor-to-ceiling in this tiny Grant Avenue storefront.

Clarion Music Center – *816 Sacramento St. at Waverly Pl.* ☎*415-391-1317. www.clarion music.com.* This music museum and performance space sells folk instruments like the Chinese *yangqin* and Japanese koto, as well as CDs and music books.

Ten Ren Tea Co. – *949 Grant Ave.* ☎*415-362-0656. www.tenren.com.* The oldest and largest U.S. outlet of a Taiwan-based tea empire, this purveyor sells loose tea as well as hot and cold cups for sipping.

Civic Center★

San Francisco's center of government occupies one of the finest groups of Beaux-Arts-style buildings in the U.S. The grandly designed complex still reflects the tenets of the turn-of-the-century "City Beautiful" urban planning movement, updated with sympathetic contemporary constructions.

A BIT OF HISTORY

San Francisco's Civic Center was not built until the early 20C, fairly late in the city's life. In order to provide a proper home for the city's government, which through the mid-19C was located around Portsmouth Square, a new city hall was planned in the vicinity of Civic Center in 1872. Endemic corruption, within both the construction industry and the city government, delayed completion for more than 25 years and vastly inflated the cost of the structure. When the great 1906 earthquake struck, the building was damaged beyond repair.

In the aftermath of the fire an idealistic group of businessmen and politicians embarked upon an ambitious scheme to create a suitable new center for the city's political and cultural life. The group of buildings that now forms the core of Civic Center was erected over the course of 20 years, beginning in 1913. First completed was the Civic Auditorium for the Panama-Pacific International Exposition of 1915. The new City Hall opened at the end of 1915, while a stately main library and federal office buildings followed soon after. The historic portion of the complex was completed with the opening of the Veterans Building and the War Memorial Opera House in 1932.

United Nations Birthplace – In 1945, the United Nations Conference on International Organization convened in the War Memorial Opera House. The United Nations Charter was signed in the Veterans Building's Herbst Theatre on June 26. Throughout subsequent decades, the Civic Center remained a locus of administration, as well as home

🚌 Bus 5–Fulton, 19–Polk or 47–Van Ness; all streetcars Civic Center station.
🚇 Civic Center station, 511.org.

ℹ️ **Info:** ☎415-391-2000. www.sftravel.com.

▶ **Location:** Civic Center is located within the triangle of Market Street, Franklin Street, and Golden Gate Avenue.

👫 **Kids:** Sound Commons in United Nations Plaza and soft-serve ice cream at Bi-Rite Cafe.

🕐 **Timing:** Civic Center can be seen in half a day; allow an additional half-day for the Asian Art Museum. Morning is a good time to visit, followed by lunch or shopping in Hayes Valley.

🅿️ **Parking:** The Civic Center Plaza Garage is located between Polk, Larkin, Grove and McAllister Sts; enter on McAllister (💰$3-6/hr; ☎415-863-1537).

😋 **Don't Miss:** The Asian Art Museum and the City Hall rotunda.

to such cultural institutions as the Louise M. Davies Symphony Hall and the War Memorial Opera House.

The area was boosted by the opening of the new Main Library in 1996, the renovation of City Hall in 1995–99, and the opening of the Asian Art Museum in the Old Main Library in 2003. Today, it remains rough around the edges, with a noticeable indigent and homeless population near the library. At the same time, the area is rapidly revitalizing with new civic projects, a vibrant Wednesday farmers market in UN Plaza, near-constant weddings taking place at City Hall, and a crop of trendy eateries along Market Street and in neighboring Hayes Valley. In 2020, the Asian Art Museum will complete a massive expansion of its galleries.

The City Beautiful

Around the turn of the 19C, civic leaders across the country joined forces to improve the quality of life in American cities. This concerted effort, known as the City Beautiful movement, brought together business leaders, politicians and architects who worked to make urban areas better places to live and work. Their efforts included such seemingly mundane projects as widening streets, installing street lights and building sewer systems, but also encompassed more singularly aesthetic goals.

The most prominent designer associated with the City Beautiful movement was Chicago architect **Daniel Burnham**, who was hired by a group of San Francisco businessmen to develop a plan that would improve the image and efficiency of the city. Over the course of two years Burnham made many trips to the city, spending untold hours in a cabin on the slope of Twin Peaks, sketching and studying the topography and character of the city below. With help from local architect Willis Polk, in 1905 he presented what became known as the **Burnham Plan**, an ambitious proposal for wide boulevards, traffic circles with streets radiating outward, and public monuments much like those of Washington DC or Paris.

The Burnham Plan was adopted with strong support, and the leveling of the city by the great earthquake and fire of 1906 seemed to offer a clean slate on which to implement it. However, concerns for private property rights and the urgency of rebuilding homes and businesses outweighed civic altruism, and reconstruction of the city in the aftermath of the disaster occurred along the old street grid. Construction of Civic Center proceeded more slowly, and today the ensemble stands as San Francisco's only realization of Burnham's grand plan.

WALKING TOUR
.8mi.

▷ Begin at United Nations Plaza, Hyde St and Fulton St.

United Nations Plaza★

Linking Market Street with the Civic Center, this plaza (1980, Lawrence Halprin) commemorates the 1945 founding of the United Nations. The plaza is bordered by parallel rows of square columns bearing names of United Nations member countries and the years in which each joined. A large fountain forms the striking centerpiece. A **sculpture (1)** of Simón Bolívar on a horse dominates the west end.

Scattered throughout the plaza, **Sound Commons (2)** is a public music and sound installation created by the Exploratorium in 2016, which includes echo tubes, xylophones, and giant chimes, staffed seven days a week by nonprofit Hunters Point Family, which employs at-risk youth and adults.

▷ Walk south on Hyde St. to Market St.

Orpheum Theatre★

1192 Market St. (at Hyde & Eighth Sts.)
& ✆415-551-2000. www.shnsf.com.
Originally designed (1926, B. Marcus Priteca) for vaudeville, this theater evokes a glorified, pre-Reformation Spain. The intricate facade is fashioned after a 13C Léon cathedral, the high vaulted lobby ceiling is reminiscent of the Alhambras. The 2,200-seat theater housed the 1970 production of *Hair*. A San Francisco landmark, it was restored in 1998 to make it a suitable venue for Broadway shows.

▷ Walk back to the Fulton St. Mall and turn left.

James Lick Memorial (3)

A gift of the James Lick Trust, established by a mid-19C developer, the work (1894, Frank Happersberger) depicts Eureka standing atop a 30ft central column.

Turn right on Larkin St.

Asian Art Museum★★★
✦see p 76

Turn left on Larkin St.

San Francisco Public Library★
100 Larkin St. ◷*Open Mon 10am–6pm,
Tue–Thu 9am–8pm, Fri noon–6pm,
Sat 10am–6pm and Sun noon–5pm.*
◷*Closed major holidays.* ✕♿🅿
✆*415-557-4400. http://sfpl.org.*
San Francisco's 376,000-square-
foot Main Library (1996, James Ingo
Freed and Cathy Simon) blends a
contemporary take on Civic Center
architecture with high technology. The
gleaming granite exterior is from the
same quarry that provided stone for
early Civic Center structures. The main
facade reveals an updated version
of Beaux-Arts classicism, while the
Hyde Street elevation has an angular,
contemporary face. The seven-story
interior, replete with catwalk bridges,
artworks and an asymmetrical skylit
atrium, boasts multimedia computers,
access to electronic databases, as well
as books and magazines.

Cross Larkin & Grove Sts.

Bill Graham Civic Auditorium
99 Grove St. www.billgrahamcivic.com.
Originally completed for the 1915 Panama-Pacific International Exposition,
the Civic Auditorium (Arthur Brown, Jr.)
has undergone many remodelings and
name changes, most recently in memory
of popular music promoter Bill Graham,
who died in 1992. The 7,000-seat, four-
story Beaux-Arts auditorium has long
been one of the city's prime performance
and event venues.

Cross Grove and Polk Sts. to City Hall.

City Hall★★
*1 Dr. Carlton B. Goodlett Pl. (bounded
by Grove, McAllister & Polk Sts. and Van
Ness Ave.).* ◷*Open Mon–Fri 8am–8pm.*
◷*Closed major holidays.* ☞*Guided
tours Mon–Fri 10am, noon and 2pm.*
♿🅿 ✆*415-554-6139. sfgov.org/cityhall*
This monumental Beaux-Arts edifice,
crowned by a magnificent dome, is often

City Hall

© Brigitta L. House/MICHELIN

considered San Francisco's most beautiful building. Designed by Arthur Brown, Jr., a graduate of the École des Beaux Arts in Paris, the building was completed in 1915 under the stewardship of populist mayor James Rolph, who vowed to stamp out the corruption that contributed to the first City Hall's demise.

The massive four-story building covers two city blocks. Its splendid dome, trimmed with gold leaf, rises to a height of 307ft, about 13ft taller than the U.S. Capitol Building in Washington DC. On the Van Ness Avenue facade, handsome Atlas-like telamones support the entrance. Doric pillars and colonnades along the porticoes, facades and dome reinforce the Classical idiom.

Damaged in the Loma Prieta earthquake of 1989, the grand edifice closed in 1995 for $300 million of seismic retrofitting and historic restoration. It reopened in 1999 floating upon 600 "base isolators" (rubber and steel discs) beneath the building that dissipate motion.

Inside, a grand ceremonial marble staircase ascends to a 181ft open rotunda, its east-facing section flanked by city government offices. The mayor's office is beneath the central pediment on the Polk Street facade, with a balcony facing east onto Civic Center Plaza. Two grand public courts with marble walls extend from the rotunda.

To the east of City Hall lies **Civic Center Plaza**, often the site of rallies, demonstrations and fiery speeches. The broad, beautifully proportioned space has been restored to its original 1912 design. Only children and families are allowed inside the creative and eye-catching **Helen Diller Family Foundation Playgrounds (4)**, which were beautifully renovated in 2018 to include towering slides, climbing structures, and swings with views of city skyline.

▶ Continue west on Grove St. Cross Van Ness Ave. and walk north.

San Francisco War Memorial and Performing Arts Center★★

Guided tours on Mondays (see Louise M. Davies Symphony Hall).

Closed major holidays. ✕ ♿ ☎415-552-8338. (see Entertainment). www.sfwmpac.org. Flanking a formal courtyard designed by Thomas Church, these twin structures erected in memory of San Francisco's war dead served for decades as the city's center for the performing arts.

War Memorial Opera House

301 Van Ness Ave.
The first city-owned opera house (1932, Arthur Brown, Jr.) hosted the plenary sessions that led to the establishment of the UN in 1945. The San Francisco Opera and San Francisco Ballet perform here in an elegantly appointed 3,176-seat auditorium. The proscenium, graced by Edgar Walter's gilded relief sculptures of two Amazons astride horses, is backed by a golden brocatelle curtain.

Veterans Building

401 Van Ness Ave.
This structure is home to city government offices and the 928-seat **Herbst Theatre**. The **San Francisco Arts Commission Gallery** (*open Tue–Sat 11am–6pm; ☎415-554-6080; www. sfartscommission.org*) is a small space that showcases work by local artists. The commission also mounts exhibits in City Hall, in the San Francisco Airport, and on MUNI bus stops throughout the city.

▶ Return to Grove St.

Louise M. Davies Symphony Hall

Van Ness Ave. and Grove St. Visit by guided tour, Mon 10am–2pm. $10 (includes tour of War Memorial Opera House and Herbst Theatre). ♿ P ☎415-552-8338 (tours); ☎415-864-6000 (tickets). www.sfsymphony.org.

In contrast to the Beaux-Arts buildings of Civic Center, this modern structure (1980, Edward Bassett) features a curving glass facade that reveals the lobby areas of the 2,743 seat hall. It is home to the San Francisco Symphony. The elegant bronze sculpture *Large Four Piece Reclining Figure* **(3)** (1973) at the entrance is by Henry Moore. Fletcher Benton's *Bal-*

anced Unbalanced T **(4)** (1981) faces Franklin Street from Goldman terrace.

ASIAN ART MUSEUM★★★

200 Larkin St. ⏱*Open Tue–Sun 10am–5pm (Feb–Sept Thu until 9pm).* ⏱*Closed Jan 1, Thanksgiving Day, Dec 25.* ⊛*$25 ($10 1st Sun of the month).* ⌇*Free guided and self-guided audio tours available.* ✕&. ☏*415-581-3500. www.asianart.org.*

The Asian Art Museum's 18,000 works span 6,000 years and include art from China, Japan, Korea, India, Southeast Asia and the Himalayas.

A BIT OF HISTORY

The collection at the Asian Art Museum was originally assembled by **Avery Brundage** (1887–1975), a Chicago industrialist who was fascinated by East Asian cultures and began collecting Japanese woodblock prints and netsuke—carved bone toggles used to fasten kimono sashes. In the 1930s his collections expanded to 3,000-year-old Chinese bronzes, Chinese ceramics and objects from Korea, Southeast Asia, India and the Middle East.

In 1959, Brundage donated a part of his collection to San Francisco on the condition that the city create a museum to house it. In 1960, voters passed a bond to fund the Asian Art Museum, which opened as a part of the de Young Museum in Golden Gate Park. In 1989, following damage to its building in the Loma Prieta earthquake, the museum relocated to the former main library at Civic Center. Italian architect Gae Aulenti, known for Paris' stunning Musée d'Orsay, designed the $160 million renovation of the Beaux-Arts-style space, preserving the marble staircase, columned loggia and great hall, while adding modern elements.

The museum continued to collect pieces after Brundage's gift, and currently holds about 18,000 works. One of the city's top art venues, it has been the site of numerous high-profile shows, including an exhibit of the famous terracotta warriors of China's first emperor in 1994. In addition to the vast historical works, the museum is a major collector of contemporary Asian art.

2018-2019 Expansion – In 2018, the Asian Art Museum began a major expansion project, the centerpiece of which is the 13,000-square-foot **Akiko Yamazaki & Jerry Yang Special Exhibition Pavilion**, named for the Yahoo co-founder and his wife, major donors to the museum. The space, slated to open in 2020, will host a robust program of temporary exhibits, with an increased focus on contemporary work. It will also feature a 7,500-square-foot rooftop terrace showcasing a collection of contemporary sculpture. The museum's educa-

South Asian Gallery, Asian Art Museum

Highlights of the Chinese Dynasties

Neolithic Period (c. 5000–16C BC): Regional cultures emerge, with distinct craft traditions in clay, stone, bone, basketry and textiles.

Shang Dynasty (1122–1028 BC): Transition to Bronze Age is marked by the rise of cities and rival clans. Remarkable piece-mold technique is invented for casting shapely bronze vessels.

Zhou Dynasty (1122–256 BC): Prosperity during unsettled era of state-making creates a market for objects of extreme technical refinement and splendor.

Qin Dynasty (221–206 BC): Short-lived dynasty marks beginnings of imperial China; the Great Wall is unified and a common script is established.

Han Dynasty (206 BC–AD 220): Major dynasty forges a single Chinese nation and imposes a long period of peace marked by expansion and the coming of Buddhism. Prosperity encourages trade along the Silk Road, bringing in foreign influences. The decorative dragon becomes prominent, along with layered and inlaid bronzework.

Six Dynasties (AD 317–589): Empire splits into rival states.

Sui Dynasty (AD 581–618): Empire is reunited; Grand Canal is built. Potters improve glazing techniques.

Tang Dynasty (AD 618–907): Expansive dynasty blossoms into powerful nation, open to foreign trade and spreading Chinese influence, especially to Japan. Aristocratic burial rites are increasingly elaborate; tomb furnishings proliferate in quality and quantity. Buddhism flourishes. AD 907–1125: Empire breaks down into individual states, including the northern **Liao dynasty** (937–1125).

Song Dynasty (AD 960–1279): Humanistic age of extreme aesthetic richness is renowned for fine and varied ceramics and painting. Nomads establish **Jin dynasty** (1115–1234) in the north, but the court moves south to Hangzhou and continues to govern as a sub-dynasty known as the **Southern Song** (1217–1279).

Yuan Dynasty (AD 1279–1368): Mongol dynasty favors blue-and-white porcelains to trade with Islamic nations.

Ming Dynasty (AD 1368–1644): Return to native rule is a classic age of blue-and-white wares.

Qing Dynasty (AD 1644–1911): Period of foreign rule under Manchus features ceramics of brilliant color and eggshell translucency. Contact with West increases.

tional programs and main galleries are also being redesigned, with a new focus on master pieces within the collection. ☺ *The museum will remain open throughout the expansion, though certain floors will be inaccessible in 2019. Closed at press time, the third-floor galleries are slated to reopen by late spring 2019. Galleries on the second floor, including the Korean and Japanese collections, will be closed throughout the summer of 2019, reopening in the fall ahead of the inauguration of the new pavilion in early 2020. Not all pieces discussed here will be on view.*

South Asian Art★★
3rd floor

The collection from India, Pakistan, Bangladesh and Sri Lanka boasts a wealth of religious statuary. The Gandhara style developed in what is now southern Afghanistan and northern Pakistan. At the crossroads between East and West, its sculpture reflects a Hellenistic and Roman style of carving, illustrated by a splendid rendition of a 2C–3C Bodhisattva. Outstanding are eight fragments of **friezes** depicting the life of Shakyamuni, the Indian prince who became the Buddha. Another prize holding is the **silver elephant throne★★** made in India c. 1870–1920.

Art of the Persian World and West Asia
3rd floor

This small gallery displays objects from present-day Iran, Iraq, Afghanistan, Turkmenistan and Uzbekistan. The works span 6,000 years from prehistoric through Islamic medieval periods. Particularly fine are the Luristani bronzes (c. 1000–650 BC) and ceramics from the 15C Timurid dynasty of Tamerlane.

Southeast Asian Art★
3rd floor

More than 500 pieces from Thailand, Burma, Laos, Cambodia, Indonesia, Vietnam, Malaysia and the Philippines include sculpture, Thai ceramics, Thai and Lao silks, weaponry (highlighted by sinuous gilt *krises,* Malay-Indonesian daggers), jewelry and manuscripts. The vivid set of nearly 200 Indonesian rod **puppets★★** is rare and beautiful.

Tibetan and Himalayan Art★
3rd floor

This fascinating gallery contains about 300 items from Nepal, Tibet, Mongolia and Bhutan, largely religious art including scriptures and gilt bronze sculptures

Buddha image (AD 338), Chinese Art Gallery

Image courtesy of the Asian Art Museum of San Francisco

of Hindu and Buddhist gods. The collection of brilliant *thangkas* (Nepalese and Tibetan scroll paintings) is one of the country's largest. Spectacular metalwork shrines produced by Newar artisans from the 8C–19C are inlaid with semiprecious stones.

Tibetan artworks, with terrifying and beautiful imagery, are unique expressions of Buddhism. Ritual implements are made of metal, gems, and human bone. Most common are the bell *(drilbu)* and thunderbolt *(dorje)*, respectively representing the feminine feature of wisdom and male feature of skillful means. Bhutan is renowned for textiles woven in cotton, wool and silk.

Chinese Art★★★
3rd and 2nd floors

Over half the museum's holdings, the Chinese collection includes bronzes, sculptures, paintings, textiles and decorative artworks. The museum's oldest pot, a small earthenware **bottle** from the Yangshou culture, dates from 4800–3600 BC. **Oracle bones**, created by priests to divine the future, are the first evidence of written language in China. Neolithic artisans produced **jades** in a doughnut shape called *bi,* still a popular finished shape for jade. Shang dynasty bronzes, made for tomb offerings, include three-legged pots called *ding,* decorated with spirals and monster heads. A highlight is a rhinoceros-shaped **ritual vessel★★** (12C BC). Depleting bronze resources caused the Han dynasty government to widely ban the ritual bronzes in tombs, resulting in use of pottery. Stoneware and lacquerware developed during this era; look for China's oldest-known (AD 1) **lacquer vessel** with a maker's mark.

Indian influences permeate early works of Chinese Buddhist art. Among them is the earliest known Chinese **Buddha image★★★** (AD 338), a gilt bronze representation of the Indian prince who became the Buddha (*on view after summer 2019*). The worldly confidence of the Tang dynasty encouraged an appreciation of simplicity, exemplified by the draperies on Buddhist images.

History of Japan

Prehistoric Age (c. 12,000 BC–AD 552): Contact with China and Korea after c. 300 BC brings new technologies to pottery; metal tools and bronze bells (dotaku) develop. In **Kofun Period** (AD 250–552), imperial Japan takes form.

Asuka to Nara Periods (552–710): Buddhism enters Japan from China via Korea. Along with religious influences, Japan imports Chinese writing, tea and styles of architecture, sculpture and painting.

Heian Period (794–1185): Capital moves from Nara to Heian-kyo (now Kyoto).

Kamakura Period (1185–1333): Rise of the warrior class of samurai. Zen (a Buddhist sect encouraging intellectual spiritualism based on meditation) arrives from southern China. The arts and the tea ceremony become secularized.

Muromachi Period (1333–1573): Under strong shogunate rule, a flourishing of Zen—and reaction against it—infuses the arts, particularly painting and the tea ceremony.

Momoyama Period (1573–1615): Warlords battle for control of Japan while Western traders and missionaries make their first landings on the Japanese coast.

Edo Period (1615–1868): The shogun Tokugawa Ieyasu moves the capital to Tokyo and seals the country from foreign arrivals; a strict class structure (samurai, farmers, craftsmen and merchants) is established. Ensuing prosperity allows the diffusion of art through a broad swath of society.

Meiji Period (1868–1912): Following the 1853–54 visit of U.S. Commodore Matthew Perry, Japan is compelled to abandon isolationist policies and open trade with the U.S. and Europe. Modernization becomes paramount after a new imperial government overthrows the weakening Tokugawa shogunate.

Their cultural dynamism also shows in secular works such as the **sancai tomb figures**—three-color ceramic statues depicting horses, Bactrian camels and foreign traders. They also developed true porcelain (a hard, white ceramic of kaolin clay) and cobalt-blue glazes. Ceramics peaked during the Song dynasty with the development of green celadon glazes, light-blue Jun ware and the opaque, glassy, blue-green glaze of Longquan ware. During this dynasty, a rougher form of pottery was introduced to Japan, carried from southern Chinese monasteries by Japanese monks.

In the Yuan dynasty, potters made glazes thicker and more opaque by adding kaolin clay. The Ming dynasty is noted for the proliferation of glazing and decorating techniques, and five-color ware. Unlike post-Renaissance art from the West, which relies on a fixed perspective, Chinese (and Japanese) **landscape painting** traditionally employs a "floating" perspective that invites the eye to enter the painting and to move from feature to feature, promoting meditation. The museum's broad collection focuses on Ming and Qing masters and includes monumental landscapes and still-life scrolls from the 13C onward.

Korean Art★
2nd floor

The Korean collection includes hanging scrolls, stoneware ceramics from the Three Kingdoms and United Silla periods (57 BC–AD 935), gold jewelry, ash-glazed funerary pottery and celadon-glazed vessels from the Koryo period (AD 918–1392). Korean potters produced many unique ceramic forms, including gourd-shaped bottles with red-pigment celadon glaze. Two slate **daggers** (c. 500–600 BC) are the museum's oldest Korean artifacts. A gilt bronze sculpture of *Amitabha Buddha* (8C) is the largest of such quality in a Western collection. Exceptional portraits include *Buddha Amitabha and Eight Great Bodhisattvas* (14C) and *A King of Hell* (16C).

Japanese Art★★
2nd floor

With more than 4,200 objects, the museum's Japanese holdings make up the most comprehensive collection of Japanese art in the U.S. Highlights are screens and scrolls, ceramics, bronzes, religious sculptures, swords and decorative arts. The museum has splendid collections of *netsuke* miniatures in horn and ivory, and Japanese calligraphy representing different styles and formats from the 12C to the 20C.

Among prehistoric treasures are earthenware pottery, bronze *dotaku* (bells), mirrors and weapons, and a wealth of *haniwa* (retaining posts for burial mounds) in the shapes of animals, houses, boats and people.

Buddhist sculpture and painting reached their zenith during the Kamakura period, as the arrival of Zen inspired artistic expression characterized by monotone landscapes. The demand for **samurai swords** pushed the manufacture of Japanese steel to a high art.

Among the impressive collection of screens are colorful Yamato-e style, monochrome Kanga landscapes, and abstract, minimalist Haboku (splashed ink) style. By the Muromachi period, painters of the Kano school—which emphasize poetic simplicity of image and line—plied their arts on large screens that were used for blocking drafts and brightening dark castles.

A traditional **Japanese tea ceremony exhibit** displays roughly formed Temmoku teaware—a reflection of the secular Japanese appreciation for *wabi* (poverty) and *sabi* (rusticity).

Many painting schools flourished during the Edo period, as did lacquerware, ceramics and stage drama. Highly decorated items from this era include *inro* (small cases for personal effects), a fine *koto* (13-stringed zither), an exquisitely lacquered palanquin, and woodblock prints.

Sunday at the Museum
1st floor

The first-floor café, which opened in 2018, is regarded as the first phase in the Asian Art Museum's $90 million renovation. Its attractive minimalist design and creative pan-Asian dishes, like kimchi fries and miso avocado toast, mirror the museum's mission to celebrate the wide range of Asian cultures represented in its collection. The ace tea selection comes from San Francisco's beloved shop The Boba Guys.

ADDITIONAL SIGHT
Patricia's Green
Fell St. & Octavia Blvd., Hayes Valley

Where there was once a freeway onramp there is today a grassy park with picnic tables, a playground, and several eye-catching works of public art, including Charles Gadeken's 50ft LED sculpture *SQUARED*, which was originally exhibited at the Coachella and Burning Man festivals. Located in the heart of the trendy Hayes Valley neighborhood, it's a good place to pick up a drink from the kiosk run by beloved Mission coffee shop Ritual, then browse the many fab independent boutiques along Hayes Street.

ADDRESSES

⚇/EAT

The Market –*1355 Market St.* ☎*415-767-5130. www.visitthemarket.com.* On the first floor of Twitter's Market Street headquarters, a bustling artisan grocery and food court caters to the local lunch crowd with poké bowls, made-to-order sandwiches, coffee from Blue Bottle, and smoothies by Project Juice, as well as a sustainable butcher shop, organic produce, and artisan bread to take home.

Bi-Rite Café – *52 Grove St.* ☎*415-710-0633. biritemarket.com.* Bi-Rite, the Mission's beloved gourmet supermarket, opened a snack bar in Civic Center Plaza in 2018. Stop by for locally roasted Sightglass coffee, kale salad, or soft-serve buffalo-milk ice cream ice.

Financial District★★

This cacophonous forest of skyscraping steel, glass, and stone represents the heart of the city's financial community. Though modern in appearance, the district stands on the city's historic core and includes some of San Francisco's oldest and most architecturally significant buildings.

A BIT OF HISTORY

While San Francisco was born in 1776 at Mission Dolores and The Presidio, the roots of the modern downtown lie beneath the Financial District, where the village of Yerba Buena grew up in the early 1840s along what was then a sheltered bayfront. In 1846 U.S. forces occupied the town at the outbreak of the Mexican-American War, and the following year Yerba Buena's name was changed to San Francisco. Irish surveyor Jasper O'Farrell laid out a street grid, designating the muddy path along the waterfront as **Montgomery Street** in honor of the commander of the U.S. forces who took the village. O'Farrell traced Market Street at a diagonal to the already established downtown grid, then laid another grid at a competing angle south of Market Street.

Until 1848, the sleepy community served as a supply center for oceangoing vessels that periodically sailed into the bay. By late 1849, with the discovery of gold in the Sierra Nevada foothills, San Francisco boomed as the principal communication and supply conduit between the mining camps and the rest of the world. Dozens of vessels that sailed into the bay were abandoned by crews who jumped ship for the gold fields. Empty boats served as impromptu warehouses and hotels. Wharves extended east of Montgomery Street to deep-water anchorage; the intervening mud flats were filled in with sand, dredgings and ship carcasses until the waterfront reached the line of the modern Embar-

🚋 California Street. 🚌 Bus 1–California, 2–Clement, 3–Jackson, 4–Sutter, 5–Fulton, 6–Parnassus, 7–Haight, 12–Folsom, 41–Union; all streetcars Embarcadero or Montgomery St. stations. 🚇 Embarcadero or Montgomery St. stations, 511.org.

📄 **Info:** www.sftravel.com.

▶ **Location:** The Financial District is concentrated in a roughly triangular area bounded by Kearny, Washington, and Market Sts.

👥 **Kids:** Children can hear the story of the Gold Rush from the seat of a stagecoach at the Wells Fargo History Museum.

🕐 **Timing:** The district is fairly deserted at night and on weekends. Visit on a weekday to see it in full swing.

🅿 **Parking:** Garage parking, though plentiful, is expensive; it's best to use the many buses, streetcars or cable cars that serve the area, or try the parking garages in nearby Chinatown. If you do drive, be alert to parking signs, as street parking is prohibited along certain thoroughfares during rush hours.

😊 **Don't Miss:** The Transamerica Pyramid.

cadero. Today very little remains of the Gold Rush city.

Wall Street of the West – San Francisco's role as financial center of the West Coast was cemented by silver. The immense fortunes engendered by Nevada's Comstock Lode during the 1860s brought financial and commercial enterprises and the new transcontinen-

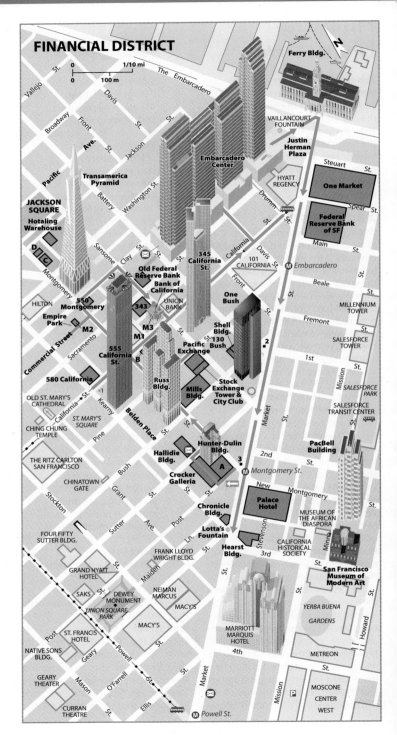

FINANCIAL DISTRICT

tal railroad to the port city. The Financial District quickly emerged as the commercial nexus of the West.

The great earthquake and fire of 1906 razed the district, but within three years it had been largely rebuilt. Many new buildings, such as the Bank of California, epitomized "City Beautiful" ideals, employing Classical motifs to imply order and substance. Another burst of construction occurred in the late 1920s, when three office towers—the Hunter-Dulin, Russ and Shell Buildings—were completed, each with features common to the early Art Deco period, such as ornamental tops and setbacks on the upper stories. The Great Depression and World War II put a temporary halt to growth, but beginning in 1959 with the Crown Zellerbach building, dozens of skyscrapers rose. The construction wave culminated in the early 1970s with the city's two signature towers, the Bank of America Center (now 555 California Street) and the Transamerica Pyramid. The swift pace of wholesale change led preservationists to lobby for protection of many older buildings, and for strict limitations on the height and bulk of new ones. This movement resulted in the **Downtown Plan** of 1985, whose mandatory guidelines put a cap on the square footage of new construction allowed annually in the Financial District. As a result, most development now has shifted south of Market Street, where the 1,070ft Salesforce Tower, slated to be completed in 2018, will surpass the Transamerica Pyramid, as the tallest building in San Francisco, and to the mid-Market corridor, where tech companies are being lured by the mayor's tax break incentives. Nonetheless, the hallowed crossing of Montgomery and California Streets remains the heart of financial San Francisco.

WALKING TOUR
2.1mi

▷ Begin at the intersection of Post, Montgomery & Market Sts.

Belden Place

A delightful surprise is this one-block-long alley, extending from Pine to Bush Streets just east of Kearny Street. A piece of Old World Europe transplanted to San Francisco, it is lined with small restaurants—French, Italian, Catalan, American—whose servers attend umbrella-covered tables, packed back-to-back, from one end of the lane to the other.

One Montgomery Street (A)

This grand banking hall rose after the 1906 quake as the headquarters of First National Bank (later merged with Crocker Bank). The original section along Post Street, once a 14-story office tower, was designed by Willis Polk; above that entrance an ornate cast-iron canopy is graced with figures that flank a shield, inscribed with the words "Systematic Saving is the Key to Success." The ornate interior **banking hall★**, now a Wells Fargo branch bank was completed by Charles Gottschalk in 1921. In the 1980s the building was incorporated into the Crocker Galleria.

From the corner, walk west on Post Street and enter the **Crocker Galleria★** (1983, Skidmore, Owings & Merrill), an small, elegant retail center that cuts through the middle of the block, with three tiers of commercial spaces topped by a barrel-vaulted glass roof (○ open Mon–Fri 7am–pm, Sat 10am –5pm; ✕ ⛶ 🅿 ✆ 415-393-1500; www. thecrockergalleria.com). Chocolatiers, bakeries, clothing boutiques and small eateries attract workers from adjacent office towers. From the upper level of the Galleria, a stairway leads to a tranquil **rooftop terrace** atop One Montgomery, a good place to enjoy a takeout lunch.

▷ Exit Crocker Galleria on Sutter St.

Hallidie Building★★
130–150 Sutter St.
One of San Francisco's most noteworthy works of architecture, the seven-story

office block was designed by Willis Polk (1918) and named for Andrew Hallidie, inventor of the cable car. Because the facade is formed by a modular grid of glass panes hanging from a concrete frame, the building is considered the world's first glass-curtain-walled structure.

▶ Walk east on Sutter St.

Hunter-Dulin Building★
111 Sutter St.
This richly detailed building—completed in 1927 by the New York firm of Schultze and Weaver, designers of the Waldorf-Astoria Hotel—combines historical styles in a freewheeling manner. The main shaft incorporates Romanesque arches and cast-iron spandrels embellished with medallions of mythical figures. Near the top, a central tower rises four floors to a mansard roof. The elevator lobby boasts a painted, beamed ceiling and inlaid marble floor. Writer Dashiell Hammett set the office of his fictional hero, detective Sam Spade, here.

▶ Walk to corner of Sutter and Montgomery Sts. and turn left.

Mills Building
220 Montgomery St.
www.themillsbuilding.com
One of the few downtown structures to survive the earthquake and fire, this stately office building (1891) reflects the Chicago-school tenets of its designer, Daniel Burnham. The first in the city to be clad in decorative terracotta, the building was reconstructed after the quake by Willis Polk. A richly ornamented Romanesque archway forms the main entrance. The 22-story tower along the Bush Street facade was added in 1931 by Lewis Hobart.

Russ Building★
235 Montgomery St.
This 31-story Gothic Revival landmark (1927, George Kelham) fills an entire block of Montgomery Street. A two-story archway entrance leads to a striking **lobby**★ that features stone vaulting

over cloister-like corridors, inlaid mosaic floors and elaborate elevator panels. Glass cases in the lobby display historic model ships from building owner Walter Shorenstein's collection.

▶ Turn right at Pine St.

Pacific Exchange Building★
301 Pine St. at Sansome St.
☛*Interior not open to the public.*
Built in 1915 to house a U.S. Treasury office, this proud structure was enlarged with a tower in 1930. Ralph Stackpole, later a Coit Tower muralist, was commissioned to sculpt the remarkable pair of Social Realist–style monumental statues flanking the entrance.

▶ Turn right at Sansome St.

The Stock Exchange Tower & City Club of San Francisco
155 Sansome St. cityclubsf.com
☛*Not open to the public. Rivera murals accessible via guided tour only, 1st and 3rd Monday of the month. Reserve at www.sfcityguides.org.*
Opened during the Great Depression, the Stock Exchange Tower (1930, Timothy Pflueger) was an office for brokers adjacent the San Francisco Stock Exchange. It was also home to The Pacific Stock Exchange Lunch Club, today The City Club of San Francisco, a members-only social and business club. The City Club's interiors are considered one of the finest examples of Art Deco style in the city.
In 1931, Mexican artist Diego Rivera was commissioned to create murals for The City Club's stairwell.
The choice of artist was controversial: the building was designed as a beacon of capitalism and Rivera was an outspoken communist supporter. The finished work, The Allegory of California, features a large female figure cradling a collection of working people. Today, the City Club is closed to the public, but guided tours allows limited access to the interiors and mural.

◔ Walk north on Sansome to California St and turn left.

555 California Street★★

555 California St. (enter via Montgomery St. plaza). ♿

One of the city's tallest building, this 52-story, dark-red behemoth (1969, Skidmore, Owings & Merrill) contains 2 million square feet of office space. Its color comes from slabs of carnelian granite that wrap the central shaft rising 780ft from street level. The broad, open plaza along California Street is anchored by *Transcendence* (1) (1969, Masayuki Nagare), a dark, polished sculpture dubbed "The Banker's Heart." From the plaza, glance north at the post-Modern design of **580 California Street** (1987, Johnson and Burgee) with its 12 faceless, hooded human figures encircling the 20th floor.

◔ Cross Montgomery St. and walk east on California St.

Merchants Exchange Building★ (B)

465 California St.

This 14-story office building (1903, Willis Polk) was the focal point of commerce in c. 1900 San Francisco. Signals from its rooftop belvedere announced the arrival of ships through the Golden Gate. Badly damaged in the 1906 fire, it was quickly restored. Prolific architect Julia Morgan maintained an office on the 11th floor for most of her 46-year career. From the Ionic columns at the entrance, walk though the barrel-vaulted elevator lobby to the commodious **Grain Exchange Hall★★**. On the walls are five murals by marine artist William Coulter. (⊶ *Closed to the public, but the hall may be included on some historical tours.*)

◔ Return to Montgomery St. and turn right.

⚮ Wells Fargo History Museum★ (M1)

420 Montgomery St. ◷*Open Mon–Fri 9am–5pm.* ◷*Closed major holidays.* ♿ ☏*415-396-2619.* *www.wellsfargohistory.com.*

Concord coaches of Wells Fargo & Co. began carrying freight and passengers in 1852. In this modern two-level gallery, Wells Fargo's inherent links to California history are told via photographs, documents, gold nuggets, bank notes and coins. Displays explore such topics as gold assaying, stagecoach robbery and telegraphing. Visitors can view a restored original coach and climb aboard a reconstructed one.

◔ Continue north on Montgomery St. and turn left onto Commercial St.

Commercial Street

Between Montgomery & Kearny Sts.

This narrow alley offers intriguing glimpses of early commercial San

The Barbary Coast Trail

Through downtown San Francisco, large bronze medallions embedded in sidewalks at street corners indicate the course of the Barbary Coast Trail. Extending 3.8mi from the Old Mint at Fifth and Mission Streets to Aquatic Park at the foot of Van Ness Avenue, this urban stroll cuts through Chinatown, Commercial Street, Jackson Square, North Beach and Fisherman's Wharf, en route linking dozens of historic sites and a handful of museums. It is a fine introduction to the Gold Rush heritage of San Francisco.

The brainchild of writer-historian Daniel Bacon, the privately sponsored trail officially opened in 1997 with implantation of the markers. (The city offered its assistance to the tourism-friendly venture by charging a $10,000 permit fee.) Walking-tour brochures, and Bacon's book, may be purchased at the **San Francisco Museum and Historical Society** (☏*415-775-1111; www. sfhistory.org*) and bookstores throughout the city.

Francisco. Before landfill extended the waterfront to the Embarcadero, this block formed the foot of Long Wharf, which ran across the mud flats along the line of present-day Commercial Street to deep-water anchorage.

Look east to see the towers of Embarcadero Center framing a fine view of the top of the historic Ferry Building, which stands at what once was the end of the wharf.

Tiny **Empire Park,** a privately owned public space, was renamed in 1999 to honor "Emperor" Joshua Norton, an eccentric bankrupted businessman who held court on Commercial Street for 20 years in the 1860s and 70s.

Pacific Heritage Museum (M2)
608 Commercial St. ◷*Open Tue–Sat 10am–4pm.* ◷*Closed major holidays and between major exhibitions.* ♿ ☏*415-399-1124.*

This small museum in a bank annex displays changing exhibits on artistic, cultural and economic themes related to peoples of the Pacific Rim. The building (1984, Skidmore, Owings & Merrill) incorporates the exterior walls and basement vaults of its 1877 predecessor, a U.S. Subtreasury building, itself erected on the site of San Francisco's first mint.

▷ Backtrack to Montgomery St. and turn left. Cross Montgomery at Clay St.

550 Montgomery
550 Montgomery St. ☏*415-956-0506* ◷*Open Mon–Fri 10am–6pm, Sat 10am-6pm.*

Originally the main San Francisco office of the Bank of Italy, the predecessor to the Bank of America, this building was declared a National Historic Landmark in 1982 as the birthplace of branch banking. The ornate lobby, replete with Carrrara marble, vaults and intricate moldings, is now home to Wingtip, a luxury men's retailer, that also operates a members-only club on the top two penthouse floors.

▷ Cross Clay St.

Transamerica Pyramid★★
600 Montgomery St. ⚏*Not open to the public. www.transamerica.com.*

Since its completion in 1972, this bold pyramid has come to symbolize San Francisco, a role similar to New York City's Empire State Building or Chicago's Willis (formerly Sears) Tower.

Designed by William Pereira to house the headquarters of the Transamerica Corporation, a leasing and financial institution, the elegant 48-story spire rises 853ft from street level to the tip of its 212ft hollow lantern. Slanted sides reduce the extent of its shadow on surrounding structures. To the east, a peaceful grove with some 40 redwood trees forms a tranquil oasis.

▷ Walk east on Clay St. and turn right onto Sansome St.

Old Federal Reserve Bank★
400 Sansome St.

This classical Beaux-Arts gem (1924, George Kelham) makes a dramatic first impression with its eight 25ft Ionic columns and the row of federal eagles perched above its portico. The building exemplifies San Francisco's banking-temple tradition. Artist Jules Guerin, chief muralist for the Panama-Pacific International Exposition of 1915, painted the impressive "Traders of the Adriatic" mural. In 1984 the Fed moved its district headquarters to Market Street.

▷ Cross Sacramento St. and continue south on Sansome St.

343 Sansome
◷*Roof garden open Mon–Fri 9am–6pm.* www.343sansome.info

On the roof of this mixed-use landmark high-rise (1908, John Galen Howard) there is a privately owned public garden, open to visitors on weekdays. From the building's lobby, take the elevators to the 15th floor for views of the Financial District and the Bay.

▷ Cross Halleck Alley, continue south on Sansome St. to California St.

Bank of California★★
400 California St.
Now Union Bank, this exquisite, classically proportioned bank (1907, Bliss and Faville) displays the resources put into rebuilding San Francisco after the 1906 Fire. A regal ceiling tops the magnificent banking hall, embellished with Corinthian pilasters.

▷ Walk east on California St.

345 California Center★
345 California St.
Two angular towers linked by a glass-enclosed "sky bridge" cap this futuristic skyscraper (1986, Skidmore, Owings and Merrill). The building incorporated the facades of earlier historic structures, including the J. Harold Dollar Building (1920) and the Robert Dollar Building (1919), former steamship-line headquarters. The top 11 stories house the luxurious Loews Regency Hotel, formerly the Mandarin Oriental *(main entrance at 222 Sansome St.).*

▷ Continue east on California St.

Embarcadero Center★
Bounded by The Embarcadero and Clay, Sacramento & Battery Sts.
☎415-772-0700 ✕♿🅿
embarcaderocenter.com.
The city's largest office and commercial complex, this series of four slab-like office towers (1982, John Portman and Assoc.) and the adjoining Hyatt Regency Hotel cover nearly 10 acres. A shopping center occupies its lower floors, running along historic Commercial Street; pedestrian bridges traverse cross streets to link the four structures. More than a dozen sculptures dot public spaces, among them works by Jean Dubuffet and Louise Nevelson.
Linked to the east tower (Four Embarcadero Center) by a pedestrian bridge, the Hyatt Regency (1973) boasts an asymmetrical 17-story **atrium★**. At the east end of the complex is brick-paved **Justin Herman Plaza ♟♟**, where the angular forms of Vaillancourt Fountain (1971) invite exploration.

▷ Cross The Embarcadero to the Ferry Building.

Ferry Building★★
♿*See THE EMBARCADERO.*

▷ Cross The Embarcadero to the south side of Market St.

One Market★
1 Market St.
Erected in stages, this office complex weds the facade of the original Southern Pacific Railroad headquarters (1916, Bliss and Faville) to a futuristically redesigned interior (1995, Cesar Pelli and Assoc.).

▷ Walk southwest on Market St. and cross Spear St.

♟♟ Federal Reserve Bank of San Francisco
101 Market St. ☞*Visit by guided tour (90 min) only; group tours Mon–Thu 9.30am and 1pm, reservation required.* ⏱*Closed major holidays.* ♿
☎*415-974-4133. www.frbsf.org.*
A vaulted loggia covers the bank's Market Street frontage, from which the bulk of the building (1982, Skidmore, Owings & Merrill) steps back in a series of terraces. In the lobby, the **The Fed Center★** exhibit offers entertaining lessons in basic economics. Using computer simulators, visitors adjust the rate of money growth, set interest rates or taxes, and gauge the effect on economy. A currency exhibit explores paper money from colonial to modern times.

▷ Continue southwest on Market St. to Battery St.

One of the city's most energetic pieces of public sculpture, the **Mechanics Monument (2)** *(median at Market and Battery Sts.)* vividly memorializes the craftsmen who built San Francisco. Created by Douglas Tilden in 1896, the sculpture was dedicated to Peter Donahue, owner of the city's first iron foundry.

▶ Cross Bush St., then Battery St. to its south side.

Shell Building★
100 Bush St., at Battery St.
Clad in light brown terra-cotta, this graceful Art Deco tower (1929, George Kelham) has a plain, 20-story central shaft that steps back to form a slender, richly ornamented top. Decorative motifs, including a large gilt shell over the entrance and shell forms covering the parapets, represent the Shell Oil Corporation, which developed the property as its Western headquarters.
Next door, at **130 Bush Street** (1910, McDonald and Applegarth), stands one of the city's narrowest office buildings. Gothic-style ornamentation covers the 10-story, bow-fronted tower that measures just 20ft wide.

▶ Continue west on Bush St. one block and cross.

One Bush Plaza★
Originally called the Crown Zellerbach Building, this distinctive tower is San Francisco's best example of International style architecture. Designed by Hertzka and Knowles/Skidmore, Owings and Merrill in 1959, modeled after the latter firm's influential Lever House in New York City, the pale green glass box stands on concrete stilts above a broad plaza. At its base is a sunken plaza anchored by a small, freestanding circular structure that houses a financial firm.

▶ Cross Sutter St., turn right on Market St. Walk southwest to Montgomery St.

An angelic female perched atop a stone shaft, above a miner waving an American flag, is the most prominent element of the **Native Sons of the Golden West Monument (3)**, which honors the establishment of California statehood in 1850. Sculpted by Douglas Tilden in 1897, the statue was originally erected farther down Market Street, then moved to Golden Gate Park before being placed at its present location, at a prominent intersection, in 1977.

▶ Cross Market St.

Palace Hotel★★
2 New Montgomery St. ✕ ♿ ▣
♺ *415-512-1111. www.sfpalace.com.*
This elegant hostelry figures prominently in San Francisco history. Constructed in 1875 by financier William Ralston as part of his plan to lure development south of Market Street, the Palace Hotel gained a reputation as the most opulent hotel in the West until it was gutted in the 1906 Fire. It reopened in 1909 with great fanfare. Rivaling the Fairmont Hotel in sophistication and luxury, the new Palace quickly became the focal point of high society. The hotel has hosted many luminaries (Warren G. Harding died here in 1923), and was restored in 1989–91 and again in 2015. Enter at 639 Market Street and stroll the main corridor to the glorious **Garden Court★★**, capped by a canopy of intricate art glass. The corridor boasts display cases with fascinating mementoes. Also worth seeing is the **Pied Piper Bar** (*off corridor near Market St. entrance*) and its famous allegorical mural of the Pied Piper of Hamelin by Maxfield Parrish, painted for the hotel's reopening in 1909.

▶ Cross Market St., turn left and continue to Kearny St.

A cast-iron column rising from a small fountain, beloved **Lotta's Fountain** (*northeast corner of Market and Kearny Sts.*) was given to the people of San Francisco by entertainer Lotta Crabtree in 1875. Every April 18 around 5am, San Franciscans congregate here to commemorate the anniversary of the great earthquake and fire of 1906.
The intersection hosting Lotta's Fountain once was the heart of the city's newspaper industry. The former **Chronicle Building** (*690 Market St.*), erected in 1889 by Burnham and Root, is the city's oldest office tower, partially destroyed in the earthquake of 1906. Across Market Street lies the **Hearst Building** (*691 Third St.*), an exuberant, Spanish Revival–style structure that was

the home of the *San Francisco Examiner* from 1911 to 1965.

ADDITIONAL SIGHT

Jackson Square★★

Bounded by Washington, Montgomery & Sansome Sts. and Pacific Ave.

Despite its name, San Francisco's oldest surviving commercial neighborhood is not a "square" but five square blocks of well-preserved mid-19C structures between North Beach and the Financial District. This former waterfront neighborhood was once the heart of the notorious **Barbary Coast**, the bawdy, Gold Rush-era district of saloons, theaters and burlesque houses that lined Pacific Avenue between Sansome Street and Columbus Avenue. The brick structures outlasted the great earthquake and fire of 1906; since the 1960s, many have been converted to upscale art galleries, design firms, and antique stores.

Today the two- and three-story buildings, with brick, cast-iron or stucco facades, create a cozily uniform departure from the neighboring towers of the Financial District. The oldest buildings lie along Montgomery Street a block north of the Transamerica Pyramid. The **Belli Building (C)** *(no. 722)* was constructed in 1849-1850 on a foundation of redwood that literally floats upon former tidelands. First a tobacco warehouse, later a raucous nightclub where Lotta Crabtree got her start, it served as the law offices of famed attorney Melvin Belli from the 1960s until it was damaged in the 1989 earthquake and has long been neglected. The attached **Belli Annex** *(no. 726)*, a three-story brick Italianate built in 1852, marks the site of the first meeting (in 1849) of the California Freemasons. Next door, the two-story **Golden Era Building (D)** *(no. 730)* was built in 1852 as the home of the West's premier literary magazine, the *Golden Era,* whose contributors included Mark Twain, Bret Harte and Joaquin Miller. Around the corner, the Italianate-style **Hotaling Warehouse** *(451–455 Jackson St.)* was constructed for whiskey distill-

ing and storage in 1866. The building was rescued from the 1906 conflagration thanks to the valiant efforts of sailors, who strung a water hose over Telegraph Hill from their ships, and local firefighters. If the liquor had exploded, Jackson Square would have gone up with it.

Pacific Avenue, the northern boundary of Jackson Square, was for years (before and after the earthquake) the rowdiest street in San Francisco.

Many of its buildings were at one time saloons, dance halls, gambling parlors, brothels or boarding houses catering to transient sailors. Painted white pilasters and naked, dancing nymphs, sculpted in bas-relief on the exterior walls of the 1907 **Hippodrome** *(no. 555)*, are a vivid reminder of its post-earthquake heyday. Early 20C dances such as the turkey trot were popularized here, to the sounds of ragtime and Dixieland jazz bands, before spreading across the country.

ADDRESSES

♈/EAT

$$ Tadich Grill – *240 California St.* ☎*415-391-1849*. **Seafood**. Fresh fish is the fare of choice at this San Francisco institution, which began during the Gold Rush as a coffee stand. Go for the charcoal-grilled sole, the cold seafood salads, and the no-nonsense service by white-jacketed waiters in long aprons.

SHOPPING

William Stout Architectural Books – *804 Montgomery St.* ☎*415-391-6757. www.stoutbooks.com.* When books and magazines overflowed his apartment, architect Stout went into business as a bookseller. A huge selection of architectural titles, as well as art, photography, and landscaping themes now overflow this charming shop.

Nob Hill★★

Nob Hill, which witnessed one of San Francisco's first infusions of wealth, today remains a vivid example of the city's diverse urban community. Cable cars trundle up and down the steep slopes, passing restored Edwardian homes and 1920s high-rise apartment buildings. Cozy bistros, corner grocery stores, and boutiques nestle together along the serene, tree-lined side streets. Sloping down to the southwest, Lower Nob Hill (often referred to as the Tendernob), bordered by Geary and Polk Streets, has a grittier feel but is filled with trendy bars and restaurants.

🚃 All lines, 511.org.

ℹ️ **Info:** www.sftravel.com

▶ **Location:** West of Chinatown, north of Union Square, and uphill from everywhere.

👨‍👦 **Kids:** The Cable Car Museum, next-best thing to a cable car ride.

🕐 **Timing:** Plan about two hours to visit Nob Hill.

🅿️ **Parking:** Be sure to check signs for scheduled street-cleaning days before taking a spot on the street.

😊 **Don't Miss:** A swooping cable-car ride up and down Nob Hill's steep flanks.

A BIT OF HISTORY

Nob Hill acquired its reputation as home to San Francisco's elite during the city's earliest years. In 1856 Dr. Arthur Hayne, a well-to-do dentist, became the first to settle on the craggy hill, erecting a modest home on the 376ft summit where the Fairmont Hotel stands today. Soon after, merchant William Walton built a grander residence at the present-day corner of Washington and Taylor Streets. By the late 1860s, a handful of millionaires had built homes near the summit, establishing it as a choice residential locale.

The exclusive cachet was ensured after cable-car lines were installed on its steep flanks in 1873, opening the door to development of formerly inaccessible summits, and construction on the crest of Nob Hill boomed. As the rest of the city battled the Panic of 1893, an economic depression affecting all industrial cities in the U.S., Nob Hill became what author Robert Louis Stevenson called "the hill of palaces," thanks in good part to a group of newly minted millionaires.

The Big Four – In 1859 four middle-class Sacramento merchants—**Leland Stanford**, **Charles Crocker**, **Mark Hopkins**, and **Collis Huntington**—together purchased a modest number of shares in what seemed at the time an impossible venture: a railway across the western U.S. A decade later the railroad was complete and their investments yielded millions of dollars. The four promptly moved to San Francisco, purchased lots on the summit of Nob Hill and built sprawling mansions ("Nob" is a contraction of "nabob," a term for European adventurers who made fortunes the Far East).

In the 1880s the Big Four were joined on the hill by two "Bonanza Kings," who had extracted huge fortunes from Nevada's Comstock silver lode in 1873. **James Fair**, a former miner, bought Dr. Hayne's property, and **James Flood** erected his Italianate brownstone mansion, today the Pacific-Union Club.

Through the late 19C, large Victorian houses appeared on the flanks of the hill, near cable-car routes established along California and Powell Streets. After its destruction by the great quake and fire of 1906, the area was rebuilt with tall, narrow Edwardian homes and high-rise apartments. Today Nob Hill maintains turn-of-the-20C charm, although many wealthier San Franciscans now live in neighborhoods to the northwest, where larger plots accommodate palatial mansions. Asian families populate the northeast slopes near Chinatown, and a large singles population occupies studios and small apartments to the southwest.

RUSSIAN HILL
NOB HILL

WALKING TOUR

▶ Begin at the southwest corner of Powell and California Sts.

.6mi. The first of the Big Four to build his mansion atop Nob Hill, Leland Stanford constructed an immense Italianate villa on a corner lot in 1876. Today it is the site of the **Stanford Court Hotel**, re-modeled in 1972 from an apartment building, and remodeled again in 2018 to include updated ecofriendly modern

decor and hip lobby whiskey bar Seven Stills. The gray stone retaining wall was built in the 1870s and was the only part to survive the 1906 fire.

▶ Walk west up California St.

InterContinental Mark Hopkins San Francisco

One Nob Hill (999 California St. at Mason St.). ✕ ♿ 🅿 ☎*415-392-3434.* *www.intercontinentalmarkhopkins.com.* In 1877 Mark Hopkins began construction of a sprawling Victorian mansion to rival Stanford's in elegance and ostentation. Hopkins died in 1878 before it was completed; in 1893 his widow donated the residence to the California School of Design. The 1906 fire razed the structure, and in 1926 the Mark Hopkins Hotel rose in its place.

The hotel is crowned by the **Top of the Mark**, a swank restaurant and bar (☞see Addresses) with panoramic **views★★★**.

☞ Cross California St.

Fairmont Hotel★★

Bounded by California, Mason, Powell and Sacramento Sts. ✕ ♿ 🅿 ☎415-772-5000. www.fairmont.com/sanfrancisco. With its opulent lobby, dignified facade and illustrious history, the Fairmont offers a glimpse of early 20C Nob Hill. Designed by James and Merritt Reid, its construction began in 1902 under the stewardship of Tessie Fair Oelrichs, James Fair's daughter. Work was nearly complete when the 1906 Earthquake struck and fire swept the hill, leaving only the granite outer walls intact. Architect Julia Morgan oversaw the restoration and completion of the building in its original Italian Renaissance style. On April 18, 1907, exactly a year after the earthquake, the Fairmont reopened, quickly becoming the city's premier hotel. In 1945, the United Nations Charter was drafted in the elegant Garden Room; commemorated by the UN-member flags above the hotel's main entrance. A modern tower was added in 1961. In the ornate main lobby, massive marble pillars and wrought-iron balconies remain from Morgan's 1906 design. Don't miss the **Tonga Room**, a tiki-themed lounge featuring Pacific Rim cuisine, umbrella drinks and regular occurring faux tropical rainstorms★.

☞ Walk west on California St.

Pacific-Union Club★

1000 California St.
⚇Not open to the public.
The only structure on Nob Hill to survive the 1906 blaze, silver baron James Flood's mansion was built in 1885 by English architect Augustus Laver at a cost of $1.5 million. Unlike other Nob Hill palaces, which were made of California redwood, Flood's 42-room Italianate home was built of Connecticut brownstone and withstood the 1906 earthquake, although the intense heat of the ensuing fire gutted the lavish interior. In 1908 architect Willis Polk added wings on two sides. Today the building is home to the exclusive Pacific-Union Club, which traces its origins to 1852.

☞ Continue west on California St. and cross Taylor St.

Grace Cathedral★

1100 California St. at Taylor St. 🕐Open 8am-8pm most days. ☞Guided tours (90 min) on select days at 10am or by appointment. Self guided tours available through the GraceGuide app ♿🅿 ($25) ☎415-749-6300. www.gracecathedral.org.
The third-largest Episcopal cathedral in the U.S. crowns the crest of Nob Hill, its French Gothic spires soaring over the city. Consecrated in 1964, the edifice occupies the lot formerly owned by Charles Crocker, whose Second Empire-style mansion stood next to his son's Victorian villa. After both homes were destroyed in the 1906 Fire, the family donated the land to the Episcopal diocese. Grace's cornerstone was laid in 1910 and construction began in 1928, but it wasn't fully completed until the 1960s. The Notre Dame-inspired design by Lewis P. Hobart was executed in steel-reinforced concrete to withstand seismic tremors. Set between the main entrance doors in the Gothic eastern portal, the bronze **Gates of Paradise** are the cathedral's most prized architectural feature. Duplicates of a set cast by Florentine sculptor Lorenzo Ghiberti, the 16ft doors are divided into ten richly ornamented panels illustrating scenes from the Old Testament. Inside the cathedral, dozens of stained-glass windows and murals depict a diversity of figures, including Robert Frost, Franklin D. Roosevelt and Albert Einstein. The alterpiece, painter Keith Haring's *A Life*

Cable Car Museum

of Christ, was dedicated in 1995. A magnificent Aeolian-Skinner organ resounds with 7,286 pipes. Two labyrinths invite exploration: an outdoor terrazo stone path to the right of the east entrance, and a second limestone labyrinth inside. A thoroughly San Franciscan institution with an inclusive ethos, Grace is committed to social justice and progressive theology, playing a vibrant, multifaceted role in the local community. Since 2012, Grace has operated an artist-in-residence program, it frequently hosts multi-faith celebrations and music concerts, and the main nave is home to a popular yoga class every Thursday night, accompanied by live music.

▶ Exit cathedral on Taylor St. and cross to the park.

Huntington Park

Banked slightly above street level, Huntington Park gracefully crowns Nob Hill. John McLaren, who designed Golden Gate Park and other Bay Area public gardens, oversaw the design and cultivation of this 1.75-acre plot, donated to the city after Collis Huntington's opulent mansion on the adjacent lot was destroyed in the 1906 Fire. Blackwood acacias and sycamores thrive here, framing the 20C replica of Rome's Tartarughe ("Tortoise") Fountain, purchased in Italy by William Crocker's wife, as the park's centerpiece.

▶ Walk east on Sacramento St. and turn left on Mason St.

▲▲ Cable Car Museum★★

1201 Mason St. at Washington St. ⊙*Open Apr–Oct daily 10am–6pm. Nov–Mar 10am–5pm.* ⊙*Closed Jan 1, Thanksgiving Day, Dec 25.* ♿ ☏*415-474 -1887. www.cablecarmuseum.com.*

This weathered brick building on the steep north slope of Nob Hill offers an up-close look at the nerve center of San Francisco's renowned cable-car system, the only one of its kind in the world. Besides serving as a powerhouse and car-storage barn, the structure houses a unique history museum.

On the upper level, a balcony overlooks the cable-car mechanism. Motors hum and giant wheels called "sheaves" rotate, powering continuous loops of cable for the system's three lines. Historical displays tell the story of the cable cars from their invention, to the present.

Among the treasured pieces is **Car No. 8**, only survivor of the Clay Street Hill Railroad, San Francisco's first cable-car line, which began operation in 1873. On the lower level, a small viewing area offers a glimpse of the room where the thick steel cables enter the building.

ADDITIONAL SIGHT

The Ritz-Carlton, San Francisco

600 Stockton St. (between California and Pine Sts.) ✕♿🅿 ☏*415-296-7465. www.ritzcarlton.com.*

Built on the Chinatown flank of Nob Hill (1909, Napoleon Le Brun & Sons) as the West Coast headquarters of the Metropolitan Life Insurance Co., the original

© plus99/iStockphoto.com

Getting A Grip: San Francisco's Cable Cars

More than 8 million visitors and San Franciscans annually ride the city's signature cable cars, a public transportation system invented and developed by Scotsman Andrew Smith Hallidie in 1873. Inspired by the work of his father, who had been awarded the world's first patent on iron-wire rope in 1835, 16-year-old Hallidie came to California in 1852, at the height of the Gold Rush, to build wire-rope transport systems for the mines. In his 20s he moved to San Francisco, where he established a wire-rope manufacturing company and developed suspension bridges and cable tramways for Nevada Comstock Lode's silver mines. In 1869 Hallidie first conceived of a similar system for public transportation. Four years and $85,000 later, the idea that had been dubbed "Hallidie's Folly" took form as a primitive cable car line that ascended Clay Street between Kearny and Leavenworth Streets at 6mph.

A testament to the quality of Hallidie's design, today's cable cars work in much the same way as those of 1873. Huge loops of steel cable run at a continuous 9.5mph beneath Powell, Hyde, Mason and California Streets, powered by electric motors. To start the car moving, the "gripman"—in the middle of the car—operates a lever that extends down through a slot in the street. At the underground end of the lever, a "grip" closes and opens like a jaw on the moving cable. The tighter the grip closes, the faster the car goes. To reduce speed, the gripman opens the grip to release the cable; brakes are applied to stop. A conductor at the rear of the car helps with braking when necessary.

Because the soft metal dies, inside the jaws of the grip, are the only contact between the cables and the cars (which can weigh up to ten tons), they must be replaced every four days. The cables, constructed of six strands of 19 wires twisted around a core of sisal rope, must be replaced every few months through a labor-intensive process of cutting and splicing each individual strand. The track is inspected daily for imperfections, as are each car's three sets of brakes: wheel brakes, track brakes and emergency brakes. This is essential, considering the harrowing 18–21 percent grades the cars negotiate.

Designated a National Historic Landmark in 1964, the system today has 40 cars operating on three lines (Powell-Mason, Powell-Hyde and California Street).

The entire system, including the powerhouse, was rehabilitated in 1982–1984, preserving this unique, characteristic part of San Francisco's past and present.

80ft cube was expanded in 1914 and 1920 with two symmetrical wings. A facade of 18 Ionic columns supports an entablature that features hourglasses and lions' heads; an allegorical figure ("Insurance") spreads its wings over two symbolic families from the portico above the entrance.

The Ritz purchased the building in the late 1980s, and the luxurious hotel opened in 1991.

ADDRESSES

ℹ/ EAT

$$ Swan Oyster Depot – *1517 Polk St.* ℰ*415-673-1101.* Jokes and shells fly at this old-time lunch counter where the crew serves up fresh clam chowder, crab legs, seafood cocktails and oysters on the half shell. Expect a line.

$$$ Top of the Mark – *InterContinental Mark Hopkins.* ℰ*415-772-5278. www.intercontinentalmarkhopkins.com.* Once a copper baron's penthouse, the Top of the Mark was redesigned in 1939 as a swank Art Deco-style bar by Timothy Pflueger, boasting gorgeous, sweeping views. Live music Wed-Sat.

North Beach ★★

Once the heart of San Francisco's Italian community and one of the city's oldest neighborhoods, this sunny district has become a prime residential haven for diverse ethnic groups. Although businesses from burgeoning Chinatown, to the south, slowly encroach across Broadway, the flavors and fragrances of North Beach's Italian roots still predominate, as evidenced by dozens of well-patronized trattorias, cafes and delicatessens. A onetime refuge for San Francisco's Beat counterculture, this neighborhood retains, to a certain degree, the close-knit character of a village.

A BIT OF HISTORY

Only the name remains of the narrow stretch of sand that once formed the area's bayside border. As early as the 1850s, land-hungry speculators began dumping tons of fill material into the shallows that once lapped present-day Bay Street, eventually erecting a flour-ishing industrial zone atop the buried beach. Rough-and-tumble tent cities appeared on the sheltered southwest slope of Telegraph Hill in the early Gold Rush years. **Little Chile**, populated by

🚋 Powell-Mason.

🚌 Bus 30–Stockton, 45–Union-Stockton or 39–Coit, 511.org.

🛈 **Info:** www.northbeachbusinessassociation.com.

▶ **Location:** North Beach nestles between bustling Fisherman's Wharf and the steep slopes of Telegraph Hill and Russian Hill.

👥 **Kids:** Coit Tower, one of San Francisco's enduring symbols.

🕐 **Timing:** Mornings bring smells of freshly roasted coffee beans; in the late afternoon the fragrance of garlic from Italian restaurants wafts over the neighborhood.

🅿 **Parking:** Street parking is difficult. Take a bus or try North Beach Garage *(735 Vallejo St. between Stockton and Powell;* ⬜*$3.50/hr).*

😊 **Don't Miss:** Filbert and Greenwich steps.

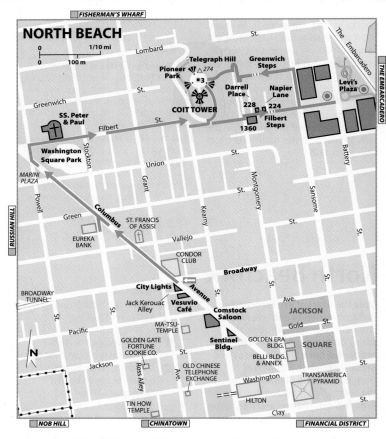

NORTH BEACH

treasure-seeking Chileans and Peruvians, sprang up near Kearny Street. Directly to the east between Broadway and Union Street stood **Sydney Town**, home of a notorious group of former Australian convicts, many of whom regularly terrorized their South American neighbors. Ships' crews carved chunks from the side of Telegraph Hill to provide ballast for their homeward voyages, the vessels having been vacated by the argonauts. The hillside scars remain visible today.

After the heady days of the Gold Rush, a polyglot mixture of newly arrived immigrants from Spain, France, Portugal, Germany and Italy moved into the valley, which subsequently became known as the **Latin Quarter**. Goats roamed the rocky crest of Telegraph Hill, where the working-class Irish had established an enclave on the eastern slope. Italian immigration, slow in the mid-19C, increased dramatically in the 1880s as successful émigrés brought their families from Europe. Newcomers from northern Italy disembarked at the foot of Sansome Street and stayed, attracted by North Beach's relatively warm microclimate, low rents and proximity to the wharves and canneries where many made their living. The Italian community gradually displaced other ethnic groups, and by 1900 the old Latin Quarter had given way to **Little Italy**.

The Best Minds of a Generation – As the children of Italian immigrants grew up, they also moved out, seeking agricultural opportunities in the rich Napa and Sonoma county farmlands. In the mid-50s, vacancies in North Beach had driven rents low enough to attract an anarchic assortment of poor and disillusioned—"beaten"—writers and artists bent on rejecting established societal and artistic norms. Calling themselves the **Beat Generation** and dubbed "beatniks" (by columnist Herb Caen), they adopted nonconformist bohemian lifestyles, smoked marijuana, drank red wine and espresso, listened to jazz and be-bop, and read poetry at favorite haunts like the Co-Existence Bagel Shop and The Place (both long since vanished). Of their principal gathering places, few remain; City Lights Bookstore, Vesuvio Café, Tosca Cafe and Caffé Trieste are rare survivors.

The movement inspired an outpouring of creative activity by its leading lights: poets Lawrence Ferlinghetti, Kenneth Rexroth, Gregory Corso and Allen Ginsberg; novelist Jack Kerouac; and visual artists Jay DeFeo and Robert LaVigne. The 1955 reading of Ginsberg's raw, apocalyptic poem "Howl" gave birth to the San Francisco Poetry Renaissance and an enduring cultural legend. "I saw the best minds of my generation destroyed by madness," Ginsberg intoned, "starving, hysterical, naked, draggin themselves through negro streets at dawn lookin for an angry fix."

Within a decade, the movement was over, ruined in part by busloads of "square" tourists who overran North Beach in their search for "cool." By the mid-60s, the best minds of the Beat Generation had either passed away or moved on.

North Beach Today – Few in the counterculture could now afford the high rents of North Beach's surprisingly uniform, three- to four-story flats and apartment houses, built in a nine-year flurry of reconstruction after the 1906 Earthquake and Fire. The northward flow of families and businesses from Chinatown, begun in the 1960s as immigration restrictions on Asians eased, continues the district's long tradition of multiethnic coexistence. Many nonresident Italian Americans still consider North Beach home, returning often to shop, dine or gather at one of the venerable institutions still operated by descendants of the original owners. Around and on Washington Square are some of North Beach's best restaurants.

WALKING TOUR
1.6mi

▶ Begin at the corner of Columbus Ave. & Broadway.

City Lights Bookstore★

261 Columbus Ave. ◷*Open daily 10am–midnight.* ◷*Closed Thanksgiving Day and Dec 25.* ✆*415-362-8193. www.citylights.com.*

Founded in 1953 by poet Lawrence Ferlinghetti, this former beatnik hangout was the first all-paperback bookstore in America. It remains one of the best-known independent shops in the U.S., as much for its history as for its meandering layout, ambience and notably excellent and diverse selection of books—some released by City Lights Publishers. In the upstairs poetry and Beat literature room, comfortable chairs encourage browsers to linger with their selections.

Across Jack Kerouac Alley from City Lights Bookstore lies **Vesuvio Café** (*255 Columbus Ave.;* ✕ ♿ ✆*415-362-3370; www.vesuvio.com*), another popular landmark of North Beach's Beat heyday. It was here that a black-clad crowd of beatniks gathered on October 13, 1955, before attending Ginsberg's now-legendary reading of "Howl" at the Six Gallery (long gone from its former Marina District location). Vivid paintings and leaded glass enliven the cafe's wood-trimmed walls, which are crammed with photos and memorabilia from the Beat era.

Just steps southeast on Columbus Avenue is the **Comstock Saloon.** (*155 Columbus Ave.;* ✕ ♿ ✆*415-617-0071; www.comstocksaloon.com*). Established at the edge of the Barbary Coast in 1907 as the Andromeda Saloon, it attracted such diverse personalities as Jack Dempsey, a 1913 bouncer who became world heavyweight boxing champion,

T'ai Chi

Early-rising visitors enjoying a morning trek through North Beach, Russian Hill, Nob Hill or other residential areas are likely to spy individuals or groups of people dressed in everyday clothes performing what appears to be a slow-motion outdoor ballet. *T'ai chi ch'uan,* an ancient, noncompetitive martial art, is practiced by many citizens as a form of exercise. The slow, meditative transitions between specified stances and positions is said to condition the body and relax the mind by harmonizing of the passive and active principles of yin and yang. Almost any serene plot can be a good place to perform this ritual, but groups tend to gather at Ina Coolbrith Park, Huntington Park, St. Mary's Square, and especially Washington Square Park.

and Baby Face Nelson, public enemy no. 1, captured at the Andromeda by the FBI in 1939. Now owned by the chic hospitality company The Absinthe Group, the bar retains many historic photos and original antiques, complimented by nightly live music, a classic-leaning cocktail program, and upscale pub food.

▶ Walk north to Broadway, turn right and cross Columbus Ave.

As you cross, glance to your right for an impressive view of the Transamerica Pyramid. The **Sentinel Building** *(916 Kearny St.),* a green, copper-trimmed, flatiron-shaped office building (1905, Salfield and Kohlberg), rises in the foreground. Filmmaker Francis Ford Coppola purchased and restored the

tower in the 1970s; Coppola also owns and operates **Café Zoetrope** *(℘415-291-1700)* on the ground floor, a wine-centric Italian restaurant with vintages from the Italy and California, including the Napa Valley's Niebaum-Coppola Estate.

Broadway

Broadway between Columbus Ave. and Montgomery St.

Though its reputation for danger, vice and sin has gentled in recent decades, the strip of sex shops and topless clubs along Broadway and Kearny Street harks back to San Francisco's less-than-savory past. Broadway's notoriety originated in the waterfront dives of Sydney Town in the 1850s, when a zone of dance halls, brothels, gambling dens and outlaw nests known as the **Barbary Coast** arose along lower Pacific Avenue, extending to present-day Jackson Square and parts of Chinatown. Sailors on shore leave enjoyed the strip's diversions at great peril: "Shanghaiing" was an all-too-common practice (the word, meaning "recruiting someone forcefully for maritime service," is said to have originated here). Civic pressure led to the cleanup of the Barbary Coast after the 1906 earthquake and fire, and bars offering exotic entertainment were restricted to Broadway, where they have persisted, mostly undisturbed, for years. Several risqué venues opened in the 1960s and early 1970s, among them the Condor Club at the intersection of Broadway, Columbus and Grant Avenues. For several decades a neon figure of **Carol Doda**, the "queen of topless

Café Zoetrope

© Anna Serrano/hemis.fr

© canbalci/iStockphoto.com

dancing," hung provocatively above the street, drawing scores of visitors. The cartoonish landmark was removed (and auctioned off piecemeal) in 1991, but several all-nude venues remain.

▷ Continue up Columbus Ave.

Columbus Avenue

Designed in 1872 as a direct path from the Financial District to the industrial zone growing along the northern waterfront, this broad, busy avenue traces the valley between Russian and Telegraph Hills, indiscriminately cutting across the city's square grid and creating several confusing six-way intersections. Called Montgomery Avenue at its construction, it was later renamed for Christopher Columbus to honor North Beach's Italian community. Today anchored by the Transamerica Pyramid, the thoroughfare extends through North Beach to The Cannery on Fisherman's Wharf. The blocks between Broadway and Filbert Street, lined with fragrant bakeries, garlicky trattorias, pungent delicatessens and aromatic cafes, preserve the soul of Italian North Beach.

▷ Continue to Stockton St. and turn left.

The melding of cultures that distinguishes present-day North Beach is clearly visible in the block of Stockton Street between Vallejo and Green Streets. Asian markets and Chinese street signs rub shoulders with old-fashioned Italian shops advertising fresh tagliarini and imported olive oil.

▷ Return to Columbus Ave. and continue northwest.

Washington Square Park★
Filbert St. and Stockton St.
5am–midnight. ♿
With a broad, sunny lawn and clusters of willow, cypress and sycamore trees, this pentagonal park occupies the heart of North Beach. The popular neighborhood gathering spot was donated to the city by its first mayor, John W. Geary, and set aside as a public park in 1847 by Jasper O'Farrell, surveyor of San Francisco's downtown street grid. After Columbus Avenue sliced off its southwest corner (now called Marini Plaza) in 1873, the park was landscaped to Victorian taste with shade trees and a broad, curving path for promenading. Hundreds of refugees camped here during the year following the 1906 earthquake and fire. Today, elderly Asians gather each morning to practice *t'ai chi*, a graceful form of martial arts (♿*see above*), and Italian retirees chat on the benches facing Union Street. Visitors and locals alike often picnic on the grassy lawn.

Saints Peter and Paul Church★
666 Filbert St., north side of Washington Sq. *Open Mon–Fri 7am–4pm, Sat–Sun 6.30am–7pm.* ♿ ☏415-421-0809. www.salesianspp.org.
Built in Gothic Revival style with Italianate details, this handsome, twin-

spired church (1924) is fondly known as the Italian Cathedral. Lawrence Ferlinghetti dubbed it "the marzipan church on the plaza," a description particularly true at night when floodlights bathe its cream-colored exterior. The imposing facade bears the opening line of Dante's *Paradiso*: "The glory of Him who moves all things penetrates and glows throughout the universe." The interior is warm and inviting, enclosed by an unusual flat ceiling of dark wood and illuminated by banks of votive candles and richly colored stained-glass windows. A spectacular, 40ft-high altar, made of Mediterranean marble and onyx, features a sculpted reproduction of da Vinci's *Last Supper.*

Screen legend Marilyn Monroe and baseball great Joe DiMaggio took wedding photos on the front steps of SS. Peter and Paul, contributing to the myth that they were married inside. DiMaggio grew up in North Beach, and as a youth in the 1930s was a member of the church's boys' club—along with New York Yankees teammates Tony Lazzeri and Frankie Crossetti.

The church reflects North Beach's multiethnic character, offering Mass in English, Italian, Latin and Cantonese.

▶ From the church, walk east up Filbert St. and climb the hill, following the "Stairs to Coit Tower" signs. To avoid the steep climb, take the 39–Coit bus from Washington Square.

Jungle City

The relative warmth of Telegraph Hill and Washington Square attracts colonies of colorful parrots, believed to be descendants of escaped household pets. The parrots now form a curious and vocal part of North Beach's landscape, their loud screeches and brilliant colors enlivening Telegraph Hill's verdant flanks and the leafy canopies of Washington Square.

Telegraph Hill★

The abrupt rise that punctuates the eastern edge of North Beach was named for a long-vanished semaphore erected atop its summit in 1850. A precursor to modern telegraph systems, the semaphore signaled the arrival of ships through the Golden Gate by varicolored flags hoisted along its two arms, positioned according to the type and nationality of the vessel. Gold Rush-era shacks and tent cities that dotted the steep, rocky flanks developed into working-class neighborhoods that persisted until the early 20C. Most of the structures on the hill (and in surrounding North Beach) burned to the ground during the 1906 Fire, but houses on the east slope were saved by determined Italian Americans, who beat back the flames with blankets soaked in red wine.

The tree-filled expanse at the hill's 274ft summit, today known as **Pioneer Park**, was donated to the city in 1876 by a group of businessmen intent on preserving the open space for future generations. The bronze statue of **Christopher Columbus (3)** at the center of the Coit Tower parking area was erected by the local Italian-American community. Panoramic **views★★** from the summit encompass major landmarks including Twin Peaks, Lombard Street, the Golden Gate Bridge, Alcatraz and the Bay Bridge. On clear days, the East Bay hills come into view. As you gaze, listen for the sounds of barking sea lions drifting up from Pier 39.

👥 Coit Tower★★★

Summit of Telegraph Hill. 🕐*Open daily April-Oct 10am–6pm, Nov-Mar, 10am-5pm. Closed Jan 1, Thanksgiving Day and Dec 25.* 🅿 ℘*415-249-0995. sfrecpark.org/destination/telegraph-hill-pioneer-park/coit-tower.* 🎫*$9 elevator fee.* 🔊*30-minute docent-guided tour available, $8.*

Towering 180ft above a 32ft rectangular base, this fluted, concrete column (1933, Arthur Brown, Jr.) was an enduring gift to San Francisco's citizens from an unusual woman who wished to add "to the beauty of the city which I have always loved." Initially infamous for the heated social controversy incited by its lobby murals, Coit Tower ranks today among the city's best-known landmarks.

"Firebelle" Lillie

When **Lillie Hitchcock Coit** (1843–1929) was a child in San Francisco, daring teams of volunteers battled the fires that regularly ravaged the city. It is said that one afternoon in the 1860s young Lillie, who had been saved from a fire as a child, came upon Knickerbocker Engine Company No. 5 struggling up Telegraph Hill en route to a blaze. Throwing down her schoolbooks, she rallied onlookers to help the firemen. In return, the company made her an honorary member. For the rest of her life, even as a wealthy widow in Paris, Coit wore a gold, diamond-studded fireman's badge everywhere she went; it was pinned to her clothing when her remains were cremated in 1929. In her will, she bequeathed $125,000 to the city, part of which paid for the statue of volunteer firemen in Washington Square Park. The bulk of the gift provided funds for Coit Tower, which, despite local lore, was not designed to resemble a firehose nozzle.

The Murals

The first major commission of the Depression-era Public Works of Art Project (PWAP), a New Deal initiative that engaged artists to decorate public

☺ **A Bit of Advice** ☺

Visiting Coit Tower

Don't drive to the top of Coit Tower; cars often wait in line over an hour to park at the summit. Instead, take the 39–Coit bus from the Union Street/Columbus Avenue stop on the south side of Washington Square or walk. The hill's flanks are steep, so wear sturdy shoes and pause frequently to rest and admire the wonderful vistas that extend over city and bay.

buildings, the 19 fresco **murals★★** in the lobby of Coit Tower were created in 1934. Working for an average of $31.22 a week, 26 local painters and numerous assistants labored for five months to produce a series of frescoes depicting contemporary life in California. While celebrating the state's abundance and diversity, the works contained powerful images that bluntly criticized the economic inequities of life during the Great Depression. The murals' left-wing content raised the hackles of San Francisco's conservative elite. Fueling the controversy, a tense labor conflict smoldered along the waterfront at the base of Telegraph Hill, erupting into the longshoremen's Pacific Maritime Strike just as work on the murals drew to a close. The sometimes-violent strike crippled the entire West Coast and caused some to

Murals, Coit Tower

© Brigitta L. House/MICHELIN

view any form of social criticism as radical agitation. Responding to civic pressure, the San Francisco Art Commission delayed the opening of Coit Tower and considered destroying the murals. After vigorous debate, only the most blatant (hammer-and-sickle) symbols of left-wing sympathy in Clifford Wight's mural (no. 4) were effaced, and the building was finally opened to the public in October 1934.

Visit

The murals display remarkable uniformity in both theme and style despite the fact that so many different artists created them. **California Industrial Scenes** (John Langley Howard) depicts the despair of the era through an image of a migrant family posing beside their disabled Model-T, while a group of well-to-do day-trippers gazes on them as if they were a tourist attraction. **The Library** (Bernard Zakheim) inspired controversy for its suggestion that the works of Karl Marx might offer a viable form of government. In **City Life** (Victor Arnautoff), perhaps the best-known mural, a bustling street scene criticizes the indifference of urban dwellers to one another.

A brief elevator ascent *(tickets from gift shop or reserve in advance at tickets. sftravel.com)* and a short flight of stairs take visitors to the observation deck. From here, panoramic **views★★★** sweep Angel Island and Marin County to the north, the Bay Bridge and Treasure Island to the east, downtown San Francisco to the south, and Russian Hill and the Golden Gate Bridge to the west.

▷ From Coit Tower, descend Telegraph Hill Ave. and turn left at Filbert St.

Filbert Steps★★

Coit Tower to Sansome St.
Concrete and wooden stairs, descending this steep section of Filbert Street, comprise one of the city's most charming pathways. At 1360 Montgomery Street (1937), the stairs pass a gleaming Streamline Moderne apartment house that appeared in the 1947 film Dark Passage as the place where Lauren Bacall's character hid an escaped convict (Humphrey Bogart). Below Montgomery Street, the wooden staircase follows lushly landscaped garden terraces named for Grace Marchant, their original designer and a longtime neighborhood resident. Those who live along the steps today cultivate her verdant legacy, and the gardens flourish year-round. Inhabitants of the treehouse-like precincts along the pedestrian streets of **Darrell Place** and **Napier Lane** occupy handsome, mid-19C wooden cottages in styles typical of the vernacular architecture of the post-Gold Rush period. Note the simple facade at **no. 228** (1869), a delicately restored example of the Carpenter Gothic style, and the cottage at **no. 224** (1859).

▷ At the bottom of the steps, cross Sansome St.

Levi's Plaza

Filbert St., between Sansome and Battery Sts.
Completed in 1982, this award-winning group of buildings (Hellmuth, Obata & Kassabaum) was designed to harmonize with the varying architectural styles of the surrounding neighborhood. Look west from the intersection of Battery and Filbert Streets to appreciate how its stacked-box profile mimics the houses marching steeply down Telegraph Hill. Administrative headquarters of Levi Strauss & Co., the complex boasts beautifully landscaped open spaces that serve as a placid haven amid the bustle of the nearby Embarcadero.

▷ Walk north on Sansome St. to Greenwich St. and turn up the steps.

The **Greenwich Steps**, while not as lushly picturesque as the Filbert Street staircase, these steps scale nasturtium-covered rocks and patches of fragrant anise along the ascent to the top of Telegraph Hill.

ADDRESSES

CAFES

NORTH BEACH CAFES

At **Caffé Trieste** (601 Vallejo St.; 415-550-1107; www.caffetrieste.com; cash only), where Francis Ford Coppola famously penned most of The Godfather screenplay, and **Mario's Bohemian Cigar Store** (566 Columbus Ave. 415-362-0536), a cup buys you a table for hours; the latter serves up the best focaccia sandwich going. Big windows at **Caffé Puccini** (411 Columbus Ave. 415-989-7033)and **Caffè Greco** (423 Columbus Ave. 415-397-6261; www.caffegreco.com) offer glimpses of daily life in North Beach, while **Réveille Coffee Co.** (200 Columbus Ave. 415-789-6258. www.reveillecoffee.com) serves third-wave coffee in its modern cafe.

NORTH BEACH PIZZA

Tony's Pizza Napoletana – 1570 Stockton St. 415-835-9888. tonyspizza napoletana.com. There's often a wait for the award-winning Neapolitan-inspired pies at lively first-come-first-served Tony's, but you can grab for a slice to go next door.

NORTH BEACH DELICATESSENS

Molinari Delicatessen – 373 Columbus Ave. 415-421-2337. molinaridelisf.com. Whiffs of Parmesan, basil, salami and olives waft from this century-old North Beach institution. Neighborhood locals pop in early to pick up handmade ravioli, cheeses, olive oils, and vinegars from Italy. Later in the morning, meats and cheese appear on the chopping block for the picnic-in-Washington Square crowds.

NORTH BEACH BAKERIES

Liguria Bakery – 1700 Stockton St. 415-421-3786. For early birds only: available in just a few flavors (including raisin, garlic, rosemary and black olive), the melt-in-your-mouth focaccia drips with olive oil and sells out early.

Stella Pastry and Cafe – 446 Columbus Ave. 415-986-2914. Opened in 1942, this tiny bakery is famed for its traditional Italian pastries, particularly its light, creamy sacripantini cake. Also on the menu are éclairs, napoleons, cannolis and all manner of cakes and tarts.

© Doug Olson/Fotolia.com

Coffee in North Beach

Black as night, strong as sin...

Long before every shopping mall and fast-food joint in America installed a coffee bar, before the Beats of the 50s were bolting shots of espresso in smoky cafes, the Italian-American residents of North Beach were drinking fine coffee. Today, with more than a dozen cafes and two traditional roasteries, North Beach is still a prime spot to enjoy some form of the bitter black liquid.

SHOP

Al's Attire – 1300 Grant Ave, 415-693-9900 alsattire.com. Formal suits, dresses, shoes, and other attire are made-to-order by Al's team of tailors in North Beach.

THEATER

BEACH BLANKET BABYLON

Club Fugazi – 678 Beach Blanket Babylon Blvd. (Green St.). 415-421-4222. www.beachblanketbabylon.com. See Paris Hilton, Donald Trump, Brad Pitt and Mr. Peanut—plus some of the most ludicrous hats ever created—on the same stage in this outrageous spoof of current events and pop culture, which has played before packed houses at the same location since 1974.

Russian Hill ★

Russian Hill rises abruptly from the landfill flats of Fisherman's Wharf and North Beach. Its precipitous flanks harbor a number of pre-1906 architectural gems and a rich history of literary activity. Topping 360ft at Vallejo Street between Taylor and Jones, and 294ft at Lombard and Hyde, the hill's two summits offer splendid views of Coit Tower, the Financial District, Alcatraz and the bay. Several secluded pedestrian stairways and paths negotiate the dips between the two peaks, making for beautiful, if vigorous, walks. Pleasant sidewalk cafes, restaurants, bars and shops on nearby Hyde and Polk Streets provide welcome places to eat, relax or browse.

🚋 Powell-Hyde or Powell-Mason.

⚅ **Michelin Map:** *See RUSSIAN HILL, NOB HILL* p89

🛈 **Info:** ☎415-391-2000. www.sanfrancisco.travel, 511.org.

▶ **Location:** Russian Hill is bounded by Francisco, Taylor, Pacific, and Polk Streets.

👥 **Kids:** Lombard Street, for the fun and the great view.

🕐 **Timing:** Plan a couple of hours to visit Russian Hill, a bit more if hill-climbing isn't your forte.

🅿 **Parking:** Street parking is available, but it's more fun to take the cable car.

👁 **Don't Miss:** Stair-streets: Vallejo Street and Macondray Lane.

A BIT OF HISTORY

According to San Francisco lore, Russian Hill was named in the mid-19C when the graves of Russian seal hunters were discovered atop the crest of present-day Vallejo Street. After thousands of people turned out to see the city's first public hanging here in 1852, Joseph Atkinson built the first house on the south side of Russian Hill. Others followed, mainly working-class families who built simple wooden residences and climbed the steep slopes on foot. By the 1880s, cable-car lines had crept up Russian Hill's flanks. Small Victorian flats were built side-by-side with simple shingled cottages. A community of writers and artists moved in, securing Russian Hill's reputation as a bohemian enclave before upscale development took root. From 1856 through the 1890s, Catherine Atkinson kept her home *(at 1032 Broadway)* open to such literary lights as Mark Twain, Ambrose Bierce and Robert Louis Stevenson. From the late 1860s until 1906, local literary maven Ina Coolbrith also hosted literary salons, inviting Twain, Bierce, Bret Harte, Charles Stoddard, George Sterling and others to her house at 1604 Taylor Street. For more than two decades after the 1906 quake and fire, the California Literary Society met in Coolbrith's upstairs flat at 1067 Broadway. In the 1940s Russian Hill provided the setting for several mystery novels, and in 1952 Beat writer Jack Kerouac spent six months on the hill, staying with friends Neal and Carolyn Cassady at 29 Russell Street and working on several novels, including *On the Road*. Unlike elite Nob Hill, Russian Hill continued to develop as a middle-class neighborhood, with small homes set relatively far apart and separated by gardens and wells. Although a few residential enclaves survived the 1906 Fire, many homes were destroyed, and the ensuing architectural ferment of 1906–20 continues to define Russian Hill's aesthetic. Two- to four-story Edwardian buildings flourished, as did a number of pueblo-style stuccoes and Spanish and Art Deco apartment towers. Several less attractive high-rises were erected in the 1960s and 70s, blocking views; a 40ft height limit was imposed in 1974. Russian Hill today is a living testament to the city's architectural diversity. Its lofty heights, well-tended homes and tranquil parks and gardens make it one of San Francisco's most picturesque neighborhoods.

WALKING TOUR

.1mi.

▶ Begin at Mason & Vallejo Sts. and walk west, climbing the left staircase.

Ina Coolbrith Park

A narrow plot of steep hillside bursting with Monterey pines, agave plants and hydrangea bushes along the Vallejo Street stairs, Ina Coolbrith Park was dedicated in 1931 as a memorial to the acclaimed poet and avatar of San Francisco's turn-of-the-20C literary community. The niece of Mormon prophet Joseph Smith, **Ina Donna Coolbrith** (1841-1928) moved west with her family as a child. During the 1860s Coolbrith wrote poetry for and helped edit *The Californian* and the *Overland Monthly*, both highly esteemed literary journals, while spearheading the vibrant local salon scene. Later, Coolbrith encouraged writer Jack London and dancer Isadora Duncan in their artistic pursuits. The state legislature named her California's poet laureate in 1919.

From the Taylor Street stairhead, Coit Tower, the Bay Bridge and Yerba Buena Island are visible to the east through the trees. Begonias, zinnias and other blooming flowers garnish the paths that zigzag across the tiny park, and benches provide a peaceful place to rest.

▶ Cross Taylor St. and continue up the Vallejo St. stairs to the summit.

Charming historic residences and outstanding eastward bay views★★ mark the summit of **Vallejo Street**. Tucked behind tall shrubbery and a redwood fence, the **Williams-Polk House★** *(1013–1019 Vallejo St.)* was designed in 1892 by Willis Polk. The house is seven stories high on the side facing Broadway *(not visible)*. Inspired by the Arts and Crafts aesthetic, Polk embellished his creation with indigenous materials. So pleased was he with his design and with the view from the house that the architect waived his fee in exchange for quarters in the eastern third of the building.

Steepest Streets of San Francisco

- Filbert between Hyde and Leavenworth – **31.5%** grade
- Jones between Union and Filbert – **29%** grade
- Duboce between Buena Vista and Alpine – **27.9%** grade
- Jones between Green and Union – **26%** grade
- Webster between Vallejo and Broadway – **26%** grade
- Duboce between Alpine and Castro – **25%** grade
- Jones between Pine and California – **24.8%** grade
- Fillmore between Vallejo and Broadway – **24%** grade

The large, shingled structure at 1020 Vallejo Street is **The Hermitage** (1982, Esherick, Homsey, Dodge & Davis). The building occupies the former site of a one-story cottage that was home to the Rev. Joseph Worcester, an early proponent of the Arts and Crafts movement in the West. (Worcester had a hand in designing the Swedenborgian Church.) Two of Worcester's original designs, the three-story, gable-roofed **Marshall Houses** *(1034 and 1036 Vallejo St.)*, both built in 1889, are the oldest shingle-style houses in the Bay Area.

▶ Continue walking west to Florence Ln. on the left.

Screened by a charming, rose-covered fence, the shingled mansion at **40 Florence Lane** (1857) is one of the oldest homes on Russian Hill, remodeled by Willis Polk in 1891, and expanded nearly a century later by architect Robert A.M. Stern.

▶ Cross the street to Russian Hill Pl.

In 1916 Polk built the houses at **1, 3, 5 and 7 Russian Hill Place** for Norman Livermore, which appear from the front as tiny Mediterranean-style cottages.

Lombard Street

© McPHOTO/age fotostock

Turn right on Jones St. and walk north to Green St.

From the corner of Jones and Green Streets, fine **views**★★ extend to the north over Alcatraz. The 1000 block of Green, known as the "Paris Block" due to its elegance, features 12 beautifully restored Victorian-era earthquake survivors, all of which are on the National Register of Historic Places. The 1857 **Feusier Octagon House** at 1067 Green was sold in 1870 to Louis Feusier; the handsome mansard roof was added several years later.

Return to Jones St. Turn left, continuing to Macondray Ln. Turn right and stroll to the wooden staircase.

Macondray Lane★

This enchanting little walking street, overhung by lush greenery, was one of Ina Coolbrith's favorite places to roam; it also appeared as "Barbary Lane" in author Armistead Maupin's serialized 1970s epic, *Tales of the City*.
The quintessential hidden garden of flowering plants and trees, turn-of-the-20C clapboard houses and modern glass condominiums share the cozily private, cobbled lane.

Return to Jones St. and continue north, turn left on Union St. Turn right on Leavenworth St. and continue to Lombard St.

👥 Lombard Street★★★

Among San Francisco's most photographed attractions, the 1000 block of Lombard Street boasts eight switchbacks in its one-block descent from Hyde to Leavenworth. The block's natural 27 percent grade was gentled to 16 percent in 1922, when cobblestones were used to pave the street. Today, roughly three-quarters of a million cars negotiate the hairpin turns each year, descending through banks of hydrangeas.
Climb the stairs flanking the curves to Hyde Street, where **views**★★ extend north and east. From here, cable cars coast down to Ghirardelli Square and the Hyde Street Pier against a backdrop of Alcatraz and Angel Island.

ADDITIONAL SIGHT

San Francisco Art Institute★

800 Chestnut St. ⏱Open Mon–Fri 9am–5pm. ✕👥 ℘415-771-7020. www.sfai.edu.
Founded in 1871, this prestigious fine-arts college occupies a Spanish Colonial Revival-style building (1926, Arthur Brown, Jr.), expanded in the béton brut style by English-born architect Paffard Keatinge Clay in 1969. A cultural center as well as a college, the institute welcomes the public to exhibits, galleries and screenings of avant-garde films. Displays of student work change regularly in its open-air courtyard; temporary exhibits are mounted in the

Walter and McBean Galleries (🕐open Tue 11am–7pm, Wed–Sat 11am–6pm). The **Diego Rivera Gallery** (🕐open daily 9am–7pm; closed major holidays) is a student-run exhibition space that features the mural *The Making of a Fresco Showing the Building of a City* (1931) by Diego Rivera, which was commissioned by SFAI President William Gerstle. In this wonderfully original and well-known meta-work, Rivera depicts himself and a team of workers painting a mural of a city; the artist is seated on a scaffold with his back to the viewer, a paintbrush in his hand. From the rooftop deck, grand **views★★** extend over Telegraph Hill and the northern waterfront.

ADDRESSES

🍴EAT

Swensen's Ice Cream – *Union St. at Hyde St.* 📞415-775-6818. When his troop sailed into the heat of the South Pacific during World War II, San Francisco's Earle Swensen volunteered to make ice cream. Upon the war's conclusion, he opened a shop in Russian Hill, in 1948. There's only room for about a dozen customers, so most eat their cones out front while waiting for the cable car.

Union Larder – *1945 Hyde St.* 📞415-323-4845 unionlarder.com. An impressive list of wines by the bottle and by the glass, craft beer, artisan cheese and house-cured charcuterie plates are served in this upscale, industrial-chic deli and wine bar. Window seats overlook the Hyde Street cable car passing by.

Union Square★

The Union Square area is San Francisco's most vibrant and prestigious urban shopping district. Dominating the square itself, major department stores stand shoulder-to-shoulder with upscale boutiques and a turn-of-the-20C hotel. To the east, designer shops crowd in beside art galleries and specialty stores, and upscale cafes set up umbrella-shaded tables along secluded pedestrian lanes. To the west is the city's theater district, where large and small venues mix with art galleries, hotels, and all-night diners.

A BIT OF HISTORY

In 1850, mayor John White Geary (1819–1873) presented the city with Union Square Park, a precious gift during the height of the Gold Rush when land was at a premium. For the next two decades the neighborhood remained largely residential, with staid Victorian homes and churches flanking the open square. Through the 1880s and 90s, the area grew increasingly commercial as merchants, attracted to the upscale, pic-

- 🚋 Powell-Hyde or Powell-Mason. 🚌 Bus 2–Clement, 3–Jackson, 4–Sutter, 30–Stockton, 38–Geary or 45–Union-Stockton; all streetcars Powell St. station. 🚇 Powell St. station, 511.org.
- ℹ **Info:** 📞415-391-2000. www.sftravel.com.
- ▶ **Location:** Bounded by Sutter, Taylor, Kearny and O'Farrell Streets.
- 👪 **Kids:** Museum of Ice Cream
- 🕐 **Timing:** Midday is a great time for people-watching as shoppers and office workers break in the park.
- 🅿 **Parking:** Union Square Garage; 💲$2.50-$6/hr).
- 😎 **Don't Miss:** A ride in the Westin St. Francis' glass elevators

turesque central square, rented the homes of wealthy residents who had relocated west to Pacific Heights. Sutter Street became the area's first fashionable shopping artery, followed by the streets flanking the square itself.

Large retail establishments began to appear in 1896 when the **City of Paris** department store took up residence at the corner of Geary and Stockton streets. Across the park at Geary and Powell, white-gloved porters opened the doors of the St. Francis Hotel for the first time in 1904. With its grand lobby and luxurious guest rooms, the St. Francis, along with City of Paris and esteemed interior-design gallery Gump's, ensured Union Square's elite cachet.

The 1906 earthquake and fire nearly razed the district, but determined entrepreneurs lost no time in rebuilding. In 1908 the City of Paris rose anew; architects Bakewell & Brown preserved much of its original design and added a stained-glass rotunda reminiscent of one in Paris' Galeries Lafayette. The St. Francis was reconstructed that same year in its original Renaissance Revival style. In the blocks east of the square, Gump's was rebuilt, and new boutiques appeared along Maiden Lane. One of the long-running survivors from that era, Gump's closed permanently in 2018. To the west, numerous theaters took root, many sporting Neoclassical facades. In the following decades, several exclusive and prestigious social clubs were founded in the area, among them the Romanesque Revival-style **Olympic Club** *(524 Post St.)*, the Moderne-influenced **Bohemian Club** *(624 Taylor St.)* and the **Metropolitan Club** *(640 Sutter St.)* for women only.

Today this preponderance of theaters and shopping destinations, along with numerous hotels, makes Union Square one of the city's liveliest districts. During the day, shoppers mob the stores around the square, especially **Saks Fifth Avenue**, **Neiman Marcus**, and **Macy's**, while flower vendors, buskers and panhandlers cram the sidewalks and traffic chokes the streets. At night, crowds shift west toward the theater district.

WALKING TOUR
.5mi.

▶ Begin at the center of Union Square Park.

Union Square Park★
Bounded by Post, Stockton, Geary, and Powell Sts.

One of the few designated parks in Jasper O'Farrell's rigid street plan, this 2.6-acre parcel was landscaped in the early 1850s and was named on the eve of the Civil War, when it hosted numerous rallies in support of the Union. In 1901 the **Dewey Monument (1)**, commemorating Admiral George Dewey's 1898 defeat of Spanish naval forces in the Bay of Manila, was erected at the center of the square. Newton Tharp designed the slender, 97ft granite Corinthian column and Robert Aitken cast the bronze figure of Victory—armed with wreath and trident—surmounting it. A five-story parking garage was built beneath the square in 1942, raising the park slightly above street level. The park fell into decline in the 1980s, but a $25 million-dollar restoration completed in 2002 spiffed up the square with new granite surfaces, steel benches and public art installations,

---

☺ Box Office ☺

If you're interested in seeing a play or performance while you're in San Francisco, be sure to visit the **TIX Bay Area** box office in Union Square Park *(Powell St. between Post and Geary Sts.;* 🕐 *open Sun-Thu 8am-4pm, Fri-Sat 8am-5pm; closed Jan 1, Thanksgiving Day, Dec 25;* 📞 *415-430-1140; www.theatrebayarea.org).* Here you can buy both advance tickets and same-day, half-price tickets—many for well under $30—to many live shows around the city. Half-price tickets go on sale at 11am every day and are available on a first-come, first-served basis. You may also order half-price tickets in advance or online through Tix in Advance *(*📞*415-433-1235; www.tixbayarea.com).*

UNION SQUARE AREA

0 ___ 1/10 mi
0 ___ 100 m

N

regenerating the economic vitality of the surrounding area.

Union Square Park has hosted many heated demonstrations over the decades, but today its palm trees and green lawns are often bustling merrily with shoppers and passersby. Music and dance performances occur regularly on the stage along the park's north side. It is home to several heart-shaped Hearts of San Francisco sculptures, a citywide public-art installation spearheaded by San Francisco General Hospital.

▷ Cross the square to the corner of Geary and Stockton Sts.

Neiman Marcus

150 Stockton St. (at Geary St.). ◑Open Mon–Sat 10am–7pm (Thu 8pm), Sun noon–6pm. ◑Closed Thanksgiving Day, Dec 25. ✕⚹.✆415-362-3900. www.neimanmarcus.com.

With its rose-colored, harlequin-patterned granite exterior and rounded glass-and-aluminum entrance corner, this post-Modern department store (1982, Johnson & Burgee) marks a sharp architectural departure from the Renaissance-style City of Paris store that stood here since 1896. The beloved City

of Paris landmark was demolished in 1981, but its exuberant stained-glass **rotunda★** was preserved above the entrance foyer, framed by enameled, wrought-iron balconies, with Paris' emblem, a sailing ship, and its motto, *Fluctuat nec Mergitur* ("He Floats but Does Not Sink").

▷ Walk north up Stockton St. to Maiden Lane.

Maiden Lane

Once flanked with low-rent brothels, Maiden Lane was reincarnated after the 1906 Fire as a quaint pedestrian street lined with maple trees, cafes, boutiques, salons and galleries. At no. 140 stands the **Frank Lloyd Wright Building★** (1949), the only structure in San Francisco designed by Wright and a forerunner to the famed architect's Guggenheim Museum in New York City. Formerly a gift shop and later an antique gallery, the space is now home to ultra-luxe Milanese menswear brand and tailor ISAIA. Today the landmark building's interiors, including its signature skylit gallery with a curvaceous interior with many circular and spiral motifs, are a stunning backdrop for the brand's handsome suits. Note the small round porticoes used as display cases, cutout porthole-like windows, and ramp spiraling up to the second floor.

▷ Return to Stockton St. and continue north.

♙♟ Ruth Asawa Fountain (2)
Stockton St. and Post St.
This playful fountain (1972) by San Francisco sculptor Ruth Asawa is a triumph of collective creativity. Asawa asked locals, including schoolchildren, to sculpt city landmarks out of baker's dough. She cast the flour-and-water bas-reliefs in metal and arranged them around the fountain's cylindrical base. Today it stands between the Grand Hyatt and the Union Square Apple Store. Apple originally planned to demolish the fountain when building its store in 2013, but changed plans after outcry from locals.

▷ Continue north to Sutter St. and turn left.

Four Fifty Sutter★
This 26-story tower (1929, Timothy Pflueger), housing medical and dental offices, is one of San Francisco's finest Art Deco skyscrapers. Mayan motifs cover the spectacular gold-painted elevator lobby, adorn the plaster ceiling

and decorate the undulating terra-cotta exterior all the way up to the top floor.

▷ Continue west to Powell St. and turn left.

Westin St. Francis Hotel★★
335 Powell St. ✈ *Self-guided walking tour maps available at concierge desk.* ✗♿️🅿 ☎*415-397-7000.*
www.westinstfrancis.com.
Internationally renowned, this elegant Renaissance and Baroque Revival structure fronts the entire west side of Union Square. Commissioned by millionaire Charles Crocker, it opened in 1904 as the Hotel St. Francis. After the 1906 Fire, Bliss & Faville rebuilt and enlarged the hotel; it resumed business in 1907.
The hotel completed a $45 million renovation in 2018, preserving its early 20C grandeur. The beautiful entrance hall, where coffered ceilings, marble-sheathed Corinthian columns and ornate balconies create a luxurious ambience. The "Magneta" grandfather clock, built in Vienna, is a favorite rendezvous point for San Francisco socialites. A 32-story tower (William L. Pereira Assoc.) was added to the rear of the hotel in 1972. Visitors who brave the vertiginous ride up in its glass exterior **elevators** ♙♟ are rewarded with expansive **views**★★

Westin St. Francis Hotel

© Brigitta L. House/MICHELIN

Geary Theater

© Marco Lorenzetti/American Conservatory Theater

of Union Square, the Financial District and the Bay Bridge.

▶ Continue south on Powell St. to Geary St. Turn right.

Theater District

Bounded by Sutter, Powell, Geary & Taylor Sts.

San Francisco's theater district contains venues ranging from spare, intimate houses to enormous, ornate, multi-balconied palaces.

Grandest among the latter are the **Geary Theater★** *(415 Geary St.)*, designed by Bliss & Faville in 1909 and home to San Francisco's renowned American Conservatory Theater company, and the adjacent **Curran Theatre★** *(445 Geary St.)*, by Alfred Henry Jacobs in 1922, today a major venue for theater and Broadway productions. Registered National Historic Landmarks, the Geary and the Curran were constructed of reinforced concrete in the Neoclassical style. The Geary's fancifully embellished terracotta columns and stolid exterior set off the Curran's Romanesque arches and mansard roof. The Curran Theatre has staged long-running Broadway shows since it opened.

Nearby is the Native Sons Building, with medallion portraits of prominent Californians embedded in the building's facade.

&Consult *Your Stay in the City for more San Francisco and Bay Area theater listings and ticket information.*

▶ Continue east on Geary St. Turn right on Grant Ave.

♣♣ Museum of Ice Cream

1 Grant Ave. ◷ *Mon-Sun 10:30am-8:30pm, advance reservations required.* ✕⟨&⟩ ☎855-258-0719 *www.museumoficecream.com.* ⟨∞⟩$38

The whimsical ice-cream-inspired exhibits at this experiential art space are designed to be interactive, fun, and supremely photogenic, with attractions like the famous rainbow-sprinkle-filled pool overseen by a cheerful onsite staff, who enthusiastically engage with visitors in addition to doling out treats like mini ice cream cones and mochi. Founded as a pop-up project in New York City before moving to other locations, the Museum of Ice Cream's San Francisco location became its first permanent space in 2018. Though its playful eye-candy ambience has made the museum a magnet for selfie-taking millennials, it is a fun and appropriate spot for kids, too—though note that the museum is adults-only after 7:30pm.

ADDRESSES

ART

49 Geary – *49 Geary St., between Grant & Kearny Sts.* Many of the city's longest-running and most prestigious galleries are located within this four-story building, including Fraenkel Gallery, Haines Gallery, and Roberto Koch. There are also several rare-book collectors and antiquarians inside.

♀/EAT

$$ John's Grill – *63 Ellis St.* ☎*415-986-3274. www.johnsgrill.com.* **American**.
The setting for author-patron Dashiell Hammet's famed The Maltese Falcon, this legitimately old-school San Francisco restaurant opened in 1908. The shrimp Louis and chicken Jerusalem are classics.

The Bayshore region of San Francisco includes some of the city's most popular attractions Fisherman's Wharf, Alcatraz and the Golden Gate Bridge—as well as the peaceful, sprawling Presidio, an 1,480-acre park with coastal trails, golf courses, and a fine arts museum. At Fisherman's Wharf, along the Northern Waterfront between Telegraph Hill and the Marina District, relics of San Francisco's maritime past occupy the city's shoreline. Farther west, the waterfront includes Crissy Fields, beloved by joggers and bikers. Views from the waterfront's splendid setting take in passing freighters, the Golden Gate Bridge, Alcatraz, and the rugged shoreline of Marin County.

Highlights

On the Waterfront

Once an industrial zone, Fisherman's Wharf is San Francisco's most popular tourist destination. Its piers offer everything from carousel rides to sea lions on Pier 39, to maritime history on Hyde Street Pier. Fisherman's Wharf also serves as the departing point for ferries to Alcatraz. This infamous 12-acre island served variously as a fortress, military prison and U.S. Federal Penitentiary until its 1972 conversion to a national park.

To the east of Fisherman's Wharf, the Embarcadero lines the waterfront along the bay. The Embarcadero was once the hub of San Francisco's shipping and transportation. Revitalization began after the 1989 Loma Prieta earthquake damaged the Embarcadero Freeway. Once the freeway was razed, massive redevelopment began, creating the palm-line boulevard, airy plazas, and green spaces that define the area today. The farmers' market at the Ferry Building has become one of the best in the country, selling local and organic produce and drawing some 25,000 visitors each week.

East of Fisherman's Wharf is the Marina District, running between the wharf and the Presidio, and from the northern waterfront to Pacific Heights. The Marina is a popular neighborhood for young, wealthy professionals. Visit on a sunny weekend and you'll see why— Union Street and Chestnut Street are both chock-full with chi-chi boutiques, bars, and wonderful restaurants.

Outdoorsy types love to bike or jog along Marina Green past Crissy Field to the Golden Gate Bridge and beyond. The Golden Gate Bridge is a major attraction. Opened in 1937 and painted bright orange, it spans the Golden Gate Strait and is the ninth-largest suspension bridge in the world. On the Golden Gate's southern side is the Presidio. Maintained by the National Park Service, the Presidio lures visitors with its lushly forested expanse as well as its rich history as a military installation.

Ferry Building Farmers' Market

© Peter Wrenn/Michelin

Alcatraz★★★

A mere 1.5mi from the comforts of San Francisco, this infamous 12-acre island, now inhabited by scores of seabirds who nest among its crumbling ruins, once held scores of prisoners incarcerated atop its sheer cliffs. Aptly nicknamed "the Rock" and isolated from shore by the cold, treacherous currents that swirl through the bay, Alcatraz served variously as a fortress, military prison, and U.S. Federal Penitentiary until its conversion to a national park and museum in 1972. A visit to Alcatraz provides a haunting journey into one of the harshest chapters of American judicial history.

A BIT OF HISTORY

For thousands of years before Spanish and Portuguese explorers first set sights on Northern California, some 10,000 indigenous people lived on the coastal area between the San Francisco Bay and Point Sur.

According to Native American oral history, the Alcatraz island was originally used to ostracize members of the tribe. It was also used for food gathering.

The first Europeans to sight the barren island were Spanish explorers José de Cañizares and Juan Manuel de Ayala in 1775. Noticing the large number of gannet-like cormorants nesting on the cliffs, they named the rocky spot *Isla de los alcatraces*, or "island of gannets."

With no freshwater and little natural vegetation, the island remained uninhabited until President Millard Fillmore designated it a military reservation in 1850.

Alcatraz' location at the mouth of the bay made it a natural choice for a fortress, and Army engineers planned to make the island one of three forts in a "Triangle of Defense" to guard the entrance of San Francisco Bay. The other two points of the triangle would be the forts at Fort Point and Lime Point, although the fort at latter was never built.

Info: www.nps.gov/alcatraz. Tickets ☎415-561-4900 or www.alcatrazcruises.com. Ticket booth located at Pier 33, Fisherman's Wharf.

Location: Ferry service to Alcatraz is provided by Alcatraz Cruises (☏see p111). Ticket prices include ferry transport, temporary exhibits ans special programs, and the cellhouse audio tour.

Timing: During peak tourist season (July and August), tours to Alcatraz are often booked weeks in advance, so reserve as early as possible or purchase tickets online. Allow a minimum of 3 hours to tour Alcatraz, including ferry trips.

Don't Miss: The excellent cellhouse audio tour, included in the ticket price.

ALCATRAZ CRUISES

Ferries depart from Pier 33 at Fisherman's Wharf �*Open mid-Mar–mid Nov daily 8.45am–3.20pm every 30–45min (evening tours daily 3:50pm and 4:45pm); rest of the year daily 8:45am–1.35pm every 20–30min (evening tours daily 3:50pm and 4:45pm). Closed Jan 1, Thanksgiving Day, Dec 25.* $38.35 ($45.50 for evening tour); children, senior, and family discounts available.

Alcatraz Cruises, LLC – Pier 33, Hornblower Alcatraz Landing. ☎415-981-ROCK (7625). www.alcatrazcruises.com

Construction on a garrison began in 1853, and was completed by December 1859. Captain Joseph Stewart took command of Alcatraz Island with 86 men of Company H, Third U.S. Artillery. Though

Alcatraz

© GoodLifeStudio/iStockphoto.com

cannons were mounted on the island, advancing military technology soon rende-red them obsolete; not one was ever fired in defense.

In 1861 Confederate sympathizers and renegade U.S. soldiers were incarcerated at the garrison. In the 1870s its walls held Native American prisoners from various Indian wars in California and the West. The largest group of Native Americans held at Alcatraz was a group of 19 Hopis held from January 3 to August 7, 1895, who were incarcerated for refusing to send their children to government-run boarding schools and for refusing to farm on individual plots away from the mesasthe isolated flat-topped, steep-sided hills on which they lived.

In 1901 the last cannons were disman-tled, and six years later regular troops abandoned the island, to be replaced by members of the U.S. Military Guard.

"Super Prison" – Mounting costs and increasing protest over conditions led to the 1933 transfer of the property to the U.S. Department of Justice, which established a federal penitentiary on the island. Banishment to the maxi-mum-security facility on Alcatraz was reserved for the most "desperate and irredeemable criminals" in the federal system, including those designated "public enemies" and deemed a danger to society, even behind bars. The ratio of one guard to every three prisoners, a strict "no talking" rule, brutal isolation

cells, and a near-impenetrable security system quickly established Alcatraz's reputation as America's bleakest prison. Some 1,545 prisoners were held at Alc-atraz over 28 years. Notorious inhabit-ants of "the Rock" included mobster Al "Scarface" Capone, bank robber George "Machine Gun" Kelly, Alvin "Creepy" Karpis, and Robert "Birdman" Stroud (who, contrary to popular lore, never kept birds here).

Over the years, 36 men tried to escape from Alcatraz in 14 attempts, all of them apparently unsuccessful. Some of the escapees were captured, some were shot, and some disappeared forever in the bay. The most notorious attempt in 1962, in which three inmates disap-peared, raised serious questions about the prison's deteriorated condition. That, combined with the high cost and the complaints of San Franciscans wor-ried about the prison, led to the decision to close Alcatraz. The prison closed on March 21, 1963.

After the last inmates were transferred in 1963, the island fell vacant until 1969, when a group of Native Americans occupied it. They cited an 1868 treaty granting them the right to claim unin-habited federal land. The occupation ended 19 months later, its goals unre-alized. The occupation did, however, kickstart the Pan-Indian Movement. On October 12, 1972, Alcatraz was des-ignated part of the Golden Gate National

Recreation Area, and was opened to the public the following year. The following year the site was opened to the public. Today, it is one of the most visited sites in the National Park Service.

VISIT

The ferry trip *(15min)* to the dock at Alcatraz offers stunning **views★★** of the city skyline, the Golden Gate Bridge and the cliffs of the island. Graffiti from the Indian occupation can be spotted on the bluffs and dock buildings. At the ferry wharf, rangers provide general information near the landing, after which visitors are free to inspect the exhibit area on the lower floor of the Barracks Building (1867), view an **orientation video** *(15min)* in the theater, or climb the steep switchback road past the ruins of the Post Exchange and Officers' Quarters to the cellhouse.

The award-winning Alcatraz **Cellhouse Audio Tour** is recommended. It covers the inside of the cellhouse (at the top of the island) during the penitentiary era (1934–1963), and is included in the ticket price. Ranger-led talks and guided strolls in otherwise inaccessible parts of the island are occasionally offered; information is available at the landing dock. Evening tours offer a more guided exploration of the cellhouse, and a darker view of prison life. A haunting view of the city skyline, sometimes as it becomes obscured by fog, contributes to the sense of isolation.

Once on the island, visitors can stay as long as they like; ferries depart for San Francisco about every 30min, and visitors can return on any ferry.

Cellhouse★★

While most of the island's buildings have been reduced to ruins and turned over to raucous flocks of seabirds, the forbidding cellhouse is intact enough to provide a chilling glimpse into the bleak life of the federal prisoners who were sentenced here. Built by convicts in 1911, it was, for a time, the largest reinforced concrete structure in the world.

Visitors enter the building near the bunker-like control center, formerly an

⊙ A Bit of Advice ⊙

Cold sea spray and strong winds often buffet the island, and pathways are rough and steep. Wear protective clothing and strong, comfortable shoes. An Easy Access Program is available for the physically impaired. See ranger at entrance to island. Also note that there is no food for sale on Alcatraz Island, so grab a bite at Pier 33 before you depart.

arsenal of arms and tear gas. Beyond the control center lies the Visitation Area, where prisoners were separated from visitors by thick plate glass and spoke over a monitored telephone.

Once inside the cavernous main room, visitors can stroll down "Broadway," the wide central passage between B and C Blocks leading to "Times Square," and step into a cramped, cold cell furnished with a regulation army cot, a folding table and chair, and a squat, open toilet. Prisoners who violated the strict rules of Alcatraz were subjected to solitary confinement in the dank isolation rooms, or "dark holes," of D Block. Robert "Birdman" Stroud was one of the Alcatraz prisoners kept in isolation. Indeed, he spent more time in isolation than any other federal prisoner in history. Stroud was incarcerated for 54 years; 43 of them were spent in solitary confinement.

Access to the recreation yard and library, now open for exploration, was a privilege awarded for good behavior. Several concrete paths lead around the perimeter of the island, though most is not accessible to the public. The main road to the cellhouse and the western road from the cellhouse to the base of the recreation yard exit are open year-round. Bird-watching enthusiasts will be pleased to find a wide variety of birds on Alcatraz. The island is now a sanctuary for seabirds and waterbirds, including cormorants, pigeon guillemots, snowy egrets and black-crowned night herons. The first half of the year offers the greatest chance for spotting them.

The Embarcadero★

A waterfront promenade stretching three miles from Fisherman's Wharf to China Basin, The Embarcadero ("boarding place" in Spanish) combines expansive views of the bay with public artworks and attractions.

A BIT OF HISTORY

The vibrant hub of San Francisco's shipping and transportation industries from the Gold Rush until the 1950s, the Embarcadero took shape in the 1850s when landfill extended the shore from its natural line along present-day Montgomery Street. As San Francisco boomed through the late 19C, sailors, longshoremen and warehouse workers frequented the growing number of gambling dens and union halls.

Ferries from points across the bay began docking here before the turn of the 20C, and the waterfront swarmed with daily commuters until 1936, when rail service and auto lanes over the new San Francisco–Oakland Bay Bridge siphoned away ferry traffic. Through the mid-20C, the Embarcadero fell into disuse as shippers gradually transferred their activities across the bay to the better-equipped Port of Oakland.

The construction of the elevated **Embarcadero Freeway**, planned as a link between the Bay Bridge and the Golden Gate Bridge, in the 1950s further diminished the waterfront's appeal by interposing a dirty concrete roadbed between the city and the bay. Construction had reached north to Broadway before massive protest halted progress in 1959. The freeway was razed after being damaged in the 1989 Loma Prieta earthquake, to many San Franciscans' glee.

A New Beginning – Ongoing redevelopment projects have revitalized this historic area. Extending 3.2mi from Fisherman's Wharf to China Basin is **Herb Caen Way**, a promenade named for the popular late *San Francisco Chronicle* columnist whose trademark ellipses punctuated many a morn-

🚍 Bus 7–Haight, 14–Mission, 21–Hayes, 31–Balboa, or 71–Haight-Noriega; all streetcars Embarcadero station. 🚈 Embarcadero station, 511.org.

♿ **Michelin Map:** *See YERBA BUENA GARDENS*.

ℹ️ **Info:** ☎415-391-2000. www.sftravel.com.

🧭 **Location:** The main Embarcadero attractions are Fisherman's Wharf, the Ferry Building, and Oracle Park. While the distances between them can be long for walkers, the Embarcadero is ideal for jogging.

👪 **Kids:** A baseball game at Oracle Park (or a tour, if you're not here on a game day).

🕐 **Timing:** You may not want to visit the Embarcadero sights together. The sights are linked to adjacent neighborhoods: Fisherman's Wharf to North Beach, the Ferry Building to the Financial District, and Oracle Park to SoMa.

🅿️ **Parking:** Very little public parking is available on the Embarcadero; drivers might try the lot at the Embarcadero Center (see FINANCIAL DISTRICT) or Fisherman's Wharf (the garage is across from Pier 39). We highly recommend the F-Market & Wharves historic streetcar, running between Fisherman's Wharf and the Castro District.

👀 **Don't Miss:** The Ferry Building—its gourmet indoor marketplace and outdoor farmer's market have become a magnet for chefs and food lovers across the Bay Area.

Historic Streetcar in front of Ferry Building
© Dorin_S/iStockphoto.com

The Historic Streetcars of the F-Market Line

San Francisco's cable cars are not the city's only rolling history: Since September 1995, a colorful fleet of historic streetcars has glided up and down Market Street, a historical grace note amid the throngs of pedestrians, cars, buses, and streetcars that swarm the bustling thoroughfare. Since 2000, these beloved antiques have traversed the shoreline along the Embarcadero from China Basin to Fisherman's Wharf, south and north of Market Street.

Elegantly streamlined and colorfully painted, PCC cars were manufactured in the U.S. from 1936 to 1952 and put into service throughout North America and Europe. The rehabilitated cars today reflect not only the Muni green-and-cream colors, but also more than two dozen color schemes of other cities where these streetcars were used, including Boston (orange, cream, and silver), Baltimore (yellow and gray), Los Angeles (red, orange, and gray), and Kansas City (cream, black, and silver). Also on the tracks are retired streetcars from cities around the world, such as England, Zürich, Melbourne, Milan, and Hiroshima.

ing read from 1938 to 1996. This long ribbon of sidewalk draws visitors and residents to enjoy glorious views of the bay, the Bay Bridge and the towers of the Financial District. The road itself is brightened by Canary Island palms and by the F-Market streetcars that rattle along its length. Fishermen gather at the end of **Pier 7** *(near Broadway)* with its old-fashioned wrought-iron railings and park benches and their expansive views of the bay.

South of the Ferry Building, brick warehouses and factories of the onetime waterfront industrial belt are reborn as residential and office spaces, some with trendy eateries. **Hills Plaza**, with its distinctive brick tower, is a noteworthy example; erected in 1924, it originally housed the headquarters for Hills Brothers Coffee Company.

New residential buildings and forward-thinking commercial complexes such as **The Yard at Mission Rock** (www.theyardsf.com), a year-round shipping container village filled with food trucks, pop-up shops and the Anchor Brewing Company beer garden located in the San Francisco Giants Parking Lot A (3rd St. and Terry Francois Blvd), continue to enliven the west side of the Embarcadero from the Bay Bridge to Oracle Park at China Basin. In late 2019 or early 2020, the area will get yet another boost with the planned opening of the **Chase Center** (www.chasecenter.com), an eleven-acre multi-use complex at Third and 16th Sts. in Mission Bay that will include new restaurants, office space, waterfront public park and the Golden State Warriors new stadium.

SIGHTS
Ferry Building★★
Embarcadero at Market St.
Open Mon–Fri 10am–7pm,
Sat 8am–6pm, Sun 11am–5pm.
Closed Thanksgiving Day, Dec 25.
✕ ♿ 🅿 415-983-8000.
www.ferrybuildingmarketplace.com.

A hugely successful renovation, completed in 2003, has brought this landmark back into the spotlight as an airy gourmet retail and restaurant complex. Designed by A. Page Brown of Colusa sandstone and anchored on 111 steel-framed concrete piers, the building was hailed at its dedication in 1898 as the most solidly constructed edifice in California, a claim that was proved when it survived the great earthquake of 1906. The Ferry Building's 240ft clock tower, designed by Willis Polk, was inspired by the Giralda of Seville and boasts four huge (and accurate) clock faces.

Until completion of the Golden Gate and Bay Bridges in the late 1930s, the Ferry Building served as San Francisco's main transportation hub. An estimated 50 million people passed through it annually, Marin County and East Bay commuters. In 1956, after ferry traffic declined, the northern half of the structure was converted into office space, and in 1962 the southern half was remodeled as well.

After an extensive four-year, $100 million renovation, the building reopened in 2003 with 65,000 sq ft of marketplace space along the first floor's central nave, now filled with dozens food producers and eclectic shops. In addition to the grab-and-go kiosks, there are several popular sit-down restaurants and cafes. Stroll behind the building to the wooden sundeck, where commuter ferries depart for Sausalito and Larkspur in Marin County. Just north, another ferry offers services to Alameda, Oakland, Tiburon and Vallejo. The tranquil monument to Mohandas K. Gandhi **(2)** was donated to the city in 1988.

Nearby, the new two-acre Rincon Park (along the waterfront at the foot of Folsom St.) was dedicated in early 2003. Marked by a bayfront promenade with **views★★** of the sparkling bay, Bay Bridge and Treasure Island, Rincon Park showcases Cupid's Span, a 60ft-tall bow and arrow made of fiberglass and steel by sculptors Claes Oldenburg and Coosje van Bruggen.

👥 Exploratorium★★★
Pier 15, Embarcadero at Green St.
Open Tue–Sun 10am–5pm, Thu
additional hours 6pm-10pm (adults
only). Closed Mon (except select
holidays), Thanksgiving Day, Dec 25.
$30 adults, $20 kids; call or check
website for periodic free admission.
✕ ♿ 🅿 415-528-4444.
www.exploratorium.edu.

This ambitious hands-on museum set in a 30,000-square ft building on Pier 15, has served as a model for similar science museums since its opening in 1969. The Exploratorium's creator, physicist Frank Oppenheimer, maintained a novel philosophy that a museum can best teach science through "hands-on" participation.

With three times more space overall than its previous home at The Palace of Fine Arts, the new Exploratorium, has 150 brand-new interactive exhibits among the more than 600 on view. These explore physics, electricity, life sciences, thermodynamics, weather, light, psychology, linguistics, sense perception and a host of other subjects. By pushing buttons, rotating wheels, peering through prisms, activating motors, engineering arches, arranging chimes, shouting into tubes, and performing a wide variety of other actions, visitors of all ages set experiments in motion, observe the results and speculate on the causes. Instructions and explanations accompany each exhibit, and staff members are available to answer questions. The building itself is a referendum on science in action. Nearly 6,000 high-efficiency solar panels installed on the roof were designed to ultimately generate 100% of the Exploratorium's electricity demand, helping it meet its goal of becoming the largest net-zero energy museum in the U.S.

Exploratorium

Long time popular exhibits include the miniature **tornado demonstration**; the photosensitive **Shadow Box**, where people's shadows are recorded on a wall, the **distorted room**, where visitors can enter an optical illusion, and the pitch-black **Tactile Dome**★ (⏱*1hr sessions begin at 10:15 daily ☎additional $15; reservations advised; ☎415-528-4444*), a multilevel crawl chamber through which visitors feel their way. In addition, the new all-glass Bay Observatory and Terrace overlooking the Bay and Outdoor Gallery, where a 150-ft-long pedestrian bridge engulfs visitors in fog every hour, provides new opportunities to observe the science of the natural world as well. Also on site are two restaurants, the **Seismic Joint Cafe** and the bay-facing **SeaGlass Restaurant** serving seasonal and sustainable comfort food with both kids and parents in mind, plus craft beer and cockails. There's also a gift shop (accessible without a ticket) stocked with unique gadgets, games, tinkering items, and books that focus on science, art, and technology.

Rincon Center★

101 Spear St. at Mission St. ⏱*Open daily.* ✕&🅿 ☎*415-777-4100.*
This complex (1989), a block south and west of the Ferry Building, boasts a panoply of stores and cafes. The former Rincon Annex Post Office (1940, Gilbert S. Underwood), which now functions as the center's **lobby,** remains its most gripping feature. Especially worthy of note are Russian-born artist Anton Refregier's **murals**★ depicting Northern California's rough-and-tumble history, from the arrival of Sir Francis Drake in 1579 until World War II. The 27 pannels were painted from 1941 to 1948 under the Federal Art Project of the Work Projects Administration. Rendered in broad, muscular strokes and bold colors that underscore Refregier's thematic emphasis on labor, struggle, and war, the panels provide an unsparing view of the wild West. Adjacent display cases present artifacts and photographs. In the lofty atrium off the lobby, an 85ft **Rain Column** (1988, Doug Hollis) forms the eye-catching centerpiece of a spacious food court.

👥 Oracle Park (formerly AT&T Park)★★

24 Willie Mays Plaza, at 3rd & King Sts. 🎧*Tours ($22) daily 10.30am and 12.30pm except on game days.Coca-Cola Fan Lot (free) open 2hrs before scheduled first pitch on days of home games, and on non-game days Sept–May Sat–Sun 10am–4pm, Apr–Aug daily 10am–4pm.* ☎*Game tickets $33–$225.* ✕&🅿 ☎*415-972-2000. www.mlb.com/giants/ballpark.*
Many baseball insiders consider San Francisco's $319 million major-league stadium to be among the finest in the world. Opened in 2000, it couples the mood of an early 20C urban ballpark, such as Boston's Fenway Park or Chicago's Wrigley Field, with modern amenities. HOK Sport designed the 40,800-seat stadium to shield players and spectators from wind and fog. Upper-level tiers offer spectacular views of the city skyline, Bay Bridge and Oakland.

The park's main entrance is at **24 Willie Mays Plaza,** where a red-brick facade rises behind William Behrends' 9ft bronze statue of the Hall of Fame outfielder, who wore the number 24 throughout his playing career (1951–73). The **Coca-Cola Fan Lot** features pop-bottle slides, a wiffleball field, speed-pitching, baserunning areas, and "the world's largest baseball glove," a sculpture of a three-finger mitt. Behind the right-field wall, 335ft from home plate, rare home runs may splash into **McCovey Cove** (named for Giants' first baseman Willie McCovey), a part of the Bay known as China Basin. Ambitious fans watch games from kayaks in the cove, hoping to fish out home run balls. In true San Francisco fashion, Oracle Park was a pioneer in bringing gourmet goodies to the ballgame, with park vendors selling local wine and craft beer on tap, artisanal crab sandwiches, slices from beloved North Beach pizzeria Tony's, Mission-style burritos, and organic fried-chicken sandwiches, in addition to more standard ballpark fare, like sausages and sodas.

ADDITIONAL SIGHTS
San Francisco–Oakland Bay Bridge★★

○*Open daily.* ⌫*$6 toll westbound only from Oakland. Nonvehicular crossing of the bridge prohibited.* ☏*511 or 511.org.*

Though often overshadowed by the celebrity of the Golden Gate Bridge, this double-deck engineering marvel is a distinctive and beloved landmark in its own right. Begun in 1933, the project was financed by a $77 million federal loan during the nadir of the Great Depression. Engineers Charles H. Purcell, Charles E. Andrew and Glenn B. Woodruff joined forces with architect Timothy Pflueger to design the bridge, which had to cross 8.4mi of water—including approaches, its span is nearly eight times that of the Golden Gate.

To traverse the distance, the bridge was conceived as two structures meeting at Yerba Buena Island, a rocky promontory midway across the bay. The western section, comprising two 2,310ft suspension bridges, joins San Francisco and the island. The roadway hangs suspended from steel cables draped between four distinctive X-braced towers; a concrete pier rises 48 stories from the floor of the bay to anchor the two suspension bridges in the center. The eastern section, joins Yerba Buena Island and Oakland. Between the two sections, a tunnel pierces Yerba Buena Island; 76ft wide and 58ft high, its diameter may be the largest of any vehicular tunnel in the world. Completed in November 1936, the original bridge carried trains on its lower level and cars on its upper level for two decades.

Safety concerns after the Loma Prieta earthquake prompted construction of a new eastern span, adjacent to the original. Opened in 2003, the new 2,047-ft-long structure, designed by T.Y. Lin International in conjunction with the engineering firm Moffat & Nichol, is the largest self-anchored bridge in the world. Though revered for its striking modern design, it cost an estimated $6.4 billion (significantly above the original estimate of $250 million), making it the most expensive public work project in California history.

The western span also received a design enhancement in 2013 with the installation **The Bay Lights★**, a generative light sculpture comprised of 25,000 individual white LEDs. Originally designed by artist Leo Villareal as a temporary work to commemorate the 75th anniversary of the bridge's opening, the now permanent art piece creates mesmerizing light patterns that can be seen from the San Francisco shoreline but remain invisible to the drivers on the road.y

Treasure Island★

Take I-80 across the Bay Bridge; exit at Treasure Island/Yerba Buena Island. ▥ *Bus 108–Treasure Island.* ☏*415-274-0660. www.sftreasureisland.org.*

Lying in San Francisco Bay midway between San Francisco and Oakland, this 400-acre man-made isle was constructed in 1938 from the rubble of the Bay Bridge tunnel to host a world fair.

Embarcadero and San Francisco–Oakland Bay Bridge viewed from Coit Tower

Today it offers stupendous panoramic views as well as charming insights into a sometimes-overlooked chapter of San Francisco history.

Opened on February 18, 1939, the **Golden Gate International Exposition of 1939–1940** drew more than 17 million visitors during its two-year run. In all, 36 nations and 31 states participated in the fair, themed "The Pageant of the Pacific" to prompt awareness of trade potential with Pacific Basin nations. World War II brought an abrupt end to the jubilant celebration of Pacific relations. Naval Station Treasure Island operated on the island from World War II until it closed in September 1997.

Today, the island is mainly residential, with a few restaurants and several wineries and bars. After nearly two decades of public planning, the island is set to add 8,000 new homes, 500 hotel rooms, 300 acres of park and open space and 100,000 office spaces to be built over the next 20 years. The development plans were approved by the city, but not without controversy: current residents will be evicted to make room for new buildings.

For now, it's worth taking a detour off the on ramp to take in the sweeping **view★★★** of the city, encompassing the Bay Bridge, the San Francisco skyline, the Golden Gate, Alcatraz, Mount Tamalpais, Angel Island and the North Bay, with the Richmond-San Rafael Bridge.

ADDRESSES

ORGANIC TREASURES

There are a multitude of local, artisan food purveyors in the Ferry Building's always-bustling central hall. **Cowgirl Creamery**'s (no. 17) delectable artisan cheeses, made in Point Reyes and Petaluma, can be sampled on site or shipped home. **Prather Ranch Meat Company**'s (no. 33) methods are certified humane and organic; the staff cheerfully educates customers about sustainable husbandry. For a loaf, a roll, or a pastry, **Acme Bread Company** (no. 15) is famed for artisan breads made from organic flours. For dessert, try a fresh galette or pastry at **Frog Hollow Farms** (no. 46) and a cup of joe at one of **Blue Bottle Coffee** espresso bar outlets (shop #7 and in the North Arcade).

SHOPPING AND CAFES

Ferry Plaza Farmers' Market – *Market St. at The Embarcadero. Open Tue and Thu 10am–2pm, Sat 8am–2pm. ☎415-291-3276. www.cuesa.org.* The city's most prestigious farmers' market brings together Bay Area farmers and artisanal food producers three days a week. Live music and cooking demos are regular fixtures on the scene.

The Java House Restaurant – *Pier 40, the Embarcadero at Townsend St. ☎415-495-7260. www.javahousesf.com.* Pick up a tasty, cheap cheeseburger or tuna sandwich, settle down on a stool and get a taste of colorful, workaday San Francisco from this shack on Pier 40 beside the South Beach yacht harbor.

Fisherman's Wharf★★★

San Francisco's colorful maritime legacy survives in this bustling district on the northeastern tip of the peninsula. A carnival atmosphere prevails on the rowdier east end of the wharf, especially at the Pier 39 marketplace, where there's a pod of vociferous and amusing sea lions, as well as a multitude of souvenir shops. Street performers and sidewalk seafood stands add to the chaos. The western end of the wharf has historic sailing ships, a maritime museum, some art galleries, a relaxing park, and two shopping centers housed in historic factories.

A BIT OF HISTORY

In 1853, **Henry "Honest Harry" Meiggs**, councilman, entrepreneur, and later the most notorious embezzler of public funds in the city's early history, constructed a wharf extending 1,600ft from Francisco and Powell Streets across North Point Cove into the bay. From its inception, Meigg's Wharf was an important center of industry. The ferry terminal to Sausalito was located at its far end, and a sawmill, a pipe works, and a junk shop crowded its length. Shipbuilding flourished and visitors came down to the wharf to enjoy bay views and the cheap beer, cracked crab and hot chowder. In the 1860s, North Point Cove from Bay Street to the current shoreline was filled with rock, creating a flat stretch of land that became a manufacturing and industrial zone. After anti-Chinese legislation in the 1870s restricted commercial opportunities for the Asians, who previously had dominated the fishing industry, Genoese immigrants took to the seas. Over time, the fishermen (*pescatori* in Italian) were outnumbered by their compatriots from Naples, Calabria and Sicily.

Today descendants of Sicilians dominate, from the fishing boats that continue to depart from here to the wildly

🚋 Powell-Hyde or Powell-Mason. 🚋 Streetcar F-Market. Bus 19–Polk, 30–Stockton, 39–Coit, or 47–Van Ness, 511.org.

ℹ️ **Info:** www.fishermans wharf.org.

▶️ **Location:** Fisherman's Wharf is centered on Jefferson St. between Grant and Hyde Sts.

👫 **Kids:** The carousel on Pier 39 and the Aquarium of the Bay.

🕐 **Timing:** In summer and on most weekends, crowds make movement difficult, especially along Jefferson Street. In winter, when crab fishing is in swing, the wharf is at its most interesting and least congested.

🅿️ **Parking:** Public transportation is the best way to get here—try the F-Market streetcars and Powell Street cable cars. For drivers, there are large garages across from Pier 39 (*Beach St. between Stockton & Powell Sts.*) and underneath Ghirardelli Square (*Beach St. at Larkin St.*), but they are expensive and often full.

😋 **Don't Miss:** Clam chowder in a bread bowl or a crab sandwich, the sea lions at Pier 39, and the historic vessels at Hyde Street Pier and Pier 45.

popular restaurants and sidewalk seafood stands that bear the names of their prominent Italian-American founders. Through the first half of the 20C, fishing remained a major industry. As maritime technology became more efficient, however, the bay and surrounding waters were overfished, forcing the boats to

Fisherman's Wharf

© Luis Fidel Ayerves/age fotostock

move farther and farther beyond the Golden Gate or to relocate altogether. By the 1950s the fleet's numbers had been severely reduced, and large sections of the old industrial zone had become run-down or abandoned.

Tidal Wave of Tourism – The opening of the National Maritime Museum in 1951 marked the beginning of the waterfront's rebirth as a tourist destination. The area boomed in the 1960s when developers began purchasing properties such as the California Fruit Canners Association building and the old Ghirardelli Chocolate Factory, converting them into showpieces.

In years since, a massive influx of tourism has sparked an explosion of related businesses, few of them linked to the maritime legacy that makes the wharf such an interesting place to visit.

Brightly lit T-shirt shops and souvenir stands line the south side of Jefferson Street along with several novelty museums aimed at capturing the tourist market, including the San Francisco outpost of the world-famous wax museum **Madame Tussauds** (👥 *145 Jefferson St.;* 🕐*Open Mon-Thu 10am–7pm, Fri-Sun 10am-8pm;* 💲*$25; $15 if purchased online;* 📞 *866-233-4240; www.madametussauds.com)* **Ripley's Believe It or Not! Museum** (👥*175 Jefferson St.;* 🕐*Open Sun–Thu 10am–9pm, Fri–Sat 10am–10pm;* 💲*$22* 📞*415-202-9850;*

www.ripleys.com/sanfrancisco), and the **The San Francisco Dungeon** (👥*145 Jefferson St.;* 🕐*Open Mon-Fri 12pm–7pm, Sat-Sun 10am-8pm;* 💲*$15;* 📞*855-753-9999; www.thedungeons.com/san-francisco),* an interactive journey through San Francisco's colorful past, led by fully costumed professional actors in immersive 360º themed sets. (*Note that tickets for these venues can often be purchased together for a discount.*) Yet underneath the honky-tonk veneer, much of the area retains its salty character of old. Visitors who step off the main path will discover a series of working piers, fabulous views of the bay, and several evocative monuments to the city's maritime past, including some interesting historic vessels.

SIGHTS

Sights below are listed from east to west.

👥 Pier 39★

Embarcadero at Beach St. 🕐*Open daily 10am–9pm (hours vary for individual shops).* ✕🚻🅿 📞*415-981-7437. www.pier39.com.*

Built over a dilapidated c.1900 pier, this festive, bilevel marketplace ranks among the top tourist destinations in the state. After the Port of San Francisco lost its shipping supremacy to Oakland in the 1970s, Pier 39 was nearly demolished, but a redevelopment (1978) attracted retailers from video arcades to candy shops, boutiques and restaurants.

At the base of the pier lies the **Aquarium of the Bay★** (👥 ⏰*Open daily 10am-6pm* ⏰*Closed Dec 25;* 🎫*$28;* ♿ ✆*888-732-3483 or 415-623-5300; www.aquariumofthebay.com*).

Visitors here may enter and view the undersea world up close with a stroll through two clear 300ft-long tunnels that burrow through tanks containing over 20,000 aquatic creatures, including Pacific octopus, eels, and sharks. There's also a series of touch pools that allow you to touch live bat rays and leopard sharks.

Adding to Pier 39's carnival atmosphere, a group of wild California **sea lions★** occupies the docks off its west side, where they are often lounging or fighting each other for a prime spot in the sun. The reason for the blubbery creatures' arrival here in 1990 is a mystery, but it is thought that they are members of the same colony that inhabits Seal Rocks, near Cliff House; their raucous barking can be heard from as far away as Telegraph Hill. Learn more about these glorious creatures at the **Sea Lion Center** (⏰*Open daily 10am-5pm.* ✆*415-289-7373; bayecotarium.org)*, located on the second level, featuring interactive displays, educational video and presentations led by aquarium naturalists.

California sea lions, Pier 39

© Robert Harding/hemis.fr

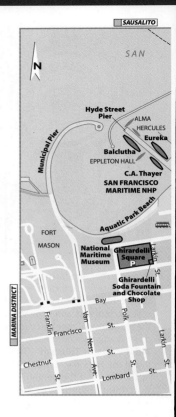

Touch a sea lion pelt then step outside to the dock overlook to see them up close. Adventurous types should visit **City Kayak** (⏰*Open Fri-Mon, 10am-5pm. Walk-in rentals available Mar-Nov noon-5pm.* ✆*888-966-0953; www.citykayak. com)*, which rents boats to kayakers of all abilities. Beginners can paddle along the waterfront and experts can venture all the way to the Golden Gate Bridge or around Alcatraz Island.

There are more than 30 different animals, including some marine creatures, to ride on the two-story open-air Italian-made **carousel** (🎫*$5)* at Pier 39, which at night is illuminated by 1,800 LED lights.

👥 Bay Cruises★

A scenic cruise on San Francisco Bay offers visitors a new perspective of the city, from a peek at the underside of the Golden Gate Bridge to wide **views★** of

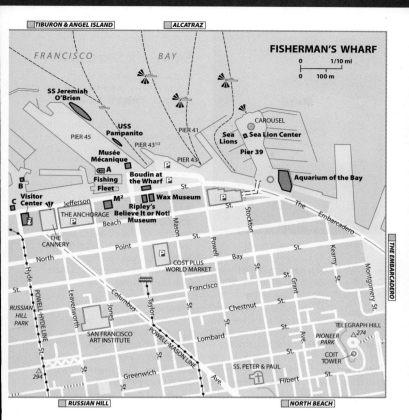

steep hills and the skyline. From the vantage point of the bay, visitors can learn about San Francisco and get a glimpse of the waterfront as a working port. The Blue and Gold Fleet's **Bay Cruise Adventure** (*Departs Pier 39 May–Sept daily 10am–6pm; rest of the year 10am–4:30pm, Sat-Sun until 5:30pm; Closed Dec 25; round-trip 1hr; English-language commentary; $30, no reservations required; 415-705-8200; www.blueandgoldfleet.com) travels west along the shoreline, circles beneath the Golden Gate Bridge and passes close to Angel Island, Alcatraz, and Pier 39's sea lions. (Mulitlingual audio tapes available for smartphones) The Red and White Fleet's **Golden Gate Bay Cruise** (*Depart from Pier 43½ May–Sept daily 9:15am–6:15pm; rest of the year daily 10am–4:15pm (earlier apply in winter; round-trip 1hr; commentary; $30 415-673-2900; www.redandwhite.com)* follows a similar route; individual headsets broadcast a well-produced narrative (available in sixteen languages).

👥 Boudin at the Wharf★

160 Jefferson St. Baker's Hall open Sun-Thu 8am–9pm , Fri-Sat 8am–10pm; museum and bakery tour Wed–Mon 11.30am–9pm; restaurant and bar daily 8am–9pm. 415-928-1849. www.boudinbakery.com.

Opened in spring 2005, this airy, 26,000sq ft shrine to sourdough bread adds a note of elegance to Fisherman's Wharf. Sporting a 30-ft-long observation window along Jefferson Street so that passersby can watch the bakers at work, the structure contains a cafe, restaurant, demonstration bakery, and museum, which offers a self-guided exploration of the history of bread-baking in San Francisco.

Clam chowder in sourdough bread

Sidewalk Seafood

A stroll along the north side of Jefferson Street between Jones and Taylor Streets leads through a symphony of smells and tastes whose overriding note is fresh seafood. The tradition of eating outdoors on the wharf dates from the early 20C, when Italian fishermen returning from early-morning runs grabbed bowls of chowder from sidewalk stands before hurrying off to sell the day's catch. In 1916, Tomaso Castagnola began offering walkaway crab cocktails to tourists who came down to see the colorful fishing fleet. His success led Italian fishing families to set up their own steaming pots along the wharf from which they sold freshly cooked Dungeness crab. Even the opening of large, full-service restaurants in the 1930s could not diminish the popularity of the sidewalk stands.

Today, a ladle of creamy clam chowder in a hollowed-out loaf of sourdough bread has become a mandatory part of the San Francisco experience. Another quintessentially San Franicsco food available at the wharf is Dungeness crab, a symbol of the local fishing industry. The season typically begins in November, when it's sold fresh from daily trapping by street vendors, many of whom make a rhythmic show of cracking the sweet crustacean's ten legs. You can either buy them cooked and steamed, or take it home raw to work your own magic.

Out of season, fresh crab is flown in, and remains a fixture on the wharf's restaurant menus.

Although nontraditional items such as pizza have recently appeared, the best fare on the wharf still comes from the sea—including shrimp or crab salad sandwiches on crusty sourdough rolls, freshly steamed Pacific rock lobster, prawn and crab cocktails, oysters, crab cakes, and an assortment of fried squid, fish, and clams.

Dungeness crabs

USS Pampanito

© ksteffens/iStockphoto.com

The Boudin family began making sourdough bread more than 150 years ago for fortune-seekers headed to the Nevada hills during the Gold Rush. The same recipe for the tart, chewy bread—unbleached flour, water, a pinch of salt, and a portion of so-called mother dough—has been used ever since. Try it Fisherman's Wharf style: hollowed out and filled with clam chowder.

♟♟ Musée Mécanique ★

Pier 45, Shed A (Embarcadero at Taylor St.). ◷*Open daily 10am–8pm.* ♿ ☎*415-346-2000. www.museemecaniquesf.com.* Formerly housed in a small gallery at the Cliff House (↻*see SUTRO HEIGHTS*), this curious collection of over 300 antique mechanical amusements includes coin-operated player pianos, mobile dioramas made entirely of toothpicks, and penny-arcade picture machines, in addition to pinball machines. Note that although there is no admission charge, most machines require one to three quarters to operate.

♟♟ USS Pampanito★★

Pier 45, Fisherman's Wharf. ◷*Open Sun-Thu 9am-6pm, Fri-Sat 9am-8pm. Call for closing times.* ☜*$20. 12 and under $10.* ☎*415-775-1943. maritime.org/uss-pampanito* A World War II, Balao-class submarine built in the Portsmouth naval shipyard in 1943, this deep-diving, 311ft vessel

made a half-dozen patrols during her two years of service in the Pacific, sinking six Japanese ships and damaging four others. In September 1944, the *Pampanito* and two other submarines jointly attacked a convoy of Japanese ships in the South China Sea carrying oil, raw rubber and other war supplies. After sinking several ships, the three subs pursued the surviving vessels out of the area. When the *Pampanito* returned a few days later, the crew spotted men clinging to pieces of wreckage; the 73 rescued were British and Australian prisoners of war who had been aboard the sunken vessels. That number—73—is commemorated on the *Pampanito's* flag, displayed on the pier. Other informative panels describe the workings of a submarine and tell the story of the *Pampanito.*

Visit

⊘ *Some physical agility is required to slip through the submarine's narrow corridors and small hatches.*
The haunting, self-guided audio tour begins on the upper deck and moves from the rear (aft) torpedo room through the maneuvering room, engine rooms, galley, control room and officers' quarters to the cramped forward torpedo room, where members of the crew slept beside the massive weapons. A former commander of the sub narrates the audio tour, his matter-of-fact voice

and understated descriptions effectively conveying the claustrophobia, fear and boredom that faced those who signed on for submarine duty. Pampanito veterans have added their personal accounts, complemented by r historic recordings.

▲▲ S.S. Jeremiah O'Brien★

Pier 45. ⏱*Open daily 9am–4pm.* ⏱*Closed Jan 1, Thanksgiving Day, Dec 25.* ⌖*$20.* ☏*415-544-0100.* *www.ssjeremiahobrien.org.*

This noble gray vessel formed part of the 5,000-ship armada that stormed Normandy Beach on D-Day in 1944. Launched on June 19, 1943, she was one of a fleet of 2,751 Liberty Ships that served as the backbone of the supply line to U.S. Armed Forces during World War II. Lovingly restored and maintained by volunteers, the ship is the only operational Liberty Ship on the West Coast. Self-guided tours cover the wheelhouse, engine room, crew's quarters, deckside guns and ship's store. On "steaming weekends" *(3rd weekend Jan–Apr, Jun–Sept & Nov)*, the crew fires up her triple-expansion steam engines, used in the blockbuster movie *Titanic* to replicate the engines of that ill-fated luxury liner.

Fishing Fleet★

North side of Jefferson St. between Jones and Taylor Sts.

The small, colorful fishing boats tied up at the docks just off Jefferson Street are remnants of an active and successful fleet that once numbered more than 450 vessels. Today the fishermen take out their vessels very early in the morning to fish for rex and petrale sole, sea bass, mackerel, sand dab, rock cod, ling cod and herring in the waters outside the Golden Gate, then return to unload their catches along this and other piers behind the Jefferson Street Lagoon. Millions of pounds of seafood still come into this port annually.

Visitors may take a self-guided tour of this active wharf area by following 30 interpretive signs describing the history and operation of the fishing industry.

A small building of brown wood with a stained-glass ship's wheel over its door rests at the foot of **Pier 45**. Erected in 1980, this **Fisherman's and Seamen's Memorial Chapel (A)** remains truly ecumenical, hosting christenings, bar mitzvahs, Latin masses, Buddhist memorials, and weddings of all sorts.

▲▲ San Francisco Maritime National Historical Park ★★

Hyde and Jefferson Sts.
⏱*Open daily 9.30am–5pm.*
🚶*Guided pier walks and boat tours daily; last entry to the ships at 4.30pm; call for schedule.* ⏱*Closed Jan 1, Thanksgiving Day, Dec 25.* ☜*$10 to board the ships;* ☏*415-447-5000.* *www.nps.gov/safr,www.maritime.org.*

Built as a ferry terminal in the years before construction of the Golden Gate and Bay Bridges, the **Hyde Street Pier** eventually became the mooring for six historic ships purchased and restored by the **San Francisco Maritime Museum**, The entire pier area, including the fleet, are maintained by the park. In addition to its six ships—three of which may be boarded and explored—the pier houses a turn-of-the-20C "ark" (a flat-bottomed houseboat that served as a summer retreat on the bay), the 1850s-era office of Tubbs Cordage, several old tug boats and a **small boat shop (B)** that offers lessons in boat building and restoration. At the corner of Jefferson and Hyde Streets, the visitor center has maps, seafaring exhibits and a schedule of the day's events. The **Maritime Store (C)** at the entrance provides information and offers a vast array of books.

Eureka★

Right side of pier.

This enormous sidewheel ferry, built in 1890 and still the world's largest wooden floating structure, could carry up to 2,300 commuters at a time. Originally named the *Ukiah*, the ship served as a railroad-car ferry until 1922, when she was rebuilt as the *Eureka* and launched as a passenger and auto ferry between Sausalito and San Francisco. After 1941 the *Eureka* plied the waters on the Oakland-San Francisco run until her giant walking-beam engine snapped in 1957.

C.A. Thayer, San Francisco Maritime National Historical Park

© Brigitta L. House / MICHELIN

Today, visitors can wander the massive decks or operate a model walking-beam that stands beside the actual four-story, steam-powered engine.

C.A. Thayer★
Across from the Eureka.
Built in 1895 to haul logs of heavy Douglas fir between Washington and California, this venerable, three-masted wooden sailing schooner is one of only two such ships in the country (the other, the *Wawona,* is berthed in Seattle). Her single deck, open hold, shallow draft, and relatively wide beam enabled her small crew to hold the 156ft craft steady in shallow, turbulent coves called "dog-holes" as timber was loaded from the bluffs above. Visitors who now descend into the ship's hold find themselves in a dark cave, its walls worn smooth by many loads of rubbing logs. Just above are the handsome captain's quarters and adjacent formal dining room. In the fore-castle, a video *(11min)* recounts the story of the ship's last voyage. Deckhands in period costume often introduce the boat to groups of schoolchildren.

Balclutha★★
End of pier on the left.
Looming over the pier, this three-masted, steel-hulled square-rigger was launched in Glasgow in 1886, rounding Cape Horn 17 times on voyages between Europe and California. A deep-sea cargo vessel measuring 301ft, the *Balclutha* carried wine, spirits, hardware and coal from European ports to San Francisco, returning to the continent loaded with California wheat. In 1904 her owners based her in San Francisco and she began a long career in the salmon industry, running cannery supplies and workers between Alaska and California. A promoter bought the ship in 1933, renamed her the *Pacific Queen,* and displayed her in various ports as a "pirate" ship. Following this ignominious stage of her career, she came to rest on the Marin mudflats, a near wreck. In 1954 the National Maritime Museum purchased and refurbished her, restoring her original name.
Today visitors admire the vast decks, inspect the bird's-eye maple cabinets and elegant Victorian furnishings of the captain's quarters. In the *Balclutha's* cavernous hold are displays of various anchors, mast riggings and rudders, ballast tubs and a model salmon cannery. Note that at press time the Balclutha had been dry-docked for restoration in Alameda; she is slated to return to the pier in 2019.

Aquatic Park Beach
This small beach fronting a grassy lawn was created in the 1930s as part of a WPA recreational complex. The beach is protected from the open water by the Municipal Pier. While most people con-

sider the waters of San Francisco Bay too cold for swimming, hearty members of the century-plus-old Dolphin Club and the South End Rowing Club still swim here daily. Line fishermen frequent the 1,850ft **Municipal Pier** (1934), along with others seeking a quiet place to stroll.

♣♣ Cartoon Art Museum (M2)

781 Beach St between Hyde and Larkin Sts. ◷ *Thu-Tues 11am-5pm .*◷*Closed Weds, Jan 1, Easter Sunday, Thanksgiving Day, Dec 25.* ⊜*$10* ♿ ☏*415-227-8666. www.cartoonart.org.* This friendly museum is the only one of its kind in the western United States. Founded in 1984 to foster appreciation of cartoon art, it was homeless until 1987, when Peanuts creator Charles M. Schulz provided it with an endowment to rent a public space. It has since amassed an 7,000-piece permanent collection, including work from the late 18C. Originally in Yerba Buena Gardens, it opened in its current space in 2017.

♣♣ Ghirardelli Square★

900 North Point St. between Polk, Larkin & Beach Sts. ◷*Hours for shops and restaurants vary.* ◷*Closed Jan 1, Thanksgiving Day, Dec 25.* ✕♿🅿 ☏*415 -775-5500. www.ghirardellisq.com.* One of the finest examples of San Francisco's dedication to preserving its historic buildings, this redbrick shopping and dining complex was once the home of the Ghirardelli Chocolate Factory. Stop by the popular **Ghirardelli Soda Fountain and Chocolate Shop★**, home of the Earthquake sundae—eight scoops, eight toppings—and many other types of chocolate confections (♣♣*1st floor of Clock Tower Building;* ◷ *open Sun–Thu 9am–11pm, Fri–Sat 9am–midnight;* ☏*415-474-3938).*

National Maritime Museum at the Aquatic Park Boathouse Building★

Beach St. at Polk St. ◷ *Open daily 10am–4pm.* ☏*415-447-5000. www.nps.gov/safr/.*

Resembling an ocean liner at berth, this unusual Streamline Moderne building (1939) houses a fine collection of maritime artifacts.Its upper floors are recessed from a flat roof to create the impression of a ship's decks, a nautical effect enhanced by railings, porthole windows and cowl ventilators that look like smokestacks. It was built as the Aquatic Park Casino, centerpiece of the WPA's never-realized recreational complex. The interior boasts undulating undersea murals by Hilaire Hiler and a terrazzo floor designed by Richard Ayer, based on a shoal chart of the bay.
In the entrance hall you'll find a large anchor, the hull of a scow schooner and three fine models (including one of the *Preussen,* a unique, five-masted square-rigger). One collection is devoted to steam-powered ocean travel from post-Civil War to the 1980s; the first floor also hosts temporary exhibits. A larger exhibition hall *(2nd floor)* focuses on the 1850s–60s—the city's early years as a sea and inland port. Fisheries, whaling, and shipbuilding are portrayed through unusual artifacts. Displays on the traditional arts of the sailor include knotting, modeling, whittling and scrimshaw carving. Large windows to the north, as well as an open observation deck *(3rd floor),* offer grand views of the historic sailing ships at Hyde Street Pier.

ADDRESSES

♀/EAT

The Fairy Codmother – *2824 Jones St.* ☏*415- 606-9349 www.codmother.com.* Just a block from the waterfront crab stands and souvenir shops, this low-key food truck serves up generous baskets of battered fish and chips, which you can eat at the shaded picnic tables onsite.

Buena Vista Cafe – *2765 Hyde St.* ☏*415-474-5044. www.thebuenavista.com.* Known as the first bar in the U.S. to serve Irish coffee (Irish whiskey, coffee and whipped cream), the Buena Vista remains a local institution. Breakfast is served all day by aproned waiters who willingly direct visitors to local attractions.

Golden Gate Bridge★★★

Stretching across the narrow strait of the Golden Gate above the swirling union of the Pacific Ocean and San Francisco Bay, this elegant Art Deco suspension bridge remains one of San Francisco's most beloved symbols.

A BIT OF HISTORY

Imagined by a madman in 1869 and proposed intermittently over the next four decades by saner visionaries, the bridge across the treacherous strait between the San Francisco Peninsula and Marin County elicited passionate emotions and aggressive resistance at every stage of its conception. Few took the idea seriously until 1916, when auto transportation was fast becoming a way of life, and San Francisco's Board of Supervisor's commissioned the first feasibility study in 1918.

Initial cost estimates for the structure ran as high as $100 million, but Joseph Strauss, a tireless and innovative engineer who already had built more than 400 bridges around the world, claimed that he could span the "unspannable" passage for a mere $27 million. Excited by Strauss' plan, citizens of counties from San Francisco to the Oregon border offered financial and political support. Two major foes, however, stood in the way—the powerful Southern Pacific Railroad (sole owner of all transbay ferry operations), which stood only to lose from Strauss' railless design, and the U.S. War Department, which feared that the bridge would hinder navigation and provide a target for enemy bombs in the event of war. Some naysayers claimed that the deep and turbulent waters of the bay were too treacherous for such an undertaking, and still others decried Strauss' estimate as being nearly $75 million too low.

For years parties on both sides wrangled. When the War Department withdrew its opposition in 1924, the Southern Pacific filed a battery of lawsuits designed to keep the project in

🚌 Bus 28–19th Ave., 29–Sunset or 76-Marin Headlands; 511.org.

♿ **Michelin Map:** *See THE PRESIDIO* pp142-143

🛈 **Info:** ☎415-921-5858. www.goldengate bridge.org.

▶ **Location:** The Golden Gate Bridge spans the mouth of San Francisco Bay, joining the northwestern tip of the San Francisco Peninsula with the Marin Headlands. Car access from US-101/Hwy. 1 or from Lincoln Blvd. 🅿$7.50 toll (southbound only). Pedestrian access to the bridge (east sidewalk only) Apr–Oct 5am–9pm, rest of the year 5am–6.30pm . Bicycle access 24hrs/day; press the button to open the remote-activated security gate during night-time hours. You can get to the pedestrian path from Fort Point National Historic Site (♿*see THE PRESIDIO*), though you'll have to make a steep climb.

🕐 **Timing:** Beautiful any time, the bridge is particularly so at sunset.

🅿 **Parking:** There are two parking lots on the San Francisco side of the bridge, one on either side of the roadbed; the east lot is metered parking and the west lot costs $5 per day at weekends; the lot is reserved for employees only on weekdays. Keep in mind that, with only 150 spots between them, the lots fill up quickly on nice days.

👁 **Don't Miss:** The walk across the span on the east sidewalk; dress warmly!

The Golden Gate Bridge

Measuring 1.7 miles from end to end (with a suspension span of 1.22 miles), the Golden Gate Bridge stood for many years as the world's longest suspension bridge until it was superseded by the Verrazano-Narrows Bridge, connecting the Staten Island and Brooklyn boroughs in New York, in 1964. Unlike more rigid types of bridges, a suspension bridge relies on gravity for its stability: the massive weight of the roadway, suspended from cables anchored on land, keeps the structure from falling. The cables provide enough flexibility for the mid-span of the bridge to deflect transversely up to 27ft in high winds without jeopardizing the structure's integrity. There are f ive main components to a suspension bridge: piers, anchorages, towers, cables and a roadway, constructed in that order.

♦ The Golden Gate Bridge's two **piers** form the bases of the towers. The Marin pier stands close to shore, but the San Francisco pier had to be poured a quarter-mile offshore in 100ft of water because the nearer bedrock was deemed unstable. An oval concrete fender, 27.5ft thick at its top and as long as a football field, surrounds this southern pier, protecting it from battering waves and collisions.

♦ The two **anchorages**, each a collection of massive concrete blocks able to withstand 63 million pounds of pull from the cables, were sunk into pits deep enough to hold a 12-story building.

♦ The twin steel **towers** rise 746ft (65 stories) above the piers, each supporting a total load of 123 million pounds from the two main cables.

♦ The massive **cables**, spun out of 80,000 miles of wire, rest in saddles at the tops of the towers and are embedded into the anchorages on land. Under normal conditions (70°F and no load on the span), the cables bend the towers toward the shore by 6in.

♦ The steel-reinforced **roadway** hangs from ropes attached to the cables at 50ft intervals.

Since the Golden Gate Bridge's inauguration, weather conditions have forced it to close only three times. The bridge is continually maintained by a team of electricians, ironworkers and painters. Since 1937, the bridge has been repainted repeatedly to prevent corrosion from salt air, fog, winds and auto exhaust. Its trademark shade, dubbed "International Orange," was selected for aesthetic reasons, and in part because of its visibility in fog.

litigation for decades. During the same period, several of the counties that had originally joined the Golden Gate Bridge and Highway District pulled out, citing danger and expense. Since no federal or state funding was to be allocated, the remaining counties faced shouldering even more of the financial burden to achieve their goal of a link to the city across the bay.

By the time the last obstacles were removed—the railroad finally dropped its lawsuits under public pressure—the Great Depression had crushed the economy and citizens couldn't afford the bonds issued for public support. Then A.P. Giannini, visionary founder of the Bank of Italy, stepped forward and announced that his bank would finance the bridge. In January 1933, nearly 12

© franckreporter/iStockphoto.com

Golden Gate Bridge

years after Joseph Strauss first submitted his proposal, groundbreaking ceremonies finally took place.

Spanning the Gate – Unemployed laborers turned out in droves to compete for plum jobs on the bridge despite the widely held belief that one life would be lost for every $1 million spent. Fortunately Strauss and his principal assistant engineer, Clifford Paine, addressed that grim prospect by enforcing unprecedented safety procedures, including safety belts, nets and filter glasses to block the blinding sun. Their stringency paid off. Over the course of the bridge's construction, the safety nets saved the lives 19 men, who became known as the "Half-Way-to-Hell Club." The first fatal accident, the toppling of a derrick onto a young steel worker, did not occur until the fourth year of construction. Then, only three months before the bridge opened, a scaffold suspended below the roadway tore loose and plummeted into the safety net, carrying a dozen men with it. The net held for an instant, then ripped open, dropping the victims into the deepest part of the channel. Two survived the plunge, but the rest were lost in the vicious currents.

Despite this tragedy, the Golden Gate Bridge was hailed as a model of safety, economy and grace at its inauguration on May 27, 1937, with the *San Francisco Chronicle* referring to its a $35 million steel harp.

A holiday atmosphere prevailed in the city on opening day. Schools, offices and stores either closed or operated on a reduced schedule. By 6am, 18,000 people were waiting to cross the bridge from both sides. The first to cross the full span was Donald Bryan, a sprinter from San Francisco Junior College. Others rollerskated, walked on stilts, played musical instruments, walked backwards or walked their pets, all setting first-time records.

In total, a crowd of more than 200,000 surged across the span on foot on opening day. Automobiles followed next, continuing a week-long round of festivities celebrating the conquest of the "unbridgeable" Golden Gate. The final cost of construction was around $35 million.

The Golden Gate Bridge has only been closed a handful of times. In addition to brief closures for visiting dignitaries President Franklin D. Roosevelt and French President Charles de Gaulle, there have been three closures due to extremely high winds. On December 1, 1951, wind gusts of up to 60mph resulted in a 3hr closure. On December 23, 1982, 70mph winds closed the bridge for 2hrs. Winds of up to 75mph on December 3, 1983 resulted in the bridge's longest closure, of 3hrs 27min. None of the winds caused damage.

Today, over 100,000 vehicles traverse the Golden Gate Bridge daily, while pedestrians and cyclists take to its sidewalks to admire its soaring towers, graceful cables and wondrous views. The busiest traffic day to date was October 27, 1989, ten days after the massive Loma Prieta earthquake, when 162,414 vehicles crossed the bridge. It celebrated its 75th anniversary in 2012 with great fanfare. The Golden Gate Bridge ranks as the world's tenth-longest suspension bridge, surpassed by spans in Japan, England, Denmark, China, South Korea and New York. The bridge makes its presence known from afar at many points in San Francisco and Marin County, especially from Land's End, the Presidio, Marin Headlands, the Marina District and Fisherman's Wharf.

VISIT

On the south side of the bridge, a cross-section of a cable, a dignified statue of Joseph Strauss, and panel displays lead from the parking area through nearly five acres of manicured gardens of annuals and perennials. Just beyond, from a series of viewing platforms, you can drink in the sight of the bridge's massive towers and cables. Three plaques commemorate distinctions awarded by the American Society of Civil Engineers. The bridge was named a California Historic Civil Engineering Landmark in 1976 and a National Historic Civil Engineering Landmark in 1984. It was also awarded a special citation for infrastructure rehabilitation in 1986.

The **The Golden Gate Bridge Welcome Center**(*Open daily 9 am–6 pm; closed Thanksgiving & Dec 25*), built as part of the bridge's 75th-year anniversary celebration in 2012, provides a wealth of historical and pratical information, plus a gift shop and public restrooms.

For most visitors, a scenic stroll across the bridge on the east sidewalk is a must (*1.7mi one way, open daily sunrise to sunset*). Be sure to wear a warm jacket to ward off stiff winds, which can be quite strong on the central span. Cyclists cross the bridge using the opposite sidewalk (*24 hours access allowed*).

At the entrance to the sidewalk, note the memorial plaque dedicated to the eleven men killed while building the bridge. Then walk to the center of the 1.7mi span for **views**★★ of Alcatraz, the Marin Headlands and the Pacific Ocean. From here, you can get a sense of Strauss' magnificent accomplishment by gazing up the sleek, looping cables that rise in a smooth arc to the top of the towers. At mid-span the bridge is 220ft above the waters of the bay.

Continue across the bridge to reach the **Vista Point** on the Marin County side. Here are lovely **views**★★ of the bridge from the north, backdropped by the forested hills of the Presidio. The sweeping perspective encompasses the entire northern waterfront of the city, as well as the San Francisco–Oakland Bay Bridge. Also on the Marin side's viewing station is the Lone Sailor Memorial, dedicated on April 14, 2002 to all of the American sea services, including the Navy, Marine Corps, Coast Guard and Merchant Marine. The memorial represents sea service members' last glimpse of America's West Coast before heading out for their service at sea.

Visitors who want even more background information can take advantage of the twice-weekly free walking tours of the bridge offered by San Francisco City Guides (415-557-4266, www.sfcityguides.org) in conjunction with the San Francisco public library.

The historic **Round House** (1938), originally built as a restaurant for passing motorists, serves affordable locally sourced Americana fare, plus snacks and coffee (*open Sat-Sun 9am–5:30pm*), On the opposite side of the bridge, the **Bridge Café** offers coffee, ice cream, and other grab-and-go options. (*open daily 9am–6pm*).

Marina District★

Ensconced on the northern waterfront between the Presidio and Fisherman's Wharf, the Marina District is a desirable residential neighborhood, especially among young professionals. Many blocks of pale, stucco facades are enlivened by an abundance of Mediterranean Revival–style architectural details, including columns, tile roofs, and arched windows and doors. The most expensive homes border the broad swath of Marina Green and overlook San Francisco Bay.

A BIT OF HISTORY

Early Spanish settlers were not attracted by the muddy, marshy inlet, although the high ground hemming it on either side greatly interested military commanders charged with guarding the Golden Gate. Soldiers established the Presidio on the rise to the west in 1776 and in 1797 emplaced a battery of five bronze cannons atop the knoll now known as Black Point, to the east. The guns were never used, but in 1850 the site caught the eye of American military strategists, who established an army reservation there. To stave off Confederate attack during the Civil War, the Union Army installed a new battery of 12 cannons. Like its predecessor, it never saw battle. Development came slowly to the mud flats, sand dunes, and marshes between Black Point and the Presidio. At the beginning of the 19C, dairy farms covered the hills and valleys to the south (present-day Cow Hollow) and a roadhouse stood on the site of the Palace of Fine Arts, an area then called Harbor View. In 1911, city boosters seeking a location for a world's fair—to promote the rebirth of the city after the 1906 earthquake and fire, and to celebrate the opening of the Panama Canal—decided upon this largely empty tract. The Army Corps of Engineers erected a seawall along the muddy waterfront and by 1913 had filled the 600 acres inside it with tons of sand and earthquake debris, creating a flat, attractive site

🚍 Bus 22–Fillmore, 28–19th Ave., 30–Stockton, 41–Union, 45–Union-Stockton, or 47–Van Ness, 511.org.

🛈 **Info:** www.sftravel.com.

▶ **Location:** The Marina is bounded by San Francisco Bay, Van Ness Avenue, the Presidio, and Lombard Street.

👪 **Kids:** Watching kites in Marina Green or combing the beach along Crissy Field.

🕐 **Timing:** Marina Green, Chestnut Street, and Union Street are pleasant for strolling by day or evening. Union Street is especially festive at Christmas time, when its Victorian houses are bedecked with white lights. Fort Mason Center's galleries are open by day, but most theater performances are held at night; call the Fort Mason box office at ✆415-345-7575 or visit www.fortmason.org for information about events and cultural offerings.

🅿 **Parking:** Street parking is usually available in the Marina District's residential areas, though time limits (usually 2-3hrs) are strictly enforced. Limited free parking is available in the Marina Yacht Harbor, along Marina Green, and at the Exploratorium. There is a paid lot for visitors to Fort Mason Center.

☻ **Don't Miss:** The Palace of Fine Arts.

for the buildings of the Panama-Pacific International Exposition of 1915. At the fair's close, its structures were all razed except the Palace of Fine Arts.

Marina District viewed from Pacific Heights
© Brigitta L. House/MICHELIN

Developers took over, building choice homes for sale. The Marina District, as it became known, gained a reputation as a desirable middle-class address.

Ironically, the same uncompacted land-fill laid down for a fair that advertised San Francisco's recovery from the 1906 earthquake proved disastrous during the Loma Prieta quake of 1989. The unstable ground beneath the Marina District liquefied during the tremor, causing several homes to collapse. Today, however, the marks of Loma Prieta are largely erased and the Marina District remains an affluent residential neighborhood distinguished by its architectural harmony, its glorious views of the Golden Gate, and its tourist attractions at Fort Mason and the Palace of Fine Arts.

FORT MASON★
Upper Fort Mason★

The gentle slope and broad crown of a low hill overlooking the bay was a logical place for a military reservation. The Army failed to occupy the attractive site for more than a decade after 1850, however, and several well-to-do civilian families, in the interim, erected homes on Black Point before Union forces repossessed the property in 1863 during the Civil War. Named in 1881 for Col. Richard Mason, California's first military governor (1847–49), the outpost formed the western command center for the U.S. Army during the Indian Wars of the late 19C. Gen. Frederick Funston's interim

government established headquarters here in the anxious hours immediately following the 1906 quake, and tents were set up on the fort's broad meadow to house refugees from the devastated areas of the city.

GGNRA Headquarters

Bldg. 201, MacArthur St. (entrance at Franklin & Bay Sts.). ○*Open Mon–Fri 8am–5pm.* ♿🅿 ☏*415-561-4700. www.nps.gov/goga.*

Built in 1901, this three-story structure served briefly as an army hospital before its conversion to administrative offices after 1906. Inside, visitors may obtain abundant maps and information on GGNRA activities, and limited material on other national parks of the West. Behind the headquarters building lies the charming **Fort Mason Community Garden**, a public plot where local residents can register for space to grow vegetables, flowers and root crops (dozens of such gardens exist in the city). Stroll along Pope Street to see examples of early military construction, including a wooden base chapel (1942). Originally a barracks, the American Youth Hostel at the head of the street dates from the Civil War period.

Black Point Battery

North end of Franklin St.

In 1797, Spanish soldiers installed five-gun Batéria San José atop this serene bluff overlooking San Francisco Bay. The homes erected—without permission—

by civilians in 1855 were confiscated by the army in 1863; several remain today along the east side of Franklin Street, used as officers' quarters.

Although the guns have been removed, Black Point Battery still offers lovely **views** east to tall-masted ships and small boats anchored off Aquatic Park, with the downtown towers and East Bay hills beyond.

The Great Meadow
Near Bay and Laguna Sts.

Site of a tent city erected to shelter thousands of refugees from the 1906 quake, this broad, undulating lawn today draws picnickers and sunbathers. In the meadow stand a statue of the Madonna **(1)** by Italian-American sculptor Beniamino Bufano and a bronze figure of Bay Area Congressman Phillip Burton **(2)**, whose efforts spearheaded creation of the GGNRA.

Fort Mason Center for Arts & Culture★★

℘415-345-7500. www.fortmason.org.
Built on landfill during the early 20C, this bayside complex of barracks, warehouses, and docks served as the official embarkation point for Americans serving in Pacific theaters of war from 1910 through the Korean War.

More than 1.5 million GIs and 23 million tons of cargo shipped out from its three sturdy docks during World War II, making Fort Mason the second largest Army port in the U.S. at that time.

The lower bayside section of Fort Mason was decommissioned for civilian use in 1962 and was completely transformed as a cultural and community complex by 1977. Today its renovated military structures (dubbed "Landmark Buildings A-E") house more than two dozen arts organizations, theaters, galleries, and restaurants, with many spots geared toward children.

In addition to the spots listed below, some venues worth visiting are the **San Francisco Children's Art Center** *(Bldg. C, 1st floor;* Mon–Sat 9am–5.30pm; *closed school holiday weeks;* ℘415-771-0292; www.children-

sartcenter.org), the **Museo Italo Americano** (B*ldg. C, 1st floor.* Open Tue–Sun noon–4pm and by appt. Mon. Closed major holidays. ℘415-673-2200. www.museoitaloamericano.org), the **Magic Theatre** (*Bldg. D, 3rd floor;* ℘415-441-8822; www.magictheatre.org), which produces innovative plays from established and emerging writers; and the **Young Performers Theatre** (*Bldg. C, 3rd floor;* ℘415-346-5550; www.ypt.org), which specializes in dramatics for children.

Additionally, the parking lot is home to a Sunday morning farmers' market and **Off The Grid**, a weekly pop-up featuring a rotating selection of food trucks, mobile bars and live bands, every Friday evening 5p,-10pm from March through late-Oct. *www.offthegrid.com.*

Golden Gate National Recreation Area

Embracing San Francisco's northern and western boundaries as well as Angel Island, Alcatraz, and a large portion of coastal Marin County, the Golden Gate National Recreation Area was established by act of Congress in 1972. The 26,000-acre system of national parks, encompassing historic landmarks, military sites, redwood forests, beaches, and undeveloped coastal lands, came about largely through the efforts of U.S. Congressman Phillip Burton, who championed the movement to preserve the area's unused military lands as parks for nature conservation and recreation. Today the GGNRA attracts more than 13 million visitors annually.

GGNRA sites described in this guide include: Alcatraz, Baker Beach, Crissy Field, China Beach, Cliff House, Fort Funston, Fort Mason, Fort Point NHS, Land's End, Marina Green, Marin Headlands, Muir Beach, Muir Woods NM, Ocean Beach, The Presidio, San Francisco Maritime NHP, Stinson Beach, Tennessee Valley.

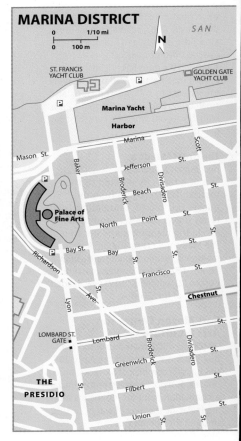

SFMOMA Artists Gallery

Bldg. A. Open Mon-Fri 9am–5pm; closed major holidays. ✆415-441-4777. www.sfmoma.org/artists-gallery.

As part of its mission to support the local art community, the San Francisco Museum of Modern Art maintains this commercial gallery space in Fort Mason, which hosts constantly rotating exhibits each year of new work by emerging and established artists.

San Francisco Art Institute★★

Pier 2. Galleries open Wed-Sun noon-7pm Closed major holidays. ✆415-641-1241. www.sfai.edu.

The San Francisco Art Institute, the oldest art school in California, opened this expansive $50 million annex to its historic main campus on Chestnut Street in Russian Hill in 2017. The vast, light-filled space on a renovated 1912 pier (*2017, Leddy Maytum Stacy*) is filled with over 160 studios for students and faculty, as well as 3,300 square feet of public exhibition space.

While visitors aren't allowed into the classrooms, private studios, or student lounges, they can enter the light-filled central atrium and public galleries via a set of glass doors on the pier (walk to the end of the pier for sweeping views of the Golden Gate Bridge and the bay). Here, frequently changing, high-quality temporary exhibits showcase work by faculty, students, and local artists.

In addition to representing a major evolution for SFAI, the campus signifies a new era for Fort Mason as an art and cultural center, now hosting dozens of student-artists who work on the premises every day.

The Interval at Long Now★

Bldg. A. Open daily 10am–midnight. ✆415- 561-6582. www.theinterval.org

Enjoy coffee or cocktails amid books, and mechanical wonders at this bar, café, and museum space that's also home to the Long Now Foundation, a forward-thinking cultural institution, founded in 1996 by a group of scientists and artists to address what they perceived to be a dangerous rise in short-term thinking and quick-fix solutions to difficult societal problems. Among the prototypes on display are a 10,000-year clock that is accurate to one day in 20,000 years and Brian Eno's ambient light-painting installation behind the bar. The foundation hosts lectures every Tuesdays at 7.30pm.

FRANCISCO BAY

Wave Organ

San Francisco Art Institute

PIER 2

PIER 3

MUNICIPAL PIER

FESTIVAL PAVILION

PIER 1

HERBST PAVILION

Black Point Battery

YOUTH HOSTEL

SFMOMA Artists Gallery

Marina Green

Blvd.

A B C D E

Fort Mason Center for Arts & Culture

AQUATIC PARK

FISHERMAN'S WHARF

Van Ness Ave.

1 Community Garden

CHAPEL

Webster St.

Beach

Buchanan St.

2 GGNRA HQ

The Great Meadow

Upper Fort Mason

Cervantes

Pierce

Fillmore St.

Blvd.

North Point St.

Bay

Francisco St.

Franklin St.

RUSSIAN HILL

MARINA

Steiner

Fillmore

GEORGE R. MOSCONE RECREATION CENTER

DISTRICT

St.

Chestnut

Street

Lombard

Buchanan

Laguna

Octavia

Gough

St.

St.

Pierce

Greenwich

Webster

Filbert

Vedanta Society

Street

2164/2166

2040

Octagon House

COW

Union

Charlton Court

HOLLOW

St.

Mary the Virgin

Green

Vallejo St.

PACIFIC HEIGHTS

Maritime Research Center

Bldg. E, 3rd floor. ⏱*by appt. only Mon–Fri 1–4.30pm.* ⏱*Closed federal holidays.* ♿🅿 ✆*415-561-7030. www.nps.gov/safr.*
Operated by the San Francisco Maritime National Historical Park, this library of maritime history maintains a collection of over 32,000 books plus oral history archives, sea chanteys, recorded interviews, vessel registers, photographs, and other nautical items centering on West Coast shipping and whaling.
The Oceanic Society maintains offices here and launches **whale-watching cruises** (⏱*see p 146*) from the harbor.

COW HOLLOW

Despite its bucolic name, Cow Hollow is best known for its charming, trendy shops and restaurants housed in attractive Victorians along bustling Union Street. Wedged below the flats of the Marina District at the foot of steeply rising Pacific Heights, the rolling "hollow" was known as Golden Gate Valley in the mid-19C, when herds of cattle from more than 30 dairy farms grazed upon its dales and hills. In the 1890s developers readily transformed Cow Hollow's pastures into a respectable neighborhood of two- and three-story wood-frame houses. Buildings along Union Street, the main thoroughfare, survived the earthquake and fire of 1906, and the area enjoyed a boom as

The Panama-Pacific International Exposition of 1915

As stewards of the West Coast's busiest port in the early 20C, San Francisco residents took keen interest in the construction of the Panama Canal. The resurrection of the city from the 1906 earthquake and fire, and increasing competition from the port at Los Angeles, heightened San Franciscans' resolve to celebrate the canal's completion in a way that would unequivocally announce that the city was rebuilt, rejuvenated and ready to resume its place as the economic and cultural center of the American Pacific coast.

On a 635-acre tract of reclaimed land, an esteemed group of architects, including Louis C. Mullgardt, Bernard Maybeck, Willis Polk, and William B. Faville, set about designing a fabulous complex of pavilions representing 25 countries and 29 states. From its opening day in February 1915, the fair dazzled the public with its attractions and architecture. Indirect lighting, an innovation of the era, accented a fantasy city of Renaissance palazzos, Spanish missions, Classical temples, and Byzantine domes. The Great Palace of Machinery was vast enough for an airplane to fly through it.

The Oregon State pavilion resembled the Parthenon, only using redwood trunks instead of marble pillars. Visitors were awed by a working scale model of the Panama Canal. At the center of the fairgrounds rose the Tower of Jewels, covered with more than 100,000 cut-glass jewels backed by tiny mirrors and suspended on wires, so that the tower appeared to shimmer in the breeze. Most beloved by San Franciscans was the Palace of Fine Arts *(www. palaceoffinearts.org)*. The fair was acclaimed far and wide as the most ambitious event ever hosted by the city, attracting nearly 20 million visitors in its ten months of operation and earning a substantial profit—but ultimately failing to lure back the shipping business lost to Los Angeles' growing port.

Constructed primarily of wood and plaster, most fair buildings were demolished at the exposition's close in December 1915. Only the Marina Yacht Harbor and the reconstructed Palace of Fine Arts remain today.

it greeted merchants and residents fleeing the burned-out areas of San Francisco. Local businesses catered primarily to neighborhood shoppers until the 1950s, when antique shops and interior decorators began renting Union Street's Victorian storefronts. Other fashionable shops and restaurants followed suit. Much of Cow Hollow's genteel, early 20C architecture survives, along with several evocative reminders of its rural past.

Union Street★

www.unionstreetsf.com.
Lined with refurbished Victorians, Union Street's eight-block retail district between Van Ness Avenue and Steiner Street invites leisurely exploration. Old houses have been converted to boutiques, galleries, arts-and-crafts shops, and small, urbane restaurants.

Particularly attractive is **Charlton Court** *(south side of Union St. between Laguna & Buchanan Sts.),* a quiet lane thought to have once served as a depot for milk wagons. The house and barn (c. 1870) of James W. Cudworth, Cow Hollow's first dairyman, still stand behind a palm tree at no. 2040. A roofed passage at no. 2164/2166 leads to an old barn and leafy carriage yard, where plants and garden ornaments are displayed for sale. Cow Hollow's most unusual building, visible to the north from the corner of Union and Webster, is the former temple of the **Vedanta Society of Northern California** (1905) *(2963 Webster St.).* Built by Joseph Leonard after a design by Swami Trigunatita, the three-story wooden building sports an ecumenical medley of ornamentation representing diverse religions and cultures.

St. Mary the Virgin Episcopal Church

2325 Union St. at Steiner St. ◷*Open Mon–Fri 9am–5pm, Sun during services.* ◷*Closed major holidays and Christmas week.* ♿ ☏*415-921-3665. www.smvsf.org.*
Partially hidden behind its fence and lych-gate, this charming church (1891) evokes the feel of an English country parsonage, though its wooden frame and redwood-shingle cladding herald the Arts and Crafts style characteristic of northern California architecture. Peace and tranquillity pervade the quiet, A-frame sanctuary and grounds. The gushing spring in the entry courtyard was used to water dairy herds, and is one of Cow Hollow's most beguiling reminders of its bucolic past.

Octagon House★

2645 Gough St. at Union St. ◷*Open 2nd & 4th Thu, & 2nd Sun of the month, noon–3pm.* ◷*Closed major holidays.* ☞*Donation requested.* ☞*Guided tours (30min) available.* ☏*415-441-7512.*
Built in 1861 by William C. McElroy, this small house was moved from a nearby lot to its present site in 1953 by the National Society of Colonial Dames of America in California, which uses it as a museum for its collection of decorative arts from the Colonial and Federal periods. The two-story structure took its curious shape from Orson Squire Fowler's popular 1848 book, *A Home for All,* which theorized that octagonal houses provided more light, space and ventilation than conventional square-cornered houses. The floor plan was substantially altered when the central stairwell was moved to the west wall by its present owners. Most of the rooms on the second floor, which is naturally lit by a central octagonal cupola that protrudes above the main roof, retain their original dimensions.

The museum displays many fine pieces of early American furniture, portraits, samplers, looking glasses, pewter and silverware, as well as examples of ceramics and other decorative items from the lively import trade during the Colonial era and early Republic.

ADDITIONAL SIGHTS
Chestnut Street

The four blocks of Chestnut Street between Divisadero Street and Fillmore Street, about halfway between Union Street and Marina Green, comprise the Marina District's main commercial avenue. A pleasant thoroughfare for shopping, dining and strolling, Chestnut Street projects a comfortable, friendly and relaxing atmosphere reminiscent of a small-town main street.

Marina Green

Encompassing an expansive stretch of Marina District waterfront between Webster and Scott Streets, this broad, 10-acre greensward is popular with locals for its stiff breezes—ideal for kite-flying, which is a popular and picturesque activity here—and for its stupendous **views**★★ of San Francisco Bay, the Golden Gate Bridge, and yachts anchored offshore.
A favored spot of sunbathers, volley-ball players, and joggers, the lawn is bordered by handsome dwellings in a diverse array of architectural styles. Most were built in the 1920s and incorporate Spanish and Italian Baroque details inspired by the 1915 Panama-Pacific International Exposition.
Enclosed by a 1,500ft jetty extending parallel to Marina Green, the **Marina Yacht Harbor** encloses a flotilla of boats, many of them belonging to members of the private St. Francis Yacht Club, which occupies an attractive, tile-roofed structure (1928, Willis Polk).

Wave Organ

St. Francis Yacht Club harbor. www. exploratorium.edu/visit/wave-organ.
Before it relocated from the Palace of Fine Arts to the Embarcadero, the Exploratorium helped build this unusual outdoor sound installation, know as the Wave Organ, at the very end of the jetty extending from Marina Green into San Francisco Bay. The work of Exploratorium artists-in-residence Peter Richards and George Gonzalez, this jumble of concrete and stone is embedded with

Palace of Fine Arts

© PhotoDisc, Inc.

Maybeck's design was purely romantic in concept, inspired largely by the work of 18C engraver Giovanni Piranesi and *The Isle of the Dead,* a 19C painting depicting a royal tomb. Maybeck himself described the building as "an old Roman ruin" and stated his intent to project sadness. Reinforcing the sense of mystery and melancholy, the female figures sculpted by Ulric Ellerhusen along the top of the peristyle face inward, their faces buried in their arms.

The building, which later housed a theater, underwent another renovation in 2010-2011. Though not generally open to the public, it continues to host ocassional concerts and speakers. Visitors can also walk around the exterior and signature 135ft tall rotunda decorated with figures of weeping women and mythical creatures that ringed the colonnade. On clear days, the swan-filled lagoon spreading from the foot of the rotunda reflects mirror images, making it one of the city's most photographed sites .

PVC organ pipes, which create eerie sounds as the water rises and falls.

Palace of Fine Arts★★

3301 Lyon St. 🕐 *Open during events.* 📞*415-563-6504*
www.palaceoffinearts.org.
This faux Roman palace, replicated from structures designed by renowned architect Bernard Maybeck to house art exhibits for the 1915 Panama-Pacific International Exposition, is one of the remaining structures from that show. The original building, designed to be impermanent, was framed in lath and chicken wire and covered with a plaster and burlap-fiber mixture called "staff," its surface sprayed to resemble travertine. When the buildings of the fair were torn down, aesthetically minded citizens lobbied to spare the Palace of Fine Arts. No efforts were made to strengthen the building, however, and it slowly disintegrated until a plan for restoration was made in 1962. Workers made casts of the columns, statuary and artistic details, and the building was entirely reconstructed in concrete and steel in 1964–1967.

ADDRESSES

🍽/EAT

Wrecking Ball Coffee – *2271 Union St. www.wreckingballcoffee.com.* There is an astonishing variety of excellent coffee made in the Bay Area, and Wrecking Ball, which roasts its beans in SoMa and sells them in a tiny shop on Union Street, is among the best. Stop into their tiny Union St cafe for an afternoon treat.

SHOP

Readers Bookstore – *Fort Mason. Landmark Bldg C, First Floor.* 📞*415-771-1076. www.friendssfpl.org.* Browse the stacks of old vinyl records and second-hand books, including a fine art-book selection, at this creaky used bookstore and adjoining cafe. All profits benefit the San Francisco Public Library.

The Presidio★★

For more than two centuries, the Presidio's privileged setting on 1,480 acres overlooking the Golden Gate earned it a reputation as the most beautiful military installation in North America. Residents and visitors are drawn to the lushly forested expanse to enjoy its handsome and eclectic mix of architectural styles, its traces of San Francisco's military history, its recreational opportunities, and the spectacular views extending from its miles of wooded trails.

Closed as an army base in 1994, the Presidio is now administered by a federal trust agency in partnership with the National Park Service. It's now home to restaurants specializing in California-centric cuisine, The Walt Disney Family Museum, and seasonal events such as Twilight, Friday evening gatherings featuring food trucks, lawn games and live music.

A BIT OF HISTORY

Selected as the site of the northernmost military installation of the far-reaching Spanish colonial empire, the Presidio (the word means "military garrison") was dedicated on September 17, 1776, by Lt. José Joaquin Moraga. Originally an adobe quadrangle about 300yds on each side located approximately where the Main Post now stands, the Presidio was San Francisco's first European settlement, predating Mission Dolores by a month. The Spanish never considered the outpost to be of primary importance despite its strategic location. Official disinterest, combined with decades of rain, earthquakes, wind and salt air, kept the fortress in a perpetual state of disrepair, even after Mexico acquired it (along with independence from Spain) in 1821.

The Presidio's outlook changed in 1846 when John C. Frémont and a group of civilians staged the capture of the crumbling, largely defenseless fort from the Mexican government. The American flag was raised over the decaying garrison

🚌 Bus 28–19th Avenue, 29–Sunset, 41–Union, 43–Masonic or 45–Union-Stockton, 511.org.

ℹ️ **Info:** ✆415-561-4323. www.nps.gov/prsf or www.presidio.gov.

▶️ **Location:** The Presidio occupies a large, roughly square area in the city's north-west corner. Pick up maps and check out the exhibits at the new **Presidio Visitor Center**, located on the Main Post parade *(Building 210 Montgomery St.).*

👪 **Kids:** Cannon drills at Fort Point; Walt Disney Family Museum, live tidepool tank at the Marine Sanctuary Visitor Center.

🕐 **Timing:** Outdoorsy types could easily spend a day exploring trails around here. History buffs can spend a few hours in the Main Post area.

🅿️ **Parking:** Follow signs for ample parking, some free and some with hourly fee. Enter by **Lincoln Boulevard** (which skirts the Coastal Defense Batteries, offering stunning bridge **views★★**) or by historic gates. The **Lombard Street Gate** *(Lombard St. at Lyon St.)* and **Marina Gate** *(Marina Blvd. at Lyon St.)* are close to the Marina District; the latter brings you by the Crissy Field Center. **The Presidio Boulevard Gate** *(Presidio Blvd. at Pacific St.)* and **Arguello Boulevard Gate** *(Arguello Blvd. at Pacific St.)* enter from the south.

🎯 **Don't Miss:** The Main Post; views from Baker Beach.

Aerial view of The Presidio

© Presidio Trust

following cession of California to the U.S. in 1848. San Francisco's growth as a commercial hub during the Gold Rush caused President Millard Fillmore to issue an executive order in 1850 reserving the property for military use. Over the next decade the fort was restored and enlarged, while other installations were erected around the bay, including Fort Point and Alcatraz.

Bulwark of National Defense – The timing of this military construction was fortuitous. Following the outbreak of the Civil War, defense of San Francisco Bay moved to top priority from the Union's point of view. Gold and silver from California and Nevada mines were at stake. The Presidio undertook a major military buildup to guard against invasion by Confederate forces.

Following the Civil War, the Presidio housed U.S. troops engaged in conflicts with the Modoc, Apache, and other Native American tribes across the West. Between 1886 and 1976, the

magnificent eucalyptus, cypress, and pine forests—in all, 100,000 trees of 200 species—were planted in military rows on the rolling lands of the base, both to beautify it and to protect its terrain from erosion. The coastal defense batteries along the bayfront also were constructed. After 1898 the Presidio served as the launching pad for American expansion into the Pacific.

The presence of a large, standing army proved vital at the time of the 1906 earthquake and fire. Presidio troops helped maintain order as martial law was proclaimed, and more than 16,000 refugees camped on the fort's open lands. When the United States entered World War I, troops trained here for combat in France. During World War II, the Presidio became headquarters for the Western Defense Command, as nearly 2 million troops shipped out from San Francisco. In the 1950s the base was named the command center for Nike missile defense of the bay and served as headquarters for the Sixth U.S. Army until 1994.

Swords to Plowshares – In 1962 the site was named a National Historic Landmark District. When the Golden Gate National Recreation Area (GGNRA) was created a decade later, Congress tagged the Presidio, whose military importance had waned, for future inclusion in the park. In 1989 the Presidio was designated for closure as part of a general defense reduction and consolidation,

PresidiGo

A free shuttle-bus service makes nearly 40 stops in the park and departs the Presidio Transit Center Mon–Fri 6.30am–7.30pm every 30min and Sat–Sun 11am–6.30pm every hour (℘415-561-5300; www.presidio.gov/shuttle).

and on October 1, 1994, the Sixth Army marched off the grounds for the last time as the Presidio came under the supervision of the National Park Service. The remnants of the earliest 18C structures were discovered beneath the Main Post parking lot in 1996, shedding new light on what was believed to be the size of the original Presidio.

Today a unit of the GGNRA, the property is managed by **The Presidio Trust**, a presidentially appointed, nonprofit board charged with maintaining the Presidio's aesthetic, ecological and historic integrity. About 80 percent of Presidio lands are under the direct aegis of the trust, while coastal areas are managed by the National Park Service. Ensuring public access to the fine Greek, Colonial, Mission, Mediterranean Revival and Victorian buildings, as well as to trails and natural habitats, is central to every decision. So, too, is protecting the rights of a community of 800 households and over 150 organizations.

Despite resistance by some preservationists, filmmaker George Lucas (Star Wars) developed the former Letterman Army Medical Center complex (1899), on the east side of the Presidio, as a campus for the digital arts, incorporating a seven-acre "Great Meadow." Today, the Yoda statue that stands outside what is now the **Letterman Digital Arts Center** (1 Letterman Dr, Building B, ℘415-746-5445), home to Lucas's Industrial Light and Magic, is a pilgrimage site for Star Wars fanatics.

ⓔ The free **PresidiGo shuttle** operates two "around the park"routes, which stop at more than 40 destinations within the Presidio. (More information at www. presidio.gov/transportation/presidigo or at the Visitors Center).

SIGHTS
Presidio Visitors Center★★
Building 210, 210 Lincoln Blvd.
ⓞOpen daily, 10am–5pm. ♿🅿
℘415-561-4323. www.presidio.gov/ places/presidio-visitor-center
Opened in February 2017 in a rehabilitated historic Colonial Revival style building on the north end of the Main Post adjacent to the Presidio transit center, the new William Penn Mott Jr. Visitor Center is the place to begin your exploration of the Presidio, Crissy Field and neighboring Golden Gate National Recreation Area. Originally built in 1900 as the Army post's guardhouse, it was converted in 1951 to house a bank and United States Post Office to serve the needs of base residents.

As part of The Presidio's post-to-park transformation, the restored two-room building, which includes the original wood floors, bead board wainscoting, sheet metal ceiling, and exposed brick walls, now serves as orientation hub for visitors, with interactive exhibits that highlight the park's natural and cultural significance and an information desk staffed by the Natural Park Service and Presidio Trust. There's also a wonderful gift shop integrated into the space, where you'll find books on local history and ecology, travel guides, maps, souvenirs, and Presidio- and San Francisco-branded apparel.

Main Post★★
Although no longer the efficient headquarters of a bustling military base, the Main Post remains the focal point of activity at The Presidio.

The stately brick **barracks★** (c.1890) stretching along Montgomery Street, on the west side of the large central Parade Ground, once housed soldiers of the Spanish-American War. One of these buildings is now the **Lodge at the Presidio**, a boutique hotel. Another is the **Society of California Pioneers Museum and Library** (101 Montgomery St. ⓞOpen Wed–Sat 10am–5pm. ⓞClosed major holidays. ♿℘415-957-1849. www.californiapioneers.org), which organizes exhibits on California history drawn from the permanent collection of 6,000 artifacts and 50,000 photographs. At the Parade Ground's southern end stands **Pershing Square**, site of the home of Gen. John "Black Jack" Pershing, later commander of the American Expeditionary Forces in Europe during World War I. Pershing's wife and daughters perished in a 1915 blaze that

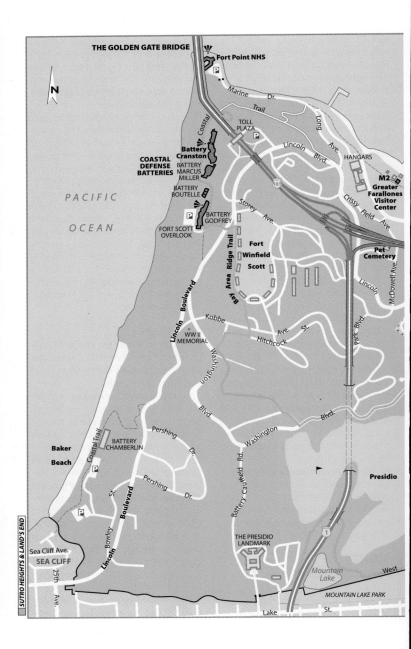

THE GOLDEN GATE BRIDGE

Fort Point NHS

Marine Dr.

Trail

TOLL PLAZA

Lincoln Blvd.

HANGARS

Battery Cranston

COASTAL DEFENSE BATTERIES

BATTERY MARCUS MILLER

BATTERY BOUTELLE

BATTERY GODFREY

FORT SCOTT OVERLOOK

M2 Greater Farallones Visitor Center

Crissy Field Ave.

Storey Ave.

Fort Winfield Scott

Pet Cemetery

Lincoln

McDowell Ave.

Bay Area Ridge Trail

Lincoln Boulevard

Kobbe

Hitchcock Ave. St.

WW II MEMORIAL

Washington Blvd.

Park Blvd.

PACIFIC OCEAN

Coastal Trail

Pershing Dr.

Battery Caufield Rd.

Washington

Blvd.

Presidio

Baker Beach

BATTERY CHAMBERLIN

Pershing Dr.

Lincoln Boulevard

Bowley St.

THE PRESIDIO LANDMARK

Sea Cliff Ave.

SEA CLIFF

25th Ave.

Mountain Lake

West

MOUNTAIN LAKE PARK

Lake St.

N

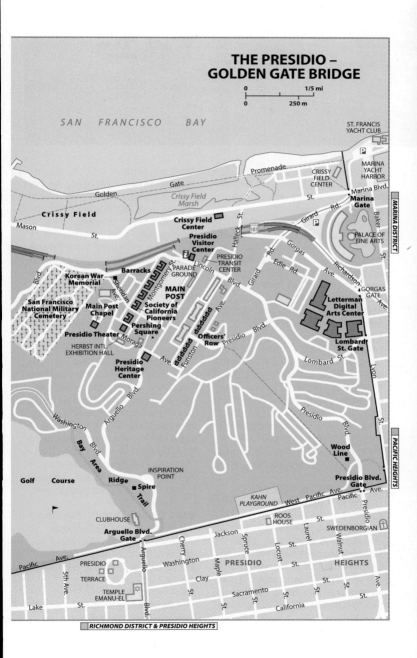

THE PRESIDIO – GOLDEN GATE BRIDGE

0   1/5 mi
0   250 m

SAN FRANCISCO BAY

ST. FRANCIS
YACHT CLUB

MARINA
YACHT HARBOR

Marina Blvd.

Promenade

CRISSY
FIELD
CENTER

Marina
Gate

Golden   Gate

Crissy Field
Marsh

Girard   Rd.

PALACE OF
FINE ARTS

Crissy Field

Crissy Field
Center

Mason   St.

Presidio
Visitor
Center

Halleck   St.

Gorgas

Edie   Rd.

Richardson   Ave.

Baker   St.

Korean War
Memorial

Barracks

Lincoln

PRESIDIO
TRANSIT
CENTER

Girard   Rd.

GORGAS
GATE

Montgomery   St.

PARADE
GROUND

Blvd.

Letterman
Digital
Arts Center

San Francisco
National Military
Cemetery

Main Post
Chapel

MAIN
POST

Society of
California
Pioneers

Ave.

Sheridan   Ave.

Blvd.

Moraga

Pershing
Square

Presidio   Blvd.

Lombard
St. Gate

Presidio Theater

Officers'
Row

Funston   Ave.

Lombard   St.

Lyon   St.

HERBST INTL.
EXHIBITION HALL

Ave.

Presidio
Heritage
Center

Presidio

Arguello   Blvd.

Blvd.

Washington

Bay

Area

Ridge

INSPIRATION
POINT

Wood
Line

Golf   Course

Trail

Spire

Presidio Blvd.
Gate

Pacific   Ave.

CLUBHOUSE

KAHN
PLAYGROUND

West   Pacific   Ave.

Pacific

Presidio

ROOS
HOUSE

Arguello Blvd.
Gate

Arguello

Jackson

Spruce   St.

Laurel   St.

SWEDENBORGIAN

Walnut   Ave.

Pacific   Ave.

5th Ave.

PRESIDIO

TERRACE

Washington

Cherry   St.

Maple   St.

Clay

Locust   St.

St.

PRESIDIO

HEIGHTS

Blvd.

TEMPLE
EMANU-EL

Clay

Sacramento

St.

St.

St.

Lake   St.

California

MARINA DISTRICT

PACIFIC HEIGHTS

RICHMOND DISTRICT & PRESIDIO HEIGHTS

147

Main Post

© Charity Vargas/Presidio Trust

destroyed the house (a son survived); a flagpole signifies its location. A nearby monument marks the corner of the original adobe and thatched-roof Presidio compound built by the Spanish in 1776. Just west, on a low rise, the **Interfaith Center** *(130 Fisher Loop; ◦ Guided tours select Sundays 11 am and 1pm, or by appointment ℘415-561-5444; www.interfaith-presidio.org)* features a 1930s WPA mural by artist Victor Arnautoff. At the east end there is a small Vietnam memorial.

Tree-lined Funston Avenue, one street east of the Parade Ground, was once reserved for officers. The Neoclassical and Italianate cottages (1862–63) at the southern corner, known as **Officers' Row★**, originally faced west but were turned towards the east in 1878 to present a more pleasant aspect to visitors. An ongoing dig by University of California archeology students has turned up 150,000 artifacts from this era.

Presidio Officers Club★

50 Moraga St. on the Main Post.
◷*Open Tue–Sun 10am–6pm.*
◦ *Guided tours Sat. 1pm.* ◷*Closed major holidays.* ♿ ℘*415-561-4400.*
www.presidio.gov/officers-club
Established in 1776 by Spanish explorers and serving as an elite gathering place for Army brass throughout the 20th century, the Officer's Club is San Francisco's most historic building. An amalgam of adobe, wood-frame, concrete, and steel structures constructed over the course of approximately 200 years, it has now been charmingly restored and serves an

interesing museum and cultural center. In the **Mesa Room**, just beside the club's main entrance, you can see the building's original adobe walls, which date from about 1800; they were unexpectedly uncovered during restoration.

The permanent exhibit at the **Presidio Heritage Gallery** chronicles the history of the park, starting with the native Ohlone people of Northern California and continuing all the way to the present day. Volunteer docents are often available to answer questions about the show. The gallery and common spaces are also frequent hosts to changing art and historical exhibits covering topics, like a 2018 show chronicling Japanese internment in California during WWII. Visitors often spend a minute or two relaxing on the couches in old-fashioned **Moraga Hall**, where, in the winter, there's often a roaring fire. Just beside it, Andy Goldsworthy's Earth Wall is displayed in the patio dining room. of upscale Mexican restaurant **Arguello** *(℘415-561-3650 www.arguellosf.com).*

Walt Disney Family Museum

104 Montgomery St. ◷*Open daily 10am–6pm, last entry at 4:45pm.*
◷*Closed Jan 1, Thanksgiving Day, Dec 25.* ($25, 6-17 yrs $15, free under 5).
🅿 ℘*415-345-6800.*
www.waltdisney.org
Visitors of all ages will delight at this interactive animation museum, set in a former barrack, that features the life and work of the man behind the mouse. interactive galleries organized chronologically showcasing his early

drawings, cartoons, films, music, along with a replica model of Disneyland, often narrated in Walt Disney's own voice. The musuem also houses a theater that screens a different Disney film each month (free with admission) and a popular onsite cafe.

San Francisco National Military Cemetery

Entrance off Sheridan St. at Lincoln Blvd.
In 1884 The Presidio's 28-acre burial ground was designated a National Military Cemetery, allowing any U.S. veteran the privilege of being buried here. At the entrance, the **Korean War Memorial,** a slab of curved black granite printed with historic photographs, is a tasteful tribute; the memorial was inaugurated in 2016, after years of struggle for recognition by veterans groups.

Within the cemetery, graves date from as far back as the Civil War. Well-known persons laid to rest here include Gen. Frederick Funston, acting Presidio commander during the 1906 earthquake and fire, and U.S. Rep. Phillip Burton, sponsor and champion of the GGNRA.

A short distance away, beneath the Crissy Field Avenue overpass leading to the Golden Gate Bridge, lies a small **Pet Cemetery** ▲♛, with whimsical, and often poignant headstones marking the graves of generations of Presidio pets.

Wood Line★

Near the trailhead departing from the Broadway Gate
⊘ *Three-mile docent-led guided Art Hikes, which visit all four Andy Goldsworthy sculptures in the park, are offered the 2nd Sat of the month, 10:30am and 1pm.*
An earthwork sculpture by noted contemporary artist Andy Goldsworthy, *Wood Line* is a 1,200-foot-long row of fallen logs, which weaves through a eucalyptus forest in the southeast corner of the park. The work, one of four Goldsworthy commissions in the Presidio, celebrates the restoration of park's trees. Not far away, the sculptor's *Spire* is a 100-foot tower created with felled Monterrey cypress.

Crissy Field

Crissy Field Ave. off Lincoln Blvd.
Gazing over this broad, flat marsh, visitors may not understand why it is widely hailed as San Francisco's most impressive environmental restoration in recent years. Yet the work done to bring it back to its natural state was tremendous. Once a soggy marsh, the field was drained and filled for the 1915 Panama-Pacific International Exposition, then covered with 70 acres of asphalt as an Army aircraft test site from 1919 to 1936. (Many original buildings still stand, including hangars that once housed cloth biplanes.) The National Park Service undertook a three-year, $32-million project to restore the original tidal marsh, beach and dunes, anchoring them with native grasses and other plants. Today the 100 acres of wild, windswept shoreline is a favorite place for walkers, joggers, bicyclists, windsurfers, and birds.

At the east end is **Crissy Field Center** (▲♛ *1199 E. Beach;* ⊘*open Mon–Fri by appointment;* ✆*415-561-7752; www.crissyfield.org),* an urban environmental education center for youth. Just past it is the **West Bluff Picnic Area,** a popular place for picnicking with a spectacular view of the Golden Gate Bridge.

▲♛ Greater Farallones Visitor Center (M2)

991 Marine Dr. ⊘*Open Wed–Sun 10am–4pm.* ⊘*Closed Jan 1, Thanksgiving Day, Dec 25.* ⊉
✆*415-561-6625. www.farallones.org.*
Exhibits describe research and conservation efforts in the 1,200sq mi sanctuary, whose boundaries embrace Marin County coastlines to the mean high-tide mark and the rocky Farallon Islands (26mi west of the Golden Gate), home to the largest concentration of breeding seabirds in the continental U.S. The sanctuary also harbors two dozen species of marine mammals.

The visitor center has a live tidepool tank; interactive computer displays outlining such sanctuary activities as whalewatching, bird watching, fishing and kayaking; and murals depicting life

A Whale of a Time

Few experiences may be more thrilling, and perhaps more unsettling, than tossing in salty swells on a small boat beyond the sight of land, surrounded by a good dozen of the largest creatures on Earth.

Such may be the predicament of those who venture into the Gulf of the Farallones National Marine Sanctuary. This stretch of sea is extraordinarily rich in krill, tiny shrimp-like crustaceans that are the favorite food of baleen whales. Blue whales, who may consume four tons in a single day, grow to 100ft long and 200 tons in weight; in summer and fall, these gargantuan creatures converge near the Farallon Islands, spouting and raising their fins and tails as they roll in the waves. Agile humpback whales may approach boats at closer proximity. In winter, gray whales, migrating between Alaska and Baja California, pass through these seas; they may be accompanied by newborn calves as they travel north in spring.

Unless you own your own boat, the only practical way to visit the sanctuary is aboard a marine research vessel. The Oceanic Society's naturalist-led *Salty Lady,* a 56ft Coast Guard certified vessel with an observation deck and limited indoor seating, accommodates 48 passengers and crew (*$128; www. oceanicsociety.org/whale-watching/farallons)*; it departs San Francisco Yacht Harbor bordering Marina Green weekend days rain or shine mid-May to Nov; call or check website for schedule. Keep in mind that the boat, though bound for the Farallon Islands, may turn back short of the avian-rich rocks, depending upon what marine life or inclement weather it encounters en route.

in the Gulf of the Farallones and Cordell Bank sanctuaries.

Coastal Defense Batteries★

Scattered along the cliffs that border Lincoln Avenue between Fort Point and Baker Beach, these crumbling concrete bunkers offer spectacular **views★★★** of the sea, the Marin Headlands and the Golden Gate Bridge. Linked by the Coastal Trail, the batteries were constructed between 1853 and 1910 to protect San Francisco Bay from invasion. As with most fortifications around the bay, their guns were never fired in defense. Stroll along the Coastal Trail south from the Golden Gate Bridge toll plaza through **Battery Cranston** (1897), Battery Marcus Miller (1891), Battery Boutelle (1900), and Battery Godfrey (1895) to the Fort Scott Overlook. At Battery Chamberlin (1902), overlooking Baker Beach farther down the Coastal Trail, the public may assist in cleaning, loading and firing a 50-ton "disappearing" gun the first full weekend of each month (*open Sat–Sun 11am–3pm).*

Baker Beach★

Bowley St. off Lincoln Ave., southwest corner of the Presidio.

Popular as much for its smooth sand as for the high dunes that protect it from all but the coldest winds, Baker Beach attracts two types of beachgoer. The southern end draws families and adolescents; the northern end, with its more dramatic view of the Golden Gate Bridge and the sage-covered cliffs, is popular with devotees of nude sunbathing—an activity tolerated (though not officially permitted) on federal land.

ADDITIONAL SIGHT

▲▲ Fort Point National Historic Site★

End of Marine Dr. Interior open Fri-Sun 10am–5pm. Exterior accessible daily. Closed Jan 1, Thanksgiving Day, Dec 25. 415-556-1693. www.nps.gov/fopo.

Tucked beneath a steel arch at the southern anchorage of the Golden Gate Bridge, this impressive, multi-storied brick-and-granite fort stands as a fine example of Civil War-era masonry and military architecture. Designed as the first of three enormous fortifications to guard the entrance to San Francisco Bay (the other two were to be built on Alcatraz Island and at Lime Point, now the northern anchorage of the bridge), Fort Point was erected in 1861 atop the site of Castillo de San Joaquín (1794), an abandoned Spanish gun battery. Master brickmasons were hired to build the structure; their fine craftsmanship remains evident throughout.

As the Civil War approached, the U.S. military, anticipating Confederate attacks on San Francisco Bay, ordered the uncompleted and unarmed fort occupied. For months a garrison stood guard over empty gun casements.

Fort Point's ordnance was never fired in defense. By 1885 its guns were considered obsolete and were removed for scrap. Long periods of minimal occupation or complete abandonment followed, with the thick walls occasionally serving as a damp, lonely barracks for unlucky companies of soldiers.

Initial plans for the Golden Gate Bridge placed Fort Point on the exact spot where Joseph Strauss, the bridge's designer, intended to sink the southern anchorage. After visiting the fort, Strauss was so impressed by the quality of its masonry that he designed a massive steel arch over the fort to preserve it.

Visit

Restored and rebuilt by the National Park Service in the 1970s, Fort Point provides visitors with a glimpse into military life on the California coast in the late 19C. Information panels throughout the building detail the history of the fort and the lives of the soldiers stationed there. Just inside the "sally port," the only entrance to the structure, lies a Spanish bronze cannon (1684), saved from Castillo de San Joaquín, and a huge 1844 Rodman cannon, typical of those that once guarded the Golden Gate (*cannon drill demonstrations are presented regularly; check at front desk for day's schedule*).

To the right of the sally port, the former sutler's store (post exchange) houses a visitor center, bookstore, and a small theater presenting slide shows and short films about the fort and the Golden Gate Bridge. Handcut granite spiral staircases lead to the upper tiers, with their intricate masonry and arching ceilings. Officers' quarters and privates' barracks are hung with historical photographs, and there are exhibits documenting the experiences of 20C African-American soldiers and the wartime contributions of American women. From the top-level barbettes, visitors can marvel at a unique and stunning **view**★★ of the underbelly of the Golden Gate Bridge.

ADDRESSES

CAFE

Transit Cafe – *215 Lincoln Blvd., Main Post. ℘415-561-4435. www.presidio.gov/places/transit.* Right near the PresidiGo shuttle stop and Visitors Center, this relaxed little eatery serves wood-fired pizzas, fresh salads, and paninis, plus strong coffee and craft beer. There are views of the bridge and bay from the sunny patio.

Arguello– *Officer's Club, 50 Moraga Ave., Main Post. ℘415-561-3650. www.arguellosf.com.* Creative Mexican food, a fine list of artisan mezcal, and a gorgeous historic setting recommend this upscale Mexican spot in the Officer's Club.

Warming Hut Cafe and Park Store – *983 Marine Dr., near Crissy Field. ℘415-561-3042.* Formerly a U.S. Engineer Storehouse, this historic 1909 wood-frame building is now a sweet café and gift shop run by the Golden Gate National Parks Conservancy. It's the perfect place to stop for a hot chocolate or a coffee during a breezy walk from Crissy Field to Fort Point.

RECREATION

House of Air – *926 Mason St. ℘415-965-2470. houseofair.com.* Bounce out excess energy during one of this massive trampoline playground's "open jump" sessions. For tots, there are designated zones for 3 to 6 year old jumpers.

San Francisco's central neighborhoods encompass a diverse group of districts, including the ritzy Pacific Heights, home to the city's social elite, and its neighbors Japantown and Presidio Heights. To the south, the sprawling Richmond district and the rolling, landscaped Golden Gate Park stretch 52 blocks from Haight-Asbhury to the Pacific Ocean. The Golden Gate Park is often considered part of the Richmond or Sunset Districts, but it is truly a neighborhood in its own right; larger than New York City's Central Park, it is home to lakes, gardens, trails, museums, windmills, a buffalo paddock, and nearly every kind of sport arena, from bocce courts to polo fields to flyfishing ponds.

Highlights

1 Enjoy 360-degree views from the **de Young Museum's observation tower** (p158)

2 Admire 20 million specimens at the **California Academy of Sciences** (p159)

3 Take in stellar views from **Twin Peaks** (p164)

4 Explore **Pacific Heights** on architectural walking tour (p169)

5 Shop **Fillmore St.** and see a movie at Japantown's **Sundance Kabuki Theater** (p170, p165)

From the Park to Pacific Heights

Stretching 3 miles inland from Ocean Beach to Stanyan Street, Golden Gate Park is a 1,017-acre rectangle greensward home to a complex of art and science museums and a wealth of recreational opportunities.

An enchantingly natural yet entirely purpose-built urban oasis of meadows, gardens, lakes and woodlands, the park is the result of careful planning by two inspired landscape architects and the labors of an army of gardeners.

Directly to the west of the park sits the Haight-Ashbury neighborhood. Although more than four decades have passed since the "Summer of Love," a 1960s counterculture ethos still clings to the Haight, which borders Haight Street between Central Avenue and Stanyan Street, just west of the Castro.

The stretch of Haight Street between Central Avenue and Stanyan Street, known as the Upper Haight, is packed with vintage boutiques and coffee houses.

Edging the Pacific Ocean and the northern side of the Golden Gate Park is the Richmond District. At the turn of the 20C, Richmond's western reaches were condemned as the Great Sand Waste until the establishment of Geary Boulevard opened the district to settlement. Today, the neighbohood is a residential haven with a middle-class small-town feel. Its population incorporates a cultural mix that is apaparent in the area's myriad restaurants, including Chinese, Thai , Burmese, Vietnamese and Korean eateries. Richmond's main thoroughfare, Clement Street teems with shops and markets hawking everything from bok choy to flip-flops. Where the Richmond meets the ocean sits the Cliff House, the ruins of Sutro Baths, and the California Palace of the Legion of Honor.

To the north and east of the Richmond, Pacific Heights sits along a high east–west ridge between Van Ness Avenue and the Presidio. This tiny residential enclave is synonymous with wealth. It offers great opportunities for strolling, eating and shopping, and holds some of the city's finest houses and loveliest views, as well as some killer steep streets.

At the south end of Pacific Heights, in a part of the city known as the Western Addition, Japantown abounds with Japanese architecture and culture. At the heart of Japantown is the Japan Center, a complex of shops, sushi bars, theaters and hotels. Crowned by a five-tiered pagoda, the center hosts celebrations such as the annual Cherry Blossom Festival in April (nccbf.org).

Golden Gate Park★★★

Encompassing more than 1,017 acres of meadows, gardens and public buildings, verdant Golden Gate Park is the largest cultivated urban park in the US. It has 27 miles of footpaths and 7.5 miles of equestrian trails, all linking an enchantingly natural, yet entirely man-made, landscape of lakes, waterfalls, swales and woods.

A BIT OF HISTORY

As San Francisco prospered in the 1860s, William Ralston and others began laying plans for a city park to rival designs for Central Park in New York City. They selected a tract of the sandy scrublands known as the Outer Lands as an affordable location. When Mayor H.P. Coon consulted Frederick Law Olmsted, designer of Central Park, the famous landscape architect eyed the dunes and advised that large trees would never grow on the site. Undaunted, city planners in 1871 contracted engineer and surveyor William Hammond Hall to build a park on the maligned tract.

Raising a bulwark behind Ocean Beach to deflect ocean winds, Hall graded the inland dunes into gentle hills and valleys, securing them by sowing barley, lupine and ammophila grass. When this natural matting had taken root, he began to plant trees. Starting on the eastern end of the park, Hall laid out roads in a meandering fashion, partly to discourage speeding but also to imitate the leisurely ambience of a rural road. By the late 1870s, the park was a resounding public success.

"Uncle John" – In 1890 Hall appointed **John McLaren** (1846–1943) as the new park superintendent. Fondly known as "Uncle John" by his staff and an admiring public, the cantankerous, Scottish-born McLaren ran Golden Gate Park with a patriarchal hand. Believing that a park should provide a refuge from city life, he fought hard against new buildings, statues and other urban encroachments for 53 years, and personally planted millions

ᴍᴜɴɪ Bus 5–Fulton, 21–Hayes or 44–O'Shaughnessy. &415-673-6864 or www.511.org for more information. A free park shuttle operates on weekends 9am-6pm.

🛈 **Info:** &415-831-2700. www.goldengatepark.com.

◖ **Location:** Golden Gate Park is three miles long and 0.5mi wide, bordered by Ocean Beach, Stanyon Street, Fulton Street and Lincoln Way. The main visitor center 🛈 is at the Beach Chalet in the park's western end (🕒open daily 9am–5pm; &415-751-2766). At the east end brochures are available at McLaren Lodge park headquarters (🕒open Mon–Fri 8am–5pm; &415-831-2700).

👨‍👦 **Kids:** California Academy of Sciences, Koret Children's Quarter, the buffalo paddock, a boat ride on Stow Lake or renting bicycles and riding through the park.

🕐 **Timing:** Visit popular attractions in the morning to avoid large crowds.

🅿 **Parking:** The Music Concourse Garage (entrance at 10th Ave. & Fulton St.) is open daily 7.30am–10pm. On weekends spots fill up quickly and street parking is difficult. John F. Kennedy Drive between Kezar Drive and 19th Avenue is closed to car traffic on Sundays.

🚫 **Don't Miss:** de Young Museum, Japanese Tea Garden, boating on Stowe Lake, the Conservatory of Flowers and the Dutch Windmill.

GOLDEN GATE PARK
EASTERN SECTION

0 — 1/10 mi
0 — 100 m

N

Shrader St.
Grove St.
Hayes St.
Fell St.
Oak St.
Page St.
Haight St.
Waller St.
Beulah St.

PANHANDLE

Stanyan St.

McAllister

Fulton

Stanyan

McLAREN LODGE

Arguello Blvd

2nd Ave.

4th Ave.

6th Ave.

8th Ave.

10th Ave.

12th Ave.

14th Ave.

16th Ave.

17th Ave.

19th Ave.

21st Ave.

23rd Ave.

Cabrillo

Fulton

Park Presidio Blvd

Conservatory Dr.

West Dr.

John F. Kennedy Dr.

Conservatory of Flowers

GIANT TREE FERNS

Lily Pond

John McLaren Rhododendron Dell

ROSE GARDEN

DE YOUNG

Hagiwara Tea Garden Ave.

MUSIC CONCOURSE

Japanese Tea Garden **3.**

Concourse Dr.

California Academy of Sciences

SPRECKELS BANDSHELL

Garden of Shakespeare's Flowers

Nancy Pelosi Dr.

Green Dr.

ROBIN WILLIAMS MEADOW

TENNIS COURTS

SHARON BLDG.

Koret Playground

Carousel

Bowling

Kezar Dr.

Alvord Lake

KEZAR STADIUM

Frederick

Carl

Arguello Blvd

3rd Ave.

Way

5th Ave.

7th Ave.

Hugo

Lincoln

Martin Luther King Jr. Dr.

URBAN FORESTRY CENTER

NURSERIES

BIG REC BALL FIELD

COUNTY FAIR BLDG

Helen Crocker Russell Library of Horticulture

San Francisco Botanical Garden at Strybing Arboretum

9th Ave.

11th Ave.

Funston Ave.

15th Ave.

2

Stow Lake

STRAWBERRY HILL
△428

PAVILION

PIONEER LOG CABIN

4.

Stow Lake Dr. E.

Stow Lake Dr.

Martin Luther King Jr. Dr.

Cross Over Dr.

Lincoln

Transverse Dr.

BOATHOUSE

Prayer Book Cross **5**

John F. Kennedy Dr.

Park Presidio Bypass Dr.

Transverse Dr.

Lloyd Lake

Portals of the Past

SPEEDWAY MEADOW

Overlook

Elk Glen Lake

Middle Drive West

Fulton

Recreation

Recreational opportunities abound in the park. Public sports facilities include baseball/softball diamonds at **Big Rec Ball Field** (*415-831-5510*) and tennis courts (*415-831-6301*) north of the **Children's Playground**. Pedal boats and row boats may be rented at **Stow Lake**, off John F. Kennedy Drive .5mi west of 10th Avenue (*open daily 10am–5pm; 415-386-2531*). The nine-hole **Golden Gate Park Golf Course** is located near 47th Ave. & John F. Kennedy Dr. (*415-751-8987*). Paved biking and skating trails ramble the park; Middle Drive West is a car-free skaters' haven on Saturdays, while a portion of John F. Kennedy Dr. is dedicated to **skaters** and bicyclists on Sundays and holidays (*rentals at several shops along Stanyan St., and behind Stow Lake Boathouse; 415-668-6699*). Extensive **hiking paths** wind through the park, and a variety of free **walking tours** are conducted year-round; call or check the website for schedule (*415-263-0991; www.sfpt.org*).

of flowers, bulbs and trees. By the time of his death at age 97, McLaren had succeeded in cultivating one of the world's most varied gardens.

The Midwinter Fair of 1894 – Four years after McLaren's appointment, journalist Michael H. de Young, inspired by the World's Columbian Exposition of 1893 in Chicago, successfully convinced city officials that San Francisco should mount its own fair at Golden Gate Park to promote the city's splendid winter climate. Five fancifully domed and spired buildings and a 266ft Electric Tower were erected around a quadrangle called the Great Court, and the California Midwinter International Exposition of 1894 (also called the Midwinter Fair) opened on January 27. All of California's

counties, four other states and more than 19 foreign countries participated, drawing some 2.5 million visitors during its six months of operation. The complex was adapted and expanded over the years to accommodate the de Young museum and the Asian Art Museum, but after suffering major damage during the 1989 Loma Prieta it was slowly dismantled, with the Asian Art Museum moving to Civic Center in 2003 and the de Young constructing an architecturally daring new home on the site in 2005.

In addition to being a leafy retreat, Golden Gate Park has had many uses during the 20C. Refugees set up temporary homes here after the 1906 earthquake. Thousands flocked here during the "Summer of Love" in 1967, when

Conservatory of Flowers

© Drew Bird/Conservatory of Flowers

hippies hung out and crowds gathered for mass celebrations and concerts at Speedway Meadow.

Today the park continues to host free music concerts at the Music Concourse and Sharon Meadow and to serve as a glorious backyard—a place for family picnics, neighborhood baseball games, outdoor sports and contemplative strolls.

SIGHTS
Conservatory of Flowers★

100 John F. Kennedy Dr. at Conservatory Dr. W. ○*Open Tue–Sun 10am–6pm.* ☛*Guided tours daily11am, 12:30pm, 2:30pm* ○*Closed major holidays except Memorial Day, July 4 and Labor Day.* ⬤*$9.* ♿ ☏*415-831-2090. www.conservatoryofflowers.org.*

This ornate Victorian glass palace shelters more than 1,700 species of rare and exotic plants under an octagonal central dome and two flanking wings. Golden Gate Park's oldest structure, the lacy white wood-frame building was prefabricated in Dublin, Ireland, modeled after the glasshouses of London's Kew Gardens; it was shipped to the San Jose estate of James Lick for installation. Arriving after Lick's death in 1876, the structure was purchased by a consortium of San Francisco businessmen led by Leland Stanford, and donated to Golden Gate Park. Seasonal blooms in formal geometric designs grace the parterres in front.

John McLaren Rhododendron Dell

John F. Kennedy Dr. at 6th Ave.
At the heart of this 20-acre, spring-blooming garden, originally planted with 850 varieties of rhododendrons, stands a **statue of John McLaren (1)** contemplating a pinecone. The life-size proportions and quiet pose contrast with the host of heroic bronze figures that surround the nearby **Music Concourse**, an ironic contradiction to McLaren's lifelong campaign to keep statues from cluttering the park's scenery.

♟♟ Koret Children's Quarter
Kezar Dr.
A pioneering concept when it opened in 1888, this municipal playground was centered on the sandstone Sharon Building, which provided refreshments, stored play equipment, and stabled goats for the kids' "barnyard."

Today the building houses the **Sharon Art Studio** (*300 Bowling Green Dr.*), a venue for art classes for children and adults (☏*415-753-7006; www.sharonart-studio.org*).

The magnificent Herschell-Spillman **Carrousel in Golden Gate Park★**its princely stable of carved wooden animals under a dome supported by 16 fluted columnswas built in 1912 and restored in 1984 (○*open daily Memorial Day through Labor Day, 10am–4.30pm; rest of the year Fri–Sun.* ○*closed Jan 1, Thanksgiving Day, Dec 25;* ⬤*$2/adult, $1/ child;* ☏*415-831-2770*).

♟♟ Japanese Tea Garden★★
Hagiwara Tea Garden Dr. ○*Open Apr-Oct daily 9am-6pm; Nov-Mar daily 9am-4:45pm.* ⬤*$9.* ♿✖🅿 ☏*415-666-3232; japaneseteagardensf.com.*

Harboring a delightful maze of winding paths, stone lanterns, ornamental ponds, bonsai, a wooden pagoda, a Zen garden and a teahouse, this tranquil, five-acre garden has been an attraction since it was built for the Midwinter Fair of 1894. The garden continued operating under the direction of master gardener Makoto Hagiwara, who also tended the tea concession and is credited with inventing the fortune cookie here in 1909.

The garden is most colorful around April, when its cherry trees burst into bloom. The exquisitely crafted ceremonial gateway at the front entrance is a traditional feature of Japanese shrines. Inside, the steeply arching wooden **Moon Bridge (2)** takes its name from the orb formed by the bridge and its reflection in the pond below. Near the center of the garden sits a 10.5ft statue of the Buddha, cast in Japan in 1790. Visitors enjoy sipping green tea and nibbling delicate cookies in the open-air **teahouse (3)**.

San Francisco Botanical Garden at Strybing Arboretum★★

Martin Luther King, Jr. Dr. at 9th Ave.
🕐*Open daily Mar-Sep 7:30am–5pm, rest of the year varies.* 🗣*Guided tours (90min), advanced reservations required.* ⚲*$9, free on the second Tuesday of every month, Jan 1, Thanksgiving, Dec 25.* 🍴🅿 ☎*415-661-1316. www.sfbotanicalgarden.org.*

This outstanding botanical collection comprises 8,000 species of plants from all over the world. The arboretum emphasizes regions of Mediterranean climate, with collections from California, the Cape Province of South Africa, southwestern Australia and Chile. Other attractions include a hillside garden of succulents; the Cloud Forests, where mist emitters supplement the fog; the Nature Trail; and the Primitive Plant Garden of moss, cycads, horsetails, gingko trees, ferns, and conifers.

The Garden of Fragrances features a wall built of stones removed from a medieval Spanish monastery purchased by William Randolph Hearst, who had it dismantled and shipped to Golden Gate Park for reassembly. A fire destroyed the crates and identifying markings, leaving a great pile of indistinguishable stones from which the Park Department has drawn over the decades.

Housed in the County Fair Building to the west of the Arboretum's main entrance, the **Helen Crocker Russell Library of Horticulture** (🕐*Open Wed–Mon 10am–4pm;* 🕐*Closed major holidays*) has more than 27,000 books and 450 plant and garden periodicals and presents quarterly exhibits of botanical prints and other art.

Garden of Shakespeare's Flowers★

Martin Luther King, Jr., Dr. and Middle Dr. E.

Established in 1928, this small English garden nurtures plants mentioned in the works of William Shakespeare. The locked box in the back wall contains a bust of the Bard, a copy from the sculpted image at the poet's tomb carved by Gerard Johnson after Shakespeare's death in 1616.

👥 Stow Lake★

Stow Lake Dr.; access from John F. Kennedy Dr. or Martin Luther King, Jr., Dr. 🕐*Boathouse open daily 10am–5pm, weather permitting.* ⚲*$28.50/hr pedal boat; $38.50/hr 4-6 person pedal boat; $22.50/hr rowboat.* 🛶♿🍴🅿 ☎*415-752-0347. www.stowlakeboathouse.com.*

The park's main irrigation reservoir surrounding Strawberry Hill is the largest of the 15 man-made lakes that dot Golden Gate Park. Swarms of waterfowl share the water with the small boats which may be rented on the northwest shore. The 428ft summit of Strawberry Hill, reached by footpath, is the highest point in the park. Constructed in 1894, a **waterfall (4)** named for industrialist Collis P. Huntington cascades 125ft from the summit to the surface of the lake. Immediately north of Stow Lake, **Prayer Book Cross**, a 57ft Celtic cross carved of sandstone, dominates the hill above **Rainbow Falls (5)** The historic boathouse snack shop serves classics such as pink popcorn and It's It Ice Cream sandwiches as well as local burgers, hot dogs, beer and wine .

DE YOUNG MUSEUM★★★

50 Hagiwara Tea Garden Dr. at John F. Kennedy Dr. 🕐*Open Tue–Sun 9.30am –5.15pm (Fri Jun–Nov until 8.45pm).* 🗣*Audio tours* ⚲*$15* 🕐*Closed Thanksgiving Day and Dec 25.* ⚲*$15 (allows same-day admission to the Legion of Honor* ♿*see SUTRO HEIGHTS and LAND'S END). Free first Tue of the month.* ♿🍴🅿 ☎*415-750-3600. www.deyoungmuseum.org.*

Survivor of a turbulent past, the de Young is today a major force on the West Coast museum scene. Its collection from the pre-Columbian era to the present traces the history of art in the Americas, complemented by significant holdings in textiles and African and Oceanic art. The collection, along with that of the Legion of Honor, belongs to the city of San Francisco; together these institude Young Museum

© Gregory Bertolini / Fine Arts Museums of San Francisco

tions form the **Fine Arts Museums of San Francisco**.

A BIT OF HISTORY

The de Young Museum was established by **Michael H. de Young**, co-founder of the *San Francisco Chronicle* and organizer of the 1894 California Midwinter International Exposition. When the fair closed, he persuaded the city's Park Commission to preserve the Egyptian Revival-style Fine Arts Building as a museum, which he filled with an eclectic assortment of artworks and natural history exhibits.

New wings were added in the 20C, one of them to house the Asian Art Museum, but the entire structure was badly damaged in the 1989 Loma Prieta earthquake. Temporary bracing couldn't solve the building's safety issues, and it was demolished in 2002. In 2003 the Asian Art Museum took up residence in the refurbished former Main Library at Civic Center, and in 2005 the de Young Museum welcomed visitors to its new home in Golden Gate Park.

Funded by $190 million in private donations, the daring building was created by Swiss architects Jacques Herzog and Pierre de Meuron, designers of London's Tate Gallery of Modern Art. A total of 950,000 pounds of copper sheaths the exterior; over the the next decade it will fade from bright copper to cinnamon, then to a rich green that will blend in with the surrounding trees.

VISIT

The interior is centered on a vast, airy lobby. Throughout, you'll find rich native woods and Italian stone, as well as two gardens with ferns and eucalyptus. Selections from the 25,000-piece permanent collection are displayed on the Concourse and Upper levels. The basement (Lower Level) has a large space for special exhibits and a gift store. On the west side of the building you'll find a courtyard cafe and sculpture park.

Enter the museum on the Concourse Level. If the line for tickets here is long, head to the Lower Level, where there's rarely any line at all. Digital screens on both floors display the day's schedule of docent-led tours and family activities. Audio tours ($8) are available at the main lobby kiosk. Be sure to treat yourself to the 360-degree views from the Observation Deck atop the de Young tower.

American Art★★
Concourse and Upper levels
Eighteen galleries are devoted to the museum's extensive collection of paint-

ings, decorative arts and sculpture. Works are arranged chronologically starting on the Upper Level, where in intimate galleries you'll find artwork from the colonial era through the Arts and Crafts movement of the early 20C. The museum's major works from this period include paintings by John Singleton Copley, Frederic Edwin Church, Mary Cassatt and John Singer Sargent, as well as furniture by the Herter Brothers and Chippendale.

The survey of American art continues on the Concourse level, whose nine light-filled galleries are designed to accommodate large-scale pieces. The collection here ranges from Grant Wood's *Dinner for Threshers* (1934) through postwar paintings by heavy-hitters like Willem de Kooning and Mark Rothko to contemporary works in new media by emerging artists. Selected pieces of sculpture, including works by Isamu Noguchi and Louise Nevelson, are on display in the Sculpture Garden. Additional galleries are dedicated to photography and works on paper.

Art of the Americas★
Concourse Level
This important collection, comprising works from Mesoamerica, Central and South America and the West Coast of North America, is housed in four large galleries. Indigenous art from the west coast of North America includes fine basketry, storage containers for inter-tribal "potlatch" gatherings, and rare 19C totem poles depicting ancestral animal spirits. A special gallery is devoted to ancient objects from Mexico, including the museum's outstanding grouping of Teotihuacan murals.

African Art★
Upper Level
The **African art** permanent collection contains pieces from 80 distinct sub-Saharan cultures, mostly West African from AD 1200 to the present. Note especially the early 20C Shrine Figure of a Seven Headed Bush Spirit, a six-foot-tall sculpture from the Niger River Delta acquired by the museum in 2004.

Oceanic Art★
Upper Level
The museum's holdings of Oceanic art come from Melanesia, Indonesia, Polynesia, the Caroline Islands of Micronesia and the Maori peoples of New Zealand. Wood carvings predominate here. The Jolika Collection of New Guinea art features more than 400 works including several towering figures, masks and ceremonial costumes.

Textile Art★
Upper Level
More than 12,000 textiles and costumes from around the world make up this collection. You'll find everything from Turkish carpets to the latest couture.

♙♙ CALIFORNIA ACADEMY OF SCIENCES★★
55 Music Concourse Drive. ○Open Mon–Sat 9.30am–5pm, Sun 11am–5pm, closes early on Thanksgiving Day, Dec 25. ⊛$39.95 ♿✕🅿 🖉415-379-8000. www.calacademy.org.

The oldest scientific institution in the West, the venerable California Academy of Sciences has since its inception aimed at exploring, explaining and celebrating the natural world. Its three branches— the **Kimball Natural History Museum**, the **Steinhart Aquarium** and the **Morrison Planetarium**—today occupy a groundbreaking new building that showcases institutional philosophy and cutting-edge technology along with the academy's ever-expanding collections.

A BIT OF HISTORY
Founded in 1853 in a surge of post-Gold Rush enthusiasm for knowledge about California's physical environment, the Academy of Sciences began as a group of naturalists who collected specimens, presented scholarly papers, and eventually began to function as a natural-history museum. In 1891 they took up residence at 833 Market Street, but after the building was destroyed by the earthquake of 1906, the academy was re-established in Golden Gate Park. The 1989 Loma Prieta inflicted enough damage to convince directors that a

new facility was needed, and Pritzker Prize-winning architect Renzo Piano was commissioned to design a building integrating all three branches of the Academy under one roof. A hallmark of Piano's 410,000sq ft, structure is a "living roof" made up of 1.7 million native Caliornia plants and 60,000 photovoltaic cells. This unique lid not only helps the building meld with its surroundings but also absorbs rainwater to decrease runoff and provides natural insulation.

VISIT

The academy is home to 38,000 live animals in addition to 46,000 million scientific specimens on display that teach visitors about the incredible variety of earth's environments. Kids will love the Africa Hall, which has a pod of 20 African penguins (feedings *10am & 3pm*), the touching tide pools, and the swamp where Claude the albino alligator lives. The aquarium itself houses an extraordinary living coral reef surrounded by 4,000 fish, representing over 900 species, the bottom of which can seen up close through underwater viewing panels on the lower level (twice daily dive shows at 11:30am and 12:30pm).

Upon entry, grab free tickets at the planetarium kiosk for one of the daily shows projected on the 75ft wide screen in what is the world's largest and advanced all-digital domes. Be sure to also factor enough time to journey through the **Rainforests of the World**, a 4-story glass sphere in the central courtyard that transports visitors from understory to canopy to root systems, check out newer installations such as the 400-piece gems and mineral exhibit as well as the Twilight Zone, featuring rarely seen species that live 200 to 500 feet below the ocean's surface.

ADDITIONAL SIGHTS IN THE PARK

The western section of Golden Gate Park, from Stow Lake to the ocean, abounds with great stretches of meadows, woods and sports facilities. Reflected in Lloyd Lake, the portico known as **Portals of**

the Past are the remains of a Nob Hill mansion destroyed in the 1906 earthquake. Halfway to the ocean from Stow Lake lies the **Polo Field** where myriad sports games are held, and runners, cyclists and equestrians use its tracks. At **Spreckels Lake,** model-boat enthusiasts launch their own radio-controlled vessels. Farther west along John F. Kennedy Drive, at the **Bison Paddock 🚹🚻**, a small herd grazes under eucalyptus trees.

In the park's northwest corner, the small **Queen Wilhelmina Tulip Gardens** *(bloom early spring)* is the setting for the **Dutch Windmill★ 🚹🚻** (1902), one of the world's largest, which pumped water for park irrigation until 1929. in the southwest corner lies its companion, The **Murphy Windmill** (1905). Both windmills have been restored for decorative purposes.

Beach Chalet★

1000 Great Highway (between Fulton St. and Lincoln S). ⏰*Open Mon-Fri 11am-9pm, Sat-Sun 10am-10pm.* ⏰*Closed Dec 25.* 🍴♿🅿

Designed by Willis Polk, this Spanish Colonial-style pavilion (1921) operated for years as a workingman's bar. Here you'll find some of the city's finest WPA-funded **murals★**, frescoes executed in 1937 by Lucien Labaudt depicting recreation. They have since been restored and the building's main floor now serves as a park **visitor center.** A banister, designed by Labaudt in the form of a serpent and carved of magnolia wood leads to the Beach Chalet Brewery and Restaurant and ocean views.

ADDRESSES

🍽 EAT

Park Chow – *1240 9th. Ave.* ✆*415-665-9912. www.chowfoodbar.com.* A half block from Golden Gate Park, this busy, friendly spot serves up healthy American comfort fare at sidewalk tables, inside by the fireplace, or up on the rooftop deck.

Haight-Ashbury★

Although almost five decades have passed since the Human Be-In and Summer of Love, a countercultural ethos still clings to Haight-Ashbury, usually called "the Haight." Named for two streets intersecting at its heart, this neighborhood draws hordes of young people to its thrift stores, bars and coffeehouses. With 90 percent of its housing stock predating 1922, the Haight also boasts some of the city's loveliest Victorian homes.

A BIT OF HISTORY

Culture... Before the early 1870s, the neighborhood was a sandy scrubland sparsely populated by farmers. But as San Francisco's population skyrocketed, the city pushed westward and the street grid was extended into what is now the Haight-Ashbury district.

As Golden Gate Park and the panhandle developed, a resort area took shape in the neighborhood surrounding Stanyan Street. Beginning in 1895 **The Chutes**, an amusement park on the south side of Haight Street between Cole and Clayton streets, drew large crowds with its vaudeville theater, zoo, carnival rides and 300ft water slide.

Property values quintupled and new homes proliferated so rapidly that the architectural style of the day, Queen Anne, still characterizes the Haight today.

〰 Bus 6–Parnassus, 7–Haight, 33–Stanyan, 37–Corbett, 43–Masonic, or 71–Haight-Noriega; streetcar N–Judah, 511.org.

🗓 **Info:** ✆415-391-2000. www.sftravel. or www.sfgate.com/ neighborhoods/sf/haight/.

▷ **Location:** Haight Street extends from the eastern edge of Golden Gate Park, just south of the panhandle.

👫 **Kids:** The Randall Museum.

🕐 **Timing:** Hang in the Haight for an hour or so, longer if you want to people watch in a coffee shop or browse through a bookstore.

🅿 **Parking:** Try for a spot on the residential lanes crisscrossing Haight Street.

◉ **Don't Miss:** Picture-postcard views from Twin Peaks and Alamo Square.

...and Counterculture – A haven for refugees fleeing the burnt-out parts of the city after the 1906 earthquake and fire, by the 1950s the neighborhood hosted an eclectic mix of students, gays, African Americans and beatniks fleeing tourist-ridden North Beach.

Residential Architecture

Hundreds of unique, eye-catching Victorian period houses, most in the Queen Anne style, adorn Haight-Ashbury. Characterized by asymmetrical massing, a panoply of external surfaces and designs, bay windows and sometimes turrets, the homes date primarily from the building boom of the 1880s and 90s. Because houses in the Haight were so much in demand, Queen Annes were frequently built in rows of four or five similar structures, but a variety of color and detailing options provided ample opportunity for homeowners to distinguish their abodes from their neighbors'. A stroll along Central Avenue or Page, Masonic or Waller streets reveals fanciful examples of Queen Annes, many restored during the gentrification trend that swept the neighborhood in the 1980s and 90s. The rows at **1214–1256 Masonic Avenue** and **1315–1335 Waller Street★** embody the spirit of the style.

© Peter Wrenn/Michelin

👥 Postcard Row: Alamo Square Victorians

The row of Victorians located at 710–720 Steiner St., between Hayes and Grove Streets, strikes a familiar chord with most San Francisco visitors. One of the most photographed vantages in the city, "Postcard Row" stands before a remarkable, snapshot-ready backdrop featuring many city landmarks, including 555 California Street and the Transamerica Pyramid. Alamo Square Park across the street allows photographers ample time to focus. The "Painted Ladies", as these houses are sometimes called, were featured in the opening scenes of the *Full House* TV show, as well as films such as *Bicentennial Man* (1999), *Invasion of the Body Snatchers* (1978) and *Junior (1994)*.

Distinguished externally by window and door treatments and by color, the three-story, wooden, gable-roofed houses were completed in 1895 and sold for $3,500 apiece by Irish-born carpenter and real-estate developer Matthew Kavanagh, who lived at no. 722 from 1892–1900. All seven homes are private, one- or two-family dwellings. The J. Frank Moroney house at no. 710 is distinguished by its jewel-encrusted stained-glass windows and ornate gable. It sold for $87,500 in 1974. In 2014, no. 722 was sold for $3.1 million.

A decade later, the Haight blossomed into a countercultural lodestar, drawing hippies from around the US with promises of mind-altering drugs and free love. An estimated 20,000 people crammed into Golden Gate Park in January 1967 for Timothy Leary and Allen Ginsberg's **Human Be-In,** an anti-establishment celebration featuring poetry readings and rock concerts. Jerry Garcia's Grateful Dead held court at 710 Ashbury Street; neighbors included Janis Joplin and members of Jefferson Airplane. These musicians invented the wandering, melodic "San Francisco Sound" that catapulted them to international fame. Haight-Ashbury reached its peak later that year during what became known as the **Summer of Love,** when some 75,000 young people flocked to the neighborhood, sleeping in Golden Gate Park and attending free concerts and parties. In 1968, many hippies left the Haight, and heroin replaced LSD and marijuana as the drug of choice. By 1971, more than a third of the shops on Haight Street were boarded up, and violent crime soared. Yet the neighborhood survived; crime dropped as incomes and property values rose. By 1980 the Haight had re-emerged as a middle-class enclave.

Today the Haight is more mainstream than it was during its late 60s heyday, with a number of upscale designer-clothing shops and restaurants serving young professionals, but disaffected youths still congregate on street corners and in Golden Gate Park, and graying hippies abound. Even as the Queen Annes are restored to their late-19C beauty, vestiges of the 60s live on.

SIGHTS
Haight Street★

Lined with coffee shops, boutiques, pubs and restaurants, Haight Street from Stanyan Street to Central Avenue is the neighborhood's main drag. The narrow sidewalks are often packed with skateboarders, shoppers and tourists; incense wafts from New Age shops; and rock music pulses from frenetic thrift stores. While the buildings here are not the district's most distinguished, some, like the colorful, curvaceous structure at **no. 1679–81** (1904, James F. Dunn), display a certain charm.

Buena Vista Park

Rising abruptly south of Haight Street, between Central Avenue and Baker Street, this sylvan hill boasts tantalizing glimpses of the city from between the trees that crowd its steep slopes. The 36.5-acre park was reserved for public use in 1867, and John McLaren supervised the planting of cypress, live oak, pine and eucalyptus trees during the early 1900s. Sweeping **views** of San Francisco's residential areas stretch away toward bay and ocean from the summit, reached after a challenging climb.

ADDITIONAL SIGHTS

St. Ignatius Church★

650 Parker Ave. at Fulton St. ⏰*Open Mon –Fri 8.30am–5pm, Sun 8.30am–noon.* ✆*415-422-2188. www.stignatiussf.org.*

This imposing domed Renaissance Revival church (1914, Charles J. Devlin), on the campus of Jesuit-affiliated University of San Francisco, features two 213ft towers flanking a facade dominated by Corinthian columns.

A campanile at the northeast corner houses a three-ton bell cast in England in 1859. In the interior, a deeply coffered ceiling and free-standing columns offer a dramatic framework for the sanctuary, whose paintings and stained-glass windows were added between 1938 and 1962.

A polychrome white-oak baldachin stands over an altar of Italian marble with Moroccan onyx inlays, containing relics of St. Ignatius.

👥 Randall Museum

199 Museum Way, Corona Heights. From Haight St., take Masonic Ave. south to Roosevelt Way; turn left, then right after three blocks on Museum Way. ⏰*Open Tue–Sat 10am–5pm.* ⏰*Closed major holidays.* ✆*415-554-9600. www.randallmuseum.org.*

This free family-oriented natural history and science museum set on a hill overlooking the city reopened in early 2017 after an $8 million-dollar renova-

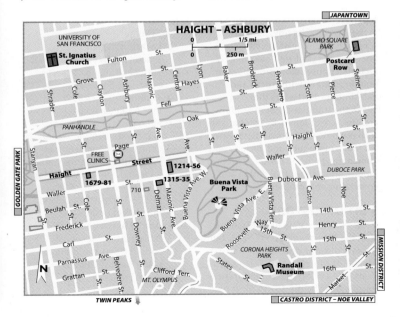

tion with refreshed interactive exhibits on earthquakes, a live-animal nursery and a brand new STEM lab.

👥 Twin Peaks★★★

From Haight St. drive south on Clayton St. to Carmel St.; cross and continue up Twin Peaks Blvd. to Christmas Tree Point. These two high points dominate the horizon west of downtown and are visible from more areas of the city than Mt. Davidson, highest point in San Francisco at 929ft. The two distinct but adjacent peaks reach 904ft (north peak) and 922ft (south peak).

Most visitors content themselves with the grand **panorama★★★** of the north and east sides of the city from the parking lot at Christmas Tree Point, although it is possible to climb up the grassy slopes of either peak for a view to the west as well. On clear days, Mt. Diablo to the east in Contra Costa County, and Mt. Tamalpais, to the north in Marin County, come into view. Architect Bernard Maybeck, who designed the Palace of Fine Arts for the 1915 Panama-Pacific International Exhibition, had grandiose plans for Twin Peaks, including a great monument at the summit with waterfalls cascading to the valley below. The plans never materialized.

Today visitors and locals throng the viewpoint, particularly on weekend afternoons. Be sure to bring a jacket as it can get extremely cold, when the fog rolls in and engulfs the view.

ADDRESSES

SHOPPING

Bound Together Anarchist Collective Bookstore – *1369 Haight St. Open daily 11.30am–7.30pm. ☎415-431-8355. boundtogetherbooks.wordpress.com.* For decades this volunteer-run outlet has supplied required reading for the counterculture: books, magazines and pamphlets on alternative thinking and the remaking of society.

Japantown

Known as Nihonmachi by local residents, Japantown is a locus of Japanese-American cultural life in the Bay Area. Its tidy, six-block core displays some of the city's finer groupings of well-maintained Victorian houses alongside modern buildings, many with stucco and half-timbered exteriors that evoke the traditional countryside architecture of Japan. By comparison with teeming Chinatown, Japantown is a much more subdued, orderly and open neighborhood centered on the Japan Center shopping, dining and entertainment complex.

A BIT OF HISTORY

A few Japanese came to San Francisco after the Meiji revolution of 1868, but arrivals did not peak until the first decade of the 20C. Anti-Asian sentiment slowed Japanese immigration considerably by the 1920s. Most new

- 🚍 **bus** 38–Geary, 2–Clement, 3–Jackson or 4–Sutter.
- ♿ **Michelin Map:** See p168.
- ℹ **Info:** www.sfjapantown.org, 511.org.
- ▶ **Location:** Japantown is bounded by Fillmore, Sutter and Laguna Streets and Geary Boulevard.
- 🕐 **Timing:** Try to arrive in time for lunch or dinner to enjoy sushi or ramen at one of the restaurants in Japan Center or Nihonmachi Mall.
- 🅿 **Parking:** Japan Center Garage is located beneath the center (entrance on Geary Blvd.; $1-$3.50/hr, partial validation from select businesses).
- 😍 **Don't Miss:** A traditional Japanese bath at Kabuki Springs & Spa, the interior of the Buddist Church of San Francsico.

arrivals settled in the South of Market area, but when that neighborhood was devastated by the earthquake and fire of 1906, residents took refuge in the Western Addition. The new community, popularly known as Little Osaka, harbored about 7,000 Japanese-American residents within a 20-block rectangle formed by Fillmore, Pine, Octavia and O'Farrell streets.

Little Osaka was abandoned during World War II when anti-Japanese hysteria following the Pearl Harbor attack culminated in Executive Order 9066, forcing the evacuation of 112,000 Japanese-Americans to internment camps. Empty residences soon were inhabited by an influx of civilian workers, many of them black, who came to fill wartime shipyard jobs. Diminished from its prewar size, Japantown took on its present appearance in the late 1960s and 70s when massive urban-renewal projects cleared blocks of Victorian housing and widened Geary Boulevard. Since then, new construction has generally echoed Japanese architectural themes. San Francisco's Japantown is one of only three Japantowns remaining in the U.S.

SIGHTS
Japan Center
Between Post, Fillmore & Laguna Sts. and Geary Blvd.
🕐*Open daily. Most shops open daily 10am–6pm, restaurantsand lounges later.* 🚫*Closed Jan 1, Thanksgiving Day, Dec 25.* ✕♿🅿 *www.sfjapantown.org.*
Reminiscent of contemporary Japanese architecture, this five-building complex (1968, Minoru Yamasaki) of shops, restaurants, cinemas and the Kabuki Hotel serves as a focal point for community celebrations. Its most striking Japanese touch is the **Peace Pagoda (1)**, inspired by the miniature round pagodas dedicated to eternal peace by Empress Koken more than 1,200 years ago in Nara, Japan. Rising 110ft above the plaza in five copper-roofed concrete tiers, the pagoda is capped by a golden ball atop a copper spire, symbolizing virtue.
From the Peace Plaza, stroll west through the Kintetsu and Kinokuniya buildings,

Visiting Japantown
Japantown comes alive in the evening when diners and moviegoers flock to its many restaurants and its celebrated **Sundance Kabuki Theatre** complex. The greatest crowds gather on festival days. During the spectacular **Cherry Blossom Festival** in mid- to late April, thousands congregate to enjoy Japanese arts and crafts, foods and music, taiko drumming, dancing and a colorful parade.

linked by an arching bridge over Webster Street. They are home to a colorful row of Japanese restaurants, music and video stores, electronics stores, shops, a Japanese bookstore and the Ikenobo Ikebana (flower-arranging) Society. The complex's westernmost building houses the **Sundance Kabuki Theatre** which screens first-run films and the annual **San Francisco International Film Festival** in April and May *(www.sundance-cinemas.com/kabuki.html)*.

Buchanan (Nihonmachi) Mall
Buchanan St., between Sutter & Post Sts. This attractive outdoor pedestrian street (1976) evokes the atmosphere of a Japanese village, with cobbled paving and "half-timbered" buildings. A small police *koban* (kiosk) stands at the Post Street end, while traditional restaurants and shops selling Japanese furniture, stationery, chinaware, gifts, kimonos and publications line its sides.

Konko Church of San Francisco
1909 Bush St., at Laguna St.
🕐*Open Mon–Sat 9.30am–5.30pm, Sun 8am–1pm, call ahead.* 📞*415-931-0453.*
With a handsome "half-timbered" exterior surface and timbers jutting from the roof, this steel-frame building (1973, Van Bourg, Nakamura & Associates) blends traditional Japanese aesthetics with modern engineering.
The interior incorporates a natural-wood Shinto altar with Christian influences such as pews. English-language services are held Sundays. Inspired by

a Japanese farmer's revelation in 1859, the Konko (Eternal Golden Light) sect of Shintoism advocates earthly happiness and respect for all life.

Sokoji-Soto Zen Buddhist Temple

1691 Laguna St., at Sutter St.
415-346-7540.
Dedicated in 1984, this overseas-mission temple building is handsomely clad with half-timbered stucco facing. Images of Koso-Dogen Zenji and Taiso-Keizan Zenji, celebrated as the founders of the Soto sect of Zen, flank the golden image of Shakyamuni Buddha at the center of the elaborate altar.

Buddhist Church of San Francisco★

1881 Pine St., at Octavia St.
Open Wed 6pm–8pm. English-language service Sun 10am. Closed major holidays. 415-776-3158.
www.bcsfweb.org.
This most exquisite of Japantown temple interiors occupies the second floor of an otherwise unprepossessing building (1938, Gentoko Shimamato). It is capped by a stupa, a bell-shaped pagoda, containing relics of the Buddha presented by the Thai royal court in 1935.
The Jodo Shinshu (True Pure Land) sect of Buddhism has long adopted such American cultural influences as pews, pulpit, and an organ, but the golden altar embodies Japanese tradition. Central is a small standing image of Amida Buddha, raising his right hand in a sign of wisdom and lowering his left in compassion. He is flanked on the right by an image of Shinran Shonin (1173–1262), founder of the Jodo Shinshu sect.

The Cathedral of St. Mary of the Assumption★★

1111 Gough St, at Geary Blvd.
Open Mon-Sat 8.30am–4.30pm. Mass Mon-Fri 8am, 12.10pm, Sat 8am, 5.30pm, Sun 7.30am, 9am, 11am, 1pm (Spanish). Docents available daily, call ahead to schedule tour. Organ recitals Sun 4pm. 415-567-2020 .
www.stmarycathedralsf.org.

Sheathed in white travertine marble and visible from miles around the city, San Francisco's third Catholic cathedral (1971) resembles a giant washing-machine agitator. It was designed by Pier Luigi Nervi & Pietro Belluschi, with McSweeney, Ryan & Lee. The building's most daring design attribute is its reinforced concrete **cupola**, formed of hyperbolic paraboloids that join to enclose a soaring atrium. At eye-level, glass panels afford fine city views. Narrow stained-glass windows rise steeply from the four compass points to meet at the cupola's apex, forming a brilliant cross 190ft above the sanctuary floor. Suspended on wires 75ft above the altar is a contemporary **baldachin**, a shimmering canopy of anodized aluminum rods designed by Richard Lippold to sparkle in the slightest breeze. A magnificent, 4,842-pipe Ruffatti organ perches on a concrete pedestal.

ADDRESSES

TAKING A BREAK

Kabuki Springs & Spa – *1750 Geary Blvd. in Japan Center. 415-922-6000. www.kabukisprings.com.* This day spa offers private traditional Japanese baths and spa treatments such as ayurvedic rebalancing and *shiatsu* massage, along with a communal bath area (bathing suit optional) for men Mon, Thu, Sat, women Wed, Fri, Sun, and coed Tue (bathing suit required).

SHOPPING

Soko Hardware – *1698 Post St. at Buchanan St. Open Mon–Sat 9am–5.30pm. 415-931-5510.* Japanese housewares such as tatami mats, wrapping paper, rice cookers and flower-arranging supplies.

New People – *1746 Post St. at Webster St. Open Mon–Sat noon-7pm, Sun noon-7pm. 415-931-5510. www.newpeopleworld.com.* Experience modern-day Japanese pop culture at this hybrid shopping complex, tea parlor, and cinema. For sale are souvenirs, anime-inspired fashion, and new and classic Japanese films.

Pacific Heights★★

Stretching along a high east-west ridge between Van Ness Avenue and the Presidio, this elegant residential neighborhood holds some of the city's finest houses and loveliest views. The name Pacific Heights connotes San Francisco wealth, and its reputation is fully deserved: no other neighborhood gives a grander vision of the life of affluent San Franciscans.

A BIT OF HISTORY

The area today known as Pacific Heights occupies a favored location equidistant from San Francisco's three main historic centers: Mission Dolores, the Presidio and the commercial area around Yerba Buena Cove (today's Financial District). Trails linking these three centers converged near the highest point of the ridge, called the divisadero, but the neighborhood's precipitous streets were not developed until late in the 19C. Improvements in public transportation, notably the invention of the cable car, brought the area within easy reach of downtown, and at the end of the 1870s Pacific Heights experienced its first of many real-estate booms.

Gingerbread Houses – While the city's most successful merchants constructed huge mansions on the eastern edge of the neighborhood (Van Ness Avenue), speculative developers began building more modest but still impressive homes. Often erecting between five and ten houses at a time, side by side on the narrow lots, contractors followed formulaic floor plans but adorned the exteriors with prefabricated decorative elements that could be ordered from catalogs. The abundance of such "gingerbread"—including fish-scale shingles, ogive-arched window frames and finely carved verge boards—earned these houses the nickname "Gingerbread Victorians," and the many examples are among San Francisco's most cherished treasures.

🚍 Bus 3–Jackson, 22–Fillmore, 24–Divisadero, 41–Union, or 45–Union-Stockton, 511.org.

ℹ **Info:** ℘415-391-2000. www.sftravel.com.

▸ **Location:** Pacific Heights is roughly bounded by Van Ness and Presidio Avenues and Pine and Vallejo Streets. The main shopping corridor is Fillmore Street between Bush and Jackson Streets. Bear the terrain in mind when planning a visit; streets ascend and descend abruptly, sometimes as much as 100ft in one block (🚶 *for a list of San Francisco's steepest streets, see RUSSIAN HILL*), so while, for example, Pacific Heights might look close to Cow Hollow on a map, it's actually a tough walk if you're headed south.

🕐 **Timing:** To get a sense of life in Pacific Heights, visit during early evening or a sunny weekend afternoon, when the people who live here jog the streets or walk their dogs. Better yet, arrive for lunch, shop and see the sights in the afternoon, then dine at a Fillmore Street bistro.

🅿 **Parking:** Though the neighborhood is easily accessible by bus, street parking is generally easier to find here than elsewhere in the city. There is a metered lot at California and Steiner Streets.

😊 **Don't Miss:** A walking tour of the Haas-Lilienthal House, an intact Victorian home open to the public.

Although many of the Van Ness mansions were dynamited by the US Army in order to create a firebreak during the

An Architectural Smorgasbord

Pacific Heights' wealthy denizens spent fortunes ensuring that their residences reflected their financial and social status. As a result, the neighborhood constitutes a showcase of design. A slow meander along its quiet streets reveals examples of almost every architectural style and period that exist in San Francisco. Because elite taste leaned toward refined Classical motifs, many architects looked to the Italian Renaissance palazzo for inspiration and followed the rules and precepts established by the École des Beaux Arts in Paris (which many of them had attended). Stone and brick were a popular building materials, and designs tended to follow one consistent historical style rather than mix aspects from different periods.

For more on Pacific Heights architecture, take the **Pacific Heights Walking Tour** offered by San Francisco Architectural Heritage every Sunday afternoon (*2hrs; meet at the Haas-Lilienthal House at 12.30pm; $8; 415-441-3000).*

1906 quake and fire, wealthy San Franciscans who had lost homes on Nob Hill and elsewhere resettled here, attracted by the neighborhood's bay views and peaceful, noncommercial ambience. Most of the district's largest homes date

from 1906–16, a time of great energy in every aspect of San Francisco's civic life. Along Broadway, for example, Comstock mining magnate James Leary Flood, whose Nob Hill residence was gutted by the fire, built a pair of mansions, each of which would cost $25–50 million today. Other bankers, industrialists and civic leaders built stately homes nearby. Only the very rich could afford to maintain such massive residences, and beginning in the 1920s apartment towers were built to lodge the city's elite on a more modest scale—though some of these buildings have come to rank among San Francisco's most desirable addresses, offering splendid views.

Today many Pacific Heights mansions house private schools or consulates, such as those of Italy *(2590 Webster St.)* and Germany *(1960 Jackson St.)*.

SIGHTS
Haas-Lilienthal House★★

2007 Franklin St., between Washington & Jackson Sts. Visit by guided tour *(1hr) Wed and Sat noon, Sun 11am, 3:30pm.* Closed major holidays and some Saturdays; call ahead. $10. 415-441-3000. www.sfheritage.org.

One of the city's few Victorian-era residences open to the public, this edifice (1886, Peter R. Schmidt) is among the last survivors of the many ornate single-family houses that once filled this neighborhood. The elegant residence typifies the aspirations of the city's upper-middle class at the end of the 19C—whereas the grandiose mansions atop Nob Hill were for the affluent elite. Constructed for William Haas, a prominent wholesaler, it passed to his daughter and son-in-law, Alice and Samuel Lilienthal, in 1916. After Alice's death in 1972, her family donated the house to the Foundation for San Francisco's Architectural Heritage, which currently maintains it. The exterior embellishments are typical of the Queen Anne style and include a variety of patterned siding, ornately bracketed gables and a deceptive corner tower with windows 10ft above the floor. The basement, once used as a ballroom, now displays photographs showing the house in its pre-1906 neighborhood context. Upper-floor rooms, including two parlors, a dining room and one of the original six bedrooms, are furnished in a range of decorative styles dating from the 1880s to the 1920s.

Spreckels Mansion★★

2080 Washington St.

Of all the many grand mansions in Pacific Heights, none is more ostentatious than the elaborate French Baroque-style palace built in 1913 for sugar magnate Adolph Spreckels and his wife, Alma de Bretteville Spreckels. Today, it is owned by famed romance novelist Danielle Steel.

The main facade consists of five arched windows separated by pairs of ornate Ionic columns. The house faces onto lushly landscaped **Lafayette Park**. The rear gardens, which drop steeply down to Jackson Street, boast a covered swimming pool.

Spreckels Mansion

© Brigitta L. House / MICHELIN

Broadway Mansions★

Broadway between Fillmore and Buchanan Sts.

These two elegant blocks of Broadway bear witness to the emergence of Pacific Heights as home to San Francisco's elite after the 1906 earthquake. One of the finest buildings in the city is the former **Flood Mansion★** *(no. 2222)*, designed by local architects Bliss and Faville in 1912 for James Leary Flood. The house is a refined and beautifully crafted version of an Italian Renaissance palazzo, its Tennessee marble hung on an earthquake-resistant steel frame. A pair of brick mansions, both dating from the same period, stand alongside the Flood Mansion; they now house private schools. Just south of Broadway, the **Bourn Mansion** *(2550 Webster St.)* was designed by Willis Polk in 1896 for William Bourn, the mining magnate for whom Polk also created the magnificent Filoli estate south of San Francisco. Designed as a pied-à-terre, the stately home contains only two bedrooms; rough clinker brick softens the Classical formality of the facade. Most unusually, the design plays down the importance of the entrance, which is set back in a deep vestibule beneath the upper-floor balcony.

In the block east of Webster lie two other remarkable mansions, the stately **Italian Consulate** *(no. 2590 Webster St.)*, and the blue-and-gray, Baroque Revival-style **Hamlin School** *(no. 2120)*. James Flood had the latter (1901) constructed on land owned by his sister, then moved to the Flood Mansion after its completion.

Fillmore Street★

Lively and inviting, Pacific Heights' commercial district lies along Fillmore Street between Jackson and Bush Streets. Impeccably turned-out locals fill the cafes, bistros and a welter of boutiques that range from frighteningly haute to more down-to-earth.

South of California Street, Fillmore runs past the Japan Center and across Geary Boulevard through the heart of the Western Addition. To the north, it reaches the edge of Pacific Heights at Broadway, where it offers one of the city's finest bay **views★** before dropping swiftly down into Cow Hollow.

Alta Plaza Park

Bounded by Jackson, Scott, Clay and Steiner Sts.

Set aside as a public park in the mid-1850s, the lush green oasis of Alta Plaza lies at the heart of Pacific Heights. Basketball and tennis courts and a children's playground occupy the center of the park, while terraces drop down on Alta Plaza's south side, forming a distinctive ziggurat of concrete and shrubbery.

The houses facing the south side are among Pacific Heights' oldest: a series of elaborate Italianate Victorian houses at **2637–2673 Clay St.**, all designed and built by the same contractor in 1875.

On the park's north side, Jackson Street features a pair of houses created by two influential turn-of-the-20C architects whose use of Classical Beaux-Arts models contrasts with the lighthearted playfulness of other Victorian-era designs. The former Music and Arts Institute at **2622 Jackson St.** was the first of architect Willis Polk's many commissions in the city. Built of stone in 1894 and styled like a Renaissance-era Tuscan villa, the house was acclaimed by *The San Francisco Examiner* as "the first Classical residence in San Francisco."

Nearby, the angular brick facade of **2600 Jackson St.** was designed by Ernest Coxhead and built in 1895 by industrialist Irving Scott for his daughter.

ADDRESSES

ⵏ/ EAT

Salt & Straw – *2201 Fillmore St.* ☏*415-829-2803, saltandstraw.com.* Even on a brisk San Francisco afternoon, the line of customers snakes out the door of this charming ice-cream shop, which serves flavors both classic and exotic, like roasted beet, sweet corn, honey-lavender, rye-and-cacao-nib sorbet on handmade waffle cones.

Richmond District and Presidio Heights

One of San Francisco's most ethnically diverse neighborhoods and a haven of the middle class, the Richmond District is a relatively flat expanse of undistinguished row houses sandwiched between Masonic Avenue to the east, California Street to the north, Golden Gate Park to the south and the Pacific Ocean to the west. Just to the north, between California Street and the Presidio, lies Presidio Heights, a wealthier residential enclave comprised largely of spacious, single-family homes.

A BIT OF HISTORY

The Richmond District and Presidio Heights both were once part of the Outer Lands, a vast expanse of scrubs and dunes. Cemeteries occupied its Eastern edge. In the final two decades of the 19C, Adolph Sutro purchased vast amounts of the sandy acreage cheaply. He built a steam railway along the present course of California Street to his Cliff House and bathhouse at Land's End. Construction in the Richmond District proceeded quickly after the 1906 earthquake. Two years later, Mayor Jim Rolph ordered all cemeteries moved south of the city to the town of Colma, spurring construction of yet more single-family row houses until the Great Depression struck in 1929. These new tracts drew residents of broad ethnic diversity, including White Russians fleeing the 1917 Russian Revolution, Jews from Eastern Europe and, after World War II, Japanese-Americans returning from internment camps. Chinese-Americans have formed the largest ethnic group since the 1970s, but the 1990s witnessed a resurgence of Russian immigration. Presidio Heights developed more slowly, as wealthy families built unique, often

palatial homes. A casual stroll along Pacific Avenue, Jackson Street and Washington Street, reveals a variety of architectural styles. Specially designed door knockers, mailboxes, gates and gardens add to the appeal.

Particularly worth noting is **Roos House** (3500 Jackson St.), a massive, half-timbered residence designed in 1909 by renowned Arts and Crafts architect Bernard Maybeck.

SIGHTS

San Francisco Columbarium

1 Loraine Ct., north of Anza St. ◷Open Mon–Fri 8 am–5pm, Sat–Sun 10am–3pm. ◷ Closed Jan 1, Thanksgiving Day, Dec 25. ♿P ✆415-221-1838. www.neptune-society. com/columbariium.

Owned by the Neptune Society of Northern California, a cremation organization, this copper-roofed, Neoclassical rotunda recalls the days when cemeteries covered the Richmond's dunes. Erected in 1898 as part of the Oddfel-

---

〽 Richmond District: bus 38–Geary, 1–California, 2–Clement or 4–Sutter. Presidio Heights: bus 3–Jackson or 43–Masonic. 511.org.

🛈 **Info:** www.sfgate.com/neighborhoods/sf/innerrichmond.

▶ **Location:** These neighborhoods lie quite near to each other, just south of the Presidio between Presidio Ave. and Park Presidio Blvd.

👪 **Kids:** The San Francisco Fire Department Museum.

🕐 **Timing:** Plan a morning here, followed by lunch on Sacramento Street.

🅿 **Parking:** Spaces are fairly easy to find along the residential streets.

😊 **Don't Miss:** Breathtaking views from the Lyon Street steps.

RICHMOND DISTRICT PRESIDIO HEIGHTS

lows Cemetery, the columbarium was spared when the graves were removed to Colma in 1914. Today it contains more than 4,400 niches, including those of several prominent San Francisco families. The flamboyant interior is adorned with a mosaic-tile floor, stained-glass windows and skylights, and brightly painted plaster filigree.

Clement Street

The more charming of the Richmond's main shopping thoroughfares (the other being highway-like Geary Boulevard), Clement Street is popular for its markets, bookshops, household-goods stores and excellent yet understated restaurants.

The 12-block stretch between Arguello and Park Presidio boulevards is sometimes known as "New Chinatown" because so many of its residents have relocated from downtown's Chinatown. But while Asian restaurants predominate, a culturally diverse community thrives on Clement Street.

Temple Emanu-El★

2 Lake St. ✆ *Visit by appt only.* ◷*Closed Jewish holidays.* ♿ ☎*415-751-2535. www.emanuelsf.org.*
Rising 150ft from the ground and visible for miles, this synagogue's spectacular, orange-tiled, Byzantine-style dome crowns a massive, architecturally unified complex of offices and meeting halls. Designed by Sylvain Schnaittacher, John Bakewell and Arthur Brown, Jr., the building was dedicated in 1926 as the third synagogue for the venerable Reform Jewish congregation, founded in San Francisco in 1850. Outside the sanctuary doors, a cloistered courtyard is dotted with plants named in the Old Testament as well as a lion-headed fountain. Visitors enter through the vestibule, its ceiling decorated with a brilliant blue and yellow fresco of a star-studded sky. The temple, which seats 1,700, is lit by two stained-glass windows representing fire (west) and water (east). Four massive bronze chandeliers symbolize the tears of the Jews. At the altar, the Ark

of the Covenant stands beneath a marble canopy, housed in a gilded bronze tabernacle box inlaid with cloisonné; the box was built in London by Californians Frank Igerson and George Dennison. The synagogue is home to the **Elizabeth S. and Alvin I. Fine Museum**, whose exhibits in the temple foyer integrate Jewish art and history into the congregational mind set. The permanent collection includes many antique ritual objects.

Presidio Terrace

Immediately north of the synagogue sits this exclusive residential enclave since 1905, with many elegant homes by noteworthy architects, including no. 15 (1905, Bakewell & Brown), no. 34 (c. 1910, George Applegarth) and no. 36 (1911, Julia Morgan).

Sacramento Street

The discreet but charming stretch of Sacramento Street between Lyon and Spruce Streets forms the elite shopping district of Presidio Heights. Its upscale boutiques, intimate restaurants and small cinema cater to a mostly local clientele.

Swedenborgian Church★★

2107 Lyon St. at Washington St.
🕐*Open Mon–Fri 10am–6pm, Sun service 11am.* 📞*415-346-6468. www.sfswedenborgian.org.*
This diminutive, lovingly crafted wood-and-brick chapel is named after Swedish scientist and philosopher Emanuel Swedenborg, who inspires the congregation. A fine example of Arts and Crafts design and construction, the church was conceived in 1895 by the congregation's founder, the Rev. Joseph Worcester. Bruce Porter sketched the design from an Italian original, while A. Page Brown served as chief architect and Bernard Maybeck as draftsman. Willis Polk designed the adjacent Parish House.
The church interior replicates the natural beauty of a California woodland. The ceiling is supported by bark-covered branches of native California madrone. Landscape painter William Keith contributed the pastoral scenes of the California

countryside along the north wall, while Porter designed the windows along the south wall. The solid chairs were built without nails, of maple wood and woven tule rushes from the Sacramento River delta. A giant clam shell near the altar is the baptismal font in which poet Robert Frost, among many others, was sanctified as an infant. Outside brick walkways frame lush gardens planted with trees from around the world.

Lyon Street Steps

Between Broadway and Green St.
Too steep for vehicular traffic, this part of Lyon Street was landscaped c. 1915 and today forms one of the city's most attractive public spaces. Dropping toward the bay from the west end of Broadway along the eastern wall of the Presidio, the steps offer a memorable **view**★★ out over the great dome of the Palace of Fine Arts across the bay to Angel Island and Mt. Tamalpais. Flower beds and other plantings soften the Beaux-Arts stairs, landings and balustrades, and benches offer a place to rest while taking in the view. The corner of Broadway and Lyon offers pedestrian access to the Presidio.

🧍🧍 San Francisco Fire Department Museum

655 Presidio Ave., between Bush and Pine Sts. 🕐*Open Thu–Sun 1–4pm.*
♿ 📞*415-563-4630 or 415-558-3546. www.guardiansofthecity.org.*
This converted firehouse garage houses a collection of historic fire engines, including the city's first hand-drawn pump cart (1849). Historical displays, photos and memorabilia, including eclectic collections of fire extinguishers, helmets, hydrants and uniforms, tell of the city's several devastating fires and heroic figures from San Francisco's firefighting past. Worth noting are the helmet that belonged to Lillie Hitchcock Coit, the eccentric booster of the San Francisco Fire Department and a certificate proclaiming her an honorary member of Knickerbocker Engine Co. Afterwards, peek into the adjacent Firehouse No. 5.

San Francisco's southern neighborhoods include the lively Castro and Mission Districts and the sprawling, industrial South of Market region. Epicenter of gay San Francisco, the Castro hums with energy night and day along its central commercial coridor, Castro Street. Its neighbor, the sunny Mission District, is San Francisco at its most bohemian, with artists, dot-commers and activists coexisting with a vibrant Latino community. San Francisco's hardscrabble history meets its high tech-present in the large heterogeneous region known as SoMa. Within SoMa, the Yerba Buena area has transformed in a major arts and cultural enclave.

Highlights

1　See a movie at the historic **Castro Theatre** (p177)

2　Chill at sunny **Dolores Park** with a burrito from a nearby tacqueria (p181)

3　Tour **Balmy Alley**'s colorful mural (p182)

4　Taste microbrews at the **Anchor Brewing Company** (p185)

5　Explore the **San Francisco Museum of Modern Art** (p189)

Castro, Mission and SoMa

The once quiet suburb of Eureka Valley adopted its present Castro character in the 1970s, when enterprising gay designers began purchasing the 19C Victorians at rock-bottom prices and fixing them up. In 1977, residents succeeded in electing neighborhood local Harvey Milk to the Board of Supervisors. Slain by a fellow supervisor the following year, Milk remains a revered figure for being the first openly gay elected official in U.S. history. Today, the rainbow flag, a universal symbol of gay pride, is everywhere; it flies over the streets and adorns the district's vibrantly painted Victorian houses.

To the east of the Castro is the Mission District, named for Mission Dolores, which anchored a small village in the early 1800s. By the turn of the 20th century, the neighborhood was mainly populated by European immigrants who worked in the warehouses, breweries and factories south of Market. Forced out of their homeland by the revolution, Mexicans began arriving in the 1920s. Central and South Americans have followed in the decades since. Though gentrification has pushed many Latinos out of the area, the stretch of 24th Street between Mission and Potrero Streets retains its Mexican character. Known as El Corazón de la Mision, or "the heart of the Mission," it's home to a large collection of Latino-themed murals.

The Mission is also home to dozens of the city's best restaurants, and plentiful bars and nightspots that draw young hipsters. Funky art galleries stand shoulder-to-shoulder with thrift shops and used bookstores, while residential blocks are lined with pastel-painted Italianate row houses, some dating as far back as the 1870s.

Northeast of the Mission is SoMa (South of Market). During the Gold Rush Days, SoMa was home to the town's weathy and elite citizens. When the 1906 earthquake destroyed most of the area, this region (bounded by 12th, Market and King Streets) and the Embarcadero then became known as South of the Slot, a reference to its location on the wrong side of the Market Street cable-car track. As manufacturing declined in the mid-20C, architects, graphic designers, software companies and publishers divvied up former industrial building and warhouses into loftlike offices. Then in 2000, the Internet bubble burst, leaving nearly half of the offfices vacant. SoMa is now booming again, eclipsing the Financial District with new construction, and the Yerba Buena area is home to such powerhouses as the San Francisco Museum of Art, Yerba Buena Gardens and the Contemporary Jewish Museum.

Castro District★ and Noe Valley★

The bustling Castro District is the heart of San Francisco's vibrant gay community, as well as the geographical center of the city. Bars, restaurants, trendy clothing stores and boutiques crowd together along Castro, Market and 18th Streets, while residential side streets lined with beautifully refurbished Victorians invite leisurely exploration.

A BIT OF HISTORY

Part of a 4,000-acre land grant given to San Francisco's last Mexican mayor, José de Jésus Noe, the present-day Castro District and neighboring Noe Valley were used primarily for cattle-ranching and sheep-grazing until shortly after the Gold Rush. In 1854, during a citywide wave of land speculation, a wealthy produce merchant named John Meirs Horner bought much of Noe's ranch, plotted a street grid, and began peddling land tracts to working-class Irish and German immigrants. By 1887 the Market Street Cable Railway extended down Castro Street, linking Eureka and Noe Valleys and opening the 21st Street summit to development.

As the district sustained only minor damage in the 1906 earthquake and fire, campgrounds for refugees were quickly erected. Many of the temporary residents opted to stay, and a tight-knit working-class community thrived well into the 1920s, when a commercial building boom graced Castro Street with the majestic Castro Theatre and several other fine structures. The Great Depression forced many landowners to divide and rent out single-family homes, and federal housing subsidies in the 1950s further encouraged the working-class families' slow march out of the city.

A New Alternative – In the early 1970s gay San Franciscans began purchasing the neighborhood's neglected Victorians and bringing them back to their

🚍 Bus 24-Divisadero; streetcars F-Market, K-Ingleside, L-Taraval, M-Oceanview or T-third Street to Castro St. station, 511.org.

♿ **Michelin Map:** See p180

ℹ **Info:** www.sfgate.com/neighborhoods/sf/castro.

▶ **Location:** The Castro District is roughly bounded by Market, Dolores, 22nd and Douglass Streets. Castro Street between Market and 19th Streets is the liveliest strip in the neighborhood, with bars, restaurants, cafes and shops. Market Street between Castro and Church Streets also has a number of restaurants and shops. In quaint Noe Valley the main drag is 24th Street between Church and Castro Streets.

🕐 **Timing:** During the day, the Castro's cafes and shops do a brisk business. At night, neon signs of bars and the spectacular Castro Theatre light up, dance music is ratcheted up a few notches and the air buzzes with palpable energy.

🅿 **Parking:** Street parking here is difficult. You're better off taking public transport, particularly the F-Market historic streetcar, which will deposit you right in the heart of the district at Castro and Market Streets. To get to Noe Valley from here, take the 24–Divisadero bus on Castro Street south (over a mammoth hill) to 24th Street.

😊 **Don't Miss:** A performance at the Castro Theatre.

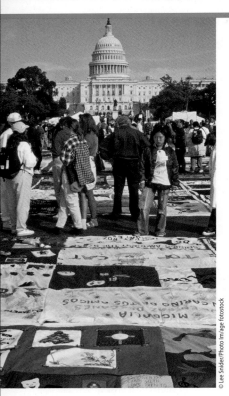

© Lee Snider/Photo Im/age fotostock

AIDS Memorial Quilt displayed in the National Mall, Washington DC in 1996

The AIDS Memorial Quilt

Invoking both an American tradition of quilting and a historic practice of honoring the dead with national monuments, the AIDS Memorial Quilt, sponsored by the NAMES Project Foundation, represents a unique, moving response to the AIDS epidemic. Composed of coffin-sized 3ft-by-6ft panels, each handmade in memory of someone who died of the virus, the quilt tours the world in sections to increase AIDS awareness and to raise funds for North American AIDS-service organizations.

The idea for the quilt originated with Cleve Jones, a San Francisco gay-rights activist. In 1985, after learning that more than 1,000 city residents had died of AIDS-related illnesses, Jones asked participants in the 1985 memorial march for Harvey Milk to carry signs bearing the names of friends and acquaintances who had succumbed to the virus. At the end of the march, the posters were affixed to the facade of the San Francisco Federal Building, and the resulting patchwork resembled a quilt.

In 1986, Jones founded the NAMES Project, and in spring 1987 he made the first cloth panel in memory of his best friend. Soon, handmade panels adorned with such diverse materials as spray paint, leather, sequins and photographs began arriving at the NAMES Project headquarters in San Francisco from all over the United States.

In October 1987, when the quilt was displayed for the first time in Washington DC, it comprised 1,920 panels and covered a space larger than a football field. A 1996 display in the capital was made up of an estimated 41,000 panels, covering roughly 29 football fields. That was the last time the quilt was displayed in its entirety. As of 2012, the quilt had more than 48,000 panels, attesting to both the devastation of the illness and the spirit and *joie de vivre* of those who have died.

🛈 *For more information, visit www.aidsquilt.org.*

former grandeur. The first gay bars appeared on Castro Street in 1972 and thanks to the social liberalization of the period and significant gains in gay civil rights, they operated largely without harassment. It soon gained a reputation for being one of the most vital gay neighborhoods in the world. In 1977 residents of the Castro were instrumental in electing **Harvey Milk** to the city's Board of Supervisors, making him the first openly gay elected official in U.S. history. Milk's life and career were cut short the following year when he and then-Mayor George Moscone were gunned down at City Hall by City Supervisor Dan White. In 1978 San Francisco passed the Gay Bill of Civil Rights, forbidding discrimination in housing and employment on the basis of sexual orientation.

Crisis struck the neighborhood in the 1980s with the onset of the AIDS epidemic. In response, public-education and human-rights organizations took root in the Castro; many still thrive. Today a friendly, upbeat ambience pervades the district. Dance music pulses in many shops, whose creative, sometimes outrageous window displays are among the most eye-catching in the city. On quiet residential streets, rainbow flags brighten the windows of pretty Victorian homes.

CASTRO DISTRICT
Castro Street

The colorful shopping strip between Market and 19th Streets has served the neighborhood since the 1850s. Named for Vincent Castro, an early Mexican rancher, the busy thoroughfare is bustling day and night.

In recent years, Market Street between Castro and Church streets has become a vibrant shopping strip. Full-grown Canary Island palm trees were planted along the median in 1994, and in 1995, the refurbished streetcars of the historic F-Market line began clanging through, balancing the trend-setting designer clothing boutiques and new restaurants with a charming touch of the past. At the southwest corner of Market and Castro streets is Harvey Milk Plaza, dedicated

© San Francisco Travel Association/Scott Chernis

Castro District at night

in late 1997 on the 20th anniversary of Milk's election to office. Above a simple memorial flies a huge eight-color rainbow flag, the universal symbol of sexual diversity that was created in the Castro. Spearheaded by the citizens group Friends of Harvey Milk Plaza, new designs for the plaza as a sweeping public space have been submitted to the city; it is slated for redevelopment, but final plans for the plaza are still in the works. Walking south, look for the rainbow crosswalks at 18th and Castro streets to find the **Rainbow Honor Walk** (*see below*). Near the same intersection, Milk lived in blue Victorian at **575 Castro Street**. His apartment was located above his first-floor camera shop, and his campaign headquarters was in the rear. Today, **Human Rights Campaign Store** (*415-431-2200. www.hrc.org*) occupies the first floor, selling branded souvenirs and clothing to support their organization's mission to promote tolerance worldwide. A mural of Milk, clad in a T-shirt adorned with a rainbow flag, gazes from an upstairs window.

Castro Theatre★

429 Castro St. Open daily, at showtimes. 415-621-6120. www.castrotheatre.com.
Declared a San Francisco Historic Landmark in 1977, this splendid Spanish Renaissance Revival theater (1922, Timothy Pflueger) is the city's finest example of early 20C movie-palace architecture.

Rainbow Honor Walk

Look for the rainbow crosswalks at the intersection of Castro and 18th streets. There you'll find the nonprofit-sponsored Rainbow Honor Walk (rainbowhonorwalk. org), a collection of bronze sidewalk placards dedicated to history's most significant lesbian, gay, bisexual, transgender, and queer people. A diverse group of poets, scientists, activists, and musicians make up the current honorees, including James Baldwin, Allen Ginsberg, and Jane Addams, with plans to expand the list to dozens more honorees.

The front exterior features Spanish Colonial-style ornamentation above the low-hanging marquee and a huge, pink-neon sign, both added in 1937. The grand 1,520-seat interior's gently curved green and gold-leaf ceiling, two-story proscenium framed by columns and an ornate lintel, and sumptuous murals create a magical ambience. Attend one of the nightly screenings to hear resident musicians playing the organ, which slowly rises from the orchestra pit. Screening Hollywood classics, kitschy cult favorites, rare foreign films and new independent movies, the Castro Theatre also hosts several annual film festivals, including the San Francisco Jewish Film Festival and Frameline, the San Francisco International LGBTQ+ Film Festival.

GLBT Historical Society Museum

5127 18th St.   *415-621-1107* Mon-Fri 10am-6pm; Sun. 11am-5pm. Closed Dec 25, Dec 31, Jan 1, Jan 22. *$5 www.glbthistory.org* A small museum chronicling San Francisco's GLBT history through artifacts, photos, and other materials from the society's extensive archives. There is a particularly moving segment dedicated to Harvey Milk's career and assassination. In addition to the main gallery, two smaller spaces are dedicated to temporary exhibits, which change frequently but often highlight work by GLBT artists or chronicle the history of specific social movements. The space also frequently hosts talks, film screenings, and other special events.

NOE VALLEY

In the lowlands south of the Castro District, Noe Valley features wide, hilly, Victorian-lined streets. Like the Castro, the neighborhood was part of José Noe's huge ranch until well into the 1850s, and harbored a thriving community of working-class immigrants through the mid-20C. In the 1970s the area gained popularity with hippies and artists. Noe Valley has recently become a desirable neighborhood for young professionals and families. **24th Street** (*between Church & Castro Sts.*), its colorful commercial thoroughfare, retains a local feel thanks to a local ordinance that restricts chain businesses in the area. During the day, the sidewalks fill with denizens walking dogs and pushing strollers; cafes overflow with latte lovers, and designer clothing shops, bookstores, flower stands and wine merchants beckon shoppers. In 2016, the neighborhood association successfully converted a 24th Street parking lot into the Noe Valley Town Square (noevalleytownsquare.com) which features a children's play area, benches, and an open plaza to accommodate the Saturday farmers' market 8am-1pm. (3861 24th St, www.noevalleyfarmersmarket.com).

ADDRESSES

SHOPPING

Omnivore Books – *4885A Cesar Chavez St.* *415-282-4712, www.omnivorebooks.com.* If you love cooking, seek out this tiny bookshop. The floor-to-ceiling collection includes new, antiquarian, and collectible books and magazines exclusively focused on food and drink. In the evenings, it hosts a robust schedule of free author and chef events.

Mission District★★

With its freewheeling, festive Latino flavor, the Mission District is one of the city's liveliest neighborhoods. It's also one of its warmest—a high ridge on the scenic western edge of the district protects the area against the chill fogs and ocean winds that afflict many other parts of the city.

A BIT OF HISTORY

In 1776, Spanish explorer Juan Bautista de Anza chose this location for a Catholic mission dedicated to St. Francis of Assisi—the origin of the city's name.

A primitive village grew up in the vicinity of the mission, but the surrounding lands remained largely uncultivated. After secularization in 1834, wealthy Californio ranchers used the property for cattle grazing, although Yankee squatters' rights prevailed after the U.S. won the Mexican-American War in 1848. During the post-Gold Rush boom in 1851, a plank road was laid through the marshy South of Market area, providing a connection to the flourishing downtown waterfront and opening the neighborhood to development.

A street grid was platted, with 16th Street serving as the main commercial thoroughfare. The Mission District mostly attracted working-class people, many from Germany and Scandinavia—and, later, Italy and Ireland—who had arrived on trade vessels and stayed on to work in the burgeoning city.

Latino Enclave – Because much of the district survived the earthquake and fire of 1906, many of those left homeless by the conflagration resettled here. Throughout the 1920s, Mexicans fleeing revolution in their homeland swelled the ranks of Latinos in the core of the Mission; in subsequent decades, new waves of Latinos replaced many European-descended families. Social and political unrest in Central and South America since the 1970s has fueled an influx of new immigrants.

MUNI Bus 14–Mission, 22–Fillmore, 26–Valencia or 33–Stanyan. 16th St. or 24th St. station, 511.org.

 Info: www.sanfrancisco. travel/neighborhood/ mission-district

 Location: The vast Mission District is roughly bounded by Potrero Avenue and Dolores, 14th and Cesar Chavez Streets. Though homey Latino eateries still dominate on 24th Street east of Mission Street, the Valencia Street Corridor, between 16th and 22nd Streets, now teems with trendy restaurants, cafes, galleries and shops. Exercise caution at night.

 Kids: A banana split royale at St. Francis Fountain.

 Timing: The Mission is fun both by day and night. To enjoy the best of both worlds, come for lunch, then visit Mission Dolores, shop on Valencia Street, see the murals on 24th Street and stay for dinner. Exuberant celebrations occur regularly, including **Cinco de Mayo** (first Sunday in May) and **Carnaval** (Memorial Day Sunday). See Calendar of Events.

 Parking: The Mission is easily accessible via public transportion; BART is particularly convenient. Street parking is sometimes possible to find (don't leave valuables in the car, though). A parking garage is at 3255 21st Street, at Mission Street.

 Don't Miss: A visit to the historic Mission Dolores and a Mission-style burrito at a taqueria before strolling down Balmy Alley to admire the vibrant murals.

The area east of Valencia and south of 16th Street today remains predominantly Latino and largely working-class, though artists and entrepreneurs have discovered the Mission, giving rise to a bustling nightlife scene on the western edge of the district, where chic new restaurants and bars sit alongside the taquerias, cafes and used bookstores.

SIGHTS
Mission Dolores (Mission San Francisco de Asís)★★

3321 16th St. at Dolores St. ◷Open daily 9am–4pm (Good Friday until noon; Easter Sunday 10am–1pm). ◷Closed Jan 1, Thanksgiving Day, Dec 25. ◸$5 donation requested. ♿♺415-621-8203. http://missiondolores.org.

Flanked by a historic cemetery and a lavishly ornamented 20C basilica, San Francisco's oldest extant structure serves as a reminder of the city's Spanish heritage and a repository of early European history. The sixth mission in the Alta California chain was first established in 1776 near the present-day corner of Camp and Albion Streets, two blocks east of its present site. A nearby lake named for Our Lady of Sorrows (Nuestra Senora de los Dolores) gave the mission its centuries-old nickname, Mission Dolores. The present chapel was completed in 1791. After secularization in 1834, the property was occupied by squatters. The Catholic Church reacquired it in 1860, erecting a series of larger churches alongside the old chapel to accommodate a growing congregation. The present **church★** (1918), with ornate Churrigueresque facade, was designated a basilica in 1952.

Visit

Remarkably sturdy, the **chapel★★** has survived major earthquakes in 1868, 1906 and 1989 as well as abandonment and neglect. Today it appears much as it did in 1791, thanks to a conscientious restoration program completed in 1995. Cement stucco covers 4ft-thick adobe walls. The ornate, hand-carved reredos and side altars were imported from Mexico in 1780, and bronze bells high in the chapel's front exterior facade were brought as gifts in 1792, 1795 and 1797. The remarkable multicolored motifs painted on the high, beamed ceiling are patterned after Ohlone basket designs.

A small passage north of the chapel contains a splendid **diorama** of the mission as it appeared in 1799; the model was created for the Golden Gate International Exposition of 1939–40. The mission's small **museum (M)** houses artifacts discovered during restorations, as well as baptismal records and vestments dating from the colonial period.

On the south side extends a tranquil **cemetery★**; here, amid verdant plantings, are buried many of San Francisco's early leaders, including Luis Antonio Arguello (1784–1830), first governor of California; and Francisco De Haro (1803–48), first mayor of San Francisco.

Dolores Street

Between 16th and 21st Sts.

Rolling hills, lofty palm trees and an eye-catching blend of architectural styles characterize this attractive stretch of Dolores Street. At 18th Street, Mission Dolores' architecture is echoed in the huge, red-tile-roofed Mission High School (1926, John Reid, Jr.). **Mission Dolores Park,** which once served as a cemetery for two Jewish temples, was laid out in 1905 and briefly served as a refugee camp for residents after the 1906 earthquake and fire. Today, the renovated 16-acre park is one of the city's most popular gathering spots, with tennis courts, a children's playground and lush lawns shaded by tall palms where picnickers and sunbath-

Mission District murals

© San Francisco Travel Association/Scott Chernis

Speaking Walls: The Murals of San Francisco

San Francisco tallies nearly 600 wall paintings within its 49sq mi. Some record traditional history. Others serve as vibrant pictorial voices for communities without expression in mainstream art institutions—groups united by race, ethnicity, class, gender or politics.

The great Mexican muralist **Diego Rivera** visited the city during the early 1930s, executing important works at the San Francisco Art Institute and the Pacific Exchange. Fresco murals at Coit Tower and the Beach Chalet reflect Rivera's influence during this period.

During the late 1960s, **David Alfaro Siqueiros** improved techniques for outdoor painting, and the Mission District witnessed an explosion of outdoor art the following decade. The fences, walls and garage doors of **Balmy Alley**, off 24th Street, were originally decorated by schoolchildren. Many Mission District artists painted their first murals in the alley, including Patricia Rodríguez, Graciela Carillo and Irene Pérez, who later founded Mujeres Muralistas, a group of women artists who pictured the beauty of their cultures.

Many of those early murals were subsequently replaced in the 1980s by the **PLACA** group—this time with themes of the struggle for peace in Central America. More recent Balmy Alley murals include portraits of Mexican art icons, a relief mural made with plywood cut-outs, and a mural tribute to Mujeres Muralistas. Maradiaga Mini-Park contains murals drawn to teach local kids about their Latin-American heritage.

Following is a brief list of some exceptionally interesting Mission District murals. For more information, drop by or call the **Precita Eyes Mural Arts and Visitors Center** *(2981 24th St. near Harrison St.;* ✆*415-285-2287; www.precitaeyes.org)* which offers lectures and walking tours of Mission District murals *(Sat–Sun at 1.30pm; $20; call or check website for details and meeting place)* as well as a useful map pinpointing more than 90 murals in the area if you wish to explore the neighborhood independently.

- *Las Lechugueras* (1983) by Juana Alicia; Taquería San Francisco, 24th and York Streets.

- *Silent Language of the Soul* (1990) by Juana Alicia and Susan Cervantes; Cesar Chavez Elementary School, Shotwell & 22nd Sts.

- *Five Hundred Years of Resistance* (1993) by Isaías Mata; St. Peter's Church, 24th St. at Florida St.

- *Maestrapeace* (1995) by various women artists; Women's Building, 3543 18th St.

Other mural locations described elsewhere in this guide include:
Balmy Alley (🔗*p183)*
San Francisco Art Institute (🔗*p106)*
Beach Chalet (🔗*p160)*
National Maritime Museum (🔗*p130)*
Coit Tower (🔗*p100)*
Rincon Center (🔗*p119)*

ers enjoy the city views on the sunny days. South of the park is **Liberty Street** (between 20th and 21st Sts.), lined with Victorians dating from the 1860s. All major styles are represented, including Italianate (no. 109), Stick (nos. 111–121), and Queen Anne (no. 123).

24th Street★

Between Mission and Potrero Sts.
On this lively, tree-lined shopping strip bright awnings shadow produce stands overflowing with tropical fruit; Spanish rolls off the tongues of shopkeepers and shoppers , and modest eateries serve up Latin American treats.
Stroll down **Balmy Alley★** (between Treat & Harrison Sts.) to admire the colorful murals adorning nearly every garage door and wall surface. Occupying an unassuming corner storefront, **Galería de la Raza** (2857 24th St. at Bryant St.; ⏱ open Wed–Sat noon–6pm; ✆415-826-8009; www.galeriadelaraza.org) has sustained and nurtured the Chicano art movement since 1970. The gallery showcases new artists along with established ones; exhibits reflect Chicano and Latino social and cultural issues.

Valencia Street★

Between 16th and 23rd Sts.
A profusion of restaurants, thrift stores, coffee shops, boutiques and bars lines this section of Valencia Street and the cross streets to Guerrero Street, transforming the working-class neighborhood into a the coolest destination in the city for well-heeled hipsters and techies.

ADDRESSES

SHOP

Creativity Explored – 3245 16th St. ✆415-863-2108. www.creativityexplored.org. A small but thought-provoking gallery showcasing colorful and inspiringly creative work by artists with developmental disabilities.

Everlane – 461 Valencia. www.everlane.com This trendy San Francisco clothier rose to fame for its transparent production model, commitment to ethical labor, and high-quality classic pieces, like cashmere sweaters and cotton tees, on sale at its flagship shop on Valencia.

♉EAT

$ La Taqueria – 2889 Mission St. ✆415-285-7117. One of the most popular burrito joints in the city, this long-running Mission spot serves simple tacos and famously rice-free burritos, with ace salsas on the side.

Creativity Explored

© San Francisco Travel Association/Scott Chernis

South of Market

San Francisco's hardscrabble history meets its high-tech future South of Market. Like New York City's SoHo (which inspired South of Market's sobriquet, "SoMa"), the area was, until recently, dominated by industrial buildings. On and around Third and Fourth Streets, **Yerba Buena Gardens** has become a prime cultural center. In the surroundng blocks, many buildings have been reborn as offices, luxury condos and sleek bars and bistros.

A BIT OF HISTORY

SoMa differs from other San Francisco neighborhoods in two major respects— its streets run at a 45-degree angle to those of the rest of the city, and its blocks are four times as big. Irish engineer and surveyor Jasper O'Farrell planned it that way in 1847 in anticipation of industrial growth, and gasworks, shipyards, refineries, foundries and breweries took root along the waterfront.

Despite all this industry, well-to-do San Franciscans built elegant Victorian mansions atop nearby Rincon Hill and an enclave of Georgian townhouses encircled a private oval common known as South Park. Encroaching development and the advent of the cable car in 1873 whisked most of the rich denizens away to the slopes of Nob Hill.

Neighborhood in Transition – After the earthquake and fire of 1906 razed the sector, SoMa's population remained largely male and working-class. After 1985 when the Downtown Plan limited skyscraper construction in the Financial District, several large office towers rose in the blocks between Mission and Market Streets. Work on Yerba Buena Gardens began in the early 1990s, and architects, artists, and filmmakers began carving up SoMa's warehouses into live/work spaces, and many dot-com companies set up shop here. After the 2001 tech-stock crash, commercial vacancy rates rose as high as 30 percent, but by mid-decade, the area was in an upswing again, thanks to resurgence of the Inter-

net economy and ambitious construction projects. SoMa has a lively after-dark scene thanks to the many nightclubs, galleries, microbreweries and bistros along 11th Street, near Folsom.

Streetcar N–Judah .
Bus 10–Townsend, 12–Folsom, 30–Stockton, 45–Union-Stockton, 47–Van Ness Embarcadero, Montgomery St., Powell St. or Civic Center stations,511.org.

Michelin Map: See Yerba Buena Gardens.

Info: 415-391-2000. www.sf.travel.com.

Location: The term SoMa applies mainly to the blocks between Market and Townsend Streets, from 11th Street to the Embarcadero. It is a huge, diverse area, with everything from avant-garde art to baseball. In this guide, we've given **Yerba Buena Gardens**, which is part of SoMa, its own chapter since it contains so many closely packed cultural attractions. Note that SoMa blocks are twice as long and twice as wide as those in other neighborhoods, with about five blocks per mile.

Timing: SoMa is best visited in the daytime with a specific destination in mind. Use caution around Sixth Street. At night, take a taxi.

Parking: There is a parking garage at Fifth and Mission Streets.

Don't Miss: Anchor Brewing Company, mecca for lovers of this tart microbrew.

SIGHTS

San Francisco Federal Building
90 7th Street, 415-436-7950 Mon.-Fri. 8am-6pm
Opened in 2007, this striking deconstructivist tower is home to San Francis-

co's federal government offices. In addition to its experimental design, there are several notable pieces of public art that were created for the building, including *Skygarden*, a site-specific installation by artist James Turrell, which illuminates a three-story opening in the building's façade until 10pm every evening.

Old Mint

88 5th St. at Mission St.
Not open to the public.
The Old Mint—known as The Granite Lady—is one of the city's finest Neoclassical buildings. Made of brick with stone facing in 1874, the structure served as a U.S. Mint until 1937, surviving the fire of 1906 when employees, with the help of soldiers and a tiny firehose, fought to save $200 million in silver and gold. It was damaged in the 1989 earthquake and closed in 1995. In 2016, the city and the California Historical Society began assessing the viability of restoring it.

South Park

Bounded by 2nd, 3rd, Brannan and Bryant Sts.
Charming cafes flank this sedate oval park nestled in a warehouse-dominated district. Designed in the 1850s to resemble a London-style garden, South Park was home to high society until the early 1870s. Writer Jack London was born nearby in 1876 (a plaque marks the site at 601 3rd St.). By 2003, it had become ground zero for the dot-com revolution (Twitter founder Jack Dorsey purportedly came up with his company's concept on the playground).

Folsom Street

A locus of activity for alternative society, this street—and those adjoining it between 6th and 11th Streets—holds a high concentration of nightclubs. The street hosts the leather-centric Folsom Street Fair the last Sunday of September, but its draw on most nights of the week is much more diverse. Ground zero for clubgoers is the area around 11th and Folsom Streets, where queues form outside SoMa institutions like the **DNA Lounge** (*375 11th St.;*

415-626-1409; www.dnalounge.com and newer bars like **Butter** (*354 11th St.;* *415-863-5964; www.smoothasbutter. com*) and **Wish** (*1539 Folsom St.;* *415-431-1661; www.wishsf.com*).

ADDITIONAL SIGHTS
Potrero Hill

This eclectic residential neighborhood features windswept streets, lovely views, hip commercial strips and historic factories. Many design studios have recently relocated along De Haro Street between 16th and Mariposa streets. **Eighteenth Street** between Connecticut and Texas streets harbors a cozy commercial strip, boasting scenic **views★** of downtown.

Anchor Brewing Company

1705 Mariposa St. Multiple guided tours (90min) offered daily. Reservations required. 415-863-8350. www.anchorbrewing.com.
Housed in an attractive Art Deco factory (1937), the Anchor Brewing Company has earned a reputation for its amber lager, which helped spark a trend toward beers from microbreweries in the US in the 1990s. Founded in 1896, Anchor was purchased in the mid-1970s by Fritz Maytag, the heir to the Maytag appliance fortune, who moved the operation to its present location. Guided tours traverse the three-story factory, followed by a tasting session in the tap room

CCA Hubbell Street Galleries

161 Hubbell St. 415-703-9500.
Tue.-Sat. noon-5pm. www.cca.edu.
In 2016, the California College of Art opened a set of beautiful light-filled galleries at the foot of Potrero Hill, maintaining a robust program of exhibitions by students, faculty and local artists.

Dogpatch

Once a largely industrial neighborhood between Potrero Hill and the harbor, Dogpatch is today a burgeoning arts district, with a number of intesting galleries and studios filling former warehouses and factories. Linked to the city center via light rail (MUNI K Ingleside, T Third St.), it's easy to visit from downtown.

Minnesota Street Project

11275 Minnesota St. &. *℘415-243-0825.* *Tue.-Sat. 11am-6pm.* *Closed Jan 1, Dec 25. minnesotastreetproject.com.* Artist studios and contemporary galleries fill three repurposed warehouse spaces (*2016, Mark Jensen*), some showing excellent work by local artists. The space also hosts frequent well-attended special events, like artist's talks, openings, auctions, CCA MFA exhibits, and the SF Art Book Fair (*sfartbookfair.com*). On the ground floor, hip Indian bar and restaurant **Besharam** (*$$$*, *℘415-580-7662 www.besharamrestaurant.com*) is a nice place for a snack post-gallery hopping, especially during afternoon happy hour.

ADDRESSES

SHOPPING

Chronicle Books – *680 Second St.* *℘415-537-4200. www.chroniclebooks.com.* Visit the colorful bookshop at the headquarters of San Francisco–based publisher Chronicle Books, which specalizes in art, design, gift books, cook books, and children's titles.

Yerba Buena Gardens★★

The contemporary heart of the South of Market district, this once-rundown industrial zone has evolved into San Francisco's cultural hub. With numerous museums, the city's main convention center, a performing-arts center, a children's museum and a high-tech shopping-and-entertainment complex, it pulses with activity from morning till night. At the core of one of the biggest urban-renewal projects in the U.S., this 5.5-acre park opened in 1993 between 3rd and 4th, Mission and Howard Streets. Adjacent neighborhoods now bustle with architecture and graphic-design firms, film- and software-production studios, trendy restaurants, and nightclubs. New high-rise office towers are also sprouting along the fringe of the Gardens.

A BIT OF HISTORY

For more than three decades, beginning in the 1960s, San Francisco's urban redevelopment agency cast its eyes south across Market Street. Resi-

- **Michelin Map:** See p188.
- Bus 14–Mission, 30–Stockton or 45–Union-Stockton. Montgomery St. or Powell St. stations, 511/org.
- **Info:** www.yerbabuena gardens.com.
- **Location:** The Yerba Buena Gardens cultural district stretches roughly from Second to Fifth Streets between Mission and Folsom Streets. Its centerpiece is the block enclosed by Mission, Howard, Third and Fourth Streets. Here you'll find the Yerba Buena Center for the Arts, a pleasant park, and the Sony–Metreon mall. A footbridge arches over Howard Street to the family-centered Rooftop at Yerba Buena Gardens.
- **Kids:** The Rooftop at Yerba Buena Gardens has ice skating, bowling, a carousel, and the Children's Creativity Museum.

Yerba Buena Center for the Arts

© San Francisco Travel Association/Scott Chernis

🕐 **Timing:** A visit could easily fill a full day.

🅿 **Parking:** There is a parking garage at Fifth and Mission Streets, but Yerba Buena Gardens' proximity to all the Market Street Muni and BART lines makes public transportation easy.

😊 **Don't Miss:** The San Francisco Museum of Modern Art's expanded collection.

dents fought planners and real-estate developers to prevent their declining community from becoming a high-rise ghetto. The first big step took place in 1981 with the completion of **Moscone Convention Center** (Hellmuth, Obata and Kassabaum) on the south side of Howard Street. Later additions came in 1988 and 1991, bringing total exhibition space to 442,000sq ft. Moscone West opened in 2003, giving the center a total of 650,000sq ft. A sports arena originally was scheduled for construction in the block north of the convention center. But citizens' voices won out, and a multicultural focus was agreed upon, with Yerba Buena Gardens as its centerpiece. Today the district boasts many

museums, a children's entertainment complex, galleries, a cineplex, an inviting park, performance spaces and more.

SIGHTS
Yerba Buena Center for the Arts★ (A)

701 Mission St. 🕐*Galleries open Tue-Sun 11am–6pm, Thu till 8pm.* 🕐*Closed major holidays and Mondays.* 🎟*$10; free 1st Tue of month.* ♿*℘415-978-2700. www.ybca.org.*

Exploring such issues as race, class, gender, history, technology and art, the changing exhibitions in this modernistic building (1993, Fumihiko Maki) reflect the cultural diversity and experimental élan of the Bay Area.

Designed to resemble an ocean liner—its tall flagpole suggesting a mast and the angled Mission Street facade recalling a stern—the $44 million structure contains a 6,700sq-ft performance space, two expansive first-floor galleries and a sculpture plaza. Upstairs, a high-tech gallery accommodates film, video and multimedia installations, while an open terrace overlooks the large downstairs gallery and spacious lobby. Galleries host temporary exhibitions of work by emerging and established artists. Immediately south of the galleries stands the 750-seat **Yerba Buena**

YERBA BUENA GARDENS – SOUTH EMBARCADERO

Center for the Arts Theater (B) (1993, James Stewart Polshek and Partners). Exposed steel cross beams emphasize its boxy, geometrical design, accented by red and yellow flourishes around the lobby and entrance.

Esplanade★ (C)

The Esplanade is a haven of gently rolling hills, trees, gardens, eclectic sculptures and an outdoor performance area. Paths meander about the ground level, which lies atop an underground extension of Moscone Center. The south side is dominated by **Revelations★**, a site-specific memorial to Dr. Martin Luther King, Jr. Behind an exhilarating waterfall, 50ft wide and 20ft high, are 12 glass panels engraved with quotations from the civil-rights leader's speeches and writings. It was the joint work of sculptor Howard Conwill, poet Estella Majoza and architect Joseph De Pace.

On a second-story terrace, the Sister City Garden features plants from the 14 international cities that nurture cultural and political relations with San Francisco.

ROOFTOP AT YERBA BUENA GARDENS★★ (D)

Fourth St. between Howard and Folsom Sts.

This $56 million children's complex, which sits atop the west wing of Moscone Center's South Hall, is one of the city's leading attractions for families. Attractions are centered around a 100,000sq ft Children's Garden, where kids can frolic on a giant play structure with tunnel-slides or get lost in a hedge labyrinth.

Yerba Buena Gardens

👥 Children's Creativity Museum

221 4th St. ⏱Open Wed–Sun 10am–4pm. ⏱For holiday closures, call or consult website. ⬦$12.95 ✕🚹 ☏415-820-3320. www.creativity.org.

Housed in a zany round building by architect Adele Naude Santos, this museum is a multimedia arts center for kids. Inside the Main Gallery you'll find a sampling of high- and low-tech tools to make digital music and videos, and to put on digital puppet shows. Creature costumes are provided so kids can be the stars. On other floors children can make a Claymation film with their own clay figures, play on a computer-generated maze and create digital art. Many of the exhibits involve making souvenirs (CDs, DVDs, artwork) to take home. Just outside the entrance, the illuminated, glass-enclosed **LeRoy King Carousel★** (⏱open 10am–5pm; ⬦$4 for two rides) features a menagerie of hand-carved animals. It was constructed in by Charles Looff in 1906 in Rhode Island.

👥 Yerba Buena Ice Skating & Bowling Center

750 Folsom St. at 3rd St. ⏱Open daily 10am–10pm; public-access hours vary depending on activity, day and season; call or visit website. ⬦Varies depending on day and season; call or visit website. ☏415-820-3532. www.skatebowl.com.

This 12-lane bowling alley and NHL-regulation indoor ice-skating rink offer hours of diversion. Skating lessons and skate rentals are available at the rink.

SAN FRANCISCO MUSEUM OF MODERN ART★★

151 3rd St. ⏱Open Fri–Tue 10am–5.00pm, Thu until 9pm. ⏱Closed Thanksgiving and Christmas Day. ⬦$25. ☞Guided tours available daily; ✕ ☏415-357-4000. www.sfmoma.org.

San Francisco's premier showcase for modern art is housed in a delightful building that seems to gaze benignly out over Yerba Buena Center for the Arts. Together these institutions form the creative heart of the district.

A BIT OF HISTORY

The present-day museum grew out of a group that started in 1871 as The San Francisco Art Association, a crew of artists and art lovers that was determined to promote artistic appreciation in the Bay Area. From 1935 until 1995, the museum was housed in the War Memorial Veterans Buildin, where it gained a reputation for presenting new and challenging works, organizing the first solo exhibitions of works by then-unknown artists Arshile Gorky, Clyfford Still, Jackson Pollock, Robert Motherwell and Mark Rothko. In 1988, the board of trustees initiated massive fund-raising efforts to construct a new home for the museum in Yerba Buena Gardens, as part of a citywide effort to revitalize the dilapidated area around Mission Street.

The Mario Botta Years – Swiss architect Mario Botta designed the museum building that opened in 1995. His striking design—a symmetrically arranged,

189

five-story stepped-back, redbrick building pierced in the center by a massive shaft and set off by stripes of alternating black and white stone—ushered in a new modern era for SFMOMA. Botta created a huge slanted skylight, and this oculus quickly became the museum's most recognizable and talked about architectural feature. Botta, who studied and worked extensively in Italy, envisioned the museum's interior street level as a modern-day piazza. He paved the space in alternating bands of polished and unpolished black marble and finished it with stone columns and two grand staircases.

Snøhetta and A New Architectural Design – The museum eventually grew out of its Botta-designed building. The museum needed to be able to better accommodate its burgeoning collection, which now included long-term loan of 1,100 works by leading postwar and contemporary artists from Gap founders Donald and Doris Fisher. After failing to win approval to build their own museum, the couple struck a deal to show it at SFMOMA.

Norwegian-American firm Snøhetta's design simultaneously integrates and maintains the most beloved elements of Botta's 1995 redbrick building, while nearly tripling its gallery space. The most striking feature of the Snøhetta expansion is its new eastern façade, a sloping white ten-story tower located just behind the original Botta building. Inspired by the fog and water of the San Francisco Bay, it's clad in more than 700 fiberglass-reinforced polymer panels, each uniquely shaped and studded with crystals, affixed to a curtain-wall system to create rippling horizontal bands.

In designing the interior of the museum, Snøhetta embraced the Norwegian lifestyle concept of *hygge*, loosely translated as "coziness," by creating what partner Craig Dykers described as "palate-cleansers," spaces where museumgoers can step aside and take a break. Warrens of intimate galleries and interpretative spaces offer visitors an opportunity to explore the collection on a human scale.

The New Collections – The expanded SFMOMA opened with exhibitions of 260 works of postwar and contemporary art from the Fisher Collection, more than 600 pieces on view for the first time, recent works commissioned for the museum, and favorites from its permanent collection. SFMOMA is now a truly world-class modern art museum. Its permanent collection of painting and sculpture represents all major movements of modern art, with significant strengths in early Modernism and works by California artists. The vastly expanded photography center houses a stellar collection featuring Alfred Stieglitz, Ansel Adams, Imogen Cunningham and other members of the Group f.64. The museum continues to shine in architecture and design, with collections from Swiss-French architect Le Corbusier and American designers Charles and Ray Eames.

VISIT

The museum offers 45,000 square feet of art-filled public spaces, free and open to all. To go into the museum, visitors must buy a ticket at www.sfmoma.org or from the second-floor ticket counter. It's nearly impossible to see everything in one go. Plan your visit using the free

HOWL, eon (I, II) (2017) by Julie Mehretu installed at San Francisco Museum of Modern Art

SFMOMA app (for iOS), which provides immersive, location-aware recordings that provide excellent insights into the collection. Connect to the museum's free WiFi and download the app (sfmoma.org/app). In addition to self-guided tours, the museum offers free public tours with various focuses (architecture, contemporary art, photography and featured exhibitions) several times a day.

There are two sets of elevators: The red elevators go only to the building's original five floors; the silver elevators access all galleries. If you're able, walk up or down a few of Snøhetta's asymmetrical staircases, which reward the effort with city views and unusual vantage points back into the building itself. Bathrooms are located on every floor, each painted a different vibrant color.

Atrium

First-time visitors are advised to enter via Third Street, where they can best experience Botta's original atriuma which leads to an expanded museum shop, theater, and the stylish restaurant In Situa, helmed by Michelin-starred chef Corey Lee. (*$$$. No ticket required.* ⏰*Open for lunch Thu-Mon 11am-3:30pm and dinner Thu-Sat 5pm-9pm and Sun 5pm-8pm*). Take a moment to gaze at the iconic oculus and the two giant paint-

ings by Julie Mehretu, commissioned for the space as part of SFMOMA's new commissioning program; they debuted in September 2017 and will be on view for several years. A second entrance through the sculpture terrace on Howard Street offers visitors a closer vantage of the glittery new façade, along with a peek into the ground floor gallery.

Second Floor

A good place to begin is in the Open Ended exhibition, a changing presentation of works from the SFMOMA collection; works follow a loosely chronological path from the beginning of the 20th century to the present. Presented in chapters, this exhibition focuses on historical periods, geographical places, shared sets of ideas and relationships between artists.

Works may change, but highlights of the collection include Henri Matisse's *Femme au chapeau* (Woman with a Hat) (1905), Georges Braque's *Violin and Candlestick* (1910), and Mark Rothko's *No. 14* (1960). You may find Jackson Pollock's immensely influential *Guardians of the Secret* (1943), Robert Smithson's *Nonsite* (Essen Soil and Mirrors) (1969), Robert Rauschenberg's *Automobile Tire Print* (1953), and Frida Kahlo's detailed portrait of herself and her husband, *Frieda and Diego Rivera* (1931), which she painted for museum trustee Albert Bender, her friend and patron. Other notable artists showcased here include Jasper Johns, Robert Rauschenberg, James Rosenquist, Picasso, Joan Míro, and Georgia O'Keeffe. There is also small gallery that rotates through the museum's works by Paul Klee, and another focused on the art of Northern California artists such as Richard Diebenkorn, David Park, and Bruce Connor.

Third Floor

Anchoring this floor is the Pritzker Center for Photography, which holds a whopping 17,800 pieces, including works by mid-20C American masters such as Ansel Adams, Diane Arbus, Margaret Bourke-White, Robert Mapplethorpe, and Alfred Stieglitz, as well as new works from artists like Cindy Sherman, Larry Sultan and Henry Wessel. The Japanese photography collection is particularly impressive.

Connecting the galleries is an innovative Photography Interpretive Gallery★ featuring self-directed activities such as "selfie" photogram stations and interactive video installations.

Take a few minutes to check out the museum's graphic design gallery before heading to one of the museum's most impressive outdoor sculpture terrace, where two massive sculptures by Alexander Calder and others are set against the backdrop of a verdant 4,400-square-foot green wall. Comprised of over 19,000 plants, including 21 species native to California, and supported by a recycled water irrigated system, it is currently the largest living wall in the United States.

Fourth Floor

This is one of the many gallery spaces displaying a rotating selection of works from the Fisher Collection by European and American artists. In luscious paint strokes, luminous planes of uniform color and dynamic constructions of wood and metal, the nearly 80 paintings and sculptures assembled illustrate artists' individual ideas about the making and meaning of abstract art. Highlights

include works by Lee Krasner, Martin Puryear, Ellsworth Kelly, Joan Mitchell and Cy Twombly. Before moving on, duck into the octagonal-shaped gallery devoted to paintings by Canadian-American Agnes Martin.

Fifth Floor

Painters and sculptors working in the 1960s and beyond that are associated with Pop, Minimalism and Figurative movements are featured here. Pieces are drawn from the Fisher Collection and the museum's permanent collection and include luminaries like Dan Flavin, Donald Judd, Sol LeWitt, Roy Lichtenstein, Claes Oldenburg, Andy Warhol and Chuck Close. Warhol and Close have intimate galleries dedicated solely dedicated to their work.

Down the hall is a light-filled sculpture gallery.

In addition to art viewing, this floor offers visitors two unique destinations. Don't miss the chance to walk across the Botta-designed **Oculus Bridge★★**, a dramatic catwalk-like steel turret bride that stretches out across the atrium. On the other side of the building, Cafe 5, serves a menu of lighter fare with a California-fusion slant.

Sixth Floor

This level demarcates the start of the new Snøhetta building. It's also where you'll find the crown jewel of the Fisher Collection—selections of its renowned post-war German art. Intimate galleries entirely devoted to Anselm Kiefer, Gerhard Richter, Sigmar Polke and Georg Baselitz will give you excuse to linger. The higher ceilings here allow for showing artworks of a larger magnitude. You'll also find a gallery displaying a rotating collection of pieces from the architecture and design departments' holdings.

Seventh Floor

Many visitors prefer to take the silver elevators to the top floor and then wend their way back down, taking in along the way the city views from the sculpture garden terraces. The terrace facing east

Alexander Calder gallery

Photo: © Iwan Baan, courtesy SFMOMA

offers knock-out views of the surrounding cityscape. This is also the best place to view the Snøhetta building itself; you can actually touch the façade's curtain wall surface.

Tucked away on this floor are a series of loft-like galleries displaying exhibitions of contemporary art.

ADDITIONAL SIGHTS
PacBell Building★
140 New Montgomery St.
⊶ Not open to the public.
This 30-story building (1925, Timothy Pflueger) was the only skyscraper south of Market for decades. It retains an elegant terra-cotta facade and brass doorways topped by ogee arches. The elegant **lobby★** features black marble walls, columns, and an intricate plaster ceiling with Asian motifs.

California Historical Society
678 Mission St. ☏415-357-1848.
◷ Open Tue–Sun 11am–5pm.
◷ Closed Jan 1, Thanksgiving, Dec 25.
☞$10. ♿ ☏415-357-1848.
www.californiahistoricalsociety.org.
The state's official historical research organization, founded in the late 19C, holds an extensive collection of books, photographs, periodicals, posters, and other artifacts chronicling California's colorful, rambunctious past. It maintains a library *(◷Wed–Fri 1pm–5pm)*, a public gallery with changing thematic exhibits, and a specialty bookshop.

St. Patrick's Catholic Church (F)
756 Mission St. ◷ Open daily 9am–1pm, 2pm-5pm. ♿ ☏415-421-3730.
www.stpatricksf.org.
Founded by Irish immigrants during the golden days of 1851, St. Patrick's first red brick church was erected on this site in 1872, and served working-class families through the late 19C. Destroyed by the quake and fire of 1906, it was rebuilt in 1909 in Gothic Revival style using many of the original bricks. Fire scars still mark some walls. Green-veined Irish marble lines the vestibule; stained-glass windows depict scenes from the life of St. Patrick; even the vestments are embroidered with Celtic patterns. Ironically, the congregation is now largely Filipino in ancestry, with a mass held in the Tagalog language daily.

Museum of the African Diaspora
685 Mission St. ◷ Open Wed–Sat 11am–6pm, Sun noon–5pm. ◷ Closed major holidays. ☞$10. ♿ ☏415-358-7200. www.moadsf.org.
Opened in 2005, this vibrant three-story museum explores the history, art, and culture of people of African heritage throughout the world, hewing in general to four universal themes in its permanent exhibits: origins, movement, adaptation and transformation. A Smithsonian affiliate, it frequently mounts high-quality contemporary-

art exhibitions, often showing work by groups who are underrepresented in traditional museums, in addition to hosting an artist-in-residence program and emerging-artist program to help nurture Bay Area creative talent.

Contemporary Jewish Museum

736 Mission St. ⏰*Open Thu-Tue 11am–5pm.* 👣*Tours Mon, Fri, Sat 11.30pm, Fri-Tue 11.30am & 1.30pm, Thu 1.30pm & 5.30pm, Sun 1.30pm.* ⏰*Closed Jewish holidays, Jan 1, Thanksgiving Day.* ♿🚭*$14, free 1st Tue of month.* 📞*415-655-7800. www.thecjm.org.*

This award-winning museum explores Jewish history and culture through a series of rotating exhibits, often showcasing contemporary art. Established in 1984, it maintains strong community ties via ongoing educational programs and a robust program of special events. The $50 million renovation of its new home (opened in June 2008), the Jessie Street Power Substation (1907, Willis Polk), was overseen by renowned architect Daniel Libeskind. The onsite deli Wise Sons serves traditional Jewish comfort food (museum admission not required.)

Millenium Tower

301 Mission St. 🔒*Not open to the public.*

Completed in 2008, the city's tallest residential building is a glassy skyscraper with multimillion-dollar penthouses overlooking the bay. In 2016, it made news after its developers disclosed that the building is both sinking and tilting in the soft subsoil beneath downtown San Francisco. Despite this rather dubious claim to fame, the building is worth noting for its shiny late-modernist design by Handel Architects, who also designed the World Trade Center Memorial in New York City.

Salesforce Tower

415 Mission St., Salesforce.com

Even before this certified LEED Platinum skyscraper opened its doors in 2018, its glassy façade and obelisk-esque silhouette had changed San Francisco's skyline dramatically. Its construction also signaled the start of a new era for increasingly populated and increasingly vertical San Francisco. The tallest building in the city, its 61 stories tower over the Transamerica Pyramid. Every night, its top floors are lit by 11,000 LED lights in an installation by artist Jim Campbell. From the "Ohana Floor" at the top of the building there are sweeping views of the Bay Area; though not open at press time, the Ohana Floor will be accessible to the public during select hours in 2019.

Salesforce Transit Center

South of Mission St. between Second St. and Beale St. ⏰*Park open Nov.-April 6am-8pm, May-Oct 6am-9pm. www.sfmta.com* ♿

A six-story transit hub spanning three city blocks, the Salesforce Transit Center was designed not just as a bus terminal but as an innovative public space. Its striking façade, comprised of almost 4,000 perforated aluminum panels, was part of Pelli Clarke Pelli Architects' design, which incorporates several important works of public art, including an LED display by Jenny Holzer. A major hub for MUNI, it will eventually link San Francisco to Los Angeles by high-speed rail.

For visitors, the highlight is the undulating 5.4-acre rooftop park, which is filled with mature trees, lawns, fountains, and benches. At press time, the transit center was closed for structural review.

ADDRESSES

RECREATION

$ SPIN – *690 Folsom St.* 📞*415-636-5995. wearespin.com.* This colorful Ping-Pong social club serves bar snacks, cocktails, and 12 tables for playing. It's kid-friendly till 9pm.

On the far western edge of the city, the oceanfront's stunning natural setting is its most enduring attraction. Beach-goers sunbathe and surf; hikers weave along wild, windswept bluffs; hang-gliders flock to Fort Funston; and music lovers picnic in Sigmund Stern Memorial Grove during free summer concerts. The Legion of Honor, the city's premier fine arts museum, spreads its colonnaded wings towards the Golden Gate from its spectacular perch in Lincoln Park. Adolph Sutro's former estate and Sutro Baths afford a glimpse into the past and sweeping views of the ocean. At the southern edge of the broad Sunset District, which spreads below Golden Gate Park, the 125-acre San Francisco Zoo attracts nearly one million visitors each year.

An Oceanfront Transformation

In 1881 "Comstock King" Adolph Sutro returned to San Francisco after making a fortune on the silver of Nevada's Comstock Lode (the first major U.S. discovery of silver and gold ore). Touring San Francisco's oceanfront on a leisurely buggy ride, Sutro chanced upon a commanding site with spectacular views and bought it immediately. While the sharp investor would eventually come to own one twelfth of all property in San Francisco—including hundreds of acres of windswept sand dunes between downtown and the ocean—he chose to make this plot his home, landscaping the grounds with imported, drought-resistant plants, decorating with hundreds of statues, and then opening the grounds to the public.

Sutro transformed San Franciscans' experience with the westernmost part of their city. He bought up the oceanfront Cliff House, which had been spoiled by a fire and an unfavorable reputation, and replaced it with an ornate castle of restaurants, galleries, parlors, private lunch rooms and panoramic views. He also built a railway that, for five cents, transported passengers from downtown to the enormously popular Sutro Baths. Completed in 1894, these baths included seven saltwater swimming pools (each with its own slide), 500 private dressing rooms and bleacher seating for 5,300.

With Sutro's lush estate, railway, baths and Cliff House, the oceanfront became a favorite leisure destination for pleasure-seeking San Franciscans.

At the time of Sutro's shorefront revitalization, the Sunset District was a windswept region of sand dunes. Developer

Highlights

1 A summer picnic at **Stern Grove** with free music (p196)

2 Watching the hang-gliders at **Fort Funston** (p198)

3 A sunset dinner with sweeping ocean views at **Cliff House** (p201)

4 Hiking the breezy **Coastal Trail** (p202)

5 Seeing one of the finest **Rodin collections** outside Paris (p205)

Aurelius Buckingham built the first row of houses on present-day Lincon Way in 1887, but it wasn't until the 1930s, with the completion of the Twin Peaks Tunnel, that a building frenzy was ignited. The 1930s also saw the initial plans designed for the San Francisco Zoo, as well as the 3-acre Sigmund Stern Memorial Grove presented to the city as a park in 1931 by Rosalie Stern in memory of her husband, who had gone on to become mayor of the city.

In the 1970s much of San Francisco's west coast, including Ocean Beach, Sutro Heights and Land's End, were acquired by the National Park Service as part of the Golden Gate National Recreation Area (GGNRA).

Today, San Franciscans still flock to these sites for leisure activities, enjoying dinner with a panoramic view at the restored Cliff House, visiting the enduring Legion of Honor at its stunning Lincoln Park perch, and touring Sutro's former estate and the ruins of the Sutro Baths.

Sunset District and Lake Merced

The Sunset District encompasses a broad, flat grid of regularly spaced residential streets with row after orderly row of tract houses. Most attractions lie along the coast or scattered around natural Lake Merced in San Francisco's southwesternmost corner.

A BIT OF HISTORY

Part of the wind and fog-scoured expanse of sand dunes known as the Outer Lands during the city's early decades, the Sunset is today a wind and fog-scoured expanse of stucco row houses erected after construction of a streetcar tunnel under Twin Peaks, opened the area in the 1930s. During the ensuing building frenzy, contractors raced each other along the newly platted streets to throw up mass-produced row houses. Although derided by architectural critics, the bungalows offered the possibility of home ownership to people of less-than-substantial means. The Sunset's two most interesting neighborhoods, **Forest Hill** *(east end of Taraval St.)* and **St. Francis Wood** *(east end of Sloat Blvd.)*, predate the Twin Peaks tunnel. The Sunset District harbors the main campus of San Francisco State University and the medical center of the University of California at San Francisco. On the district's southern border is Lake Merced, a recreation destination for its golf course and biking and running trails. The area's most visible landmark is the city's tallest structure, **Sutro Tower,** a pronged, red-and-white-striped television transmitter atop Mt. Sutro, which rises above the district on the northeast.

SIGHTS

⚎ Ocean Beach★

Great Highway from Balboa St. to Fort Funston. www.nps.gov.

This expansive beach creates a broad, sandy seam between the city and the

🚍 Bus 18-46th Ave., 23-Monterey, 28-19th Ave., 29-Sunset, or 48-Quintara-24th St.; streetcar L-Taraval, M-19th Ave., or N-Judah, 511.org.

ℹ **Info:** www.sftravel.com.

▶ **Location:** The Sunset District extends south from Golden Gate Park and from the Pacific coast inland to about Stanyan Street.

⚎ **Kids:** The San Francisco Zoo, of course, but also the intriguing Cayuga Playground.

🕐 **Timing:** Fog shrouds the area pretty much round-the-clock; try an early-afternoon visit if you wish to avoid it.

🅿 **Parking:** Sights have parking lots, except for Sigmund Stern Grove.

😊 **Don't Miss:** A stop at Fort Funston to see hang-gliders taking off.

Pacific Ocean. Pounding surf and a dangerous undertow make swimming here unwise, although surfers often paddle out from the beach at the foot of Taraval Street. A paved **promenade**, landscaped with dune-stabilizing grasses and shrubs, extends north 3mi from Sloat Boulevard to just south of Cliff House, making the beach popular with bikers and runners.

Sigmund Stern Memorial Grove

19th Ave. and Sloat Blvd.

😊 *There is no public parking lot, and street parking is limited.* 🕐*Open daily sunrise–sunset.* ✕🅿 𝒫*415-252-6252. www.sterngrove.org.*

Presented to the city as a park in 1931 by Rosalie Stern in memory of her husband Sigmund, this 33-acre sylvan "grove" lies at the bottom of an east-west-running ravine. Redwoods and fragrant eucalyptus trees hem the sides of the narrow valley surrounding Stage Meadow, which forms a natural amphitheater. Free musical performances are staged as part of a popular, long-running concert series endowed by Mrs. Stern in 1938. Music lovers of every stripe bring blankets and picnic fare to enjoy concerts in a range of musical styles from jazz to opera. Just east of Stage Meadow sits the dignified, Victorian **Trocadero** (1892), built by earlier landowner George M. Greene and popular as a saloon before Prohibition.

♣♣ San Francisco Zoo & Gardens★

Sloat Blvd. at 45th Ave. ◐*Open daily 10am–4pm.* ⊗*$22, children 4–14 $16.* ✖🅿 ✎*415-753-7080. www.sfzoo.org.*
Set on 100 acres on the southern fringe of the Sunset District, San Francisco Zoo & Gardens attracts almost one million visitors each year. Its original plan took shape in the 1930s with Works Progress Administration buildings. Over the years, many updates to exhibits, structures and gardens have kept the zoo looking and feeling current.
In 1997, San Franciscans approved a $48 million bond to rebuild two-thirds of the zoo by 2004, focusing on more naturalistic habitats for its 1,000 denizens. The Lipman Family Lemur Forest debuted In 2002, harboring five species of this primate from Madagascar. In 2004, the zoo introduced a three-acre African Savanna exhibit with giraffes, zebras, kudus and ostriches. Grizzly Gulch opened in 2007, providing a spacious habitat and incredible viewing opportunities for the public. The South American Tropical Rainforest and Aviary opened in 2015, completely transforming a WPA building to house a wide variety of birds and reptiles. In 2016, the zoo introduced Mexican gray wolves to Wolf Canyon and built a habitat for a leaping species of lemur known as sifaka.

Visit

Just past the entrance, the **Children's Zoo** features meerkats and prairie dogs, an insect zoo, terrariums at kids' eye level, and a petting barnyard where human youngsters can make friends with domestic animals. Admire the

*Sumatran Tiger,
San Francisco Zoo and Gardens*

Chilean flamingos, then continue to the superb **Primate Discovery Center★**, where 15 species of rare and endangered monkeys and prosimians cavort and swing in open atriums. A spur trail leads to **Jones Family Preserve**, a lushly landscaped, one-acre domain home to a six-member society of lowland gorillas.
For a glimpse of animal life below the Equator, stroll left from the main entrance to the Australian Walkabout, an outdoor habitat for kangaroos, wallabies, wallaroos and emus. Nearby are **Koala Crossing**, patterned after an Outback station, and **Puente al Sur** ("Bridge to the South"), featuring Latin American creatures like capybaras, giant anteaters, and guanacos. At **Hearst Grizzly Gulch**, watch a pair of grizzly bear sisters swim and fish *(◐feedings daily 10:30am)*. Stop by the nearby Wolf Canyon to check out three wolf brothers who are helping rebuild the population of endangered Mexican gray wolves. Visitors to **Penguin Island** can view the world's most successful breeding colony of Magellanic penguins. Detour to the **black rhinoceros** enclosure which recently lost beloved member Elly, one of the most prolific breeders in the country: she gave birth to more than a dozen calves, many of them moved to other zoos to contribute to the captive gene

pool. Stop by the sifaka exhibit to see how these endangered lemurs effortlessly leap and jump great distances. Before departing, take a spin around the track on **Little Puffer** (≈$5), a miniature turn-of-the-20C steam train gleamingly restored and brought back from premature retirement.

Fort Funston

Enter from Rte. 35 (Skyline Blvd.) just south of John Muir Dr. Bus 18-46th Ave. 415-561-4323.

This expansive former military post overlooking the Pacific Ocean was established in 1898 during the Spanish-American War but never tested in combat. The fort was renamed in 1917 in honor of General Frederick Funston, the Presidio co-commandant who organized military forces to maintain order in San Francisco in the aftermath of the 1906 earthquake and fire. With the approach of World War II, heavy cannonry was installed; Battery Richmond Davis, built in 1938, held two 16in guns. In a strategy worthy of Lewis Carroll, destination-less "roads" were created within Funston's grounds at this time to confound any invaders arriving by sea. Today the former military lands (decommissioned in 1963) are managed by the Golden Gate National Recreation Area as a 250-acre park. Ice plants cloak the dunes atop bluffs that rise 200ft above a clean sand beach; these dunes are considered among the finest hanggliding spots in the U.S. Visitors gather on a viewing deck to watch the aerialists in flight. The north end of the park is a stopover for migratory Central and South American bank swallows, which burrow into the bluffs and nest there from April through July. At that time, the habitat is closed to public visitation.

Visit

The scenic **Sunset Trail** *(.75mi)* meanders atop the windswept dunes and past Battery Davis before looping back to the parking lot. Long-distance hikers may link this trail to other sections of the Coastal Trail for a 4.7mi walk to Cliff House.

San Francisco State University

1600 Holloway Ave. at 19th Ave. Bus 18-46th Ave. or 29-Sunset; streetcar M-19th Ave. 415-338-1111. www.sfsu.edu. Founded in 1899 as a teacher-training college, this was the first normal school in the U.S. to require a high-school diploma for admission. The college had a high national profile during the late 1960s, as student protests against racial discrimination, the Vietnam War, the military draft and "irrelevant" college classes culminated in November 1968 in the longest campus strike in history. Acting university president S.I. Hayakawa refused to give in to the students, and strife finally ended in March 1969 with both sides claiming victory. A lasting legacy was the establishment of the nation's first School of Ethnic Studies and an expanded Black Studies Department. Today the 141-acre campus claims more than 30,000 students.

An emphasis on multiculturalism is evident at the **Fine Arts Gallery** *(Fine Arts Building, 1600 Holloway Ave., Room 238; Open Tue–Fri 11am–4pm; closed major holidays and school recess; 415-338-6535. gallery.sfsu.edu.),* whose changing exhibits feature contemporary art, historical examinations of diverse California art, and student art. Two Ruth Asawa sculptures flank the lobby. Inquire in the gallery for a map to campus sculptures.

The Poetry Center and American Poetry Archives *(Humanities Bldg., 1600 Holloway Ave open Mon–Thu 10am–6pm; closed major holidays; 415-338-2227. poetry.sfsu.edu.),* founded in 1954 with a gift from W.H. Auden, harbors the world's largest videotaped collection of poets and authors reading their own works—more than 2,000 in all. It hosts more than 30 readings and lectures each year. The **Sutro Library** *(1630 Halloway Ave, room 610; open Mon–Fri 10am–4pm; closed major holidays; 415-469-6100. library.sfsu.edu),* located on the fifth and sixth floor of the J. Paul Leonard Library, contains Adolph Sutro's collection of 90,000 rare books and 100,000 pamphlets, as well as several hundred Japanese ukiyo-e woodblock prints, Shakespeare folios, and antique maps, among other treasurse.

👥 Cayuga Playground

Cayuga & Naglee Aves., one block west of Alemany Blvd. 🚍 *Bus 29-Sunset.*
This urban oasis, the work of gardener Demetrio Braceros, uplifts an otherwise-downtrodden neighborhood. From the stumps of fallen trees, Braceros carved likenesses of the Virgin Mary and Jesus, Michael Jordan, Princess Diana and others, including a menagerie of animals. He also wove branches into fences, railings and benches; designed two walking paths, the Garden of Eden Trail and the New Trail of Hope; planted flowers, vegetables and fruit trees, and inscribed rocks with inspirational messages.

Sutro Heights and Land's End★★

The rugged northwest corner of San Francisco, between Ocean Beach and Lincoln Park, has drawn visitors to its rocky cliffs and sheltered coves since Ohlone Indians camped here. Comprising ghostly ruins, a historical roadhouse, trails and breathtaking views, this stretch of the Golden Gate National Recreation Area (GGNRA) provides an impressive natural refuge. Its highlight is the Legion of Honor, San Francisco's preeminent repository for European art, which enjoys a spectacular setting amid the Monterey pines and cypresses of Lincoln Park, overlooking the rugged shores of the Golden Gate.

A BIT OF HISTORY

Settlement came slowly to San Francisco's coastline. In the early days of the gold rush, a few intrepid Europeans tried to homestead here, but it wasn't until the mid-1850s that Seal Rock House, an early precursor to today's Cliff House, was constructed near the shore, drawing city dwellers on Sunday beach outings. In the mid-1860s, prominent San Francisco families adopted the area as their summer playground. However, in the last two decades of the 19C the area lost its upper-class cachet, largely thanks to a populist-minded entrepreneur.

🚍 Bus 18–46th Ave. or 38–Geary, 511.

ℹ️ **Info:** 📞415-561-4323. www.parksconservancy.org.

🧭 **Location:** The area occupies the northwestern corner of the city. Paths lace the unspoiled green expanses; a golf course lies in the southeastern corner of Lincoln Park.

👥 **Kids:** The Camera Obscura provides a fun science lesson.

🕐 **Timing:** The Cliff House has a wall of west-facing windows overlooking the ocean. Views are particularly glorious at sunset.

🅿️ **Parking:** Spaces just in front of Cliff House tend to fill quickly, but lots may be found above Sutro Baths on Merrie Way; across Point Lobos Avenue from Merrie Way; and at Fort Miley beside the USS *San Francisco* memorial. There is also parking at the Legion of Honor.

😊 **Don't Miss:** A hike along the Coastal Trail; the walk is bracing but not difficult, and the views are stellar. Wear sturdy shoes.

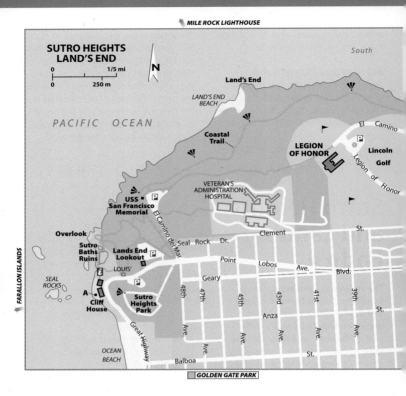

Sutro Baths

Adolph Sutro's most beloved contribution to San Francisco was the fabulous Sutro Baths, an elaborate and luxurious public swimming facility the millionaire erected among the rocks below his Sutro Heights estate. In 1891, construction began on the three-story, glass-domed structure, designed to utilize tidal ebb and flow to fill and empty its pools. After its completion in 1894, citizens paid 5 cents to travel out to the baths on Sutro's own railroad. From the Greek-inspired entrance portal, they descended a grand stairway bounded by palm trees to a cavernous main hall with seven saltwater swimming pools, ranging in temperature from bathwater-warm to ocean-cold. Patrons could change into rented woolen swimming suits in one of 500 private dressing rooms, lounge on bleachers seating 5,300 people, dine in any of three restaurants, or simply wonder at an astounding display of curiosities collected by the Comstock King. There were seven slides, one for each pool, and 30 swinging rings strung above the 1.8 million gallons of water.

Despite their enormous popularity, the baths operated at a financial loss, and in 1934 Sutro's heirs covered part of the swimming pools with a skating rink and basketball courts. After World War II, the deteriorated pools were closed. The skating rink continued to operate until 1966, when plans were made to demolish the structure and build apartments on the site. A fire of unexplained origin hastened the building's demise but the apartments were never built and the National Park Service acquired the property in 1980.

The Comstock King – In 1851, Prussian-born **Adolph Sutro** (1830–98) arrived in San Francisco in search of Gold Rush riches. After establishing himself as a tobacconist, the self-educated engineer relocated in 1860 to Virginia City, Nevada, where fortunes were being made from the Comstock Lode's silver. Mining proved treacherous due to poor ventilation and water in the shafts, so Sutro designed a 4 mile-long passage beneath the silver vein, wrangling for nearly 15 years with banks, mine owners and investors over funds. When the Sutro Tunnel finally opened, its engineer was dubbed the Comstock King.

A shrewd businessman, Sutro sold his shares in the tunnel just prior to the crash of the mine stock in 1880. Returning to San Francisco, he quickly invested his fortune in land, eventually coming to own one twelfth of all the property in the city, including hundreds of acres of windswept sand dunes between downtown and the ocean. His enormously popular Sutro Baths, his lush estate atop Sutro Heights, his five-cent railway and his rebuilt Cliff House ballooned the oceanfront's fame as a favorite leisure destination for pleasure-seeking San Franciscans of every economic stripe.

A Popular Playland – By 1921 a beach-side entertainment zone of dance halls and rides had sprung up between Sutro Heights and Golden Gate Park. Renamed **Playland-at-the-Beach** in 1928, the strip resounded with shrieks of pleasure from the Big Dipper roller coaster and sprightly music from a Looff carousel (*since restored and moved to the Rooftop at YERBA BUENA GARDENS*). Streetcars brought revelers from downtown to whoosh down the Fun House slide and munch on hot dogs and ice-cream cookie sandwiches.

By the mid-20C Playland had fallen into seediness; it succumbed to the wrecking ball in 1972. In the mid-1970s much of San Francisco's west coast, including Ocean Beach, Sutro Heights and Land's End, were acquired by the National Park Service as part of the GGNRA. Today this region's dramatic natural beauty has again become its central attraction.

SUTRO HEIGHTS
Cliff House★★

1090 Point Lobos Ave. ✕ ♿ 🅿 *415-386-3330. cliffhouse.com.*

Renovated in the early 2000s, the historic Cliff House offers both casual and upscale dining, as well as panoramic views, from its perch atop a high bluff overlooking the Pacific Ocean.

The present building is the third incarnation of a roadhouse erected in 1863 by real-estate tycoon Charles Butler, who hoped to spark Coney Island-style development of the adjacent coastal area. By the 1880s it had acquired a reputation as a gambling hall to which "gentlemen" repaired for afternoon trysts. Adolph Sutro, who bought the property in 1881, remade it as a family resort, building the Sutro Railroad to transport the general public to and from the city.

This first Cliff House burned on Christmas Day 1894, but Sutro lost no time in hiring architects Emile Lemme and C.J. Colley to design its replacement: a flamboyant, many-spired confection resembling a French chateau. Critics decried Sutro's extravagance, but the public loved the ornate castle and its restaurants, art galleries, luxurious parlors with panoramic ocean views, private lunch rooms and observation tower 200ft above the sea. Its glory was short-lived, however—the building survived the 1906 earthquake only to succumb to fire the next year.

In 1909 the **Reid Brothers**, architects of the Fairmont Hotel (&see NOB HILL), designed the third Cliff House. It was abandoned in the mid-20C until the National Park Service acquired it in 1977. For years it housed the Musée Mécanique of antique arcade games, but in the early 2000s the museum moved to Fisherman's Wharf and the Cliff House was expanded and restored.

👥 Camera Obscura (A)

1096 Point Lobos Ave. ⏱*Open daily 11am–5pm.* ⏱*Closed rainy & foggy days.* ⬤*$3.* ♿📇 ✆*415-750-0415.*

Housed in a small building on the grounds of the Cliff House, this curious walk-in "camera" employs a mirror and two opposing lenses to magnify and project views of the surrounding area onto a 6ft parabolic screen. The motorized contraption completes a 360° rotation every 6min.

Sutro Baths Ruins★

Access by footpath from Louis' Restaurant or steps from the end of the Merrie Way parking lot. www.sutrobaths.com.

The haunting vestiges of the Sutro Baths lie in a cove just north of Cliff House. Lupine and ice plants cover the hills surrounding the concrete foundations that hardly evoke the magnificence of the structure they once supported, a giant public bath that was built in 1896 then burned to the ground in 1966.

A tunnel, which once dumped dirt from the baths, pierces the bluff to the north, leading to a stretch of craggy coastline. Above the tunnel, a path leads to an **overlook** from which the remains of long-grounded ships can be spotted.

Lands End Lookout

⏱*Open daily 9am–5pm.* ⏱*Closed Thanksgiving and Dec 25.* ♿📇 ✆*415-426-5240. https://www.nps.gov/goga/planyourvisit/landsend.htm.*

This visitor center and vista point, which opened in 2012, is perched on a rocky point overlooking the sea. Stop here to learn more about the natural and cultural history of the area and pick up a map identifying visitor highlights, trails and parking. There's also a cafe, gift shop and public restrooms.

Coastal Trail★★

🚶 *3.4mi loop from the Golden Gate Bridge to Lands End. Trail head near Cliff House. www.nps.gov/goga.*

This well-maintained path provides an invigorating walk along a wild, heavily wooded shoreline boasting spectacular **views★★★** of the ocean, the Golden Gate Bridge and the Marin Headlands. For part of its length, the lower trail follows an old railroad bed atop sheer bluffs that plunge abruptly to swirling waters. Eucalyptus trees scent the hills rising to the south, while Monterey pines and firs hold the crumbling cliffs in place. Stairs scale the steeper inclines, and smaller trails lead off the main path, one of them to the secluded Land's End Beach. The main trail, narrow and winding in places, leads to a viewing platform overlooking the posh Sea Cliff neighborhood. Descend the steps to the overlook for a lovely view of rocky Eagle's Point. The return route leads up from the overlook to follow a wide, paved berm along El Camino del Mar through the **Lincoln Park Golf Course**★ (34th Ave. and Clement St., P ℘415-221-9911). These city-owned public links, landscaped by John McLaren in 1909, boast spectacular views. Pass to the right of the Legion of Honor through a parking lot above the golf course to rejoin the footpath, which leads to the trail's end at the Fort Miley parking lot. Across from here, part of the bullet-torn bridge of the **USS San Francisco** commemorates the commander and crew of this vessel, which was heavily damaged in the naval Battle of Guadalcanal (1942).

Sutro Heights Park★

Point Lobos Ave. at 48th Ave.

The grounds of Adolph Sutro's former estate occupy a striking promontory overlooking Cliff House and Ocean Beach. Although the residence was demolished in 1939, the property remains a paradise of well-tended lawns and stately groves of distinctive trees. Sutro chanced upon the commanding site in 1881 and purchased it forthwith. The original small cottage was enlarged to a comfortable, though not opulent, country home. Sutro lavished his attention on the grounds, importing drought-resistant flowers and trees from all over the world, including Norfolk Island pines, Canary Island date palms and Monterey cypresses. He designed a wind-powered watering system, built a glass conservatory for delicate plants, and installed more than 200 statues.

Ever the populist, Sutro placed a sign at the entrance inviting the public "to walk, ride, and drive therein." After his death in 1898, Sutro's daughter Emma continued this open-door policy, bequeathing the estate to the city in 1938. In 1976, the National Park Service acquired Sutro Heights.

Two stone lions, copies of originals now housed in Park Service archives, flank the park's entrance. To the left of the

broad driveway, figures of a stag and the goddess Diana rise among the foliage. Sutro's glass conservatory (now demolished) stood to the east of the circular drive that served as a carriage turnaround. A white Victorian gazebo—originally the property's wellhouse—lies to the west on a grassy lawn where intricate carpets of brightly colored flowers once flourished.

Follow the wide dirt path past the gazebo, veering left off the main driveway to Sutro's now-overgrown viewing parapet to enjoy some of the area's finest ocean **views**★★; on the clearest days, the Farallon Islands can be spied 26mi offshore.

LEGION OF HONOR★★★

100 34th Ave., Lincoln Park. ○*Open Tue–Sun 9.30am–5.15pm.* ○*Closed Thanksgiving, Dec 25.* ⌖*$15 (free 1st Tue of the month); includes same-day admission to the de Young Museum; $2 discount for bus riders with proof.* ⌖*Docent-led guided tours available daily, free with museum admission. Audio tours $8.* ✕⌖P ℘*415-750-3600. legionofhonor.famsf.org.*

A gift to San Francisco from **Alma de Bretteville Spreckels**, this museum houses her personal collection of sculptures by Auguste Rodin, plus a treasury of European, particularly French, art, spanning some 4,000 years.

Together, the Legion of Honor and the de Young museum (⌖*see GOLDEN GATE PARK*) form the Fine Arts Museums of San Francisco.

A Bit of History

Born in San Francisco to impoverished European immigrants, Alma de Bretteville (1881–1968) inherited the energy of her hardworking mother and the imagination of her father, who instilled in her pride in the faded nobility of the French de Bretteville lineage.

Alma grew into a statuesque, willful, mostly self-educated woman who defied convention in many ways. After several years of a socially unacknowledged liaison, she married sugar magnate **Adolph Spreckels** in 1908, and in

Court of Honor floor plan:

- 7 — 18c Furniture 9a, 9b, 9c
- 8 — Rodin Sculpture
- Rodin Sculpture
- 10
- 11 — Period Ceramics, Salon Dore
- 13 — 18C - 19C British Art
- 12
- Italian, French and Spanish Mannerism and Baroque Art — 6
- 14 — Dutch and Flemish Art
- 5
- 15
- 4
- 16 — European Neoclassicism
- 3 — Temporary Exhibitions
- 17 — 19C European Art
- 2
- 18
- COURT OF HONOR — *The Thinker*
- 1 — Temporary Exhibitions
- 19 — Impressionism and Post-Impressionism
- Entrance

Pacific International Exposition's French Pavilion, itself a version of the Hôtel de Salm, a 18C Parisian residence designated by Napoleon in 1804 as the Palais de la Légion d'Honneur. On Armistice Day 1924, the new museum was dedicated to the 3,600 Californians who had perished in World War I.

The Collection – Dance-related art and European decorative arts initially formed the core of the museum's holdings, along with one of the finest collections of works by French sculptor Auguste Rodin (1840–1917) outside the Musée Rodin in Paris. Alma, introduced to Rodin in 1914, acquired many of the pieces during the artist's lifetime, when his sculptures were cast by his favorite *fondeur*, Alexis Rudier. The museum now owns 106 sculptures by Rodin, of which the most famous, *The Thinker* (1880), greets visitors in the Court of Honor.

In 1950, the Legion received the city-owned **Achenbach Foundation for Graphic Arts**.

This immensely important body of works on paper today numbers 90,000 prints, drawings, photographs, and illustrated books, including the 3,000-work

1914 she met and fell under the influence of American-born dancer Löie Fuller, the toast of Belle Epoque Paris, who convinced her to become a patron of the arts with Löie as her chief adviser. In 1915 plans to build the Legion of Honor were set into motion.

The building (1924, George Applegarth) was modeled after the 1915 Panama-

Legion of Honor

archive of Crown Point Press and special collections of theater and dance designs, Asian miniatures and prints, and early photography.

Visit

Arrayed with neoclassical symmetry around the central rotunda, the main-floor galleries present a selective, chronologically organized survey of medieval to modern European art, including paintings, sculptures, textiles and decorative arts. Large galleries on the terrace (lower) level host temporary exhibitions; works from the Achenbach Foundation for Graphic Arts; and Greek, Etruscan, Roman and Egyptian antiquities and porcelain collections.

A bookstore, cafe and theater are also located on the lower level. **Audio tours** (🎧$8) present collection highlights.

Medieval Art, Mannerism and Baroque Art

Galleries 1–5.

The progressively idealized human form and increasingly secular subject matter of High Renaissance art yielded around 1520 to the figural elongation and harsh coloring associated with Mannerism. El Greco was a master of this style: In his *St. John the Baptist* (c. 1600), a strange play of light, like that of an electrical storm, charges the picture and the elongated central figure.

The Baroque style emerged in Rome around 1600 as a conscious reaction to the artificiality of the Mannerist style, and reflects the period's scientific discoveries, such as the inventions of the telescope and microscope. Representation of movement in space and time, and a fascination with light effects and the emotional state, contribute to the style's vigor and theatricality. Worth note are the Georges de la Tour companion portraits, *Old Man and Old Woman* (c.1618); and *Samson and the Honeycomb* by Il Guercino (c.1657), which exemplifies the Baroque style with rounded forms, individualized faces, blowing trees, and a sumptuous play of light.

The Rococo Style

Galleries 6 and 7.

The Rococo style flourished in mid-18C France. Jean-Antoine Watteau, François Boucher, Jean-Honoré Fragonard and Venetian painter Giovanni Battista Tiepolo all employed a profusion of ornament, asymmetrical motifs, pastel colors and exquisite craftsmanship to create an ambience of pleasure. A **marquetry table** (1680–90) is attributed to French cabinetmaker André-Charles Boulle, who was retained by Louis XIV to create pieces to ornament Versailles.

Salon Dore

Gallery 11

The Salon Doré from the Hôtel de La Trémoille is one of the finest examples of French Neoclassical interior architecture in the United States. Richly carved and ornately gilded, it was designed during the reign of Louis XVI. As a result of being moved no fewer than seven times between 1877 and today, its appearance and presentation had been greatly changed from its original aspect.

From 2012 to 2014 curators, conservators, and architects reinstated the room's original floor plan, restored the gilding and paint, repaired and replaced key carved elements, and installed an 18th-century parquet floor, a coved ceiling, windows, and new lighting.

Rodin Sculpture

Galleries 8, 10 and 12.

Gallery 10 displays large casts of great works by Auguste Rodin, widely considered the "father of modern sculpture." Look for the justly famous *Burghers of Calais* (cast c. 1889), *The Kiss* (cast c. 1887) and *The Three Shades* (cast c. 1880). Rodin's raw, unfinished bases proclaim his struggle to wrest form and meaning from mass—a stylistic trait shared by the sculptor's inspiration, Michelangelo. Sculptures by Rodin contemporaries share gallery 12. Galleries 9 and 11 are period spaces displaying 18C furniture and ormolu-mounted ceramics. The display of works by Rodin were slated to be rearranged in a new installation in early

2017 on the occasion of the centenary of the artist's death.

18C–19C British Art
Gallery 13.
Founded in 1768, the Royal Academy of the Arts moved to elevate British painting. Guided by its president, Sir Joshua Reynolds, the academy championed history painting but also encouraged portraiture and landscape. Reynolds' *Anne, Viscountess Townshend* (1779) places the subject against a carved relief suggesting ancient Greece. By the early 19C, landscape painting, thanks in particular to Thomas Gainsborough (*Landscape with Country Carts*, c.1784) and John Constable, emerged as the primary genre. Later artists such as John Martin interpreted the elements in a more dramatic manner. Examples of *chinoiserie* decoration include a scarlet-lacquered bureau-cabinet and a commode by Pierre Langlois.

17thC European Art
Galleries 14 and 15.
Protestant Holland and Catholic Flanders split politically in the early 17C, forging divergent artistic styles. In the Netherlands, Rembrandt's school documented the citizenry and their surroundings in portraits, still lifes, landscapes and genre paintings. One fine Rembrandt painting portrays sea captain *Joris de Culerii* (1632). Artists near Flanders continued under the patronage of monarchy and Church, employing richer colors and concentrating on religious subjects. Anthony van Dyck's *Portrait of a Lady* (c.1620) communicates the aristocratic status of its subject, while *The Tribute Money* (c.1612) by Flemish master Peter Paul Rubens employs sumptuous color and drama, expressing a Counter-Reformation mission to attract the faithful. Smaller Dutch pictures, such as Willem van Aelst's remarkable still life *Flowers in a Silver Vase* (1663), detail everyday life in a commercial center, while Flemish works express a connection to aristocracy. Frans Pourbus the Younger's *Portrait of a Lady* (1591), though restrained, depicts rich, fashionable clothing.

European Neoclassicism
Gallery 16.
The excavations of Pompeii and Herculaneum in the mid-18C inspired new enthusiasm for antiquity, expressed in art through the sober elevation of civic virtue and public morality. Jacques-Louis David became a foremost exponent of the new classicism following the exhibition of his *Oath of the Horatii* at the Paris Salon of 1785; two of his paintings are in this gallery. Pierre-Henri de Valenciennes' *A Capriccio of Rome with the Finish of a Marathon* (1788) reflects the classical landscape tradition of the 17C master Poussin. Fine French silver by Martin-Guillaume Biennais and Henri Auguste is also on view here.

19C Painting and Victorian Art
Galleries 17 and 18.
Reflecting radical changes in social, political and intellectual spheres, a wide variety of artistic styles rapidly evolved during Europe in the 19C. Jean-Baptiste-Camille Corot pioneered landscapes based on sensations of light and color, influencing the Barbizon School and later the Impressionists. *Equestrian Portrait of Charles V* (c. 1814) by Théodore Géricault displays the restless searching and dash of Romanticism, and Jean-Léon Gérôme's *The Bath* (c. 1880–85) reveals a new exoticism. Tapestries by William Morris, founder of the Arts and Crafts movement in England, hang here.

Impressionism and Post-Impressionism
Gallery 19.
In the late 19C, painters began developing a new visual vocabulary to record their scrutiny of nature and contemporary life. Depicting the transient moment with spontaneous brushwork, blurred outlines and colors in vibrant interrelation, the Impressionists were rejected by the Paris Salon of 1873; in response, they mounted their own, immensely influential exhibition. Realism and themes of modern urban life absorbed artists such as Edgar Degas and Edouard Manet. Works by Pierre-August Renoir, such as *Landscape at*

Gallery 18, Legion of Honor

© Steve Whittaker/Fine Arts Museums of San Francisco

Beaulieu (1893), show the dissolution of outline into warm color. *Eiffel Tower* (1889) reveals Georges Seurat's experimentation with pointillism. Paul Cézanne's *Forest Interior* (c. 1898) anticipates Cubism, rendering a scene from more than one viewpoint.

A great wave of artistic experimentation broke over Europe soon after the beginning of the 20C, inaugurating movements such as Cubism, Futurism, German Expressionism and Surrealism. Anchored by a late Claude Monet *Water Lilies* (c. 1914–17), the gallery showcases two of Pablo Picasso's stylistic transformations; two paintings demonstrating Henri Matisse's mastery of abstract design and color; and works by other innovative 20C artists such as Georges Braque and Salvador Dalí. A black lacquer and straw table and chairs by Armand-Albert Rateau are also on view.

ADDITIONAL SIGHTS
Sea Cliff★
Enter from El Camino del Mar at 27th Ave.

Curving, sloping streets accommodate this secluded residential enclave's rolling terrain, winding among luxurious Mediterranean-style homes sheathed in brick or pale stucco. Most buildings here date from the 1920s. An early local example of planned residential development, the quiet, elegant neighborhood is one of the city's most desirable addresses.

👥 China Beach
End of Seacliff Ave. off El Camino del Mar at 27th Ave. 🅿 *Parking available at beach entrance or on El Camino del Mar.*

Fringing a gentle cove, this pleasant strip of sand is one of the few places in the city where swimming is safe, though its cold ocean waters tempt few. Sheltered from the Golden Gate's incessant winds by a jutting headland, the beach was nicknamed for Chinese fishermen who camped here in the 19C. Shower rooms, a broad deck and a small area with tables and barbecue grills make China Beach a favored place for sunning and recreation.

ADDRESSES

CAFE
$ Legion of Honor Café – 📞*415-750-7639.* Lunch on sandwiches, salads, and soups, or nibble on artisan cheeses and delicious desserts at this beautiful terrace-level cafe, with indoor and patio dining.

Vineyard, Napa Valley
© Peter Wrenn/Michelin

EAST BAY

A short hop across the San Francisco–Oakand Bay Bridge or ride on the BART from San Francisco, the neighboring cities of Berkeley and Oakland have their own charms. Berkeley is home to the storied University of California at Berkeley campus, Alice Waters' Chez Panisse restaurant, an impressive botanical garden and the lovely Tilden Park. A newly revitalized Oakland boasts a downtown with historic theaters, a thriving restaurant and gallery scene, the Oakland Museum of California, and an attractive waterfront.

Highlights

Berkeley

Synonymous with the renowned University of California at Berkeley, this bohemian college town is a small city with a big reputation for political activism. The Free Speech Movement was launched on Berkeley's campus in the 1960s, and political protests are still common here, while the concepts of green and sustainable are taken very seriously. Cruise Telegraph Avenue to experience student life, cheap eats, great book and music shops. Berkeley has long enjoyed a reputation for attracting intellectuals, idealists, and eccentrics whose diverse tastes have left their mark on the city's history, architecture and ambience. Alice Waters, a New Jersey native who graduated from UC Berkeley in 1967, changed America's food scene in 1971 when she opened Chez Panisse, which still occupies the same Arts and Crafts–style bungalow on upper Shattuck Avenue.

Oakland

Named for its expansive growth of oak trees, Oakland was incorporated in 1852 as a quiet bedroom community for the woollier metropolis across the bay. Today, this workaday city is experiencing a renaissance. Businesses have replaced vacant warehouses on downtown blocks, and new office towers and condominium communities have sprung up—with more development on the way, thanks in part to then-mayor Jerry Brown, who reinvigorated downtown with his 10K initiative. Despite some persistent problems with crime, you'll now find a wide range of ethnic restaurants, cafes, and fine-dining establishments, along with new nightclubs and bars, local farmers' markets, and revitalized shopping districts luring residents and visitors to its Downtown and Uptown neighboods, and around Lake Merritt. Another Downtown draw is Jack London Square, a sparkling, pedestrian-friendly complex of shops, restaurants, and entertainment and cultural attractions that nestles along the Oakland Estuary at the site of the once-gritty dock area. The square is named for author Jack London, who spent his early years in Oakland. One of London's favorite watering holes, Heinold's First and Last Chance Saloon, still operates as a bar, though it now ranks on the National Register of Historic Places.

Upscale Rockridge has emerged between Berkeley and Oakland to unite these two metropolitan areas: blocks of restaurants, bars, locally owned boutiques and spas are found on the streets radiating from College Ave. Near uptown, the Temescal neighborhood has also become a locus for dining, art, and nightlife in Oakland.

ADDRESSES

🏨 STAY

$$$ Hotel Durant – *2600 Durant Ave., Berkeley. ☎510-845-8981. www.hotel durant.com. 143 rooms.* You can almost hear ghosts of students past charge through this renovated six-story 1928 hotel, next to the University of California campus. Historic late-19C and early 20C photos line corridor walls.

$$$$ Claremont Hotel, Club & Spa – *41 Tunnel Rd., Berkeley. ☎510-843-3000. www.claremontresort.com. 279 rooms.* A 20-minute drive from downtown San Francisco, the fairy-tale-like Claremont Resort and Spa was considered a country getaway when it opened in 1915. Now a Farimont property, it boasts a fitness center, full-service spa, tennis club, pools and day camp for kids.

🍽 EAT

$$$$ Chez Panisse – *1517 Shattuck Ave., Berkeley. ☎510-548-5525. www.chez panisse.com. Closed Sun.* **Californian**. In 1971, California cuisine was born in the kitchen of this Craftsman-style restaurant, still owned and operated by Alice Waters. It remains a destination for food lovers today. At the main restaurant, just-picked organic greens and baby vegetables pair with free-range meat and fresh fish to create stellar prix-fixe menus. Upstairs, the more casual Café at Chez Panisse serves simpler—and less expensive—fare for bothlunch and dinner.

$$ Comal – *2020 Shattuck Ave. ☎510-926-6300. comalberkeley.com.* **Mexican**. Mexican food with a California twist has made this dinner-only Berkeley spot a new Bay Area staple, with dishes like duck enchiladas in guajillo salsa and tacos stuffed with a version of Yucatec slow-cooked pork served in the warm wood dining room. Reservations are only accepted for 5:30pm seating.

$ Cosecha – *Swan's Market, 907 Washington St. ☎510-452-5900.* **Mexican**. In historic Swan's Market in Downtown Oakland, this casual counter-service spot serves Cali-Mexican snacks, like wild shrimp tacos and handmade quesadillas stuffed with sweet potato. Other popular market eateries include izakaya **AS B-dama** ($ ☎510-251-1113) and Caribbean spot **Miss Ollie's** ($ ☎510.285.6188. www.realmissolliesoakland.com).

$$ Dyafa – *44 Webster St. ☎510-250-9491. www.dyafaoakland.com.* **Middle Eastern**. With windows overlooking the twinkling harbor in Jack London Square, this Middle Eastern spot stands out among the neighborhood's many restaurants. Pile up the table with shareable small plates of hummus, blistered asparagus, bulgur-lamb kibbes, fattoush salad, and sumac-spiced chicken.

$$ Homestead –*4029 Piedmont Ave. ☎510-420-6962. homesteadoakland.com.* **New American**. On a pretty stretch of Piedmont Ave, this cozy California-style restaurant's constantly changing dinner menu is a glory of locally inspired dishes, like quiche with nettles, fire-cooked pork, and roasted kale sprouts, as well as truly memorable sourdough bread (also a staple of their breakfast menu).

DRINK

$ New Parkway Theater *474 24th St. ☎510-658-7900. www.thenewparkway.com.* At this fun movie house in Uptown Oakland, you can watch a new or classic film in comfy couch seats or a vintage lounger accompanied by a plate of mac-and-cheese and a local craft brew.

$$$ Yoshi's – *510 Embarcadero West. ☎510-238-9200. www.yoshis.com.* One of the top spots for live music in the Bay Area, this Japanese restaurant in Jack London Square presents many of the biggest names in contemporary jazz.

Yoshi's
© Yoshi's

Berkeley★★

The ultimate college town, Berkeley is remarkable for its intellectualism, political awareness and vibrant artistic and culinary communities. The hub of the action is the University of California— known as "Cal" or UC Berkeley—which has a student body of 42,000. But other forces are at work too: Though their student days are long past, hippies and activists from the 1960s have stayed on, giving the area around Telegraph Avenue a laid-back feel. A recent tide of sophisticated San Franciscans have fueled the growth of a "Gourmet Ghetto" on Shattuck Avenue, anchored by Alice Waters' legendary Chez Panisse restaurant. For those who like to stroll or bicycle, the beautiful, tree-filled neighborhoods of Claremont, Elmwood and the North Berkeley hills are well worth exploring.

A BIT OF HISTORY

Like Oakland, the lands of present-day Berkeley pastured cattle before becoming part of Luis María Peralta's Rancho San Antonio in 1820. The land was eventually overtaken by squatters. In 1852, Francis Kittredge Shattuck subdivided lands along the middle course of Strawberry Creek into farms. The nearest town, Ocean View, sprang up more than a mile away along the bay shore. Not until the 1860s, when a site on the upper forks of Strawberry Creek was selected for an institution of higher learning, did shops and hotels begin to sprout along Shattuck's farm road, today's **Shattuck Avenue**.

In 1866 the fledgling community at the edge of the undeveloped campus was named after the Irish bishop and philosopher George Berkeley (1685–1753), author of the oft-quoted line, "Westward the course of empire takes its way." For the next four decades, after it merged with Ocean View, the town grew up steadily around "Cal," as the university is called. In the aftermath of San Francisco's great earthquake and

🚉 Berkeley station
www.actransit.org
511.org.

▶ **Population:** 122,324

📋 **Info: Berkeley Visitor Information Center** (2030 Addison St. 🕐 open Mon–Fri 9am–5pm; closed major holidays; ♿ 𝒫510-549-7040 or 800-847-4823; www.visitberkeley.com), or **UC Berkeley Koret Visitor Center** (2227 Piedmont Ave. at California Memorial Stadium; 🕐 open Mon–Fri 8.30am–4.30pm, Sat–Sun 9am-1pm; closed major holidays and on football home game days). ♿ 𝒫510-642-5215; visit.berkeley.edu).

▷ **Location:** University Ave. leads from the bayshore east to the UC campus; Shattuck Ave. runs north-south at the campus' western edge. The campus lies between the flatlands, where streets are on a grid, and the foothills, where they follow the contours of the hills.

👫 **Kids:** Tilden Park hosts a petting zoo and miniature train rides.

🕐 **Timing:** Berkeley's eateries hum day and night. Check the Berkeley Repertory Theater's schedule to catch a play.

🅿 **Parking:** The only garage on campus open to the public is located at the California Memorial Stadium, 2175 Piedmont Avenue. Most street parking is metered. We recommend taking BART to the Berkeley Station, then walk to campus.

☺ **Don't Miss:** The campanile and a stroll in the UC Berkeley botanic gardens.

SOLANO AVENUE

TILDEN REGIONAL PARK

LAKE ANZA BOTANIC GARDEN

TILDEN REGIONAL PARK

NORTH BERKELEY

CODORNICES PARK

Berkeley Municipal Rose Garden

Rose Walk

La Loma Steps

Buena Vista Way

La Vereda Rd.

Gourmet Ghetto

Lawrence Hall of Science

SPACE SCIENCES LABORATORY

4TH STREET

LAWRENCE BERKELEY LAB

UC Botanical Garden

UNIVERSITY OF CALIFORNIA, BERKELEY

THE CAMPANILE

Bancroft Way

Centennial Dr.

First Church of Christ, Scientist

People's Park

CLARK KERR CAMPUS

CLAREMONT CANYON REGIONAL PRESERVE

GARBER PARK

Judah L. Magnes Museum

ELMWOOD

Claremont Resort

BERKELEY

0   1/4 mi
0   500 m

CLAREMONT

Tunnel Rd.

OAKLAND

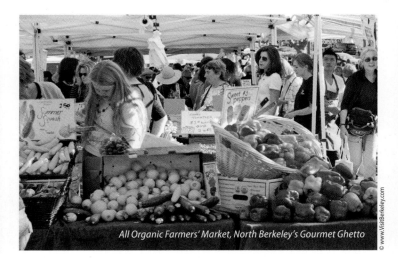

All Organic Farmers' Market, North Berkeley's Gourmet Ghetto

© www.VisitBerkeley.com

fire of 1906, a tidal wave of new settlers flooded Berkeley.

Cultural Ferment – Berkeley has long enjoyed a reputation for attracting intellectuals, idealists and eccentrics whose diverse and often highly cultivated tastes have left their mark on the city's history, architecture and ambience. While Beaux-Arts aesthetics and pockets of greenery became the hallmark of campus architecture in the early 20C, builders beyond the university property integrated leafy yards and landscaped footpaths with neighborhoods of highly original and imaginative architecture. A gastronomic version of this passion for art and nature swept Berkeley in 1971 when Alice Waters opened her famed Chez Panisse restaurant, giving rise to California Cuisine and lending the moniker **Gourmet Ghetto** to upper Shattuck Avenue *(between Rose and Virginia Sts.)*. Today Berkeley revels in its numerous fine restaurants—including a rich array of ethnic eateries—located on Shattuck and in the neighborhoods along **Solano Avenue**★ in north Berkeley, **Telegraph Avenue**★ just south of the UC campus, and behind the early 20C storefronts of the **Elmwood** shopping district *(along College Ave. at the intersection of Ashby Ave.)*. Bookstores, cinemas, cafes and craft shops also thrive in these areas.

In particular, the erstwhile industrial sector along **Fourth Street** *(north of University Ave.)* has become a popular shopping area with an upscale edge. Berkeley's penchant for idealism fueled the student protest movements of the 1960s, spreading its reputation as a hotbed of radicalism. Though now considerably mellowed from the late 70s and early 80s—when the city government cultivated its own foreign policy, promoted itself as a model for socialism, and was widely referred to as "the People's Republic of Berkeley"— the city today retains many reminders of its radical heyday.

UNIVERSITY OF CALIFORNIA, BERKELEY★★

The first and most prestigious campus of the acclaimed University of California system, UC Berkeley is noteworthy for its varied architecture and profuse landscaping, its outstanding museums and research collections, its notoriety in the 1960s and 70s as a hotbed of student activism, and its myriad contributions to human knowledge, especially in the field of nuclear physics.

A BIT OF HISTORY

The university owes its creation to clergymen scholars from the eastern U.S., led by the Rev. Samuel Hopkins Willey and the Rev. Henry Durant, who chartered the College of California in Oakland in 1854. Seeking to expand two

Campanile of UC Berkeley, San Francisco Bay in the background

© Rafael Ramirez/Fotolia.com

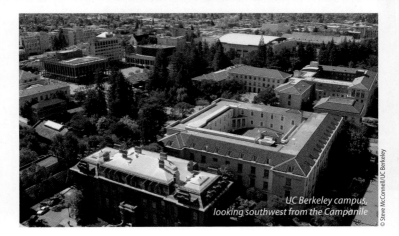

*UC Berkeley campus,
looking southwest from the Campanile*

© Steve McConnell/UC Berkeley

years later, the trustees acquired lands on the twin forks of Strawberry Creek, officially dedicating their enterprise in 1861 at **Founders' Rock (1)**, still visible on campus today *(corner of Hearst Ave. & Gayley Rd.)*.

In 1864, landscape architect Frederick Law Olmsted was commissioned to plan the college grounds and an adjacent residential neighborhood. Olmsted aligned the campus on an east-west axis, but a shortage of funds curtailed construction of this initial plan. In 1867, the college merged with the state-sponsored Agricultural, Mining and

Mechanical Arts College, and the new institution was dedicated the following year as the University of California.

Athens of the West

At the turn of the 19C, noted philanthropist and university regent **Phoebe Apperson Hearst** financed a competition to expand construction of the main campus "with landscape gardening and architecture forming one composition." Supported by Hearst's money and state funds, architect John Galen Howard set out to make Berkeley the "Athens of the West," establishing Beaux-Arts

UNIVERSITY OF CALIFORNIA, BERKELEY

Heyns Reading Room, Doe Library

© Steve McConnell/UC Berkeley

as the hallmark architectural style with a phalanx of white granite buildings sporting red-tile roofs and Neoclassical ornamentation. In the course of expansions during the first half of the 20C, campus architecture diversified with the addition of buildings by such noteworthy architects as Bernard Maybeck, Julia Morgan, George Kelham and Arthur Brown, Jr.

In addition to its 178-acre main campus, the university embraces 1,054 acres in the steep Berkeley Hills, including lands occupied by the Lawrence Berkeley Lab (⚮ *not open to the public*). Founded by Ernest O. Lawrence (1901–1958) as the Radiation Laboratory in 1936, the laboratory housed several progressively more powerful cyclotrons that fueled profound breakthroughs in 20C physics, including Glenn Seaborg's 1941 discovery of plutonium, an event that heralded the Atomic Age.

Today, with 5 undergraduate colleges and 9 graduate schools, over 2,300 fulltime faculty members and an ethnically diverse student body that numbers some 42,000, UC Berkeley ranks among the nation's leading universities. Many of its graduate programs are annually rated at or near the top of national standings, and Berkeley graduates earn more PhDs than those of any other American university. Nine Nobel laureates are among the current faculty, with seven more laureates represented in the school's alumni. The campus is an active center of culture and sport; the year's biggest sporting event is the November football game against cross-bay archrival Stanford University—called, simply, The Big Game.

VISIT

Most of UC Berkeley's buildings lie within the rectangle described by Oxford Street, Hearst Avenue, Gayley Road and Bancroft Way. Nearby paid parking garages *(www.ci.berkeley. ca.us)* include the Center Street Garage (between Shattuck and Milvia), the Allston Way Parking Garage (between Shattuck and Milvia), and the Oxford Garage (on Kittredge west of Oxford), but they are still several blocks away from campus. The parking garage at the California Memorial Stadium located on the eastern edge of campus is a better option for those with their own car as it is the only public parking garage that allows hourly parking to non-Cal Permit holders on the upper Cal Campus. Additionally, it is also adjacent to the campus's new **Visitor Center,** making it a fine place to orient yourself. The center also offers daily **guided tours** *(2227 Piedmont Ave. ℘510-642-5215).* We recommend you consider public transportation or ride-sharing services that will drop you off.

The Berkeley BART station is only one block from campus UC Berkeley runs shuttles buses Mon-Fri from the Berkeley BART station to the perimeter of the main campus and from the main campus to the Lawrence Hall of Science (℘510-642-5149,; www.pt.berkeley.edu/around/beartransit/daytime).

The Free Speech Movement

As early as the 1930s, UC students had railed against social injustice. But political events of the 50s and 60s stirred a stronger reaction and fueled Berkeley's reputation for radical behavior.

The first rumblings of the Free Speech Movement began with opposition to the House Un-American Activities Committee hearings of Sen. Joseph McCarthy and the would-be invasion of Cuba's Bay of Pigs during the Kennedy Administration. Soon civil-rights marches and Vietnam War protests catapulted the city to the forefront of national attention. On Sept. 30, 1964, the university's Board of Regents called in police to break up a peaceful sit-in demonstration by students of Sproul Plaza. Subsequent years were marked by a campaign of harsh reprisals against students who dared to declare their right to self-expression. Governor Ronald Reagan sent riot police and the National Guard to squelch demonstrations with tear-gas assaults, mass arrests and even a 17-day campus occupation.

Conflict reached its apex in spring 1969, when Berkeley residents attempted to turn an abandoned piece of university land, three blocks south of the campus, into "Power to the People Park." Trees and flowers were planted in April, but a month later, the Regents re-staked their claim by having fences built around the park. Rioting predictably ensued, with hundreds injured and one man killed by a stray bullet. The fence was not removed until 1972. People's Park is today an unstated and unspectacular memorial to that epoch.

WALKING TOUR

▶ Begin at West Gate (Oxford St. between University Ave. and Center St.).

Planted in 1877, the **Eucalyptus Grove** on the south side of University Drive contains the tallest hardwood trees in North America. Some measure nearly 200ft high.

Valley Life Sciences Building★

The largest academic building in the nation when it was completed (1930, George Kelham), this massive pseudo-Egyptian "temple" to science supports dense rows of immense pilasters; it is intriguingly decorated with bas-relief tableaux, American bison skulls, saber-tooth tiger heads, griffins and other designs. The interior houses laboratories and world-class natural-history specimen collections, including the **Museum of Paleontology★ (M1)** ♿♨(◷ *open during academic session Mon–Thu 8am–10pm, Fri 8am–5pm, Sat 1pm–5pm, Sun 1–10pm; call for hours in summer;*

♿ ✆*510-642-1821; www.ucmp.berkeley. edu).* Though only a small portion is on public display, this is one of the oldest (1921), largest and most important research collections in the country, with more than five million invertebrates and 135,000 catalogued vertebrate specimens, including the largest triceratops skull ever found, an ichthyosaur skeleton and the assembled skeleton of a *Tyrannosaurus rex.* Specimens are on view in the Wallace Atrium and on the second floor; consult the museum's website for more extensive online exhibits.

▶ Walk east of the building on the pedestrian walkway, past the flagpole. Beyond California Hall, turn uphill toward the Campanile.

Campanile Way passes among a quartet of monumental Neoclassical structures, all designed by John Galen Howard, including **California Hall (A)** (1905), **Durant Hall (B)** (1912) and **Wheeler Hall (C)** (1918), headquarters of the English department. The grandest of the four structures, **Doe Library★** (1911; additions in 1917 and 1995) recalls a

Roman temple with a Corinthian colonnade on its northern facade.

On the ground floor, the wood-paneled **Morrison Library** (1928) provides a cozy haven for casual readers. Upstairs, note the barrel-vaulted Reference Room and the old circulation hall with its magnificent coffered bronze ceiling and suspended lamps.

Bancroft Library(D)

Open during academic session Mon–Fri 10am–5pm, between sessions Mon–Fri 1–5pm. ♿ *510-642-3781. http://bancroft.berkeley.edu.*

This annex (1948, Arthur Brown, Jr.) on the east side of the Doe Library stores rare books, manuscripts, archival materials and special collections, including the country's largest assemblage of manuscripts, notebooks and papers belonging to author Mark Twain. The Bancroft is famed for its holdings of Western Americana. Treasures periodically rotated through the library anteroom include paintings of the old West, first editions and printed posters.

South of the Bancroft Library stands the oldest building on campus, the red-brick **South Hall (E)** (1873, David Farquharson), built in the French Second Empire style. Once the university president's office, the building now houses the School of Information.

▷ Ascend the stairs to the Campanile.

👥 The Campanile (Sather Tower)★★

Open Mon–Fri 10am–3.45pm, Sat 10am–4.45pm, Sun 10am–1.30pm, 3–4.45pm. Closed Dec 25–Jan 1. 👓 *$2.*

Modeled on the bell tower in Venice's St. Marks Square, this 307ft, steel-framed, granite-clad shaft (1914, John Galen Howard) is crowned by a quartet of obelisks surmounted with bronze urns, and a soaring central spire capped by a bronze lantern. A memorial to university benefactor Jane K. Sather, the Campanile houses a carillon of 61 bells. From its open-air observation platform, arched windows frame panoramic **views**★★ of

the Berkeley hills, downtown Oakland, San Francisco Bay and the intriguing geometry of the campus. When school is in session, carillonists at a keyboard play the bells from an enclosure at the platform's center in a fascinating, if deafening, performance (*concerts Mon-Fri 7:50am, noon, 6pm; Sat noon, 6pm; longer concert Sun 2pm*).

▷ Walk north from the Campanile, turning right at the first corner.

Hearst Memorial Mining Building

This granite-clad Beaux-Arts building (1907, John Galen Howard and Julia Morgan) was named for Sen. George Hearst, who made his fortune in mining. The facade bears three archways and a row of corbels carved to resemble men and women straining to support the massive wooden cornices. It houses offices, laboratories and classrooms.

▷ Walk south across Mining Circle and cross University Dr.

The route passes the back of **Le Conte Hall (F)**, the physics building where J. Robert Oppenheimer (1904–67), Edward Teller and other physicists drafted a blueprint of the first atomic bomb in the summer of 1942.

▷ Turn right, then left, crossing Strawberry Creek under an arch with a Latin inscription, and over a concrete footbridge.

At the lush green known as Faculty Glade, a path beside Strawberry Creek leads east behind the partially wood-shingled **Faculty Club (G)** (1902, Bernard Maybeck), which blends beautifully with the surrounding oaks, laurels and redwoods. After crossing and recrossing the creek on adjacent bridges, pass behind the redwood log **Senior Hall (H)** (1906, John Galen Howard) and turn left onto a path that leads past the cabin to the brown-shingled **Women's Faculty Club (J)** (1923, John Galen Howard), ensconced in a pretty English garden.

Hearst Greek Theater

▶ Pass along the front of the club, climb steps and cross to ascend a broad stairway on the north side of Cheit Hall.

The assemblage of buildings constituting the **Haas School of Business★** (1995, Moore/Ruble/Yudell/VBN) projects the atmosphere of a prosperous quarter in a north German city, complete with street lamps, gabled roofline, multi-paned windows and an enclosed parapet walk above its arching western gateway. Pass under the eastern portal arch to Piedmont Avenue, and look left to the concrete, Tudor Revival "castle" of **Bowles Hall (K)** (1929, George Kelham), rising magnificently on a hillside and surmounted by chimneys, gables and steep red-tiled roofs.

Hidden by trees a little farther to the north, the 8,500-seat outdoor (1903, John Galen Howard and Julia Morgan) was modeled after the ancient amphitheater at Epidarus.

Directly across the street stands **California Memorial Stadium** (1923, John Galen Howard), home field for the Cal Bears football team. The stadium is also the new headquarters for the U.C. campus **Koret Visitor Center** (◷open *Mon–Fri 8.30am–4.30pm, Sat-Sun 9am–1pm, closed major holidays and on foot-*

ball home game days; ⟵*Guided tours daily at 10am, subject to change; online reservations required.* ♿ ℘*510-642-5215; visit.berkeley.edu).*

▶ Turn right and walk to Bancroft Ave.

International House (L)
2299 Piedmont Ave. ✕♿ ℘*510-642-9490. http://ihouse.berkeley.edu.*
Iberian flourishes highlight this residential and cultural center (1930, George Kelham), the Berkeley branch of a movement to encourage cultural exchange between Americans and foreigners. A Moorish domed tower and balconies dominate the exterior. Many of the large public rooms reveal traditional Spanish decorative elements such as red-tile floors, carved-wood doors and iron chandeliers.

▶ Walk five minutes along up Bancroft Ave. past the Law Library. You will see the Heart Museum on your right.

Phoebe A. Hearst Museum of Anthropology (M2)
102 Kroeber Hall. ◠*$6* ♿ ℘*510-642-1191; hearstmuseum.berkeley.edu*
Among the country's most significant anthropological museums, the Hearst was established around a core collec-

219

Sather Gate

© Spencer Grant/age fotostock

tion obtained in a series of expeditions funded by Phoebe Hearst, starting in 1899. Today the **collections**★ have grown to contain nearly four million objects from around the world, with emphasis on California archaeology, ancient Peru, Classical Greece and Italy, ancient Egypt, Central American textiles and ethnological artifacts from West Africa, Oceania and the Arctic and sub-Arctic regions.

The Museum's public gallery is temporarily closed for renovation and will reopen for visitors in Spring 2019. Visitors who come in 2019 will see awe-inspiring objects such as a 7,000-pound ancient Egyptian sarcophagus lid covered with hieroglyphic spells, a West African chicken-shaped coffin and California Indian basketry. Museum exhibits are always interactive, with a variety of exciting learning opportunities where visitors can contribute their views on crucial current questions of culture and identity.

Rising across the courtyard northeast of Kroeber Hall, the 10-story concrete **Wurster Hall (N)** (1964, DeMars, Escherick, Olsen) is a striking example of the Brutalist style.

▷ Passing between Morrison and Hertz Halls, turn left at Faculty Glade and follow the creek downstream.

Pause at the wall of the old brick powerhouse to admire Byzantine-inspired mosaics created in 1936 by WPA-sponsored artists Helen Bruton and Florence Swift.

▷ Continue west to Sproul Plaza.

Sather Gate

Spanning the broad pedestrian entrance to the main campus, this monumental, filigreed bronze gateway (1910, John Galen Howard) arches between four granite pillars capped by banded glass globes.

Telegraph Avenue once met the campus at Sather Gate, but the commercial zone was cleared to Bancroft Avenue in the 1950s and replaced in 1960 by Sproul Plaza. Best known as the site of student protests in the 1960s and 70s, the plaza draws students, musicians, protesters, political campaigners, street preachers and eccentrics of every stripe. Commemorating its revolutionary birthright, a 6ft circle at the center of the plaza is ceremonially declared an extraterritorial zone "not subject to any entity's jurisdiction."

On the plaza's east side stands Sproul Hall, which houses university administrative offices.

The Martin Luther King, Jr. Student Union complex on the west side contains food services, bookstores, sundry shops. To the west is Zellerbach Auditorium, a 2,000-seat auditorium that's home to CalPerformances, which presents ballet, symphony, and other theatrical performances to the pubic. (*101 Zellerbach Hall; ☎510-642-9988*).

ADDITIONAL SIGHTS ON CAMPUS

UC Berkeley Art Museum and Pacific Film Archive★

2155 Center St at Oxford St.
🕐*Open Wed, Th & Sun 11am–7pm, Fri & Sat until 9pm.* 🕐*Closed university holidays.* 🍽*$13. (free first Thu of the month).* ✕⚹ ✆*510-642-0808. bampfa.org.*

Housing one of the largest university art collections in the U.S., the UC Berkeley Art Museum was born in 1963 when Abstract Expressionist painter Hans Hofmann (1880–1966), having left Nazi Germany with the aid of two UC professors, donated 45 paintings and $250,000 to the university. In addition to Hofmann's work, the permanent collection grew to be 19,000 pieces strong in 20C art, pre-20C European painting, Asian ceramics and painting, and a mix of contemporary art and sculpture.

In 1997, the university discovered the building did not meet current seismic standards and set out to construct a new museum near its western entrance.

Reopened on Jan 31, 2016, the new BAMPFA building, designed by architecture firm Diller Scofidio + Renfro, incorporates a 1939 Art Deco-style former University of California printing plant with a bold stainless-steel clad structure. Windows along the Center Street facade of the former printing press building have been enlarged, allowing passersby to look into the building and see the Art Wall, a 60-by-25-ft interior surface for temporary art installations, that overlooks the multilevel performance space. Babette, BAMPFA's popular cafe, cantilevers over Center Street, offering sweeping views toward the Golden Gate and the Berkeley hills. Master woodworker Paul Discoe has fabricated joinery elements that add natural warmth to the building. The craftsman has built the stepped seating of the performance space, the admissions desk, and the counter and shelving units in the BAMPFA store using wood that was salvaged from the Canary Island pine trees that were removed from the building site prior to construction. The building totals 83,000 square feet, with 25,000 square feet of gallery space. Visitors can enjoy two film theaters, a performance forum, four study centers for art and film, a reading room, an art-making lab, a cafe, and an outdoor LED screen and viewing plaza.

Associated with the museum, the renowned **Pacific Film Archive★** preserves 16,000 films, videos and rare prints of classic films emphasizing Japanese, Soviet and American art cinema. In 2009 the archive was selected to house the Film Arts Foundation's media archive, posters and publications. Screenings are held year-round at its new 232-seat state of the art theater Wed-Sun. (*210 Oxford St., free same-day gallery admission for film ticket holders* (✆*510-642-1124;* 🍽*$12).*

UC Botanical Garden★

200 Centennial Dr. 🕐*Open daily 9am–5pm.* 🕐*Closed 1st Tue of each month, Jan 1, Martin Luther King Jr. Day, Thanksgiving Day, Dec 24, 25 & 31.* 🍽*$12 (free 1st Wed of the month).* 👣*Guided tours (1hr) available Thu–Sun 1.30pm.* ⚹🅿 ✆*510-643-2755. http://botanicalgarden.berkeley.edu.*

One of the largest and most diverse collections in the United States, some 16,000 plants of more than 10,800 spe-

UC Botanical Garden

cies grace the slopes of Strawberry Canyon in a sylvan setting above the main campus. Most of the garden is organized geographically, representing flora of Asia, Africa, the Mediterranean and Europe, New Zealand, Australia, Meso-America, North America and California. Thematic gardens nurture palms and cycads, old roses and Chinese medicinal herbs. A sequoia forest and redwood grove are located across Centennial Drive.

👥 Lawrence Hall of Science

1 Centennial Dr. 🕐*Open Tue-Sun 10am–5pm and select holidays.* 🕐*Closed Thanksgiving Day, Dec 24- 25.* 👓*$12; children ages 3–18 $10;* ✕🅿 🖉*510-642-5132. www.lawrencehallofscience.org.*
Dramatically situated high in the Berkeley hills, this futuristic museum (1968, Anshen and Allen) celebrated its 50th anniversary in 2018. Dedicated to teaching children about physics, biology, chemistry, navigation, mathematics, computers and lasers, the museum offers interactive exhibits, laboratories, and a comprehensive program of classes. Highlights include a live animal discovery center, a stop-motion movie studio and a tinkering station. Some activities, such as National Geographic 3D Theater films and interactive Planetarium shows require purchase of a separate ticket; (*check the website for times and prices*). The **view**★★ from the front patio overlooks much of the northern Bay Area. On weekdays, free shuttle service links Lawrence Hall of Science to Hearst Mining Circle (🕐*operates Mon–Fri 7:30am–7pm;* 👓*$1;* 🖉*510-643-7701*).

SIGHTS IN BERKELEY

Telegraph Avenue★

Between Bancroft and Dwight Ways.
From morning through late evening this compelling thoroughfare flows with students, bibliophiles, crafts sellers, street people and tourists, all of whom frequent its many coffeehouses, bookstores, eateries and shops.
East of the avenue, sandwiched between Dwight Way and Haste Street, **People's**

Park remains a potent symbol of Berkeley radicalism. Seized from the university by students and political activists in 1969, the park sparked a series of riots between police and protesters before a sort of truce was reached, in which the city of Berkeley manages the property in partnership with the university. Some space today has been turned into community gardens. While not without historical importance, People's Park is not a traditional park destination, as, sadly, this urban section of Berkeley is frequented by the homeless.

First Church of Christ, Scientist★★

2619 Dwight Way at Dana St.
👁*Visit by guided tour (45min) only 1st Sun of each month 12.15pm. Public services Sun 11am.* ♿🅿 🖉*510-845-7199. www.friendsoffirstchurch.org.*
Designated a Berkeley landmark in 1974, Bernard Maybeck's masterwork (1910) harmonized a wealth of styles, yet copied none, in a unique Arts and Crafts structure of unsurpassing beauty and serenity. The church fuses multiple rooflines with Spanish tiles and rectangular, fluted columns, and the sunken auditorium, in the shape of a Greek cross, is naturally lit by side windows and diagonally spanned with arching beams. The milled woodwork in the ceiling beams and furnishings were designed by Maybeck himself.

The Magnes Collection of Jewish Art and Life★

2121 Allston Way.
🕐 *Tue–Fri 11am–4pm August-mid-June.* 🕐*Closed major & Jewish holidays, and during school breaks.* 🖉*510-643-2526. www.magnes.org.*
Recently relocated near the university campus, the 15,000-piece Magnus Collection of Jewish Art and Life is the nation's third-largest museum of Jewish history and art. Named for a prominent San Francisco rabbi, the museum sponsors changing exhibits *(main level)* highlighting painting and sculpture, photography, works on paper, books, and digital media by 19C, 20C and 21C

Jewish artists. Galleries on the upper level are reserved for rotating exhibits of ceremonial and cultural items from the museum collections, including Hanukkah lamps, Torah arks, and Sephardic artifacts from around the world.

Claremont Club & Spa★

41 Tunnel Rd., end of Ashby Ave.
🕐*Open daily.* ✕♿🅿 *☏510-843-3000.*
www.fairmont.com/claremont-berkeley.
Looming like a white castle in the hills between Berkeley and Oakland, this stately old hotel (1915, Charles Dickey) forms the centerpiece of an upscale resort, now a Fairmont property. A reputation for dullness dogged the hotel for many years, largely because laws forbade the sale of liquor within a mile of the UC Berkeley campus. An enterprising student actually measured the distance in 1936 and discovered that the southern end of the hotel lay beyond the mile radius; the following year, the Terrace Lounge opened on the "wet" side of the invisible line.

👥 Tilden Regional Park

From Berkeley take Spruce St. north to Grizzly Peak Blvd., cross and make a sharp left on Cañon Dr. Follow signs to the Nature Area.
🕐*Open daily dawn–dusk.* △✕♿🅿
☏510-544-2747. www.ebparks.org.
Sprawling over 2,079 acres on the eastern side of the ridge above Berkeley, this predominantly undeveloped preserve offers varied attractions to people of all ages, including swimming and fishing in **Lake Anza,** golf, picnicking, group camping, hiking trails, a petting zoo, a carousel and miniature train rides. Also here are the biking and walking paths of the 740-acre **Tilden Nature Area** (🕐*open daily 5am–10pm, check website for ongoing restoration project updates and closures;* ♿🅿 *☏510-544-2233),* whose Environmental Education Center hosts a wide variety of naturalist programs. Next door stands the Little Farm (🕐*open daily 8.30am–4pm),* which delights kids with its live animals.
Also within the park, the 10-acre **Botanic Garden** (🕐*open daily June–*

Sept 8.30am–5.30pm, Oct–May 8.30am–5pm; closed Jan 1, Thanksgiving and Dec 25. ☏510-544-3169) cultivates the world's largest collection of California native plants. Landscaped on picturesque terraces along the banks of Wildcat Creek, the garden's more than 1,500 species are divided into 10 separate sections that correspond with geographical regions of the state.

Northgate

This neighborhood was named for its location just outside the north entrance to Cal's campus. Above the first block of Euclid Avenue, lined with pleasant shops and restaurants, the rise where Ridge Road intersects with Le Conte Avenue has been dubbed "Holy Hill" for its concentration of theological schools.
Paramount among the venerable institutions is the Graduate Theological Union *(2465 Le Conte Ave.),* a Georgian Revival mansion built of red clinker-brick in the 1920s. Of note is its **Flora Lamson Hewlett Library (P)** *(2400 Ridge Rd.; ☏510-649-2500),* one of the country's largest theological collections. Walter J. Ratcliff's Holbrook Building *(1798 Scenic Ave.),* an impressive Tudor Revival structure, is part of the Pacific School of Religion, oldest seminary in the western U.S. Its **Badè Museum of Biblical Archaeology (M3)** displays a fine collection of Old Testament (1000–800 BC) antiquities. They were excavated in the early 20C by Dr. William Badè at Tell en-Nasbeh (thought to have been the biblical Mizpah of Benjamin) in Israel (🕐*open Fri 10am–2pm* 🕐*closed major holidays, last week in Dec; guided tours by reservation at least 2 weeks in advance;* ♿*☏510-849-8286; http://bade.psr.edu).*
Thornberg Village★, better known locally as Normandy Village *(1817–1839 & 1781–1783 Spruce St.),* lies two blocks west of Holy Hill. Erected in 1927–28 in "Hansel and Gretel" style by William R. Yelland, the residential complex is a storybook fantasy of Gothic arches and towers, eccentrically peaked rooflines, gargoyles, and meandering stairways.

© www.VisitBerkeley.com

Berkeley Municipal Rose Garden

North Berkeley Hills

Long a magnet for well-educated residents, the steep hills north of the UC Berkeley campus earned their reputation for high aestheticism after the turn of the 20C. Encouraged by the Hillside Club, a social organization with strong interests in preserving the natural beauty of the hills, developers introduced landscaped footpaths to complement the Arts and Crafts and brown-shingled houses that dominated the neighborhood. When a wildfire destroyed 500- 600 neighborhood homes in 1923, many residents rebuilt in an eclectic array of period revival styles inspired by Norman castles, Swiss chalets, Spanish missions, Italian villas, and Japanese and Greek temples.

Today the area offers pleasant if strenuous strolls along its streets and paths, including **Rose Walk** *(linking Euclid & LeRoy Aves.)* and **La Loma Steps** *(between LeRoy Ave. & Buena Vista Way).* At the heart of the neighborhood, the four-acre **Berkeley Municipal Rose Garden★** *(Euclid Ave. north of Bayview Pl.)* flourishes on terraces that descend down the canyon of Codornices Creek.The garden, one of the first Civil Works Progress Projects, was conceived in 1933 and com-

pleted in 1937. Today, it contains over 1,500 rose bushes of 250 species. One spectacularly eccentric house, the **Hume Cloister (Q)** *(2900 Buena Vista Way)*, replicates a 13C French monastery. An even more unusual structure, the **Temple of the Wings (R)** *(2800 Buena Vista Way)* with Corinthian colonnades joined to a central dance stage, was designed by Bernard Maybeck in 1914.

ADDRESSES

CAFE

Peet's Coffee & Tea – *2124 Vine St. ℘510-841-0564. www.peets.com.* Berkeley-born Peet's has been serving gourmet roasts in North Berkeley since the 1960s. Visit the original six-decade-old flagship of the popular Emeryville-based chain.

℘/EAT

The Cheese Board Collective – *1504 Shattuck Ave. ℘510-549-3183 cheeseboardcollective.coop.* North Berkeley's famed worker-owned bakery and cheese monger opened in 1971 with a gourmet ethos and a revolutionary collective approach. Today, it's a gourmet ghetto institution.

Oakland★

Directly across the bay from San Francisco, linked to it by the San Francisco-Oakland Bay Bridge, bustling Oakland boasts a large and busy port, gleaming waterfront, and civic-center districts. Also found here is an exceptional museum and a profusion of ambitiously restored mid-19C–20C residential and commercial buildings.

A BIT OF HISTORY

Part of a 44,800-acre ranch from 1820 to the Gold Rush, Oakland was incorporated on May 4, 1852. The arrival of the **transcontinental railroad** in 1869 established the city as a regional transportation hub, and businesses sprang up along 8th, 9th and Washington Streets—the area today known as Old Oakland. When the 1906 earthquake and fire devastated San Francisco, Oakland sheltered more than 150,000 refugees, many of whom elected to remain. Skyscrapers grew up along Broadway through the early 20C, and in 1936 the city was joined to San Francisco by the Bay Bridge, the largest civil engineering project of the time. Oakland's population grew by a third during the years of World War II when the Kaiser Shipyards attracted thousands of workers. With the end of the war, however, came economic decline and social unrest. In the 1960s Oakland suffered through race riots and rising rates of urban poverty and violent crime. Natural disasters also took their toll—the Loma Prieta earthquake of 1989 collapsed the "Cypress Structure" section of the double-deck I-880 freeway through West Oakland, while a devastating hill fire in 1991 razed substantial residential areas.

A Gradual Rebuilding – Although vacant storefronts continue to haunt Broadway, major civil-engineering programs have brought a measure of recovery to downtown. The expanded, modernized **Port of Oakland** now ranks among the top 20 in the world. In addition, the opening of eight BART stations in Oakland in 1974, the re-establishment of passenger

🚉 12th Street/City Center or Lake Merritt station. Alameda/Oakland ferry to Jack London Square, 511.org.

▸ **Population:** 425,000

🛈 **Info:** ☏510-839-9000. www.oaklandcvb.com, www.oaklandnet.com.

◖ **Location:** Most Oakland sights are located along the waterfront and within the square formed by I-880 and I-980 and Lake Merritt. All are within (lengthy) walking distances of each other. You'll need a car or public transporation to get to the Additional Sights.

👥 **Kids:** The Chabot Space & Science Center and the Oakland Zoo are geared toward families. Children's Fairyland is fun for very young visitors.

🕐 **Timing:** Downtown Oakland bustles only during weekday business hours, the best time to visit the area. The waterfront area is a pleasure to explore on foot throughout the day. Visit farmers' market in Old Oakland (Fridays) and Grand Lake (Saturdays).

🅿 **Parking:** Parking is available in downtown Oakland garages. BART's 12th Street/City Center station is convenient to downtown, Chinatown, and Old Oakland. The Lake Merritt station accesses the Oakland Museum of California and the south side of Lake Merritt. Jack London Square offers abundant garage parking.

♿ **Don't Miss:** The Oakland Museum of California.

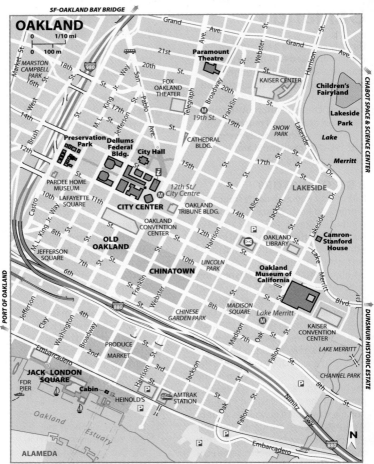

ferry service to San Francisco in 1989, and the completion of a new Amtrak passenger station in 1995 renewed Oakland's traditional role as a Bay Area transportation center. The City Center and Jack London Square areas underwent massive redevelopment in the 1980s, thanks in part to former Mayor Jerry Brown, whose 10K Initiative catalyzed retail interest downtown. Meanwhile, the city has aggressively preserved its rich architectural heritage, buying and refurbishing scores of Victorian and 20C houses and commercial buildings in Old Oakland and Preservation Park.

Today, Oakland is as hot as ever, and hordes of Bay Area residents priced out of San Francisco have fled to "Oaktown" as a more affordable (and sunnier) alternative. As a result you find gentrified neighborhood shopping precincts, such as **Piedmont Avenue** (*between MacArthur Blvd. and Pleasant Valley Ave.*) and **College Avenue** in the Rockridge district, and vibrant nightlife corridors such as **Uptown** (*between 27th St, San Pablo Ave, City Center, and Harrison St*) filled with hip restaurants, bars, and music venues.

A good way to experience Oakland's burgeoning art scene is to check out **First Fridays**—hosted by **Art Murmur** since 2006—a free monthly gallery walk on the during which local galleries throughout the city collectively open to the public and hold artists receptions (*first Friday of the month 6pm-9pm*), and **Saturday Stroll**, a more intimate guided tour of local galleries (*every Sat 1pm-5pm*); *www.oaklandartmurmur.org.*

DOWNTOWN

12th St./City Center station.

Free 90min guided walking tours of downtown Oakland are offered May– Oct Wed & Sat at 10am; reservations recommended but not required. *510-238-3234. www.2oaklandnet.com/ walkingtours.*

City Hall

1 Frank Ogawa Plaza. *Open Mon–Fri 9am–5pm.* *Closed major holidays.* *510-444-2489.*

The present-day center of downtown Oakland was ordained by city planners to be the dynamic intersection where Broadway, San Pablo Avenue and 14th Street converged.

Since the opening of City Center in the 1980s, the focus of business has shifted one block south. A vaulting symbol of the city's progressive spirit, when it was completed in 1914 (Palmer, Hornbostel & Jones), City Hall's 18-story shaft rises from a three-story Beaux Arts podium, capped by a Baroque-style clock tower. Inside, an elegant staircase leads from the lobby to a third-floor Council Chamber.

Oakland City Center★

Between Broadway and 12th, 14th, and Clay Sts. *510-830-1650. www.oaklandcitycenter.com.*

The pleasantly landscaped John B. Williams Plaza conducts pedestrians via escalators upward from the sunken BART station to this open-air mall.

At its center stands a brightly painted metal **sculpture (1)** by Roslyn Mazzilli entitled *There* (1988). The title is a jocular allusion to Gertrude Stein's famous (and usually misinterpreted as spiteful) observation—"There is no there there"—following a visit to her childhood hometown. To the west, three-story rows of modern commercial

buildings frame a view of the Federal Building's twin towers.

East from the plaza, sight lines converge on the 21-story **Oakland Tribune Building** (*13th and Franklin Sts.*). The jaunty landmark (1923, Edward Foulkes), housed the offices of *The Oakland Tribune* until the newspaper moved to Jack London Square in 1992.

Ronald Y. Dellums Federal Building★

Between 12th, 14th, Clay & Jefferson Sts. This monumental, twin-towered structure is the largest building in Alameda County. Completed in 1993, the limestone-clad towers are linked by a 75ft glass rotunda that serves as a lobby. A marble-and-granite map of the Bay Area spreads across the rotunda floor.

Preservation Park

13th St. and Martin Luther King, Jr. Way. *510-874-7580. www.preservationpark.com*

These 16 splendidly landscaped Victorian homes were relocated from their original sites and restored as a charming office park. Labels recount the history of each of the houses, which span the decades from about 1870 to 1910.

Worth a special visit is the Italianate **Pardee Home Museum★** (*672 11th St. at Castro St.; visit by guided tour (1hr) only Sat 10.30am & 2nd Sun of month 2pm (call ahead);* *closed major holidays;* *$5;* *510-444-2187; www.pardeehome.org*), family mansion of two Oakland mayors: Enoch Pardee and, later, his son George. Built in 1868, the mansion is maintained as it was in 1981 at the death of George Pardee's daughter. Tours reveal a hodge-podge of furnishings and thousands of *objets d'art.*

Old Oakland★

Bounded by Broadway and 7th, 10th, and Washington Sts. *Farmers' market held Fri 8am–2pm on 9th St. between Broadway and Clay St.* *Free walking tours of the downtown district are available through City of Oakland every Wed and Sat. May-Oct, which include entry to Preservation Park https://www.oaklandca.gov/topics/walking-tours*

This restored historic district formed the heart of downtown Oakland during the 1870s. Today it remains an extraordinary grouping of 19C commercial buildings. The shops, hotels and restaurants were built between 1868 and 1880 for the throngs of travelers passing through the Central Pacific passenger depot at 7th and Broadway (terminus of the first transcontinental railroad). The sturdy, two- and three-story structures were restored in the 1980s and are splendid showcases of Victorian craftsmanship. The site was restored and achieved historic preservation status and rebranded as **Swan's Market** *(9th and Washington Sts.;* ⏰*open Mon–Sat 9am–10pm)*, a popular ethnically diverse culinary marketplace teeming with quick-service restaurants, produce and fish markets, butcher shops and other stalls.

Oakland Chinatown

Bounded by Broadway and 7th, 10th & Harrison Sts.

Although the first Chinese immigrants arrived in Oakland in the early 1850s, they gathered in the present nine-square-block quarter during the 1870s. Unlike its San Francisco counterpart, Oakland's Chinatown does not court tourists, although many visitors enjoy exploring the bustling array of shops and restaurants. If you happen to be in town during the last weekend in August, be sure to drop by the Oakland Chinatown StreetFest *(www.oaklandchinatownstreetfest.com)*, when hundreds of vendors draw thousands of visitors with calligraphy and origami demonstrations, face painting, barbecue, music and other attractions.

Paramount Theatre★★

2025 Broadway. 🚇*19th St.* 👁*Visit by guided tour (2hrs), held 1st & 3rd Sat of month 10am.* 👓*$5.* ⏰*Closed major holidays.* ✆*510-893-2300. www.paramounttheatre.com.*

This monumental movie palace (1931, Timothy Pflueger) is one of the nation's finest examples of Moderne design. The building's resplendent Art Deco detailing describes flowers, foliage, birds and people in addition to the more abstract designs typical of the style. Authentically restored in 1973, it is now owned by the city as a performing-arts facility. The exterior boasts two majestic tile mosaics of puppeteers, divided by the towering Paramount sign. The amber-colored *Fountain of Light* dominates the lobby; the glass sculpture appears to be rising in spectacular billows toward a green-lit grillwork ceiling. With seating for nearly 3,000 people, the lavish auditorium features a gold-lit filigreed ceiling, and paneled side walls sculpted in bas-relief scenes of maidens and warriors. Ralph Stackpole sculpted the horsemen on the orchestral panel above the stage. A Wurlitzer organ mounted on a hydraulic lift rises to stage level for performances. Also worth a gaze are the splendidly decorated men's and women's restrooms and the curving foyers. Nearly as fantastic is the nearby **Fox Oakland Theater** *(1897 Telegraph Ave., www.thefoxoakland.com)*. Built in 1928 (Diggs, Weeks & Day), this exotic, Moorish-style movie palace conjures visions of Arabian Nights. In its day, it was said to have been grander than anything on Hollywood Boulevard.

The theatre was restored and reopened in late 2008 as a live-performance venue; it also houses the charter high school Oakland School for the Arts.

WATERFRONT

Southwest of downtown.

👥 Jack London Square★

Along the Embarcadero from Clay to Alice St. ⏰*Farmers' market Sun 9am–2pm.* 🅿✕♿✆*510-645-9292. www.jacklondonsquare.com.*

Stretching along the busy Inner Harbor of the Oakland Estuary southeast of Broadway, this once-gritty dock area has been developed as an attractive, pedestrian-friendly complex, with an impressive farmers' market, now operated by CUESA (Center for Urban Education about Sustainable Agriculture), which also runs the Ferry Plaza Market in San Francisco. In addition to shops, restaurants, hotels, cinemas, and a yacht harbor, it has become the East Bay's hippest nightlife district. Oakland's passenger lines, Oakland Estuary water-taxi service, and ferries from San Francisco converge near the marina.

The square was named for writer Jack London, who lived in Oakland as a boy and young man. His adventurous spirit is recalled in the historic **Jack London Cabin**, a reconstruction from original timbers of the rustic, single-room log cabin that London occupied during the winter of 1897–98 while prospecting for gold in the Yukon Territory.

Near the cabin stands one of London's favorite watering holes, **Heinold's First and Last Chance Bar** *(48 Webster St.; ℘510-839-6761; www.heinoldsfirstand lastchance.com)*, built in 1883 from the timbers of a whaling ship. Heinold's was also patronized by authors Ambrose Bierce, Joaquin Miller and, for a short time, Robert Louis Stevenson. Still operating as a bar, it was declared a National Literary Monument in 1997.

A floor contorted by the 1906 earthquake (and never repaired) holds three small tables and a half-dozen barstools; wonderful historical photos cover the walls.

USS Potomac
FDR Pier, end of Clay St. (Visitor center opposite at 540 Water St.). ◷*Open Mon-Fri 9am-4pm; dockside tours (45min) Wed, Fri and Sun 11am–2.30pm.* ◷*Closed mid-Dec–mid-Jan or inclement weather.* ⊜*$10. History cruises (2hrs and 3hrs) mid-June–mid-Nov alternating Thu and Sat by reservation* ⊜*$55–$75. Blues cruises two Sundays a month ($55).* ⊜*$55. ℘510-627-1215. www.usspotomac.org.*
Franklin Delano Roosevelt's presidential yach, aka The Floating White House, is berthed at Jack London Square. The 165ft former Coast Guard cutter was built in 1934 and officially recommissioned as a U.S. Navy vessel for the use of the Commander in Chief two years later. Today the *Potomac* has been renovated to match its appearance when it served

as a presidential retreat on the Potomac River and along the Atlantic seaboard. Points of interest include the Presidential Cabin, the engine room and a radio room from which Roosevelt made a national broadcast on March 29, 1941.

LAKE MERRITT AREA
East of downtown.
🚉*Lake Merritt station.*

Lake Merritt
Bounded by Lakeside Dr. and Grand and Lakeshore Aves.
The shores of this 155-acre saltwater tidal lake offer a haven of green serenity near the bustling heart of the city. The shimmering expanse of water was a marshy tidal slough until 1869, when Dr. Samuel Merritt, an ex-mayor who owned land on its shores, dammed the outlet at 12th Street to create the lake. In 1870, he successfully lobbied the California legislature to declare it an official wildlife refuge. Although many private landowners built mansions at its edge, the city eventually secured the properties and turned them into public parkland. A pleasant esplanade winds around the lake's 3.5mi shoreline, broadening on the northern side into **Lakeside Park** *(Bellevue & Grand Aves.)* This lush oasis of 122 oak-shaded acres includes a bandstand, show gardens, and **Children's Fairyland** ♟♙ *(699 Bellevue Ave.;* ◷*open 10am–4pm daily Jun–Aug, Wed–Sun Apr–May & Sept–Oct, Fri–Sun Nov–Apr;* ◷*Thanksgiving, Dec 24–25, Dec 31-Jan 5 and during inclement weather;* ⊜*$12;* ✕♿🅿 *℘510-452-2259; www.fairyland.org)*, a 10-acre amusement park for the very young.

♟♙ Oakland Museum of California★★
1000 Oak St. ◷*Open Wed–Thu 11am–5pm, Fri 11am-10pm, Sat-Sun 10am-5pm.* ◷*Closed Jan 1, Jul 4, Thanksgiving Day, Dec 25.* ☞*Guided tours Fri-Sun (check website).* ⊜*$15.95 (free 1st Sun of month).* ✕♿🅿 *℘510-318-8400. http://museumca.org.*
A city showpiece, this 7.7-acre cultural complex celebrates California's natural

and human history and its art. A setting for public art and celebration, the museum's innovative gardens—a geometric weave of landscaped passages, courtyards, terraces and stairways—encourage visitors to explore the building from its sunken central lawn court to its scenic rooftops.

In the early 1960s, city officials and private individuals launched a massive public campaign to build a grand new museum complex that would help revive inner-city Oakland. The facility consolidated three existing collections—the Snow Museum, which focused on natural history; the Oakland Public Museum, devoted to Native Californian ethnology and the state's pioneer history; and the Oakland Art Museum.

Internationally acclaimed architect Eero Saarinen was the leading candidate to design the museum when he died unexpectedly in 1961. His colleague Kevin Roche was then chosen to undertake the project. With assistance from architectural technologist John Dinkeloo, Roche created a series of tiered horizontal galleries around a central courtyard, overhung with terraced roof gardens. Composed solely of reinforced concrete, plate glass and wood, the building's strongly angular lines are graced by statuary and softened with flowers, shrubs and trees—including orchard varieties like olive and pear that recall the state's important agricultural roots. The museum opened in 1969 to

rave reviews, with *New York Times* critic Ada Louise Huxtable calling it "one of the most thoughtful revolutionary structures in the world."

The three main departments—natural sciences, history and art—occupy the principal halls on three separate levels of the building. In 2010, the Art and History Galleries reopened after an expansion and renovation designed by Kevin Roche which showcases new acquisitions. The **Great Hall** features major traveling exhibitions, art shows and temporary presentations drawn from the museum's own collections. On Fridays evenings 5pm-9pm, admission is half price and the museum host special programs and food trucks.

Gallery of California Natural Sciences★

1st level.

Inspired by Elna Bakker's book *An Island Called California,* this hall (also known as the Hall of California Ecology) is arranged to guide visitors on a walk eastward through central California to experience the astounding breadth and richness of the state's geography and biodiversity. Detailed dioramas of native flora and fauna re-create eight distinct biotic zones that stretch across the middle of the state: the Coastline, the foggy Coastal Mountains, the dry Inner Coast Ranges, the Central Valley, the Sierra Slope, the High Sierra, the sagebrush deserts of the Great Basin, and the rocky

Gallery of California Natural Sciences

© Odell Hussey/Oakland Museum of California

Kings River Canyon *(1878) by William Keith, Gallery of California Art*

© Odell Hussey/Oakland Museum of California

Mojave Desert. Located off the main hall is the Aquatic California Gallery, where realistic displays in resin illustrate life in the state's coastal and delta waters, salt marshes and freshwater streams.

Gallery of California History★
2nd level.
This hall displays 2,200 artifacts and artworks arranged chronologically to explore the theme of "Coming to California." Exhibits explore the story of California, from the incredible diversity of early Native American culture, to the Gold Rush and growth of San Francisco, through the rise of Los Angeles and Hollywood, to the tumultuous decades of the 1960s and 70s. It concludes with a frequently updated and rotating gallery space that addresses current issues and contemporary perspectives. The gallery also features multimedia viewing and listening stations, and offers visitors chances to share their own stories.

Gallery of California Art★★
3rd level.
Installed thematically with a focus on "California's Land, People, and Creativity," this light-infused gallery is devoted to works by artists who have lived, worked or studied in California. The collection contains paintings, sculptures, drawings, prints, photographs and mixed-media works from the early

19C to the present. Of special note are the 19C California landscapes, including paintings of the Sierra Nevada by Thomas Moran, Albert Bierstadt, Thomas Hill and William Keith. The museum holds the largest collection of work from California Arts and Crafts practitioners Arthur and Lucia Kleinhans Mathews. California Impressionist works are represented by Guy Rose, Joseph Raphael and E. Charlton Fortune, and by the Oakland-based "Society of Six" landscapists: William Clapp, August Gay, Selden Gile, Maurice Logan, Louis Siegriest and Bernard von Eichman.

The collection includes works by Richard Diebenkorn, Elmer Bischoff, David Park and other adherents to the Bay Area Figurative movement, as well as by Abstract Expressionists Clyfford Still, Mark Rothko, Sam Francis, Frank Lobdell and Hassel Smith. Later 20C works by Wayne Thiebaud, Robert Bechtle, David Hockney and Bruce Conner share space with contemporary sculptures by Deborah Butterfield, Manuel Neri and ceramist Robert Arneson.

The museum owns the world's largest collection of Dorothea Lange's photographs and negatives, and photography by Eadweard Muybridge (an early San Francisco panorama) and such group f.64 members as Edward Weston, Ansel Adams and Imogen Cunningham.

Mountain View Cemetery

5000 Piedmont Ave. *510-658-2588* *Open Mon-Fri 8:30am-4:30pm, Sat-Sun 10am-4pm. Docent-led historical tours available, consult website for upcoming programs. www.mountainviewcemetery.org*

In the hills above the picturesque Piedmont neighborhood, this public cemetery was designed by Frederick Law Olmsted, the famous landscape architect behind Central Park in New York City. Established in 1863, it's the resting place for a number of famous locals, including architects Julia Morgan and Bernard Maybeck, and serves a diverse community. .

Filled with winding roads, grassy slopes, old-growth oak trees, and quiet gardens, the grounds invite both wandering and contemplation. A particular draw are the breathtaking views of Oakland, the Bay, and San Francisco from the ridge at the top of the cemetery. Open to the public seven days a week, the cemetery also runs special events, including free themed tours of the site and an annual pumpkin patch for local kids.

ADDITIONAL SIGHTS

Chabot Space & Science Center★

10000 Skyline Blvd. Exit I-580 at Park Blvd.; continue east across Rte. 13, then right on Mountain Blvd. Climb to ridgetop, then right on Skyline Blvd. Open Wed–Sun 10am–5pm and federal holidays. Closed July 4, Labor Day, Thanksgiving Day, Dec 25. Museum (includes two planetarium shows) $18; children ages 3–12, $14. 510-336-7373. www.chabotspace.org.

Thirteen years in the making, this impressive 86,000sq ft hilltop center occupies 13 acres of parkland. Within are an acclaimed planetarium and theater, hands-on exhibits and science labs, and powerful telescopes that invite public access. The surrounding site has an amphitheater and a natural garden. To the right of the main entrance, in the East Building, the 241-seat **Ask Jeeves Planetarium** can project up to 9,000 stars with fiber-optic technology and

its Zeiss projector. Among the center's hands-on exhibits is **Destination Universe**, which lets kids crawl into a black hole and see what happens when galaxies collide. **One Giant Leap: A Moon Odyssey** allows them to try their hand in landing the original space roadster (a Mercury space capsule).

A sky bridge leads to the West Building. Solar and meridian-transit **telescopes★** are attached to this building; beyond is Leah, the historic 8in refractor telescope, moved from the original 1883 Oakland Observatory. Weekend viewing *(free)* is offered at a 20in refractor nicknamed "Rachel." A 36in telescope, Nellie, is located in a rolling-roof observatory that offers 180-degree views of the heavens.

Oakland Zoo

9777 Golf Links Rd., just east of I-580. Open daily 10am–4pm. Closed Thanksgiving & Dec 25. $24; $20 children ages 2–14. 510-632-9525. www.oaklandzoo.org.

Set inside 490-acre Knowland Park, this small zoo boasts more than 660 native and exotic animals. Among the most popular are chimpanzees, elephants and lions, as well as sun bears in Rain Forest Canyon. In addition to traditional viewing opportunities and children's zoo, thrillseekers can head to Adventure Land, where they can ride a rollercoaster, carousel, and, a 2/3-size replica of a **Civil War-era train** (*open daily 10am–4pm; $1.75 each or 16 rides for $24*) pulled by a steam locomotive, or take the 15min **Sky Ride** (*open Sat–Sun 11am–4pm; $3*) enjoying a birds-eye view of the bison, tule elk, and the Bay Area skyline.

Dunsmuir Historic Estate★

2960 Peralta Oaks Ct., off 106th Ave. south of Knowland Park. Mansion visit by guided tour only Apr–Sept Wed 11am; $5. 510-615-5555. www.dunsmuir-hellman.com.

Built by Alexander Dunsmuir, son of a wealthy British Columbia coal baron, this historic 50-acre estate is one of Oakland's unsung highlights. Dunsmuir had the house built in 1899 as a wed-

Going The Distance exhibit, Chabot Space & Science CenterCenter& Science Center

ding gift for his wife, Josephine; but on the couple's honeymoon in New York, Alexander took ill and died. Josephine lived in the house for fewer than two years before her own death. The estate was purchased by the City of Oakland in the early 1960s.

Visit

House tours begin at the quaint **Dinkelspiel House**, built for the Hellmans' daughter Florence in the early 1930s. The long driveway to the mansion leads through a meadow landscaped in part by John McLaren, best known for his work in Golden Gate Park. A new pavilion above the meadow is a venue for concerts and other special events.

The centerpiece of the estate is 37-room **Dunsmuir House**, built in Neoclassical Revival style with symmetrical facades, hipped or gabled roofs and Palladian windows. Measuring more than 16,000sq ft in three stories, the house has a Tiffany-style dome, 10 fireplaces and inlaid parquet floors.

Roads lead south to a historic farm area. Of note is the **Carriage House,** with mahogany-paneled walls and wrought-iron horse feeders.

Oakland Aviation Museum

8252 Earhart Rd, Building 621, North Field, Oakland Airport. ◷*Open Wed –Sun 10am–4pm.* ⊜*$15.* ♿ 🅿 ☎*510-638-7100. www.oakland aviationmuseum.org.*

This vintage (1940) hangar, built as a training facility for World War II aircraft mechanics, is home to this surprising museum. On display are Naval fighters and a sister craft to the L-10 piloted by Amelia Earhart. The impressive Ahrens Collection offers 1/72 scale-model U.S. military aircraft; other exhibits feature women and African American aviators, aerial photography, air racing, and Col. Jimmy Doolittle's 8th Air Force.

Outdoors is the Short Solent four-engine Flying Boat *(tours Sat and Sun only 10am, 11am, 1pm, 2pm and by appointment* ⊜*$7),* built in 1946. Almost 90ft long, with the tip of its tail 37ft above the ground, the plane was designed to take off and land exclusively in water. Converted to luxury passenger service in 1949, it became the property of reclusive billionaire Howard Hughes in 1959. It was restored after his death.

USS Hornet Sea, Air & Space Museum★★

Pier 3, Alameda. Take Atlantic Ave. north off Webster St. (Rte. 61) and follow signs. ◷*Open daily 10am–5pm (last entry 4pm).* ◷*Closed Jan 1, Thanksgiving Day, Dec 25. Currently closed while undergoing renovations until spring 2019.* ⊜*$20.* ✕ 🅿 ☎*510-521-8448. www.uss-hornet.org.*

Step back in time at this small museum dedicated to the historic World War 2 U.S. Navy carrier. Commissioned in November 1943, the Essex-class aircraft carrier was the eighth in a line of U.S. naval vessels to be named *Hornet*. With a length of 894ft, the 41,200-ton ship was designed to carry up to 3,400 service-men and an attack force of F6F Hellcat fighters, TBM Avenger torpedo bombers and SB2C Helldiver dive bombers.

Steaming from Pearl Harbor in March 1944, the USS *Hornet* moved quickly to the forefront of the Pacific war. In action at Iwo Jima in June 1944, air crews shot down 67 Japanese aircraft, commencing an extraordinary string of victories that earned the ship seven battle stars, and her pilots Navy records for the number of planes shot down in one month (255) and in a single day (72).

At the invasion of Okinawa in April 1945, the *Hornet* scored the first crippling hits on the largest battleship of its day, the 72,000-ton *Yamato*, which was sunk in the battle. The *Hornet* ended the war with a combat record of 1,420 aircraft, 42 cargo ships, 10 destroyers, a carrier, a cruiser and a battleship destroyed.

in 1969 the Hornet retrieved the crew of Apollo 11 upon their return from the first manned moon mission.

The splashdown in the Pacific was witnessed live by President Richard Nixon from the *Hornet's* bridge. Later that year, the *Hornet* also retrieved the returned astronauts of *Apollo 12*. The ship was decommissioned in June 1970 and declared a National Historic Landmark in 1991.

Visit

Boarding the ship on its vast **Hangar Deck**, where aircraft were stored between sorties, you may view a short orientation program and peruse a gal-lery of historic photographs before com-mencing self-guided tours.

At mid-ship, a set of painted footprints marks the first steps of Apollo 11's lunar astronauts back on "earth," when they walked from the retrieval helicopter to quarantine in a customized trailer; an adjacent exhibit highlights that event. A 5min **flight simulator** (⌐$6), equipped with computer-generated film and hydraulic lifts, lets you experience the sensation of launching and landing an aircraft on a carrier deck.

Steep, narrow ship ladders climb to the sprawling **Flight Deck,** above which rises the massive "Island" or control tower. You may climb to the Navigation Bridge, where the captain and officers piloted the ship, and the Flag Bridge, where the fleet admiral commanded a task force of support ships. From the Primary Flight Control Bridge overlooking the runways in the aft of the control tower, the "Air Boss" monitored the takeoffs and landings of aircraft.

Descending to the **Second Deck**, below the Hangar Deck, you may tour the refurbished officers' quarters, lounge and dining hall, the Marine Detachment quarters, the enlisted men's mess and the engine room.

ADDRESSES

⊻/EAT

$-$$ The Hive – *2325 Broadway. Hours vary by shop. hiveoakland.com.* One of the best reasons to visit this multifaceted live-work-gather space in Uptown Oakland is to drink a craft beer in the heated patio at Drake's Brewery. Other draws include trendy Indian restaurant Dosa, an artisanal Firebrand Breads bakery, and an ice-cream cart by Humphry Slocombe, best known for its bourbon-spiked "secret breakfast" flavor.

$ Blue Bottle Coffee – *300 Webster St. ℘510-653-3394. bluebottlecoffee.com.* The Bay Area's most beloved coffee company roasts its beans in Jack London Square. Stop by Blue Bottle headquarters to sample brews or sign up for one of the tastings and educational courses they offer onsite (check website for details).

ART

Betti Ono – *1427 Broadway, Oakland, CA 94612. ℘510-473-5919. bettiono.com.* One of the many excellent galleries in Downtown Oakland, Betti Ono specializes in local emerging artists.

East Bay Area

East of the ridge line backdropping Berkeley and Oakland lies a series of hills and valleys overshadowed by regal Mt. Diablo. Martinez, Concord, Walnut Creek, Alamo, Danville and other pleasant suburban communities spread over the valley floors, while exclusive developments extend higher into the grassy hills. The historic Solano County towns of Vallejo and Benicia guard either end of narrow Carquinez Straits in the northeast part of San Francisco Bay.

SIGHTS
👫 Mount Diablo State Park★

North Gate Rd., 35mi from San Francisco. From Oakland, take Rte. 24 east through Caldecott Tunnel to Walnut Creek. Continue east on Ygnacio Valley Rd. for 2.5mi; take a right on Walnut Ave., which turns into North Gate Rd. after 1.5mi and leads another 12mi to the summit. ◷*Park open daily 8am–dusk.* ◷*Closed during very high fire-risk days; call in advance for information.* ◠*$10/car.* △ ♿ 🅿 ☏*925-837-2525. www.mdia.org.*

The sweeping panoramic **view★★★** from the 3,849ft summit of Mt. Diablo is said to encompass more than 40,000sq mi. That would make it the second most extensive view over land from any point on earth, after Africa's Mt. Kilimanjaro.

On clear days, the naked eye can easily pick out such far-flung landmarks as San Francisco (27mi west), the Farallon Islands (62mi west), Mt. Lassen (165mi northeast), the Sacramento River Delta to the north, and the long wall of the Sierra Nevada range to the east. A good pair of binoculars can bring Yosemite National Park's El Capitan (130mi east) into focus. From this remarkable vantage point, Colonel Leander Ransom in 1851 established the Mt. Diablo Base and Meridian, used to make the first surveyed maps of Northern California and Nevada. A year later, R.D. Cutts mapped the state's northern waterways for the Coast Survey from here.

📄 **Info:** www.sfgate.com/neighborhoods/eb.

◑ **Location:** Sights in this section are located north and east of Berkeley and Oakland; all lie within 40mi from San Francisco.

👫 **Kids:** Six Flags Discovery Kingdom, the perfect combination of sea creatures, wildlife and thrill rides.

◷ **Timing:** Rush-hour traffic into San Francisco in the morning and back out in the evening will slow your transit time to these sights, so plan accordingly and avoid peak traffic hours if you can.

☻ **Don't Miss:** The Blackhawk Museum, a must for auto and design buffs.

Both survey marks still can be seen upon the rock now enclosed by the small **Summit Museum Visitor Center** (◷*open daily 10am–4pm;* ☏*925-837-6119*), built of locally quarried sandstone by the Civilian Conservation Corps in 1940.

Exhibits within the museum focus on Mt. Diablo's geology and its natural and human history; telescopes mounted on an observation deck assist viewing of distant sites. ☻ *Note: summer fogs often obscure views.*

On the mountain's flanks are extensive outcrops of fossilized seashells and prehistoric mammal bones. The park is also home to some 400 plant species, as well as deer, cougar, coyote, bobcat and about 200 species of birds, including bald eagles. Mt. Diablo offers camping, picnicking, hiking on more than 150mi of trails, and climbing in the weird sandstone formations known as **Rock City**. The Mitchell Canyon section of the park also has a visitor center (◷*open Sat–Sun and some holidays spring and summer 8am–4pm, fall and winter 9am–3pm*).

👥 Lindsay Wildlife Museum

1931 First Ave., Walnut Creek, 45mi from San Francisco. From Oakland, take Rte. 24 east, turning north on I-680. Turn left at the Treat/Geary Exit onto Geary Rd.; left again on Buena Vista Ave.; then right on First Ave.

🕐*Hours Wed-Sun 10am-5pm; hours vary.* 🕐*Closed Mon, Tue, week following Labor Day.* 🎟*$10, children 2–17 $8.* ♿🅿✆*925-935-1978. www.wildlife-museum.org.*

This small community-oriented natural-history museum is both an educational center and the largest wildlife-rehabilitation hospital in the U.S. Native injured animals that cannot be returned to the wild live out their days here, under conditions carefully designed to satisfy both their physical and psychological needs. Eagles, hawks and other raptors roost on perches, while squirrels, coyotes and other mammals cavort below eye level. Live reptiles and amphibians, as well as mounted insect collections, introduce yet more local fauna.

Eugene O'Neill National Historic Site★★

Kuss Rd., Danville, 28mi from San Francisco. From I-680 east of Oakland (between Rte. 24 & I-580), exit at Sycamore Valley Rd.; National Park Service van picks up visitors at Museum of San Ramon Valley in Danville for drive to Tao House.

👥*Visit by guided tour (2.5hrs) only, Wed–Fri and Sun 10am and 2pm (shuttle pickup times), reservations required. Also open Sat for self-guided tours without reservation.* 🕐*Closed Jan 1, Thanksgiving Day, Dec 25.* ♿ ✆*925-838-0249. www.nps.gov/euon.*

Situated on a scenic knoll in the shadow of the Las Trampas wilderness, this modest yet comfortable dwelling was home for more than six years to playwright **Eugene O'Neill** (1888–1953). Author of nearly 60 plays, winner of four Pulitzer Prizes for drama, and the only American playwright to win the Nobel Prize for Literature (in 1936), O'Neill is one of the nation's most influential dramatists.

Tragedy and Triumph

The son of a successful traveling actor, O'Neill was born in a New York City hotel and raised largely "on the road" by a loving but troubled family. O'Neill's personal life was filled with difficulties. His mother was addicted to morphine and his brother to alcohol. Both of his sons, Eugene Jr. (1910–50) and Shane (1919–77), committed suicide and he was bitterly estranged from his daughter, Oona (1925–91), following her 1943 marriage to much-older comic actor Charlie Chaplin.

Suffering from tuberculosis, alcoholism and severe depression himself, O'Neill overcame his afflictions to find fulfillment first as a seaman and ultimately as a playwright. His heavily autobiographical tragedies helped transform American theater from an arena of pure entertainment into a high art form. O'Neill's six years at **Tao House**, a then-remote home he built with his third wife—Carlotta (née Hazel Tharzing, 1888–1965), an actress and a former Miss California—were among the happiest and most productive of his life.

In 1936, the intensely private O'Neills bought 158 acres of almond and walnut orchards on the flank of Las Trampas Ridge, attracted by the site's remoteness and its handsome views of Mt. Diablo and the San Ramon Valley.

Designed by architect Frederick Confer, their white, two-story Monterey-style house was built of concrete blocks intended to resemble adobe brick, with a black-tile roof and verandas on the second floor. The couple christened their home Tao House after Carlotta's taste for chinoiserie and Eugene's interest in the Taoist philosophy. Here O'Neill wrote six plays, including four of his greatest: *The Iceman Cometh, Hughie, A Moon for the Misbegotten* (whose intended setting is thought to be the old barn on this property) and his masterpiece, *A Long Day's Journey into Night.*

O'Neill's degenerative illness and an inability to hire local assistance during World War II forced the couple to sell the house in February 1944 and return to the East Coast, where the playwright

Tao House living room, Eugene O'Neill National Historic Site

NPS photo/Luther Bailey

died in 1953. After the property became a National Historic Site in 1980, the National Park Service began efforts to restore the home and furnishings.

Visit

On the downstairs floor, guided tours lead through the kitchen, living room, guest room (which hosted Bennett Cerf, Somerset Maugham and John Ford), and "Rosie's Room," named for O'Neill's cherished player piano. Upstairs are O'Neill's writing den, which he furnished in a style fitting for a shipboard cabin, and the couple's bedrooms—the writer's still containing his original bed, an antique Chinese opium couch from Gump's. The 13-acre site also preserves the pool built for the playwright, an avid swimmer, and the grave of the O'Neills' beloved Dalmatian dog, Blemie.

👥 Blackhawk Museum★★

3700 Blackhawk Plaza Cir., Danville, 33mi from San Francisco. Exit I-680 at Sycamore Valley Blvd. (which becomes Camino Tassajara) and continue 5mi to Blackhawk Plaza.
🕐*Open Wed–Sun 10am–5pm.*
🕐*Closed Jan 1, Thanksgiving Day, Dec 25.* 💲*$15.* 🔊*Guided tours (1hr) available Sat–Sun 2pm.* ♿ 🅿 *℘925-736-2280. www.blackhawkmuseum.org.*
At the eastern end of Blackhawk Plaza —a beautiful, Mediterranean-style luxury shopping complex landscaped with a cascading artificial creek—rises

the rose-granite and glass facade of this museum. It displays a rotating collection of more than 40 historically significant restored vintage automobiles spanning the 1890s through the 1960s. Informatively labeled and attractively arranged through two levels, the rare and historic vehicles are presented as works of art. From the ground floor, an interior hall leads to the Moving Inspirations Art Galleries, comprising nearly 4,000 pieces of automotive art and memorabilia.

John Muir National Historic Site★

4202 Alhambra Ave., Martinez, 30mi from San Francisco. Take I-80 northeast from Oakland to Rte. 4 East; exit at Alhambra Ave. and turn left.
🕐*Open daily 10am–5pm. Guided tours daily 2pm, with additional tours Sat-Sun 11am.* 🕐*Closed Jan 1, Thanksgiving Day, Dec 25.* 🍴♿🅿 *℘925-228-8860. www.nps.gov/jomu.*
This comfortable home surrounded by orchards formed part of the 2,600-acre fruit ranch owned by **John Muir** (1838–1914). The legendary conservationist resided here during the final decades of his life, tending orchards and writing works that have since become landmarks of the environmental movement. Born near Dunbar, Scotland, Muir arrived in Wisconsin with his family at the age of 11. Detesting the drudgery of farm work, he eventually departed to pursue the life of a wandering botanist, walking

first to the Gulf of Mexico in 1867, where he took ship passage for San Francisco. His many visits to the Sierra Nevada invoked a lifelong love for rugged wilderness. A fine scientist and gifted writer, Muir published observations of nature that attracted a following among East Coast readers and opened minds to the then-novel idea of conserving wilderness lands.

Muir helped found and served as the first president of the Sierra Club, and eventually prevailed upon the U.S. Congress to bolster the young National Parks movement with new or expanded parklands in the Sierra Nevada and elsewhere.

Visit

Built in 1882 by Muir's father-in-law, Dr. John Strentzel, this two-story, Italianate frame residence was John Muir's home from 1890 until his death. The house reflects the Victorian proclivities of the Strentzel family more than Muir's own simple tastes. The conservationist wrote many of his influential books in the second-floor "scribble den," which retains his original desk and objects collected on his trips throughout the U.S.

Muir himself planted the large *Sequoia giganteum* (giant sequoia) that grows sturdily near the northwest corner of the house. The park also preserves a number of grape vines and fruit trees, and beyond, 326 acres of land on Mt. Wanda. Beyond the orchard stands the **Martinez Adobe** (1849), received by Vicente Martínez as part of an early 19C land grant of 17,750 acres.

A film on Muir's life is shown in the visitor center. Muir and his family are interred in a nearby private graveyard.

Benicia

34mi from San Francisco.
Take I-80 northeast from Oakland across the Carquinez Bridge, then east on I-780 to 2nd St. exit in Benicia. ℘707-745-2120. www.beniciachamber.com.
Established on part of General Mariano Vallejo's vast land holdings, this small, friendly community on the north shore of the Carquinez Straits was named for

Vallejo's wife. The town—second to be incorporated in the state—grew up along 10 blocks of First Street north of the waterfront, today a pleasant boulevard of cafes and shops. From February 11, 1853, to February 25, 1854, Benicia served as the California state capital. **Benicia Capitol State Historic Park** *(115 West G St.; ◷open Thu noon-4pm, Sat–Sun 10am–5pm; ◷ closed Jan 1, Thanksgiving Day, Dec 25; ⊕$3; ℙ ℘707-745-3385; www.parks.ca.gov)* preserves the old brick statehouse, furnished as it may have been during its one-year tenure.

Benicia Arsenal

From 1st St. drive east on Military East, pass through the old army gate. Follow signs to the Camel Barn and Clocktower.
The U.S. Army founded a military reservation in Benicia in 1849, establishing the Benicia Arsenal the following year. One of four U.S. arsenals at the time, it served until it was deactivated in 1964, after which it was converted to the Benicia Industrial Park. Many of the old military buildings today house offices and artists' studios, some of which are open to the public.

Among historic reminders of the army's presence are the oldest military cemetery in the Pacific states (1849), the turreted arsenal storehouse known as the Clocktower (1859), the commandant's house, and the **Benicia Historical Museum** *(2060 Camel Rd.; ◷open Wed–Sun 1–4pm; ⊕$7 (free 1st Wed of month); ♿ ℙ ℘707-745-5435; www. beniciahistoricalmuseum.org)*, where the army auctioned camels in 1864 after experimenting with them as pack animals in the North American deserts.

Port Chicago Naval Magazine National Memorial

Concord Naval Weapons Station, 38mi from San Francisco. Take I-80 northeast from Oakland to Rte. 4 East; exit at Port Chicago Hwy. and proceed to main gate.
◤Visit by guided tour (1hr) only Thur–Sat 12.45pm (2wk advance reservation required). ◷Closed Jan 1, Thanksgiving

Day, Dec 25, during Concord Naval Station operations. ♿🅿 ✆925-228-8860. www.nps.gov/poch.

This somber memorial was dedicated on July 17, 1994, on the 50th anniversary of a World War II munitions explosion that killed 320 mostly African-American military and civilian workers. Wayside exhibits line a brick walkway that leads to the Suisun Bay tidal basin, where the memorial stands. Names of all victims are etched into its polished black granite. Inland, a chapel and visitor center contains further exhibits.

Vallejo Naval & Historical Museum

734 Marin St., Vallejo.

🕐Open Mon–Fri 10am–2pm. Sat 10am-4pm. ⊚$5. ♿🅿 ✆707-643-0077. www.vallejomuseum.org.

Located in the former Vallejo City Hall (1927), this fine small museum has five galleries that recount regional history. It highlights the naval presence with a submarine periscope installed through the roof for a 360-degree view.

Two-to-three-hour walking tours of the **Mare Island Naval Shipyard** are arranged through the museum. The U.S. Navy purchased Mare Island in 1852 and assigned David Farragut ("Damn the torpedoes, full speed ahead") as its first commandant. The base grew to become the largest ship construction and repair site in the world. Tours take in 19C–20C housing of many styles, a hospital complex, dry docks and other facilities.

👥 Six Flags Discovery Kingdom★

1001 Fairgrounds Dr., Vallejo, 30mi from San Francisco. Take I-80 northeast from Oakland and exit at Rte. 37. Or take Blue & Gold Fleet ferry from Pier 41 (San Francisco) to Vallejo with shuttle service to the park.

🕐**Park** open daily mid-May–Labor Day; Sat–Sun early Sept–April; hours and additional days of operation vary seasonally; check website. ⊚$70.99; children under 4ft $50.99. ✕♿🅿($30). ✆707-643-6722. www.sixflags.com/discoverykingdom.

This 160-acre landscaped park contains a zoo, an oceanarium and an amusement park, while entertaining and educating visitors about conservation issues with various shows and exhibits. Begun as a modest theme park 25mi south of San Francisco, it was renamed Marine World Africa USA in 1972 and relocated in 1986 to Vallejo. The Six Flags chain of theme parks acquired the park in 1999.

Visit

A visit to the Discovery Kingdom is best structured around live animal performances in various outdoor amphitheaters (shows last 2–30min; map and schedule available at entrance). ⊙Entrance to these attractions requires additional pass purchase.

Prominent are the bottle-nosed acrobats of **Dolphin Harbor** who dive, cavort and splash the audience in the aptly-named show **Drench** and the **Wildlife Theater**, where the presentation of exotic animals from around the world furthers appreciation for endangered species. There also are seal, sea-lion and tropical-bird displays. Visitors pass through a transparent viewing tunnel as sharks swim overhead in **Shark Experience★**; hand-feed giraffes at the **Giraffe Dock**; watch frisky walruses through a glass-walled tank at the **Walrus Experience★**; and explore the steamy jungle setting of the **Butterfly Habitat★**. The **Odin's Temple of the Tiger★** provides an underwater viewing window on 400-pound Bengals. **Looney Tunes Seaport** is a children's ride and amusement area. Among the most popular rides are the **V2: Vertical Velocity**, which spirals riders to speeds of up to 70mph in less than 4 seconds; and **Monsoon Falls**, in which rafters plunge over a 55ft rapid. The nine roller-coasters are even better known; they include **Medusa**, which travels at 65mph through seven inversions; **Superman Ultimate Flight**, that simulates flying, and the new **Wonder Woman Lasso of Truth,** a gigantic pendulum ride that takes riders sky high while rotating counterclockwise (slated for early-mid 2017).

MARIN COUNTY

Introduced by the windswept ridges, sheltered valleys, and sandy coves of the Marin Headlands, Marin County lies just over the Golden Gate Bridge from San Francisco. Here, surrounded on three sides by water, you'll find uparalleled natural sites such as the wave-lashed sands of Point Reyes National Seashore, the lofty peak (2,571ft) of Mount Tamalpais, and the majestic stands of redwoods (one of only two stands of virgin growth in the National Park Service) at Muir Woods National Monument. Western Marin County in particular remains a favorite desination for day and weekend trippers from San Francisco, especially Sausalito, Point Reyes and Muir Woods.

Highlights

1 Admire classic views of San Francisco from **East Fort Baker** (p243)

2 Drive the amazingly scenic **Conzelman Road** (p245)

3 Walk beneath awe-inspiring redwoods at **Muir Woods** (p249)

4 Wild, windswept views at **Point Reyes Lighthouse** (p253)

5 Stroll along stylish Bridgeway Boulevard in **Sausalito** (p258)

History

The uplift of the coast ranges some 25 million years ago established a new coastline for California. Today's many marine terraces, marking the shoreline of millenia past, are a visible legacy of this dramatic uplift that continues to raise the mountains. The ruggedness of these shores ensured their isolation for centuries after initial European exploration in the 16C. Despite the claims of Sir Frances Drake for England in 1579, the coast Miwok, Pomo, Yuki, and other tribes lived virtually untouched by the outside world until 1812, when the Russians established a colony at Fort Ross. Though Russian efforts were short-lived, they provoked greater interest in northern California from Mexican authorities. Mexicans grazed cattle here after they threw off the Spanish yoke in 1821. Meanwhile, Americans logged the redwood forests to near depletion into the early 20C. During World War II, defenses were built along the Marin Headlands, and the Marinship naval shipyard employed thousands of workers. By the latter half of the 20C, Marin County had become synonymous with the California lifestyle. Little wonder that director George Lucas chose the region as the pastoral home for Skywalker Ranch, his celebrated movie and audio post-production facility.

Houseboats, Sausalito

© Eddie Hernandez Photography/iStockphoto.com

Visiting Today

Marin County's natural beauty, coupled with the laid-back atmosphere of the rural towns, provide a welcome break from the dynamism of San Francisco city life. Not to mention the fact that this area makes a great launching point for exploring the wineries of the Sonoma Valley. Sausalito is a favorite excursion for both residents and visitors, lying just a short drive or ferry ride across the bay from San Francisco. The most appealing way to get here—on a nice day—is to hop aboard a ferry from the city. Once you disembark, it's an easy stroll along Bridgeway Boulevard, the community's commercial spine, where you'll find upscale shops and gorgeous views. Restaurants on the water offer vistas that stretch across the bay to Tiburon and Angel Island. On the land side, tiers of pricey private residences climb down the steep slopes to the bay.

Keep traveling north on Highway 101 to discover charming towns like Mill Valley and Larkspur or detour along the coast to bohemian Inverness and Tomales Bay. Also in Marin Country is the Muir Woods National Monument. The 560-acre plot of Coast Redwoods was named for Scottish immigrant, John Muir, the revered naturalist and pioneer in the U.S. forest conservation movement—which celebrated its 100th anniversary in 2008.

ADDRESSES

🏨 STAY

$$$$ The Inn Above Tide – *30 El Portal, Sausalito; ☎415-332-9535, www.innabovetide.com.* The suites at this luxury inn, all of which boast spectacular views of the water, were updated in 2018 with custom art and furniture. Seals and pelicans glide past private balconies as sailboats materialize from the bay's haunting fog.

$$$ Mill Valley Inn – *165 Throckmorton Ave., Mill Valley. ☎415-389-6608. www.marinhotels.com. 25 rooms.* French doors open onto private decks or balconies overlooking a redwood grove or the streets of charming Mill Valley. Breakfast, included in the room rate, is served on an outdoor terrace.

$$$$$ Manka's Inverness Lodge- *30 Callendar Way, Inveness. ☎415-669-1034. www.mankas.com. 6 rooms, 2 cabins and 1 house.* After this 1917 hunting and fishing lodge, built in the Arts and Crafts style, burned to the ground in 2006, the owners lovingly rebuilt it with a stylish cabin-in-the-woods aesthetic.

$$$ Nick's Cove *23249 Highway 1, Marshall. ☎415-663-1033 nickscove.com. 12 cottages.* Sleep in a cozily decorated stilted cabin, warmed by a wood stove and perched over Tomales Bay, at this West Marin charmer, also home to an old-school-style waterfront restaurant (*$$. Sun–Thu 11am-8pm, Fri–Sat 11am-9pm*) popular with oyster-crazed locals.

🍽 EAT

$$ Buckeye Roadhouse – *15 Shoreline Hwy., Mill Valley. ☎415-331-2600. www.buckeyeroadhouse.com.* **American**. Classic American cooking is given a gourmet touch in this handsome 1937-vintage lodge, where the smell of wood smoke permeates the air. Come for a plate of bingo oysters and a martini.

$$ Fish *350 Harbor Drive, Sausalito 415-331-3474. www.331fish.com.* **Seafood**. Ultra-fresh local catch is prepared in sandwiches, chowders, and tacos at this superlative counter-service spot, where draft beer is served in mason jars and the dining room is a cluster of first-come-first-serve picnic tables overlooking the famous houseboats in Sausalito's harbor.

$$$ Sir and Star – *1000 Sir Francis Drake, Olema. ☎415-663-1034. sirandstar.com.* **Californian**. The bounty of surrounding Point Reyes farmland is duly reflected in the menu at this elegant country restaurant, where coastal cauliflower soup, a heritage lamb chop, and glass of red make a charming conclusion to a day on the coast.

$ Terrapin Crossroads –*100 Yacht Club Drive, San Rafael. ☎415-524-2773* **Californian**. There are live bands in the bar every night, wine on tap and California-style cuisine in the family-friendly restaurant, an onsite concert hall, and an outdoor stage for summer festivities at this lively music and gathering spot owned by former Grateful Dead bassist Phil Lesh.

Marin Headlands★★

Rising north of the Golden Gate, these 15 square miles of pristine coastal lands encompass windswept ridges, sheltered valleys, sandy coves and scattered vestiges of the area's military history. Protected since 1972 as part of the Golden Gate National Recreation Area (and by the U.S. Army before that), the Marin Headlands offer unequaled views of the city-fringed bay, the Golden Gate Bridge elegantly overlapping San Francisco's skyline, and the vast Pacific Ocean stretching away to the western horizon. Hiking, biking, fishing, and camping opportunities abound.

A BIT OF HISTORY

The headlands' strategic importance became evident to U.S. Forces soon after their takeover of California in 1846. A fort was planned at Lime Point (today the north pier of the Golden Gate Bridge) to complement Fort Point and Alcatraz in guarding the mouth of the strait. The fort was never built, but other defenses—batteries, bunkers and gun emplacements—appeared along the bluffs. Many installations rapidly grew obsolete, to be replaced by newer armaments at Forts Baker, Barry and Cronkhite. No gun was ever fired in defense, and today the grounds of the forts harbor a multitude of abandoned coastal defense installations ranging from post-Civil War earthen bunkers to Cold War-era Nike missile sites.

Thickly covered with coastal grasses, sagebrush, coyote brush and oak woodlands, the headlands are a wilderness providing habitat for lizards and snakes, elusive bobcats and foxes, and blacktailed deer. In spring, lupine, Indian paintbrush and other colorful wildflowers decorate the hillsides, and in fall, various species of raptors pass by on their annual migration to winter nesting grounds in the south—sometimes up to as many as 100 hawks fly overhead each hour. Lagoons and coves attract stately egrets and herons, while fleets of brown pelicans patrol the coastal waters. The seas cliffs are renowned by geologists for their pillow bassalt exposures; offshore rocks provide haven for seals, sea lions and nesting shorebirds.

🚌 Bus 76-Headlands (Saturday, Sundays and holidays only); 511.org

ℹ️ **Info:** ☎415-331-1540; www.nps.gov/goga/marin-headlands.htm.

▶ **Location:** By car, follow US-101 north across the Golden Gate Bridge and exit at Alexander Ave. (2mi); follow Marin Headlands signs.

👫 **Kids:** Geared especially for kids under 10 years old, the popular Bay Area Discovery Museum has imaginative exhibits on the local environment.

🕐 **Timing:** In summer, ocean-born fogs pour over these hills, freshening the air but obscuring the stunning views of the bridge, bay and city. In fall and spring—the best seasons to visit—the hills bask in sunshine. If possible, avoid crowds by going mid-week; Sundays are especially popular.

🅿️ **Parking:** There are free parking lots at nearly all the sights in the Marin Headlands.

👁 **Don't Miss:** The classic views south overlooking the Golden Gate Bridge from Conzelman Road and the bluffs of East Fort Baker.

Marin Headlands

© mtilghma/iStockphoto.com

SIGHTS
Fort Baker

From San Francisco, follow US-101 north across the Golden Gate Bridge to the Alexander Ave. exit, just past Vista Pt. At Bunker Rd., turn left and follow signs to the Bay Area Discovery Museum.
Named in honor of Col. Edward Dickinson Baker, a Civil War hero and friend of Abraham Lincoln, this attractive group of buildings and batteries was the first military post on the north side of the Golden Gate. Eight small batteries were constructed between 1873 and 1943, including the still-visible Battery Yates (1905) near Cavallo Point—the easternmost tip of Horseshoe Cove.

Formerly home to the Army's 91st Division Reserve, the section east of the bridge, called **East Fort Baker**, now hosts a U.S. Coast Guard station, the Presidio Yacht Club and the Bay Area Discovery Museum (below). Stroll the bluffs overlooking Horseshoe Cove for dramatic **views★★** of the Golden Gate Bridge.

The **Bay Trail***(.25mi)* along the shore east of Cavallo Point offers views of the East Bay, Angel Island and Alcatraz while skirting the habitat of the endangered Mission Blue butterfly.

**MARIN HEADLANDS
MOUNT TAMALPAIS**

Father of the National Parks

United State Mint image

When William Kent donated land for Muir Woods National Park in 1908, he insisted that the park be named after California's most famous and beloved naturalist, John Muir.

Born in Dunbar, Scotland in 1838, Muir emigrated to America with his family in 1849. In the fields and woods of Wisconsin's countryside, Muir cultivated a deep love of the natural world.

In 1867, following a recovery from an eye injury, Muir set out to explore the natural world. After traveling throughout the US and Central America, he entered Yosemite's high country in 1868 and fell in love. He would go on to write, "Then it seemed to me the Sierra should be called not the Nevada, or Snowy Range, but the Range of Light...the most divinely beautiful of all the mountain chains I have ever seen."

Muir became the valley's most devoted champion. In 1875 he wrote an article proposing that Yosemite be declared a national park, and in 1890 Congress passed the Yosemite National Park bill, setting aside the wilderness around Yosemite Valley and Mariposa Grove. In 1905, after lobbying by Muir and others, California ceded the valley and Mariposa Grove to the federal government to be incorporated in the park.

In addition to Yosemite, Muir helped create the Sequoia, Mount Rainier, Petrified Forest and Grand Canyon national parks. He is also credited with the 1892 founding of the Sierra Club, a preeminent organization dedicated to preservation and expansion of wildlife and wilderness areas. In 2005, California honored Muir by commemorating him on California's State Quarter.

Muir's prolific writings about his travels and naturalist philosophy continue to inspire readers to explore the country's wilderness.

Half Dome, Yosemite National Park

© Tomas Nevesely/iStockphoto.com

Conzelman Road leading to Point Bonita

© Peter Dean/iStockphoto.com

👥 Bay Area Discovery Museum★ (M)

East Fort Baker, 557 McReynolds Rd., Sausalito. 🕐*Open Tue–Fri 9am–4pm, Sat 10am–5pm, Sun 9am–5pm.* 🕐*Closed major holidays and 10 days in Sept.* 👁️*$13.95 (free 1st Wed of month).* ✕♿🅿️ 🕿*415-339-3900.* *www.baykidsmuseum.org.*

With a stunning location in a cluster of historic Army buildings in Fort Baker, this excellent and highly interactive children's museum has hands-on indoor and outdoor exhibits scattered throughout a eucalyptus-cloaked 2.5-acre space. For older children, the **Fab Lab** is a high-tech maker space filled with 3-D printers, laser cutters, and vinyl cutters. For the littlest visitors, the **Tot Spot** has a miniature river to splash in, costumes and puppets, and other stimulating multi-sensory games. At the **Bay Hall**, kids can sail the seas or fish for salmon on the Discovery Boat, or play with a huge wooden train set. Though the focus is on kids, adults will enjoy the museum's sublime setting, with views of the fog rolling in over the Golden Gate Bridge.

Conzelman Road★★★

From Fort Baker, return to Alexander Ave., turn right toward US-101, pass under the freeway and continue to Conzelman Rd., following signs for Marin Headlands.

This gloriously scenic route snakes along the Headlands' rugged bluffs past abandoned military batteries. Turnouts provide opportunities to drink in outstanding **views★★★** of San Francisco Bay, the Golden Gate Bridge and the Pacific.

Stop at **Battery Spencer** *(.25mi)*, a massive concrete casement built in 1896 to house three cannons, for a formidable city view framed by the looming north pier of the Golden Gate Bridge.

From mid-August to mid-December, **Hawk Hill★** *(1.75mi)*, draws legions of birders to witness the southward migration of raptors—eagles, hawks and falcons—plying the only such flyway on the West Coast. Just below it, the **Battery Construction 129** the highest gun battery in the U.S., was begun in 1942 to house a 16in gun capable of firing shells over 20mi.

Beyond Battery 129 the road crests and becomes a winding one-way passage that curves down along the precipitous edge of a high sea cliff. Entering decommissioned Fort Barry, it heads past Battery Rathbone-McIndoe (1905) to Batteries Alexander (1905), Wallace (1918) and Mendell (c. 1905). From the latter, views extend west and north over the coastal headlands, guano-covered Bird Rock, Rodeo Valley and the stark barracks and buildings of Fort Cronkhite. Point Bonita can be seen due south of Battery Mendell.

Ohlones and Coast Miwoks

When the Spanish explorers arrived in the 18C, the Bay Area supported some 7,000–10,000 people, and was North America's most densely populated region north of Mexico. The **Coast Miwok** dwelt north of the city, in present-day Marin and western Sonoma counties. Their rich cultural heritage included basket-making, dances, ceremonies, and a complex and intricate language. Their diet included large game, seafood, buckeye nuts, clover, honey, and dried kelp. The **Ohlone**, or Costanoans, inhabited areas on the San Francisco Peninsula, east of the bay and south to Big Sur. The semi-nomadic people lived in light and portable structures built of tule, and moved according to ancient seasonal patterns of hunting and gathering for foods such as acorns, berries and salmon. Their deep connection to the natural world was expressed in creation myths enacted in songs, dances, and games.

👥 Point Bonita Lighthouse★

From the end of Conzelman Rd., follow lighthouse signs to trailhead for a hike (.5mi) to Point Bonita (sturdy shoes advised). ⏰*Open Sat–Mon 12.30–3.30pm.* 🚶*Guided tours (45min) 12.30pm.* 🅿 ☎*415-331-1540. www.nps.gov/goga/pobo.htm.*

Perched on the rocky tip of Point Bonita, this lighthouse has helped guide mariners through the Golden Gate since 1855. Though automated in 1981, the it still employs its original Fresnel lens, through which beacons of light were beamed to 19C passenger ships, lumber schooners and naval fleets of both world wars. Extensive restorations to the lighthouse were completed in 1996.

👥 Marin Headlands Visitor Center★

Building 948, Fort Barry, Sausalito. From Conzelman Rd. take Field Rd. to the corner of Bunker Rd. ⏰*Open Wed–Mon 9.30am–4.30pm.* ⏰*Closed Tues, Thanksgiving, Dec 25.* 🚶*Call ahead for schedule of guided tours (1–2hrs).* ♿🅿 ☎*415-331-1540. www.nps.gov/ goga/marin-headlands.htm.*

Located in Fort Barry's former post chapel (1941), this ranger station mounts excellent, hands-on natural history displays and exhibits on the human inhabitants of the headlands—Coast Miwok, 19C vaqueros (Mexican and Native American cattle ranchers), Portuguese dairy ranchers, lighthouse keepers, and soldiers. Browse the well-stocked bookstore for field guides and maps. Near the visitor center lies Missile Site SF 88L, a former **Nike missile site**, one of several around the bay. Its original but unarmed Nike missiles are open to the public on weekends; there is a special open house with Army veterans on the first Sat of each month (⏰*open Thu, Fri, Sat 12.30–5.30pm;* ♿🅿 ☎*415-331-1543).*

Headlands Center for the Arts

944 Simmonds Road, Sausalito. Take a left onto Bodsworth Rd. and another left onto Simmonds Rd. ⏰*Open Sun-Thu noon–5pm.* ♿🅿 ☎*415-331-27870. www.headlands.org.*

This multidisciplinary arts center in Fort Barry operates a robust international artist-in-residence program. Stop in for a coffee and biscotti in the Mess Hall, then take a turn around the Project Space gallery to see what current residents are creating, or visit during one of the center's frequent speakers, public dinners, or open-studio events.

Fort Cronkhite & Rodeo Beach

Follow Bunker Rd. to Mitchell Rd. and continue along Rodeo Lagoon to beach parking lot.

Named for a World War I commander, the fort houses gun batteries and a Nike missile. It is one of the best examples of mobilization posts in the country. Visitors can walk around the barracks, mess halls and supply buildings, which overlook the crashing waves of Rodeo Beach.

Mount Tamalpais★★

The geographic focal point of southern Marin County, kingly Mt. Tamalpais *(tam-ul-PIE-us)*—known locally as Mt. Tam—towers majestically over San Francisco from the north. Its rocky, 2,571ft summit affords some of the Bay Area's finest views, while its flanks harbor an extraordinary abundance of trails, meadows, forests and other enticements to delight lovers of natural beauty and outdoor sports. Largely undeveloped, its terrain protected as state and national parklands or county watershed, it has been a treasured recreation resource for Bay Area urbanites for more than a century.

A BIT OF HISTORY

Coast Miwok tribes made their home on the bay and ocean fringes of Mt. Tamalpais for at least 3,000 years prior to European exploration and settlement of the area. The mountain itself was considered sacred. In 1772, Spanish explorers Don Pedro Fages and Padre Juan Crespí named the mountain La Sierra de Nuestro Padre de San Francisco ("The Mountain of Our Father of San Francisco"). Its present name is thought to have been derived from the Coast Miwok words *tamal,* meaning "bay," and *pa* (later corrupted by the Spanish to *pais*), meaning "mountain."

Trail, Rail and Carriage – In the decades following the Gold Rush, residents and visitors looked to the mountain for leisure and recreation. Hiking trails were established, and in 1884 a wagon road to the west peak was built. By 1896 tourists could ascend from the foothill town of Mill Valley to the summit aboard the steam-powered Mill Valley and Mt. Tamalpais Scenic Railway (later known as the Mt. Tamalpais and Muir Woods Railway). Dubbed the "Crookedest Railroad in the World," the train chugged along a steep 8.2mi route, negotiating 281 curves. In 1907, a "gravity car" line to

Michelin Map: See p243.

Info: ☎415-388-2070. www.parks.ca.gov.

Location: To get to Mt. Tam from San Francisco, take US-101 north over the Golden Gate Bridge to the Mill Valley/Stinson Beach exit and turn left onto shore-hugging Rte. 1 (Shoreline Hwy.). Turn right on Panoramic Highway and follow the signs to Mt. Tamalpais. The **Muir Woods Road** branches off the Panoramic Highway.

The park can be reached by public transportation via West Marin Stagecoach. ☎511 or 415-455-2000. marintransit.org/stage.html.

Kids: A walk under the mighty redwoods at Muir Woods National Monument.

Timing: The mountain is a favored recreation destination, and each season has advantages. In spring, myriad small creeks run full, grassy ridges wear a lush green coat, and wildflowers festoon the slopes. In summer, thick fogs can blanket the mountain's lower slopes; yet the summit is often sunny with extraordinary views of fog-wrapped San Francisco Bay. Fall and winter tend to be cool.

Parking: On mountain lots ($8/ car) are East Peak, Rock Spring, Pantoll Ranger Station, Bootjack Picnic Area and Mountain Theater.

Don't Miss: To enjoy the awe-inspiring Muir Woods redwoods, head there early or late in the day.

Muir Woods was installed, wherein passengers glided silently down from the summit to the Muir Woods Inn before hiking or riding horse-drawn carriages to the redwood forest. The railway ceased operation in 1930.

The work of preserving Mt. Tamalpais' unspoiled beauty was initiated by **William Kent,** an ardent and wealthy Marin County conservationist and state representative. Kent's donations and political lobbying helped create Muir Woods National Monument and Mount Tamalpais State Park.

A nature lover's paradise, Mt. Tamalpais is blessed with abundant wildlife and a tremendous variety of vegetation. Some 300 species of birds have been spotted here, including red-tailed hawks, turkey vultures, black ravens, Stellar's jays, quail, wrens and pileated woodpeckers. Black-tailed deer, Western gray squirrels, Sonoma chipmunks and brush rabbits all make their homes here. Nocturnal bobcats are present but rarely seen, and sightings of mountain lions and coyotes have been reported, though most were hunted out in the early 1800s.

SIGHTS
Mount Tamalpais State Park★★
801 Panoramic Hwy, Mill Valley, 18mi from San Francisco.
🕐*Park open daily 7am–sunset.*
🕐*Closed during high fire-risk days. Maps and recreation information available at Pantoll ranger station (*🕐*open summer daily 8am–dusk, rest of the year hours vary) and Mt. Tamalpais Interpretive Association's East Peak Visitor Center (*🕐*open Sat–*

Sun 11am-4pm). ⊗*$8/car.* △ 📞*415-388-2070. http://parks.ca.gov.*

The park began as a 200-acre gift from William Kent and was later enlarged through the efforts of local hiking clubs. Today it completely surrounds Muir Woods National Monument. Nature lovers flock to Mt. Tam's trails year-round, and summer brings theatergoers to the Mountain Theatre, a woodsy amphitheater with terraced stone seats, which mounts popular musicals on weekends in May and June (*E. Ridgecrest Blvd., just east of intersection with Pantoll Rd.;* 📞*415-383-1100; www.mountainplay.org*).

East Peak
From the Pantoll ranger station, take Pantoll Rd. to Ridgecrest Blvd. and continue toward the summit.

Numerous turnouts, picnic spots, trailheads and scenic overlooks mark the long ascent to a parking area a quarter-mile below the top of Mt. Tamalpais. From here, cities, towns and majestic bay appear as if on a giant raised relief map, backdropped to the east by Mt. Diablo, 35mi away. The 360-degree panorama is one of the finest **views★★★** in the Bay Area. On exceptionally clear winter days, the snow-capped Sierra Nevada mountains are visible 140mi to the east, as are Mt. St. Helena to the north and the Farallon Islands to the west.

Vegetation at this elevation consists mostly of the brushy mix of scrub oak and red-barked manzanita known as chaparral. From the East Peak parking lot, a short but rocky and strenuous path (*.3mi*) leads to the summit fire lookout, rebuilt in 1937 by the Civilian Conservation Corps (⊶ *closed to the public*). The

A Cradle for Mountain Biking

In the early 1970s, a group of local bicycle enthusiasts began modifying and equipping their traditional balloon-tired "cruiser" bikes to withstand travel across Mt. Tamalpais' rugged trails and fire roads. Riding and racing such bikes became a local passion, and the ensuing years brought increasing technological innovations that resulted in today's sophisticated "mountain bikes." Mt. Tamalpais continues to attract a steady stream of bicycling enthusiasts, many of whom make the strenuous ascent to the summit on the unpaved Old Railroad and Eldridge grades.

⚑ **Verna Dunshee Trail** *(.7mi)* makes a level, paved loop around the summit. Many trails guide hikers and cyclists to East Peak and other points around the park. One of the more popular mountain-bike routes starts from a trailhead at **Mountain Home Inn,** a bed-and-breakfast lodge built on the site of a historic railroad inn *(810 Panoramic Hwy.; park in public lot across from the inn)*. The path ascends on unpaved fire roads that follow, in part, the old railway grade. Hikers may prefer to start higher on the mountain, at Pantoll, where several possible routes lead to the summit. Another popular destination is the **West Point Inn** (1904), a rustic wooden structure situated on a ridge just below the summit. Hikers, equestrians and bicyclists congregate here to relax on the shady veranda and take in panoramic **views**. From the inn, the Old Railroad Grade continues to East Peak.

⚏ MUIR WOODS NATIONAL MONUMENT★★★

17mi from San Francisco.
Take US-101 north to Rte. 1 (Shoreline Hwy.); continue to Panoramic Hwy. and follow signs to Muir Woods.
🕐*Open daily 8am–sunset.* 🎫*$10.*
✕♿🅿 *Advance reservations required for parking or shuttle service, book at gomuirwoods.com or 800-410-2419. $8.50 per vehicle.* ☎*415-388-2596. www.nps.gov/muwo.*
Situated on the slope of Mt. Tamalpais along Redwood Creek, Muir Woods harbors one of the largest stands of ancient coast redwoods in the Bay Area. The tranquil grove of majestic red-barked trees, some 1,100 years in age, attracts more than 1.5 million visitors annually.

A Tree-Lover's Monument

The world's tallest trees, coast redwoods *(Sequoia sempervirens)*, can attain heights equal to that of a 36-story building. They are among the few conifers that can sprout from knotty outgrowths, called burls, as well as reproduce by seeds. The absence of resin in the trees' 6in- to 12in-thick bark, coupled with the high tannin content of the wood, ren-

Muir Woods National Monument

© Damien Michelin

ders them resistant to fire, insect damage and disease, enabling them to live for hundreds of years. Muir Woods is a relatively young grove; its oldest trees are more than a millennium old. California's tallest, oldest redwoods thrive north of here in the Redwood Empire. Prior to the arrival of Europeans on the west coast, millions of acres of primeval redwood forest blanketed the coastal reaches of California and southern Oregon; aggressive logging has since wiped out all but 150,000 acres. Much of Mt. Tamalpais' virgin redwood forest was logged in the years following the Gold Rush, but the trees in present-day Muir Woods escaped the lumbermen's saws and axes, owing to their relative inaccessibility. The forest became a national monument in 1908 after William Kent donated 295 acres of land in Redwood Canyon to the federal government in 1907, insisting that the park be named for conservationist John Muir. In a letter of thanks to Kent, Muir wrote, "This is the best tree-lover's monument that could possibly be found in all the forests of the world."

Visit

The redwoods found in Muir Woods are epic, but so are the crowds, particularly during the high season. As of January

2018, all visitors are required to make advance reservations for the Marin Transit shuttle to the park (see below) or for a space in the onsite parking lot. Spots are reserved for a 30-minute window, but, once parked, vehicles may stay in the lot until closing. Marin Transit operates weekend park-and-ride shuttle service from Sausalito and Marin City to Muir Woods year-round, and weekday service from June to August (*$3 round trip, check routes and schedules at gomuirwoods.com*). Visitors who hike or cycle to the park do not require a reservation. Note that there is no cell phone service or WiFi at Muir Woods.

From the visitor center and adjacent bookstore , six miles of trails (some paved) wind about the forest floor, following the paths of Redwood Creek and Fern Creek. The **Main Trail** 🚶 *(1mi)* crosses over a series of wooden bridges, looping under a dense canopy of mature redwoods that rise like spires toward the heavens. Amid groves of living trees, trunks of fallen giants lie in various states of decay in a lush undergrowth of sword ferns, azaleas and horsetail, a primitive plant whose ancestry dates back 300 million years. Muir Woods' most impressive trees stand in **Cathedral Grove** and **Bohemian Grove,** site of the park's tallest tree (unmarked), measuring 253ft.

The Main Trail connects to the Hillside Trail *(1.9mi loop)* or to the Ocean View, Lost and Fern Creek trails *(3.1mi loop)*. Trails also connect with unpaved hiking trails in Mount Tamalpais State Park.

ADDITIONAL SIGHTS
Muir Beach Overlook
17mi from San Francisco.
Take US-101 to Rte. 1 (Shoreline Hwy.); from Muir Woods, take Frank Valley Rd. 2.5mi and turn right on Rte. 1.
Steps lead down to a railed promontory that affords sweeping **views**★★ of the coast to the north and south. Hooded concrete burrows on the bluff behind the promontory were installed during World War II; signs illustrate how they were designed to target enemy vessels. South of the overlook, Shoreline High-

way passes **Muir Beach**, a small, scenic stretch of sand situated at the mouth of Redwood Creek. Tables and grills make this an excellent spot to relax, though dangerous tides and currents make swimming inadvisable.

Stinson Beach
Rte. 1, 5mi north of Muir Beach.
Called Willow Camp in the late 19C, this charming beach town is a popular stop for coastal travelers, with its assortment of restaurants and art galleries, bookstore, surf shop and outdoor theater. The excellent **beach**★★, one of the largest in the area, is the town's principal attraction, though its surf is rough and the weather is often overcast. Spectacular on a sunny day, one of the area's most picturesque hiking trails, **Steep Ravine**,*(3mi each way)*, runs from Pantoll Ranger Station to Stinson Beach, alongside redwood-fringed Webb Creek.

👥 Audubon Canyon Ranch
4900 Shoreline Hwy. (Rte. 1), 3.5mi north of Stinson Beach.
🕐*Open mid-Mar–mid-Oct, call for hours.* 🚫*$15 donation suggested.*
🅿 📞*415-868-9244. www.egret.org.*
The Martin Griffin Preserve, overseen by the nonprofit organization Audubon Canyon Ranch, is a 1,000-acre bird sanctuary and protected wetland located in a woodsy canyon adjacent Bolinas Lagoon. It's home to one of the coast's most important nesting sites for great blue heron, great egret, and snowy egret. During the spring and summer months, the center's grounds and trails are open to hikers and birdwatchers. A small onsite museum mounts exhibits on local geology and natural history.

Bolinas
5mi north of Stinson Beach.
Take first left turn off Rte. 1 north of Bolinas Lagoon.
In a captivating setting on an off-the-beaten-path peninsula between the Pacific Ocean and Bolinas Lagoon, this picturesque community has in recent decades developed a reputation as an insular outpost of counterculture. Set-

tled in 1835 on the Baulenes Rancho land grant, the town boomed during the Gold Rush when schooners came here to load timber destined for building sites in San Francisco. Today, the quaint downtown features a charming bar, a health-food store, several cafes and the small **Bolinas Museum** *(48 Wharf Rd.; open Fri 1–5pm, Sat–Sun noon–5pm; closed Jan 1, Dec 25; 415-868-0300. www.bolinasmuseum.org).*

ADDRESSES

EAT

$$ The Pelican Inn – *10 Pacific Way, Muir Beach. 415-383-6000. www.pelican inn.com.* This thoroughly British country inn ($$$) and pub was created by a fourth-generation pub owner from Surrey, England. Pub fare and British and Irish brews are served in a low-beamed dining room and at a Tudor-style bar.

Point Reyes National Seashore★★

Windy, wave-swept and often cloaked in fog, the Point Reyes Peninsula is an enchantingly varied expanse of wilderness. Jutting from the west Marin County pasturelands into the Pacific Ocean, this 30-mile coastal wedge harbors long sandy beaches, lush forests, rugged sea cliffs and vast wetlands, all populated by diverse animal, bird and marine life. Laced by close to 150 miles of trails, the 102 square-mile peninsula was designated a National Seashore in 1962.

A BIT OF HISTORY

Formed by the San Andreas Fault, the Point Reyes Peninsula rides on the eastern edge of the Pacific tectonic plate, creeping northwesterly at about 2in per year, while the adjacent North American plate travels westward at a slower rate. The two plates meet in a rift zone that runs south through the Olema Valley and northwest beneath narrow Tomales Bay, which separates the peninsula from the rest of Marin County. The jut of land was thrust more than 16ft northwest of the mainland by the great earthquake of 1906. A legacy of the peninsula's ancient journey along the San Andreas Fault is its granite back-bone, **Inverness Ridge**, which has geo-logic origins in the Tehachapi Mountains

- **Info:** 415-464-5100. www.nps.gov/pore.
- **Location:** The Point Reyes Peninsula lies some 40mi north of San Francisco. From the city take US-101 north to Mill Valley/Stinson Beach exit (Rte. 1); continue on Shoreline Hwy. (Rte. 1) to Bear Valley Rd. (27mi). Alternatively, continue north on US-101 to the Greenbrae exit (10mi) to Sir Francis Drake Blvd. west, turn right on Rte. 1 and take the first left onto Bear Valley Rd.
- **Kids:** Kule Loklo, a re-created Miwok village.
- **Timing:** Weather conditions can change dramatically from one area to the next on the peninsula; visitors should always be prepared for cool winds and damp conditions. The autumn months are usually mildest. Winter, the rainiest season, is the best time to see migrating gray whales.
- **Don't Miss:** Point Reyes Lighthouse for its wild, windswept views. Also, the Earthquake Trail, for intriguing glimpses of terrain disrupted by the 1906 earthquake.

300mi to the south. Five million years ago, the peninsula occupied the site of present-day Monterey Bay; someday it will be an island sliding toward the Gulf of Alaska.

"White Bancks and Cliffes" – For thousands of years, Point Reyes was home to Coast Miwok Indians. The peaceable Miwoks harvested acorns and berries, fished for shellfish and salmon, and hunted deer and elk. In summer 1579, Francis Drake, an English explorer sponsored by Queen Elizabeth I, turned south from his search for a Northwest Passage and anchored his ship, the *Golden Hind*, for repairs in the vicinity of Point Reyes. The "faire and good baye" he described is thought to be the protected bay now known as Drakes Bay. Drake claimed his landfall for England, calling it "Nova Albion" after "the white bancks and cliffes" (resembling the blanched palisades of England's Dover coast) that rise over Drakes Beach.

In the next decades the area was visited by Spanish explorers, including Sebastián Vizcaíno, who in 1603 named it La Punta de Los Reyes or "Point of the Kings." In 1792, British Captain George Vancouver gave Drakes Bay its name. But Francis Drake's claim to Nova Albion was never upheld by Vancouver or other English visitors. The area became a distant colony of Spain. After Mexican independence in 1821, Point Reyes became a center for cattle ranching, remaining so after the U.S. takeover of California. In the 1950s, development threatened the peninsula, but fierce preservation efforts led to the creation of the Point Reyes National Seashore in 1962.

Numerous historic cattle ranches, dating from the 1850s to 1870s, continue to operate within the park's boundaries, and drivers must be ready to pause for herds crossing the roads.

SIGHTS
BEAR VALLEY AREA
👥 Bear Valley Visitor Center★
Bear Valley Rd., Olema ⏲*Open Mon–Fri 9am–5pm, weekends, holidays 9am–5pm.* ⏲*Closed Dec 25.* ♿🅿 ☏*415-464-5100.*

Rangers on duty at this attractive, barn-like park headquarters provide information, answer questions and post times and meeting places for guided hikes and other interpretive programs. Spend time in the center's fine **exhibit hall,** where displays on coastal wetlands, birdwatching hot spots, marine mammals and cultural history provide an introduction to the peninsula.

From the Visitor Center parking lot, the pleasant, easy **Earthquake Trail★** 👥 🚶 *(.6mi)* invites strollers to see the dramatic effects of ground-shifting that took place during the 1906 quake, whose epicenter was in this rift zone. One spot on the trail shows how a wooden fence split and separated as it rode with the moving ground.

Also leading from the parking lot, the **Woodpecker Nature Trail** 👥 🚶 *(.7mi)* offers a quick introduction to the natural wonders of Point Reyes.

👥 Morgan Horse Ranch
⏲*Open Wed-Sat 7.30am–5.30pm, Sun-Tue 8.30am–4.30pm.* 🅿

Situated just behind the Visitor Center, this 100-acre ranch maintains a herd of more than a dozen compact, muscular Morgans used by park rangers for backcountry patrol. A self-guided tour of the ranch (including a blacksmith's shop, pole barn and stables) trots visitors through two centuries of history about the Morgan, the first American breed of horse.

👥 Kule Loklo
A short walk *(.5mi)* from the Visitor Center, this re-created Coast Miwok village offers a glimpse into the lifestyle and culture of the peninsula's native inhabitants. The village's structures, built according to authentic Miwok techniques, include redwood-bark shelters, an underground sweat lodge and a ceremonial dance house. At the time of Francis Drake's visit, some 100 Miwok villages similar to this one were scattered across present-day Marin and south Sonoma Counties.

Bear Valley Trail★

🚶 *8.2mi round-trip. Trailhead near Visitor Center.*

Hikers, bikers, joggers and equestrians range this wide, easygoing path along Coast Creek. Traversing redwood forests and picnic-perfect Divide Meadow, the trail ends at the Arch Rock **viewpoint** overlooking the ocean and the eponymous formerly ached rock structure, which collapsed in 2015. Several more-strenuous trails branch off the Bear Valley Trail, including the Sky, Glen and Old Pine trails; the Coast Trail intersects it near Arch Rock.

Limantour Beach

From the Visitor Center, drive 1.5mi north on Bear Valley Rd. Turn left on Limantour Rd. and continue 6mi.

This splendid curve of land along Drakes Bay is famous for its fine **views** of the white cliffs of Point Reyes. At the northern end, the shoreline narrows to form Limantour Spit, which separates the wildlife-rich waters of Limantour Estero (*estero* is Spanish for "estuary") from the deeper waters of Drakes Bay. From September through May, Limantour Estero and nearby Drakes Estero are major wintering and migratory grounds for shorebirds and seabirds.

POINT REYES PENINSULA AREA

The tip of Point Reyes, stretching some 15mi into the Pacific Ocean, has for centuries constituted a severe hazard for mariners. Numerous ships have met their demise here, lost in the dense fogs and stormy weather that frequently drape the exposed jut of land. High winds and heavy surf rake the northwest-facing bluffs; beaches and estuaries on the southeast side enjoy sheltered conditions. When visiting this area, note that the closest gas is located in Point Reyes Station, about 20mi from the lighthouse.

Drakes Beach

Take Sir Francis Drake Blvd. and follow signs for the Lighthouse, turn left on Drakes Beach Road 🕐*Sunrise*
to midnight. ♿ 🅿 📞*415-669-1250.*

Here, visitors enjoy one of the peninsula's most scenic stretches of sand, sheltered from pounding surf and stiff ocean winds. White sandstone cliffs line the shoreline. The adjacent estuary attracts birds (and birdwatchers) year-round, and the onsite **Kenneth C. Patrick Visitor Center** mounts exhibits on the marine ecosystem of Drakes Bay

The Great Beach

Follow Sir Francis Drake Blvd. southwest 4.7mi from Mt. Vision Rd.; turn right at sign to North Beach.

Also known as Point Reyes Beach, this splendid 12-mi strip comprising **North Beach** and **South Beach** faces northwest—directly into the strongest winds and roughest surf of the open ocean. The beaches offer glorious walks, but strong currents make them unsafe for swimming, surfing or wading. When the surf is especially high, rangers will warn visitors against walking on the sand altogether.

👥 Point Reyes Lighthouse★★

From Bear Valley Visitor Center, follow Sir Francis Drake Blvd. 22mi to the end. 🕐*Open Fri–Mon 10am–4.30pm, weather permitting.* 🕐*Closed Tue–Thu; Dec 25.* 🅿 *From parking lot, .5mi walk to visitor center & lighthouse.* 📞*415-669-1534. www.nps.gov/pore.*

Perched halfway down the sheer south face of precipitous Point Reyes headland—one of the foggiest and windiest points in the continental U.S.—this beacon guided countless mariners for more than a century, from 1870 to 1975. A steep staircase of 308 steps *(closed when winds exceed 40mph)* descends to the station, where visitors can admire the three-ton Fresnel lens cast in 1867 (🕐*Fri–Mon 2:30-4pm)*. The entire lighthouse was extensively renovated in 2018; today, the brass-mounted light, still fully operational, is visible for more than 24 nautical miles. On clear days, the headlands offer excellent **views★★★** of the coast, the Farallon Islands to the southwest and distant

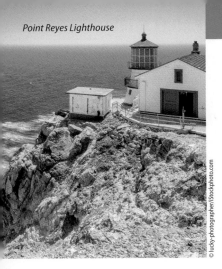

© lucky-photographer/iStockphoto.com

San Francisco. The spot is popular with birders and whale-watchers, who congregate here to spy gray whales as they pass close to shore during their annual migration season *(Dec–Apr)*. Sea lions and seals perch on rocky abodes just east of the point. Chimney Rock is one of the best places to spot elephant seals in the Bay Area.

TOMALES POINT AREA

Dairy and cattle ranches blanket the peninsula's northern point, set between the Pacific Ocean to the west and Tomales Bay to the east.

♟♟ Pierce Point Ranch

From Bear Valley Visitor Center, take Sir Francis Drake Blvd. north 7.5mi. Turn right on Pierce Point Rd. and continue to its end. ○*Open dawn–dusk.* ♿🅿

Established in 1858 by Vermont dairy farmer Solomon Pierce, this pastoral spread of farm buildings remains the only one of the park's 26 historic dairy and cattle ranches open to the public. A self-guided tour leads among the ranch buildings, while exhibits describe such farm activities as butter churning and hay collecting.

The wide, mile-long stretch of **McClures Beach** *(turn left at end of Pierce Point Rd.; follow steep .5mi dirt path to beach)* is bounded by granite outcrops. At the south end, a narrow passageway through the rocks *(accessible only at low*

tide) opens onto a pocket beach where cormorants nest on Elephant Rock.

The lands surrounding the beach and the ranch today form a 2,600-acre reserve for a flourishing herd of some 440 **tule elk**, reintroduced in 1978; these animals once roamed the entire peninsula before being hunted out in the late 19C. More than 150 white-spotted **axis deer** graze on the moors between Marshall Beach Trail and Estero Trail; a similar number of **fallow deer** (many with pure white coats) range over the peninsula.

♟♟ Tomales Bay State Park

1208 Pierce Point Rd., 4mi north of Inverness. ○*Open Fri–Mon 8am–sunset.* ⊚*$8/car.* ⚠♿🅿 ☏*415-669-1140. http://parks.ca.gov.*

Tiny **Heart's Desire Beach** and Shell Beach offer excellent opportunities for swimming and wading in sheltered Tomales Bay. Follow interpretive signs along the **Nature Trail** *(.5mi)* to Indian Beach, where a traditional native shelter can be visited.

ADDITIONAL SIGHT

Point Reyes Station

2mi north of Olema by Rte. 1.

This charming town grew up as a dairy center and stop along the North Pacific Coast Railroad. Although bakeries, restaurants, art galleries and antique shops now occupy some of its late-19C structures, dairy ranchers still swap stories at the local diner and load up supplies at the feed barn, preserving the community's bucolic atmosphere.

EXCURSION

SONOMA COUNTY COAST

North of Point Reyes Station, Highway 1 snakes along the precipitous Pacific coastline for 74mi before entering Mendocino County (⚓ *see The Green Guide California).* Spectacular views abound of steep, rocky cliffs pummeled by roiling surf. Sleepy seaside towns and state parks punctuate the wild shoreline, which nurtures a variety of birds and marine animals.

Bodega Bay

34mi north of Point Reyes Station.
The second-largest salmon port on the Pacific coast bears the name of Spanish explorer Juan Francisco de la Bodega y Cuadra, who reached its sheltered anchorage in October 1775. Commercial fishing took off in the 1940s; today, the waterfront bustles with the comings and goings of some 300 boats. From the bluffs atop **Bodega Head** *(3mi off Hwy. 1 on Eastshore Rd., north of Bodega Bay)*, on the far side of the bay, stretch splendid **views★** of the coast from Point Reyes to Fort Ross. Between January and May, the bluffs are popular with whale-watchers.

Six miles east in **Bodega** is the building *(17110 Bodega Lane)* that served as the schoolhouse in Alfred Hitchcock's classic film *The Birds* (1962). Originally the Potter School (1873), the Italianate structure is now a private residence.

Sonoma Coast State Beaches★

Extending 18mi, Bodega Head to Meyers Gulch, just north of Jenner. ⏱*Open daily.* ⌖*$8/car.* ⛺♿🅿 📞*707-875-3483. http://parks.ca.gov.*
This spectacular strip of coast affords striking seascapes and numerous opportunities for fishing, hiking, camping, sunbathing and beachcombing. Rocky outcrops separate the 15 small, sandy crescents that punctuate the shoreline. Some of the most dramatic **views★** are from **Duncan's Landing** *(5mi north of Bodega Dunes).*
One of the most accessible of the Sonoma Coast beaches is **Goat Rock Beach★** *(8mi north of Bodega Dunes)*, at the mouth of the Russian River, where visitors enjoy a unique **view** of river and ocean, barely separated by a narrow spit of sand. From November to March, throngs of resident harbor seals vie with fishermen to catch schools of salmon that return each year to spawn.
Turnouts abound on this stretch of highway. North of Jenner, the road is a series

of switchbacks above the ocean *(average speed 25mph).* Several miles south of Fort Ross, the road flattens out and marine terraces appear on the left.

Fort Ross State Historic Park★★

19005 Coast Hwy 1, Jenner, 22mi north of Bodega Bay. ⏱*Grounds open daily dawn–dusk. Visitor center open daily 10am–4.30pm.* ⏱*Closed Thanksgiving Day, Dec 25.* ⌖*$8/car.* ♿🅿 📞*707-847-3286. http://parks.ca.gov.*
Built high on a desolate promontory above an azure cove and flanked by mountains to the east, Fort Ross provided a base from which Russian colonists hunted sea otters for their valuable pelts and supplied food to Russia's more remote outposts in Alaska.
Settlement Rossiia (Russia), as the colony was christened, was established in 1812 by members of the Russian-American Company. The first colonists, a group of 25 Russians and 80 Alaskan Aleuts (recruited for their skill in hunting sea otters), negotiated with the resident Kashaya Pomo Indians for land before constructing the garrison. Several hundred people subsequently led a peaceful existence cultivating the land and its resources, but by the mid-1830s, California's sea otter population was decimated and the colony abandoned.

Fort Ross State Historic Park

© jmoon17/iStockphoto.com

The present fort has been partially restored to its early appearance. A short, paved loop trail *(.5mi)* leads from a **visitor center**—offering displays on the history of the fort and earlier Pomo tribes—through a cypress grove to the fort. Constructed of redwood and modeled after traditional edifices in Siberia, the stockade contains six structures of clean, simple lines. Most buildings are replicas; only the **Rotchev House** *(north wall)* is partially original. The **officials' quarters** *(southwest wall)* display artifacts evoking the fort's early days.
The small **chapel**—first Russian Orthodox church in North America outside Alaska—boasts a distinctive, hexagonal tower and round cupola. This building is the third incarnation of the original structure that was erected in 1825 but collapsed during the 1906 earthquake.

Salt Point State Park

9mi north of Fort Ross. ⊙*Open daily dawn–dusk. Visitor Center open Apr–Oct weekends 10am–3pm.* ⊛*$8/car.* ⊙*Closed during inclement weather.* ⚠ 🅿 ℘*707-847-3221. http://parks.ca.gov.* Named for the substance that Native Americans once collected from submarine crevices for preserving seafood, this 6,000-acre park runs along 4mi of coastline. Divers favor the site for its underwater **Gerstle Cove Marine Reserve**. Off the shores of the cove, seals sun themselves on glistening rocks.
The adjacent **Kruse Rhododendron State Reserve** *(entrance 3mi north of Salt Point)* protects 317 acres studded with thickets of coast rhododendron that succeeded vegetation razed years ago by a forest fire. This site is best visited from April to June, when the towering rhododendrons burst into bloom.

ADDRESSES

🍴/EAT

The Marshall Store – *19225 Highway 1, Marshall.* ℘*415-663-1339.* Every weekend, crowds descend on the string of no-frills oyster shacks that hug the shoreline east of Point Reyes Station, including charmingly low-key, first-come-first-serve The Marshall Store, where you can order a plate of the freshest imaginable oysters in a range of preparations while gazing out at the waters where they were harvested.

Cowgirl Creamery – *80 Fourth Street, Point Reyes Station.* ℘*415-663 9335 www.cowgirlcreamery.com.* Though now headquartered in Petaluma, this beloved Bay Area cheesemaker got its start in Point Reyes Station. The original creamery, located in a former hay barn, is now a retail shop and deli where you can pick up picnic provisions, like sandwiches, salads, and wheels of the company's beloved Mt Tam, an organic triple cream cheese.

RECREATION

Five Brooks Ranch – *8001 Highway 1, Olema.* ℘*415-663-1570. fivebrooks.com.* Guided trail rides throughout Point Reyes and horseback-riding lessons.

Sausalito★

Nestled into the bay side of the Marin Headlands, just a few miles north of the Golden Gate Bridge, this upscale residential community draws throngs of visitors on sunny days and weekends. Sausalito's winding streets, quaint boutiques and lush hillsides dotted with attractive homes and gardens create a relaxed yet cultured ambience, and its privileged setting affords some of the finest views of San Francisco and the bay islands.

A BIT OF HISTORY

On the afternoon of August 5, 1775, the Spanish supply ship *San Carlos,* under the command of Lt. Juan Manuel de Ayala, dropped anchor just outside the Golden Gate. Ayala's first mate and six crew members, sent ashore to explore potential anchorage sites, became the first Europeans to enter the bay from the sea. Ayala named their chosen anchorage after the trees they found growing along freshwater streams (the Spanish word *sauces* means "willows").

Sausalito's first Anglo settler, **William Richardson,** arrived in San Francisco Bay in 1822 at age 27, while serving as first mate on a British whaler. In 1825, having acquired Mexican citizenship, Richardson married the daughter of the *comandante* of the Presidio. Through family connections, he later acquired title to the 19,572-acre Rancho del Saucelito, which stretched from the Marin Headlands to Stinson Beach on the west side of the peninsula. In 1849, after the U.S. takeover of California, his property came under dispute and he was forced to sell the southern portion of the land.

Railroad and Shipping Hub – In 1875, the North Pacific Coast Railroad extended its tracks from San Rafael to Sausalito. Trains carrying lumber from the northern redwood forests halted here to unload their cargoes onto a fleet of ferryboats that carried travelers and commerce between rural Marin County and booming San Francisco.

▶ **Population:** 7,061

▤ **Info:** ☎415-289-4117. www.sausalito.gov.

◐ **Location:** Sausalito lies just north of Golden Gate Bridge, along the eastern side of the Marin County peninsula. Driving from San Francisco, take US-101 over the Golden Gate Bridge to the Alexander Ave. exit, just past Vista Point; continue 2mi to Bridgeway Blvd. The ferry (♨*see Addresses*) is an excellent option for a visit to Sausalito; the trip takes about 30min and the Sausalito ferry landing is conveniently located downtown within walking distance of shops and restaurants.

👫 **Kids:** Budding dam-builders will love the Bay Model Visitors Center of the U.S. Army Corps of Engineers.

◉ **Timing:** Sausalito's scenery, shops and eateries make it a great day trip from San Francisco. For a stroll in the residential neighborhoods along Bulkley Avenue, come in the morning; afternoon is best for leisurely exploration of Bridgeway's shops and boutiques.

🅿 **Parking:** Street parking and public lots fill to capacity on weekends, forcing drivers to park on residential streets high on the hillsides. Consider visiting during the week if you're behind the wheel.

☻ **Don't Miss:** A walk on Bulkley Avenue, for a sense of the Sausalito lifestyle.

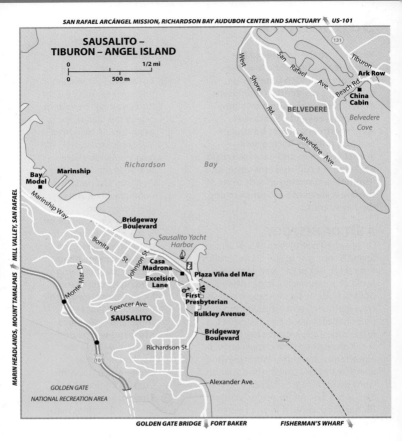

SAN RAFAEL ARCÁNGEL MISSION, RICHARDSON BAY AUDUBON CENTER AND SANCTUARY ⚓ US-101

SAUSALITO – TIBURON – ANGEL ISLAND

In 1942, three months after the U.S. entered World War II, the U.S. Maritime Commission hired the W.A. Bechtel Company to construct a new West Coast shipyard capable of quickly building standard **Liberty Ships** and oil tankers. Bechtel selected 210 acres of undeveloped Sausalito waterfront as the site of the new facility, known as Marinship; in 1942–43, 75,000 men and women poured into the town to build vessels for the American war effort.

Beginning just before the war—in the years following the 1937 completion of the Golden Gate Bridge—Sausalito also experienced an influx of writers, artists, poets and other free-spirited souls. They found inexpensive refuge in the hulks of retired ferryboats and in houseboats made from the hulls of old military landing craft. The close-knit community of "floating home" dwellers persists today, continuing the 1890s tradition of houseboating on Richardson Bay.

SIGHTS
Bridgeway Boulevard★

This attractive thoroughfare skirting Sausalito's waterfront was originally called Water Street. The name was changed to Bridgeway in 1937, as highway engineers had planned to route Golden Gate Bridge automobile traffic directly through Sausalito. An alternate route above the village was ultimately selected and Bridgeway instead became the anchor of a charming district of restaurants, cafes, galleries, shops and inns like the **Casa Madrona Hotel and Spa** *(801 Bridgeway; ☎415-332-0502; www. casamadrona.com)*, a restored Victorian

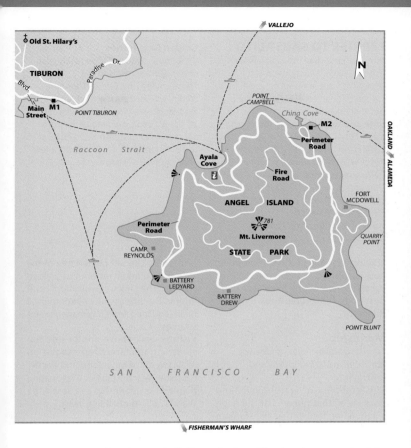

villa (1885) nestled on the wooded hillside overlooking the yacht harbor.

Near the ferry landing, across from the Mission-style Sausalito Hotel and The Inn Above Tide, is tiny **Plaza Viña del Mar**. The plaza honors the city of Viña del Mar, Chile, one of Sausalito's two sister cities (the other is Sakaide, Japan). South of the ferry landing, Bridgeway's wide sidewalks offer delightful **views★★**.

Sausalito Visitor Center & Historical Society

780 Bridgeway. ◔*Open Tue–Sun 11.30am–4pm.* ◔*Closed major holidays.* ♿ ℙ ℰ*415-289-4117. www.sausalitohistoricalsociety.com.* Occupying a former ice house, this small museum's displays trace the history of Sausalito from the days of the Coast Miwok to the present. Look for photographs of the Golden Gate Bridge under construction and portraits of such famous residents as actor Sterling Hayden; Sally Stanford, a San Francisco madam who became mayor of Sausalito; and infamous rum-runner and bank robber "Baby Face" Nelson.

Bulkley Avenue

From Bridgeway, follow Princess St. (first street south of Plaza Viña del Mar) to Bulkley Ave. and turn right. A walk up shady Bulkley Avenue, through the hills that backdrop Sausalito's waterfront, brings visitors to elegant homes and contemporary compounds embellished by elaborate gardens and forests of pine, oak, acacia and eucalyptus trees. The **First Presbyterian Church** (1909, Ernest Coxhead) is a

FERRIES TO SAUSALITO

Although the drive from San Francisco to Sausalito is fairly quick and undeniably scenic, parking in Sausalito can be difficult to find. Ferries are a good alternative.

Blue and Gold Fleet ferries depart from Pier 41 at Fisherman's Wharf *Open daily year round; times vary. Check website for current schedule. No service Thanksgiving Day, Dec 25. Duration 30min. $12.50 each way, children, $7.50 each way. Blue & Gold Fleet 415-705-8200. www.blueandgoldfleet.com.*

Golden Gate ferries depart from the Ferry Building. *Open daily year round. No service Jan 1, Thanksgiving Day, Dec 25. Duration 25min. $12.50 each way, children ages 5-18 $6.50 each way Golden Gate Ferry 415-921-5858. goldengateferry.org. 511.org.* A visitor information kiosk at the ferry landing provides brochures and other Sausalito information.

striking example of the Shingle style; note its intricate wooden exterior. Just past the church, tiny **Excelsior Lane** descends the precipitous slope to Bridgeway.

Marinship

From downtown, follow Bridgeway north 1mi to Marinship Way and turn right.

This complex of warehouses and docks is all that remains of the huge shipbuilding facility that transformed Sausalito during World War II. In 1942 and 1943, more than 90 vessels were constructed here, including 15 Liberty Ships, 62 T-2 oil tankers and 16 Navy oilers, all in record time.

Bay Model Visitor Center of the U.S. Army Corps of Engineers★

2100 Bridgeway. Open Tue–Sat 9am–4pm. 415-332-3871.

Located in a former Marinship warehouse, this 1.5-acre scale model of the San Francisco Bay and Sacramento-San Joaquin Delta was originally conceived to test the effect on the shallow bay of proposed dams. The dams were never built. Today the model serves as an educational and interpretive tool to simulate the tides, currents, salinity and other water-flow aspects of the vast estuary system; it is normally in full operation on Fridays and Saturdays, demonstrating the passage of a 24hr period in

just 15min. The self-guided tour of the model includes an introductory video ("Water: The Link to Civilization") and interactive displays on environmental issues and long-term bay management strategy.

Visitors walk above and beside the sprawling miniature representation of 343sq mi of bay, delta and Pacific coastline. Near the lobby is a fascinating **display★** on Marinship and Sausalito's World War II shipbuilding years.

ADDRESSES

SHOP

Heath Ceramics – *400 Gate Five Road, Sausalito; 415-332-37325. www. heathceramics.com.* Heath Ceramics' line of handcrafted tableware, mugs, and tile has been produced in Sausalito since 1948, and its factory store a veritable pilgrimage site for design lovers today. Reserve in advance for weekly tours (see website for times).

EAT

Cibo – *1201 Bridgeway, Sausalito; 415-331-2426. www.cibosausalito.com.* A savory brunch menu, California-style salads, panini sandwiches, and perfectly pulled espressos have made this half-day cafe popular with Sausalito locals. Right on the water, the outdoor tables are always packed on a sunny day.

Tiburon★
Angel Island★★

A breezy maritime ambience, a historic Main Street, a bustling waterfront promenade and popular restaurants lure visitors to this charming bayside village at the southern tip of the Tiburon peninsula.

A BIT OF HISTORY

Lt. Juan Manuel de Ayala, the first European to visit the area, named Punta de Tiburon (Shark Point) during his 1775 voyage to explore and chart San Francisco Bay. Tiburon formed part of an 1834 Mexican land grant, and in 1884 became a busy railroad town when a branch line of the San Francisco and North Pacific Railroad was built along the peninsula, making it possible to travel from San Rafael and the Redwood Empire to San Francisco via train and ferry. Today, roads and a bike path along Richardson Bay mark the route of the long-defunct railroad.

SIGHTS
Main Street

False-fronted buildings on charming Main Street evoke the atmosphere of the late 19C. Walkways skirt the shore, and ferryboats docking from San Francisco and Angel Island add to the hubbub. West of downtown, Main Street turns sharply north to become pleasant **Ark Row**, where trees shade a charming collection of grounded houseboats, or "arks," that once floated on the bay as summer residences.

The China Cabin★

52 Beach Rd. Turn west from Tiburon Blvd. ○Open Apr–Oct Sat–Sun 1–4pm; rest of the year by appointment only. ◠Donations requested. ℘415-435-1853. www.landmarkssociety.com.
Resting atop pilings in Belvedere Cove, this beautiful, Victorian-era social salon was salvaged from the *SS China* (1866), a sidewheel steamer that once traversed the Pacific Ocean from San Francisco to

- **Michelin Map:** See SAUSALITO pp258-259.
- **Info: Tiburon** ℘415-435-7373; www.townoftiburon.org. **Angel Island** ℘415-435-1915; www.parks.ca.gov.
- **Location:** The easiest and most scenic route to Tiburon is by ferry. Blue and Gold Fleet ferries depart from San Francisco's Ferry Building and Pier 41 at Fisherman's Wharf daily (◠$12.50 each way; ℘415-705-8200; www.blueandgoldfleet.com). The journey takes about 30min direct, and 45 minutes on boats stopping in Sausalito or Angel Island. If you are driving from San Francisco, take US-101 north 6mi to the Tiburon Blvd. (Rte. 131) exit; continue 4mi to the town center.
- **Timing:** Weekends bring throngs of visitors to Main Street; in the evening relax on the outdoor deck of a waterside restaurant.
- **Parking:** Parking lots are located on Tiburon Blvd. next to the Boardwalk Market; on Main St. next to the Tiburon Playhouse theater; and at Point Tiburon.

Hong Kong and Yokohama for the Pacific Mail Steamship Company.
The interior, restored to its full, gilded grandeur, offers a tantalizing glimpse of the elegance and luxury of 19C social salons.

Old St. Hilary's

201 Esperanza St. From Tiburon Blvd. turn east on Beach Rd. and follow signs across Mar West St. (.7mi). ○Open

261

Arks Around the Bay

Through the late 19C and early 20C, numerous San Franciscans spent their summers aboard floating homes known as "arks," moored off the shores of Sausalito and other southern Marin County towns such as Tiburon. Popular summer retreats, these quaint structures enhanced the good life on San Francisco Bay and Richardson Bay. Some of them have been preserved on land as shops and homes on Bridgeway (north end of Sausalito Yacht Harbor) and "Ark Row" (downtown Tiburon). A refurbished ark is displayed at the Hyde Street Pier in San Francisco.

Apr–Oct Sun 1–4pm; rest of the year by appointment only. ⟳Donations requested. ♿🅿 *415-435-1853. www.landmarkssociety.com.*
Perched on a hillside above town, this former Roman Catholic church (1888) represents an excellent example of the Carpenter Gothic style. The historic landmark is surrounded by **St. Hilary's Preserve**, which protects 217 species of wildflowers, two-thirds of them native to the Tiburon Peninsula. Scenic paths lead through the preserve, where the wildflowers bloom for much of the year.

Richardson Bay Audubon Center and Sanctuary

376 Greenwood Beach Rd., 3.2mi west of downtown off Tiburon Blvd. ⏰Open Mon–Fri 9am–5pm. 415-388-2524. www. richardsonbay.audubon.org.
Administered since 1961 by the National Audubon Society, this bayside refuge comprises 11 acres of land and 900 acres of San Francisco Bay, and is used by the society to educate people about natural history, particularly waterfowl. Grounds include a .5mi mountain trail, a redwood grove, a hummingbird garden and four bird watching platforms with scopes. The centerpiece of the property is the 1876 **Lyford House** (🔊tours by *appointment only)*, an 1876 Victorian built by a prominent 19C doctor.

ANGEL ISLAND STATE PARK★★

Access from San Francisco's Pier 41 on Fisherman's Wharf via Blue and Gold Fleet ferry (25min each way; ⟳$9.75 one way; 415-705-5555; www.blueandgoldfleet.com); a ferry also connects the island to Tiburon (10min each way; ⟳$15 round trip; includes park admission fee; cash only. 415-435-2131; www.angelislandferry. com). Alcatraz Cruises, Alcatraz-Angel Island combo tour ($76, daily departures 9:30am and 9:40am, www. alcatrazcruises.com) ⏰Open daily 8am–sunset. △✖♿ 415-435-5390. www.angelisland.org, www.parks. ca.gov.
This hilly, forested island, separated from Tiburon by tide-swept Raccoon Strait, is a peaceful oasis in San Francisco Bay. Over its long history of human habitation, the 750-acre island—the largest in the bay—has served as a Coast Miwok haven, a Spanish land-grant cattle ranch, a U.S. military base, a quarantine station and an immigration facility. The island was named Isla de Los Angeles by Lt. Juan Manuel de Ayala in 1775. After years of military use and a period (1910–40) as an immigration station, the island was declared surplus property by the federal government in 1948. In 1963 the entire island (except a Coast Guard installation at Point Blunt) became part of California's state park system. Today it draws tourists to its beautiful trails, bay views, campsites and picnic spots.

VISIT
Ayala Cove

Ferries dock at this cozy little cove named for Lt. Juan Manuel de Ayala, who anchored his ship here for a month in 1775. The cove's broad sweep of lawn is a popular picnic spot. Stop at the state park **visitor center** (⏰*open daily;* 415-435-5390) for information and exhibits on the island's history.

Perimeter Road

5mi loop. Trailhead to left of Ayala Cove.
This mostly paved road rings the island's forested flanks and offers an easy, scenic stroll past military installations and garrisons recalling the island's human history. From various points along the road, **views★★★** take in the jagged San Francisco skyline, ship-like Alcatraz and the Golden Gate Bridge spanning the mouth of San Francisco Bay. From the main path, spur roads and trails lead to several fine beaches and enclaves of historic buildings. At China Cove (North Garrison), a barracks that formerly housed Chinese, Russian, Japanese and South American immigrants today houses a small **museum★ (M2)** (☞visit by 45min guided tour only; call for schedule 📞415-435-5390). The **Fire Road** 🏃 (3mi loop) circumscribes the island at a higher elevation, providing bikers and hikers a more challenging route.

Mt. Livermore

The 781ft summit of the island's central peak, accessible from Ayala Cove by the moderately strenuous Northridge *(2mi)* and Sunset *(2.5mi)* trails, offers an unobstructed **panorama★★★** sweeping over San Francisco, the bay and the communities surrounding it. The mountain was named for Caroline Livermore, leader of the movement to preserve Angel Island.

ADDITIONAL SIGHTS

San Rafael Arcángel Mission

5th Ave. & A St. in San Rafael. Take US-101 north to Central San Rafael exit. 🕐*Chapel open daily 6.30am–6.30pm, museum open Wed-Fri 11am–4pm, Sat-Sun 10am–3pm.* 🕐*Closed major holidays.* ☞*Guided tours available on request; call ahead.* 💰*Donations requested.* 📞*415-454-8141.*
The 20th and penultimate mission of the California chain was founded in 1817 as an *asistencia* to Mission Dolores in San Francisco. The branch mission was used as a sanitarium for San Francisco parishioners in failing health, and was named for the patron saint of bodily

healing. The buildings were razed in 1870; the current replica on the site dates from 1949.

Marin County Civic Center

3501 Civic Center Drive, San Rafael. 📞*415-473-3762.* 🕐*Open Mon–Fri 8.30am-4.30pm.* 🕐*Closed Sat–Sun, major holidays.* ☞*Docent-led tours every Wed and Fri. at 10:30,* 💰*$10; self-guided tours via iOs and Adriod app Marin County Civic Center by Frank Lloyd Wright.*
The only civic project ever designed by American architect Frank Lloyd Wright, Marin County's courthouse, government office, and jail are housed within this hugely original building, today a National Historic Landmark. Outside, the earthy color scheme and massive rotunda mimic the palette and shapes of Marin County's hillsides—though Wright, who died before the project was complete, is said to have opposed the idea of painting the rotunda blue. Inside, long sunlit atriums are filled with plants, golden spheres, terrazzo stairs and retro gold grillwork.
It's worth visiting the onsite café *($, Mon–Fri 7am-4pm)*, which is frequented by government workers and attorneys, for the views from its terrace.
There are frequent arts and cultural events at the 2000-seat Veterans' Memorial Auditorium onsite, and the county farmers market, the third biggest in the state, takes over the Civic Center parking lot from 8am-1pm every Thu and Sun.

ADDRESSES

RECREATION

The **Angel Island Company** rents bicycles from a kiosk in Ayala Cove *($50/day* 📞*415-435-2131; angelisland.com).* Bicycles can also be brought on ferrries to the island.
Sea Trek offers **sea kayak** tours from Sausalito to Angel Island *($95 reservations required;* 📞*415-332-8494; www.seatrek.com).*

WINE COUNTRY

Lying inland within a two-hour drive of San Francisco, the Napa Valley and Sonoma County thrive on the abundant sunshine and fertile soil that produce grapes for some of North America's finest wines. Though vineyards flourish along many of California's inland coastal areas from Eureka to San Diego County, and even as far east as the foothills of the Sierra Nevada, these areas just north of San Francisco have garnered a reputation as the state's preeminent winemaking regions. Visitors and locals flock here, drawn by the temperate climate, varied natural beauty and acclaimed wineries that make the Wine Country one of California's foremost tourist destinations.

Highlights

1. Sonoma **farmers' markets** (p267)
2. Pair wine with art at the **Hess Collection Winery** (p273)
3. Cooking demonstration at the **Culinary Institute of America** (p276)
4. Sterling's **aerial tramway** (p278)
5. Tour the lush **Luther Burbank Home and Gardens** (p286)

From Criollas Cuttings to a Gastronomic Center

Cuttings of Criollas grapevines first traveled to Alta California with missionary Franciscan padres during the late 17C. Wines made from these "mission" grapes were used mostly for trade or sacramental purposes. In the early 1830s, Frenchman Jean-Louis Vignes established a vineyard near Los Angeles using European grapevines *(Vitis vinifera)*, and by the mid-19C winemaking had become an important California industry. After various ups and downs over the past 150 years, wine country seems to be on firmer ground. In recent decades the Napa and Sonoma Valleys have experienced tremendous development. The late 20C and 21C witnessed an explosion of small-scale operations, some housed in old wineries updated with state-of-the-art equipment.

Researchers at the University of California at Davis' renowned Department of Viticulture and Enology develop new methods of grape cultivation and winemaking, while trade associations work to promote California wines throughout the world.

Today the Wine Country has become a center for fine wine as well as gastronomy. Trendy restaurants shine like stars in the culinary firmament, and in 1995 the renowned Culinary Institute of America installed a campus in the former Christian Brothers/Greystone Cellars winery. Recent years have seen the rise of showplace operations—among them Opus One, Clos Pegase, Artesa and the Hess Collection Winery—that combine wine production with the display of fine art and innovative architecture.

A Bit of History

In 1857 **Agoston Haraszthy** (1812–69), a Hungarian immigrant, purchased a 400-acre estate in Sonoma County, named it Buena Vista, and cultivated Tokay vine cuttings imported from his homeland. The grapes flourished, inspiring Haraszthy to redouble his efforts at producing premium wines in northern California, experimenting with assorted varieties of *vinifera* cuttings and trained area grape growers. The quality of California wines steadily improved.

Boom and Bust – Haraszthy's discoveries created a boom in the wine industry throughout the Napa and Sonoma Valleys in the last decades of the 19C. Among the wineries established during this period were **Gundlach-Bundschu (1)** (1858), **Charles Krug (2)** (1861), and **Schramsberg Vineyards** (1862), first of the region's hillside wineries to hew storage caves out of rock. **Beringer**, **Beaulieu** and **Inglenook**, renowned names of the present-day wine industry, were also established during this period. As the 19C drew to a close, northern California grapevines fell prey to the root louse phylloxera; entire vineyards were decimated. Researchers discovered they could combat phylloxera by replanting vineyards with disease-resistant rootstocks from the midwestern U.S., onto which *vinifera* cuttings had been grafted. The wine industry achieved a modicum of recovery by the early 20C only to be faced with another setback: on January 29, 1919, the U.S. Congress ratified the 18th Amendment prohibiting the manufacture, sale, importation and transportation of intoxicating liquors.

Prohibition – Prohibition brought California's winemaking industry to a near-standstill. Licenses were granted to only seven California wineries to produce wines for sacramental and medicinal use. Home production of "non-intoxicating" grape juice for private consumption was also permitted. In 1933, when Prohibition was repealed, wine growers began rebuilding their industry. The Great Depression slowed the recovery, and it was not until the early 1970s that the demand for fine table wines rose and California's wine industry was fully re-established.

The Art of Winemaking

The Wine Country is organized into **Approved Viticultural Areas**, each suitable for the cultivation of certain types of grapes. Growing conditions vary depending on soil type and climate. Volcanic activity in the region has produced porous soils in which wine grapes thrive, but minerals, soil depth and moisture vary from region to region. **Weather** is considered the most important factor affecting the cultivation of wine grapes, which require a long growing season of hot days and cool nights. In the Wine Country, grapes ripen slowly from April to October, giving flavors and acids plenty of time to develop. The average annual rainfall of 33in occurs mostly in winter. Differences in elevation, proximity to the sea and exposure to sun, fog and wind create numerous microclimates.

The Wine Country's current production is based primarily on descendants of European *vinifera* cuttings. Best adapted to Wine Country growing conditions is the **Cabernet Sauvignon**, a small, blue-black grape from the Médoc district of France's Bordeaux region that produces a rich, full red wine. Burgundy's **Pinot Noir** grape is used for both table wine and California sparkling wine. Other red wine grapes from Europe include **Cabernet Franc**, **Petite Sirah**, **Napa Gamay** (derived from France's Gamay Beaujolais) and **Zinfandel**.

Some of California's finest white wines are made from **Chardonnay**, the premier white grape of France's Chablis and Burgundy regions. Chardonnay produces a dry, richly flavored wine. The **Sauvignon Blanc**, used in the making of French Sauternes and Pouilly-Fumé, grows well in Wine Country's cooler areas. **Pinot Blanc** is an important ingredient in many sparkling wines. Other white European varieties include **Riesling** and **Chenin Blanc**.

From Vine to Barrel to Bottle – Once grapes have achieved desired levels of sugar and acid, they are picked by hand or machine and placed into a stemmer-crusher, where paddles remove the stems and break the skins to produce a soupy mixture of seeds, skins and juice called **must**. In the making of white wines, the must is pressed immediately, usually in a device known as a **bladder press**. The pressed juice is clarified, inoculated with yeast, transferred to tanks, and left to ferment. During **fermentation**, which can last three days to six weeks, the yeast organisms consume the sugar in the grapes, creating ethyl alcohol, carbon dioxide and heat. If left unchecked, this heat can speed the fermentation process, completing it before desired flavors have had time to develop, so modern fermentation tanks are equipped with cooling sheaths to control temperature. In making red wines, fermentation occurs before pressing so that the skins and seeds impart rich, dark colors and tannins to the fluid.

After fermentation, impurities are removed by filtration, centrifuging or **racking** (in which wine is transferred from tank to tank, leaving settled sediments behind). In the last clarification, called **fining**, substances such as clay,

Area Code: 707

GETTING THERE

BY BUS – **Golden Gate Transit** buses run between San Francisco and many cities in Sonoma County (*415-455-2000; www.goldengate.org*).

BY TRAIN – **Sonoma-Marin Area Rail Transit** (*707-794-3330, sonomamarintrain.org*) connects Marin County with Petaluma and Santa Rosa, with plans to extend service to Healdsburg and Windsor.

BY CAR – Consult individual entries for directions to the **Napa Valley, Sonoma Valley** and the **Upper Sonoma-Russian River Region.** Drinking wine and navigating the rural roads of Wine Country is a risky proposition, and police officers regularly pull over drivers. We recommend you designate a non-drinking driver or hire one of the many private ride services and taxis that operate in the area. In adition to Uber and Lyft, which operate in most parts of Napa and Sonoma Valley, you can arrange drop off and pick up with the following companies. **In Napa Valley: Platypus Tours** *(707-253-2723; www.platypustours.com);* Yellow Cab of Napa *(707-226-3731; www.yellowcabnapa.com)*, and Beau Wine Tours & Limousine Service) *(707-257-0887; www.beauwinetours.com).* In Sonoma county, Sonoma Taxi Service *(707-889-1266; www.sonomataxi.net)*, Vern's Taxi Service *(www.vernstaxi.com, 707-938-8885)*, Pure Luxury Transportation Service Inc. *(800-626-5466; www.pureluxury.com)*, Leone Wine Tours *(707-331-8991; www.leonewinetours.com)*, and CWT Transportation *(707-253-1300; www.californiawinetours.com).*

GENERAL INFORMATION

WHEN TO GO – The best times to visit are in the spring, when yellow mustard plants blossom in the vineyards before the summer's heat sets in; and in the fall, when temperatures are comfortable, the sun infailably shines, and winemakers begin the harvest and crush (pressing of grapes). Advance reservations are recommended for lodging and attractions during peak season.

VISITOR INFORMATION – The following agencies provide maps and information on recreation, accommodations and seasonal events: **Visit Napa Valley** *(600 Main St., Napa; 707-251-5895; www.visitnapavalley.com)*; **Napa Valley Vintners Association** *(P.O. Box 141, St. Helena; 963-3388; napavintners.com)*; **Sonoma Valley Visitors Bureau** *(453 1st St. E., Sonoma & 23570 Arnold Dr.; and Cornerstone Sonoma, 23570 Arnold Drive. 866-996-1090; www.sonomavalley.com)*; **Sonoma County Tourism Bureau** and **Sonoma County Vitners** *(400 Aviation Boulevard, Suite 500; 707-522-5800; www.sonomacounty.com)*; **Russian River Wine Roads** *(1437 Grove Street, Healdsburg; 707-433-4335; www.wineroad.com).* Order the **Napa Valley Guide** *($6.95),* which includes information on lodging, dining and shopping, at 855-0847-6272 or www.napavalleyguidebook.com, or download a free pdf at www.visitnapavalley.com. For local events and news, **Sonoma Magazine** (www.sonomamag.com) is available at many local newsstands, or free online or at most winecountry visitors centers.

ACCOMMODATIONS – Charming **bed-and-breakfast inns** can be found in towns along Rte. 29 (Napa Valley), Rte. 12 (Sonoma Valley) and US-101 (Russian River Valley). Larger **hotels** are located in Napa, Sonoma and Santa Rosa. In addition to national services, wine-country-specific B&Bs, hotel reservations, and vacation rentals can be booked via the **Napa Valley Welcome Center** (*251-9188 or 855-333-6272*) and

Stay Sonoma Valley (℘800-969-4667; www.staysonomavalley.com). Year-round **camping** is available at Bothe-Napa Valley State Park (℘942-4575), Sugarloaf Ridge State Park (℘833-5712), and at Lake Sonoma (℘433-2200).

gelatin or egg whites may be introduced; sediments and impurities adhere to these materials, which are then easily removed. Many wines are **barrel-aged** in white-oak barrels; aging can last months or several years. Certain varieties require a blending stage in which wines are mixed to achieve desired flavors. Some wines are bottled before the final aging period.

ADDRESSES

RECREATION

Ballooning – Balloon tours *(3–5hrs)* depart at dawn and fly year-round. Prices are generally about $200/person. Advance reservations required. Napa Valley companies include **Napa Valley Aloft** (℘855-944-4408. *www. nvaloft.com)* and **Calistoga Balloons** (℘942-5758; *www.calistogaballoons.com)* and **Napa Valley Balloons Inc.** (℘800-253-2224; *http://napavalleyballoons.com)*. Sonoma County companies include **Wine Country Balloons and Tours** (℘538-7359; *winecountryballoons.com*.

Biking – Rent a bike *($45/day)* or book a full or half-day cycling tour *(starting at $139 for half day)* with **Napa Valley Bike Tours**, which has a branch in Napa *(950 Pearl St, Napa, ℘707-944-2953 napavalleybiketours.com)* and in Younteville *(6500 Washington St, Younteville; ℘707-251-8687)*. In Sonoma, **Wine Country Cyclery** *($10/hour or $30/day, 262 W Napa Street, Sonoma. 707-996-6800; www.winecountrycyclery.com)* rents bikes one block from the Town Square. **Get-Away Adventures** leads weekend and day **bicycle tours** (℘800-499-2453; *www.getawayadventures.com)*, "sip 'n' cycle" winery tours, and multi-sport hiking, cycling and kayaking trips in the wine country *(starting at $150, equipment provided)*.

Flying –Take an aerial tour of the wine country in vintage biplanes or veteran military aircraft with **Vintage Aircraft Company**; prices depend on plane, but start at $175 for a 20-minute single-passenger flight *(vintageaircraft.com)*.

Farmers Markets – These bustling markets offer local produce, poultry and other farm products:

Napa Downtown Farmers' market *(195 Gasser Drive, Napa; Sat. 8:30am-1pm; napafarmersmarket.com)*.

Calistoga Farmers' Market *(1235 Washington St, Calistoga; ℘707-942-8892; Sat 9am-1pm)*.

Valley of the Moon Farmers Market *(Sonoma Plaza; May–Sept Tue. 5:30pm-dusk; http://www. sonomaplazamarket.org)*.

Healdsburg Farmers' Market *(1 block west of plaza, North and Vine Sts. May–Nov Sat 8:30am-noon; www. healdsburgfarmersmarket.org)*.

🍴 STAY

$$ The Lodge at Sonoma – *1325 Broadway. ℘707-935-6600. www. marriott.com* - Clean, well-priced, and spacious guestrooms keep this attractive Marriott-owned property perpetually booked, but locals come here for the excellent in-house restaurant, **Carneros Bistro and Wine Bar** (℘707-931-3405. *New American)*, known for its thoughtful wine list and locally sourced food, elegant yet comfortable atmosphere, and winningly friendly service.

$$$ Harvest Inn – *1 Main St, St. Helena ℘707-963-9463 www.harvestinn.com* Wake to a view of dawn breaking over the fields of grape vines in this cozy St. Helena bed and breakfast, nestled between wineries and redwood trees. At night, sip a glass of Napa red beside the in-room brick fireplace.

WINE COUNTRY

$$$ Hotel Olea – *5131 Warm Springs Road, Glen Ellen. ℘707-996-5131. oleahotel.com.* In the charming hamlet of Glen Ellen, this boutique inn was fully renovated after the 2017 Sonoma County fires, with modern but cozy guestrooms shaded by old-growth oak trees. A chef-designed breakfast is included in the price, as are the complimentary wine and snacks in the homey fireplace-warmed lobby.

$$$ El Dorado Hotel and Kitchen *405 1st Street W, Sonoma. ℘707-996-3030. www.eldoradosonoma.com.* This hotel feels surprisingly tucked-away, despite its heart-of-it-all location on Sonoma's main plaza. Subdued second-floor guestrooms overlook downtown or the onsite pool. First-floor Californian restaurant, **El Dorado Kitchen**, is a lively spot for dinner and drinks.

$$$ Autocamp *14120 Old Cazadero Rd, Guerneville. ℘888-405-7553 autocamp.com. $190-300.* The magic of camping with a modern twist: this hotel is a cluster of luxuriously decorated airstreams and canvas tents, nestled within a grove of Russian River Valley redwood trees.

$$$$ Senza Hotel – *4066 Howard Ln., Napa. ℘707-253-0337. www.senzahotel.com. 26 rooms.* This recently renovated luxurious bed-and-breakfast complex sprawled across two acres is a lovely rural option. New amenities include a spa, heated outdoor pool with cabanas, remodeled hot tub, and outdoor fireplace.

$$$$$ The Francis House – *1403 Myrtle St, Calistoga. ℘707-341-3536. thefrancishouse.com. 5 rooms.* A crumbling 1886 wine country estate was lavishly restored and reopened as an intimate inn, with luxurious guestrooms outfitted with vintage furnishings and surrounded by lush landscaping and herb gardens.

ⵛ EAT

$$ Angele – *540 Main St., Napa. ℘707-252-8115. www.angelerestaurant.com.* **French**. Set in a repurposed boathouse with a charming patio overlooking the Napa River, this bistro serves classics like croque monsieur and roasted quail.

$$ Mustards Grill – *7399 St. Helena Hwy., Yountville. ℘707-944-2424. www.mustardsgrill.com.* **Contemporary**. A long-standing favorite, this ranch-style restaurant draws winemakers and industry VIPs for its fresh cuisine and top-notch wine list. The menu ranges across American regional dishes to Asian-inspired new classsics.

$$$ The Girl and the Fig – *110 West Spain St. ℘707-938-3634. www.thegirlandthefig.com.* **French**. The quintessential California wine-country restaurant, this all-day eatery uses fresh greens, local meats, and artisan cheeses to create its appealing French-inspired menu, served in a convivial dining room on Sonoma's square. Locals gather at the in-house bar for a glass of wine from the reasonably priced Rhone-centric wine list.

$$$ Salt and Stone – *9900 Sonoma Highway, Kenwood. ℘707-833-6326. www.saltstonekenwood.com.* **New American** There's a relaxed elegance to the bar and dining room at this country restaurant, where local wines are served alongside American classics like crab cakes, fresh oysters, charcuterie, and roast lamb.

$$$ Bouchon – *6534 Washington St., Yountville. ℘707-944-8037. www.thomaskeller.com.* **French**. This adorable, lively little bistro run by Thomas Keller oozes charm, with a rustic French menu.

$$$$$ French Laundry – *6640 Washington St., Yountville. ℘707-944-2380. www.thomaskeller.com.* **Contemporary French**. Set in a century-old stone building, this gastronomic destination is considered by some the best restaurant in the U.S. Chef Thomas Keller's nightly nine-course tasting menus showcase masterfully prepared imaginative cuisine. Optional sommelier matches wines on request. Reserve two months ahead.

$$$$ La Toque – *1314 McKinstry St., in the Westin Verasa Napa, Napa. ℘707-257-5157. www.latoque.com. Dinner only.* **Contemporary French**. The nightly changing five-course prix-fixe menu (often featuring foie gras) is paired with stellar international wines.

$$$$ Single Thread – *131 North St, Healdsburg. ℘707-723-4646. www.singlethreadfarms.com.* **Californian**. A deep commitment to hospitality and rigorous attention to the season drive this unique restaurant's meticulously designed eleven-course tasting menu, which changes weekly to align with the micro-seasons and the havest from Single Thread Farm.

Reading a Wine Label

Who made the wine and where was it bottled? Where and when were the grapes grown? How much alcohol is contained therein? The label on a bottle of wine says all of this and more. Labeling information is regulated by the U.S. Treasury Department's Bureau of Alcohol, Tobacco and Firearms, and certain elements are required by law.

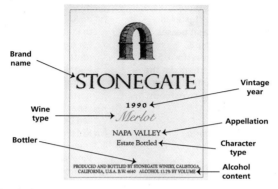

Brand name ──→

Wine type ──→

Bottler ──→

←── **Vintage year**

←── **Appellation**

←── **Character type**

←── **Alcohol content**

Required elements

Brand name – May be the name of the producer, or a secondary or special brand name of the producer.

Wine type – If 75 percent of the grapes used in the wine are of one type, such as Chardonnay, Zinfandel or Pinot Noir, that name must appear on the label as the name of the wine. Otherwise the wine may be called "table wine" or take a generic name such as Burgundy or Chablis.

Appellation – This is the geographic origin of the grapes used in making the wine. In order for the name of an Approved Viticultural Area, such as Napa Valley, to appear on the label, 85 percent of the grapes used must come from that particular area. If the appellation is a county such as Napa or Sonoma, the grape content from that appellation must be 75 percent. If the appellation is the state of California, the wine must be produced entirely from California-grown grapes.

Bottler – The name of the bottling winery may be different from that of the brand name. "Produced and Bottled by" indicates that at least 75 percent of the wine was fermented by the bottler. "Made and Bottled by" indicates that at least 10 percent of the wine was fermented by the bottler.

Alcohol content – Table wines may contain 7–14 percent alcohol by volume; aperitif wines 15–24 percent; dessert wines 14–24 percent or greater. There is no requirement for sparkling wines.

Optional elements

Vintage year – The year in which the grapes were grown may only appear on a label if 95 percent of the grapes used in the wine were harvested that year.

Character type – Additional information such as "Estate Bottled" indicates that the vineyard is managed by the winery, and that the vineyard and the winery are located within the stated appellation.

Vineyard – If the label indicates a specific vineyard, 95 percent of the grapes used must come from that vineyard.

Napa Valley★★

Cradled between two elongated mountain ranges, this world-renowned valley extends roughly 35 miles in a northerly direction from San Pablo Bay to Mt. St. Helena. The Napa Valley is home to some of California's most prestigious wineries, many of them clustered thickly along Route 29 as it passes through the towns of Napa, Yountville, Oakville, Rutherford, St. Helena and Calistoga. Others dot the more tranquil Silverado Trail to the east and the intervening crossroads.

SIGHTS
Described from south to north.

Napa

Originally settled in 1832, this small city on the banks of the Napa River experienced its first significant population boom as a resort town during the post-Gold Rush period. Riverboat captains and bankers established businesses and elegant Victorian residences through the late 19C, transforming Napa into an active shipping and administrative center. Now Napa County's largest city, with nearly 80,000 residents, it still serves as a gateway for the valley's wines and agricultural goods, but now boasts a revitalized riverfront area teeming with new restaurants and hotels. A magnitude 6.0 earthquake centered in Napa in Aug 2014 caused an estimated $380 million dollars of loss valley wide, but the local economy is once again booming.

Downtown

1st and 2nd Sts. between Main and Randolph Sts.

At the friendly heart of downtown Napa, the venerable **Goodman Building** (1901), with its gray stone facade *(1219 1st St.)*, is now home to the research library and museum of the Napa County Historical Society, which just returned to the site after being displaced by the 2014 earthquake. Just across the street and one block north, an enormous contemporary **Clock Tower** overlooks the

---

⌖ **Michelin Map:** See p272.

ℹ **Info:** ℘707-226-5813 www.visitnapavalley.com.

▸ **Location:** From San Francisco (55mi), drive north on US-101; exit at Rte. 37 and drive east to Rte. 121. Turn left (north) on Rte. 121 and continue to Rte. 29 north. For a quicker if less scenic route, drive north on I-80 to Rte. 37 west and continue to Rte. 29 north. Auto traffic, especially on weekends, can be heavy.

👥 **Kids:** A ride on the aerial tramway at Sterling Vineyards.

🕑 **Timing:** To fully experience the region's relaxed pace and easygoing character, it's best to select no more than two or three wineries per day for tasting and tours. Travelers on tight schedules should bear in mind that although the Wine Country is blessed with lots of lush vegetation, inspiring vistas and an enviable climate, tourist attractions other than wineries are few. Visitors for whom wines and winemaking hold limited appeal should plan less time to visit the region.

🏆 **Don't Miss:** At least one winery tour and tasting.

---

site where the first Magnavox speaker was invented in 1915 (a bronze sculpture of a vintage speaker commemorates the achievement). Other noteworthy buildings include the stately, ornate **Winship-Smernes Building** *(948 Main St.)* and the **Italianate Napa Opera House** *(1030 Main St.; ℘707-880-2300; www.nvoh.org)*. Constructed in 1879 and

Goodman Building, downtown Napa

© Peter Wrenn/MICHELIN

closed in 1914, the Opera House was reopened in 2003 after massive renovation and is now used as a multidisciplinary performance space.

Oxbow Public Market★★

610 and 644 1st St. at McKinstry St.
The centerpiece of the burgeoning Oxbow district is the **Oxbow Public Market** (*Open weekdays 9am-9pm, weeeknds 10am-9pm, merchant hours vary* . 🅿 *707-226-6529. www.oxbow-publicmarket.com)*, which celebrated its 10th anniversary in 2017. Founded by the former project manager of the San Francisco Ferry Building, this local-focused culinary marketplace has more than two dozen shops, restaurants and kiosks selling fresh-picked produce, exotic spices, oysters, coffee and pastries, local cheese, and ice cream. For snacks, some standout spots include **Three Twins Ice Cream, The Model Bakery**, and **Ritual Coffee Roasters**. There are frequent public events and happy hour specials, but you can also just drop in for a glass of rosé and tacos with housemade tortillas to enjoy on the patio overlooking the Napa River.

CIA at Copia (Culinary Institute of America)★

500 1st St., Napa. 707-967-2500. www.ciaatcopia.com. Check website for classes and special events.
Beside the **Oxbow Public Market** in the former Copia facility, the new public-facing campus for the Culinary Institute of America is an ambitious 80,000-sq-ft food-and-wine destination, which debuted in 2016. Inside, there is a 72-seat theater that hosts demonstration-style cooking and wine classes, a collection of public art (some with food-realted themes), and a spacious home and kitchen shop. There are a wide range of classes offered in the center's test kitchen, with topics, from making éclairs to the history of Napa Valley wines. Visitors can also dine at The Restaurant at CIA Copia, which serves Mediterranean-inspired California cuisine.

di Rosa Center for Contemporary Art★★

5200 Sonoma Hwy. (Rte. 121), Napa. Open Wed–Sun 10am–4pm. Docent-led guided tours daily free with admission; reservations advised. $18. Closed most federal holidays. 🅿 707-226-5991. www.dirosaart.org.
This stunning art and nature preserve showcases the land's natural beauty and its owner's formidable art collec-

Wineries described in this section have been selected and rated on their historic, architectural and cultural merits.
For a comprehensive, updated listing of wineries throughout Napa, consult the website *www.visitnapavalley.com*

NAPA VALLEY AND
SONOMA VALLEY
🍇 Described winery

(Map of the Napa Valley and Sonoma Valley region showing the following labeled locations:)

CLEAR LAKE

Mt. St. Helena
4343

Robert Louis
Stevenson
State Park

★ Old
Faithful
Geyser

GEYSERVILLE

128

★ Sharpsteen Museum

Clos Pegase ★

★ Calistoga

Sterling ★★

Schramsberg

Petrified
Forest

Bothe-Napa
Valley

Culinary Institute of
America at Greystone

Bale Grist
Mill SHP

Robert Louis Stevenson
Silverado Museum

★★ Beringer

Auberge
du Soleil

★ St. Helena

Hall
Winery

Mumm Napa

Sugarloaf
Ridge

Rutherford

St. Supéry ★★

2730
Mt. Hood

★★ Inglenook

Lake
Hennessey

SANTA
ROSA

Annadel

Kenwood

★ Robert
Mondavi

Oakville

Yountville

Stag's Leap

Mt. Veeder
2677

Domaine
Chandon

Napa Valley
Museum

★ Jack London
SHP

Glen Ellen

★★ Hess Collection

2180
Sonoma Mtn.

★ San Francisco
Solano

Buena
Vista ★★

NAPA

CIA at
Copia

★ Lachryma Montis

Sebastiani ★

Goodman
Bldg.

Oxbow
Public
Market

★★ SONOMA

Milliken Pk.
743

★★ Petaluma Adobe
SHP

Train
Town

Artesa

SANTA ROSA

PETALUMA ★

★★ di Rosa
Preserve

116

121

0   5 mi
0   10 km

↑ Marin French Cheese Company   ↓ SAN FRANCISCO   VALLEJO ↓

★UPPER SONOMA – RUSSIAN RIVER REGION

↑ WINTERS

Iron Mtn.
2287

Lake
Berryessa

Pope Cr.

Las Posadas

Atlas Pk.
2663

Silverado Trail

Napa

SAN FRANCISCO

---

tion. Son of a U.S. ambassador to Italy, René di Rosa began acquiring works by undiscovered artists in the 1950s. In 1960, he bought an abandoned 460-acre vineyard here, converting the 1886 stone winery into his home.

Di Rosa and his wife amassed a personal collection of more than 2,000 works by 800 Bay Area artists working in all mediums, including Robert Arneson, Joan Brown and Bruce Conner. In addition to showcasing the di Rosas' work in two constantly changing galleries, there are often special events, speakers, and opening parties onsite.

Artesa Vineyards and Winery

1345 Henry Rd., Napa 🕐 *Open daily 10am–5pm.* 🕐 *Closed Jan 1, Thanksgiving Day, Dec 24–25.* 🎫 *$35-$75 tasting fee. Reservations recommended.* ♿ P 📞 *707-224-1668. www.artesawinery.com.*

In 1872 the Codorniu family of Barcelona became Spain's first producers of sparkling wine made in the méthode

Méthode Champenoise

Most sparkling wines produced in the Wine Country are made by the méthode champenoise developed in 17C France by Dom Perignon, a Benedictine monk. In this process, a still wine traditionally blended from Pinot Noir and Chardonnay grapes is inoculated with yeast and sugar, bottled, capped and allowed to ferment a second time. The carbon dioxide gas retained in the bottle infuses the wine with bubbles, creating pressures of up to 110 pounds per square inch inside the bottle. The bottle is then stored on its side for as many as six years to let the wine age. Following aging, the wine is clarified by "riddling," a painstaking process of turning and lifting the bottles daily, bit by bit, until they are nearly upside down, so that yeast and sediments gather in the neck. The wine must then be "disgorged": The neck of the bottle is immersed in a brine solution so that the sediments within it freeze; when the bottle is then uncapped, pressure from within forces out the plug of frozen sediment. A *dosage* of sugar and brandy or other wine is added to the bottle before final corking and labeling.

champenoise tradition. Their Napa Valley operation, which shifted its focus to still wines in 1997 and changed its name to Artesa (meaning "craftsman") in 1997, occupies an innovative contemporary structure (1991, Domingo Triay) at the foot of Milliken Peak. Sloping, grass-covered earth berms bury the winery's walls, maintaining consistently cool temperatures in storage and production areas within. Galleries around a serene courtyard hold 16C–17C European winemaking equipment and changing displays of works by local artists. There are a variety of tasting experiences, some of which include a tour of the facilities ($45) or tapas ($60), as well as the classic tasting at the beautiful Foyer Bar ($35).

The Hess Collection Winery★★

4411 Redwood Rd. ○*Open daily 10am–5pm (galleries close 5:30pm).* ○*Closed Jan 1, Dec 25, Easter Sunday.* ☞*$25 tasting fee.* ♿🅿 ☎*707-255-8584. www.hesscollection.com.*

Nestled in a remote southwestern corner of the Napa Valley on the slope of Mt. Veeder, this beautifully renovated structure contains a fine private art collections open to the public, as well as a state-of-the-art winemaking facility. The original stone structure (1903) was acquired by the Christian Brothers in the early 1930s to house the Mont LaSalle winery. In 1983, Swiss entrepreneur Donald Hess leased the property, transforming the upper floors into galleries to exhibit his outstanding collection of works by contemporary American and European artists.

Through wide windows in the stairwells, visitors strolling through the sweeping galleries glimpse the steel tanks and ultra-modern bottling room of the winery.

Yountville

This small community of 3,000, ranging along the east side of Route 29, was named for George C. Yount (1794–1865), a North Carolina frontiersman who

Vineyards, Artesa Vineyards and Winery

© gcosoveanu/iStockphoto.com

Domaine Chandon

© M. Linda Lee/MICHELIN

established vineyards here in 1836 on a portion of the 11,814 acres granted him by the Mexican government.

Today Yountville's charming inns, trendy boutiques and excellent eateries make it a popular base for visitors to the southern Napa Valley. It's perhaps best known as the home of Thomas Keller's The French Laundry, a long-running and award-winning French restaurant in a rustic stone cottage.

Napa Valley Museum★

55 Presidents Cir., Yountville. Open *Wed–Sun 11am–4pm.* Closed major *holidays and during installations.* $10 ♿ 🅿 ☎ *707-944-0500.* *www.napavalleymuseum.org.*

The highlight of this regional museum (1998, Fernau and Hartman) is permanent exhibit **Land and People of the Napa Valley**, that describe the artistic, cultural and environmental heritage of the region. The main and spotlight galleries hosts an ever-changing array of exhibitions that explore topics as diverse as beer to video games.

Domaine Chandon★★

1 California Dr., Yountville. Open *daily 10am–5pm.* Closed Jan 1, *Thanksgiving Day, Dec 25.* $20–35 *tasting fee.* 🍴♿🅿 ☎ *888-242-6366.* *www.chandon.com.*

The beautiful France-meets-California setting at this Yountville winery was commissioned by Moët-Hennessy, owners of France's famed Moët et Chandon. The modern structures of gray concrete harmonize with the sweeps and curves of the surrounding terrain; the arched ceilings are reminiscent of traditional wine caves in France's Champagne region. In the entrance hall, an attractive gallery highlights skills and trades related to winemaking.

Here, you can sip sparkling and still wines by the glass, by the bottle or in a tasting flight on the grounds of this lush winery, where, refreshingly, reservations are not required and tastings are still reasonably priced. During the summer, many visitors take a glass of bubbly to the picnic tables scattered across the landscaped lawn.

Stag's Leap★

6150 Silverado Trail, Napa. Open *daily, by reservation only.* 🌿*Estate tour and tasting (Daily 10am, 1pm and 3pm;* $75) Closed *Jan 1, Thanksgiving Day, Dec 15.* ♿🅿 ☎ *707-257-5790.* *www.stagsleap.com*

Located in the Stag's Leap district, the award-winning wines produced at this 100-year-old vineyard have long been considered among the best in Napa, particularly the robust cabernets, in addition to petit verdot, merlot and chardonnay.

Located down a long rural road and surrounded by gardens, the old stone manor house where wines are served resembles a castle, and was once a hub of socialites and stars who orbited around Horace Chase, Stag's Leap's first owner, in the 19thC. Space is limited; reservations are required for all tastings and tours.

Mumm Napa★

8445 Silverado Trail, Rutherford.
🕐*Open daily 10am-6pm.* ≪*$25-35 tasting fee.* 🍷*Guided tours (Daily 10am, 11am, 1pm, 3pm* ≪*$40 tasting and flute included).* 📱*707-967-7700. www.mummnapa.com.*
On hot summer afternoons, locals and visitors gather to sip cold glasses of sparkling wine, shaded by umbrellas and oak trees, on the patio at Mumm, which overlooks the rolling vineyards of Rutherford. Here, the well-priced table-service tastings will take you through a flight of Mumm's esteemed bubbly, which was first created using the Champagne method by Mumm Napa's founding winemaker Guy Devaux. You can also order a glass to sip along with an artisan cheese, nut, and fruit plate.

Hall Wines★

401 St. Helena Highway South, St. Helena. 🕐*Open daily 10am-5:30pm.* 🍷*Guided tour available.* 🕐*Closed major holidays.* ≪*$40 tasting fee.* ✕&📱 ✆*707-967-2626. www.hallwines.com.*
The floor-to-ceiling windows in the tasting room and visitor's center at this upscale Napa winery overlook fields of grape vines stretching to the foot of the Mayacama Mountains to the west. With this bucolic backdrop, knowledgeable servers will take you through a lively tasting of Hall's signature Bordeaux-style varietals; the winery is best known for its award-winning cabernet sauvignons.

Owned by Craig and Kathryn Hall, the contemporary tasting room doubles as an art gallery, showcasing the couple's nice collection of contemporary work; the giant silver rabbit at the entrance is a work by artist Lawrence Argent and a well-known St. Helena landmark.

Inglenook★★

1991 St. Helena Hwy. (Rte. 29), Rutherford. 🕐*Open daily 10am–4:30pm.* 🕐*Closed Jan 1, Easter Sunday, Thanksgiving Day, Dec 25.* ≪*$20-35(including tour).* &📱 ✆*707-968-1161. www.inglenook.com.*
The stone winery (1882) at the center of the Inglenook Estate was owned by Gustave Niebaum, a Finnish sea captain and enterprising founder of Inglenook Wines (1879). Most of Niebaum's property, including his Victorian home and 1,600 acres of adjacent land, was purchased in 1975 by filmmaker Francis Ford Coppola (The Godfather trilogy) and his wife, Eleanor, who brought wine-making back to the chateau. The estate was renamed in 2002 after its flagship wine, and later, in 2011, after the original estate.

Guests can sample Inglenook wines, including the flagship Rubicon, which is made from predominately Cabernet Sauvignon grapes grown on the estate, in the elegant Pennino Salon from 11am to 4pm every day ($45), or join the weekly food-and-wine pairing at the chateau ($165).

Robert Mondavi Winery★

7801 St. Helena Hwy. (Rte. 29), Oakville. 🕐*Open 10am–5pm.* 🕐*Closed Jan 1, Easter Sunday, Thanksgiving Day, Dec 24-25.* ≪*$25-$50 tasting fee.* 🍷*Guided tours (30min–1.5hrs; ≪$40); reserve.* &📱 ✆*888-766-6328. www.robertmondaviwinery.com.*
Established in 1966, Robert Mondavi is possibly the most famous name in California wine. Today, the Mondavi grounds are almost always overflowing with visitors sipping flights, picnicking in the gardens, and touring the fermentation facilities and barrel-aging room. Going beyond the usual offerings, Mondavi runs bicycle tours of the vineyards, twilight walks with wine tastings, and guided tours and tastings in Mandarin, Cantonese, Spanish, Japanese and French. If you want to keep it simple, no reservations are required for the walk-

in tastings (*$25-50 depending on your choice of wines*), which run all day.

Despite the crowds, Mondavi remains a reliable pick for a first-time visit to Napa, as it's still a great spot to try distinctively California-style wines. It's also a beautiful spot. Constructed in 1966, the striking main building on the property anticipated a new generation of modern wineries designed to showcase art, architecture and wine. Sculptor Beniamino Bufano's figure of St. Francis with outstretched arms greets visitors beneath the monumental arched entry to the complex, and temporary exhibits of works by local artists are regular features at the winery. A popular Summer Music Festival and a winter concert series are held here annually.

St. Supéry★★

8440 St. Helena Hwy. (Rte. 29), Rutherford. ◕*Open daily 10am–5pm.* ◕*Closed major holidays.* ☛*Guided tours (1r–1.5hrs;* ☜*$40–$65); reserve.* ☜*$35 tasting fee.* ♿ 🅿 ☏*707-963-4507. www.stsupery.com.*

In addition to tastings of St. Supéry's estate-grown wines, this renovated modern winery offers offers a range of educational experiences; for example, guests can try their hand at blending a white to taste using the winery's Sauvignon Blanc and Sémillon (*$60, including 750ml bottle to take home*), or they can sign up for an intensive look at grape varietals with the winery's viticulturist (*$75, includes tasting*).

An onsite art gallery features changing exhibitions throughout the year.

Notably, the winery received Napa Green Winery designation in 2012, indicating that it is growing grapes with a rigorous focus on sustainability and green practices.

St. Helena★

Rte. 29, 12mi north of Napa.

A picturesque main street graces this charming town of 5,800 at the heart of the Napa Valley. Plentiful and widely varied accommodations and stellar restaurants, and a central location close to a number of popular wineries make St. Helena an excellent base for exploring the entire valley.

Robert Louis Stevenson Silverado Museum★

1490 Library Ln., St. Helena ◕*Open Tue–Sat noon–4pm.* ◕*Closed federal holidays.* ☜*Donation suggested.* ♿ 🅿 ☏*707-963-3757. stevensonmuseum.org.*

Housed in a pleasant gallery within the town library building, this small, memorabilia-packed museum is devoted to the life and works of Robert Louis Stevenson (1850–94), renowned and beloved author of such popular 19C stories as Treasure Island, Kidnapped and A Child's Garden of Verses. Stevenson honeymooned in a cabin on the slopes of Mt. St. Helena in summer 1880 and immortalized this Napa experience in his book The Silverado Squatters.

The museum's holdings—comprising photographs, books, manuscripts and the author's personal artifacts—are considered second in importance only to the Stevenson collections at Yale University's Beinecke Library.

Beringer Vineyards★★

2000 Main St. (Rte. 29), St. Helena. ◕*Sun-Thu 10:30am–4:30pm; Fri-Sat 10:30am-5pm* ☛*Guided tours available (30min–1hr;* ☜*$35–$55, tasting included).* ◕*Closed Jan 1, Thanksgiving Day, Dec 25.* ☜*$25 tasting fee.* ♿ 🅿 ☏*707-257-5771. www.beringer.com.*

The Napa Valley's oldest continuously operating winery was established in 1876 by Jacob and Frederick Beringer, German immigrants who arrived in the U.S. in the 1860s. The brothers' winery escaped the worst of the legislative strictures of Prohibition because they acquired a license to produce wine for religious and medicinal purposes. Extending into the sloping hillside behind the complex are over 1,000ft of tunnels where the temperature remains a constant 58°F, an ideal environment for aging wine.

The centerpiece of the property is the stately **Rhine House** (1883), constructed

The Silverado Quaffer

When Robert Louis Stevenson honeymooned in the Napa Valley in 1880, he expressed his affection for the region's fledgling wine industry in word and taste. "I was interested in California wine," he wrote in *The Silverado Squatters*. "Indeed, I am interested in all wines, and have been all my life, from the raisin wine that a schoolfellow kept secreted in his play-box up to my last discovery…

"Wine in California is still in the experimental stage; and when you taste a vintage, grave economical questions are involved… Meanwhile, the wine is merely a good wine; the best that I have tasted better than a Beaujolais, and not unlike."

Stevenson was particularly fond of the **Schramsberg Vineyards** *(1400 Schramsberg Lane off Petersen Lane west of Rte. 29; ℘707-942-4558; www. schramsberg.com).* "Mr. Schram's place… is the picture of prosperity," the author scribed. "I was tasting wines in the cellar. To Mr. Schram this was a solemn office; his serious gusto warmed my heart; prosperity had not yet wholly banished a certain neophite and girlish trepidation, and he followed every sip and read my face with proud anxiety. I tasted all, I tasted every variety of Schramberger, red and white Schramberger, Burgundy Schramberger, Schramberger Hock, Schramberger Golden Chasselas, the latter with a notable bouquet, and I fear to think how many more."

by Frederick Beringer as his residence. Modeled after the Beringer ancestral home in Germany, the 17-room mansion features elegant woodwork, inlaid floors and exceptional **stained-glass windows★**.

The Culinary Institute of America at Greystone

2555 Main St. (Rte. 29), St. Helena. ◷*Open daily 10am–6pm.* ⏷⏷*Guided tours available (* ⊜*$10).* ◷*Closed Thanksgiving and Dec 25.* ✕&🅿 *℘707-967-1100. www.ciachef.edu.*
The massive stone **building★** looming over Rte. 29 was erected in 1889 by William Bourn as Greystone Cellars, a cooperative effort by Napa Valley winegrowers in need of aging and storage facilities. The largest freestanding stone building in California when it was built, the winery changed hands several times before being purchased in the 1950s by the Christian Brothers, a Catholic teaching order.

Today the building houses the West Coast campus of the renowned Culinary Institute of America, which offers continuing education for professionals in the food, wine, health and hospital-ity fields, in addition to offering popular culinary and wine classes to the public (see website for details). Visitors may take a self-guided tour of the historic building, which houses a **corkscrew collection★** of more than 1,800 wine openers, some dating from the 18C, assembled by Brother Timothy, cellarmaster of Christian Brothers. Also check out the Spice Islands Marketplace *(open daily 10:30am–6pm. ℘707-967-2309)*, stocked with every cooking gadget and book imaginable, in addition to rare spices.

♟♟ Bale Grist Mill State Historic Park

3369 St. Helena Hwy. (Rte. 29), St. Helena. ◷*Park open Sat–Sun 10am–5pm.* ◷*Closed major holidays.* ⊜*$5.* &🅿℘*707-963-2236. www.napavalleystateparks.org.*
From the parking area, a pleasant, sylvan path leads to this charming historic **grist mill★**, powered by a 36ft waterwheel. Established in 1846 by Edward T. Bale, an Englishman who married a niece of Gen. Mariano Vallejo, the mill ground into flour the grain harvested by Napa Valley farmers. The wooden mill

and waterwheel, which ceased operation about 1905, are partially restored. Docent tours and an audiovisual presentation provide a good introduction to the milling process, and demonstrations allow a look at the mill in action (call for demonstration schedule). Visitors can purchase flour and cornmeal milled on site.

Sterling Vineyards★★

1111 Dunaweal Ln., Calistoga. Open Mon–Fri 11am–4pm, Sat–Sun 10am–4pm. Closed Jan 1, Thanksgiving Day, Dec 25. $35 includes tramway, wine tasting and self-guided tour; ⌖ P 800-726-6136. www.sterlingvineyards.com

Perched like a secluded Greek monastery on a 300ft knoll rising abruptly from the valley floor, this complex of pristine white buildings (1969, Martin J. Waterfield) is one of the Napa Valley's architectural grace notes.

Visitors ascend to the winery from the parking area by a hushed ride on the vineyard's **aerial tramway** ▲▲, from which tranquil views extend over the surrounding area. At the summit, follow informative panels on a self-guided tour through the winery, across terraces with **views★** of the northern Napa Valley, and under campaniles representing a contemporary take on traditional mission-style bell towers.

Clos Pegase★

1060 Dunaweal Ln., 6.8mi north of St. Helena via Rte. 29 (entrance on left). Open daily 10am–5pm. Guided tours Fri, Sat, and Sun 10am (60-90 mins); $55 including tasting. Closed Jan 1, Easter Sunday, Thanksgiving Day, Dec 25. $30-45 tasting fee. ⌖ P 707-942-4981. www.clospegase.com

Housed in a harmonious sprawl of terra-cotta and earth-toned structures at the base of a small volcanic knoll, Clos Pegase (1987, Michael Graves) is a striking example of the Napa Valley's variety of architectural styles.

The monumental winery complex reveals architect Graves' signature view of themes from classical antiquity, reflected in oversized columns, triangular pediments and an open central atrium. Selections from owner Jan Shrem's private art collection appear throughout the winery, even in the 20,000sq ft of storage caves hewn into the knoll of volcanic tufa. Shrem's residence, also designed by Graves, crowns the knoll (not open to the public).

Calistoga★

Rte. 29, 6mi north of St. Helena.

Founded in 1859 in the shadow of Mt. St. Helena and at the very top of the Napa Valley, this residential and resort town of 5,200 unites the flavor of the late-19C frontier era with 20C modernity. Thermal activity in the area, manifested in numerous geysers and hot springs, fueled Calistoga's development as a resort where tourists flocked to "take the waters"; local Native Americans had long sworn by their medicinal properties.

According to legend, Calistoga founder **Sam Brannan** (1819–88) stumbled upon the town's name by confusedly (some say drunkenly) declaring it "The Calistoga of Sarafornia" (Saratoga of California) after upstate New York's famed Saratoga Hot Springs.

Today, hot-spring spas and bottled mineral water continue to fuel the town's popularity. False-front facades along **Lincoln Avenue**, the town's main thoroughfare, provide a charming frontier flavor, as does the historic **Railroad Depot** *(1458 Lincoln Ave.).* Erected in 1868 to serve the long-defunct Napa Valley Railroad Company, the structure now houses shops, a restaurant. The visitor center is now located at 1133 Washington St. (707-942-6333).

▲▲ Sharpsteen Museum★

1311 Washington St., Calistoga. Open daily 11am–4pm. Closed Thanksgiving Day, Dec 25. $3 donation requested. ⌖ P 707-942-5911. www.sharpsteenmuseum.org

The highlight of this small museum is an intriguing assemblage of miniature **dioramas** re-creating scenes of Calistoga's colorful past.

Founded in 1979 by Ben Sharpsteen—one of Walt Disney's original 11 animators and later an Oscar-winning producer—the museum also features a collection of early 19C photos, a restored stagecoach and assorted artifacts pertaining to the town's history.

Adjoining the museum building is a **cottage** from Sam Brannan's resort, relocated from its original site and fully refurbished to appear as it would have during Calistoga's resort heyday.

👥 Old Faithful Geyser★

1299 Tubbs Ln., Calistoga.
🕐*Open Mar-Sept 8.30am-7pm; Oct-Feb 8:30am-5pm;. ⊚$15.*
✕ 👤 🅿 ✆*707-942-6463.*
www.oldfaithfulgeyser.com.

Located at the foot of Mt. St. Helena, this privately owned geyser is one of the world's three known "faithful" geysers, so named for their regular eruptions (the others are located at Yellowstone National Park and in New Zealand). Approximately every 40 minutes, the geyser spews a column of superheated water some 60ft into the air in a splendid shower of droplets and steam. There is also a small petting zoo on site.

👥 Petrified Forest★

4100 Petrified Forest Rd, Calistoga.
🕐*Open Jun–Sept daily 10am–7pm; Oct–May daily 10am–5pm.* 🕐*Closed Thanksgiving Day, Dec 25.* ✎*Guided tours (1.5hr) available 11am, 1pm, 3pm ⊚$12.* 👤 🅿 ✆*707-942-6667.*
www.petrifiedforest.org.

A circuit trail through this small, privately owned forest winds past the stone remnants of giant redwoods that were petrified more than three million years ago when Mt. St. Helena erupted, covering the surrounding area with ash and molten lava. Among the highlights is The Giant, an ancient redwood 60ft long and 6ft in diameter.

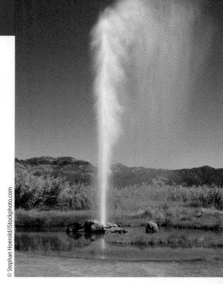

© Stephan Hoerold/iStockphoto.com

Old Faithful Geyser

Robert Louis Stevenson State Park

Highway 29, 7mi north of Calistoga.
🕐*Open daily dawn–dusk.* 🅿 ✆*707-942-4575. www.parks.ca.gov.*

This largely undeveloped park provides an excellent opportunity for hikers and bikers to explore the rugged, picturesque slopes of Mt. St. Helena (4,343ft). On its ascent to the summit, a trail passes the site (near an abandoned silver mine) where Robert Louis Stevenson and his wife, Fanny Osborne Stevenson, spent their honeymoon in 1880.

After one mile, the trail emerges from the forest to join an unpaved fire road up to the summit; from the road, sweeping **views**★★ extend over the northern Napa Valley and beyond. Another trail winds six miles east below cliffs of volcanic origin.

Silverado Trail★

Running parallel to Route 29 along the eastern edge of the Napa Valley between Napa and Calistoga, this scenic road offers a tranquil alternative to the often traffic-choked main highway. Its many dips and curves accommodate the rolling terrain at the base of the ridges bordering the valley, and acres of serene vineyards are punctuated by numerous wineries. Several crossroads link the pastoral Silverado Trail with Route 29.

Sonoma Valley★★

The Sonoma Valley is agriculturally and topographically more diverse than the Napa Valley. Anchored by the historic town of Sonoma, the valley dominates the southern portion of Sonoma County, where vineyards and wineries abut orchards and fields. The region enjoys a reputation for excellent produce and other farm products, as well as for wines. The county is home to 17 official American Viticultural Appellations (AVAs) and over 400 wineries.

SIGHTS
Sonoma★★

Site of the California mission chain's northernmost and final outpost, this charming community of about 11,000, set amid the sun-soaked orchards and vineyards of the Sonoma Valley, is the Wine Country's most historically significant town. Sonoma was born in 1823 with the founding of the San Francisco Solano Mission. Nearby, the Mexican government established a military outpost to guard against the threat of Russian encroachment from Fort Ross, 30mi north. After missions were secularized in 1834, Gen. Mariano Vallejo was assigned to oversee distribution of the mission lands and to establish a pueblo at Sonoma.

The town's central plaza was the scene on June 14, 1846 of the **Bear Flag Revolt**, an uprising of American settlers disgruntled with Mexican control of California. Hoisting a white flag with a brown bear and a star, the group proclaimed California an independent republic. A month later, U.S. Forces captured Monterey, declared California a U.S. possession, ending the short-lived republic. Formally incorporated in 1850, Sonoma flourished as a supply and trade center for the area's farms and nascent winemaking industry.

The town retains the charming flavor of that period. Several noteworthy exam-

- ⏱ **Michelin Map:** See p281.
- ℹ **Info:** ℘707-996-1090; www.sonomavalley.com.
- ◗ **Location:** From San Francisco (49mi), take US-101 north; exit at Rte. 37, continue to Rte. 121 and turn left (north). Continue to Rte. 12. Most wineries lie in the vicinity of Sonoma and along or near Rte. 12 as it leads through the town of Sonoma to Santa Rosa and to the Upper Sonoma-Russian River Region.
- 👪 **Kids:** Train Town: a giant model train that you can ride on.
- 🕐 **Timing:** For a perfect day in Sonoma, try to see the historic sights early, then have a picnic lunch, followed by a leisurely afternoon in the wineries.
- 👁 **Don't Miss:** Farmers' markets abound in this area, revealing the local passion for the gourmet, the organic and the homegrown. The ones on the plazas in Sonoma and Healdsburg are particularly enticing.

ples of 19C residential architecture grace the streets south and west of the plaza, displaying elements of the Mission, Bungalow and Monterey Colonial styles.

Sonoma State Historic Park★★

🕐*All sights open daily 10am–5pm.* 🕐*Closed Jan 1, Thanksgiving Day, Dec 25.* ☏*Guided tours available Fri-Sun 11am–3pm.* 💲*$3 ticket includes same-day admission to all sights (purchase at any sight or at Petaluma State Historic Park, below).* 🅿 ℘*707-938-9560. www. parks.ca.gov; www.parks.sonoma.net.* Headquartered near the Toscano Hotel, the park maintains and operates the town's key historic sites, including the

San Francisco Solano Mission, the Sonoma Barracks, the Toscano Hotel, the Vallejo Home and Petaluma Adobe.

Plaza★

Bounded by Spain St., 1st St. W., Napa St., and 1st St. E.

Laid out by Mariano Vallejo in 1835, Sonoma's eight-acre plaza is the largest of its kind in California. Anchored at its center by the **City Hall** (1908), an eye-catching Mission Revival

structure of roughly hewn basalt, the plaza today is attractively landscaped, laced with walkways and dotted with duck ponds, benches and play areas.

On the east side of the Plaza, the **Sonoma Valley Visitor Center** (*453 1st St. E., ☏707-996-1090; www.sonomavalley. com*) is lodged in a restored Carnegie Library building (1913). A dramatic bronze **statue (1)** near the northeast corner depicts a soldier raising the Bear Flag, commemorating the 1846 revolt. Shady yews, sycamores and plane trees create a peaceful atmosphere amid the bustle of surrounding streets.

San Francisco Solano Mission★

E. Spain St. and 1st St. E. ☞Guided tours Fri–Sun 11am-3pm. ♿ ☏707-938-9560.

Founded in 1823 by Father José Altamíra, California's final mission was part of a Mexican government effort to strengthen its holdings against potential Russian invasion. The original wooden church and other structures, destroyed during an uprising in 1826, were replaced by adobe buildings. The mission operated until secularization in 1834, when Mariano Vallejo dismantled the property and erected a parish chapel on the site of the original church.

About half of the original mission complex remains standing. It includes the chapel and part of the priests' quarters, restored around 1912. Displays of period furnishings and artifacts retell mission history. In the restored chapel, the Stations of the Cross and framed paintings are authentic to the mission period.

Across Spain Street *(no. 217)* stands the **Blue Wing Inn** (1840), an attractive, symmetrical adobe structure that formerly served as a saloon and hotel.

Sonoma Barracks★

Spain St. and 1st St. E. ☞Guided tours Sat–Sun 11am-3pm ☏707-939-9420.

This spacious, two-story adobe structure (1841), its wide balcony overlooking the plaza, housed Mexican troops stationed here to guard Sonoma. Following U.S. occupation of California, the barracks served various American regiments during the Mexican-American War. Now a museum of the historic park, the barracks contains displays illustrating aspects of Sonoma's history, including artifacts from the various periods of Mexican and American settlement.

Adjacent to the barracks lies the historic **Toscano Hotel** (*☞guided tours Sat–Sun 1pm–4pm),* built as a general store in the 1850s and converted to a boardinghouse in the 1880s for Italian immigrants working in nearby quarries. Today the wood-frame building's fancy Victorian furnishings belie its rough-and-tumble origins. Visitors can peek into cramped upstairs sleeping rooms and explore the restored kitchen and dining room room.

Lachryma Montis (Vallejo Home)★

West Spain St. and 4th St. West ☞Guided tours weekends 1pm-4pm. ☏707-938-9559.

The elegant Gothic Victorian home (1852), set amid attractive landscaped grounds, was named "tear of the mountain" in Latin for the mountain spring on the property. It served as the final home of Mariano Vallejo (1807–90), one of Mexican California's most powerful figures. The four-bedroom house is furnished to reflect the period when Vallejo lived there, and a small interpretive center displays artifacts from the 19C.

The Adobe (Three Sticks Winery)★

143 W. Spain St. ◷*Mon-Sat 10am-4pm. By appointment only.* ◷*Closed major holidays.* ◎*$40-$80 tasting fee.* ℘*707-996-3328 ext. 105 www.threestickswines.com*

Just off the town's main square, the historic Vallejo-Castañeda hacienda, the oldest continuously occupied residence in Sonoma, was built in 1842, when California was a part of Mexico. Once the property of Captain Salvador Vallejo, brother of Mariano Vallejo, the building was purchased in 2012 by the owners of artisan winery Three Sticks, who extensively restored the property, including the original murals on the walls. First used only for private tastings for winery members, it is now open to the public for wine tastings (advance reservation required), with knowledgeable hosts who are as well versed in Sonoma history as they are in wine-making.

Buena Vista Winery★★

18000 Old Winery Rd. ◷*Open daily 10am–5pm.* ◷*Closed Jan 1, Thanksgiving Day, Dec 25.* ◎*$20 tasting fee.* ◞*Guided tours available (Daily 11am, 2pm, with reservation.* ◎*$40, including tasting).* ℗℘*800-926-1266. www.buenavistawinery.com*

Sonoma County's first premium winery, founded in 1857 by early entrepreneur Agoston Haraszthy is set on a rolling site amid eucalyptus, oak and bay laurel trees.

Visitors may peer through an iron gate into Haraszthy's renowned **wine cellars**, dug into the limestone hill behind the winery by Chinese laborers in 1863. The stone **Press House** (1862), reputed to be California's oldest remaining winery building, today boasts a refurbished interior; the wooden beams are original.

Sebastiani Vineyards★

389 4th St. E. ◷*Open daily 10am–5pm.* ◞*Guided tour (90min; Wed-Sun 11am.* ◎*$45).* ◷*Closed major holidays.* ◎*$15-25 tasting fee.* ♿℗ ℘*707-933-3230. www.sebastiani.com.*

This sprawling stone winery incorporates sections of a livery stable purchased by Italian immigrant Samuele Sebastiani in 1904, that he transformed into a wine cellar throughout the first half of the 20C. The reception room displays rudimentary casks, crushers and other equipment from the early part of the century. Visitors on tour see Sebastiani's two 60,000-gallon oak fermentation tanks, reputed to be the largest in the world outside of Heidelberg, Germany.

Ram's Gate Winery★★

28700 Arnold Dr. ◷*Open Thu-Mon 11am–6pm by appointment.* ◞*Guided tour available (90min.* ◎*$65).* ◷*Closed major holidays.* ◎*$40 tasting fee.* ♿℗℘*707-721-8700. www.ramsgatewinery.com.*

Small-lot Chardonnay and Pinot Noir, chic architecture, and sweeping vineyard views makes this relatively young winery a top stop for any oenophile. The winery offers a range of experiences, from a tasting flight to food-an-wine pairings, all of which take place in architect Howard Backen's modern building, which is meant to conjure up old farmsteads.

👥 Train Town

20264 Broadway. ◷*Daily 10am–5pm.* ◷*Closed Thanksgiving Day, Dec 25 and during heavy rain.* ◎*Free general admission, train rides $7.50; all other rides $3.75* ♿℗ ℘*707-938-3912. www.traintown.com.*

An old-fashioned carousel and a working scale-model railroad make Train-Town a fine destination for families with small children. Passengers sit on benches in low, open-top train cars for a 20min ride through ten acres of landscaped countryside with bridges, tunnels, waterfalls and miniature buildings. The train stops midway at a petting zoo.

Sonoma Valley vineyards

Glen Ellen

About 8 miles north of Sonoma on Highway 12.

A picturesque hamlet bordered by Sonoma Creek, Glen Ellen is home to Jack London State Historic Park (*see below*) and a number of excellent wineries, in addition to boasting a number of nice places to eat, drink, and sleep in this oak-filled 800-person community.

Jack London State Historic Park★★

2400 London Ranch Rd., Glen Ellen.
🕐*Open daily 9am–5pm; cottage noon–4pm.* 🚶*Free guided tours (Sat-Sun 11am, 1pm; 1–2hrs) available.*
🅿️♿*$10/car.* ✆*707-938-5216. www.jacklondonpark.com.*

Sprawling among peaceful hills in the shadow of Sonoma Mountain is the 800-acre "Beauty Ranch," home of writer Jack London (1876–1916) during the last years of his life. Today a state park, the ranch commemorates this beloved American author of novels *The Call of the Wild* (1903) and *The Sea Wolf* (1904).

Sailor on Horseback

Born illegitimately in San Francisco in 1876, Jack London was raised in Oakland, where as a boy he labored in the city's canneries and mills. His huge capacity for hard work and his love of adventure were united with a voracious appetite for books. He joined a sealing expedition to Siberia and joined the Klondike Gold Rush in 1897. Forced by scurvy to return to Oakland the following year, London directed his energies to writing stories

of his adventures in the far north. His first short story, published by the *Overland Monthly,* earned him only $5 but launched a hugely successful career as a novelist, foreign correspondent, short-story writer and lecturer.

In 1905 London, by then renowned as an author and advocate of socialism, purchased a rundown ranch in the hills near Glen Ellen and settled there with his second wife, Charmian. In 1911 the Londons began construction of Wolf House, a massive four-story mansion of hand-hewn lava boulders and redwood logs. Its 26 rooms and nine fireplaces occupied 15,000sq ft. On the night of August 22, 1913, a month before the couple was to move in, a fire roared through the house, leaving only stone walls. Crushed, the Londons never rebuilt Wolf House, but continued to live in a small cottage on the ranch. Jack London died there in 1916 at the age of 40 of uremic poisoning.

Visit

Erected by Charmian London in 1919 as her residence, with the intention of making it a museum to honor her husband, the rustic stone **House of Happy Walls★ (A)** today serves as the park visitor center. The massive building contains memorabilia of both Londons, including artifacts from the author's life and work, letters, photographs, clothing and objects amassed during the couple's world travels, notably Pacific meanderings aboard their boat, the *Snark*.

A trail (🚶*1.2mi round-trip; trailhead at House of Happy Walls*) winds through rolling meadows and forests to the ghostly ruins of **Wolf House★**, in the heart of a glade overlooking a peaceful valley. A short detour leads to the Londons' gravesite atop a peaceful hill. The **Beauty Ranch Trail★** (🚶*.5mi loop; accessible from the upper parking lot)* wanders about the property past stables, silos, a piggery and the Londons' modest cottage (☞$3).

More extensive hiking trails lead throughout the park and up the steep slope of Sonoma Mountain *(summit on private property)*.

Petaluma Adobe State Historic Park★★

3325 Adobe Rd., Petaluma, via Rte. 116. 🕐*Open Tue–Sun 10am–5pm.* 🕐*Closed Jan 1, Thanksgiving Day, Dec 25.* ☞$3 *(includes admission to Sonoma State Historic Park).* 🅿 ✆707-762-4871. www.petalumaadobe.com

In 1834, Mariano Vallejo established a 100sq mi ranch headquarters on this hilltop site overlooking the rolling Sonoma County countryside. Rancho Petaluma thrived, producing cattle, horses, sheep and crops of grain until Vallejo leased out the property in September 1850.

Today the restored two-story dwelling, one-half its original size, re-creates the atmosphere of a prosperous 19C ranch with interpretive displays and period furniture. In the courtyard stand hive-shaped ovens once used to prepare meals for the adobe's residents.

Petaluma★

12mi west of Sonoma via Rte. 116 west from Rte. 12. Tourist information ✆877-273-8258. www.visitpetaluma.com.

Set aside the Petaluma River in a fertile valley 40mi north of San Francisco, this agricultural town of nearly 60,000 grew from a hunters' camp to a grain-shipping port in 1852. The **Great Petaluma Mill** *(Petaluma Blvd. N. and B St.; restored as a shopping complex)*, once the region's largest feed mill, survives as a testimony to the city's early industry. Dubbed the "World's Egg Basket," Petaluma shipped as many as 600 million eggs per year until high labor and feed costs caused

the decline of the poultry industry after World War II.

The city today remains a dairy center, with many cheese producers, including the Bay Area's beloved Cowgirl Creamery, operating here.

The **Old Petaluma** historic district *(north of B St. along Petaluma Blvd. N. and Kentucky St.)* reflects the town's Victorian heritage with its cast-iron architecture. Petaluma's finest row of ironfront architecture *(Western Ave. between Kentucky St. and Petaluma Blvd.)* is bounded on the north corner by the Italianate **Mutual Relief Building** (1885) and on the south by the **Masonic Hall** (1882), topped by a landmark clock tower. Nearby, the **McNear Building** *(15–23 Petaluma Blvd. N.)*, with its elegant row of second-story arches, actually incorporates two structures; the original (1886) and the addition (1911) were owned by one of Petaluma's first families. Garlands, wreaths and marbled columns constitute some of the rich detail that distinguishes the facade of the Old Opera Housea *(149 Kentucky St.)*, built in 1870 to host minstrel shows and theater productions.

Free walking tours of the historic downtown, led by costumed docents (🚶*Guided tours May–Oct Sat 10.30am)*, depart from the **Petaluma Historical Library and Museum** *(20 4th St.;* 🕐*open Thu–Sat 10am–4pm, Sun noon–3pm;* 🕐*closed major holidays;* ✆707-778-4398; www.petalumamuseum.com). The 1906 Classical Revival building's free-standing, stained-glass dome is the largest in California. The **Heritage Wall** (1998, Steve della Maggiora) muralizes Petaluma history on a wall of a building *(Petaluma Blvd. N. and Washington St.)* that once housed the world's only pharmacy for chickens.

ADDRESSES

🍽/EAT

El Molino Central – *11 Central Ave, Boyes Hot Springs.* ✆707-939-1010. www.elmolinocentral.com. Sonoma locals come to this delightful Mexican spot to stock up on handmade corn tortillas and butternut-squash-stuffed tamales, but you can also snag a seat at one of the first-come-first-served patio tables to dine on the seasonal selection of moles, tacos, and enchiladas.

SHOPPING

Cornerstone Sonoma *23570 Arnold Drive, Sonoma. 707-933-3010. www. cornerstonesonoma.com.* This multifaceted wine country marketplace features several tasting rooms from local winemakers, art galleries and design shops, a café, a demonstration kitchen for culinary events, and a test garden run by Oakland-based Sunset Magazine. You'll also find an information kiosk operated by the Sonoma Valley Visitor's Center (*Daily 10am-5pm. ☎707- 996-1090*).

Hosts who are as well versed in Sonoma history as they are in wine-making.

Upper Sonoma-Russian River Region★

This region of northern Sonoma County comprises three principal wine areas: the **Russian River Valley,** the Dry Creek Valley and the Alexander Valley. Smaller areas include Knight's Valley, Green Valley, Northern Sonoma and Chalk Hill. The Russian River Valley follows the curving path of the Russian River as it meanders south through Healdsburg and veers west toward the coast, passing picturesque wineries, vineyards and brooding stands of redwood trees. Swimming and kayaking are popular sports on the river where it passes through the resort communities of Forestville, **Guerneville**, Monte Rio and Duncans Mills, and the surrounding forests offer ample opportunities for hiking and camping. Hemmed by majestic mountain ridges, the **Alexander Valley** extends along the Russian River east and north of Healdsburg. Small, rustic wineries dot the curves and corners of Route 128 as it wanders across a pastoral landscape of vineyard-covered foothills. The 20 mile-long valley was named for Cyrus Alexander, a Pennsylvania trapper who settled here in the 1840s. The delightful **Dry Creek Valley★** extends from the Warm Springs Dam on Lake Sonoma to just south of Healdsburg. Approximately 12 miles long, the narrow valley is laced with small, winding roads that meander among vineyards, beneath canopies of trees and across the valley floor. Zinfandel grapes have been grown here, and in the Alexander Valley, for more than a century.

- **Michelin Map:** See p286.
- **Info:** ☎707-869-9000. www.russianriver.com.
- **Location:** The region lies northwest of the Napa and Sonoma Valleys, linked to San Francisco by US-101. From San Francisco take US-101 north to Santa Rosa (49mi) or to Healdsburg (64mi).
- **Kids:** The Charles M. Schulz Museum, mecca for fans of the beloved *Peanuts* comic strip.
- **Timing:** If you're in Healdsburg around lunchtime, the town's main plaza is an excellent spot for an alfresco picnic.
- **Don't Miss:** Luther Burbank Home and Gardens, birthplace of the Santa Rosa plum, among other fruits and vegetables.

SIGHTS
Santa Rosa
26.5mi southeast of Sonoma.

The sprawling city of 175,000 is the commercial hub and seat of Sonoma County. Incorporated in 1858, it boomed after the opening of the Golden Gate Bridge in 1937. Native sons include botanist Luther Burbank (1849–1926) and cartoonist Charles Schulz (1922–2000), as well as collector Robert Ripley (1893–1949) of *Believe It or Not!* fame.

US-101 bisects the old and new sections of town. Santa Rosa's historic district, known as **Railroad Square** *(bounded by 3rd, Davis and 6th Sts. and the railroad tracks)*, is west of the freeway; it comprises a charming cluster of restored brick and stone buildings constructed in 1870 to serve the Santa Rosa and North Pacific Railroad.

Today the square is an attractive group of offices, specialty shops, boutiques, restaurants and inns; a visitor center occupies the former train depot *(9 4th St.; Open Mon–Sat 9am-5pm, Sun 10am-5pm. 707-577-8674; www.visit-santarosa.com).*

East of US-101 and the Santa Rosa Plaza mall is the downtown area, centered on **Courthouse Square** *(Mendocino and Santa Rosa Aves. at 3rd and 4th Sts.).* Framed by fountains, the grassy swath is a popular site for outdoor concerts. Northeast of downtown are lovely residential streets lined with well-preserved late-19C Victorian homes.

Luther Burbank Home & Gardens★
Sonoma and Santa Rosa Aves., Santa Rosa. Gardens open daily 8am-dusk. Tours, museum, and gift

shop *Apr–Oct Tue–Sat 10am–4pm, Sun 11am-3pm* 🚶‍♂️*Home visit by guided tour only (👁️$10).* ♿ ☎️707-524-5445. *www.lutherburbank.org.*

Visitors can tour the modest home of the renowned botanist, who moved to Santa Rosa from Massachusetts in 1875, or stroll among lush gardens, which today feature many of Burbank's experimental hybrids, including some 100 varieties of roses. Burbank's extensive experiments in plant hybridization—resulting in such now-commonplace strains as the Russet Burbank potato, the Shasta daisy and the Santa Rosa plum—produced more than 800 new varieties of fruits, nuts and vegetables and earned him a reputation as magician of the botanical world.

In the renovated carriage house, displays tell the story of Burbank's life and work. The simple furnishings of his charming Greek Revival home bear witness to the horticulturalist's simple lifestyle, although he clearly had many high-powered friends: photos show him with the likes of Henry Ford, Thomas Edison, Jack London and Helen Keller.

Church of One Tree
Juilliard Park, across Santa Rosa Ave. from Burbank Home, Santa Rosa. 🔒*Closed to the public.*

Constructed of boards from a single 275ft redwood tree, this now-dilapidated Gothic Revival church formerly housed a small museum dedicated to the life and discoveries of native-son Ripley, creator of *Believe It or Not!*

Sonoma County Museum★ (M1)
425 7th St., Santa Rosa. 🕐*Open Tue–Sun 11am–5pm.* 🕐*Closed major holidays.* 👁️*$10.* ♿ ☎️707-579-1500. *www.sonomacountymuseum.org.*

Santa Rosa's former post office (1909), designed in the Classical Revival style, showcases the art, history and culture of Sonoma County. Historical exhibits cover the period from the early 18C, when Miwok, Pomo and Wapo peoples occupied the area, through the growth of the wine industry and recent population growth. Landscapes by William Keith and Thomas Hill are among works

presented in the California Gallery of 19C painting. The museum also boasts the largest private collection of works (more than 100 drawings, sculpture, collages and photographs) by site-specific artists Christo and Jeanne-Claude.

👥 Charles M. Schulz Museum and Research Center (M2)
1 Snoopy Pl., off W. Steele Ln. and Hardies Ln, Santa Rosa. 🕐*Open Memorial Day–Labor Day Mon-Fri 11am-5pm, Sat-Sun 10am-5pm. Rest of the year closed Mon, Tue.* 🕐*Closed major holidays.* 👁️*$12, children 4–18 $5.* ♿🅿️ ☎️707-579-4452. *www.schulzmuseum.org.*

For nearly 50 years, until his death in early 2000, Santa Rosa resident Charles Schulz wrote and illustrated the popular comic strip, Peanuts. Opened in 2002, the museum celebrates the Peanuts characters through rotating exhibits of 6,000 original comic strips, while also telling the story of Schulz's life and career, while. A 100-seat auditorium presents daily screenings of the Peanuts animated shows.

👥 Snoopy's Gallery and Gift Shop
1665 W. Steele Ln., Santa Rosa. 🕐*Open daily 10am–6pm.* 🕐*Closed major holidays.* ♿🅿️ ☎️707-546-3385 or 800-959-3385. www.snoopygift.com.*

Lovers of *Peanuts* enjoy a visit to this gallery, where memorabilia, cartoons, and original drawings are displayed.

👥 Redwood Empire Ice Arena
1667 W. Steele Ln., Santa Rosa. 🕐*Open daily 9am–7pm.* 🕐*Closed major holidays.* ✖️♿🅿️ ☎️707-546-7147. *www.snoopyshomeice.com.*

Schulz himself directed the construction of this Swiss chalet-style arena in 1969. It hosts concerts, hockey games and ice shows, and is open for public skating *(rentals available;* 🕐*call or visit website for schedule).*

Healdsburg★
15mi northwest of Santa Rosa.

Founded in 1857 by Harmon Heald, a migrant farmer-turned-merchant, tranquil Healdsburg (HEELDS-burg) sits at the confluence of the Alexander, Dry Creek and Russian River valleys. Several excellent restaurants and inns make it an ideal starting point for forays into these areas. At the heart of this town of 11,600 is picturesque, one-acre **Plaza Park** *(Healdsburg Ave. and Plaza, Center and Matheson Sts.)* Just off the plaza lies **SHED**, a stylish well-stocked culinary and gardening retail shop, locavore cafe, and fermentation bar, that also hosts classes *(25 North St., Healdsburg.* ○*open Wed-Mon 10am-9pm.* ✆*707-431-7433. www.healdsburgshed.com).*

Healdsburg Museum (M3)

221 Matheson St., 2 blocks east of the plaza. ○*Open Wed–Sun 11am–4pm.* ○*Closed major holidays.* ♿🅿✆*707-431-3325. www.healdsburgmuseum.org.* Housed in a beautifully preserved former Carnegie Library, this small museum contains a collection of artifacts from indigenous peoples and from California's Mexican period. Highlights include photographs, Pomo Indian baskets, grinding rocks and weapons, bringing to life upper Sonoma's colorful history.

Lake Sonoma★

11mi north of Healdsburg by Dry Creek Rd. 🧗△*(*☍*$10–$40; reservations* ✆*877-444-6777).* 🅿✆*707-431-4553. www.parks.sonoma.net.* Nestled in the coastal foothills of northern Sonoma County, this elongated lake was created in 1983 when the Warm Springs Dam was constructed at the confluence of Warm Springs and Dry creeks. Now a popular recreation area, Lake Sonoma offers a plethora of activities including boating, swimming, fishing, picnicking, hiking and camping in and around its sapphire waters.

👥 Visitor Center and Fish Hatchery★★

3333 Skaggs Springs Rd., Geyserville. ○*Visitor center open daily.* ✆*707-431-4533. www.spn.usace.army.mil/lake_sonoma/vcandfh.htm.* Displays of craftwork and artifacts in the Visitor Center exemplify the traditions and beliefs of the indigenous Pomo people. Panels illustrate local geological formations and thermal activity. The state-of-the-art hatchery building, created by the U.S. Army Corps of Engineers to mitigate environmental disruption of Dry Creek caused by the Warm Springs Dam, offers a rare opportunity to observe the spawning and hatching of steelhead trout and coho (silver) and chinook salmon. Fish climb a "ladder" into the hatchery where they are held, sorted and spawned—activities visible from a mezzanine-level interpretive center.

Lake Sonoma Overlook

2.5mi from Visitor Center via Stewarts Point Rd.; follow signs. Designed in harmony with its natural surroundings, the wood-timbered overlook offers soaring **views★★** of the lake, dam and surrounding mountains, including Mt. St. Helena in neighboring Napa Valley.

👥 Armstrong Redwoods State Reserve★

2mi north of Guerneville on Armstrong Woods Rd. ○*Open daily 8am—one hour past sunset; visitor center open daily 11am–3pm.* ✆*707-869-2958.* ☍*$8/car.* 🅿✆*707-869-2015. www.parks.ca.gov* Lush, dense forests of varied species of trees surround a 500-acre grove of ancient redwoods that survived 19C logging operations thanks to conservationist efforts of Col. James Armstrong. Today the grove forms the heart of an 800-acre state park with some of Sonoma County's finest surviving redwood trees. A self-guided nature trail (.5mi) passes through fern-laced glades.

WINERIES

Simi Winery★

16275 Healdsburg Ave., Healdsburg. ○*Open daily 10am–5pm.* ☍*$15 tasting fee.* ☍*Guided tour available (daily 11am, 2pm.*☍*$30)* ○*Closed Jan 1, Easter Sunday, Thanksgiving Day, Dec 25.* ✕♿🅿✆*800-746-4880. www.simiwinery.com.*

Founded in 1883 by Italian immigrants Giuseppe and Pietro Simi, this winery today boasts some of the oldest vines and stone cellars in California alongside an ultra-modern winemaking facility. The massive stone cellars were built in two phases, visible in the building's two types of stonework. In the mid-1880s, Chinese workers constructed the original south side, as well as railroad tracks that still run through the middle of the property. (They were once used to ship bottles directly from the cellars.).

The north side was constructed in 1904 by Italian masons under the direction of Isabel Simi, Giuseppe's daughter, who (according to local lore) took over management of the winery at age 14. Legend has it that after Prohibition, with the winery all but bankrupt, Isabel rolled a barrel onto the old highway and offered free sips of wine, thereby establishing California's first tasting room.

A guided tour takes visitors through the historic stone cellars and into a high-tech fermentation center.

© M. Linda Lee/MICHELIN

Ferrari-Carano Winery vineyards

Ferrari-Carano Winery★

8761 Dry Creek Rd. ◷*Open daily 10am–5pm.* ☞*$15-25 tasting fee.* 👣*Guided tours (Mon–Sat 10am, reservation required).* ◷*Closed major holidays.* 𝄞*707-433-6700. www.ferrari-carano.com.*

Five acres of stunning parterre gardens surround a spectacular Italianate villa on this fine estate.

Visitors enter through wrought-iron gates, meandering along garden paths, past a rippling stream. An Italian courtyard provides the formal entrance to the Renaissance-style Villa Fiore (1997), its stone columns and arches rising above the Dry Creek Valley. From the tasting room and wine shop, a curving stone staircase descends to a vaulted, cobblestone-floored viewing area, revealing more than 1,100 French oak barrels aging fine red wines.

Korbel Champagne Cellars★

13250 River Rd., 2.5mi northeast of Guerneville. ◷*Open 10am–5pm.* 👣*Winery tour daily 11am–4pm.* ◷*Closed major holidays.* 👣👤📶 𝄞*707-824-7000. www.korbel.com.*

Korbel dates from the late 1870s, when Czech immigrants Anton, Francis and Joseph Korbel planted grapevines on the site. In 1886 they built a large, handmade-brick building for the production of brandy and sparkling wine. The highlight of a visit to Korbel is an informative guided tour covering both historic and contemporary processes of méthode champenoise sparkling-wine production. Enjoy a wander through the 250-variety antique rose garden on the slope below the Korbel family home.

Francis Ford Coppola Winery★★

300 Via Archimedes, Geyserville. ◷*Open daily 11am–6pm.* ◷*Closed major holidays.* 👣*Winery tour (45mins) daily 11.30am, 1pm & 2pm* ☞*$20).* 👤📶 𝄞*707-857-1400. www.francisfordcoppolawinery.com.*

Looking every bit like a stage set, this namesake winery owned by Francis Ford Coppola boasts rooms filled with the director's film memorabilia, as well as bocce courts and two giant swimming pools with private cabins (◷*open spring through fall;* ☞*$35 day pass; reservation required months in advance*) where you can take a dip after a grueling day of tastings (*$30-40 tasting fee; complimentary pours of their Rosso & Bianco wines*). An onsite restaurant, Rustic (◷*open daily 11:00am - 9:00pm; 707-857-1485*) serves the director's own pizza and other Italian favorites.

The Bay Area bedroom communities south of San Francisco range down the east side of the Santa Cruz Mountains sandwiched between US-101 and I-280. From north to south, Millbrae, Burlingame, San Mateo, Redwood City, Palo Alto, Mountain View, Los Altos and Santa Clara stretch down toward San Jose, California's third-largest city, located in the Santa Clara Valley along Coyote Creek and the Guadalupe River. Cutting-edge technology is one of the reasons to visit the valley, but by no means the only one. San Jose offers a wealth of cultural attractions, from the downtown historic district—which dates back to 1777—to the 132,000sq ft Tech Museum of Innovation.

Highlights

1. Visit Stanford campus' **Rodin collection** (p293)
2. Wander the 16-acre **botanical gardens** at **Filoli** (p295)
3. Play with interactive exhibits at the **Tech Museum of Innovation** (p296)
4. Learn about semiconductors at the **Intel Museum** (p301)
5. Observe sea elephants at the **Año Nuevo State Reserve** (p305)

Silicon Valley

The self-proclaimed capital of Silicon Valley, San Jose was founded in 1777 as El Pueblo San Jose de Guadalupe, by Lieutenant Jose Joaquin Moraga on order of the Viceroy of New Spain, as the first civilian settlement in Nueva California (later Alta California). Then, it served as an agricultural community providing fruit, vegetables, wheat and beef during the Spanish conlonial and Mexican periods to the military personnel at the nearby Presidio of San Francisco and Presidio of Monterey.

Agriculture remained the city's chief industry from the 1850s until the mid-20C. After World War II, a population explosion in the area spurred rapid development and urbanization. By the 1950s, electronics industries began to supplant the orchards and ranches. Beginning with the development of the semiconductor industry in the mid-20C, innovative new enterprises arose in the Bay Area to fill the growing demand for electronic products. By the 1970s, Silicon Valley, which included such computer giants as Hewlett-Packard, Apple Computer, Intel and a host of semiconductor laboratories, had moved well beyond their humble garage beginnings to become the dominant industry in San Jose and the neighboring communities.

In the late 1990s, a new breed of technology-based companies came to town. Known as dot-coms, these Internet companies and their stock prices rocketed in the short term, making millionaires of many investors as well as many stock option-holding employees, until the bubble burst in March 2000.

Today, IT professionals in the Silicon Valley—home to giants like LinkedIn, Apple, Oracle, Google, Facebook, Evernote and Yahoo!, —rank among the highest paid in the country.

The local braintrust includes Stanford University in Palo Alto, with its lovely Richardsonian Romanesque–style buildings roofed with tiles and surrounded by eucalyptus, bay and palm trees.

Established by railroad magnate Leland Stanford in 1891, Stanford University boasts a distinguished tenure-line faculty that includes Nobel laureates, Pulitzer Prize winners and recipients of the National Medal of Science.

San Mateo County Coast

From the San Francisco city limits, Hwy. 1 stretches beside the Pacific Ocean through the rural and almost totally undeveloped coastline of San Mateo County, 70 percent of which is dedicated open space.

The beaches here sprawl—from wide-open sandy strips, to hidden rocky coves—and each is wildly different from the next. Small towns and lush, green farms dot the countryside.

ADDRESSES

🏠 STAY

$$ Costanoa – *2001 Rossi Rd., Pescadero, Hwy. 1.* ✆*650-879-1100. www.costanoa. com. 52 units.* A "base camp for coastal adventures" near the Año Nuevo State Reserve, Costanoa offers three types of accommodation—a stylish 40-room lodge, a set of cabins favored by families and couples, and a handful of tent bungalows. A general store and spa complete the complex.

$$$ Dream Inn – *175 W Cliff Dr, Santa Cruz.* ✆*844-510-17460.www. dreaminnsantacruz.com52 units.* There's an ocean view from every room at this renovated motor inn, located right on Cowell Beach in Santa Cruz. Funky retro decor compliments the building's old-style architecture.

$$$ Hotel De Anza – *233 W. Santa Clara St., San Jose.* ✆*408-286-1000 or 800-843 -3700. www.hoteldeanza.com. 100 rooms.* Built in 1931 and fully renovated six decades later, the historic De Anza retains an Art Deco-era appeal. Rooms are spacious and contemporary; guests get a morning paper with their coffee and are invited to "raid the pantry" for late-night deli snacks!

$$$$ Stanford Park Hotel – *100 El Camino Real, Menlo Park.* ✆*650-322-1234. www.woodsidehotels.com. 163 rooms.* Near Stanford University, this handsome inn boasts.rooms with vaulted ceilings, granite fireplaces, English yew-wood armoires and writing desks, and courtyard views. Its warm decor and guest library contribute to a high-brow academic flavor.

🍴 EAT

$ Palo Alto Creamery – *566 Emerson St., Palo Alto.* ✆*650-323-3131. www. paloalto creamery.com.* **American**. This 1923 soda fountain keeps its menu and prices as authentic as its atmosphere. Cheeseburgers, milkshakes, meatloaf and fried chicken.

$$ Vung Tau – *535 Santa Clara St., San Jose.* ✆*408-288-9055. www.vungtau restaurant.com.* **Vietnamese**. Elegant decor, hospitable service and a massive menu of authentic offerings such as hearty *bun bo hue* makes this a favorite among South Bay business types by day and Vietnamese families at night.

$$ Evvia Estiatorio – *420 Emerson St., Palo Alto.* ✆*650-326-0983. www.evvia.net.* **Greek**. No stodgy Balkan eatery, Evvia's open kitchen focuses on Californian approaches to Aegean classics. You'll get spanakopita (spinach pie) and moussaka (lamb-eggplant casserole), to be sure, but also octopus with roasted bell peppers and salmon with a tomato-ouzo sauce.

$$ Moss Beach Distillery – *140 Beach Way, off Hwy. 1, Moss Beach.* ✆*650-728-5595. www.mossbeachdistillery.com.* **American**. Built in the 1920s as a Hollywood retreat, this historic building became a Prohibition-era hideout for bootleggers. It's now a steak-and-seafood eatery (the Sunday Brunch draws raves) where diners can take in beautiful sunsets while whale-watching from an outdoor patio.

$$$$ Manresa – *320 Village Ln., Los Gatos.* ✆*408-354-4330. www.manresa restaurant.com. Wed–Sun dinner only.* **Contemporary**. Hidden down a narrow side street, this celebrated tasting menu restaurant, reopened after a kitchen fire, is back firing on all cylinders. Chef David Kinch's ever-changing nightly tasting menu, presented as an alphabetized list of ingredients, are both once cerebral, luxurious and delicious. Whimsical dishes, such as a sampler of savory petite fours, red pepper pates de fruits, black olive madeleines, or green garlic panisse with Meyer lemon curd and tahini, offer an illusory play on the palate.

Tech Museum of Innovation

© Tech Museum of Innovation

Palo Alto★

An affluent college town of about 65,000, Palo Alto derives its name from the twin-trunked coast redwood under which Gaspar de Portolá camped on his 1769 expedition. Now single-trunked and timeworn, El Palo Alto, "the tall tree," still stands in a small park by the railroad tracks off Alma Avenue. It remains the official symbol of Stanford University.

STANFORD UNIVERSITY★★

Circled by Campus Dr. E. & W., west of El Camino Real (Rte. 82) via Palm Dr. From San Francisco drive south on US-101 and exit west at Embarcadero Rd., which becomes Galvez St. as it enters campus. Visitor information center at 295 Galvez St. (⏱Open Mon–Fri 8.30am–5pm, Sat–Sun 10am–5pm; ⏱ Closed during Dec-Jan recess, see website for exact dates. ☕Free campus tours (1hr) depart from visitor center early Jan–late Dec. Self-guided tours also available via website. ✕♿P ☎650-723-2560. www.stanford.edu.

Established by railroad magnate Leland Stanford, this renowned institution sprawls across 8,180 acres. Its gracious, Spanish-flavored Richardsonian Romanesque buildings are shaded by eucalyptus, bay and palm trees.

Born in New York state, the university's founder, **Leland Stanford** (1824–93), moved to California during the Gold Rush, became state governor, then president of the Central Pacific Railroad, a risky venture that earned him a fortune. In 1884 Stanford and his wife, Jane, lost their only child, 15-year-old Leland, Jr., to typhoid fever. The bereft couple, declaring that "the children of California shall be our children," set out to establish a university on the grounds of their Palo Alto ranch. Architect Charles Allerton Coolidge and landscape architect Frederick Law Olmsted jointly conceived the campus plan and the low, arcaded buildings of the university, which opened in 1891. Two years later, Stanford

Info: ☎650-324-3121. www.paloaltochamber.com.

Location: Palo Alto is located about 33mi south of San Francisco via US-101, between the marshlands of southern San Francisco Bay and the Santa Cruz Mountains.

Timing: Plan about a day to enjoy the sights in Palo Alto.

Parking: There are metered spaces for visitors at various locations throughout the Stanford campus, and a visitor lot behind Memorial Auditorium. Other Palo Alto sights offer free parking.

Don't Miss: The Cantor Arts Center, with its impressive collection of Rodin scuptures.

died at age 69 and the 1890s financial depression threatened the existence of the university. By the early 20C, with the economic crisis resolved, Stanford University was on its way to becoming a celebrated academic institution.

The northwest corner of that campus still holds the **Red Barn** (*Fremont and Electioneer Rds.*), original Victorian stables built by Leland Stanford more than a century ago.

The campus remains a leading academic and research center, with more than 10,000 students. Among its 1,910 faculty are 17 Nobel laureates and 16 recipients of the National Medal of Science.

The Stanford's Visitor's Center offers a twice-daily walking tours, which visits the university's main sights, including the Quad, White Plaza, and Memorial Church. They also offer several themed tours for prospective students and visitors, including the Arts and Humanities Tour, which takes you to Stanford's most important museums and performance venues, including the Cantor Arts Center and the Rodin Sculpture Garden.

Advance reservations are required for all tours; book online.

😊 *While most students navigate Stanford's sprawling campus on bicycle, visitors can jump on the free student shuttle, the Marguerite (transportation. stanford.edu), when traveling between far-flung sights. Alternatively, the Visitor's Center offers a golf-cart tour ($5, fee waived for people with disabilities), which whizzes around the campus in an hour.*

Main Quadrangle★

From downtown Palo Alto, Palm Drive leads to the historic heart of campus. The expansive, tiled courtyard is bordered by the university's 12 original colonnaded buildings and anchored by magnificent **Stanford Memorial Church★★** (🕐 *open Mon–Fri 8am–5pm, Sun 11.30am–3.30pm.* 🕐 *closed major holidays;* 📞*650-723-1762).* Built in 1903 by Jane Stanford to commemorate her husband, the church features elaborate Byzantine-style mosaics, stained glass and three renowned organs equipped to play Renaissance and Baroque music.

Hoover Tower★

🕐*Observation deck open daily 10am–4pm.* 🕐*Closed between academic quarters.* 👁$4, cash only. ♿ 📞*650-723-2053.*

The landmark 285ft campanile houses part of the Hoover Institution on War, Revolution and Peace, a public-policy research center inspired by university alumnus Herbert Hoover. Two museum galleries *(both sides of entrance hall)* are devoted to the considerable accomplishments of Hoover and his wife, Lou Henry Hoover. The top of the tower features a 48-bell carillon and an observation deck offering panoramic views of the campus.

Cantor Arts Center★

Lomita Dr. and Museum Way. 🕐*Open Wed–Mon 11am–5pm, Thu 11am–8pm.* 🕐*Closed major holidays.* ✖♿🅿📞*650-723-4177. www.museum.stanford.edu.*

This university museum houses a dazzling, eclectic collection of 40,000 pieces of ancient to contemporary sculpture, paintings, crafts and ceremonial artworks from Africa, Oceania, Asia, Europe and the Americas. Noted for its cultivated eclecticism, it is renowned for its collection of 200 Rodin sculptures, the world's largest outside Paris.

The Cantor's precursor was founded by Leland and Jane Stanford as a memorial to their son, an amateur collector of eclectic tastes. Leland, Jr.'s well-rounded collections formed the nucleus of the museum (1894, Percy and Hamilton), designed after the National Archaeological Museum of Athens and built of reinforced concrete.

Although Jane Stanford bolstered the collection by donating 15,000 additional objects before her death in 1905, the early museum closed after suffering heavy damage in the earthquake of 1906. The museum was revived in the 1950s, but severe structural damage during the Loma Prieta earthquake of 1989 again forced its closure. The university responded with an ambitious campaign to retrofit the original 72,000sq ft building, while architect James Polshek & Partners designed a rectangular, 42,000sq ft addition of steel, glass and stucco. It reopened in 1999.

It is now a premier university teaching museum that illustrates comparative objets d'art from a broad spectrum of cultures and eras, in addition to mounting interesting contemporary exhibits that draw audiences from across the Bay Area.

Visit

Designed by Venetian artist Antonio Paoletti, the 13 mosaics across the front facade of the original building illustrate the progress of civilization through learning and arts. Three pairs of massive entry doors, each weighing 600 pounds, are encased in bronze panels depicting examples of ancient architecture. Flanking the entrance, the two original wings exhibit the Classical, historical and international collections, while the new addition—behind the entry hall—houses contemporary art and rotating exhibits. Two courtyards are devoted to sculpture.

Stanford Alumnus: Herbert Hoover

One of Stanford University's most illustrious alumni was Herbert Hoover (1874–1964), a member of the institution's first class in 1891 and a graduate in geology. Hoover traveled the globe as a mining engineer for nearly two decades—managing mines in Russia, China, Burma and Australia—before entering public life in 1914, when he established a humanitarian relief organization in Europe. His role as an adviser to President Woodrow Wilson led to his appointment as secretary of commerce in the Harding and Coolidge administrations of the 1920s. Hoover subsequently was elected U.S. President in 1928 and served one term.

In 1945, Hoover was called back to public service by President Harry Truman to coordinate dispersal of food to 28 nations during a postwar famine. He served as an adviser to President Dwight Eisenhower in the 1950s.

Before he died at age 90, Hoover wrote more than 30 books and expanded a world-renowned library that he had established at Stanford in 1919. He maintained an office on the 11th floor of the Hoover Tower, built in 1941.

A central gallery behind the entrance lobbies acknowledges the museum's origin in the **Stanford Family Collection**. It includes family portraits, curios from young Leland's collections, the boy's death mask, and the **Golden Spike** from the ceremonial completion of the first transcontinental railroad.

Rodin Sculpture Garden★
Located on the southwest side of the Cantor Center, this one-acre garden displays 20 large-scale bronze casts by French sculptor Auguste Rodin, including his famed *The Gates of Hell* (1880–1900). A half-dozen casts from Rodin's series *The Burghers of Calais* are also displayed in a courtyard on the Serra Street side of the Main Quad.

Elsewhere on campus are sculptures by such prominent artists as Joan Miró, Alexander Calder and Henry Moore. A free *Guide to Outdoor Sculpture* is available at the art museum and the campus visitor information booth.

Stanford Linear Accelerator Center
2575 Sand Hill Rd., Menlo Park. ◐*Closed to the public except for public lectures and guided tours (1.5hrs) offered two Fridays a month 1:30pm, by reservation only. Registration opens on the last Friday of every month at 9 am and fill up quickly.* ♿ 🄿 *www.slac.stanford.edu.*

Operated by the university for the U.S. Department of Energy, SLAC opened in 1961 as a research facility in particle physics. Within this 480-acre facility, which includes a 2mi-long linear accelerator, scientists probe the structure of matter on atomic and subatomic levels with x-rays and particle beams.

EXCURSIONS

NASA Ames Research Center
Moffett Field, Mountain View.
From US-101, take Moffett Field exit; turn right to main gate, then left on R.T. Jones Rd. to Gate 17C. ◐*Visitor center open Tue–Fri 10am–4pm; Sat–Sun noon–4pm.* ◐*Closed major holidays.* ☎*650-604-6274. www.arc.nasa.gov.*
Founded in 1939 at a former naval air field as an aircraft research laboratory, this 430-acre facility has been a part of the National Aeronautics and Space Administration since 1958. Now the hub of NASA information technologies, Ames is also the lead NASA agency in the study of gravity, astrobiology and Mars exploration, to name but a few. The center is home to the world's largest wind tunnel, several advanced flight simulators, and an Immersive theater with a 14ft by 36ft wide screen that screens videos about Mars missions, simulated flights through the Milky Way, and other scientific discoveries. The onsite **gift shop** (*Mon.-Fri 10am-6pm*) opened in 2018;

it's the place to pick up a totally unique souvenir for the science lover in your life, like a model satellite, photos of space or NASA-branded apparel.

Filoli★★

13mi north of Palo Alto at Woodside and 30mi south of San Francisco. Take I-280 to Edgewood Rd.; exit west, turn right on Cañada Rd. and continue 1.3mi to gate. ⏲*Open Tue–Sim 10am–5pm.* ⏲*Closed major holidays.* ⚏*$25.* ✖♿🅿 ✆*650-364-8300, ext. 507. www.filoli.org.*

Sunken garden, Filoli

Nestled into the inland side of the Coast Range's heavily wooded foothills, this 654-acre just celebrated its 100th anniversary in 2018. Its elegance exemplifies the gracious lifestyle made possible at the turn of the 20C by fortunes derived from mining, real-estate speculation, water development and agriculture.

The formal Italian Renaissance gardens and U-shaped, "Modified" Georgian Revival mansion (1915–17, Willis Polk) were commissioned by William Bourn II (1857–1936), owner of the Empire Mine in Grass Valley; at the time, the Empire was California's most productive hard-rock gold mine. Bourn was also president of the Spring Valley Water Company, consisting of Crystal Springs Lake and its adjacent lands. Filoli (named for a favorite Bourn credo, *Fight for a just cause; Love your fellow man; Live a good life*), with its large, mature trees spreading shadows over acres of well-kept lawns, still exudes settled rural wealth.

After the deaths of Bourn and his wife in 1936, Filoli was acquired by its only other owner, William P. Roth, who died in 1963. His widow donated Filoli to the National Trust for Historic Preservation in 1975.

Mansion★★

The ground floor features furniture and art from both the Bourn and Roth families; an extensive collection of 17C–18C Irish and English furnishings and decorative arts bequeathed by Melville Martin in 1998; and pieces on loan from the Fine Arts Museums of San Francisco. House tours commence in the Reception Room, where a 17ft by 33ft Persian carpet (19C), woven over three generations, covers the floor. The kitchen features an impressive ship's stove acquired in 1942 from the Matson Navigation Company, owned by Lurline Roth's father. The grand ballroom, with its 22ft ceilings, is adorned with Ernest Peixotto murals (1925) depicting Ireland's Lakes of Killarney and Muckross House, an 11,000-acre estate given by the Bourns to their daughter on her marriage in 1910.

Gardens★★★

Designed by Bruce Porter with continuing assistance from Isabella Worn, this 16-acre botanical wonder (1917–20) successfully combines the formal with the natural. Planned as a sequence of outdoor "rooms," each with its own horticultural and seasonal delights, the gardens are aligned along the same north-south axis as the house, extending the lines of the mansion's hallway.

Some of the most interesting plants were gifts or purchases from foreign governments, disposing of display specimens after the 1915 Panama-Pacific International Exposition.

Many of the column-shaped Irish yews, used as pillars in Filoli's garden "architecture," started as cuttings from the yews at Muckross.

San Jose★

Now California's third largest city with well over one million residents, the self-proclaimed "capital of Silicon Valley" bustles with high-tech prosperity. In San Jose's revitalized downtown, stately old buildings sit alongside modern high-rises amid palm-lined plazas and avenues. The city boasts a number of unusual museums, from innovative new ones to "mysterious" older ones.

A BIT OF HISTORY

Spanish administrators chose this site in the fertile Santa Clara Valley in 1777 for the founding of the first civilian settlement in Alta California. The new farming community on the banks of the Guadalupe River supplied food to soldiers in San Francisco and Monterey. Twenty years later, the San José Mission was founded 13mi to the north. In 1849, three years after the American takeover of California, members of the state's Constitutional Convention chose San Jose as the state capital, an honor it held for several months before the seat of government was moved to Vallejo.

From the mid-19C to mid-20C, agriculture remained San Jose's chief industry. Abundant flowering orchards attracted weekend tourists who came from throughout the Bay Area to enjoy "the Garden City in the Valley of Heart's Delight."

In the postwar period, the character of Santa Clara County changed dramatically as structures housing electronics industries began to sprout in place of the orchards, and by the late 1960s "Silicon Valley" had encompassed San Jose. Such computer giants as IBM, Hewlett-Packard, Apple, Novell and Adobe Systems developed facilities in the city and in neighboring communities.

🚌 Fremont Station
⚐ **Michelin Map:** See inside back cover.
🛈 **Info:** ☏408-295-9600. www.sanjose.org.
▶ **Location:** The downtown heart of San Jose, focused around **Plaza de Cesar Chavez** *(Market St. & Park Ave.)*, site of frequent civic festivals, bustles seven days a week.
👥 **Kids:** There's lots for kids to do in San Jose, including the Children's Discovery Museum, the Tech Museum of Innovation, the Winchester Mystery House with its confounding twists, turns and stairways, and the quaint Happy Hollow Park and Zoo.
🕐 **Timing:** San Jose swarms during the week; try to plan a weekend visit, when traffic is lighter and parking lots are less crowded.
🅿 **Parking:** Parking is available at many downtown garages. The **Valley Transportation Authority (VTA)** light-rail system *(☏408-321-2300; www.vta.org)* runs 24 hours daily, linking most hotels and attractions at a nominal cost.
☺ **Don't Miss:** The Tech Museum of Innovation, a fitting introduction to the sights of Silicon Valley.

SIGHTS
👥 Tech Museum of Innovation★★

201 S. Market St. at Park Ave, San Jose.
🕐*Open daily 10am–5pm.* 🕐*Closed Dec 25.* 🎟*$29 combo IMAX show and museum admission, $23 for students, seniors and children museum* ✕♿☏*408-294-8324. www.thetech.org.*

Celebrating its 20th anniversary in 2019, this state-of-the art, interactive exhibit hall (popularly known as "The Tech") is designed to encourage the spirit of innovative curiosity characteristic of the original techno-tinkerers of Silicon Valley. Housed in a domed, mango-colored building with azure highlighting, The Tech is entertaining for all ages, and seeks to inspire the innovator in everyone though run and engaging challenges. Exhibits explore robotics, cyber security, bioengineering, space exploration, wearable technology, and innovations in technology that saves lives.

Established in 1990, the museum increased its size six-fold (to 132,000sq ft) when it moved to its present site in 1998. A fascinating mobile sculpture, George Rhoads' *Science on a Roll,* enlivens the side-entrance sidewalk on Park Avenue, where crowds gather outside to watch a continuous sequence of clanging and clattering billiard balls travel by ramps and elevator through a precisely synchronized mechanical maze.

Visit

The main entrance is on the middle floor of a three-story atrium. The Tech has recently revitalized its galleries with new and relevant exhibitions. In Cyber Detectives, visitors play games to pick up important skills in staying safe online before going on a mission to catch a cyber criminal. In Social Robots, budding engineers learn about circuitry while building a robot. In Body Metrics, visitors try wearable technology that measures their heart rate, muscle tension and brainwaves and encourages them to explore their biometric data. Innovations in Healthcare highlights the engineering design process of inventors saving lives with technology. The Tech is also the first museum in the country to feature the jaw-dropping Anatomage Table, where users can virtually dissect a 3D human body, a high-tech tool used by doctors and medical students today. The Tech also features the first interactive exhibit about DIY bio in the world. BioDesign Studio is designed to empower visitors to use biology as technology. Visitors code their own creature and then unleash it into a digital world displayed on a stunning curvedmonitor wall. Guests also get their hands on real lab equipment to mix different strands of colorful DNA and experiment with emerging biotechnology like using mushroom root as sustainable building materials. Visitors create their own mushroom brick and learn about ways companies are using bioengineering to make the world a better place.

Check out The Tech Studio, a makerspace where visitors are challenged to create solutions using tech like making 3D printed prosthetics or designing devices that harness the wind. Staples like the JetPack chair and earthquake simulator also excite theimagination of young visitor. The Tech is home to the Hackworth IMAX Dome Theater that screens educational films and the occasional Hollywood blockbuster on a hemispherical screen that engulfs the audience with images and sound.

The Tech recently opened a 280-seat IMAX "dome theater," where laser shows, blockbuster films, and educational videos are screened.

San Jose Museum of Art

110 S. Market St., San Jose. ⏰*Open Tue–Sun 11am–5pm, until 8pm on the 3rd Thu of the month.* ⏰*Closed Jan 1, Thanksgiving, Dec 25.* ⊚*$10.* ✕ & ☏*408-271-6840.*
www.sjmusart.org.

Established in 1933 in an old sandstone Richardsonian Romanesque post office (1892) and expanded in 1991 with a modern wing of glass, aluminum and concrete, the museum faces Fairmont Plaza. At any one time, four major exhibits are presented; rotated quarterly on a staggered schedule, they may feature cutting-edge paintings, sculpture, photographs and installation art by California artists, as well as nationally significant traveling shows. Three Dale Chihuly glass chandeliers above the main entrance are among the 1,400 works of 20C and 21C art in the museum's permanent collection. Wall text is in Vietnamese and Tagalog as well as Spanish and English, is testimony the ethnic diversity in the South Bay area.

Cathedral Basilica of Saint Joseph

80 S. Market St., San Jose.
🕐*Open daily.* ✆*408-283-8100.*
www.stjosephcathedral.org.
Founded in 1803 as a small adobe church, hub of the first Catholic parish in California, this beautiful building was constructed in 1877 by Brian Clinch—a devout architect who read the New Testament in Greek. The cathedral was dedicated as a minor basilica in 1997. The impressive interior is worth a visit.

San Jose Museum of Quilts & Textiles

520 S. 1st St., San Jose. 🕐*Open Wed–Fri 11am–4pm, Sat-Sun 11am-3pm (1st Fri of month 7–11pm).* 🕐*Closed major holidays and between shows.* 💰*$8 (pay what you can 1st Fri).* ♿✆*408-971-0323. www.sjquiltmuseum.org.*
The oldest quilt museum in the United States offers regularly changing exhibits of works by traditional and contemporary quilt and woven tapestry artists. Costumes and dolls from various ethnic communities suggest the diversity of design and craft traditions.

👥 Children's Discovery Museum of San Jose★

180 Woz Way, San Jose. Exit I-280 at Bird Ave. 🕐*Open Tue-Fri 10am-4pm, Sat 10am-5pm, Sun noon-5pm* 🕐*Closed Jan 1, Thanksgiving Day, Dec 25.* 💰*$15.* ✗♿✆*408-298-5437. www.cdm.org.*
Housed in a whimsical purple structure (1991, Ricardo Legorreta) that resembles building blocks, this bilingual (English-Spanish) museum dominates Guadalupe River Park. Hands-on exhibits and programs are geared to families and school-age children. Highlights include **Streets**, an intersecting corridor demonstrating the workings of urban infrastructure; a hands-on exploration of the physics behind **Bubbles**, interactive arts and nature exhibits; and activity areas designed to teach cultural diversity. A theater features a variety of performers.

Peralta Adobe and Fallon House Historic Site★

175 W. St. John St. at San Pedro St.
🌿*Visit by guided tour (90min) only, by appointment.* ♿ ✆*408-287-2290. www.historysanjose.org.*
Ensconced amid the modern structures of downtown, an early 19C adobe and a luxurious Italianate mansion recall San Jose's Spanish Colonial beginnings and its early 19C growth.
Erected for Thomas Fallon, a flamboyant former guide with the Frémont party who had married a Californio land-grant heiress, Fallon House was the grandest residence in San Jose when it was completed in 1855. Among other luxurious accoutrements, the mansion boasted marble fireplaces, elaborately decorated ceilings and woodwork carefully painted to look like oak. After serving as a hotel and a restaurant through the early 20C, it was acquired by the city and painstakingly restored. The lower level contains an excellent small museum detailing San Jose's development from Spanish Colonial pueblo through the American period.
Across the street, the modest Peralta Adobe was the residence of Luís María Peralta, a high-ranking pueblo official and wealthy landowner. The bedroom of the structure appears as it would have around 1800 (note the intriguing, suspended cradle), while the living room, or *sala*, is more elaborately furnished as it would have been around 1840.
Currently only accessible on guided tours, the site is currently working on plans to open to the public on a regular basis.

👥 Kelley Park

1300 Senter Rd. at Story Rd., San Jose
🕐*Open daily 8am until 30min after sunset.* ✗♿🅿
The former orchard estate of Judge Lawrence Archer, a San Jose mayor, and his daughter and son-in-law, Louise and Frank Kelley, this 156-acre park on Coyote Creek contains a variety of attractions. **Happy Hollow Park and Zoo** (👥🕐*open daily 10am–5pm, Mar–Aug, until 4pm weekdays Sept–mid-Nov,*

closes earlier in spring and winter, check website for hours, 🕐*closed major holidays;* ⬠*$14.25;* 🅿*$10;* ✆*408-794-6400; www.hhpz.org)* harbors more than 150 animals, including a jaguar and a pygmy hippo; children's rides, and a puppet theater. Broad shaded lawns attract throngs for weekend picnics. There's also a Greek-style amphitheater and a miniature train linking the zoo and the historical museum.

History Park at Kelley Park★
1650 Senter Rd. at Phelan Ave. 🕐*Open Mon–Fri noon–5pm, Sat–Sun 11am-5pm, individual business hours vary, check the website.* 🕐*Closed major holidays.* ✕🅿✆*408-287-2290. www.historysanjose.org.*

This 14-acre complex, with paved streets and a running trolley, evokes life in San Jose around the turn of the 20C. The park comprises some two dozen historic homes and shops, a third of which are re-creations; the rest were relocated from their original sites. Two or three shops are open each day on a rotating schedule and staffed by docents.

It's hard to miss the 115ft reproduction of the **San Jose Electric Tower**, a fanciful metal-beamed pyramid of street lights; and the **H.H. Warburton Doctor's Office**, with its medical and dental paraphernalia.

Other highlights include the **Print Shop**, demonstrating traditional typesetting and printing techniques, and a brick reproduction of the city's **Chinese Temple**, featuring an elaborately carved Cantonese wooden altar from the original 1880s temple.

Japanese Friendship Garden★
🕐*Open daily 10am–sunset.* ♿🅿*$10;* ✆*408-277-5254.*

The meticulously landscaped 6.5 acres, built in the early 1960s, are modeled after Korakuen Garden in Okayama, Japan, San Jose's sister city. Paths wind past stone lanterns, a small pagoda and a variety of flora, including flowering cherry trees and carefully placed conifers. On the upper level, a large pool—populated by brightly colored koi, turtles, ducks and blue herons—is spanned by a lovely Moon Bridge. A waterfall pours over ornamental rocks into a lower pool, site of a teahouse. The shapes of the two ponds resemble the Japanese characters for *kokoro*, a word designating heart and soul.

Overfelt Gardens
2145 McKee Rd., San Jose. 🕐*Open daily 10am–dusk.* ♿🅿✆*408-251-3323.*

This 33-acre park was the home of Mildred Overfelt (1873–1967), whose father established a prosperous grain and dairy farm here in the 1850s. The original ranch house still stands. The Chinese Cultural Garden has a 30ft statue of Confucius overlooking a reflecting pond, and pavilions dedicated to statesmen Sun Yat-sen and Chiang Kai-shek.

👤👤 Winchester Mystery House
525 S. Winchester Blvd. 👀*Visit by guided tour only, call or consult website for schedules.* ⬠*$20* ✕♿🅿 ✆*408-247-2000. www.winchestermysteryhouse.com.*

This strange, rambling 160-room Victorian hodgepodge is the creation of Sarah Winchester, widow of rifle magnate William Wirt Winchester (portrayed by Helen Mirren in the movie *Winchester* (2017). After purchasing an eight-room San Jose farmhouse in 1884, she added to it compulsively until her death in 1922. Local legend avers that Mrs. Winchester was guided in her architectural excesses by the ghosts of those who had lost their lives to Winchester firearms. Now largely unfurnished, the house is notable for its collection of Tiffany and European **art glass**. The **Winchester Firearms Museum** on the grounds displays an international collection of pistols and rifles.

👤👤Rosicrucian Egyptian Museum★
1660 Park Ave at Naglee Ave. 🕐*Open Wed–Fri 9am–5pm, Sat–Sun 10am–6pm.* 🕐*Closed Mon–Tue & major holidays.* ⬠*$9.* ♿🅿✆*408-947-3635. www.egyptianmuseum.org.*

Modeled after the Temple of Amon at Karnak, the exterior is dominated by a columned entryway and gold-paneled doors incised with hieroglyphs. The interior features one of the most extensive displays of Egyptian and Mesopotamian artifacts in the Western United States, numbering some 5,000 pieces. Note in particular the display on mummification *(gallery A)*, with painted coffins; **sarcophagi**; human and animal remains, including an unsheathed, mummified body; and a full-scale reproduction of a Middle Kingdom **Rock Tomb** (↩*visit by guided tour only)*.

Displays of Egyptian pottery, jewelry, glass, funerary objects, writing implements and statues of deities *(galleries B, C & D)* range from the pre-Dynastic period (4800 BC) to the Coptic period (late 2C–mid-7C AD) and include Babylonian, Sumerian and Assyrian cylinder seals and cuneiform tablets.

The museum is located on the edge of **Rosicrucian Park**, a five-acre city block filled with statues, gardens and Egyptian- and Moorish-style buildings that serve as headquarters for the English Grand Lodge of the nonsectarian Rosicrucian Order, AMORC (Ancient and Mystical Order Rosae Crucis). The grounds now house research and administrative buildings, an auditorium, a **planetarium** and the museum, with many events and exhibits geared toward families.

EXCURSIONS

Santa Clara

2.5mi northwest of downtown San Jose.
The city of Santa Clara was founded in 1777, when the Santa Clara de Asís Mission (*see below*) was founded, for which the city was named.

Santa Clara de Asís Mission

Santa Clara University, 500 El Camino Real, Santa Clara. ◷*Open daily sunrise–sunset.* ◷*Closed Dec 26–Jan 1.* ♿▣*408-554-4000. www.scu.edu/mission.*
Established on the banks of the Guadalupe River in 1777, the eighth California mission was founded as an additional outpost in the vicinity of San Francisco Bay, but was moved in 1781 to its present site on higher ground. Padre

Junípero Serra officiated at the laying of the cornerstone for an impressive adobe church that was completed in 1784. Surrounded by fertile lands, the mission prospered until an earthquake destroyed the complex in 1812. A new church, completed in 1814, served first as a mission, then as a parish chapel, until it was destroyed by fire in 1926. The current building resembles the original 1784 adobe.

Visit – Offset by a campanile, the **church** exterior features statues of saints and a roof covered in clay tiles gleaned from the ruins of earlier mission structures. Today encased in redwood, the wooden cross standing in front of the church dates to the 1777 founding of the mission. The painted ceiling of the Victorian-style interior replicates the original design of Mexican artist Augustín Davila.

The simple **St. Francis Chapel** *(behind the main sanctuary)* contains an original wall, ceiling and floor. Left of the church lies a landscaped **quadrangle** where olive trees, roses and wisteria survive from the mission days.

Across from the entrance to the mission lies the **De Saisset Museum** (◷*open Tue–Sun 11am–4pm;* ◷ *closed Jul–Sept, major holidays;* ✆*408-554-4528; www.scu.edu/deSaisset)*, a university museum devoted to world art and California history. The main level features temporary exhibits of selections from the museum's permanent collection of 16C–20C European and American art; Asian art and African art.

There are free docent tours available with advance reservations.

Triton Museum of Art★

1505 Warburton Ave. at Lincoln St., Santa Clara, 2 blocks north of El Camino Real. ◷*Open Tue–Sun 11am–5pm.* ♿▣*408-247-2438. www.tritonmuseum.org.*
Ensconced in a tranquil seven-acre park, this modern museum displays an eclectic collection of Native American and Western art in three skylit galleries. The **Austen D. Warburton Collection**

of **American Indian Art and Artifacts★** spans several centuries of basketry, pottery and other artifacts from California, Southwest and Pacific Northwest tribal traditions. Selections from the permanent collection, displayed in a gallery to the right of the central rotunda, include a 19C Albert Bierstadt landscape, an 18C William Hogarth engraving and a 17C Rembrandt etching. Temporary exhibits emphasize the diversity of contemporary art in the San Francisco Bay Area. A sculpture garden nestles outside the museum walls.

Intel Museum★★

2200 Mission College Blvd., Santa Clara. ○*Open Mon–Fri 9am–6pm, Sat 10am–5pm.* ○*Closed major holidays.* 🚻🅿 *℘408- 765-5050. www.intel.com*
As the world's largest semiconductor company, the Intel Corporation invented the technology—in 1968—that put computer memory on tiny silicon chips rather than in magnetic fields. This museum allows visitors to go behind the scenes of a Silicon Valley facotyr. Interactive exhibits here in the company headquarters walk visitors through the principles of transistor technology, from identification of conductors to chip design and production. Displays showcase the use of these chips in personal computers, as well as future practical applications.

👥 California's Great America

4701 Great America Parkway, Santa Clara. Exit US-101 at Great America Pkwy., 6mi north of San Jose.
○*Open late-Mar–Oct daily from 10am; late-Nov-Dec 30 5pm-10pm; closed Dec 24-25, check website for additional closures.* ○*Closing times vary.* ✏*$42.99 (purchase online for best prices)* ✕🚻🅿 *℘408-988-1776. www.cagreatamerica.com.*
This 100-acre amusement park, originally opened in 1976, is a favorite of roller-coaster fanatics. Favorite rides include the Gold Star and Flight Deck roller coasters and the 224ft **Drop Tower**. Other seasonal attractions include Boomerang Water Park *(open*

Memorial Day-mid-Sept), and Winter Fest *(late Nov--Dec 30, 5pm-10pm).* The park also has a dedicated family ride area, several shops and cafe, and hosts a full schedule of live entertainiment.

San Carlos

27mi northwest of San Jose.
Exit US-101 at Redwood Shores Pkwy and drive east; turn right on Airport Rd. and right on Skyway Rd. San Carlos means 'City of Good Living'.

👥 Hiller Aviation Museum

601 Skyway Rd. ○*Open daily 10am–5pm.* ○*Closed Jan 1, Easter Sunday, Thanksgiving Day, Dec 25.* ✏*$16. ℘650-654-0200. www.hiller.org.*
Exhibits proceed chronologically through the history of manned flight, with special emphasis on the greater Bay Area. One of the earliest aircraft displayed is the 1883 **Gull,** a fully controllable glider invented by John J. Montgomery, a Santa Clara University engineering professor. Montgomery later was killed testing his third glider prototype in 1911—the same year the **Curtiss-Pusher** landed and took off from the first "aircraft carrier," the USS *Pennsylvania,* in San Francisco Bay. Further exhibits progress from early fixed-wing aircraft to blended and oblique wing designs, and include such innovations as the Flying Platform and the high-altitude Boeing Condor. Many of the aircraft on display have been refashioned by resident craftsmen, whose projects may be viewed through the windows of the Restoration Workshop.

Fremont

19mi northeast of San Jose.
Exit I-680 at Mission Blvd (Rte 238).
Fremont was founded from five other towns in 1956. Fremont is now a metropolitan, ethnically rich city with all the conveniences that provides.

San Jose Mission

43300 Mission Blvd. at Washington Blvd., Fremont. ○*Open daily 10am–5pm.* ○*Closed Jan 1, Easter Sunday,*

Don Edwards, San Francisco Bay National Wildlife Refuge

© André Stanescu/iStockphoto.com

Thanksgiving Day, Dec 25.
$5 donation requested. &510 -657-1797. www.missionsanjose.org.
The 14th mission in the California chain was founded by Padre Fermín Lasuén in 1797. The mission's first permanent adobe church was completed in 1809. Before secularization in 1834, San José was one of the most prosperous missions in California.

During the Gold Rush, the mission served as a rooming house and general store for gold seekers. In 1858 the mission complex was returned to the Catholic Church, but a massive earthquake ten years later destroyed the old adobe church, and a wooden Gothic-style structure was erected in its place. In the early 1980s work began on the careful reconstruction of the original adobe that occupies the site today.

Within the simple, unadorned exterior walls, the church interior reflects the 1833–40 period, featuring an ornate gold-leaf replica of the reredos and historic **statuary**. Note the statue of St. Joseph (c.1600) from Spain and that of the Virgin (18C) from Mexico; rear side altars display statues of Christ (early 19C) and St. Bonaventure (1808). The hammered copper baptismal font (1830s) was painted by Augustín Davila, painter of the interior of the original church.

A small garden separates the church from the original adobe **padres' quarters**, which now house a museum featuring Native American and church artifacts.

Don Edwards San Francisco Bay National Wildlife Refuge★

Marshlands Rd., Fremont.
From I-880 or Rte. 84 at east end of Dumbarton Bridge, take Thornton Ave. to refuge road. Visitor center open Wed–Sun 10am–5pm. Closed major holidays. & 510-792-0222. www.fws.gov/refuge/don_edwards_ san_francisco_bay.

The largest urban wildlife refuge in the U.S. sprawls across 20,000 acres of salt marsh, tidal sloughs, mudflats and rolling hills at the southern end of San Francisco Bay. More than 200 species of waterfowl, shorebirds and migratory birds live, breed and feed in the refuge, dedicated in 1972 and renamed for a former congressman in 1995. From the bluff-top **Visitor Center**, an extensive system of trails follows boardwalks and bridges across tidal flats. Within the center are excellent interpretive exhibits on life in the refuge, as well as an auditorium and observation deck. More trails extend through managed wetland habitat from an **Environmental Education Center** *(Los Esteros Rd., Alviso; from Rte. 237, turn right at Zanker Rd. for 2mi; open Sat–Sun 10am–5pm; call to verify; 408-262-5513).*

Ardenwood Historic Farm

34600 Ardenwood Blvd., Fremont, just north of Rte. 84. Farm and house open Tue–Sun 10am–4pm (no special programs in winter). $3 ($6 Apr–Nov Thu–Fri & Sun). Closed Thanksgiving Day, Dec 25. & 510-544-2797. www.ebparks.org/parks/ardenwood.
Here you can see (and participate in) the common activities of a late-19C farm. George Washington Patterson built a home here in 1857; as his property grew into a prosperous estate, his house was expanded in Queen Anne style in 1889 and surrounded by elaborate Victorian gardens. Many original buildings, including the **house** *(visit by guided tour only Apr–Nov; 510-791-4196),* remain standing. Weekend programs include the planting, tending and harvesting of organic crops, and demonstrations of cooking, farm chores and blacksmithing.

San Mateo County Coast

Untouched by the sprawl of the city to its north or the urbanized peninsula area to its east, coastal San Mateo County is geographically isolated by the San Gregorio and Santa Cruz mountain ranges and protected against development by the relative lack of a practical commuter route. Route 1 narrows to two lanes as it runs south from Pacifica through the farming and fishing villages of Moss Beach, Princeton, San Gregorio and Pescadero. South of Half Moon Bay, the east side of the highway skirts a undulating landscape of flowers, wholesalers' greenhouses, and rows of artichoke plants; pumpkin patches dot the landscape in the fall. To the west extend ocean beaches, superb spots for strolling, tidepooling and wildlife observation. From January to April, **gray whales** may be seen migrating offshore.

The notorious stretch of highway known as **Devil's Slide** forms a gateway to the coast from San Francisco. South of Point San Pedro, the highway narrows and swerves around steep cliffs dramatically striated with rock layers upthrust from ancient marine sediments. Severe rock slides often closed the roadways. After years of fighting between environmentalists and state officials, ground was broken in 2005 to build a series of two tunnels to bypass the treacherous stretch. With the completion of the tunnels in Mar 2013, the old Devil's Slide highway has been converted into a trail for hikers and bicyclists.

SIGHT
👫 CuriOdyssey
1651 Coyote Point Dr., San Mateo. Exit US-101 via Poplar Ave. or Dore Ave. 🕐*Open Tue–Sat 10am–5pm, Sun noon–5pm.* 🕐*Closed major holidays.*

⚬ **Michelin Map:** See inside back cover.

▯ **Info:** www.parks.ca.gov (for state parks).

▷ **Location:** From San Francisco drive south on Hwy. 1 (19th Ave.) or Rte. 35 (Skyline Blvd.), which intersects Hwy. 1 south of Daly City. To return to San Francisco, either retrace the route or take Rte. 92 east from Half Moon Bay, then continue north on I-280. In the driving tour (p298), mileage to each sight is calculated from the preceding sight.

👫 **Kids:** The fascinating tidepools at Fitzgerald Marine Reserve.

🕐 **Timing:** Plan a leisurely half-day to do the drive itself. You'll need more time if you'd like to relax on a beach or two.

🅿 **Parking:** The car fee at park entrances allows same-day entrance to other state parks.

🚫 **Don't Miss:** Reservations are necessary to visit the wildlife protection areas at Año Nuevo State Reserve during the breeding season from December through March; the spectacle is well worth the effort of advance planning.

$13.50, 11 youth 13–17 $9.50; children 2–12 $8.50. 📞*650-342-7755. www.curiodyssey.org.*

Geared toward teaching children the natural environment of the Bay Area, this interactive museum offers an exploration "from the mountains to the bay" with small animals and an aquarium. A wildlife habitat features more than 40 species of indigenous live animals and a 4,000sq ft aviary with dozens of native

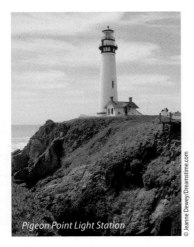

Pigeon Point Light Station

© Jeanne Dewey/Dreamstime.com

California birds. Coyote Point and the adjacent Coyote Point Recreation Area has nature trails, a beach, a saltwater marsh, picnic grounds and a marina.

🚗 DRIVING TOUR

66mi coastal drive south along the West Coast down Hwy. 1.

Sanchez Adobe Historic Site

1000 Linda Mar Blvd., Pacifica, 9mi south of San Francisco via Hwy. 1. ⏱Open Tue–Thu 10am–4pm, Sat–Sun 1–5pm. ☎650-359-1462. www.historysmc.org.
Reflecting many periods of California history, this adobe was built in 1848 as the home of Don Francisco Sanchez. Artifacts recall the site's prior use as an Ohlone village, a Spanish mission farm and a cattle ranch; it later became a general's residence, a hotel, a Depression-era speakeasy and an artichoke

😊 A Bit of Advice 😊

Though the ocean can look tantalizing on a hot day, swimming is inadvisable along the San Mateo County Coast due to cold water and hazardous surf; beware sneaker (large coastal) waves when venturing close to shore.

storage facility. Restored in 1953, it has been refurbished and is open for self-guided tours.

Point Montara Lighthouse

5mi south. 16th St. off Hwy. 1, Montara. ⏱Open daily 8am–sunset. ☎650-728-7177. www.parks.ca.gov.
Built in 1875 as the Point Montara Fog Signal and Light Station, this picturesque beacon house—a naval training base during World War II—has been a youth hostel since 1980.

👥 James V. Fitzgerald Marine Reserve★

2mi south. California Ave. at N. Lake St., Moss Beach, west of Hwy. 1. ⏱Open daily dawn–dusk. 🅿 ☎650-728-3584. www.fitzgeraldreserve.org.
Extensive shale reefs bridge the expanse between land and sea, creating tidepools richly populated with myriad marine life, including limpets, barnacles, mussels, sea urchins, starfish, anemones, chitons, hermit crabs, sponges and abalone. Rangers help visitors search the wonders of the pools and lead explorations during low tide. A small visitor center identifies specimens.

Pillar Point Harbor

3mi southeast.
A granitic headland extends from the coast here, creating a sheltered harbor that serves as an anchorage for local fishermen. Fresh fish is sold daily from boats and fish markets, and simple seafood restaurants serve up steaming chowder, seafood cocktails and fresh fish and chips. Whale-watching trips depart from the wharf during the season (⏱ ☎415-256-9604; www.oceanicsociety.org/whale-watching/gray-whale-watching.)

👥 Francis Beach

5mi south. Foot of Kelly Ave. in Half Moon Bay, .6mi west of Hwy. 1. ⏱Open daily 8am–sunset. 🚗$10/car. ⛺($35-50) 🅿 ☎650-726-8819. www.parks.ca.gov.
The Half Moon Bay State Beach system extends 4mi to the north of this flat,

sandy expanse, and includes Venice and Dunes beaches. Francis Beach provides a welcome departure from the coast's typically rocky beaches. Dune grasses fringing the shoreline provide habitat for snowy plovers. Picnic tables overlook the ocean from the day-use area, and a Coastside Trail (3mi) lures hikers and bikers. The skull of a blue whale entangled in a fisherman's net in 1988 is visible near the entry booth. A **visitor center**, with exhibits on regional history and natural resources, is open on Sat–Sun.

San Gregorio State Beach

12mi south. Open daily 8am–sunset. *$8/car.* *650-879-2170. www.parks.ca.gov.*
This broad, sandy beach lies at the mouth of San Gregorio Creek. Walk north at low tide to see dramatic, cavelike erosion at the base of the sandstone bluffs, or stroll atop to spot whales in season.

Pescadero State Beach

4.4mi south. Open daily 8am–sunset. *$8/car.* *650-879-2170. www.parks.ca.gov.*
From the bluffs that loom over this popular beach, views extend west over the Pacific and the San Mateo County coastline. East of Route 1, extensive walking trails penetrate the **Pescadero Marsh Natural Preserve,** a 510-acre freshwater/brackish coastal marsh. Migratory birds plying the Pacific Flyway stop here to rest, drawing flocks of birdwatchers, especially in late fall and early spring.

Pebble Beach

2.2mi south. Open daily 8am–sunset. *$8/car.* *650-879-2170. www.parks.ca.gov.*
Breaking waves here deposit glistening, many-colored pebbles onto the beach from an offshore quartz reef *(note: it is illegal to remove pebbles).* This part of the coast bears spectacular displays of **tafoni**—lacy, filigree-like formations wrought by erosion on the face of weathered stone. Pebble Beach is the northernmost unit of **Bean Hollow State Beach**, accessible from here by car or via a 12-station clifftop nature trail *(1mi).*

Pigeon Point Light Station★

3.6mi south. Grounds open daily 8am–sunset. Guided tours (30min) Thu–Mon 10am–4pm, weather permitting. Lighthouse closed to the public. *650-879-2120. www.parks.ca.gov.*
Built in 1871, this starkly graceful lighthouse tower was automated in 1926. The lantern room contains the original Fresnel lens, a device consisting of 1,008 glass prisms that shape light from a central lamp into a horizontal beam intense enough to be visible many miles out at sea. Although the lighthouse is closed to the public, the point offers lovely views of the coast and surrounding landforms. A self-guided tour of the grounds explains the light station's past. The lighthouse outbuildings today house a unit of the American Youth Hostel Association.

Año Nuevo State Reserve★

7mi south. Open daily 8am–sunset. Rookery open Apr–Aug 8.30am–3.30pm; Sept–Nov 8.30am–3pm (visitor permit required; issued at reserve). Closed 1st 2 weeks in Dec. *$10/vehicle, $7 guided tour.* Access by guided tour (2hr 30min) only Dec 15–Mar 31 Mon–Fri 9am–5pm, Sat–Sun 9am–3pm; reserve 8 weeks in advance. *650-879-2025 or 800-444-4445. www.parks.ca.gov.*
This 4,000-acre coastal reserve encompasses a rocky offshore island and a wildly beautiful promontory of bluffs and beaches. The promontory is the largest mainland rookery between Baja and northern California for **northern elephant seals**. From December through March, the seals gradually congregate here, the females coming ashore to give birth to single pups and joining "harems" dominated by massive 2.5-ton alpha bulls. Violent clashes between males over harem control are common. In spring and summer, seals again come ashore to molt.

Continue about 21mi along the Coast Road (Highway 1) until it becomes Mission St. into Santa Cruz.

Santa Cruz Beach Boardwalk

© VSCC and Beach Boardwalk

Santa Cruz

70mi south of San Francisco.
Take US-101 S. to Mountain View; Rte. 85 S. toward Los Gatos, then Rte. 17.

The archetypical California beach community (pop. 50,000), Santa Cruz curves around the northern end of Monterey Bay. Founded in 1791 with the Santa Cruz Mission, it became a seaside resort after the railroad arrived in the late 19C.
🛈 *Visitor information:* ✆831-425-1234; www.santacruzca.org.

The **Santa Cruz Beach Boardwalk**★★ (👤🕐*open Memorial Day–Labor Day daily 11am, Sept–Apr Sat–Sun & holidays noon;* 🕐*closing hours vary;* ✆831-423-5590; *www.beachboardwalk.com)*, built in 1904, remains the oldest amusement park in California. Its renovated boardwalk features turreted and brightly painted buildings and rides fronting a wide bay beach *(swimming inadvisable because of dangerous currents)*. Both the **Giant Dipper** (1924)—a .5mi-long wooden roller coaster—and the **Looff carousel** (1911)—are national historic landmarks.

Goodman once performed with their big bands. A few blocks west, the **municipal wharf** is lined with tackle shops and eateries.

Santa Cruz Surfing Museum inside the Mark Abbott Memorial Lighthouse

© VSCC and Paul Schruab

North of the waterfront, in the Mark Abbott Memorial Lighthouse *(West Cliff Dr.)*, stands the **Santa Cruz Surfing Museum**, with an informative exhibit on West Coast shark attacks, and various models of surfboards (*open Jul 4–Labor Day Thu–Tue 10am–5pm, rest of the year Thu–Mon noon–4pm; closed Jan 1, Dec 25; donations accepted; 831-420-6289; www.santacruzsurfingmuseum.org).*

The **Santa Cruz Museum of Natural History** *(1305 E. Cliff Dr.)*, on a cliff above the bay, covers the natural history of the area and includes an exhibit of artifacts detailing the Ohlone Indians' way of life (*open Tue–Fri 11am–4pm, Sat-Sun 10am-5pm, free 1st Fridays. $4; 831-420-6115; www.santacruzmuseums.org).*

Santa Cruz Mission and State Historic Park *(Mission Plaza off School St. From Rte. 1 N turn right on Mission St., then left on Emmet St.; open Mon, Thu–Sat 10am–4pm, Sun noon–4pm; 831-425-5849; www.santacruzstateparks.org)* preserves the site of the original mission (1791). The 12th mission was the smallest of all. After achieving a peak population of 531 neophytes, it declined slowly; only a seven-room **barracks** (1824) remains from the original complex.

The **University of California, Santa Cruz★** *(follow Bay St. northwest to main entrance on Coolidge Dr.)* is renowned for its architecture and spectacular **setting★★** in the lush hills amid redwood trees. Eight campuses surround an academic and administrative core that serves some 17,000 students. In 1965 the state university system carefully integrated 14 original structures from the 1860s Cowell Ranch into the new campus.

Just west of the city, **Natural Bridges State Beach★** *(West Cliff Dr at Swanton Rd open daily 6am–dusk. 831-423-4609)* is a popular local spot where natural rock formations once formed a series of bridges, some of which have collapsed. From there, it's a short drive to the excellent kid-friendly **Seymour Marine Discovery Center (***100 McAllister Way Tue-Sun 10am–5pm$9 831-459-3800; seymourcenter.ucsc. edu)*, fun by the UC Santa Cruz Marine Biology Department, where children can view sea creatures and even pet sleeping sharks.

Six miles north of Santa Cruz is **Henry Cowell Redwoods State Park★** *(Rte. 9; open daily 6am–dusk; $6/vehicle; 831-438-2396; www.parks.ca.gov).* Trails weave through this 1,760-acre tract of redwoods bisected by the San Lorenzo River, The **Redwood Grove Trail** *(.8mi; begin south of parking lot)* loops past the park's largest trees.

Roaring Camp Railroads

Roaring through the Cowell Redwoods, the **Roaring Camp Railroads (***Graham Hill Rd., Felton; open daily 9am-5pm; closed Dec 25; 831-335-4484; www. roaringcamprr.com)* offers two old-time rail excursions. The narrow-gauge steam-train tour *(6mi, 75min; $27, $20 for children)* snakes through the redwood forest to the summit of Bear Mountain. The beach train crosses forests, trestles, gorges and a tunnel en route to the Santa Cruz Boardwalk operates weekends Apr-May, daily Jun-mid Aug*(3hrs; $31).*

Pier 39, Fisherman's Wharf
© Jon Arnold Images/hemis.fr

Where to Stay

San Francisco is a treasure trove for aficionados of small, European-style "boutique" hotels whose rates range from moderate to pricey. But there is something for everyone here, with nearly 33,000 hotel rooms in the city—small private hotels for the budget traveler, hostels for the backpack crowd, and large luxury hotels, at which rates for standard rooms may start at $300.

The high price of real estate coupled with tremendous demand makes for what can be astronomical room rates. San Francisco proper is small and thus land is limited. You can often pay substantially less for more space by staying in Oakland and taking BART into the city. An alternative to hotels is Airbnb (www.airbnb.com), on which locals rent out private rooms and entire apartments.

The properties listed below were selected for their ambiance, location and/or value for money. Prices reflect the average cost for a standard double room for two people in high season. In off-season, hotel rooms can cost half of what they would in high season. Quoted rates don't include an additional 14% occupancy tax, plus a 0.195 percent California Tourism fee, and a 1.5-2.25% Tourism Improvement District assessment (depending on the location) levied on San Francisco hotels room.

🛏Additional hotels are listed throughout this guide. See Index for a complete listing of places to stay.

$$$$$	over $350
$$$$	$250–$350
$$$	$175–$250
$$	$100–$175
$	less than $100

CASTRO DISTRICT

$$ Inn on Castro– *321 Castro St. & 4080 18th St. ℰ415-861.0321. www. innoncastro.com. 8 rooms.* A largely gay and lesbian clientele frequents this bed-and-breakfast inn in a Edwardian house in the heart of the Castro. Rates include a complimentary full breakfast buffet served in the parlor.

CIVIC CENTER/TENDERLOIN

$$ The Inn at the Opera – *333 Fulton St. ℰ415-863-8400 or 800-729-7182. www.shellhospitality.com. 48 rooms. Restaurant $$$.* This Wyndham-owned small hotel is popular among musicians and stage performers, owing to its location a block from the War Memorial Opera House. The 18 simple yet tastefully decorated suites include refrigerators, wet bar areas and microwaves for après-theater snacking. Rates include a continental breakfast and WiFi.

Phoenix Hotel

© Nick Simonite/Phoenix Hotel

$$ Phoenix Hotel – *601 Eddy St. ℰ415 -776-1380 or 800-248-9466. www. phoenixsf.com. 44 rooms.* Since its stylish renovation in the 1990s, this former motel has been a popular stop for touring bands and visiting rockers. Rooms, many of which overlook the palm-tree-fringed swimming pool, retain a bit of mid-century cool, and the low-lit onsite bar, Chambers, is packed with shelves of vinyl records.

$$ Sleep Over Sauce – *135 Gough St. ℰ415-621-0896 or www.sleepsf.com. 8 rooms.* A self-billed urban guest house in the heart of Hayes Valley can be rented out by the room or the entire house. Don't look for a front desk. Guests check in at the bar of their popular late-night restaurant Sauce located on the ground floor.

FINANCIAL DISTRICT

$$ Hyatt Regency San Francisco – *5 Embarcadero Center. ℘415-788-1234 or 800-633-7313. www.hyatt.com. 802 rooms.* An architecturally acclaimed hotel with a 17-story central atrium at the foot of Market Street, the Hyatt is tied to the Embarcadero Center by a pedestrian bridge. Every room has a city or bay view.

FISHERMAN'S WHARF

$ Hostelling International– Fisherman's Wharf – *Bldg. 240, Fort Mason. ℘415-771-7277. www.sfhostels. com. 160 rooms.* Few youth hostels offer the views afforded by this one, perched on a bluff in Fort Mason, overlooking San Francisco Bay with the Golden Gate Bridge in the distance. There are two other Hostelling International locations, Downtown and near the Civic Center.

$$$ Argonaut – *495 Jefferson St. ℘415-563-0800 or 800-790-1415. www.argonauthotel.com. 252 rooms.* This maritime-themed hotel has an ideal location next to Ghirardelli Square, the cable-car turnaround and Fisherman's Wharf. Some rooms offer views of the bay and Alcatraz; all are soundproofed and include flat-screen TVs and free Wi-Fi.

Suite, Argonaut

© Argonaut

$$$ Hotel Zoe – *425 North Point St. ℘415-561-1100 or 800-648-4626. www. hotelzoesf.com.* This stylish maritime-themed hotel has an ideal location for first-time San Francisco visitors, just beside Ghirardelli Square, the cable-car turnaround and Fisherman's Wharf. Some rooms offer views of the bay and Alcatraz; all are soundproofed and have flat-screen TVs and free Wi-Fi.

JAPANTOWN

$$$ Hotel Kabuki – *1625 Post St., Japan Center. ℘415-922-3200 or 800-533-4567. www.jdvhotels.com. 218 rooms.* After completing a $31 million renovation in 2018, the long-running Kabuki Hotel joined the ranks of San Francisco's most stylish accommodations, with minimalist yet chic décor inspired by traditional Japanese design, an onsite Zen garden, and a collection of vintage art that celebrates San Francisco's unique blend of cultures.

$$ The Buchanan – *1800 Sutter St. ℘855-454-4644. www.thebuchanan hotel.com. 131 rooms.* The central Japantown location makes this Kimpton-owned property convenient for explorations across the city, and rooms on the upper floors have beautiful city views along with attractive dark-hued interiors.

MARINA/COW HOLLOW

$$ Hotel del Sol *3100 Webster St. ℘415.921.5520. www.jdvhotels.com* An old-school 1950s motor lodge was doused in a rainbow of color during its recent redesign, when rooms were dressed up with vibrant orange walls, retro-style blue couches, and mulitcolor bedspreads. A favorite with families, it's kid- and pet-friendly, plus there's a heated pool, flat-screen TVs in every room, and bicycle rentals onsite. From here, it's an easy walk or ride to a plethora of Cow Hollow restaurants, Chestnut Street, and the waterfront.

NOB HILL

$$$ The Ritz-Carlton – *600 Stockton St. ℘415-296-7465 or 800-241-3333. www. ritzcarlton.com. 336 rooms. Restaurant.* **$$$$**. For pure luxury and upscale service, the Ritz-Carlton reigns supreme. The lobby is decorated with a rich collection of 18–19C antiques and paintings; guestrooms have been carefully restored with European charm and luxury in mind.

$$$$ The Fairmont – *950 Mason St. ☎415-772-5000 or 866-540-4491. www.fairmont.com/san-francisco. 606 rooms. Restaurant $$$.* This grand hotel, which underwent a $21 million dollar renovation in 2014, has a rich history that includes the 1906 earthquake and creation of the United Nations in 1945. Handsomely appointed rooms are in the original main building and in a 1961 tower that offers extensive views across the city. Don't miss happy hour at the exotic **Tonga Room & Hurricane Bar** with its thatched umbrellas and simulated rain storms.

$$$ Mark Hopkins InterContinental – *999 California St. ☎415-392 3434 or 885-424-6835. www.intercontinental markhopkins.com. 380 rooms.* Opened in 1926 on the crest of Nob Hill, this grand, historic hotel stands on the site of the former mansion of "Big Four" Mark Hopkins. Elegantly traditional rooms feature a rich palate of golden yellows and sienna, dark woods and marble bathrooms with black granite vanities. Come evening, the 19th floor supplies dancing, sweeping views and a massive cocktail menu at the legendary Top of the Mark lounge.

$$ Stanford Court Hotel – *905 California St. ☎415-989-3500. 393 rooms. Restaurant $$$.* Built on land that was part of Leland Stanford's Nob Hill estate, this historic hotel hurtled into the current century after a complete redesign in 2018. Though the building dates from the early 20th century, the rooms and common areas now boast a clean, modern décor and there are tech-friendly touches like loaner iPads and GoPro cameras available for guests. Its lobby bar, **Seven Stills on Nob Hill**, is notably excellent, serving craft beer and whiskey made in San Francisco.

NORTH BEACH

$$ Hotel Bohème – *444 Columbus Ave. ☎415-433-9111. www.hotelboheme.com. 15 rooms.* Reflecting the bohemian tastes of the Beat Generation in 1950s San Francisco, this quaint boutique hotel at the foot of Telegraph Hill is dedicated to the spirit of Jack Kerouac, Lawrence Ferlinghetti and their cohorts. Colorful rooms occupy a three-story building erected in the 1880s and are equipped with private bathrooms and free Wi-Fi.

$$$$ Washington Square Inn – *1660 Stockton St. ☎415-981-4220. www.wsisf.com. 16 rooms.* A intimate European-style inn at the foot of Telegraph Hill in the heart of bohemian North Beach, this charming bed-and-breakfast offers antique furnishings and afternoon tea, plus evening wine and hors d'oeuvres. Enjoy a complimentary continental breakfast downstairs at an antique table overlooking the square.

$ Green Tortoise – *494 Broadway. ☎415-834-1000 or 800-867-8647. www.greentortoisesf.com. 40 rooms (110 beds).* Operated by a long-distance budget bus service for backpack travelers, this clean, spacious hostel has private rooms and dorms (some co-ed) with up to eight bunks. Free daily breakfast is included, and there's a big kitchen where guests can store food and prepare meals.

THE PRESIDIO

$$$$ Inn at the Presidio – *42 Moraga Avenue on the Main Post. ☎415-800- 7356; www.innatthepresidio.com. 22 rooms.* Built in 1903 as officer's quarters, this three-story Georgian-Revival style brick building, listed on the National Register of Historic Places, is the first public hotel to open in The Presidio. It features an inviting front porch, breakfast dining hall and an outdoor deck with a fire-pit. View rooms face the verdant park landscape, while many of the suites and bay rooms on the top floor have views of the Golden Gate Bridge.

$$$$ Lodge at the Presidio – *105 Montgomery St., ☎415-561-1234, www.presidiolodging.com. 42 rooms.* On the northern edge of the Presidio's verdant parkland, a historic military barrack was elegantly restored and reopened as the Lodge at the Presidio, a handsome 42-room boutique hotel where understated interiors allow the property's spectacular views of the Golden Gate Bridge, the San Francisco Bay, and the surrounding skyline to take center stage.

S&R Lounge, Hotel Zetta
© Hotel Zetta

PACIFIC HEIGHTS

$$$$$ Hotel Drisco – *2901 Pacific Ave.* *800-634-7277. hoteldrisco.com.* *48 rooms.* After a stunning 2018 renovation, sophisticated guestrooms at this historic hotel are luxuriously outfitted and notably stylish, but they still pay homage to the old Eduardian building with elegant bespoke furniture and mutede colors. Located in a quiet corner of Pacific Heights, rooms on upper floors have breathtaking city views.

$$$$ Laurel Inn – *444 Presidio Ave.* *415-567-8467. www.jdvhotels.com.* *49 rooms.* With patterned carpets, retro-style armchairs, and art on the walls, there's a funky-sweet feeling in all of the light-filled guestrooms at the Laurel Inn, some of which boast kitchenetters and pretty city views. The lower Pacific Heights location puts you within walking distance of Divisadero Street, the newest hot spot for city dining.

SOMA/YERBA BUENA

$$$$ St. Regis – *125 3rd St.* *415-284-4000 or 877-787-3447. st-regis.marriott.com. 306 rooms.* Occupying the first 20 floors of a handsome highrise, the St. Regis epitomizes elegance from the minute guests enter the lobby dominated by a striking 16ft open fireplace. Spacious rooms overlook Yerba Buena Gardens or have expansive city views, and all come equipped with rainforest showers and flat-screen TVs.

$$$ Palace Hotel – *2 New Montgomery St.* *415-512-1111 or 888-627-7196. www.sfpalace.com. 553 rooms. Restaurant $$.*
Renovated from head to toe in 1991 and again in 2015, this elegant Market Street landmark (circa 1875)—now a Starwood hotel—bridges the gap between the 19C and the 21C. Its centerpiece is the sumptuous **Garden Court** known for its marble pillars, stained-glass domed ceiling and Austrian crystal chandeliers. Luxurious rooms are appointed with 14ft ceilings, marble baths and down comforters. Next to the heated indoor lap pool are a whirlpool and 24hr gym.

$$$ Westin San Francisco Market Street – *50 Third St.* *415-937-7000-or 888-627-8546. www.westinsf.com. 676 rooms. Restaurant $$$.* Towering 36 stories above Yerba Buena Gardens at the heart of the city's dynamic cultural district, lies this contemporary hotel with rooms that boast floor-to-ceiling windows, an indoor infinity pool, and a state-of-the-art gym and spa.

$$$$ Hotel Zetta – *55 Fifth St.* *415-543-8555. www.viceroyhotelsandresorts.com/en/zetta. 214 rooms. Restaurant $$.* Just steps from the Westfield Shopping Centre, Moscone Center, and SFMOMA, this boutique hotel lures culture seekers and hip business travelers. The rooms have no bathtubs but loads of modern high-tech amenities. Don't miss its London-inspired brasserie, Cavalier.

$$ Hotel Via –*138 King St.* *415-200-4977. www.hotelviasf.com. 159 rooms.* Just a few steps from Oracle Park in the South Beach district, this new boutique hotel has pleasingly minimalist rooms with subdued color schemes, city views, and espresso makers, plus an amiable staff and a low-key rooftop bars with beautiful vistas of the ballpark and skyline.

UNION SQUARE

$$$$ The Marker – *501 Geary St. ℘415-292-0100 or 866-622-5284. www. themarkersanfrancisco.com. 201 rooms. Restaurant $$.* This rebranded Theater District boutique hotel (formerly The Monaco), a remodeled 1910 Beaux Arts classic, offers high-tech ammenities along with luxe linens, along with eight new spa room suites with soaking tubs and in-room spa treatments. Adult coloring books, lobby social hours, and a new bar-driven restaurant Tratto have enlivened the property.

$$$$ Hotel Zeppelin – *545 Post St. ℘415-563-0303 or 866-271-3632. www. viceroyhotelsandresorts.com/en/zeppelin. 164 rooms. Restaurant $$.* Just walking distance from Union Square, this hip boutique offering, which replaced the Prescott Hotel in 2016, caters to a young clientele. Rooms range from diminutive cubbies to an 1,800-sq-ft suite with its own outdoor deck. Rooms are eclectically furnished with everything from retro record players lamp to USB-equipped nightstands. Swing by the ground-floor playroom for a game of shuffleboard or the cocktail-driven Rambler restaurant.

$$$ The Clift Royal Sonesta – *495 Geary St. ℘415-775-4700 or 800-697-1791. www.sonesta.com. 363 rooms.* Dark meets light, antique goes modern, and eccentric cajoles conservative at this high-style hostelry. Built in 1913 and reconceived for the 21st century by Philippe Starck, it features elegantly sleek public areas and guestrooms swathed in quiet tones of foggy gray, beige and lavender. The legendary **Redwood Room lounge** features original 1933 paneling and a long bar carved from a single tree.

$$$ Proper Hotel – *1100 Market St. 415-735-7777. www.properhotel.com. 131 rooms.* A landmark Flatiron building on Market Street opened as the ultra-stylish Proper Hotel in 2018, with interiors by designer Kelly Wearstler. Décor in the guestrooms is a perfectly ecclectic collection of wallpapers, vintage-inspired lamps, and graphic throw rugs. Economical but stylish bunkbed rooms are fun for friends traveling together. Downstairs, the all-day bar and restaurant Villon is already a city hot spot.

$$$ Hotel Spero – *405 Taylor St. ℘415-885-2500 or 866-289-6561. www.hotelspero.com. 236 rooms.* The former Hotel Serrano, a historic San Francisco property, was reborn after a $16 million renovation as the Hotel Spero in 2018. Today, the building's historic Spanish colonial-style architecture is complimented by contemporary guestrooms. Serious eco-conscious renovations, like soap recycling, reusable water bottles, and environmental bath products, add to the charm.

$$$ Westin St. Francis – *335 Powell St. ℘415-397-7000 or 800-937-8461. www. westinstfrancis.com. 622 rooms. Restaurant $$$$.* Occupying a Renaissance- and Baroque-revival structure built in 1904, this landmark hotel facing Union Square is renowned for its legendary service and its storied spot in San Francisco history. A $45 million renovation of the 12-story building was completed in early 2018, modernizing the guestrooms with a subtle palette and new furnishings, but history (as well as the famous glass elevators) remains the property's selling point.

$$$ The Handlery Union Square Hotel – *351 Geary St. ℘415-781-7800 or 800-995-4874. www.handlery.com. 377 rooms. Restaurant $$.* A four-generation family operation that opened in 1948 (on the site of a 1908 hotel), The Handlery is a gracious, centrally located inn with unpretentious rooms and a mid-city rarity: an outdoor heated swimming pool.

$$$ Orchard Hotel – *665 Bush St. ℘415-362-8878 or 888-717-2881. www. theorchardhotel.com. 104 rooms. Restaurant $$.* Perched on the flank of Nob Hill a few blocks above Union Square, this very comfortable, eco-friendly hotel offers modern amenities, friendly service, and delicious organic cuisine.

The Handley Union Square Hotel

© Darren Edwards/The Handley Union Square Hotel

$$$ Kimpton Sir Francis Drake Hotel
– *450 Powell St. ☎415-392-7755 or 800-795-7129. www.sirfrancisdrake.com. 416 rooms. Restaurant $$$.* A renovated 1928 classic whose 21st-floor penthouse holds one of San Francisco's longstanding nightclubs, Harry Denton's Starlight Room, the Drake rests on the cable-car line one block from Union Square. Chandeliers hanging from the gold-leaf lobby ceiling lend an atmosphere of grandeur.

Kimpton Sir Francis Drake Hotel

© Kimpton Hotels & Restaurants

$$$ Hotel Triton
– *342 Grant Ave. ☎415-394-0500 or 800-800-1299. www.hotel triton.com. 140 rooms.* A colorful avant-garde boutique hotel facing Chinatown Gate, this property recently completed a top-to-bottom renovation. The redesigned lobby, which debuted in 2018, features original art and a vintage mural that was accidentally uncovered during the building's renovation. Rooms are a mix of splashy colors and cozy furnishings, custom designed for the hotel.

$$ Tilden Hotel
- *345 Taylor St. ☎415-673-2332. www.tildenhotel.com. 118 Rooms. Restaurant $$.* Though it has changed names many times since it first opened in 1928 (most recently, in 2017, from the Mark Twain Hotel to the Tilden), this historic hotel has continued to operate in the Tenderloin for almost a century. After its most recent renovation, the rooms and common spaces have an grown-up minimalist look. For a memorable night in, the hotel's acclaimed in-house cocktail bar The Douglas Room also handles room-service.

$ Hotel Beresford
– *635 Sutter St. ☎415-673-9900 or 800-533-6533. www. beresford.com. 114 rooms. Restaurant $$.* This pleasant small Victorian hotel attracts budget-conscious travelers with its clean, well-priced, old-fashioned rooms. A similarly priced sister hotel, the Hotel Beresford Arms *(701 Post St.; ☎415-673-2600; 95 rooms)*, is three blocks away.

$ Hostelling International–Downtown
– *312 Mason St. ☎415-788-5604 or 800-464-4872. www. sfhostels.com. 230 beds.* Five floors of four-bed dormitory rooms, as well as private doubles, draw international budget travelers to this pleasant hostel off Union Square. Amenities include free Wi-Fi, a kitchen, lounges, and laundry facilities.

Where to Eat

Choosing a restaurant in San Francisco can be overwhelming. So great is the variety of eateries here, so outstanding is their quality, that dining has become a recreation in itself. Don't assume you won't be able to get a reservation: hundreds of Bay Area restaurants list their availability on www.opentable.com, a site which allows you to view menus and reserve with a mouse click.

Additional restaurants are listed throughout this guide. See Index for a complete listing of eateries.

$$$$	over $75
$$$	$50–$75
$$	$25–$50
$	less than $25

CASTRO DISTRICT

$$$ Frances – *3870 17th St. Dinner only. 415-621-3870. www.frances-sf.com.* **Contemporary**. Chef-owner Melissa Perello's relaxed resto has quickly become one of the hardest reservations in the city. The selective, daily-changing menu of contemporary California fare might feature smoked steelhead trout, ricotta gnocchi, or lamb with butter beans and artichoke.

$$ Starbelly – *3583 16th St. 415-252-7500. starbellysf.com.* **Californian.** This unpretentious eatery has become a Castro mainstay thanks to its convivial atmosphere and delicious California-style salads, pizzas, and small plates. The restaurant, which got a full liquor license (and new cocktail menu) in 2018, always reserves tables for walk-ins, inside and on the heated patio.

CHINATOWN

$$$ Mister Jiu's – *28 Waverly Pl. Dinner only. 415-857-9688. www.misterjius.com.* **Chinese**. Rising chef Brandon Jew breathes new life into this restored historic Chinatown banquet hall with high-end Chinese dishes infused with California sensibilities such as wontons with Monterey squid and tea-smoked Liberty Farm duck.

$$ Trestle – *531 Jackson St. Dinner only. 415-772-0922. trestlesf.com.* **American**. In a town overun with high-priced restaurants, dinner-only Trestle's $38 prix fixe is a refreshing alternative. The menu, which changes nightly, showcases impeccably procured farm-to-table food and value-driven wines.

$$ Z&Y – *655 Jackson St. 415-981-8988. www.zandyrestaurant.com.* **Chinese**. Savory tongue-numbing Sichuan dumplings, noodles, and soups are served at this Chinatown mainstay. Across the street, there's a more upscale ambience at **Z&Y Bistro** (*$$,606 Jackson St. 415-986-1899. www.zybistro.com. Chinese.*), opened by the same chef in 2018. Here, you'll find vegetable-centric Asian fusion dishes, as well as signature plates from the original Z&Y, like chicken with explosive peppers.

CIVIC CENTER/HAYES VALLEY

$$ Cala *149 Fell St. 415-660-7701. www.calarestaurant.com.* **Mexican.** A blend of traditional Mexican flavors, California produce, and straight-up culinary creativity come together at Cala, an ultra-buzzy Hayes Valley restaurant from well-known Mexico City–based chef Gabriela Cámara. The airy main dining room is only open for dinner, but tacos are served from restaurant's back door at lunchtime.

$$ Monsieur Benjamin – *451 Gough St. Dinner only. 415-403-2233. www.monsieurbenjamin.com.* **French.** With the convivial ambience and rich food typical to Parisian bistros, Monsieur Benjamin fills up at dinner, when French classics like veal sweetbreads, foie gras and braised rabbit are served in a contemporary dining room, with floor-to-ceiling windows overlooking busy Gough Street.

Rich Table – *199 Gough St. Dinner only. 415- 355-9085. www.richtablesf.com* With tables made of salvaged wood, a hip Hayes Valley zip code, and super-creative food—think aged-beef wontons, dried porcini doughnuts, sardine chips—Rich Table is a new-school San Francisco classic.

$ Souvla *517 Hayes St. ☏415-400-5458. www.souvla.com.* **Greek**. Greek-style spit-fired meats, like pork belly and feta-brined free-range chicken, are wrapped into pita sandwiches or served in salads at this bustling all-day counter-service spot, which has now expanded to several San Francisco neighborhoods.

$$$ Zuni Café – *1658 Market St. Closed Mon. ☏415-552-2522. www.zunicafe.com.* **Mediterranean**. A San Francisco institution for four decades, Zuni serves hearty French and Italian dishes infused with California flavors. The brick-oven-roasted chicken and the Caesar salad are local classics. The wedge-shaped, glass-enclosed space has an oyster-and-champagne bar that's popular for people-watching.

EMBARCADERO

$$$ Boulevard – *1 Mission St. at Steuart St. www.boulevardrestaurant.com. ☏415-543-6084.* **Californian**. This Belle Epoque stunner in the 1889 Audiffred Building with windows framing the Bay Bridge showcases pioneering chef Nancy Oakes' Californian cuisine. Look for Dungeness crab in season and oven-roasted meats, paired with stellar wines and gracious service.

$$$ The Slanted Door – *1 Ferry Building, No. 3. ☏415-861-8032. www.slanteddoor.com.* **Vietnamese**. This long-running Ferry Building restaurant offers fresh, Vietnamese-inspired cuisine grapefruit and jicama salad, spring rolls stuffed with pork, shrimp and mint, and fresh Dungeness crab with cellophane noodles.

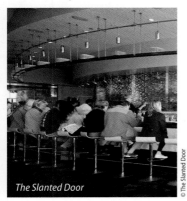

The Slanted Door
© The Slanted Door

FINANCIAL DISTRICT

Caviar tarte, Quince
© Quince

$$$$ Quince – *470 Pacific Ave. Dinner only. Closed Sun. ☏415-775-8500. www.quincerestaurant.com.* **Italian**. Chef-owner Michael Tusk's impeccably sourced and inspired nightly tasting menus always include ethereal house-made pasta. Stellar wines, stylish furnishings and unfailing service make it a true destination. Its casual sister restaurant next door, Cotogna, is a terrific, more affordable choice for lunch or dinner. .

$$ Sam's Grill and Seafood – *374 Bush St. Closed Sat & Sun. ☏415-421-0594. samsgrill-sf.com.* **Seafood**. Founded in 1867 as an open-air market, Sam's is today a no-nonsense bar and grill serving fresh fish and two-martini lunches to business people. Gruff veteran waiters add to the atmosphere.

FISHERMAN'S WHARF

$$$$ Gary Danko – *800 North Point St. Dinner only. ☏415-749-2060. www.garydanko.com.* **Contemporary**. Celeb chef Danko's culinary creations take center stage at his posh restaurant near Fisherman's Wharf. Design-your-own tasting menus (*$83 for 3-courses, $101 for 4, $119 for 5*) allow you to sample his wizardry in dishes like Moroccan spiced squab. A 2,000-bottle wine list and ninja servers makes it a celebration destination.

$$ Alioto's – *8 Fisherman's Wharf at foot of Taylor St. ☏415-673-0183. www.aliotos.com.* **Seafood**. Founded as a fish stall in 1925, Alioto's remains a Sicilian family venture. The "fastest crab-cracker on the bay" lures tourists inside, where diners enjoy views of the Golden Gate with their fresh fish.

GOLDEN GATE PARK

$$ Beach Chalet Brewery and Restaurant – *1000 Great Hwy., Ocean Beach.* 🖉*415-386-8439. www.beach chalet.com.* **California**. Built by Willis Polk in 1925 as a tea house, this San Francisco landmark now features a bustling cafe on the top floor (with ocean views) and a Golden Gate Park visitor center and cafe on the ground floor. Menu items upstairs, like fried calamari and black Angus steak, are designed to go with the house-made brews. The ground-floor Park Chalet serves pizza and BBQ fare.

HAIGHT-ASHBURY

$$ Magnolia *1398 Haight St. 415-864-7468. magnoliabrewing.com.* **American**. After two decades, this gastropub and independent brewery has become a staple in the Haight-Ashbury, thanks to its signature cask-aged brews and beer-friendly comfort food, like fish and chips or wedge salads. A second Magnolia taproom opened in the hip Dogpatch neighborhood (*2505 3rd Street.* 🖉*415-864-7468*) in 2018.

$$ Thep Phanom – *400 Waller St. Dinner only.* 🖉*415-431-2526.* **Thai**. Dishes like *ped sawan (*boneless duck in honey sauce on spinach) and "The Dancing Lady" (stuffed jumbo prawns with crab meat) result in lines out the door at this homey converted Victorian in the Lower Haight.

JAPANTOWN/WESTERN ADDITION

$$ Che Fico – *838 Divisadero St.* 🖉*415-416-6959 www.chefico.com.* **Italian**. The second-floor dining room at this Divisadero hot spot is always packed with locals hungry for the handmade pappardelle, oven-blistered squash-topped pizza, house-cured charcuterie, and fried risotto that have made Che Fico a new San Francisco institution.

$ Mifune – *1737 Post St.* 🖉*415-922-0337. www.mifune.com.* **Japanese**. This acclaimed noodle house serves 55 hot and cold varieties of

udon and soba in a stark, red and black minimalist environment.

$$ Nopa – *864 Divisadero St.* 🖉*415-864-8643.* **Californian**. The epitome of San Francisco cool, this restaurant on the edge of the Panhandle wins fans with its locavore food and drink offerings, stylish digs (including a communal table for walk-ins) and late night hours.

Nopalito *306 Broderick St.* 🖉*415-437-0303. www.nopalitosf.com.* **Mexican** Braised-pork tacos, tamales stuffed with shrimp and mole, handmade quesadillas, and other Mexican snacks are prepared with fresh local ingredients and plenty of love at this casual spot by the Nopa team. There's a second branch in the Inner Sunset (*1224 9th Ave.* 🖉*415-233-9966*).

$$$ State Bird Provisions – *1529 Fillmore St.,* 🖉*415-795-1272. www. statebirdsf.com.* **American**. The crowds line up early and never stop at this festive restaurant with dim-sum like carts whizzing through the simple storefront hawking eclectic seasonal small plates including its namesake fried quail dish with provisions.

Seafood cart, State Bird Provisions

© Ed Anderson/State Bird Provisions

MARINA DISTRICT/COW HOLLOW

$$$$ Atelier Crenn – *3127 Fillmore St. www.ateliercrenn.com.* **Modernist**. Helmed by one of the most talented chefs in the business, Dominique Crenn's inspired fine-dining restaurant is a critical darling and one of the toughest reservations in the city, with only eight tables in the dining room. You'll also need reservations for intimate **Bar Crenn**

Delfina

© Eric Wolfinger/OpenKitchenPhotography/Delfina

(*$$$ 3131 Fillmore St. ✆415-440-0460. www.barcrenn.com*), the chef's wine-centric Parisian-style salon next door.

$$ Greens – *Fort Mason Center, Bldg. A, ✆415-771-6222. www.greensrestaurant. com*. **Vegetarian**. Opened in 1979, this upscale vegetarian restaurant gets much of its produce from the Zen Center's Green Gulch Farm in Marin County. Seasonal fare like heirloom tomato salad and linguine with chanterelles are served with a view of the Golden Gate Bridge. For a quick lunch, stop by the to-go counter.

Greens

© Nader Khouri/Greens Restaurant

$$ Radhaus – *Landmark Building A, Fort Mason Center for Arts and Culture. ✆415-445-4556. radhaussf.com*. **German**. There's an open kitchen and windows overlooking the Golden Gate Bridge at this industrial-chic German-inspired restaurant in Fort Mason, a popular spot for a sunny weekend brunch of savory bread pudding, pork sausages, freshly made pretzels, and suds from the fine selection of German brews.

MISSION DISTRICT

$$ Delfina – *3621 18th St. Dinner only. ✆415-552-4055. www.delfinasf.com*. **Italian**. Craig and Anne Stoll continue to draw enthusiastic crowds to their Mission eatery—still mobbed after all these years. The ambience is comfortably chic, uplifting and lively (though loud), but the soul-warming Tuscan cuisine is the reason for the masses.

$$ Foreign Cinema – *2534 Mission St. ✆415-551-648-7600*. **Californian**. A hip clientele pack this ultra cool restaurant (and its adjacent bar, Laszlo) for Mediterranean-inflected California cuisine and house-made pop tarts for Sunday brunch, best enjoyed in the courtyard where they screen foreign and domestic flicks.

$$$$ Lazy Bear – *3416 19th St. Dinner only. ✆415-874-9921. www.lazybearsf.com*. **Contemporary**. This ultra-creative and critically acclaimed restaurant, which got its start as an underground supper club in 2009, is fine dining with a dinner party feel: here, a nightly set-course menu is served at two communal tables of diners, who are encouraged not only to chat with each other but to check out what's happening in the open kitchen.

$$$ Rintaro – *82 14th St. ✆415-589-7022. izakayarintaro.com*. **Japanese**. A California take on traditional Japanese cooking, Rintaro's kitchen makes udon and tofu by hand, sources pasture-raised chicken for its juicy yakitori, and the wasabi root served with ultra-fresh sashimi is grown in nearby Half Moon Bay.

$ Stonemill Matcha – *561 Valencia St. 415-796-3876. stonemillmatcha.com.* **Japanese**. The civic obsession with matcha hits its apex at this modern Mission tea room, where bright-green stone-ground Japanese tea powder is sprinkled onto ice cream, served in milky ginger-spiked lattes, and baked into a daily assortment of treats, like panna cotta, in an inviting Zen-like space.

$$ Tartine Manufactory – *595 Alabama St.* 415-757-0007. *www.tartinebakery. com.* **Californian**. Beloved bakery Tartine (*600 Guerrero St,* 415-487-2600) is a San Francisco institution, drawing ceaseless crowds for its famed morning buns and bread pudding. Now, diners can enjoy even more Tartine at this all-day eatery, which draws on the original's artisan ethos with seasonal dishes like celery soup, charred broccolini, and koji-smoked pork chop, served with craft cocktails and local wine.

Tartine Manufactory

© Tartine Manufactory

NOB HILL

$$$$ Acquerello – *1722 Sacramento St.* 415-567-5432. *www.acquerello.com. Dinner only. Closed Sun–Mon.* **Italian**. The sun-soaked colored walls and whispering patrons lend a soothing beauty to this chapel-cum-restaurant. Chef Suzette Gresham-Tognetti's high-end contemporary Italian pre-fixes are elevated with carefully curated Italan wines parirings.

$$$ Liholiho Yacht Club – *871 Sutter St.* 415-440-5446. *www.liholihoyachtclub. Dinner only. Closed Sun.* **Californian**. Chef-partner Ravi Kapur's patchwork upbringing blending Hawaiian, Indian, Chinese, and Californian ingredients leads to a deeply personal and delicious menu with the likes of beef-tongue bao and house-made spam with uni. Inventive bar snacks and island cocktails are the draw at its basement bar, Louie Gen-Gen Room *(by reservation only)*.

NORTH BEACH

$$$ Tosca Cafe – *242 Columbus Ave.* 415-986-9651. *www.toscacafesf.com.* **Italian**. Opened before the Prohibition, this historic bar has been revived by a duo of NYC restaurant vets, who present bold Italian-American dishes, like spicy bucatini all'Amatriciana and roast chicken for two. Be sure to order the house "cappuccino" (hot chocolate and steamed milk spiked with brandy). Expect a wait.

PACIFIC HEIGHTS

$$$ Sorrel – *3228 Sacramento St. Dinner only. 415-525-3765. www. sorrelrestaurant.com.* **Italian**. The blend of Californian and Italian food, a signature of the San Francisco dining scene, has been perfected at elegant Pacific Heights restaurant Sorrel, where flawless seafood risotto or the signature dry-aged duck for two cater to a sophisticated crowd.

$$ SPQR – *1911 Fillmore St.* 415-771-7779. *www.spqrsf.com.* **Italian**. An outstanding wine list and lovingly prepared Italian-inspired cuisine draw locals to this elegant but comfortable Pacific Heights restaurant. A variety of cold, hot and fried appetizers precedes the housemade pastas and bold entrees such as almond crusted sturgeon with sausage and orange butter.

RICHMOND DISTRICT

$$ Fiorella – *2339 Clement St.* 415-340-3049. *www.fiorella-sf.com.* Serving Neapolitan-style pizza, creative salads, and a petit list of pastas in a low-key, amiable setting, this neighborhood restaurant is invariably packed with Richmond locals sipping on generously served glasses of Italian wine.

$$ Ton Kiang – *5821 Geary Blvd. 415-752-4440. www.tonkiang.net.* **Chinese**. Clay-pot casseroles (rock cod with tofu, braised oxtail with carrot and celery), flavorful steamed dim sum, and regional Hakka specialties at dinner draw long lines here.

RUSSIAN HILL

$$ Belcampo – *1998 Polk St. 415-660-5573. belcampo.com.* **American**. This attractive butcher shop and ranch-to-table restaurant serves an abbreviated menu featuring the company's organic California-raised meats. Burgers, made from their sustainably raised beef, are the highlight.

$$$$ La Folie – *2316 Polk St. Closed Sun. 415-776-5577. www.lafolie.com.* **French**. One of the last bastions of high-end French cuisine, chef-owner Roland Passot still dazzles with 3-5-course prix fixe dinners which may include roast quail or butter-poached lobster. An adjacent lounge serves upscale nibbles and bubbles.

SOUTH OF MARKET

$$ The Perennial – *59 9th Street. Dinner only. 415-500-7788. www. theperennialsf.com.* **Californian**. The rigorous focus on sustainable food has brought The Perennial to some interesting places: a restaurant-run greenhouse, nose-to-tail meat from eco-focused farms, and fresh bread made from Kernza grain. Fortunately, good eating isn't an afterthought: the California-style food and cocktails are ace, with a good value prix fixe option.

$$ Yank Sing–*101 Spear St. 415-781-1111. www.yanksing.com.* **Chinese**. Though prices are higher than those of its Chinatown counterparts, this sprawling Chinese operation *(with a sister branch at 49 Stevenson St.)* is the best place in town for traditional and inventive dim sum, wheeled around by an efficient headset-wearing staff.

SUNSET

$$$ Outerlands – *4001 Judah Street 415-661-6140. outerlandssf.com.* **New American**. The restaurant that put the Outer Sunset on the city's dining map remains a reliably delicious, low-key, local-centric spot for comforting California-style food, just a few blocks from the beach. Food is as rustically pretty as the weathered-wood-walled dining room.

UNION SQUARE AREA

$$ Del Popolo – *855 Bush Street 415-589-7940. www.delpopolosf.com.* **Italian**. Del Popolo's wood-burning oven once circled the city in a food truck. Today, it's the centerpiece of a cozy pizzeria near Union Square, where addictive Neapolitan pies are served alongside creative small plates, like wood-fired barbecue carrots and little gem caesar.

$$ Kin Khao – *55 Cyril Magnin St, 415-362-7456. kinkhao.com.* **Thai**. At this modest restaurant in the Parc 55 Hotel, exceptional Thai flavors are fused with locally sourced ingredients, like roasted trout in red curry, or Napa Valley shelling beans tossed with lime, mint, and chili. Just off Union Square, it's often packed with locals sipping cool Thai-inspired cocktails.

Kin Khao

© Kin Khao

$ Sears Fine Food – *439 Powell St. 415-986-0700. www.searsfinefood.com.* **American**. An anachronism on the currently dining scene , this American diner remains a local insitution for its signature dish, 18 delicate Swedish pancakes (served all day) and waitresses who call you hon. There are also standard breakfasts like eggs Benedict and Blue Plate dinner specials like meatloaf.

Entertainment

PERFORMING ARTS

The Bay Area is blessed with a great wealth and variety of performing-arts offerings. Nearly 100 live-performance theaters mount stage productions performed by traveling Broadway companies and respected regional and local groups.

Acclaimed dance, symphony and opera companies perform at Civic Center venues.

The main theater district is centered just west of Union Square, while stages at Yerba Buena Gardens and Fort Mason Center host a variety of music, film, theater and dance.

Rock and alternative music play at bars and nightclubs as well as at stadiums and arenas.

Public literary readings light up bookstores, cafes and other locales. Check *SF Weekly* and *www.sfgate.com/entertainment* for current listings.

TICKETS

Popular events may sell out months in advance, so it is wise to buy tickets early. Full-price tickets can be purchased directly from the venue's box office or from one of the brokers listed below (a service charge of $1-$7 may be added to the price).

Brokers may have tickets available when the box office is sold out, but expect to pay for it. Hotel concierges may also be able to help secure tickets.

TIX Bay Area offers half-price tickets starting at 11am for selected events on the day of the show. Purchases must be made in person from the box office in Union Square on Powell St. between Post and Geary (open daily 8am–6pm), online at *www.tixbayarea.com* or by telephone: 415-433-7827. You can also buy tickets for cultural events through **City Box Office** (weekdays 9.30am-5pm and Sat noon-4pm. 180 Redwood St, Ste 100. 415-392-4400. www.cityboxoffice.com) or **Ticketmaster** (www.ticketmaster.com).

BALLET

San Francisco Ballet

301 Van Ness Ave. 415-865-2000. *www.sfballet.org*. Directed by Helgi Tomasson, the company stages classically inspired contemporary ballet works as well as traditional classical repertoire during its February–May season (plus winter *Nutcracker Suite* performances) at the War Memorial Opera House.

CLASSICAL MUSIC

San Francisco Symphony

201 Van Ness Ave. 415-864-6000. *www.sfsymphony.org*. Led by maestro Michael Tilson Thomas, the orchestra performs classical repertoire and 20C and contemporary pieces during its September–June season at Davies Symphony Hall. Families should check out the Music for Families series.

Philharmonia Baroque

401 Van Ness Ave. 415-252-1288. *www.philharmonia.org*. The ensemble performs Baroque works (Bach, Corelli, Rameau) on period instruments at the Herbst Theatre and venues in Berkeley, Palo Alto and Contra Costa.

San Francisco Contemporary Music Players

415-278-9566. *www.sfcmp.org*. This award-winning contemporary chamber music ensemble showcases new (within the last 10 years) music with its innovative concert series at various venues throughout the city.

Sound Box

300 Franklin St. 415-503-5299. *sfsoundbox.com*. A 500-seat craft-cocktail-serving space with an avant-garde audio system, Sound Space hosts experimental and contemporary classical music performances, some accompanied by dance or light show. It is located in Davies Symphony Hall.

THEATERS

Visit *www.theatermania.com*. for comprehensive listings of performances throughout the Bay Area.

San Francisco Opera's War Memorial Opera House

© David Wakely Photography/San Francisco Opera

American Conservatory Theater

415 Geary Blvd. ✆415-749-2228. www. act-sf.org. The city's longstanding resident theater company mounts classic and new works (*Speed-the-Plow*, *Blood Knot*, *Sweeney Todd*) in the former Geary Theater (1910, Bliss & Faville). Its sister outpost, The Strand Theater (1127 Market St.) located in a restored historic movie theater across from Civic Center's UN Plaza, mounts additional productions, including commissioned new work, cabaret and theater performances by A.C.T. students.

Curran Theater

445 Geary Blvd. ✆415-746-1799. sfcurran.com. Broadway traveling shows (*Harry Potter, Dear Evan Hansen*) are staged at this Downtown theater, owned by Tony Award-winning producer Carole Shorenstein Hays and was fully restored in 2016. Other Broadway productions, like Anastasia and Hamilton, come to nearby **Golden Gate Theater** *(1 Taylor St. shnsf.com)* and the **Orpheum Theater** *(1192 Market St. shnsf.com)* respectively.

Magic Theater

Fort Mason Center Building A ✆4415-441-8822. www.magictheatre.org. This local institution based in Fort Mason has been staging highly acclaimed plays and nurturing talents like David Mamet and Octavio Solis since 1967.

San Francisco Playhouse

✆450 Post St., 415-677-9596. www.sfplayhouse.org. Located in the heart of the Union Square Theater District, San Francisco Playhouse is the city's Off-Broadway company, an intimate alternative to the larger more traditional Union Square theater scene.

OPERA

San Francisco Opera

301 Van Ness Ave. ✆415-864-3330. www.sfopera.com. An active performance repertoire staged at the War Memorial Opera House includes the traditional (*La Bohème, Tosca, Porgy and Bess*) and the groundbreaking (*The Bonesetter's Daugher*, with a libretto by Amy Tan).

Pocket Opera

✆415-972-8930. www.pocketopera.org. Director emeritus Donald Pippin's company makes opera clear, accessible and affordable through small scale productions (*Cosi Fan Tutte, Xerxes*) held at various venues.

San Francisco Nightlife Websites

- www.yelp.com
- www.7x7.com/music-nightlife
- www.sfweekly.com
- www.thrillist.com/san-francisco
- www.sfgate.com/entertainment
- www.sfstation.com/clubs

THEATER FESTIVALS

Shakespeare in the Park

℘415-558-0888. www.sfshakes.org. The San Francisco Shakespeare Festival's professional troupe mounts free performances on the Main Lawn at the Presidio's Parade Grounds.

NIGHTLIFE

San Francisco's nightlife is as diverse as its population, and ranges from elegant Nob Hill piano bars to clubs offering live music and jazz. Venues blur the line between dance club, bar and live-performance spot, showcasing up-and-coming bands on some nights and celebrity DJs on others.

Though clubs of every stripe can be found throughout the city, Folsom Street and Howard Street in the South of Market draw late-night (make that early-morning) crowds to techno/hip-hop dance clubs where bouncers may scrutinize the too-casually dressed. The Mission District is home to a slew of hipster dives and DJ bars, which draw a young crowd. The nearby Castro is the city's hub for gay bars. On the other end of the city, North Beach is a mix of historic pubs, comedy venues, dives and strip clubs. To party with a preppy crowd of affluent young professionals, head to the Marina's sports bars, wine bars and lounges. For swank, Nob Hill is your neighborhood.

Drinks are taken seriously in San Francisco and priced accordingly. Creative cocktails from mixologists can start at around $15 and cover charges can run as high as $50 for the biggest clubs, though many bars have no cover. Proof of age (21) is required to enter all clubs.

🖐Consult the arts and entertainment sections of the publications listed above for detailed listings of live performances and events.

BARS

ABV

3174 16th St. www.abvsf.com
This sleek Mission cocktail bar has an appealing list of proprietary cocktails with an emphasis on highballs, wine on tap and a substantial list of mezcal, Japanese whiskey, and rare Scotches.

Alembic

1725 Haight St. ℘415-666-0822. www.alembicbar.com. The mixologists at this hip upper Haight haunt are are experts at their art, mixing up Sazeracs, pisco sours and Blood and Sands (scotch whiskey, cherry brandy, sweet vermouth and orange juice) in dark moody surroundings. Inventive bar food rounds out the offerings.

Black Cat

400 Eddy St. ℘415-358-1999. blackcatsf.com. There's live jazz every night at this Tenderloin hot spot, a contemporary take on San Francisco's historic supper clubs. You'll find low lighting, old-fashioned leather couches, and classic cocktails upstairs; there are generally excellent groups playing in the concert hall below.

Bourbon & Branch

501 Jones St., at O'Farrell. ℘415-346-1735. www.bourbonandbranch.com. This sultry speakeasy in the Tenderloin has no sign (look for the door below the Anti-Saloon League sign) and you have to ring a buzzer to get in. It was one of the city's first speakeasy-style bars and a vanguard of the genre. Reservations are required.

Mikkeller Bar

34 Mason St. ℘415-984-0279. www.mikkellerbar.com. An chic 80-seat beer hall set in a 106yr-old brick

building in the Tenderloin features 42 taps and a dizzying array of bottled beers from the best breweries in the world.

Pacific Cocktail Haven

580 Sutter St. 415-398-0195. pacificcocktailsf.com. At this amiable and unpretentious bar near Union Square, the star of the show here is the creative tropical drinks, which might include such unusual additions as curry or black sesame.

Pagan Idol

75 Bush Street 415-985-6375. www.paganidol.com San Francisco's long tiki bar tradition continues to thrive at this Financial District bar, where a combination of kitschy elements, like an erupting volcano, are complimented by truly stellar rum-based cocktails and an upbeat post-workday crowd.

Rickhouse

246 Kearny St. 415-398-2827. www.rickhousebar.com. A prime place for post-work mingling, this down-town bar is packed with professionals on weeknights. The small loft often has more breathing room.

Smuggler's Cove

650 Gough St. 415-869-1900. www.smugglerscovesf.com. Expect everything from pirate ship decor to flaming cocktails and punch bowls at this tiny tiki bar in Hayes Valley stocking over 400 rare rums.

The Snug

2301 Fillmore St. 20th St. 415-562-5092 . www.trickdogbar.com. A pretty bar in Pacific Heights with stellar cocktails, a big list of craft beers on tap, and a relaxed neighborhood ambience, despite it being overseen by a seasoned bar team.

Trick Dog

3010 20th St. 415-471-2999. www.trickdogbar.com. Hipsters of all ages cram into this bi-level cocktail den in the Mission run by ace mixologists who whip up inventive cocktails. Although the crowds are a constant, the cleverly themed drink collections menus change every few months. Upscale bar food is served till closing.

Violet's Tavern

2301 Clement St. 415-682-4861. www.violets-sf.com. This low-lit Richmond-district tavern has become a trend-setting destination for its beautifully prepared cocktails, freshly shucked oysters, upscale comfort food, and warm local vibe.

COMEDY

Cobb's Comedy Club

915 Columbus Ave. 415-928-4320. www.cobbscomedyclub.com. Some of the biggest names in standup have headlined at this 400-seat club, which runs shows Wed-Sat. Seating is first-come, first-served, and there's a full dinner menu.

The Marsh

1062 Valencia St. 415-282-3055. www.themarsh.org. Thought-provoking standup comedy, plays and other performances fill the bill at this intimate theater in the Mission District.

Punch Line

444 Battery St. 415-397-7573. www.punchlinecomedyclub.com. The seating is tight, but the cover price is right (plus a 2-drink minimum) at this proving ground for live standup, where big names work out new material.

DANCE CLUBS

1015 Folson

1015 Folsom. 415-991-1015 1015.com. Electronic music superstars play for a packed house at this preeminent San Francisco nightclub.

Temple

540 Howard St. www.templesf.com. Expect electronic music upstairs and hip hop downstairs on most nights at this 20,000-square-foot nightclub tricked out with immersive lighting and an interactive dance floor. Brace yourself for a steep cover and a long wait unless you're on a guest list. It's one of the few clubs that stays open past 2am.

Harry Denton's Starlight Room

450 Powell St, in the Sir Francisc Drake Hotel. 415-395-8595. www.harry denton.com. Dress to the nines for your trip to this 21st-floor cocktail lounge, with its breathtaking views, retro feel and sizeable dance floor.

LIVE MUSIC VENUES

Indie and Avant-Garde

Amnesia – *853 Valencia St. 415-970 -0012. www.amnesiathebar.com.* Red-tinted lighting and an eclectic array of music ranging from Gypsy to indie make for a funky night at this ultra-laid-back bar and concert space. Fans flock to weekly bluegrass and karaoke nights.

The Chapel – *777 Valencia St. 415-551-5157. www.thechapelsf.com.* A unique live music venue in a former funeral parlor, with a focus on alternative rock and dance. The same team operates bar **Curio** (*775 Valencia St. 415-551-7306 curiobarsf.com*) next door, which serves burgers and ultra-fun cocktails to an always full house.

The Independent – *628 Divisadero St. 415-771-1421. www.theindependent sf.com.* This spot seems to top everyone's list for great new bands, indie favorites and a happening crowd.

Rickshaw Stop – *155 Fell St. 415-861-2011. www.rickshawstop.com.* A younger crowd energizes this intimate club, which books up-and-coming bands before they hit big. It's warm in there, so dress cool.

Slim's – *333 11th St. 415-255-0333. www.slims-sf.com.* American roots music is often on the roster at this ever-popular South of Market nightclub. Decor is sparse and seating is limited, but the bands are worth it.

Jazz and Blues

Biscuits & Blues – *401 Mason St. 415 -292-2583. www.biscuitsandblues.com.* Quality live blues and southern soul food make an great combination at this ultrahip belowground club near Union Square.

Boom Boom Room – *1601 Fillmore St. 415-673-8000. www.boomboom blues.com.* Chicago and New Orleans-style jazz and blues rule the scene at this laid-back jazz bar in Japantown.

SFJAZZ Center – *201 Franklin St. 866-920-5299. www.sfjazz.org.* The first free-standing building in America built for jazz, this $64-million dollar music venue in the Hayes Valley that debuted in 2013 hosts a who's who of legendary and rising jazz artists. Circular stadium means there's not a bad seat in the house.

Rock and Pop

Great American Music Hall – *859 O'Farrell St. 415-885-0750. www.musichallsf.com.* Ornate decor neatly jives with modern accoutrements at this lovely early 20C music hall in the Tenderloin. You'll see a variety of bands ranging from rock to folk.

Bottom of the Hill – *1233 17th St. 415-621-4455. www.bottomofthehill.com.* Advance tickets are recommended for the straight-up rock gigs as well as indie and punk bands at this smallish club in out-of-the-way Potrero Hill.

The Fillmore – *1805 Geary Blvd. 415-346-6000. www.thefillmore.com.* Made famous by Bill Graham in the mid-1960s with acts such The Grateful Dead and Jefferson Airplane, The Fillmore continues to draw major rock and pop acts.

Shopping

From large complexes incorporating national chains, restaurants and entertainment venues, to intimate rows of boutiques scattered throughout the city, San Francisco satisfies the most ardent shopper. Most stores accept major credit cards and travelers checks, but not out-of-state checks. Many shops extend their hours during the holiday season (Nov–Dec).

MAIN SHOPPING AREAS

Union Square Area – San Francisco's leading shopping district, this area is home to major city department stores. **Nordstrom** (℘415-243-8500) is in the **Westfield San Francisco Centre** (865 Market St.; ℘415-512-6776), home to more than 200 shops and major chains. Next door in the Westfield' extension lies **Bloomingdale's** (℘415-856-5300), a Burke Williams spa, a movie theater, and a food court. Other major Union Square stores are **Macy's** (170 O'Farrell Sts.; ℘415-397-3333), **Neiman Marcus** (150 Stockton St.; ℘415-362-3900), **Saks Fifth Avenue** (384 Post St., **Brook's Brothers** (240 Post St.; ℘415-402-0476), and **Barneys New York** (77 O'Farrell St.; ℘415-268-3500). Designer and specialty shops like **Emporio Armani** (1 Grant Ave.; ℘415-677-9400), **Tiffany & Co.** (350 Post St.; ℘415-781-1000), and the **Apple Store** (300 Post St. ℘415-486-4800) are found along and around Grant Avenue, Post Street, Sutter Street and Maiden Lane. Also nearby Union Square are home furnishing chains such as **Crate & Barrel** (55 Stockton St.; ℘415-982-5200) and **Williams Sonoma** (340 Post St.; ℘415-362-9450), and bargain chains selling trends **Forever 21** (2 Stockton St.; ℘415-765-9908), **H&M** (150 Powell St.; ℘415-986-4215), and **Zara** (250 Post St.; ℘415-399-6930).

Financial District – The city's major business district boasts the **Embarcadero Center** (next to Justin Herman Plaza), a 10-acre office-and-retail complex incorporating more than 100 shops and restaurants. Nearby, the **Ferry Building Marketplace** (One Ferry Bldg) is home to several dozen specialty food boutiques, as well as **The Gardener** (℘415-981-8181), **Sur La Table** (℘415-262-9970), and **Heath Ceramics** (℘415-399-9284).
The Crocker Galleria (50 Post St.) contains nearly 30 designer and specialty shops. More than 25 fine modern design and **antique** shops, along with numerous art galleries are located in the Jackson Square Historic District near Jackson and Montgomery Streets (www.jacksonsquaresf.com).

Chinatown – Haggle at an open-air market along Stockton Street, or admire luxurious silks and jades at Grant Avenue shops, in this colorful, bustling micro-city. Pharmacies sell traditional Asian herbal remedies, and a plenitude of restaurants offer dim sum and other Chinese delicacies. Grant Avenue is one of the best places in the city to find cheap souvenirs. Of the many overstuffed souvenir shops **Old Shanghai** (645 Grant Ave. ℘415-362-5750) is among the best, stocking paper lanterns, Chinese shoes, and other inexpensive imports.

Fisherman's Wharf – Three retail centers punctuate this festive strip of souvenir shops and novelty museums. **Anchorage Square** has more than 50 shops and restaurants and a 24-hr parking garage. (℘415-775-6000); **Ghirardelli Square** features more than a dozen shops and restaurants (℘415-775-5500); and **Pier 39** boasts more than 50 specialty and gift shops (℘415-981-7437).

Hayes Valley – Just a few blocks from the Civic Center, Hayes Street and environs are ground zero for locally owned independent boutiques, many with a notably San Francisco aesthetic and, often, upscale prices.

Some boutiques specialize in eco-conscious clothing, like brand **Amor Verte** (*437 Hayes St.* 📞*415-800-8576. amourvert.com*), which produces clothes sustainable fabrics, like mulberry silk.

For handmade jewelry, tees, and cool gifts, try **Gather** (*541 Octavia St.* 📞*415-799-7130. www.gathersf.com*). Get West Coast streetwear at **Seldom Seen** (*522 Octavia St.* 📞*415-757-0915. seldomseen.com*) or **Rand + Statler** (*425 Hayes St.* 📞*415-634-0881. www. randandstatler.com*) a high-quality flannel at San Francisco–based **Pladra** (*325 Hayes St.* 📞*650-714-7135. pladra.com*).

The Marina and Cow Hollow – The shopping scene in the northwest part of San Francisco is dominated by two main streets. **Union Street** from Van Ness Avenue to Steiner Street forms the commercial heart of Cow Hollow, while **Chestnut Street** between Divisadero and Fillmore Streets is the main retail section of the Marina. Both are host to dozens of clothing, jewelry and beauty boutiques, as well as antique stores, salons, cafes and restaurants. Among the most popular boutiques on Union Street is **Ambiance** (*1864 Union St.;* 📞*415-923-9796; also at 1458 Haight St.;* 📞*415-552-5095; 3985 24th St.;* 📞*415-647-7144; and 756 Irving St;* 📞*415-661-1663*) offering trendy clothing, shoes and accessories. On Chestnut, **Marine Layer** (*2209 Chestnut St;* 📞*415-400-4136*) is a casually cool San Francisco–based clothier that sells hip plaids, soft tees, and knit sweaters for men and women.

Mission District – **Valencia Street** is the main thorouhgfare in the Mission's shopping district, but you'll find local clothing and jewelry designers, art galleries, and bookshops along cross streets, too. Design shops and clothing boutiques like **Gravel & Gold** (*3266 21st St.,* 📞*415-552-0112*), **Betabrand** (*780 Valencia St.;* 📞*415-692-7433*), and **Le Pointe** (*301 Valencia St., 415-400-4275*) will outfit you for a night out in the city. The lively area also abounds with vintage and secondhand shops, from large catch-all stores to intimate boutiques with a finely edited selection. Farther down Valencia are unique stores such as **Paxton Gate** (*824 Valencia St.;* 📞*415-824-1872*), which offers everything from garden tools to art to taxidermy supplies and the pirate supply store at **826 Valencia** (*826 Valencia St.;* 📞*415 642-5905*). In the emerging south Mission, check out the **Heath Ceramics Showroom** (*2900 18th St.,* 📞*415-361-5552. www. heathceramics.com*), which shares a space with Tartine Manufactory. True to the neighborhood's ethnic makeup, you'll also find stores selling Latin American imports, including jewelry and clothing.

South of Market – A bargain hunter's dream, this area boasts dozens of outlet centers, resale shops and design showrooms, such as **Rolo Garage** (*1301 Howard St. at 9th St.;* 📞*415-578-7139*) which stocks the latest urban fashions at great discount.

OTHER SHOPPING AREAS

In addition to the areas described above, charming neighborhood shopping areas offer a pleasant mix of small boutiques, specialty shops, bookstores, restaurants and cafes.

◆ **Fillmore Street** (Pacific Heights) *Jackson to Bush Sts. & Union to Greenwich Sts.* Fillmore Street reflects the affluence of Pacific Heights residents, housing numerous fashionable boutiques, with high-end shops such as **Sunhee Moon** (*1833 Fillmore St.;* 📞*415-928-1800*). Also here are eclectic home furnishing stores like **Nest** (*2300 Fillmore St.;* 📞*415-292-6199*), the modern **Zinc Details** (*1633 Fillmore St.;* 📞*415-776-2700*) and **Jonathan Adler** (*2133 Fillmore St.;* 📞*415-563-9500*).

- **Haight Street** (Haight-Ashbury) *Stanyan St. to Central Ave.* Haight Street is home to a number of funky clothing boutiques and secondhand shops such as **Held Over** *(1543 Haight St.; 415-864-0818)* and **Crossroads** *(1519 Haight St., ✆415-355-0555; also at 1901 Fillmore St., ✆415-775-8885)* as well as music stores like **Amoeba** *(1855 Haight St.; ✆415-831-1200),* housed in a former bowling alley. In the Lower Haight, east of Divasdero Street, boutiques like **Upper Playground** *(220 Fillmore St.; ✆415-861-1960)* cater to a more hipster millennial clientele.

- **24th Street** (Noe Valley) *Church to Douglass Sts.* Noe Valley denizens converge on 24th Street to shop and dine. The small main drag features specialty food shops and a handful of small boutiques.

- **Castro Street** (Castro District) *Market to 20th Sts.* As the city's LGBT hub, it's no surprise that the Castro is home to a number of trendy menswear stores, such as preppy-chic **Unionmade Goods** *(493 Sanchez St, ✆415-861-3373. unionmadegoods.com).* There are numerous erotic retail shops such as **Does Your Mother Know** *(4141 18th St.; ✆415-864-3160).*

- **Sacramento Street** (Presidio Heights) *Spruce to Baker Sts.* Sacramento Street caters to a largely local, affluent crowd. Here you will find women's and children's boutiques, as well as high-end home furnishings.

- **Polk Street** (Russian Hill) *Broadway to Filbert St.* The main street of tony Russian Hill, Polk Street offers a handful of small boutiques, including vintage-inspired **Belle Cose and Molte Cose** *(2036–2044 Polk St.; ✆415-474-3494).*

ART GALLERIES

San Francisco's greatest concentration of galleries can be found along Sutter, Post and Geary Streets in the blocks north and immediately south of Union Square, especially Sutter between Stockton and Mason Streets.

49 Geary Street is home to, among others, the Stephen Wirtz, Gallery Paule Anglim, Gallery Wendi Norris and Fraenkel galleries. SoMa galleries worth checking out include the **Gagosian Gallery,** Gallery 16 and **Crown Point Press** *(20 Hawthorne St.; ✆415-974-6273; www.crownpoint.com).*

DoReMi, the nickname for a 10-square-block area that touches parts of Dogpatch, Potrero Hill and the Mission, is another vibrant up-and-coming area for galleries. At the foot of Potrero Hill, **Catherine Clark Galley** *(248 Utah St. ✆415-399-1439. cclarkgallery.com)* shows high-profile contemporary work, not far from the **CCA Hubbell Street Galleries** *(161, 151, & 131 Hubbell St.)* run by the California College of Art. In Dogpatch, converted warehouses are now a multi-gallery space called **The Minnesota Street Project** *(1275 Minnesota St. minnesotastreetproject.com)* has some of the most interesting contemporary proposals in the city; the **Museum of Craft and Design** *(2569 Third St. ✆415-773-0303. sfmcd.org)* is just a few blocks away. You'll also find a number of interesting designers at work in this area, particularly at the **American Industrial Center** *(2345 3rd St., 415-621-1920. aicproperties.com);* home to **Bryr Studio** *(✆415-374-7323. www.bryrstudio.com),* which which creates bespoke clogs.

SF Arts *(www.sfarts.org)* has updated listings of current exhibits. Commercial galleries' hours vary widely, with many of them closing Sundays and/or Mondays. Most open between 10am and 11am and close between 5pm and 6pm. On the first Thursday of the month, many Downtown San Francisco galleries stay open later, until 7:30pm for a casual open house.

Galleries in the DoReMi neighborhood such as the Minnesota Street Project also stay open until 7pm *(www. firstthursdayart.com)*.

ANTIQUES

In addition to the Crocker Galleria and Jackson Square in the Financial District, a number of antique shops are sprinkled throughout the city, including the following.

African Outlet (Bay View) *4942 3rd St.* 415- 864-3576.

Past Perfect (Richmond and Haight) *6101 Geary Blvd. and 854 Stanyan St* 415-929-2288 and 415-418-6754).

Schein & Schein (North Beach) *1435 Grant Ave.* 415-399-8882. *www.scheinandschein.com.*

Timeless Treasures (Pacific Heights) *2176 Sutter St.* 415-775-8366. *www.timelesstreasuressf.*

BOOKSTORES

Adobe Books & Arts Cooperative (Mission) *3130 24th St.* 415- 864-3936. *www.adobebooks.com.*

Book Passage (Embarcadero). *1 Ferry Building.* 415-835-1020. *www.bookpassage.com*

City Lights Bookstore (North Beach) *261 Columbus Ave.* 415-362-8193. *www.citylights.com.*

Dog Earned Books (Mission). *900 Valencia.* 415-282-1901 *www.dogearedbooks.com*

Green Apple Books and Music (Richmond) *506 Clement St.* 415-387-2272. *www.greenapplebooks.com.*

Omnivore Books (Noe Valley) *3885A Ceasar Chavez St.* 415-282-4712

Willam Stout Architectural Books (North Beach) *804 Montgomery St.* 415-391-6757. *www.stoutbooks.com.*

MUSIC

101 Music (North Beach) *513 Green St.* 415-392-6369.

Amoeba Music (Haight) *1855 Haight St.* 415-831-1200. *www.amoebamusic.com.*

Aquarius Records (Mission District) *1055 Valencia St.* 415-647-2272. *www.aquariusrecords.org.*

Explorist International (Mission) *3174 24th St.* 415- 678-5691.

Groove Merchant (Haight) *687 Haight St.* 415-252-5766.

Jack's Record Cellar (Haight) *254 Scott St.* 415-431-3047.

Originals Vinyl (Lower Haight) *701 Fillmore St* 415-660-8779.

Rooky Ricardo's (Haight) *448 Haight St.* 415-864-7526. *www.rookyricardos.com.*

Rasputin Music (Haight St.) *1672 Haight St.* 415-863-2448. *www.rasputinmusic.com.*

Vinyl Dreams (Lower Haight) *593 Haight St.* 415-379-0974 *vinyldreams.storenvy.com.*

MARKETS

Farmers' markets abound throughout San Francisco and the Bay Area, packed with fresh (mostly organic) produce, meats, breads, cheeses and prepared foods from local producers. Some feature live music, cooking demos and craft booths. For the most complete listing, check out websites like www.pcfma.org.

Ferry Plaza Farmers' Market *Ferry Plaza. Sat 8am–2pm, Tue & Thu 10am–2pm.*

Fort Mason Center Farmers' Market *2 Marina Blvd. Sun 9:30am–1:30 pm.*

Heart of the City Farmers' Market *U.N. Plaza, Civic Center. Sun 7am–5pm, Wed 7am–5:30pm.*

Castro Farmers' Market *Market Street at Noe Street. Mid-Mar– mid Dec, Wed 4–8pm.*

Sports

SPECTATOR SPORTS

Tickets for professional sporting events can be purchased at the venue, or through Ticketmaster.

Oracle Park (formerly AT&T Park), home to the San Francisco Giants baseball team, is located at the south end of The Embarcadero within walking distance of the Ferry Building. **The Oakland-Alameda County Coliseum,** typically known as the Oakland Coliseum for short, hosts the home games of the Oakland Raiders (football) and the Oakland Athletics (baseball). Next door, **Oracle Arena** has served as home to the Golden State Warriors (basketball) since 1972. However, the Raiders are expected to relocated to Las Vegas, Nevada in 2020, and the Warriors are slated to relocate to the **Chase Center,** a sprawling waterfront development at San Francisco's Mission Bay by the start of the 2019-20 season. To reach the Oakland Coliseum by **car** from San Francisco, cross the Oakland Bay Bridge and take I-580 to I-980 to I-880 south to 66th Ave. exit. By rail, take the 🚇 Fremont line to the Coliseum stop, where a walkway leads to the stadium. To catch the San Francisco 49ers football team, you'll have to head south to **Levi's Stadium,** a luxury 68,500-seat facility which opened in Santa Clara in July 214. Take US-101 south 43 miles to the Great America Parkway exit. The San Jose Sharks (hockey) hold court at the **SAP Center**

Wille Mays statue, Oracle Park

in downtown San Jose, about 48 miles south of San Francisco. From San Francisco, take I-280 to CA-87 S.

WORKING OUT

The following fitness clubs open their facilities to nonmembers, and have locations throughout the city. Check websites for hours and addresses.

ACTIVE SPORTS CLUBS

www.activesportsclubs.com. $20 per day. Locations in Nob Hill, Union Square and The Embarcadero.

24-HOUR FITNESS

www.24hourfitness.com. $20 per day. 10 locations throughout San Francisco.

YMCA

www.ymcasf.org. $15-$20 per day nonmembers; $5 for members. 15 locations throughout San Francisco.

SPORT/TEAM	Season	Home Stadium	✆ Information
Major League Baseball	Apr-Oct	(81 home games)	
San Francisco Giants (NL)		Oracle Park	415-972-2000
Oakland Athletics (AL)		Oakland Coliseum	510-568-5600
National Football League	Sept-Dec	(8 home games)	
San Francisco 49ers		Levi's Stadium	415-464-9377
Oakland Raiders		through 2020	800-724-3377
National Basketball Assn.	Nov-Apr	(41 home games)	
Golden State Warriors		(Chase Center from 2020)	510-986-2200
National Hockey League	Oct-Apr	(41 home games)	
San Jose Sharks		SAP Pavilion	408-287-7070

INDEX

INDEX

INDEX

INDEX

INDEX

🛏 STAY

🍷 EAT

MAPS AND PLANS

MAP LEGEND

★★★ **Highly recommended**
★★ **Recommended**
★ **Interesting**

Selected monuments and sights

⇒ ═══ Tour with departure point

⚓ Mission

⛪ ⚲ Church, chapel

B Letter locating a sight

▪ ▲ Other points of interest

▪ Statue, monument

⁂ ⱴ Panorama – View

▬▬▬ Building described – Other

▪ Small building

⚑ Lighthouse

◎ Fountain

🛈 Visitor information

▬▬▬ Park described – Other

▬▬▬ Wooded park described – Other

▬▬▬ Cemetery described – Other

Special symbol

▦ ········· Cable car terminus, line

Additional symbols

═══ Highway, interchange

═══ Toll road, bridge

═ ─ ─ Tunnel with ramp

──► One way street

═══ Pedestrian street – Steps

═══ Shopping street

✈ 🚌 Airport – Bus station

⛴ 🚢 Passenger ferry – Cruise

● Subway station

🎁 Gift shop

🚻 Restrooms

⬍ Elevator

🅿 ✉ Parking – Post office

═╪═ Gate

► ⬭ Golf course – Stadium

🛡 Interstate Highway

44 US Highway

55 Other Route

All maps are oriented north, unless otherwise indicated by a directional arrow.

MICHELIN

travelguide.michelin.com
www.viamichelin.com

MAPS OF CANADA, AND USA

Map 585 Western USA, Western Canada

Large-format map providing detailed road systems; includes driving distances, interstate rest stops, border crossings and interchanges.
◆ Comprehensive city and town index
◆ Scale: 1 : 2,400,000 (1in = approx.38mi)

Map 761 USA Road Map

Covers principal US road network while also presenting shaded relief detail of overall physiography of the land.
◆ State flags with statistical data and state tourism office telephone numbers
◆ Scale: 1 : 3,450,000

ROUTE PLANNING

Michelin is pleased to offer a route planning service at
www.viamichelin.com

Choose the shortest route, a route without tolls, or the Michelin recommended route to your destination; you can also access information about hotels and restaurants from *The Michelin Guide*, and tourist sites from *The Green Guide*.